THE LITTLE, BROWN READER

THE
LITTLE,
BROWN
READER

Sixth Edition

Edited by

MARCIA STUBBS
Wellesley College

SYLVAN BARNET
Tufts University

■ HarperCollins*CollegePublishers*

Sponsoring Editor: Patricia Rossi
Developmental Editor: Judith Leet
Project Coordination, Text and Cover Design: PC&F, Inc.
Photo Researcher: Leslie Coopersmith
Production/Manufacturing: Michael Weinstein/Paula Keller
Compositor: PC&F, Inc.
Printer and Binder: Courier Companies, Inc.
Cover Printer: The Lehigh Press, Inc.

For permission to use copyrighted material, grateful acknowledgment is made to the copyright holders on pp. 887–893, which are hereby made part of this copyright page.

THE LITTLE, BROWN READER, Sixth Edition

Library of Congress Cataloging-in-Publication Data

The Little, Brown reader / edited by Marcia Stubbs, Sylvan Barnet. —
    6th ed.
        p.   cm.
    Includes index.
    ISBN 0-673-52211-3 (student edition) ISBN 0-673-52212-1 (teacher edition)
    1. College readers.   I. Stubbs, Marcia.   II. Barnet, Sylvan.
PE1122.L56 1992
808'.0427–dc20   92-7468
                                                                     CIP

92 93 94 95 9 8 7 6 5 4 3 2 1

CONTENTS

1 A WRITER READS

2 A READER WRITES

3   A WRITER COMPARES VIEWPOINTS

4   A NOTE ON READING (AND WRITING ABOUT) PICTURES

5 ALL IN THE FAMILY

6 TEACHING AND LEARNING

*fiction
**poetry

7   WORK AND PLAY

*fiction

8   OPEN FOR BUSINESS

*fiction
**poetry

**poetry

9 NETWORKS

10 LAW AND ORDER

*fiction
**poetry

11   IDENTITIES

12   ARTICLES OF FAITH

*fiction
**poetry

13 CLASSIC ESSAYS

*fiction
**poetry

RHETORICAL CONTENTS

Analogy

Analysis or Classification

Cause and Effect

Comparison and Contrast

Definition

Description

Diction

Evaluation

Examples, Illustrations

Exposition

Irony

Journal and Personal Report

Narration

Persuasion

Style

PREFACE

Books have been put to all sorts of unexpected uses. Tolstoy used Tatishef's dictionaries as a test of physical endurance, holding them in his outstretched hand for five minutes, enduring "terrible pain." Books (especially pocket-sized Bibles) have served as armor by deflecting bullets. And they have served as weapons: two hundred years ago the formidable Dr. Johnson knocked a man down with a large book.

In a course in writing, what is the proper use of the book in hand? This anthology contains some one hundred and twenty essays, together with a few poems, stories, and fables, and numerous "Short Views," that is, paragraphs and aphorisms. But these readings are not the subject matter of the course; the subject matter of a writing course is writing, particularly the writing the students themselves produce. The responsibilities we felt as editors, then, were to include selections that encourage and enable students to write well, and to exclude selections that do not.

To talk of "enabling" first: Students, like all other writers, write best when they write on fairly specific topics that can come within their experience and within their command in the time that they have available to write. A glance at the first three thematic sections of our table of contents will reveal the general areas within which, we believe, students can find topics they have already given some thought to and are likely to be encountering in other courses as well: family relationships, love and courtship, schools, work, sports, and play. Although the next two sections ("Open for Business" and "Networks") are also on familiar subjects — entrepreneurship, language, and popular culture — the selections themselves offer ways of thinking about these subjects that may be less familiar. Television commercials and films, for example, can be thought of as networks that articulate and transmit values implicit in a culture. The next three sections are about areas of experience that, while hardly remote from students' interest, are perhaps more difficult for all of us to grasp concretely: the tension between civil rights and liberties and the need for law and order, matters of gender and ethnic identity, and the nature of religious faith—Hebrew, Christian, Muslim, Buddhist, and Native American. In these sections, therefore, we have taken particular care to exclude writing that is, for our purposes, too abstract, or too technical, or too elaborate. Finally, we conclude with "Classic Essays," ranging from Jonathan Swift to Alice Walker.

As editors we have tried to think carefully about whether selections we were inclined to use—because they were beautifully written or on a stimulating topic—would encourage students to write. Such encouragement does not come, we feel, solely from the subject of an essay or from its excellence; it comes when the essay engenders in the reader a confidence in the writing process itself. No one quality in essays automatically teaches such confidence: not length or brevity, not difficulty or simplicity, not necessarily clarity, and almost certainly not brilliance. But essays that teach writing demonstrate, in some way, that the writers had some stake in what they were saying, took some pains to say what they meant, and took pleasure in having said it. The selections we include vary in length, complexity, subtlety, tone, and purpose. Most were written by our contemporaries, but not all. The authors include historians, sociologists, scientists, saints, philosophers, and undergraduates, as well as journalists and other professional writers. And we have included some pictures in each section. The pictures (beautiful things in themselves, we think) provide immediate or nearly immediate experiences for students to write about. (Two essays about family photographs, written by students, give some indication of ways in which one can write about pictures.) But we hope that everything here will allow students to establish helpful connections between the activities that produced the words (and pictures) in these pages and their own work in putting critical responses to them on paper.

Although any arrangement of the selections—thematic, rhetorical, alphabetical, chronological, or random—would have suited our purposes, we prefer the thematic arrangement. For one thing, by narrowing our choices it helps us to make decisions. But more important, we know that in the real world what people write about is subjects, and we don't want to miss any opportunity to suggest that what goes on in writing courses is something like what goes on outside. The thematic categories are not intended to be rigid, however, and they do not pretend to be comprehensive; some of the questions following the selections suggest that leaping across boundaries is permitted, even encouraged. And, for instructors who prefer to organize their writing course rhetorically, we have added a selective table of contents organized rhetorically. Finally, we append a glossary of terms for students of writing.

A Note on the Sixth Edition

"Never read a book that is not old." Thus Emerson. It's good advice, but we are of course pleased that when *The Little, Brown Reader* was published it immediately found a receptive audience. Second, third, fourth, and fifth editions allowed us to strengthen the book by adding some recent essays, and now the publisher has asked for a sixth edition in order to meet the needs of instructors who wish to continue to use the book but who also want something new. William Hazlitt, Emerson's older contemporary, said that he always read an old book when a new one was published. We hope that this new edition allows instructors to read both at once. Although we have retained those essays and the special features (for instance, the brief headnotes and the questions at the end of each essay) that in our experience and the experience of many colleagues have consistently been of value to instructors and to students, we have also added much new material, (including 40 new essays).

Exactly what is new? First, there are now four introductory chapters on writing. These discuss not only annotating, summarizing, and outlining one's reading, but they also discuss keeping a journal, and drafting and revising essays. It is worth mentioning, too, that these chapters include five essays by students, three with the students' preliminary notes.

Second, we have substituted many new readings within the thematic chapters (for instance, there are five new essays in "All in the Family"), and we have added two new sections, "Identities" (on gender and ethnicity) and "Classic Essays." Because some forty readings are new to this edition (including works by Zora Neale Hurston, Jean-Bertrand Aristide, Robert Bly, Lorene Cary, James H. Cone, Gish Jen, Amy Tan, Renita Weems, Letty Cottin Pogrebin, Benjamin Franklin, Derek Bok), instructors can, if they wish, build an entire course around fresh material.

Acknowledgments

As usual, we are indebted to readers-in-residence. Morton Berman, William Burto, and Judith Stubbs have often read our material and then told us what we wanted to hear.

We are grateful to colleagues and students at Wellesley College— Samantha Campbell, Michael David Coogan, Katheryn H. Doran, Lidwien Kapteijns, Cheryl Lee, Louise Marlowe, Nadia Medina, Sally Merry, Celia Rothenberg, and Winifred Jane Wood—who suggested materials or who otherwise assisted us with this new edition.

We are grateful also to colleagues at other institutions who offered suggestions for the sixth edition:

Betty Bamberg	University of Southern California
Peggy F. Broder	Cleveland State University
Domenick Caruso	Kingsborough Community College
Benjamin A. L. Click, III	Pennsylvania State University
Geraldine DeLuca	Brooklyn College
Joanna Gibson	Texas A&M University
Shelby Grantham	Dartmouth College
Douglas Hesse	Illinois State University
Cynthia Lee Katona	Ohlone College
Robert F. Lucid	University of Pennsylvania
Cecelia Martyn	Montclair State College
Anne Matthews	Princeton University
Lori Ann Miller	University of California/Irvine
Michael G. Moran	University of Georgia
Thomas E. Recchio	University of Connecticut
William E. Rivers	University of South Carolina
Don Share	Boston University
Ronald E. Smith	University of North Alabama
Carla J. Valley	University of Wisconsin—LaCrosse
Richard J. Zbaracki	Iowa State University

People at HarperCollins have been unfailingly helpful; we would especially like to thank Judith Leet and Patricia Rossi.

We are again indebted to Virginia Creeden, who effectively handled the difficult job of obtaining permission for copyrighted material.

We thank those instructors who generously offered suggestions based on their classroom experience with the first five editions: Bonnie Alexander, Kenneth Alrutz, Marianne Antczack, Norman Sidney Ashbridge, Andrew Aung, Donald Babcock, James Barcus,

Lloyd Becker, Frank Bidart, Joseph Blimm, Frank Bliss, Beverly Boone, Grant Boswell, George Branam, Eric D. Brown, Lillian Broderick, Ruth Brown, Jean Young Brunk, Beth Burch, Debra L. Burgauet, Anne Burley, Carol Burns, D. G. Campbell, J. V. Chambers, John Clifford, Ann Connor, Anne Cooney, Kenneth Cooney, Marion Copeland, Robert Cosgrove, Helene Davis, Donald DeSulis, William Devlin, John A. R. Dick, Fiona Emde, Robert Erickson, Richard Fahey, Evelyn Farbman, Michael Feehan, Linda Feldmeier, Gretchen Fillmore, Sister Jeremy Finnegan, Kathleen P. Flint, Martha Flint, William Ford, Joseph S. Frany, James French, Charles Frey, Yvonne Frey, David Gadziola, George Griffith, George D. Haich, Steve Hamelman, Bettina Hanlon, Brian O. Hannon, Hymen H. Hart, Pat Hart, Steven Harvey, Mal Haslett, Stephen Hathaway, Mark Hawkins, George Hayhoe, Zelda Hedden-Sellman, Ruth C. Hage, Kathryn Hellerstein, Dr. Elbert R. Hill, Maureen Hoal, David Hoddeson, Kathryn Holms, John Howe, William Howrath, Morris Husted, Lois B. Janzer, Johanna Jung, F. A. Kachur, Michael Kalter, Robert D. Keohan, Richard Kirchoffer, Walt Klarner, Robert Knox, Karl Kumm, Sandra M. Lee, Dorinda Lemaire, Claudia Limbert, Joyce D. Lipkis, William E. Lucas, William Lutz, Celia Martin, Marie M. McAllister, Anne McCormich, Charles McLaughlin, Garry Merritt, George Miller, John Milstead, Mary F. Minton, Chris M. Mott, Abigail Mulcahy, John Nesselhof, Robert Ohafson, Terry Otten, Jewyl Pallette, Linda Pelzer, Richard Prince, Richard Priebe, Phyllis Reed, Karyn Riedell, Leo Rockas, Duncan Rollo, Harriet Rosenblum, Ronald Ruland, Ralph St. Louis, Jack Selzer, Mary Shesgreen, Emerson Shuck, Carol Sicherman, James Smith, Larry Smith, Mark Smith, Harry Solomon, John Stahl, Judith Stanford, Carol Starikoff, Petra Steele, William B. Stone, Mary Lee Strode, William L. Stull, Tereatha Taylor, David Templeman, Elizabeth Tentarelli, Robert Thompson, Leatrice Timmons, Pamela Topping, Marilyn Valention, J. Keith Veizer, Harvey Vetstein, Brother Roland Vigeant, Lorraine Viscardi, Anthony Vital, Carolyn Wall, Don Wall, Doug Watson, Mary Weinkauf, Mark Wenz, Michael West, Richard Whitworth, Lyn Yonack, Lee Yosha, and Thomas Young.

We owe a special debt to Professor John Harwood and other teachers in the composition program at Pennsylvania State University for suggesting ways in which *The Little, Brown Reader* can be used in a course that emphasizes persuasive writing.

Marcia Stubbs
Sylvan Barnet

1
A WRITER READS

One reads well only when one reads with some personal goal in mind. It may be to acquire some power. It may be out of hatred for the author.

Paul Valéry

Good writers are also good readers—of the works of other writers and of their own notes and drafts. The habits they develop as readers of others—for instance evaluating assumptions, scrutinizing arguments, and perceiving irony—empower them when they write, read, and revise their own notes and drafts. Because they themselves are readers, when they write they have a built-in awareness of how their readers might respond. They can imagine an audience, and they write almost as if in dialogue with it.

Active reading (which is what we are describing) involves writing at the outset: annotating a text by highlighting or underlining key terms, putting question marks or brief responses in the margin, writing notes in a journal. Such reading, as you already may have experienced, helps you first of all to understand a text, to get clear what the writer seems to intend. Later, skimming your own notes will help you to recall what you have read.

But active reading also gives you confidence as a writer. It helps you to treat your own drafts with the same respect and disrespect with which you read the work of others. To annotate a text or a draft is to respect it enough to give it serious attention, but it is also to question it, to assume that the text or draft is not the last word on the topic.

But let's start at the beginning.

Previewing

By previewing we mean getting a tentative fix on a text before reading it closely.

If you know something about the **author,** you probably already know something about a work even before you read the first paragraph. An essay by Martin Luther King, Jr., will almost surely be a deeply serious discussion centering on civil rights, and, since King was a Baptist clergyman, it is likely to draw on traditional religious values. An essay by Woody Allen or one by Annie Dillard will almost surely differ from King's in topic and tone. Allen usually writes about the arts, especially the art of film, and Dillard writes highly personal meditations, often on the sacredness of nature. All three writers are serious (though Allen also writes comic pieces), but they are serious about different things and serious in different ways. We can read all three with interest, but when we begin with any one of them, we know we will get something very different from the other two.

King, Allen, and Dillard are exceptionally well known, but you can learn something about all of the authors represented in *The Little, Brown Reader* because they are introduced by means of biographical notes. Make it a practice to read these notes. They will give you some sense of what to expect. You may never have heard, for example, of J. H. Plumb, but when you learn from the note that he was a professor of history at the University of Cambridge and that he also taught in American universities, you can tentatively assume that the essay will have an historical dimension. Of course, you may have to revise this assumption—the essay may be about the joys of trout fishing or the sorrows of being orphaned at an early age—but in all probability the biographical note will have given you some preparation for reading the essay.

The **original organ of publication** may also give you some sense of what the piece will be about. The essays in *The Little, Brown Reader* originally were published in books, magazines, or newspapers, and these sources (specified, when relevant, in the biographical notes) may in themselves provide a reader with clues. For instance, since *The American Scholar* is published by Phi Beta Kappa and is read chiefly by college and university teachers or by persons with comparable education, articles in *The American Scholar* usually offer somewhat academic treatments of serious matters. They assume that the readers are serious and are capable of sustained intellectual effort. Whereas a newspaper editorial runs about 1000 words, articles in *The American Scholar* may be fifteen or so pages long.

Some journals have an obvious political slant, and the articles they publish are to some degree predictable in content and attitude. For instance, William Buckley's *National Review* is politically conservative. Its subscribers want to hear certain things, and *National Review* tells them what they want to hear. Its readers know, too, that the essays will be lively and can be read fairly rapidly. Similarly, subscribers to *Ms.* expect highly readable essays with a strong feminist slant. When *Ms.* published an essay called "Why I Want a Wife," the very title probably aroused the reader's suspicion. The suspicion was confirmed when the reader noted that the author is a woman, but if a reader missed this clue, the first paragraph indicates the author's satiric intent. (The essay is printed in this book, on page 104.)

The **form,** or **genre** (a literary term for type or kind of literature), may provide another clue as to what will follow. For instance, you can expect a letter to the editor to amplify or contradict an editorial or to comment approvingly or disapprovingly on some published news item. It will almost surely be concerned with a current issue. Martin Luther King, Jr.'s "Letter from Birmingham Jail," a response to a letter from eight clergymen, is a famous example of a letter arguing on behalf of a current action.

The **title,** as we have already noted, may provide a clue. Again, King provides an example; even before studying "I Have a Dream," a reader can assume that the essay will be about King's vision of the future. Other examples of titles that announce the topic are Alexandra Armstrong's "Starting a Business" and Paul Robinson's "TV Can't Educate." These titles are straightforward and informative, but suppose you pick up an essay called "Do-It-Yourself Brain Surgery"? What do you already know about the essay?

Skimming

"Some books are to be tasted, others to be swallowed, and some few to be chewed and digested." You may already have encountered this wise remark by Francis Bacon, a very good reader (and a good writer too, though he did not write Shakespeare's plays). The art of reading includes the art of skimming, that is, the art of gliding rapidly over a piece of writing and getting its gist.

Skimming has three important uses: to get through junk mail and other lightweight stuff; to locate what is relevant to your purpose in a mass of material, as, for instance, when you are working on a research paper; and (our topic now) to get an overview of an essay, especially to get the gist of its argument. Having discovered what you can from the name of the author, the title of the work, and the place of publication, you may want to skim the essay before reading it closely.

The **opening paragraph** will often give you a good idea of the **topic** or general area of the essay (for instance, the family), and if the essay is essentially an argument, it may announce the writer's **thesis,** the point that the writer will argue (for instance, that despite the high divorce rate, the family is still in good shape). Here is an example from Barbara Ehrenreich's "The 'Playboy' Man and the American Family." (The entire essay is printed later in this chapter.)

As a scapegoat for social pathology, feminism ranks with creeping socialism, godless atheism, and other well-known historic threats to public order. We have, in the last decade alone, been accused of causing male impotence, encouraging sexual perversity, and undermining our colorful national tradition of sex roles. In most cases, we're happy to take the credit, but there's one charge that can still make strong women cringe: the accusation that feminism "destroyed the family" or is deeply and wickedly "antifamily" even when we are talking about wholesome domestic issues like child care for working parents or who folds the clothes.

Now, this paragraph may cause some difficulties—a reader may, for instance, not be clear about the meaning of "social pathology" in the first sentence; but probably the gist is clear: because the charge that "feminism 'destroyed the family'" is so often made, it needs to be discussed. Taking the opening paragraph in connection with the title—"The 'Playboy' Man and the American Family"—a reader assumes that the essay will be concerned with the man's role in the destruction of the family. The thesis is not explicitly announced, but even a skimming of this paragraph may suggest to the reader that the writer will reject the charge against feminism.

If the first paragraph does not seem especially informative (it may be a sort of warmup, akin to the speechmaker's "A funny thing happened to me on my way here"), look closely at the second. Then, as you scan subsequent paragraphs, look especially for **topic sentences** (often the first sentence in a paragraph), which summarize the paragraph, and for passages that follow **key phrases** such as "the important point to remember," "these two arguments can be briefly put thus," "in short," "it is essential to recall," and so on. Ehrenreich's second paragraph, for instance, begins by saying "The real issue . . . is . . ." The **final paragraph** probably will reformulate the writer's thesis. When you read Ehrenreich's essay, you'll notice that her final paragraph begins thus:

> The problem, and it is a big one, is that men may have won their freedom before we win our battle against sexism.

Later, when you reread her essay carefully, you'll be on the lookout for the evidence that supports this view.

As you scan an essay, you'll find it useful to highlight phrases or sentences, or to draw vertical lines in the margin next to passages that seem to be especially concise bearers of meaning. In short, even while you are skimming you are using your pen.

If the essay is divided into sections, **headings** may give you an idea of the range of coverage. You probably won't need to high-light them—they already stand out—but there's no harm in doing so.

When you skim you are seeking to get the gist of the author's thesis or **point.** But you are also getting an idea of the author's **methods** and the author's **purpose.** For instance, skimming may re-veal that the author is using statistics (or an appeal to common sense, or whatever) to set forth an unusual view. When Ehrenreich begins by saying that "feminism ranks with creeping socialism, godless atheism, and other well-known historic threats to public order," she is using sarcasm. Why is she using sarcasm? For at least two rea-sons: to ridicule the opposition and to entertain her readers. Skim-ming reveals Ehrenreich's *attitude* as well as her purpose and au-dience. It reveals that she is probably talking to an audience of like-minded people and is chiefly giving them encouragement to maintain their view.

Another author, however, may assume that the audience needs to be educated to the real facts. Such a writer will probably take less for granted—for instance, he or she will carefully define terms—and will take pains to seem to be scrupulously fair. Or skimming may reveal that the author is not especially concerned with persuad-ing the reader but is more concerned with sharing an emotional ex-perience.

During this preliminary trip through a piece of writing, you may also get some idea of the personality of the writer. More precisely, since you are encountering not the writer in the flesh but only the image that the writer presents in the essay, you may form an im-pression of the **voice,** or **persona,** that speaks in the essay. Some-thing of Ehrenreich's persona is evident in a line such as "feminism ranks with creeping socialism, godless atheism, and other well-known historic threats to public order," where we probably hear a tone of ridicule. We will return to this important matter later, on page 23.

Let's look at an essay by J. H. Plumb, who, as you already know, was a professor of history both in England and in the United States. We suggest that in your first reading you skim it, perhaps highlight-ing, underlining, or drawing vertical lines next to passages that strike you as containing the chief ideas. To this extent you are reading for information. But because you have ideas of your own, and because you do not accept something as true simply because it appears in print, you may also want to put question marks or expressions of doubt ("Really?" "Check this") in the margin next to any passages that strike you as puzzling. Further, you may want to circle any words that you are not familiar with, but at this stage don't bother to look them up. In short, run through the essay, seeking to get the gist and briefly indicating your responses, but don't worry about getting every detail of the argument.

J. H. Plumb

The Dying Family

I was rather astonished when a minibus drove up to my house and out poured ten children. They had with them two parents, but not one child had them both in common as mother and father, and two of them belonged to neither parent, but to a former husband of the wife who had died. Both parents, well into middle age, had just embarked, one on his fourth, the other on her third marriage. The children, who came in all sizes, and ranged from blonde nordic to jet-haired Greek, bounded around the garden, young and old as happy as any children that I have seen. To them, as Californians, their situation was not particularly odd; most of their friends had multiple parents. Indeed to them perhaps the odd family was the one which Western culture has held up as a model for two thousand years or more—the lifelong union of man and wife. But it took me a very long time to believe that they could be either happy or adjusted. And yet, were they a sign of the future, a way the world was going?

Unlike anthropologists or sociologists, historians have not studied family life very closely. Until recently we knew very little of the age at which people married in Western Europe in the centuries earlier than the nineteenth or how many children they had, or what the rates of illegitimacy might be or whether, newly wed, they lived with their parents or set up a house of their own. Few of these questions can be answered with exactitude even now, but we can make better guesses. We know even less, however, of the detailed sexual practices that marriage covered: indeed this is a subject to which historians are only just turning their attention. But we do know much more of the function of family life—its social role—particularly if we turn from the centuries to the millennia and pay attention to the broad similarities rather than the fascinating differences between one region and another: and, if we do, we realize that the family has changed far more profoundly than even the bus load of Californians might lead us to expect.

Basically the family has fulfilled three social functions—to provide a basic labor force, to transmit property and to educate and train children not only into an accepted social pattern, but also in the work skills upon which their future subsistence would depend. Until very recent times, the vast majority of children never went to any school: their school was the family, where they learned to dig and sow and reap and herd their animals, or they learned their father's craft of smith or carpenter or potter. The unitary family was particularly good at coping with the small peasant holdings which covered most of the world's fertile regions from China to Peru. In the primitive peasant world a child of four or five could begin to earn its keep in the fields, as they still can in India and Africa: and whether Moslem, Hindu, Inca or Christian, one wife at a time was all that the bulk of the world's population could support, even though their religion permitted them more. Indeed, it was the primitive nature of peasant economy which gave the family, as we know it, its wide diffusion and its remarkable continuity.

Whether or not it existed before the neolithic revolution we shall never know, but certainly it must have gained in strength as families became rooted to the soil. Many very primitive people who live in a pre-agrarian society of hunting and food-gathering often tend to have a looser structure of marriage and the women a far greater freedom of choice and easier divorce, as with the Esquimaux, than is permitted in peasant societies. There can be little doubt that the neolithic revolution created new opportunities for the family as we know it, partly because this revolution created new property relations. More importantly it created great masses of property, beyond anything earlier societies had known. True, there were a few hunting peoples, such as the Kwakiutl Indians, who had considerable possessions—complex lodges, great pieces of copper and piles of fibre blankets, which periodically they destroyed in great battles of raging pride—but the property, personal or communal, of most primitive hunting people is usually trivial.

After the revolution in agriculture, property and its transmission lay at the very heart of social relations and possessed an actuality which we find hard to grasp. Although we are much richer, possessions are more anonymous, often little more than marks in a ledger, and what we own constantly changes. Whereas for the majority of mankind over this last seven thousand years property has been deeply personal and familial: a plot of land, if not absolute ownership over it, then valuable rights in it; sometimes a house, even though it be a hovel by our standards; perhaps no more than the tools and materials of a craft, yet these possessions were the route both to survival and to betterment. Hence they were endowed with manna, bound up with the deepest roots of personality. In all societies the question of property became embedded in every aspect of family life, particularly marriage and the succession and rights of children. Because of property's vital importance, subservience of women and children to the will of the father, limited only by social custom, became the pattern of most great peasant societies. Marriage was sanctified not only by the rites of religion, but by the transmission of property. Few societies could tolerate freedom of choice in marriage—too much vital to the success or failure of a family depended on it: an ugly girl with five cows was a far fairer prospect than a pretty girl with one. And because of the sexual drives of frail human nature, the customs of marriage and of family relationships needed to be rigorously enforced. Tradition sanctified them; religion blessed them. Some societies reversed the sexually restrictive nature of permanent marriage and permitted additional wives, but such permission was meaningless to the mass of the peasantry who fought a desperate battle to support a single family. And, as we shall see, the patterns of family life were always looser for the rich and the favored.

But a family was always more than property expressed clearly and visibly in real goods; it was for thousands of years both a school and a tribunal, the basic unit of social organization whose function in modern society has been very largely taken over by the state. In most peasant societies, life is regulated by the village community, by the patriarchs of the village, and the only officer of the central government these villagers see with any regularity is the tax-gatherer; but in societies that have grown more complex, and this is particularly true of the West during the last four hundred years, life has become regulated by the nation state or by the growth in power and importance of more generalized local communities—the town or county.

This has naturally weakened the authority of heads of families, a fact that can be symbolically illustrated by change in social custom.

No child in Western Europe would sit unbidden in the presence of its parents until the eighteenth century: if it did it could be sure of rebuke and punishment. No head of a household would have thought twice about beating a recalcitrant young servant or apprentice before the end of the nineteenth century. For a younger brother to marry without the consent of his eldest brother would have been regarded as a social enormity; and sisters were disposable property. All of this power has vanished. Indeed the family ties of all of us have been so loosened that we find it hard to grasp the intensity of family relationships or their complexity, they have disintegrated so rapidly this last hundred years. Now nearly every child in the Western world, male or female, is educated outside the family from five years of age. The skills they learn are rarely, if ever, transmitted by parents: and what is more they learn about the nature of their own world, its social structure and its relationships in time outside the family. For millennia the family was the great transmitter and formulator of social custom; but it now only retains a shadow of this function, usually for very young children only.

Although the economic and education functions of the family 8 have declined, most of us feel that it provides the most satisfactory emotional basis for human beings; that a secure family life breeds stability, a capacity not only for happiness, but also to adjust to society's demands. This, too, may be based on misjudgment, for family life in the past was not remarkable for its happiness. We get few glimpses into the private lives of men and women long dead, but when we do we often find strain, frustration, petty tyranny. For so many human beings family life was a prison from which they could not escape. And although it might create deep satisfactions here and there, the majority of the rich and affluent classes of the last four hundred years in Western Europe created for themselves a double standard, particularly as far as sex was concerned. In a few cities such as Calvin's Geneva, the purity of family life might be maintained, but the aristocracies of France, Italy and Britain tolerated, without undue concern, adultery, homosexuality and that sexual freedom which, for better or worse, we consider the hallmark of modern life. Indeed the family as the basic social group began firstly to fail, except in its property relations, amongst the aristocracy.

But what we think of as a social crisis of this generation—the rapid growth of divorce, the emancipation of women and adolescents, the sexual and educational revolutions, even the revolution in eating which is undermining the family as the basis of nourishment, for over a hundred years ago the majority of Europeans never ate in public in their lives—all of these things, which are steadily making the family weaker and weaker, are the inexorable result of the changes in society itself. The family as a unit of social organization was remarkably appropriate for a less complex world of agriculture and craftsmanship, a world which stretches back some seven thousand years, but ever since industry and highly urbanized societies began to take its place, the social functions of the family have steadily weakened—and this is a process that is unlikely to be halted. And there is no historical reason to believe that human beings could be less or more happy, less or more stable. Like any other human institution the family has always been molded by the changing needs of society, sometimes slowly, sometimes fast. And that bus load of children does no more than symbolize the failure, not of marriage, but of the role of the old-fashioned family unit in a modern, urbanized, scientific and affluent society.

Even a quick skimming reveals that Plumb offers, as you anticipated he would, an historical view. He begins with a glance at one contemporary family, but you probably noticed that by the second paragraph he speaks as an historian, tracing the origins and development of the institution of the family.

Highlighting, Underlining, Annotating

Now that you have the gist of Plumb's essay, go back and reread it; this time, highlight or underline key passages as though you were marking the text so that you might later easily review it for an examination. Your purpose now is simply to make sure that you know what Plumb is getting at. You may strongly disagree with him on details or even on large matters, and you would certainly make clear your differences with him if you were to write about his essay; but for the moment your purpose is to make sure that you know what his position is. See if in each paragraph you can find a sentence that contains the topic idea of the paragraph. If you find such sentences, mark them.

Caution: Do not allow yourself to highlight or underline whole paragraphs. Before you start to mark a paragraph, read it to the end, and then go back and mark what you now see as the key word, phrase, or passage. If you simply start marking a paragraph from the beginning, you may end up marking the whole; and thus you will defeat your purpose, which is to make highly visible the basic points of the essay.

You may also want to jot down, in the margins, questions or objections, and you may want to circle any words that puzzle you.

Time's up. Let's talk about the underlinings and highlightings. No two readers of the essay will make exactly the same annotations. To take a small example, a reader in Alaska would probably be more likely to mark the passage about "the Esquimaux" in paragraph 4 than would a reader in St. Louis, but here is what one reader produced.

note first person

new (California) style

(I) was rather astonished when a minibus drove up to my house and out poured <u>ten children.</u> They had with them two parents, but <u>not one child had them both in common as mother and father,</u> and two of them belonged to neither parent, but to a former husband of the wife who had died. Both parents, well into middle age, had just embarked, one on his fourth, the other on her third marriage. The children, who came in all sizes, and ranged from blonde nordic to jet-haired Greek, bounded around the garden, young and old as happy as any children that (I) have seen. To them, as <u>Californians,</u> their situation was <u>not particularly odd;</u> most of their friends had multiple parents. Indeed to them perhaps the odd family was the one which Western culture has held up as a <u>model for two thousand years or</u> more—the <u>lifelong union of man and wife.</u> But it took me a very long time to believe that they could be either <u>happy or adjusted.</u> And yet, were they a sign of the future, a way the world was going?

} old style

who says they are happy?

first person again, but less "personal"

Unlike anthropologists or sociologists, (historians) have not studied family life very closely. Until recently <u>we</u> knew very little of the age at which people married in Western Europe in the centuries earlier than the nineteenth or how many children they had, or what the rates of illegitimacy might be or whether, newly wed, they lived with their parents or set up a house of their own. Few of these questions can be answered with exactitude even now, but <u>we</u> can make better guesses. <u>We</u> know even less, however, of the detailed sexual practices that marriage covered: indeed this is a subject to which historians are only just turning their attention. But <u>we</u> do know much more of the function of family life—its social role—particularly if we turn from the centuries to the millennia and pay attention to the broad similarities rather than the fascinating differences between one region and another: and, if we do, we realize that the family has changed far more profoundly than even the bus load of Californians might lead us to expect.

change

Basically the family has fulfilled three social functions—to provide a basic labor force, to transmit property and to educate and train children not only into an accepted social pattern, but also in the work skills upon which their future subsistence would depend. Until very recent times, the vast majority of children never went to any school: their school was the family, where they learned to dig and sow and reap and herd their animals, or they learned their father's craft of smith or carpenter or potter. The unitary family was particularly good at coping with the small peasant holdings which covered most of the world's fertile regions from China to Peru. In the primitive peasant world a child of four or five could begin to earn its keep in the fields, as they still can in India and Africa; and whether Moslem, Hindu, Inca or Christian, one wife at a time was all that the bulk of the world's population could support, even though their religion permitted them more. Indeed, it was the primitive nature of peasant economy which gave the family, as we know it, its wide diffusion and its remarkable continuity.

3 functions

1. provides labor

2. transmits property

3. educates children

?

? couldn't wives earn their keep?

not also religious teachings?

Whether or not it existed before the neolithic revolution we shall never know, but certainly it must have gained in strength as families became rooted to the soil. Many very primitive people who live in a pre-agrarian society of hunting and food-gathering often tend to have a looser structure of marriage and the women a far greater freedom of choice and easier divorce, as with the Esquimaux, than is permitted in peasant societies. There can be little doubt that the neolithic revolution created new opportunities for the family as we know it, partly because this revolution created new property relations. More importantly it created great masses of property, beyond anything earlier societies had known. True, there were a few hunting peoples, such as the Kwakiutl Indians, who had considerable possessions—complex lodges, great pieces of copper

?

and piles of fibre blankets, which periodically they destroyed in great battles of raging pride—but the
property, personal or communal, of most primitive
hunting people is usually trivial.

Of course different readers will find different passages of special
interest and importance. Our personal histories, our beliefs, our
preconceptions, our current preoccupations, to some extent determine how we read. For instance, when they come to the fifth paragraph some readers may mark Plumb's sexist language ("mankind"),
and some may highlight the assertion that "Marriage was sanctified not only by the rites of religion, but by the transmission of
property." Readers who are especially interested in class relations
might also highlight and underline this sentence:

The patterns of family life were always looser for the rich and the
favored.

Notice, by the way, that although Plumb makes this assertion he
does not offer a value judgment. A reader might mark the sentence
and add in the margin: *Still true, and outrageous!* Or, conversely, a
reader may feel that the statement is false, and might write, *Really???*,
or even *Not the rich, but the poor (free from bourgeois hangups) are sexually freer.*
    As these last examples indicate, even when you set out simply
to make a few notes that will help you to follow and to remember
the essayist's argument, you may well find yourself making notes
that record your *responses* (where you agree, what you question),
notes that may start you thinking about the validity of the argument.
    As we have already said, *what* you annotate will partly depend
on what interests you, what your values are, and what your purpose is. True, you have read the essay because it was assigned, but
Plumb's original readers read it for other reasons. It appeared first
in a magazine and then in a collection of Plumb's essays. The original readers, then, were people who freely picked it up because they
wanted to learn about the family or perhaps because they had read
something else by Plumb, liked it, and wanted to hear more from
this person.
    Imagine yourself, for a moment, as a reader encountering this
essay in a magazine that you have picked up. If you are reading
because you want to know something about the family in an agrarian

society, you'll annotate one sort of thing; if you are reading because as a child of divorced parents you were struck and possibly outraged by his first paragraph, you'll annotate another sort of thing; if you are reading because you admire Plumb as an historian, you'll annotate another sort of thing; and if you are reading because you dislike Plumb, you'll annotate something else. We remind you of a comment by Paul Valéry, quoted at the beginning of this chapter: "One reads well only when one reads with some quite personal goal in mind. It may be to acquire some power. It can be out of hatred for the author." An exaggeration, of course, but there is something to it. (In the Book of Job, Job wishes that his "adversary had written a book.")

Summarizing and Outlining

In your effort to formulate a brief version of what an essayist is saying, you may want to write a summary, especially if you found the essay difficult. A good way to begin is to summarize each paragraph in a sentence or two, or in some phrases. If you summarize each paragraph, when you finish you have at hand—without any additional work—an outline of the essay. Here is a student's outline of Plumb's essay.

1.   minibus in California: ten children and two parents, but not one child was child of both adults. Different from traditional family. Sign of the way the world is going.
2.   many things not known about the past (age of marriage, sexual practices), but something known of the function of family life.
3.   Three functions: providing a labor force, transmitting property, educating and training children. Peasant families today.
4, 5.   After neolithic (agricultural?) revolution, family strengthened because people rooted to the soil (produced masses of property: land, house, or tools of a craft). Transmission of property sanctified marriage.
6, 7.   family was also school and basic social unit. Head of the household ruled (chose the mate for a child, etc.). In modern societies government has taken over many functions of patriarchs.

8. Despite loss of functions, most of us still
    feel that a family breeds stability, happi-
    ness. May be a misjudgment; family often
    was a prison. And for last 400 years the
    rich created a double standard, at least
    for sex.

9. decline of family (divorce, emancipation of
    women and adolescents, etc.) is result of
    historic change in society itself. Family
    appropriate for agricultural society, but
    less in industrial and urban societies.
    Busload of kids symbolizes not the failure
    of marriage but the loss of role for
    old-fashioned family in a modern society.

Especially if an essay is complex, writing a summary of this sort
can help you to follow the argument. Glancing over your notes, you
probably can see, fairly easily, what the writer's *main* points are,
as distinct from the subordinate points and the examples that clarify the points. Furthermore, since your summary is now a paragraph
outline, you can look it over to see not only what it adds up to, but
also how the writer shaped the material. Producing a summary,
then, may be an activity that is useful to you when you are *reading*
an essay. It will almost surely help you to grasp the essay and to
remember its argument. And if you are *writing* about the essay,
perhaps to take issue with it or to amplify a point that it makes,
you may have to include in your essay a brief summary so that your
readers will know what you are writing about.

How long should the summary be? Just long enough to give
readers what they need in order to follow your essay. If in a fairly
long essay you are going to take issue with several of Plumb's points,
you may want to give a fairly detailed summary, perhaps a page
long.

For a short essay, however, something like the following passage might be appropriate:

In "The Dying Family" J. H. Plumb argues that
when society was primarily agricultural, the family
provided education and training, a labor force, and
a way of transmitting property. In today's industri-
alized society, however, these functions are largely
provided by the government, and the traditional family is no longer functional.

(For further discussion of summaries, see the entry on page 884–85 of this book, in "A Writer's Glossary.")

Questioning the Text

We have already said that you will probably find yourself putting question marks in the margins next to words that you don't know and that don't become clear in the context, and next to statements that you find puzzling or dubious. These marks will remind you to take action—perhaps to check a dictionary, perhaps to reread a paragraph, or perhaps to jot down your objection in the margin or at greater length in a journal.

But analytic readers also engage in another sort of questioning, though they may do so almost unconsciously. They are almost always asking themselves—or, rather, asking the text—half-a-dozen questions. You'll notice that these questions concern not only the writer's point but also the writer's craft. By asking such questions, you will learn about subject matter (for instance, about the history of the family in Plumb's essay) and also about some of the tricks of the writer's trade (for instance, effective ways of beginning). If you read actively, asking the following questions, you will find that reading is *not* a solitary activity; you are conversing with a writer.

1. What is the writer's thesis?
2. How does the writer support the thesis?
3. What is the writer's purpose (to persuade, to rebut, to entertain, to share an experience, or whatever)?
4. How do the writer's audience and purpose help shape the writing? (The place of publication is often a clue to the audience.) For instance, does the writer use humor, or on the other hand does the writer speak earnestly? Are terms carefully defined, or on the other hand does the writer assume that the audience is knowledgeable and does not need such information?
5. What is the writer's tone?

These questions will help you to understand what you are reading and how writers go about their business. But you are also entitled to evaluate what you are reading, hence some other questions, of a rather different sort:

6. How successful is the piece? What are its strengths and weaknesses? What do I especially like or dislike about it? Why?

We recommend that when you read an essay you ask each of these questions, not, of course, during an initial skimming, but during a second and third reading, that is, after you have some sense of the essay.

These questions can almost be boiled down to one question:

What is the writer up to?

That is, a reader who is not content merely to take what the writer is handing out asks such questions as, Why *this* way of opening? Why *this* way of defining the term? Of course, the assumption that the writer has a purpose may be false. (We are reminded of a comment that Metternich, the keenly analytic Austrian statesman and diplomat, uttered when he learned that the Czar had died: "I wonder why he did that.") Yes, the writer may just be blundering along, but it's reasonable to begin with the assumption that the writer is competent. If under questioning the writer fails, well, you have learned that not everything in print is worthy.

A Second Essay

Let's look at the whole of an essay we began earlier, "The 'Playboy' Man and the American Family," by Barbara Ehrenreich, coauthor of *Remaking Love* and author of *The Hearts of Men: American Dreams and the Flight from Commitment*. The essay first appeared in *Ms.* in June, 1983. (You'll notice that some of the statistics are out of date, especially the statement in paragraph 8 that women's earnings average out to only a little more than $10,000 a year.) We suggest that you read it once straight through to get the gist and then reread it carefully, highlighting or underlining key passages and jotting queries and comments in the margins or on a piece of paper. And then, either to clarify your understanding of the essay or simply as an exercise, write a summary of each paragraph.

Barbara Ehrenreich

The "Playboy" Man and the American Family

As a scapegoat for social pathology, feminism ranks with creeping socialism, godless atheism, and other well-known historic threats to public order. We have, in the last decade alone, been accused of causing male impotence, encouraging sexual perversity, and undermining our colorful national tradition of sex roles. In most cases, we're happy to take the credit, but there's one charge that can still make strong women cringe: the accusation that feminism "destroyed the family" or is deeply and wickedly "antifamily" even when we are talking about wholesome domestic issues like child care for working parents or who folds the clothes.

The real issue in the debate over the family, it turns out, is *marriage* (heterosexual, monogamous, and so on), and when the critics charge feminists with being "antifamily," they mean we are responsible for "broken" homes, the 50 percent divorce rate, unwed mothers, and sometimes the entire "me generation."

The notion that women, and feminists in particular, have been waging war on matrimony departs so far from common experience and cultural memory as to deserve the status of whimsy. True, many women initiate divorces, and not only because their husbands are drunks and batterers. True, too, that a few brave women, from Emma Goldman on, have taken a principled stand against marriage as an unwelcome intrusion of government into their private lives. But the truth is that if either sex has been in revolt against marriage, it is men, and that the male revolt against marriage started long before our own rebellion as feminists.

When I was growing up in the 1950s, male hostility to marriage   4 and the responsibilities of breadwinning was an accepted fact of life. In the comics, Daisy Mae kept in training all year to catch L'il Abner on Sadie Hawkins Day, and poor, beaten-down Dagwood slaved away at the office to keep Blondie supplied with new hats. From a male perspective, which was pretty much the only one around, marriage was a "trap" for men and a lifelong sinecure for women. Even after they were "caught," men tried to escape in minor ways—

into baseball, golf, hunting, bowling, poker games, or the ideal, female-free world of Westerns.

This flight from "maturity," as concerned psychiatrists dubbed it, is one of the most venerable themes in American literary culture. In American mythic tradition, women are the civilizers and entrappers; men the footloose adventurers. Our heroes chase across the sea after great white whales, raft down the Mississippi, or ride off into the sunset on horseback. Cooper's *Deerslayer* traveled light; Davy Crockett didn't fuss over mortgage payments; and Rip Van Winkle, not quite so enterprising, went to sleep for 20 years to escape a nagging wife.

But it was in the 1950s that male hostility to marriage began to take a more urgent and articulate tone. There were low rumblings against gray-flannel "conformity"—a code word for male acquiescence to marriage and breadwinning—but in an America that was busily purging itself of Communists, bohemians, and similar deviants, no viable alternative was offered. Until Hugh Hefner's *Playboy*, which began publication in 1953. From the first feature article in the very first issue, *Playboy*'s writers railed against "gold-digging women"—wives, ex-wives, and would-be wives—all of them bent on crushing "man's adventurous, freedom-loving spirit." Marriage was an "estate in which the sexes . . . live half-slave and half-free," the slave-half being, of course, the husbands who toiled away while their wives spent their time "relaxing, reading, watching TV, playing cards, socializing. . . . " No man had to put up with this, *Playboy* told its readers: Why sign on for a life contract with one woman when there were so many Bunnies to sample? Why settle for "conformity, togetherness . . . and slow death" when you could have a bachelor apartment, a stereo, and a life of sybaritic thrills? By 1956, nearly a million loyal male readers were getting this manifesto of the male revolt.

All this, I emphasize, was going on at a time when there were fewer open feminists in the entire land than there are today in, say, the executive ranks of the Mormon Church. Married women by the thousands felt trapped and desperate too, but they weren't seething with a subversive zeal to "destroy the family" or smash the institution of marriage. In fact, when it came to marriage, Hefner was the radical; Friedan the conservative. Her manifesto of female discontent (*The Feminine Mystique*, published a full 10 years after the first issue of *Playboy*) argued that wider opportunities for women would strengthen marriage, since divorce reflected "the growing aversion and hostility that men have for the feminine millstones hanging around their necks. . . ." Friedan, and most of the feminists who followed, wanted a more equal, companionate marriage; Hefner and his followers simply wanted *out*.

There should be no mystery why, over the years, women have had a disproportionate investment in marriage. Women's earnings average out to a little more than $10,000 a year each—nowhere near enough to support a single in a swinging lifestyle, much less a single mother and her children. For most women, the obvious survival strategy has been to establish a claim on some man's more generous wage, i.e., to marry him. For men, on the other hand, as *Playboy*'s writers clearly saw, the reverse is true: not counting love, home-cooked meals, or other benefits of the married state, it makes more sense for a man to keep his paycheck for himself, rather than sharing it with an underpaid or unemployed woman and her no doubt unemployed children. A recent study by Stanford University sociologist Lenore J. Weitzman suggests the magnitude of men and women's divergent interests: upon divorce, a woman's standard of living falls, on the average, by 73 percent for the first year, while the standard of living of her ex-husband *rises* by 42 percent. For men, the alternative to marriage might be loneliness and TV dinners; for women it is, all too often, poverty.

By the standards of the 1950s, today's men are in many respects "free" at last: 7.3 million of them live alone (nearly half of them in the "never married" category) compared to 3.5 million in 1970. (The number of women living alone has also increased, but at a much lower rate, because single women are far more likely to live with children than single men.) If a man remains single until he is 28 or even 38, he may be criticized by girlfriends for his "fear of commitment," but he will no longer be suspected of an unhealthy attachment to his mother or a latent tendency to you-know-what. If he divorces his middle-aged wife for some sweet young thing, he may be viewed not as a traitor to the American way, but as a man who has a demonstrated capacity for "growth."

At the risk of sounding "antifamily," I must say that I do not think these changes, and the male revolt that inspired them, are an altogether bad thing. As feminists, we have always stood for men's as well as for women's liberation, which includes their right to be something other than husbands and breadwinners. As my son's mother, I know that I want him to grow up to be a loving and responsible adult, but I also know that it would be heartbreaking to see him "tied down," as the expression goes, to a lifetime of meaningless, uncreative jobs in order to support a family. So my purpose in recalling the recent history of men's revolt is not to say, "So there, blame *them!*"

The problem, and it is a big one, is that men may have won their freedom before we win our battle against sexism. Women might like to be free-spirited adventurers too, but the female equivalent of "playboy" does not work well in a culture still riddled with misogyny. We still earn less than men, whether or not we have men to help support us. Which is only to say that the feminist agenda is as urgent as ever, and those who are concerned about "the family" should remember that we—and our sisters and daughters and mothers—are members of it also.

Let's assume that you have read Ehrenreich's essay at least twice and that you may have written a paragraph outline. You'll recall that earlier we suggested a reader may profitably put certain questions to the text. Here, again, are those questions.

1. What is the writer's thesis?
2. How does the writer support the thesis?
3. What is the writer's purpose (to persuade, to rebut, to entertain, to share an experience, or whatever)?
4. How does the writer shape the purpose to the audience? (The place of publication is often a clue to the audience.) Does the writer use humor, or on the other hand does the writer speak earnestly? Are terms carefully defined, or on the other hand does the writer assume that the audience is knowledgeable and does not need elementary information?
5. What is the writer's tone?
6. How successful is the piece? What are its strengths and weaknesses? What do I especially like or dislike about it?

Here are a few additional questions, which this time specifically refer to Ehrenreich's essay. You might jot down your responses and later compare them with those of another reader.

1. *Ms.*, in which this essay originally appeared, addresses primarily women's issues. Is Ehrenreich's tone hospitable to male readers as well? Or is she likely to offend them?
2. Ehrenreich calls attention to the hostility to marriage displayed in comic strips and in *Playboy*. Do you think that such writings

are to be taken seriously, or are they merely harmless jokes? On what do you base your response?

3. Reread the essay closely and jot down some brief notes concerning the precautions Ehrenreich takes to make her position appear reasonable. If you can't find such material, do you regard her position as unreasonable?

If there are fundamental differences between your responses and those of a classmate, try to account for them. (The differences are probably due to your different personalities and interests, but you may find that you have fewer disagreements after discussion.)

A Note about Tone and Persona

Perhaps you know the line from Owen Wister's novel, *The Virginian*: "When you call me that, smile." Words spoken with a smile mean something different from the same words spoken through clenched teeth. But while speakers can communicate by facial gestures, body language, and changes in tone of voice, writers have only words in ink on paper. Somehow the writer has to help us to know whether, for instance, he or she is solemn or joking or joking in earnest.

Consider again the first paragraph of Barbara Ehrenreich's "The 'Playboy' Man and the American Family":

> As a scapegoat for social pathology, feminism ranks with creeping socialism, godless atheism, and other well-known historic threats to public order. We have, in the last decade alone, been accused of causing male impotence, encouraging sexual perversity, and undermining our colorful national tradition of sex roles. In most cases, we're happy to take the credit, but there's one charge that can still make strong women cringe: the accusation that feminism "destroyed the family" or is deeply and wickedly "antifamily" even when we are talking about wholesome domestic issues like child care for working parents or who folds the clothing.

Let's look at this paragraph, sentence by sentence. Ehrenreich *could* have begun,

> It is the view of some people that feminism is no less a cause of evils in our society than is a tendency toward socialism, the loss of religious faith, and other forces that in the course of history have caused harm to the commonweal.

Notice, for a start, the difference between "feminism is no less a cause . . . than is . . ." and Ehrenreich's "feminism ranks with . . ." The verb *ranks* gives her version an energy that the revision, with its colorless *is*, does not have.

The colorless or, we might say, voiceless revision is perhaps something that a reader might encounter in a sociology textbook, but it is not the sort of writing that people willingly read. What are some things that can be said about the voice evident in the original paragraph?

1. The words "social pathology" (roughly, diseases of society) indicate an educated speaker, someone familiar with academic language. The terms "creeping socialism" and "godless atheism" are clichés, words used in past decades by right-wing journalists and speakers. We might for a moment be surprised to find these canned terms in the mouth of an academic speaker, until we realize that they are used jokingly. Since *Ms.* is, roughly speaking, a liberal publication (at least so far as right-wingers see it), the words must be used ironically. In fact, even if the essay had not appeared in *Ms.*, a reader would know that the writer is being ironic; anyone who today uses these old-fashioned words must be speaking with tongue in cheek.

2. In the second sentence when the speaker says "We have . . . been accused," by "we" she of course means women who are feminists — women such as those who read *Ms.* — and so she is establishing a comforting bond between herself and her readers. This bond is strengthened when she lists the (in her view) absurd charges that she and her readers have been accused of — causing "male impotence, [and] encouraging sexual perversity. . . ." In the words "undermining our colorful national tradition of sex roles" we again hear irony, for feminists find conventional American sex roles oppressive rather than "colorful."

3. In the third sentence, in simple and direct language the speaker further emphasizes the bond with her feminist readers ("In most cases, we're happy to take the credit"), but she also jokes a bit. When she says that one accusation "can still make strong women cringe," she is playfully using a cliché that is commonly used of men ("can make strong men cringe"). But by the end of the paragraph she makes it clear that, for all of her joking, she is serious about serious matters, such as "child care for working parents."

What sort of person is Ms. Ehrenreich? Or, more accurately, what sort of persona does she convey in the essay? (As a person she presumably is many things. She may, for instance, be a loving parent, a careful editor of other people's prose, a good—or a bad—cook, and so on. Since we don't know her, we can't presume to say what sort of person she may be, but we can say what sort of *persona* she conveys in the essay.) But first, how do readers form an impression of a persona? By listening, so to speak, with a third ear, listening for the writer's attitude toward 1) himself or herself, 2) the subject, and 3) the audience. Still, different readers will of course respond differently. To take a simple example, readers who do not wish to hear arguments criticizing certain male attitudes will almost surely find the writer of the essay unfair, unwomanly, naive, crude, hysterical, or all of the above. But we think that most readers will agree with us in saying that Ehrenreich conveys the persona of someone who is 1) educated, 2) at least moderately witty, 3) not inclined to put up with nonsense, and 4) eager to address an important issue. It's our guess, too, that Ehrenreich hoped to be seen as this sort of person. If readers of her first paragraph conclude that she is conceited, unfunny, hostile to all men, a liberal who doesn't know what she is talking about, a threat to society, and so on, she has failed terribly, because she has turned her readers away.

There is a lesson for writers, too. When you reread your own drafts and essays, try to get out of yourself and into the mind of an imagined reader, say a classmate. Try to hear how your words will sound in this other person's ear; that is, try to imagine what impression this reader will form of your attitude toward yourself, your subject, and your reader.

2
A READER WRITES

All there is to writing is having ideas. To learn to write is to learn to have ideas.

Robert Frost

So far the only writing that we have suggested you do is in the form of annotating, summarizing, and responding to some basic and some specific questions about the essayist's thesis and methods. All of these activities help you to think about what you are reading. "It is thinking," the philosopher John Locke wrote, "that makes what we read ours." But of course ultimately your thoughts will manifest themselves in your own essays, which probably will take off from one or more of the essays that you have read. Before we discuss writing about more than one essay, let's look at another essay, this one by C. S. Lewis (1898–1963).

Lewis taught English literature at Oxford and at Cambridge, but he is most widely known not for his books on literature but for his books on Christianity (*The Screwtape Letters* is one of the most famous), his children's novels (collected in a seven-volume set called *The Chronicles of Narnia*), and his science fiction (for instance, *Perelandra*). Lewis also wrote autobiographical volumes and many essays on literature and on morality. The essay printed here—the last thing that he wrote—was published in *The Saturday Evening Post* in December 1963, shortly after his death.

C. S. Lewis

We Have No "Right to Happiness"

After all," said Clare, "they had a right to happiness."

We were discussing something that once happened in our own neighborhood. Mr. A. had deserted Mrs. A. and got his divorce in order to marry Mrs. B., who had likewise got her divorce in order to marry Mr. A. And there was certainly no doubt that Mr. A. and Mrs. B. were very much in love with one another. If they continued to be in love, and if nothing went wrong with their health or their income, they might reasonably expect to be very happy.

It was equally clear that they were not happy with their old partners. Mrs. B. had adored her husband at the outset. But then he got smashed up in the war. It was thought he had lost his virility, and it was known that he had lost his job. Life with him was no longer what Mrs. B. had bargained for. Poor Mrs. A., too. She had lost her looks—and all her liveliness. It might be true, as some said, that she consumed herself by bearing his children and nursing him through the long illness that overshadowed their earlier married life.

You mustn't, by the way, imagine that A. was the sort of man who nonchalantly threw a wife away like the peel of an orange he'd sucked dry. Her suicide was a terrible shock to him. We all knew this, for he told us so himself. "But what could I do?" he said. "A man has a right to happiness. I had to take my one chance when it came."

I went away thinking about the concept of a "right to happiness."

At first this sounds to me as odd as a right to good luck. For I believe—whatever one school of moralists may say—that we depend for a very great deal of our happiness or misery on circumstances outside all human control. A right to happiness doesn't, for me, make much more sense than a right to be six feet tall, or to have a millionaire for your father, or to get good weather whenever you want to have a picnic.

I can understand a right as a freedom guaranteed me by the laws of the society I live in. Thus, I have a right to travel along the public roads because society gives me that freedom; that's what we mean by calling the roads "public." I can also understand a right as a claim guaranteed me by the laws, and correlative to an obligation on someone else's part. If I have a right to receive £100 from you, this is another way of saying that you have a duty to pay me £100. If the laws allow Mr. A. to desert his wife and seduce his neighbor's wife, then, by definition, Mr. A. has a legal right to do so, and we need bring in no talk about "happiness."

But of course that was not what Clare meant. She meant that he had not only a legal but a moral right to act as he did. In other words, Clare is—or would be if she thought it out—a classical moralist after the style of Thomas Aquinas, Grotius, Hooker and Locke. She believes that behind the laws of the state there is a Natural Law.[1]

---

[1] **Thomas Aquinas . . . Natural Law** Lewis names some philosophers and theologians from the thirteenth through the eighteenth century who believed that certain basic moral principles are evident to rational people in all periods and in all cultures. (Editors' note)

I agree with her. I hold this conception to be basic to all civilization. Without it, the actual laws of the state become an absolute, as in Hegel. They cannot be criticized because there is no norm against which they should be judged.

The ancestry of Clare's maxim, "They have a right to happiness," is august. In words that are cherished by all civilized men, but especially by Americans, it has been laid down that one of the rights of man is a right to "the pursuit of happiness." And now we get to the real point.

What did the writers of that august declaration mean?

It is quite certain what they did not mean. They did not mean   12
that man was entitled to pursue happiness by any and every means—including, say, murder, rape, robbery, treason and fraud. No society could be built on such a basis.

They meant "to pursue happiness by all lawful means"; that is, by all means which the Law of Nature eternally sanctions and which the laws of the nation shall sanction.

Admittedly this seems at first to reduce their maxim to the tautology that men (in pursuit of happiness) have a right to do whatever they have a right to do. But tautologies, seen against their proper historical context, are not always barren tautologies. The declaration is primarily a denial of the political principles which long governed Europe: a challenge flung down to the Austrian and Russian empires, to England before the Reform Bills, to Bourbon France.[2] It demands that whatever means of pursuing happiness are lawful for any should be lawful for all; that "man," not men of some particular caste, class, status or religion, should be free to use them. In a century when this is being unsaid by nation after nation and party after party, let us not call it a barren tautology.

But the question as to what means are "lawful"—what methods of pursuing happiness are either morally permissible by the Law of Nature or should be declared legally permissible by the legislature of a particular nation—remains exactly where it did. And on that question I disagree with Clare. I don't think it is obvious that people have the unlimited "right to happiness" which she suggests.

For one thing, I believe that Clare, when she says "happiness,"   16
means simply and solely "sexual happiness." Partly because women like Clare never use the word "happiness" in any other sense. But

[2] **England . . . France** England before the bills that liberalized representation in Parliament in the nineteenth century, and France before the French Revolution of 1789–99 (Editors' note)

also because I never heard Clare talk about the "right" to any other kind. She was rather leftist in her politics, and would have been scandalized if anyone had defended the actions of a ruthless man-eating tycoon on the ground that his happiness consisted in making money and he was pursuing his happiness. She was also a rabid teetotaler; I never heard her excuse an alcoholic because he was happy when he was drunk.

A good many of Clare's friends, and especially her female friends, often felt—I've heard them say so—that their own happiness would be perceptibly increased by boxing her ears. I very much doubt if this would have brought her theory of a right to happiness into play.

Clare, in fact, is doing what the whole western world seems to me to have been doing for the last forty-odd years. When I was a youngster, all the progressive people were saying, "Why all this prudery? Let us treat sex just as we treat all our other impulses." I was simple-minded enough to believe they meant what they said. I have since discovered that they meant exactly the opposite. They meant that sex was to be treated as no other impulse in our nature has ever been treated by civilized people. All the others, we admit, have to be bridled. Absolute obedience to your instinct for self-preservation is what we call cowardice; to your acquisitive impulse, avarice. Even sleep must be resisted if you're a sentry. But every unkindness and breach of faith seems to be condoned provided that the object aimed at is "four bare legs in a bed."

It is like having a morality in which stealing fruit is considered wrong—unless you steal nectarines.

And if you protest against this view you are usually met with 20 chatter about the legitimacy and beauty and sanctity of "sex" and accused of harboring some Puritan prejudice against it as something disreputable or shameful. I deny the charge. Foam-born Venus . . . golden Aphrodite . . . Our Lady of Cyprus[3] . . . I never breathed a word against you. If I object to boys who steal my nectarines, must I be supposed to disapprove of nectarines in general? Or even of boys in general? It might, you know, be stealing that I disapproved of.

The real situation is skillfully concealed by saying that the question of Mr. A.'s "right" to desert his wife is one of "sexual morality."

---

[3] **Foam-born Venus . . . Aphrodite . . . Cyprus** The Roman goddess Venus was identified with the Greek goddess of love, Aphrodite. Aphrodite sprang from the foam (*aphros*), and was especially worshipped in Cyprus. (Editors' note)

Robbing an orchard is not an offense against some special morality called "fruit morality." It is an offense against honesty. Mr. A.'s action is an offense against good faith (to solemn promises), against gratitude (toward one to whom he was deeply indebted) and against common humanity.

Our sexual impulses are thus being put in a position of preposterous privilege. The sexual motive is taken to condone all sorts of behavior which, if it had any other end in view, would be condemned as merciless, treacherous and unjust.

Now though I see no good reason for giving sex this privilege, I think I see a strong cause. It is this.

It is part of the nature of a strong erotic passion—as distinct from   24
a transient fit of appetite—that it makes more towering promises than any other emotion. No doubt all our desires make promises, but not so impressively. To be in love involves the almost irresistible conviction that one will go on being in love until one dies, and that possession of the beloved will confer, not merely frequent ecstasies, but settled, fruitful, deep-rooted, lifelong happiness. Hence *all* seems to be at stake. If we miss this chance we shall have lived in vain. At the very thought of such a doom we sink into fathomless depths of self-pity.

Unfortunately these promises are found often to be quite untrue. Every experienced adult knows this to be so as regards all erotic passions (except the one he himself is feeling at the moment). We discount the world-without-end pretensions of our friends' amours easily enough. We know that such things sometimes last—and sometimes don't. And when they do last, this is not because they promised at the outset to do so. When two people achieve lasting happiness, this is not solely because they are great lovers but because they are also—I must put it crudely—good people; controlled, loyal, fairminded, mutually adaptable people.

If we establish a "right to (sexual) happiness" which supersedes all the ordinary rules of behavior, we do so not because of what our passion shows itself to be in experience but because of what it professes to be while we are in the grip of it. Hence, while the bad behavior is real and works miseries and degradations, the happiness which was the object of the behavior turns out again and again to be illusory. Everyone (except Mr. A. and Mrs. B.) knows that Mr. A. in a year or so may have the same reason for deserting his new wife as for deserting his old. He will feel again that all is at stake. He will see himself again as the great lover, and his pity for himself will exclude all pity for the woman.

Two further points remain.

One is this. A society in which conjugal infidelity is tolerated   28
must always be in the long run a society adverse to women. Women,
whatever a few male songs and satires may say to the contrary, are
more naturally monogamous than men; it is a biological necessity.
Where promiscuity prevails, they will therefore always be more often
the victims than the culprits. Also, domestic happiness is more
necessary to them than to us. And the quality by which they most
easily hold a man, their beauty, decreases every year after they have
come to maturity, but this does not happen to those qualities of
personality—women don't really care twopence about our *looks*—
by which we hold women. Thus in the ruthless war of promiscuity
women are at a double disadvantage. They play for higher stakes
and are also more likely to lose. I have no sympathy with moralists
who frown at the increasing crudity of female provocativeness.
These signs of desperate competition fill me with pity.

Secondly, though the "right to happiness" is chiefly claimed for
the sexual impulse, it seems to me impossible that the matter should
stay there. The fatal principle, once allowed in that department, must
sooner or later seep through our whole lives. We thus advance
toward a state of society in which not only each man but every impulse in each man claims *carte blanche*.[4] And then, though our technological skill may help us survive a little longer, our civilization
will have died at heart, and will—one dare not even add
"unfortunately"—be swept away.

Responding to an Essay

After you have read Lewis's essay at least twice, you may want to
jot down your responses to the basic questions that we introduced
on page 17 and reprinted on page 22 after Barbara Ehrenreich's essay.
Here they are yet again, slightly abbreviated:

1. What is the writer's thesis?
2. How does the writer support the thesis?
3. What is the writer's purpose?
4. How does the writer shape the purpose to the audience?
5. What is the writer's tone?
6. How successful is the piece? What are its strengths and weak-
    nesses?

---

[4] *carte blanche* full permission to act (French for "blank card") [Editors' note]

And here, to help you to think further about Lewis's essay, are some specific questions:

1. Having read the entire essay, look back at Lewis's first five paragraphs and point out the ways in which he is not merely recounting an episode but is already conveying his attitude and seeking to persuade.
2. Lewis argues that we do not have a "right to (sexual) happiness." What *duty* or *duties* do we have, according to Lewis?
3. In paragraph 25 Lewis writes:

   When two people achieve lasting happiness, this is not solely because they are great lovers but because they are also—I must put it crudely—good people; controlled, loyal, fairminded, mutually adaptable people.

   If you know of a couple who in your opinion have achieved "lasting happiness," do you agree with Lewis's view that their achievement is largely due to the fact that they are "good people"?
4. Evaluate Lewis's comment in paragraph 28 on the differences between men and women.

If you find yourself roughing out responses to any of these questions, you may be on the way toward writing a first draft of an essay.

The Writing Process

An essay is a response to experience. J. H. Plumb saw (or says that he saw) a busload of people and was prompted to think about them and ultimately to write an essay on the family (page 7); Barbara Ehrenreich heard people complaining about feminism and was prompted to write a response (page 19); C. S. Lewis heard (or says that he heard) someone utter a comment about a right to happiness, and he was set to thinking and then to writing about it (page 28). Their essays came out of their experience. By "experience" we do not mean only what they actually saw (since we can suspect that Plumb and Lewis may have invented the episodes they use at the start of their essays); their experience included things they had read about and had reflected on. After all, Plumb's bus, Ehrenreich's report of antifeminist objections, and Lewis's report of Clare's remark were at most only triggers, so to speak. A good deal of previous experience a good deal of later experience, chiefly in the form of reading and of thinking about what they had read, went into the production of their essays.

In short, writers record their responses to experience. You have been actively reading their responses—engaging in a dialogue with these authors—and so you have been undergoing your own experiences. You have things to say, though on any given topic you probably are not yet certain of *all* that you have to say or of how you can best say it. You need to get further ideas, to do further thinking. How do you get ideas? The short answer is that you will get ideas if you engage in an imagined dialogue with the authors whom you are reading. When you read an essay you will find yourself asking such questions as: What evidence supports this assertion? Is the writer starting from assumptions with which I don't agree? Why do I especially like (or dislike) this essay?

Many writers—professionals as well as students—have found it useful to get their responses down on paper, either as annotations in the margins or as entries in a journal, or both. Here, as a sample, are the annotations that one student jotted next to Lewis's third and fourth paragraphs.

It was equally clear that they were not happy with their old partners. Mrs. B. had adored her husband at the outset. But then he got smashed up in the war. It was thought he had lost his virility, and it was known that he had lost his job. Life with him was no longer what Mrs. B. had bargained for. Poor Mrs. A., too. She had lost her looks—and all her liveliness. It might be true, as some said, that she consumed herself by bearing his children and nursing him through the long illness that overshadowed their earlier married life.

Loaded word. Makes her too calculating

These examples are caricatures. They really defeat L's purpose.

You mustn't, by the way, imagine that A. was the sort of man who nonchalantly threw a wife away like the peel of an orange he'd sucked dry. Her suicide was a terrible shock to him. We all knew this, for he told us so himself. "But what could I do?" he said. "A man has a right to happiness. I had to take my one chance when it came."

Is CSL making him too awful?

Annotations of this sort often are the starting point for entries in a journal.

Keeping a Journal

A journal is not a diary, a record of what the writer did during the
day ("Today I read Lewis's "We Have No 'Right to Happiness'");
rather, a journal is a place to store some of the thoughts that you
may have scribbled on a bit of paper or in the margin of the text—
for instance, your initial response to the title of an essay or to something you particularly liked or disliked. It is also a place to jot down
further reflections. You can record your impressions as they come
to you in any order—almost as though you are talking to yourself.
Since no one else is going to read your notes, you can be entirely
free and at ease. The student whose annotations we reproduced a
moment ago wrote the following entry in his journal:

```
I find Lewis's writing is very clear and in its way
persuasive, but I also think that his people--A and
B and Clare--are not real people. They are almost
caricatures. Anyway, he certainly has chosen people
(or invented them?) who help him make his case. What
if Mrs. B's husband had been a wife-beater, or maybe
someone who molested their daughter? Would Lewis
still think Mrs. B was wrong to leave Mr. B?
```

A second student wrote a rather different entry in her journal:

```
Lewis at first seems to be arguing against a "right
to happiness," but really he is arguing against
adultery and divorce, against what we can call the
Playboy morality. He's talking about what Barbara
Ehrenreich talked about when she said that in the
Playboy world if a man "divorces his middle-aged
wife for some sweet young thing, he may be viewed
not as a traitor to the American way, but as a man
who has a demonstrated capacity for growth."
```

Here is a third entry:

```
Terrific. That story about A and B really got to me.
But is it true? Does it matter if it isn't true?
Probably not; there are people like the As and the
Bs. Lewis really is awfully good at holding my in-
terest. And I was really grabbed by that business
about a right to happiness being as strange as a
right to be six feet tall. But my question is this:
```

```
I agree that we don't have a right to be six feet
tall, but why, then, do we have any rights? Lewis
talks about Natural Law, but what is that? Is the
idea of one husband and one wife "Natural Law"? If
so, how come so many societies don't obey it? When
Bertrand Russell talks about natural instincts and
emotions "which we inherit from our animal ances-
tors," is this like Natural Law?

Still, I think Lewis is terrific. And I think he is
probably right about the difference between men and
women. It seems obvious to me that men care more
about a woman's looks than women care about a man's
looks. How can this be checked?)
```

You might even make a journal entry in the form of a letter to the author or in the form of a dialogue. Or you might have Mr. A. and Mrs. B. give *their* versions of the story that Clare reports.

Questioning the Text Again

We have already suggested that one way to increase your understanding of an essay and to get ideas that you may use in an essay of your own is to ask questions of the selection that you have read. Let's begin by thinking about the questions we asked following C. S. Lewis's "We Have No 'Right to Happiness'" (page 33). All of these could provide topics for your own essays. Some were questions that might be asked of any essay, you'll recall—about the author's thesis, the way in which the author supports the thesis, the author's purpose, the author's persona or tone, and your evaluation of the essay. And there were questions specifically about Lewis's essay, concerning Lewis's comments on rights and his comments about the differences between men and women.

Probably the most obvious topic for an essay such as Lewis's is

What is the author's thesis, and how sound is it?

One student formulated the thesis as follows:

```
We not only do not have a "right" to sexual hap-
piness, but we probably cannot achieve lasting
happiness if we allow sex to govern behavior that
```

otherwise "would be condemned as merciless, treacherous and unjust."

An essay concerning Lewis's thesis might be narrowed, for example to

> Does Lewis give a one-sided view of divorce?

or

> Does Lewis underestimate (or overestimate) the importance of sexual satisfaction?

But other topics easily come to mind, for instance:

1. Lewis's methods as a writer
2. The logic of Lewis's argument

Take the first of these three, Lewis's methods, a topic of special interest if you are trying to become a better writer. One student who planned to write about this topic made the following notes.

Jottings and Lists

(Parenthetic numbers refer to Lewis's paragraphs.)

1. purpose is obviously to persuade. How does he do it?

2. very informal manner
   a) begins by telling of a conversation he had (1)
   b) often uses "I"; for instance, "I went away thinking"
            (5); "this sounds to me" (6); "I can understand" (7); "I was simple-minded enough to believe" (18). So the tone is personal, as if he and the reader were having a conversation.

3. though informal, seems very educated
   a) cites authorities, apparently philosophers, in parag. 8 (check these names); refers to

Austrian, Russian, English, and French history (14)
   b) educated vocabulary ("tautologies" in parag. 14)

4. but also uses easy examples: Mr and Mrs A and Mr and Mrs B in first paragraph; stealing fruit (19-21)

5. makes the abstract clear by being concrete. In parag. 18, when he says that our impulses have to be controlled, he says, "Absolute obedience to your instinct for self-preservation is what we call cowardice. . . ."

6. sentences are all clear. Some are very short ("I agree with her," 9), but even the long sentences--several lines of type--are clear. Give one (or maybe two) examples?

7. in next to last parag, frankly speaks as a male: "domestic happiness is more necessary to them [that is, women] than to us." And "the quality by which they [that is women] most easily hold a man," and "women don't really care twopence about our looks" (all in 28). Sense of a man talking heart-to-heart to men. But how might it strike a woman? Sexist? Ask Jane and Tina.

You may prefer to record your thoughts in the form of lists:

```
methods
     examples
     anecdote about A and B (par. 1)
     stealing fruit (19-21)
informal style
     uses "I" (many places)
     also uses "we"
clear sentences (give examples)
vocabulary
     usually simple words
     a few hard words ("tautologies" in 14)
beginning: an individual listening
end: rather authoritative; generalizes about men vs
women
```

Further thinking and further readings of Lewis's essay, produced more evidence, and of course the material then had to be reorganized into a clear and effective sequence, but these notes and lists were highly promising. The student who wrote them was well on the way to writing a strong first draft.

After converting his notes into a draft, and then revising the draft, an interesting—yet rather common—thing happened. The student found himself dissatisfied with his point. He now felt that he wanted to say something rather different. The annotations and the drafts, it turned out, were a way of helping him to get to a deeper response to Lewis's essay, and so he rewrote his essay, changing his focus. But we are getting ahead of our story.

Getting Ready to Write a Draft

After jotting down notes (and further notes stimulated by rereading and further thinking) you probably will be able to formulate a tentative thesis, a point, such as "Lewis argues with great skill," or "Lewis does not make clear the concept of Natural Law," or "Lewis generalizes too freely," or "Lewis has a narrow idea of why people divorce." At this point most writers find it useful to clear the air by glancing over their preliminary notes and by jotting down the thesis and a few especially promising notes—brief statements of what they think their key points may be. These notes may include some key quotations that the writer thinks will help support the thesis.

Draft of an Essay

On "We Have No 'Right to Happiness'"

When I first read the title of C. S. Lewis's essay I was interested and also somewhat resistant. Without having given much thought to it, I believe that I do have a right to happiness. I don't want to give up this right or this belief. Still I was intrigued to know what Lewis has to say. After reading the essay it seemed entirely reasonable to say that

if there is a right to happiness there are also
limits to it. So I decided to look at how Lewis
managed to make me change my mind, at least part
way.

C. S. Lewis is persuasive especially because of
three things. First, although Lewis (a professor) is
obviously very learned, he uses an informal manner
that sounds very natural and honest. Second, he
gives clear examples. Three, his sentences are always clear. This is true even when they are not especially short. All of these things combine together
to make his essay clear and interesting. Lewis is an
Englishman, not an American.

Lewis's informal manner, especially seen in his
use of the first person pronoun, appears right away.
In the second sentence, when he says "We were discussing something. . . ." He uses "I" in the fifth
paragraph and in many later paragraphs.

Another sign of Lewis's informality is his use
of such expressions as "It might be true, as some
said," and "You mustn't, by the way, imagine," and
"for one thing." It sounds like an ordinary person
talking, even though Lewis also mentions the names
of philosophers in paragraph 8, and in paragraph 14
mentions several historical matters.

Next I will deal with Lewis's examples. The examples help him to be clear to the reader. The essay
begins with a story about four people. Two said they

had a "right to happiness." In this story Lewis lets us see two people (Mr. A and Mrs. B) who behave very badly. They justify their behavior simply by saying they have a right to happiness. They behave so badly--Mr. A deserts the wife who nursed him through a long illness, and Mrs. B deserts her husband, who is a wounded veteran--that just to hear them talk about a "right to happiness" is almost enough to make you say they should not be happy and they certainly do not have a right to happiness. The example of Mr. and Mrs. A and Mr. and Mrs. B is the longest example that Lewis gives, but Lewis several times gives short examples. These short examples make his point clear. For instance, when he wants to show how silly it is to treat sex differently from all other impulses, he says that it is "like having a morality in which stealing fruit is considered wrong--unless you steal nectarines."

Another thing Lewis does to persuade the reader is to write very clear sentences. Some of his sentences are long--about three lines of print--but the reader has no trouble with them. Here is an example of this sort of sentence.

A right to happiness doesn't, for me, make much more sense than a right to be six feet tall, or to have a millionaire for your father, or to get good weather whenever you want to have a picnic.

```
        The only thing that causes any trouble is a

few unfamiliar words such as "tautologies" (para-

graph 14) and "tycoon" (paragraph 16), but you can

understand the essay even without looking up such

words.
```

Revising and Editing a Draft

To write a good essay you must be a good reader not only of the essay you are writing about but also of the essay you yourself are writing. We're not talking about proofreading or correcting spelling errors, though of course you must engage in those activities as well.

Revising. In revising their work, writers ask themselves such questions as

Do I mean what I say?
Do I say what I mean? (Answering this question will cause you to ask yourself such questions as: Do I need to define my terms, add examples to clarify, reorganize the material so that a reader can grasp it?)

During this part of the process of writing, you do your best to read the draft in a skeptical frame of mind. In taking account of your doubts, you will probably unify, organize, clarify, and polish the draft.

1. **Unity** is achieved partly by eliminating irrelevancies. In the second paragraph of the draft, for example, the writer says that "Lewis is an Englishman, not an American," but the fact that Lewis is English is not clearly relevant to the student's argument that Lewis writes persuasively. The statement should be deleted—or its relevance should be demonstrated.
2. **Organization** is largely a matter of arranging material into a sequence that will assist the reader to grasp the point. If you reread your draft and jot down a paragraph outline of the sort shown on page 15, you can then see if the draft has a reasonable organization, a structure that will let the reader move easily from the beginning to the end.

3. **Clarity** is achieved largely by providing concrete details, examples, and quotations to support generalizations and by providing helpful transitions ("for instance," "furthermore," "on the other hand," "however").

4. **Polish** is small-scale revision. For instance, one deletes unnecessary repetitions. In the first sentence of the second paragraph, "C. S. Lewis" can effectively be changed to "Lewis"—there really is no need to repeat his initials—and in the second sentence of the second paragraph "Lewis" can be changed to "he." Similarly, in polishing, a writer combines choppy sentences into longer sentences and breaks overly long sentences into shorter sentences.

Editing. After producing a draft that seems good enough to show to someone, writers engage in yet another activity. They edit; that is, they check the accuracy of quotations by comparing them with the original, check a dictionary for the spelling of doubtful words, check a handbook for doubtful punctuation—for instance, whether a comma or a semicolon is needed in a particular sentence.

A Revised Draft

Persuasive Strategies in C. S. Lewis's
~~On~~ "We Have No 'Right to Happiness'"

When I first read the title of C. S. Lewis's essay I was interested and also somewhat resistant. Without having given much thought to it, I believe that I do have a right to happiness. I don't want to give up this right or this belief. Still I was intrigued to know what Lewis has to say. After reading the essay it seemed entirely reasonable to say that if there is a right to happiness there are also limits to it. So I decided to look at how Lewis managed to make me change my mind, at least part way.

C. S. Lewis's "We Have No 'Right to Happiness'" is surprisingly persuasive — "surprisingly" because I believe in the right to happiness, which is mentioned in the Declaration of Independence. Lewis, an Englishman writing in an American magazine, probably knew he was facing an audience who did not hold his view, and he apparently decided to begin by stating his position as directly as possible in his title: "We Have No 'Right to Happiness'." How does he win his reader over?

C. S. Lewis is persuasive because in addition to thinking carefully he writes effectively. Three features of his writing especially contribute to his effectiveness.

~~C. S. Lewis is persuasive especially because of three things.~~ First, although Lewis (a professor) is obviously very learned, he uses an informal manner that ~~sounds very natural and honest.~~ *helps to establish a bond between him and his reader.* Second, he gives clear examples. ~~Three~~, *Third,* his sentences are always clear, ~~This is true~~ even when they are not especially short. All of these things combine ~~together~~ to make his essay clear and interesting. ~~Lewis is an Englishman, not an American.~~

Lewis's informal manner, especially seen in his use of the first person pronoun, appears right away/ ~~In~~ *in* the second sentence, when he says "We were discussing something. . . ." He uses "I" in the fifth paragraph and in many later paragraphs.

Another sign of Lewis's informality is his use of such expressions as "It might be true, as some said," and "You mustn't, by the way, imagine," and "for one thing." It sounds like an ordinary person talking, even though Lewis also mentions the names of philosophers in paragraph 8, and in paragraph 14 mentions several historical matters.

~~Next I will deal with~~ *As for* Lewis's examples~~,~~/. ~~The~~ *which* ~~examples~~ help him to be clear, ~~to the reader. The~~ *the story of Mr. + Mrs. A and* ~~essay begins with a story about four people.~~ *Mr. + Mrs. B is a good illustration.* ~~Two~~ *Mr. A and Mrs. B,* *both of whom believed they* said they_ had a "right to happiness~~,~~/;" ~~In this story Lewis lets us see two people (Mr. A and Mrs. B) who~~ behave very badly. ~~They justify their behavior simply by saying they have a right to happiness.~~ They behave so badly--Mr. A deserts the wife who nursed him through a long illness, and Mrs. B deserts her husband, who is a wounded veteran--that just to hear them talk about a "right to happiness" is almost enough to make you ~~say they should not be happy and they certainly do not have a right to happiness~~ *doubt that there can be such a right.* The example of Mr. and Mrs. A and Mr. and Mrs. B is the longest example that Lewis gives, but ~~Lewis~~ *he* several times gives short examples~~,~~/ ~~These short examples~~ *that* make his point clear. For instance, when he wants to show how silly it is to treat sex differently from all other impulses, he says that it is "like having a morality in which stealing fruit is considered wrong--unless you steal nectarines."

Lewis's third persuasive technique

~~Another thing Lewis does to persuade the reader~~
is to write very clear sentences. Some of his sentences are long--about three lines of print--but the
reader has no trouble with them. Here is an example
of this sort of sentence.

A right to happiness doesn't, for me, make much
more sense than a right to be six feet tall, or
to have a millionaire for your father, or to get
good weather whenever you want to have a picnic.

*The sentence is fairly long, partly because
the second half gives three examples, but
because these examples are given in a
parallel construction ("to be," "or to have,"
"or to get") the reader easily follows the
thought.*

True,
~~The only thing that causes any trouble is~~ a few
unfamiliar words such as "tautologies" (paragraph
14) and "tycoon" (paragraph 16), *may cause a bit of trouble* but ~~you~~ can under-
a reader
stand the essay even without looking up such words.

*Of course Lewis has not absolutely proved
that there is no "right to happiness," but
he has made a good, clear case. The
clarity, in fact, is part of the case.
Everything that Lewis says here seems so
obvious that a reader is almost persuaded
by Lewis's voice alone.*

Rethinking the Thesis: Preliminary Notes

You'll probably agree that the student improved his draft, for instance by deleting the original first paragraph and replacing it with a more focused paragraph. But, as we mentioned earlier, when the student thought further about his revision he was still dissatisfied with it because he no longer fully believed his thesis.

He found that although he continued to admire Lewis's persuasive techniques, he remained unpersuaded by Lewis's argument. He therefore felt obliged to change the thesis of his essay from (approximately) "Lewis's chief persuasive techniques are . . ." to "Although Lewis is highly skilled as a persuasive writer, even his rhetorical skill cannot overcome certain weaknesses in his thesis."

Here are some of the annotations that the student produced after he recognized his dissatisfaction with his revised draft.

Mr. and Mrs. A and B may or may not be real people,
    but they certainly <u>seem</u> UNREAL: too neatly
    suited (all good or bad) to L's purpose.

> <u>The villains</u>: Mr. A (he tosses out his
> wife after she loses her looks, despite
> the fact that she wore herself out with
> his children and nursed him through long
> illness; even after wife commits suicide
> he doesn't see that he continues to talk
> selfishly); Mrs. B (she leaves her hus-
> band when he gets wounded and he loses
> his "virility" and loses his job). Aren't
> these people a bit too awful? Are they
> really typical of people who divorce?
>
> <u>The heroes--or saints</u>? Mrs. A (nursed
> husband through long illness, wore self
> out with the children); Mr. B (injured in
> war; loses job).

> CLARE: she also seems too suited to CSL's the-
> sis; she's pretty terrible, and stupid too

LEWIS ON DIVORCE: he seems to think it is always
    motivated by a desire for sex, and that it is

always wrong. But what if a husband abuses his
wife--maybe physically, or maybe verbally and emotionally. Maybe chronic alcoholic, refuses treatment, etc. Or what if wife abuses husband--probably
not physically, but verbally, and maybe she assaults
kids. Or take another angle: what if woman married
at too young an age, inexperienced, married to escape from an awful family, and now finds she made a
mistake? Should she stay married to the man for
life? In short, does Lewis see divorce from enough
angles?

First five paragraphs are extremely interesting, but
are unfair for three reasons:

1) Lewis loads the dice, showing us goodies and
   baddies, and then says (par. 5) that they set
   him to thinking about the "right to
   happiness";
2) he overemphasizes the importance of sex,
   neglects other possible reasons why people
   divorce;
3) his discussion of "natural law," is not
   convincing to me. I simply am not convinced that there is a "Law of Nature"
   that "eternally sanctions" certain
   things.

SEXIST??? Although CSL seems to be defending women
(esp. par. 28, in which he says that promiscuity
puts women at a double disadvantage), there is something sort of sexist in the essay, and I imagine
that this will turn off women, and maybe even men.
I know that I'm a little bothered by it.

The Final Version

We won't take you through the drafts that the student wrote, but
in reading the final version on page 50 you will notice that although
some of the points from the draft are retained, the thesis, as we said,
has shifted. Notice, for instance, that the first paragraph of the revised draft is used in the final version but with two significant

changes: in the first sentence the student now adds that he finds Lewis's essay "finally unconvincing," and in the last sentence of the paragraph he implies that he will discuss why the essay is "not finally convincing."

Jim Weinstein
Professor Valdez
English Composition 12
2 February 1992

Style and Argument:
An Examination of C. S. Lewis's
"We Have No 'Right to Happiness'"

   C. S. Lewis's "We Have No 'Right to Happiness'" is, though finally unconvincing, surprisingly persuasive--"surprisingly" because I believe in the right to happiness, which is mentioned in the Declaration of Independence. Lewis, an Englishman writing in an American magazine, probably knew he was facing an audience who did not hold his view, and he apparently decided to begin by stating his position as directly as possible in his title: "We Have No 'Right to Happiness.'"[1] How does he nearly win his reader over? And why is he not finally convincing?

---

   [1]Lewis's essay appears in Marcia Stubbs and Sylvan Barnet, eds., The Little, Brown Reader, 6th ed. (HarperCollins, 1993), pp 28-33. All quotations are from this source.

Lewis is highly (though not entirely) persuasive because he writes effectively. Three features of his writing especially contribute to his effectiveness. First, although Lewis (a professor) is obviously very learned, he uses an informal manner that helps to establish a bond between him and his reader. Second, he gives clear examples. Third, his sentences are always clear, even when they are not especially short. All of these things combine to make his essay clear and interesting--and almost convincing.

His informal manner, especially his use of the first-person pronouns, appears right away in the second sentence, when he says "We were discussing something. . . ." He uses "I" in the fifth paragraph and in many later paragraphs. Another sign of his informality is his use of such expressions as "It might be true, as some said," and "You mustn't, by the way, imagine." It sounds like an ordinary person talking.

Most of his examples, too, seem ordinary. They make his points seem almost obvious. For instance, when he wants to show how silly it is to treat sex differently from all other impulses, he says that it is "like having a morality in which stealing fruit is considered wrong--unless you steal nectarines" (p. 31). The touch of humor drives the point home.

Still, although Lewis seems thoughtful, and he makes his argument very clear, the essay somehow

does not finally persuade. The trouble may largely
be Mr. and Mrs. A and B, but there are other
difficulties too.

Mr. and Mrs. A and B are just too simple a
case, too neat an illustration. Lewis of course
wanted to make a clear-cut case, but a reader does
not really believe in these people. They are caricatures: Mr. A tosses out his wife after she loses
her looks (and she lost them not only through the
natural process of aging but through taking care of
the family), and Mrs. B leaves her husband, a
wounded veteran. Of course it is conceivable that
there really were a Mr. A and a Mrs. B, but surely
the pros and cons of divorce ought not to be based
on cases like this, where it is so clear that Mr. A
and Mrs. B are irresponsible. They are, one might
say, as morally stupid as Clare is. But the fact
that these people are selfish and stupid and that
they each get a divorce does not prove that only
selfish and stupid people seek divorce.

Nor do the experiences of the A's and the B's
show that people who seek a divorce always are
seeking sexual pleasure. We can imagine, for instance, a woman married to a wife-beater. Does she
not have a right to be free of her abusive husband, a "right to happiness"? Nor need we limit our
case to physical abuse. A husband (or a wife) can
abuse a spouse verbally and emotionally and can

be impossibly neglectful of the children. Or we
can imagine a couple who married when very young--
perhaps partly for the sake of defying their parents, or maybe in order to escape from a bad family
situation. In any case, we can imagine that one member of the couple now sees that a bad mistake was
made. Need they stay tied to each other?

Lewis's essay is powerful, partly because
it clearly advances a thesis that must seem strange
to many Americans; and it is interesting, partly
because Lewis makes his points clearly, and he seems
to be such a thoughtful and decent person. But in
the end the essay is not convincing. It is just a
little too simple in its examples and in its suggestion that people who claim a right to happiness
are really just saying that they want to get
divorced so they can live legally with another
sexual partner.

A Brief Overview of the Final Version

1. First, a mechanical matter: The student has added a footnote,
   telling the reader where the essay can be found and explaining
   that all quotations are from this source.
2. The title, though not especially engaging, is informative—more
   so than, say, "On an Essay by C. S. Lewis." Readers know that
   the writer will discuss Lewis's style and argument in a particular essay.
3. The student's final essay is *not* simply a balanced debate, a statement of the pros and cons that remains inconclusive. Rather,

the student argues a thesis: Although Lewis's essay is in some ways admirable, it remains unconvincing.

4. The student's thesis is stated early, in fact in the first paragraph. It's almost always a good idea to let your reader know early where you will be going.

5. Quotations are used as evidence, not as padding. See, for example, paragraphs 3 and 4.

6. The writer has kept his reader in mind. He has not summarized Lewis's essay in needless detail, but, on the other hand, he has not assumed that the reader knows the essay inside out. For instance, he does not simply assert that Mr. A behaves very badly; rather, he reminds us that Mr. A rejects his wife after she loses her looks. When he uses a quotation, he guides the reader to where in Lewis's essay the quotation can be found.

7. He also keeps the reader in mind by using helpful transitions. In paragraph 2 notice "First," "Second," and "Third"; in paragraph 5, "Still" indicates a reversal of direction. Notice, too, that key words and phrases are repeated. Repetition of this sort, like transitions, makes it easy for the reader to follow the writer's train of thought. In the second paragraph, for example, he cites Lewis's "informal manner," as the first of three points of style. His next paragraph begins, "His informal manner. . . ." Similarly, the last sentence of paragraph 3 contains the words "ordinary person." The next paragraph begins, "Most of his examples, too, seem ordinary."

8. So far we have talked about what is in the essay. But what is *not* in it is also worth comment. In the final essay the student does *not* include all of the points he jotted down in his preliminary notes. He does not take up either Natural Law or the issue of sexism, probably because he felt unsure about both. Notes are points of departure; if when you get going you find you are going down a blind alley, don't hesitate to go back and drop the point.

A Checklist for Analyzing and Evaluating an Essay That You Are Writing About

When you read, try to read sympathetically, opening yourself to the writer's vision of things. But when you have finished a sympathetic reading, and an attentive reading, and you have made various sorts of notes, probably including an outline and a summary of the essay you are reading, you are ready to *analyze* the writer's methods and to *evaluate* the piece.

In **analyzing,** you will examine the relationships between the parts; that is, you will ask such questions as:

What is the *topic* of the essay? Try to state it, preferably in writing, as specifically as possible. For example, broadly speaking, one might say that the subject of Lewis's essay is the right to happiness, but within this subject his topic, more specifically, is sexual freedom. Plumb's subject is the family, and his topic is the historical changes that the family has undergone.

What is the essay's *thesis* (either stated or implied)? If you have located a *thesis sentence* in the essay, underline it and write *thesis* in the margin. If the thesis is implied, try to formulate it in a sentence of your own.

What does the title do? What *purpose* does it suggest the writer holds?

What is the function of the opening paragraph (or paragraphs)? What claim on our attention or beliefs does it make?

What speaker or *persona* (see page 6) does the writer create, and how does the writer create it?

What is the tone? Does the tone (page 23) shift as the essay progresses? If so, why?

What *audience* is the writer addressing? The general, literate public, or a more specialized group?

How is the argument set forth? By logic? By drawing on personal experience? What evidence is there that the writer is an authority on the topic? Are there other appeals to authority? What other kinds of evidence support the essay's claim? What are the author's underlying assumptions? Are they stated or implied, and are they acceptable to you, or can you challenge them?

If there is a formal, explicit conclusion, underline or restate it. If the conclusion is not stated, but is implied, what does the writer want us to conclude?

In **evaluating,** you will ask such questions as:

Is the essay as clear as it can be, given the complexity of the material? For instance, do specific examples help to make the generalizations clear? Are crucial terms adequately defined? If the thesis is not explicitly stated, is the essay unclear or is it perhaps better because of the indirectness?

If the conclusion is not stated but implied, why does the writer not
    state it?
Is the argument (if the essay is chiefly an argument) convincing,
    or is it marred by faulty thinking? If statistics are used, are they
    sound and relevant? If authorities are quoted, are they indeed
    authorities (rather than just big names) on this topic?
Is the essay interesting? If so, in what ways, and if not, why not—
    which gets us back to analysis. If there are passages of undis-
    guised argument, for instance, are they clear without being repe-
    titious and boring? Do specific examples clarify and enliven
    general assertions?
If the essay includes narrative or descriptive passages, are they per-
    tinent? Should they have been amplified, or should they have
    been reduced or even deleted?
How is the essay organized? Is the organization effective? Does the
    essay build to a climax?

Another way of thinking about the criteria for evaluating an
essay is this:

Is the essay persuasive (whether because of its logic or because of
    the power of the speaker's personality)? and,
Does the essay give pleasure?

Don't hesitate to demand that an essay give you pleasure. The
author probably thought that he or she was writing well, and certainly hoped to hold your interest throughout the essay and to make
you feel that you were learning something of interest. In short, the
author hoped that you would like the essay. You have every right
to evaluate the essay partly by considering the degree of pleasure
that it affords. Of course, in your essay you cannot simply say that
you enjoyed an essay or that you were bored by it. You will have
to support your assertions with reasons based on evidence. To support your assertions you must have read the writer's words carefully, so we are back to an earlier point: the first thing to do if you
are going to write about a piece of writing is to read it attentively,
pen or pencil in hand.
    As you read and reread the material that you are writing about,
subjecting it to the kinds of questions we have mentioned, your
understanding of it will almost surely deepen. You will probably

come to feel that it is better—or worse—than you had thought at first, or in any case it is somewhat different.

As you prepare to write your own essay, and as you draft it, you are learning, feeling your way toward a considered analysis. All writers are in the position of the little girl who, told by an adult that she should think before she spoke, replied, "How do I know what I think until I say it?" But once having said something— whether in a mental question to yourself or in a note or a draft— you have to evaluate your thought, and improve it if it doesn't stand up under further scrutiny.

3
A WRITER COMPARES VIEWPOINTS

Writing about Opposed Arguments

Your instructor will probably ask you to read more than one essay in some section of this book. The chief reason for such an assignment, of course, is to stimulate you to think about some complex issue. After all, no one essay on any topic of significance can claim to say all that needs to be said about the topic. Essays that advocate similar positions on, say, capital punishment may, because of slightly different emphases, usefully supplement one another; and even two radically opposed essays may both contain material that you find is essential to a thoughtful discussion of the topic.

Let's say that you read an essay supporting the death penalty. Perhaps, as an aid to grasping the author's argument, you prepared a summary of the essay, and you notice that the writer's chief points are these:

1. the death penalty serves as a deterrent
2. justice requires that murderers pay an appropriate price for their crimes.

These basic points probably are supported by some evidence, but you have been reading critically, and you have wondered whether this or that piece of evidence is compelling. You have also wondered if more can't be said on the other side—not only by specific refutation of certain arguments, but perhaps also by arguments that the first essayist has not raised. You turn to a second essayist, someone who opposes the death penalty, and who (you find when you summarize the essay) in effect offers these arguments:

1. the death penalty does not serve as a deterrent
2. if the death penalty is inflicted mistakenly, the error cannot be corrected
3. the death penalty is imposed unequally; statistics indicate that when blacks and whites are guilty of comparable offences, blacks are more likely to be sentenced to death.

It is now evident that the two writers are and are not talking about the same thing. They are talking about the death penalty, but for the most part they are not confronting the same issues. On one issue only, deterrence, do they face each other. On this issue you will want to think hard about the evidence that each offers. Possibly you will decide that one author makes a compelling case at least on this issue, but it is also possible that you will decide that the issue cannot be decided. Or you may find that you can make a better case than did either writer.

Think about the other arguments offered—on the one hand that justice requires the death penalty, and on the other hand that it can be mistakenly inflicted and that it is awarded unequally. You will not only want to think hard about each of these points, but you will also wonder why only one of the two essayists took them up. Is one or the other argument so clearly mistaken that it is not worth discussing? Or is a particular argument one that can't be proved either true of false? Or are the writers working from different *assumptions* (unexamined beliefs). For instance, the writer who argues that the death penalty is capriciously enforced may assume that race prejudice cannot be overcome, whereas a writer who rejects the argument may assume that the courts can and will see to it that the death penalty is imposed impartially. As a critical reader, you will want to be alert to the assumptions that writers make. You'll have to ask yourself often, *What assumption lies beneath this assertion?*— that is, what belief is so firmly held, and is assumed to be so self-evident, that the writer does not bother to assert it? Do I share this assumption? Why?

If you are asked to compare two opposed essays, you will probably want to point out where the two face each other and where they don't. You will probably also want to offer an evaluation of the two. Or, depending on the assignment, you may use the two merely as a point of departure for your own essay on the topic. That is, you may want to draw on one or both—giving credit, of course—and then offer your own argument.

Writing about Essays Less Directly Related

Let's assume that your instructor has asked you to read Plumb's "The Dying Family" (p. 7), Ehrenreich's "The 'Playboy' Man and the American Family" (p. 19), and Lewis's "We Have No 'Right to Happiness'" (p. 28), and has asked you to compare two of the three. These essays all concern family relationships, but they do not take distinctly different positions on a single controversial topic.

Notes and Journal Entries

Let's say that you settle on Plumb and Lewis, specifically on their attitudes toward their material. Perhaps your first thought is that Lewis very obviously offers value judgments, whereas Plumb, as an historian, simply reports what has happened in history.

On rereading the two essays, you may find yourself making notes somewhat like these notes that a student made:

```
1. Some of Plumb's assumptions
      family evolves; history a process (not static,
         not cyclical)
      idea of parents wedded until death no longer
         needed in our urban, industrial society
      happiness not increasing or decreasing

2. I'm surprised to find so many assumptions in
   the writings of a historian. I thought history
   was supposed to be an account, the "story" of
   what happened; in Social Studies we learned
   history is "value-free"

3. Some of Lewis's assumptions
      Lewis very clearly makes assumptions, for in-
      stance belief in the existence of "natural law"
      (parag. 8), and belief that "domestic happiness
      is more necessary to them than to us" (to women,
      than to men), par. 28. Also assumes that women
      don't care much about men's looks (28)--but is
      this true? How might someone be able to prove
      it?

4. Big difference between Plumb and Lewis on as-
   sumptions. I think that Plumb makes assumptions
   but is hardly aware of them, whereas Lewis makes
   them and puts them right upfront. With Lewis we
   know exactly where he stands. For instance, he
   obviously believes that we can use our free will
   to behave in ways that he considers proper. He
   even talks about "good people; controlled,
   loyal, fairminded" (25). (It's hard to imagine
   Plumb talking about "good people"; he only
   talks about whether people are "happy" or
   "stable.") Lewis pretty clearly believes not
   only that it's our job to act decently, but that
   we can act decently. Seems not to accept the
```

idea that we can be overwhelmed by passion or by
the unconscious. Probably very antiFreud. Anyway, his position is clear (and I agree with
it). With Plumb we can hardly argue--at least I
can't--since I'm not a historian. I don't know
if what he says about the past really is true,
but his opening paragraph strikes me as completely made up.

5. Attitudes toward change in family:
For Lewis, a moralist, breakdown of family is a
disaster; for Plumb, a fact of social evolution

One student, whose thoughts were something like those that
we have just presented, wrote two entries in his journal.

Plumb: as I see it, he makes assumptions that pretty
much go against what Lewis is arguing. Plumb looks
at this family in California, and he says they are
happy and he thinks everything is just fine. Well,
maybe not fine, but at least he says that these
children seem "as happy as any children that I have
seen." I'm not so sure they are as happy as most. I
know (from my own experience and from what I hear
from friends) what divorced kids go through. Divorce
may be normal (common, ordinary), but is it right?
It seems to lead to so much unhappiness (for parents
and children). Putting aside my own feelings, I can
certainly see that my parents aren't especially
happy with their new families. But there is Plumb,
with his happy busload. Is he kidding? Or trying to
fool us?

Lewis: Lewis says we have no right to happiness--no
right to divorce, remarry several times, and have
families like that busload of people Plumb talks
about. Lewis seems to be saying that divorce is
morally wrong. Why? What are his reasons? I think he
gives two: 1) it makes people unhappy (for instance,
Mr. B, the wounded veteran, must have been miserable
when Mrs. B left him), and 2) it is against "Natural
Law." But, come to think of it, what is Natural
Law? What makes divorce contrary to Natural Law? Is
it really "unnatural"? Why? Lots of religions--
maybe most of them--accept divorce. And certainly

```
governments accept it. So what makes it unnatural?
What is it that Bertrand Russell said about our
animal instinct? Check this.
```

The next day, after rereading Lewis's essay and the two entries, he wrote two additional entries in his journal:

```
I think that I agree with Lewis that we don't have a
right to happiness, just as we don't have a right to
be rich and handsome. But I wish Lewis had given
some clear reasons instead of just saying that we
have to remain for life with one spouse, even if we
see that we have made a bad choice, because "Natural
Law" tells us that we can't change. Come to think of
it, Lewis does give some reasons against giving sex
a special privilege: we hurt others, and we kid our-
selves if we think each passion will last.
```

```
Both Lewis and Plumb use short stories to make their
points: Plumb's busload of Californians, Lewis's Mr
and Mrs A and Mr and Mrs B. Suppose these stories
aren't true, and Lewis and Plumb made these stories
up. Does that matter?
```

The Final Version

Drawing on this material, the student drafted and revised an essay and then submitted it to peer review. Then, in the light of the comments and further thinking, he wrote the final version, which we give here. Our marginal comments summarize some of the strengths that we find in the finished essay. (*Note:* The original essay was, of course, double-spaced.)

Title gives a clue to topic

```
          Two Ways of Thinking
          about Today's Families
```

Opening paragraph names authors and essays, and indicates thesis—that the essays strongly differ

```
     J. H. Plumb in "The Dying Family"
and C. S. Lewis in "We Have No 'Right
to Happiness'" both note that today's
families often consist of adults who
have been divorced. But that is about
as much as they would agree on. Judg-
ing from an example Plumb gives of a
minibus with ten happy children, none
```

of whom had both parents in common, Plumb thinks there is no reason to regret, much less to condemn, the behavior that presumably has produced this sort of family. And judging from the examples Lewis gives of Mrs. B who left her wounded husband and of Mr. A who left his worn-out wife, Lewis thinks that the pursuit of happiness--sexual happiness at the expense of marriage--is immoral.

Clear transition ("Despite these great differences")

Details support generalization

Despite these great differences, there are interesting similarities in the essays. The essays are both by Englishmen, are about the same length, were both written around the middle of the twentieth century, and both begin with an example. Plumb begins with his minibus of ten children and two adults, Lewis with his Mr. and Mrs. A and Mr. and Mrs. B. Certainly both examples are striking. I'm not sure that, on rereading the essays, I believe either example is real, but they caught my attention. I must say, however, that I have more trouble believing in Plumb's happy busload than in Lewis's two couples. Putting aside my own experience as the child of divorced parents (each of whom has remarried), ten children--not two of whom have the same two parents--just seems like too many.

Again a clear transition ("In addition to")

In addition to these relatively superficial resemblances, there is also a deeper resemblance. Plumb and Lewis are both talking about the great change in sexual behavior that came about in the twentieth century, especially in the middle of the century when divorce became respectable and common. But there is a big difference in their response. Plumb, writing as a historian, tries to understand why the change came about. Having concluded that the family no longer serves the purposes that it served in earlier periods, Plumb is not disturbed by the change. He ends his essay by saying, "And that busload of children does no more than symbolize the failure, not of marriage, but of the role of the old-fashioned family unit in a modern, urbanized, scientific and affluent society" (11). Lewis, on the other hand, writes as a moralist. He tries to understand why the A's and B's of this world do what they do, and he sees that they behave as they do because of "the sexual impulse" (32). But Lewis does more than see what they do; he judges what they do, in particular he judges behavior against what he calls "Natural Law" (29) and "the Law of Nature" (30). And he makes it clear that he is not speaking only of sexual behavior. After saying that women are at a disadvantage in a society that tolerates conjugal infidelity, he makes a final point that goes far beyond matters of sex:

> Secondly, though the "right to happiness" is chiefly claimed for the sexual impulse, it seems to me impossible that the matter should stay there. The fatal principle, once allowed in that department, must sooner or later seep through the whole of our lives. (33)

For Plumb, then, the family is something produced by history, and it changes as history goes on. For Lewis, the family--two adults wedded

Marginal notes (left column):

Quotation is used as evidence to support student's assertion that Plumb "is not disturbed"

Cites evidence

Quotation of more than four lines is indented 5 spaces at left

Transition ("for Plumb, then") by means of brief summary

Parallel construction
("For Plumb . . . For
Lewis") highlights
similarities and
differences

for life--is something in accordance
with Natural Law, and since this law
does not change, the nature of the
family does not change, or, rather,
should not change. This difference
between the essays, of course, is far
more important than all of the
similarities. Each essay is interesting to read, and maybe each is even
convincing during the moments that
someone is reading it, but finally
the essays are strongly opposed to
each other, and it is impossible to
agree with both of them.

Student briefly offers
objections to each
essay

Discloses reasons

How is a reader to decide between the two essays? Doubtless the
earlier experience of a reader predi-
sposes that reader to believe certain
things and not to believe other
things. Reading Plumb's essay, I
find, drawing on my experience, that
I cannot believe in his busload of
happy children. Plumb does not seem
to be aware that children are greatly
pained by the divorce and remarriage
of their parents. In short, Plumb
seems to me to be too satisfied that
everything is just fine and that we
need not regret the loss of the old-
style family. On the other hand,
Lewis does not think that everything
is just fine with the family. He sees
the selfishness behind the "right to
[sexual] happiness" that for the most
part has destroyed the old-fashioned
family. But Lewis rests his case
entirely on Natural Law, something
that perhaps not many people today
believe in.

Student imaginatively
extends the dis-
cussion

I can imagine Lewis and Plumb
meeting, and having a debate. Lewis
points out to Plumb that divorce
causes more unhappiness than Plumb
has admitted, and Plumb points out
to Lewis that if modern divorce

causes much suffering, there must
also have been much suffering when
parents did <u>not</u> get divorced. Plumb
and Lewis each grant the truth of
these objections, and then, in my imagined debate, Plumb says to Lewis,
"Furthermore, you build your case on
'Natural Law,' but I don't think
there really is any such thing. I
will grant that Mr. A and Mrs. B seem
irresponsible, but I won't grant that
married adults must for their entire
lives remain with each other." Lewis
replies: "If you don't think that
some things are right--always right--
and that some things are wrong--
always wrong--what guides actions?
You seem to care whether or not people are happy. But isn't it clear to
you that some people seek their own
happiness at the expense of others?
What gives them such a right? If you
don't believe in natural law, what do
you believe in? Where do "rights"
come from?

Transition and con-
clusion about the two
essays   And so the debate ends, not so
much because they differ about
whether people today are happier than
people in the past, but because they
differ in their assumptions. Plumb's
assumption that history determines
the rightness or wrongness of the family is unacceptable to Lewis, and
Lewis's assumption that the family is
based on natural law is unacceptable
to Plumb.

Student introduces a
personal note, but re-
lates it closely to the
two readings   What is my own position? For the
moment, I find <u>both</u> assumptions unac-
ceptable. Intellectually I feel the
force of Plumb's argument, but my experience tells me that he accepts the
change in the family too easily. Intellectually I feel the force of
Lewis's argument, but somehow I cannot convince myself that there is

such a thing as natural law. Still, of the two writers, I feel that Lewis has a clearer picture of what people are like. I do know lots of people like Mr. and Mrs. A and Mr. and Mrs. B, but I don't know that busload of California kids.

Concludes with suc-cinct references to both essays

Works Cited

Documentation

Lewis, C. S. "We Have No 'Right to Happiness.'" The Little, Brown Reader. Ed. Marcia Stubbs and Sylvan Barnet. 6th ed. New York: HarperCollins, 1993. 28-33.

Plumb, J. H. "The Dying Family." The Little, Brown Reader. Ed. Marcia Stubbs and Sylvan Barnet. 6th ed. New York: HarperCollins, 1993. 7-11.

Using Quotations

Our marginal comments briefly call your attention to the student's use of quotations, but here we remind you of procedures for using quotations. These procedures are not noteworthy when handled properly, but they become noticeable and even ruinous to your essay when bungled. Read over the following reminders, check them against the student's essay that you have just read, and consult them again the first few times you write about an essay.

1. *Quote.* Quotations from the work under discussion provide indispensable support for your argument.
2. *Don't overquote.* Most of your essay should consist of your own words.
3. *Quote briefly.* Use quotations as evidence, not as padding.
4. *Comment on what you quote;* immediately before or immediately after the quotation. Make sure your reader understands why you find the quotation relevant. Don't count on the quotation to make your point for you.
5. *Take care with embedded quotations* (quotations within a sentence of your own). A quotation must make good sense and must fit grammatically into the sentence of which it is a part.

Incorrect:

```
Plumb says he was "astonished when a minibus drove
up to my house."
```

(In this example, the shift from Plumb to "my" is bothersome, especially since the student uses the first person in his essay.)

Improved:

```
Plumb says that he was "astonished" when he saw a
minibus arrive at his house.
```

Or:

```
Plumb says, "I was astonished when a minibus drove
up to my house."
```

Incorrect:

```
Plumb implies he is well read because "Unlike an-
thropologists or sociologists, historians have not
studied family life very closely."
```

Improved:

```
Plumb implies he is well read in his assertion that
"Unlike anthropologists or sociologists, historians
have not studied family life very closely."
```

6. Don't try to fit a long quotation into the middle of one of your own sentences. It is almost impossible for the reader to come out of the quotation and pick up the thread of your sentence. It is better to lead into a long quotation with "Plumb says:" and then, after quoting, to begin a new sentence of your own.

7. *Quote exactly.* Any material that you add (to make the quotation coherent with your sentence) must be in square brackets. Thus:

```
Plumb says that he "was rather astonished when a
minibus drove up to [his] house and out poured ten
children."
```

An ellipsis (any material that you omit from a quotation) must be indicated by three spaced periods:

```
Plumb says he "was rather astonished when a minibus
drove up . . . and out poured ten children."
```

If you end the quotation before the end of the author's sentence, add a period and then three spaced periods to indicate the omission:

```
Plumb says he "was rather astonished when a minibus
drove up. . . ."
```

8. *Quote fairly.* It would not be fair, for instance, to say that Lewis says, "After all, . . . they had a right to happiness." The words do in fact appear in Lewis's essay, but he is quoting them in order, ultimately, to refute them.
9. *Identify the quotation* clearly for your reader. Use such expressions as "Lewis says," "Plumb argues."
10. *Identify the source of quotations* in a list called Works Cited.
11. *Check your punctuation.* Remember: Periods and commas go *inside* the closing quotation marks, semicolons and colons go outside. Question marks and exclamation points go inside if they are part of the quotation, outside if they are your own.

A Checklist for Editing: Thirteen Questions to Ask Yourself

1. Is the title of my essay at least moderately informative?
2. Do I identify the subject of my essay (author and title) early?
3. What is my thesis? Do I state it soon enough (perhaps even in the title) and keep it in view?
4. Is the organization reasonable? Does each point lead into the next, without irrelevancies and without anticlimaxes?
5. Is each paragraph unified by a topic sentence or a topic idea? Are there adequate transitions from one paragraph to the next?
6. Are generalizations supported by appropriate concrete details, especially by brief quotations from the text?
7. Is the opening paragraph interesting and, by its end, focused on the topic? Is the final paragraph conclusive without being repetitive?

8. Is the tone appropriate? No sarcasm, no apologies, no condescension?
9. If there is a summary, is it as brief as possible, given its purpose?
10. Are the quotations accurate? Do they serve a purpose other than to add words to the essay?
11. Is documentation provided where necessary?
12. Are the spelling and punctuation correct? Are other mechanical matters (such as margins, spacing, and citations) in correct form? Have I proofread carefully?
13. Is the paper properly identified—author's name, instructor's name, course number, and date?

4
A NOTE ON READING (AND WRITING ABOUT) PICTURES

I am after the one unique picture whose composition possesses such vigor and richness, and whose content so radiates outwards from it, that this single picture is a whole story in itself.

Henri Cartier-Bresson

The Language of Pictures

It may sound odd to talk about "reading" pictures and about the "language" of pictures, but pictures, like words, convey messages. Advertisers know this, and that's why their advertisements for soft drinks include images of attractive young couples frolicking at the beach. The not-so-hidden message is that consumers of these products are healthy, prosperous, relaxed, and strongly attractive to people of the opposite sex.

Like compositions made of words—stories, poems, even vigorous sentences—many paintings are carefully constructed things, built up in a certain way in order to make a statement. To take an obvious example, in medieval religious pictures Jesus or Mary may be shown larger than the surrounding figures to indicate their greater spiritual status. But even in realistic paintings the more important figures are likely to be given a greater share of the light or a more central position than the lesser figures. Such devices of composition are fairly evident in paintings, but we occasionally forget that photographs too are almost always constructed things. The photographer—even the amateur just taking a candid snapshot—adjusts a pillow under the baby's head, or asks the subject to smile or to lean against a tree, and then the photographer backs up a little and bends his or her knees before clicking the shutter. Even when photographing something inanimate, the photographer searches for the best view, waits for a cloud to pass, and perhaps pushes out of the range of the camera some trash that would spoil the effect of a lovely fern growing beside a rock. Minor White was speaking for almost all photographers when he said, "I don't take pictures, I make them."

And we often make our photographs for a particular purpose—perhaps to have a souvenir of a trip, or to show what we look like in uniform or at our job, or to show grandma what the new baby looks like. We take pictures of all sorts of subjects for a variety of reasons, but because most of the photographs that amateurs take are of family members, this chapter will include two essays in which students analyze family pictures. Before we give these essays, however, we want first to set forth some questions that may help you think about pictures. Then, as an example of reading the language of pictures, we reproduce a famous photograph by Dorothea Lange along with some comments on it by students.

What are some of the basic things to look for in understanding the language of pictures? One can begin almost anywhere, but let's begin with the relationship among the parts:

Do the figures share the space evenly, or does one figure overpower another, taking most of the space or the light?

Are the figures harmoniously related, perhaps by a similar stance or shared action? Or are they opposed, perhaps by diagonals thrusting at each other? Speaking generally, diagonals may suggest instability, except when they form a triangle resting on its base. Horizontal lines suggest stability, as do vertical lines when connected by a horizontal line. Circular lines are often associated with motion, and sometimes—especially by men—with the female body and with fertility. These simple formulas, however, must be applied cautiously, for they are not always appropriate.

In a landscape, what is the relation between humans and nature? Are the figures at ease in nature, or are they dwarfed by it? Are they earthbound, beneath the horizon, or (because the viewpoint is low) do they stand out against the horizon and perhaps seem in touch with the heavens, or at least with open air? Do the natural objects in the landscape somehow reflect the emotions of the figures in it?

If the picture is a portrait, how do the furnishings and the background and the angle of the head or the posture of the head and body (as well, of course, as the facial expression) contribute to our sense of the person portrayed?

What is the effect of light in the picture? Does it produce sharp contrasts, brightly illuminating some parts and throwing others into darkness? Or does it, by means of gentle gradations, unify most or all of the parts? Does the light seem theatrical or natural, disturbing or comforting? If the picture is in color, is the color realistic or is it expressive, or both?

You can stimulate responses to pictures by asking yourself two kinds of questions:

1. *What is this doing?* Why is this figure here and not there, why is this tree so brightly illuminated, why are shadows omitted, why is this seated figure leaning forward like that?
2. *Why do I have this response?* Why do I find this figure pathetic, this landscape oppressive, this child revoltingly sentimental but that child fascinating?

The first of these questions, "What is this doing?," requires you to identify yourself with the artist, wondering perhaps whether the fence or the side of the house is the better background for this figure, or whether both figures should sit or stand. The second question, "Why do I have this response?," requires you to trust your feelings. If you are amused or repelled or unnerved or soothed, assume that these responses are appropriate and follow them up, at least until further study of the work provides other responses.

Thinking about Dorothea Lange's
Migrant Mother, Nipomo, California

Let's look now at a photograph by Dorothea Lange, an American photographer who made her reputation with photographs of migrant farmers in California during the depression that began in 1929. Lange's *Migrant Mother, Nipomo, California* (1936) is probably the best-known image of the period. One of our students made the following entry in his journal. (The student was given no information about the photograph other than its title.)

This woman seems to be thinking. In a way, the picture reminds me of a statue called The Thinker, of a seated man who is bent over, with his hand touching his forehead. But I wouldn't say that this photograph is really so much about thinking as it is about other things. I'd say that it is about several other things. First (but not really in any particular order), fear. The children must be afraid, since they have turned to their mother. Second, the picture is about love. The children press against their mother, sure of her love. The mother does not actually show her love--for instance, by kissing them, or even hugging them--but you feel she loves them. Third, the picture is about hopelessness. The mother

FSA Photo/Library of Congress

doesn't seem to be able to offer any comfort. Probably they have very little food; maybe they are homeless. I'd say the picture is also about courage. Although the picture seems to me to show hopelessness, I also think the mother, even though she does not know how she will be able to help her children shows great strength in her face. She also has a lot

of dignity. She hasn't broken down in front of the
children; she is going to do her best to get through
the day and the next day and the next.

Another student wrote:

I remember from American Lit that good literature is
not sentimental. (When we discussed the word, we
concluded that "sentimental" meant "sickeningly
sweet.") Some people might think that Lange's picture, showing a mother and two little children, is
sentimental, but I don't think so. Although the
children must be upset, and maybe they even are crying, the mother seems to be very strong. I feel that
with a mother like this, the children are in very
good hands. She is not "sickeningly sweet." She may
be almost overcome with despair, but she doesn't
seem to ask us to pity her.

A third student wrote:

It's like those pictures of the homeless in the
newspapers and on TV. A photographer sees some man
sleeping in a cardboard box, or a woman with shopping bags sitting in a doorway, and he takes their
picture. I suppose the photographer could say that
he is calling the public's attention to "the plight
of the homeless," but I'm not convinced that he's
doing anything more than making money by selling
photographs. Homeless people have almost no privacy,
and then some photographer comes along and invades
even their doorways and cardboard houses. Sometimes
the people are sleeping, or even if they are awake
they may be in so much despair that they don't
bother to tell the photographer to get lost. Or
they may be mentally ill and don't know what's
happening. In the case of this picture, the woman
is not asleep, but she seems so preoccupied that
she isn't aware of the photographer. Maybe she
has just been told there is no work for her, or
maybe she has been told she can't stay if she
keeps the children. Should the photographer have

```
intruded on this woman's sorrow? This picture
may be art, but it bothers me.
```

All of these entries seem to us to be thoughtful, interesting, and helpful, though of course even taken together they do not provide the last word. Here are a few additional points. First, it happens that Lange has written about the picture. She said that she had spent the winter of 1935–36 taking photographs of migrants, and now, in March, she was preparing to drive five hundred miles to her home when she noticed a sign that said, "Pea-Pickers Camp." Having already taken hundreds of pictures, she drove on for twenty miles, but something preyed on her mind, and she made a U-turn and visited the camp. Here is part of what she wrote.

> I saw and approached the hungry and desperate mother, as if drawn by a magnet. I do not remember how I explained my presence or my camera to her, but I do remember she asked me no questions. I made five exposures, working closer and closer from the same direction. I did not ask her name or her history. She told me her age, that she was thirty-two. She said that they had been living on frozen vegetables from the surrounding fields, and birds that the children killed. She had just sold the tires from her car to buy food. There she sat in that lean-to tent with her children huddled around her, and seemed to know that my pictures might help her, and so she helped me. There was a sort of equality about it. . . . What I am trying to tell other photographers is that had I not been deeply involved in my undertaking on that field trip, I would not have had to turn back. What I am trying to say is that I believe this inner compulsion to be the vital ingredient in our work.

Lange does not say anything about posing the woman and her child, and we can assume that she had too much decency to ask a woman and children in these circumstances to arrange themselves into an interesting pictorial composition. Furthermore, it seems obvious that unlike, say, a figure in a wedding portrait, the woman is not striking a pose. She has not deliberately prepared herself for a picture that will represent her to the public. Nevertheless, the composition—the way things are put together—certainly contributes to the significance of the picture. Of course the subject matter, a mother with children, may suggest the traditional Madonna and Child of the Middle Ages and the Renaissance, but the resemblance is not just in the subject matter. Lange's photograph may remind us of paintings in which the Madonna and the infant Jesus form a unified composition, their heads and limbs harmonizing and echoing each other. The photograph, with its near-balance—a child on each side, the mother's bare left arm balanced by the child's bare arm, the mother's hand at one side of her neck echoed by the child's hand at the other side—achieves a stability, or harmony, that helps make the painfulness of the subject acceptable. That is, although the subject may be painful, it is possible to take some pleasure in the way in which it is presented. That the faces of the children are *turned away* probably helps make the subject acceptable. If we saw not only the woman's face but also the faces of two hungry children, we might feel that Lange was tugging too vigorously at our heartstrings. Finally, speaking of faces, it is worth mentioning that the woman does not look at us. Of course we don't know why, but we can guess that she takes no notice of us because she is preoccupied with issues far beyond us.

Writing about Family Photographs: Two Essays by First-Year Students

You may well take a course in college that is partly or largely concerned with reading images. Art history courses obviously have this concern, but other courses too may ask you to study pictures. A sociology course may ask you to examine such a topic as the images of brides in popular magazines, a religion course may ask you to examine images of deities in a certain culture, and a course in advertising will certainly ask you to write about visual ads. It may be mentioned, too, that much of what we know about the past—for instance about Pre-Columbian society in the New World—depends on the interpretation of images. And, of course, some careers are based on the interpretation of images, for instance of aerial photographs and of x-rays. There are good reasons, then, to develop some skill in analyzing pictures, but perhaps the best reason is that it's fun to think about pictures.

At the beginning of each thematic chapter of this text, you'll find four pictures, which we hope that you will enjoy looking at and thinking about. Like the Short Views, which also introduce each chapter, the pictures offer occasions for reflecting on the chapter's theme—family, education, work, business, and so on—and you may find yourself referring to them in journal entries or essays that you

write. Or, they may themselves be subjects of essays, a good way to practice consciously reading images.

Another good way to practice thinking about images is to analyze a snapshot or family photograph that you own, the sort of picture many of us took with us when we left home for college, or carry with us in our wallets. The two essays that we print below are analyses of family photographs written by students in response to an assignment by Nadia Medina, the instructor in a writing class whose theme, like that of our first thematic chapter, was the family.

First, the assignment:

Select a family photograph and write a paper in which you both analyze and describe the relationship of the people as they are revealed in the picture. You are welcome, indeed encouraged, to use your personal knowledge of the circumstances under which the photograph was taken, or the occasion that it celebrates, to add to your analysis. Any other material can be included (as, for example, what happened afterwards), but your paper should be anchored in the photograph itself.

Cheryl Lee
February 17, 1992
Writing 1250
Medina

The Story behind the Gestures:
A Family Photograph

At the close of my graduation ceremony, my
entire family gathered together to immortalize the
special moment on film. No one escaped the flash of
my mother's camera because she was determined to
document every minute of the occasion at every possible angle. My mother made sure that she took pictures of me with my hat on, with my hat off, holding
the bouquet, sitting, standing, and in countless
other positions. By the time this family picture was
taken, my smile was intact, frozen on my face. This
is not to say that my smile was anything less than
genuine, for it truly was a smile of thankfulness
and joy. It is just that after posing for so many
pictures, what initially began as a spontaneous
reaction became a frozen expression.

The viewer should, however, consider not so
much the frozen expressions of those in the photograph, but rather the fact that the picture is
posed. A posed picture supposedly shows only what
the people in the picture want the viewer to see--in
this case, their happiness. But ironically the photograph reveals much more about its subjects than

the viewer first imagines. The photograph speaks of
relationships and personalities. It speaks about the
more intimate details that first seem invisible but
that become undeniable through the study of
gestures.

In the photograph, the most prominent and symbolic of gestures is the use and position of the
arms. Both my father and mother place an arm around
me and in turn around each other. Their encircling
arms, however, do more than just show affection;
they unify the three figures into a close huddle
that leads the viewer's eye directly to them as opposed to the background or the periphery. The
slightly bended arms that rest at their sides act as
arrows that not only reinforce the three figures as
the focal point but also exclude the fourth figure,
my brother, from sharing the "spotlight." Unlike the
other members of the family whose arms and hands are
intertwined, Edwin stands with both hands down in
front of him, latching onto no one. The lack of
physical contact between the huddled figures and
Edwin is again emphasized as he positions himself
away from the viewer's eye as he stands in the
periphery.

Edwin's position in the photograph is indica-
tive of him as a person, for he always seems to isolate himself from the spotlight, from being the
center of attention. Thus, it is his decision to

escape public scrutiny, not the force of my parents'
arms that drives him to the side. His quiet, humble
nature directs him away from even being the focal
point of a picture and leads him towards establishing his own individuality and independence in
privacy. His long hair and his "hand-me-down"
clothes are all an expression of his simply being
himself. The reason behind his physical independence
is the emotional independence that he already possesses at the age of sixteen. He stands alone because he can stand alone.

While Edwin stands apart from the other three
figures, I stand enclosed and protected. The lock of
arms as well as the bouquet restrain me; they dissuade me from breaking away in favor of independence. Although my mother wants me to achieve the
same kind of independence that Edwin has achieved,
she works to delay the time when I actually will
move away to the periphery. Perhaps my being the
only daughter, the only other female in the family,
has something to do with my mother's desire to keep
me close and dependent as long as possible. Her arm
reaches out with bouquet in hand as if to shield
me from the world's unpleasantness. Even though
my father also holds onto me with an encircling arm,
it is my mother's firm grip that alone persuades
me to stay within the boundary of their protective arms.

Her grip, which proves more powerful than my father's hold, restrains not only me but also my father. In the picture, he falls victim to the same outstretched hand, the same touch of the bouquet. Yet this time, my mother's bouquet does more than just restrain; it seems to push my father back "into line" or into his so-called place. The picture illustrates this exertion of influence well, for my mother in real life does indeed assume the role of the dominant figure. Although my father remains the head of the household in title, it is my mother around whom the household revolves; she oversees the insignificant details as well as the major ones. But my father doesn't mind at all. Like me, he also enjoys the protection her restraining arm offers. It is because of our mutual dependence on my mother that my father and I seem to draw closer. This dependence in turn strengthens both of our relationships with my mother.

At the time the picture was taken, I seriously doubt that my mother realized the significance of her position in the picture or the import of her gestures. All of us in fact seem too blinded by the festivity of the occasion to realize that this photograph would show more than just a happy family at a daughter's graduation. The family photograph would inevitably become a telling portrait of each member of the family. It would, in a sense, leave us vulnerable to the speculative eyes of the viewer, who in carefully examining the photograph would recognize the secrets hidden in each frozen expression.

In thinking about Cheryl Lee's essay, you might ask yourself these questions:

1. Is the essay devoted chiefly to analyzing a picture or is it devoted chiefly to exploring Lee's feelings about the picture?
2. What is the function of Lee's opening paragraph? What is your response to her statement that the family gathered together "to immortalize" her graduation? What is the effect of "with my hat on, with my hat off"? How would you characterize the writer of this paragraph?
3. Do you think that Lee's interpretation is probably sound, or do you think that she reads too much (or too little) into the picture? Support your view.
4. Evaluate the final paragraph as a final paragraph.

Here is an essay by a second student, writing on the same assignment.

Samantha Campbell
Writing 1250
April 9, 1991

My Father's Photograph

I am asleep. And very little; little and asleep. I am on my back, my little head turned to the side and on my face is the emotionless solemnity of baby dreams. My left hand rests on a little

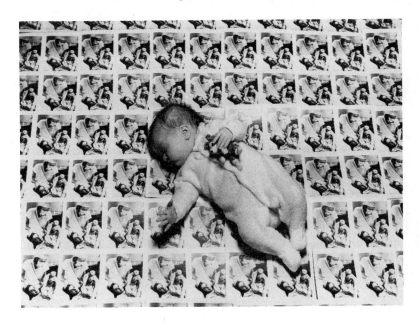

stuffed kangaroo doll, and my right hand is open so
you can see all my pretty little fingers. I am wearing a little white terrycloth suit that snaps all
the way up the front. My hair looks dark in the
black-and-white photograph, but I am told it was
quite red when I was just born.

   I am the only person in this picture; without
the background collage it would be a boring shot,
documenting that indeed I did sleep as a newborn
child. The precise rows of small photographs on
which I lie are what makes the person flipping
through my baby book stop to look more closely.
There are seven slightly tilted horizontal rows of
these identical pictures. If you stare at them long

enough they become a series of black-and-white patterns, an oddly frenetic patchwork quilt. They are
leftover birth announcements showing the photograph
taken in the delivery room minutes after I was born,
picturing my mother, my father, and me. In each tiny
picture mother is lying down and holding me up; she
is smiling at the camera, looking a bit tired but
genuinely pleased. My father, standing, rests his
hand on her long, straight, dark hair, and peers
down through his glasses at me, the little baby. He
wears antiseptic surgical garb so that he will not
breathe on me or transmit to me any unclean particles that I should be spared, at least for a while.

It is a nice picture, the birth announcement
photo. The doctor apparently had a good sense of artistic composition; the arrangement is circular, the
figures appear interwoven, bonded and linked. And
the entire shot, me resting on this careful grid-
work, is interesting too. Pretty creative of my
father (the biological one)!

But I've never liked it, and I love looking at
old pictures of myself and my family. This photo has
always disturbed me in a vague sort of way. It's
hard and it's cold. It's all stark and unflinching
lines. The background must have taken an awfully
long time to lay out; I can just see my father,
squinting, leaning over the floor, meticulously
spacing the old announcements so that they are

equidistant and straight. Like his bottles of vitamins and his comb and his brush and his toothbrush
and his dental floss and his lotions and his after-
shave all perfectly aligned near the bathroom sink
that whenever I see them make me want to scream and
pound the counter so hard they all jiggle and
vibrate and maybe fall over and then finally settle
disrupted and just a little just a little bit
crooked.

I can see him taking me out of my crib when I'm
sleeping and gingerly putting me down, very very
careful not to disturb his delicate configuration
(but I can see that the photo right under my cheek
is the tiniest bit misaligned). I'm sure he put the
kangaroo under my hand, reached quickly for the
camera and took picture after picture. I know he
changed my position, gave me different toys to hold,
because I have seen similar shots where I, the composition, and the angle have been manipulated, very
slightly. One roll of film, two? Photograph after
photograph of a little baby asleep on a crafted
crazed collage. I don't like it.

It must be the feeling behind it, because in a
way I can appreciate the originality. Objectively I
like the pictures. But I cannot be objective when it
comes to my father because I do not like what he
does and I do not like who he is. I have been physically separated from him most of my life, and I grow

more apart from him every year. But I cannot be objective because I do not like his constantly calculating mind, his absolute egomania, his entire
system of values. And I do not like the way he uses
me and talks to me and has ideas about me.

"Blood, Samantha," he says, strong gravelly
voice. "That's what it's all about. You see, you can
have your friends, that's good, friends are important and other people are important. But you have
only one mother and one father. You are connected to
your family, your real family, by blood. That's forever, kid." I've heard variations on a blood theme
for years and years, especially since my mother remarried and I gained not only a stepfather but also his
entire family to whom I have been very close.

So I know my father loves this picture, because
it is dripping with blood. He repeats himself over
and over here. "This is you with your mother and
father, this is you with your father and mother,
this is blood. There you are in the midst of it, on
top of it, you sleep with it. This is it." Here is
what I say: "No. This is not me who I am, this is me
what I was, which is an infant who can be (damnit)
used to do whatever a parent wants to do. No, it's
not me. And I don't care about the integration of
figures here, the circular image of mother father
child. I don't care that I have mother's birth blood
on my body or yours running through my veins or half

your chromosomes or eyebrows shaped like yours I
don't care I really don't. And you can't make me."

This is not a picture of love, of adoration of
a child just born. It is a picture of cold cleverness and colder ideas. It is manipulated, I am
manipulated. I feel used, like I have been before:
as a weapon against my mother when he took me away
from her (twice), or as the smiling, blond, childish
centerpiece of a casual business meeting. He likes
to show me off, to show people what he has created,
his own blood. This is not love. People tell me,
"But he really loves you, look what he sent you, see
how he calls you all the time and wants to see you
and . . ." I can't make them understand that this is
not love; I know it is not.

If you really look at the birth announcement
photograph, you see that the circle is not perfect.
My mother is the one who holds me. My father,
masked, is not touching me; his hand drops to his
side. My mother looks outward towards the photographer; she's not trapped here in this circle.
And me, well, I'm just a baby. A new, little thing
of flesh and yes, blood, but it is me what I was and
not me who I am. And I am not part of this photograph, this dead collage with the living child on
top of it. This perfect, pretty, artful creation of
a man who is only my father.

We can ask of this essay questions similar to those we asked of Cheryl Lee's essay.

1.   Is the essay chiefly devoted to analyzing a picture, or is it chiefly devoted to exploring Campbell's feelings about the picture?
2.   What is the function of Campbell's opening paragraph? What is the effect on you of the first sentence—very short—and of the second—also short, and marked by the repetition of "little." Notice, too, that except for the second sentence, all of the sentences in this paragraph begin with "I am," or with "My." How would you characterize the writer of this paragraph?
3.   Do you think that Campbell's interpretation is probably sound, or do you think that she reads too much (or too little) into the picture? Or do you think that our opinion about the validity of the interpretation is irrelevant? Support your view.
4.   Evaluate the final paragraph as a final paragraph.

Last Words

If your instructor asks you to write about a picture—perhaps one in this book—and if even after thinking about the questions on pages 75–76 you don't quite know where to begin, you may want to think about it partly in terms of one of the following remarks by distinguished photographers. (But remember: a remark need not be true just because it was made by someone who is highly regarded as a photographer.)

> A great photograph is a full expression of what one feels about what is being photographed in the deepest sense, and is, thereby, a true expression of what one feels about life in its entirety.
>
> Ansel Adams

> It's the subject-matter that counts. I'm interested in revealing the subject in a new way to intensify it.
>
> Harry Callahan

> Documentary photography records the social scene of our time. It mirrors the present and documents for the future. Its focus is man in his relations to mankind.
>
> Dorothea Lange

Photography is the simultaneous recognition, in a fraction of a second, of the significance of an event as well as of the precise organization of forms which give that event its proper expression.

Henri Cartier-Bresson

I am a passionate lover of the snapshot because of all photographic images it comes closest to truth. The snapshot is a specific spiritual moment. . . . What the eye sees is different from what the camera records. Whereas the eye sees in three dimensions, images are projected on a surface of two dimensions, which for every image-maker is a great problem. The snapshooter disregards this problem, and the result is that his pictures have an apparent disorder and imperfection, which is exactly their appeal and their style. . . . Out of this imbalance, and out of this not knowing, and out of this real innocence toward the medium comes an enormous vitality and expression of life.

Lisette Model

Or you might begin by thinking about a statement by Janet Malcolm, who in *Diana and Nikon* (a book about photography) said:

If "the camera can't lie," neither is it inclined to tell the truth, since it can reflect only the usually ambiguous, and sometimes outright deceitful, surface of reality.

5
ALL IN THE FAMILY

Sonia
Joanne Leonard, 1966

Faith Ringgold © 1973, Family of Faith Ringgold, Woman, "Mrs. Brown and Catherine," Tapestry, pieced fabric, acrylic painted on canvas. Private collection, NY, Courtesy of the Bernice Steinbaum Gallery

The Acrobat's Family with a Monkey
Pablo Picasso, 1905

Why One's Parents Got Married
R. Chast

Short Views

After a certain age, the more one becomes oneself, the more obvious one's family traits become.
          Marcel Proust

All happy families resemble one another; every unhappy family is unhappy in its own fashion.
          Leo Tolstoy, *Anna Karenina*

On Tuesday, March 31, he and I dined at General Paoli's. A question was started, whether the state of marriage was natural to man. Johnson. "Sir, it is so far from being natural for a man and woman to live in a state of marriage, that we find all the motives which they have for remaining in that connection, and the restraints which civilized society imposes to prevent separation, are hardly sufficient to keep them together." The General said, that in a state of nature a man and woman uniting together would form a strong and constant affection, by the mutual pleasure each would receive; and that the same causes of dissension would not arise between them, as occur between husband and wife in a civilized state. Johnson. "Sir, they would have dissensions enough, though of another kind. One would choose to go a hunting in this wood, the other in that; one would choose to go a fishing in this lake, the other in that; or, perhaps, one would choose to go a hunting, when the other would choose to go a fishing; and so they would part. Besides, Sir, a savage man and a savage woman meet by chance; and when the man sees another woman that pleases him better, he will leave the first."
          James Boswell

Marriage is the best of human statuses and the worst, and it will continue to be. And that is why, though its future in some form or other is as assured as anything can be, this future is as equivocal as its past. The demands that men and women make on marriage will never be fully met; they cannot be.
          Jessie Bernard

A slavish bondage to parents cramps every faculty of the mind; and Mr. Locke very judiciously observes, that "if the mind be curbed and humbled too much in children, if their spirits be abased and broken much by too strict an hand over them, they lose all their vigour and industry." This strict hand may in some degree account for the weakness of women; for girls, from various causes, are more kept down by their parents, in every sense of the word, than boys. The duty expected from them is, like all the duties arbitrarily imposed on women, more from a sense of propriety, more out of respect for decorum, than reason; and thus taught slavishly to submit to their parents, they are prepared for the slavery of marriage. I may be told that a number of women are not slaves in the marriage state. True, but they then become tyrants; for it is not rational freedom, but a lawless kind of power resembling the authority exercised by the favourites of absolute monarchs, which they obtain by debasing means.
     Mary Wollstonecraft

Nobody who has not been in the interior of a family can say what the difficulties of any individual of that family may be.
     Jane Austen, *Emma*

When I was young enough to still spend a long time buttoning my shoes in the morning, I'd listen toward the hall: Daddy upstairs was shaving in the bathroom and Mother downstairs was frying the bacon. They would begin whistling back and forth to each other up and down the stairwell. My father would whistle his phrase, my mother would try to whistle, then hum hers back. It was their duet. I drew my buttonhook in and out and listened to it—I knew it was "The Merry Widow." The difference was, their song almost floated with laughter: how different from the record, which growled from the beginning, as if the Victrola were only slowly being wound up. They kept it running between them, up and down the stairs where I was now just about ready to run clattering down and show them my shoes.
     Eudora Welty

Lewis Coser

Lewis Coser, born in Berlin in 1913, was educated at the Sorbonne in Paris and at Columbia University, where he received a Ph.D. in sociology in 1954. For many years he taught at the State University of New York, Stony Brook, where he held the title Distinguished Professor. The passage given below is from a textbook designed for college students.

The Family

Following the French anthropologist Claude Lévi-Strauss, we can define the family as a group manifesting these characteristics: it finds its origin in marriage; it consists of husband, wife and children born in their wedlock—though other relatives may find their place close to that nuclear group; and the members of the group are united by moral, legal, economic, religious, and social rights and obligations. These include a network of sexual rights and prohibitions and a variety of socially patterned feelings such as love, attraction, piety, awe, and so on.

The family is among the few universal institutions of mankind. No known society lacks small kinship groups of parents and children related through the process of reproduction. But recognition of the universality of this institution must immediately be followed by the acknowledgment that its forms are exceedingly varied. The fact that many family organizations are not monogamic, as in the West, led many nineteenth-century observers to the erroneous conclusion that in "early" stages of evolution there existed no families, and that "group marriage," institutionalized promiscuity, prevailed. This is emphatically not the case; even though patterned wife-lending shocked the sensibilities of Victorian anthropologists, such an institution is evidently predicated on the fact that men have wives in the first place. No matter what their specific forms, families in all known societies have performed major social functions—reproduction, maintenance, socialization, and social placement of the young.

Families may be monogamous or polygamous—there are systems where no man is entitled to several wives and others where several husbands share one wife. A society may recognize primarily the small nuclear, conjugal unit of husband and wife with their immediate descendants or it may institutionalize the large extended family linking several generations and emphasizing consanguinity more than the conjugal bond. Residence after marriage may be-matrilocal, patrilocal or neolocal; exchanges of goods and services between families at the time of marriage may be based on bride price, groom price or an equal exchange; endogamous or exogamous regulations may indicate who is and who is not eligible for marriage; the choice of a mate may be controlled by parents or it may be left in large measure to the young persons concerned. These are but a few of the many differences which characterize family structures in variant societies.

Topics for Discussion and Writing

1. At the end of paragraph 2, Coser writes: "No matter what their specific forms, families in all known societies have performed major social functions—reproduction, maintenance, socialization, and social placement of the young." What does "socialization" mean? How does it differ from "social placement of the young"? What specific forms does each take in our society?

2. What examples can you give of "moral, legal, economic, religious, and social rights and obligations" (paragraph 1) that unite members of a family?

3. Compare Coser and Plumb (pages 7–11) on the social functions of the family. According to Plumb, what responsibility does the family in our society have in performing the social functions Coser lists? How do other institutions compete with the family in performing some of these functions?

4. As you read other selections in this chapter (and in Chapter 11) what variations in form of the family do you encounter? Are there any variations in form Coser did not mention or anticipate?

Judy Brady

Judy Brady was born in San Francisco in 1937. She received a bachelors degree from the University of Iowa in 1960 and wanted to do the graduate work that would qualify her for teaching in a university, but her male teachers discouraged her. "Why I Want a Wife" originally appeared in the first issue of Ms.

Why I Want a Wife

I belong to that classification of people known as wives. I am A Wife. And, not altogether incidentally, I am a mother.

Not too long ago a male friend of mine appeared on the scene fresh from a recent divorce. He had one child, who is, of course, with his ex-wife. He is looking for another wife. As I thought about him while I was ironing one evening, it suddenly occurred to me that I, too, would like to have a wife. Why do I want a wife?

I would like to go back to school so that I can become economically independent, support myself, and, if need be, support those dependent upon me. I want a wife who will work and send me to school. And while I am going to school I want a wife to take care of my children. I want a wife to keep track of the children's doctor and dentist appointments. And to keep track of mine, too. I want a wife to make sure my children eat properly and are kept clean. I want a wife who will wash the children's clothes and keep them mended. I want a wife who is a good nurturant attendant to my children, who arranges for their schooling, makes sure that they have an adequate social life with their peers, takes them to the park, the zoo, etc. I want a wife who takes care of the children when they are sick, a wife who arranges to be around when the children need special care, because, of course, I cannot miss classes at school. My wife must arrange to lose time at work and not lose the job. It may mean a small cut in my wife's income from time to time, but I guess I can tolerate that. Needless to say, my wife will arrange and pay for the care of the children while my wife is working.

I want a wife who will take care of *my* physical needs. I want a wife who will keep my house clean. A wife who will pick up after my children, a wife who will pick up after me. I want a wife who will keep my clothes clean, ironed, mended, replaced when need be, and who will see to it that my personal things are kept in their proper place so that I can find what I need the minute I need it. 4

I want a wife who cooks the meals, a wife who is a *good* cook. I want a wife who will plan the menus, do the necessary grocery shopping, prepare the meals, serve them pleasantly, and then do the cleaning up while I do my studying. I want a wife who will care for me when I am sick and sympathize with my pain and loss of time from school. I want a wife to go along when our family takes a vacation so that someone can continue to care for me and my children when I need a rest and change of scene.

I want a wife who will not bother me with rambling complaints about a wife's duties. But I want a wife who will listen to me when I feel the need to explain a rather difficult point I have come across in my course of studies. And I want a wife who will type my papers-for me when I have written them.

I want a wife who will take care of the details of my social life. When my wife and I are invited out by my friends, I want a wife who will take care of the babysitting arrangements. When I meet people at school that I like and want to entertain, I want a wife who will have the house clean, will prepare a special meal, serve it to me and my friends, and not interrupt when I talk about things that interest me and my friends. I want a wife who will have arranged that the children are fed and ready for bed before my guests arrive so that the children do not bother us. I want a wife who takes care of the needs of my guests so that they feel comfortable, who makes sure that they have an ashtray, that they are passed the hors d'oeuvres, that they are offered a second helping of the food, that their wine glasses are replenished when necessary, that their coffee is served to them as they like it. And I want a wife who knows that sometimes I need a night out by myself.

I want a wife who is sensitive to my sexual needs, a wife who makes love passionately and eagerly when I feel like it, a wife who makes sure that I am satisfied. And, of course, I want a wife who will not demand sexual attention when I am not in the mood for it. I want a wife who assumes the complete responsibility for birth control, because I do not want more children. I want a wife who will remain sexually faithful to me so that I do not have to clutter up my intellectual life with jealousies. And I want a wife who understands that *my* sexual needs may entail more than strict adherence to monogamy. I must, after all, be able to relate to people as fully as possible.

If, by chance, I find another person more suitable as a wife than the wife I already have, I want the liberty to replace my present wife with another one. Naturally, I will expect a fresh, new life; my wife will take the children and be solely responsible for them so that I am left free.

When I am through with school and have a job, I want my wife to quit working and remain at home so that my wife can more fully and completely take care of a wife's duties.

My God, who *wouldn't* want a wife?

Topics for Discussion and Writing

1. Does the second sentence of the essay mean anything different from the first? If so, what? If not, why is it there?
2. Describing a recently divorced man, Brady says in paragraph 2: "He had one child, who is, of course, with his ex-wife." What information does "of course" convey? What attitude or tone?
3. If the constant repetition of "I want a wife who . . . " is not boring, what keeps it from being boring?
4. Brady is attacking sexual stereotyping. Do you find in her essay any assumptions or details that limit the stereotyping to an economic class or to an ethnic or racial group? Explain.

Julie Matthaei

Julie Matthaei teaches economics at Wellesley College and is active with the Economic Literacy Project of Women for Economic Justice of Boston. She is the author of An Economic History of Women in America *and is working on a book entitled* Beyond Sex and Blood: Economy, Family, and the Breakdown of the "Natural" Family.

Political Economy and Family Policy

Our current, "natural" family system, based on biological similarities and differences, is in crisis. Not only are its institutions breaking down, they are also under attack as unjust, unequal, and unfree. The "natural" family system needs to be replaced by a consciously social family system; this means socializing parenting costs and pursuing policies which attack the sexual division of labor and better integrate economic and family life.

The family plays a central role in the distribution of income and wealth in our society, reproducing class, race, and gender inequalities. This paper will 1) present a radical and feminist analysis of the "traditional" family system, 2) discuss the recent breakdown of this system, 3) present a radical and feminist critique of the traditional family system, and 4) indicate social policies which would build a family system more consistent with the principles of equality, freedom, and social justice.

The "Natural" Family

The development of capitalism and wage labor in the nineteenth-century U.S. brought with it new familial institutions. The family continued to be patriarchal—ruled by the husband/father—but was less defined by and involved in commodity production, either as a family firm, or as a family enslaved to producing for others. The family emerged as an increasingly personal and feminine sphere, physically separate and distinct from the competitive and masculine economy (Matthaei 1982). Since, in the nineteenth century, "scientific" explanations of social life were replacing the former religious ones, the new familial institutions were viewed as "natural," and stress was placed on their determination by biological similarities and differences. This "natural"[1] family system has three, interconnected parts:

1. *"Natural" Marriage.* Marriage is seen as a union of naturally different and complementary beings: men/males and women/females (biological sex and social gender are equated). Men and women are believed to be instinctually heterosexual; those who form homosexual liaisons are viewed as unnatural and perverted.[2] Men are seen as natural bread-winners, competing in the economy, and women as natural homemakers, caring for their husbands and children in the home, and segregated into dead-end, low paid "women's jobs." Forced into this sexual division of labor, men and women need one another to be socially complete, and in order to undertake the essential function of marriage, which is seen as . . .

2. *"Natural" Parenting.* Parenting is seen as the biological production of offspring, a process in which adults pass on their identities and wealth to their children, to "their own flesh and blood." Children

---

[1] Natural is in quotes because the "natural" family system is actually a social product.
[2] In contrast, previous times viewed homosexual attractions as natural (and shared by all) but immoral and not to be acted on (Weeks 1979).

are seen as the responsibility and property of their parents. Women/ females are seen as naturally endowed with special maternal instincts which make them more qualified than men/males for parenting.

3. *"Natural" Community.* Connected to the view of family life as natural is a white racist view of society which divides people into races and views whites as the biologically superior race. Whites rationalize their political and economic domination of people of color not only as natural but also as part of "white man's burden to civilize the savages."[3] Races and white supremacy are perpetuated as social entities by the prohibition of racial intermarriage; by the passing down of wealth or poverty, language and culture to one's children; and by racially segregated institutions such as housing and job markets.

The Breakdown of the "Natural" Family System

In the last fifteen years, the "natural" family system has been breaking down and coming under increasing attack by feminists and others.

1. *Married women have entered the labor force and "men's jobs" in growing numbers, challenging the "natural" sexual division of labor.* Now over half of married women are in paid jobs at any one time. Women are demanding entry into the better-paid "men's jobs," and pressing their husbands to do "women's work" in the home. The "natural" marriage union between a bread-winning husband and a homemaking wife has become the exception rather than the rule, characterizing only 29% of husband/wife couples in 1985 (Current Population Reports March 1985).

2. *Married women's labor force participation has created a crisis in day care: there is a severe shortage of day care facilities, especially affordable ones.* In New York, for example, between 830,000 and 1.2 million preschool and school-age children vie for the fewer than 135,000 available licensed child care placements (Select Committee on Children 1987). The shortage of day care, combined with the absence of flexible jobs, forces parents to use make-shift arrangements: 2.1 million or 7% of 5–13 year olds whose mothers work outside the home are admittedly left unsupervised; actual numbers are much higher (Children's Defense Fund 1987).

---

[3] Similarly, whites in the Eugenics movement argued that poor whites had inferior genes, and worked to limit their reproduction (Gould 1981).

3. *Growing numbers are not living in husband/wife families*; only 57% of all households include married couples. Adults are marrying later, spending more time living alone (23.4% of all households) or with friends or lovers. Homosexuality appears to be on the rise, and gays are coming out of the closet and demanding their rights. Marriages have become very unstable; divorce rates more than tripled between 1960 and 1982, more than doubling the number of female-headed households (1986 and 1987 Statistical Abstracts).

4. *"Natural" parenting is on the wane.* Divorces create "unnatural" [8] female-headed households, most with dependent children. Unwed mothering has increased to comprise 1 in 5 births and over half of all births among blacks (1987 Statistical Abstract). Remarriages create "unnatural" families, with step-parents and -siblings. More "unnatural" is the trend for sterile couples, gays, and singles to obtain children through artificial insemination, surrogate mothers, and inter-country inter-racial adoptions.

What do these trends mean? Members of the so-called Moral Majority interpret them as the breakdown of *the* family; their solution, embodied in the Family Protection Act of the late 1970s and early 1980s, is to put the "natural" family back together: encourage marriage; discourage divorce, unwed mothering, homosexuality; and get married women out of men's jobs and back into the home. The radical perspective is the opposite; the "natural" family is only one of many possible family systems, a very oppressive and ineffective one at that, as the next section will show. Growing numbers are rejecting the "natural" family system, and trying to create alternative family structures. What society needs is a radical family policy to focus and facilitate this process of dismantling of the old family system and constructing a new and more liberated one.

The Radical Critique of the "Natural" Family

The radical critique of the "natural" family has many prongs. All of these are underlain by a common claim—the "natural" family is not natural, necessary, or optimal, and a more adequate family system needs to be developed.

1. *The "natural" family system is not natural.* Biological differences in skin color or sex organs, and biological similarities between parent and child, do not necessitate a particular family form, or hierarchy

and difference between the sexes and races. Past family systems have been very different from the "natural" family.[4] It is not nature but our society which is producing and reproducing the "natural" family, and its associated institutions of gender and race difference and inequality, through parenting practices, laws, labor market structures, and culture.

2. *The "natural" family system is classist and racist.* The conception of the "natural" family is generated by the dominant culture of upperclass, native-born whites, who then claim it applies to all. Since being a man means bread-winning and supporting a homebound homemaker and children, men without "family wage" jobs due to unemployment, class, or race discrimination are seen (and often see themselves) as less than manly. Black women, forced into the labor force to compensate for their husbands' lack of economic opportunity, are viewed as unfeminine, castrating "matriarchs," and the extended and chosen family system which blacks have developed to combat poverty and economic insecurity is condemned as deviant (Stack 1974). The inability of the poor to properly parent their children because of their meager resources is seen as a fault in their characters, and they are criticized for having children at all, as if the poor do not have a right to parent.

3. *The "natural" family system impoverishes female-headed households.* Women and children face high risks of poverty. Married women are to specialize in unpaid homemaking and mothering, complementing their husbands' bread-winning. Divorce or widowhood leaves women with little access to income, but with major if not full emotional and financial responsibility for the children.[5] "Women's jobs" do not pay enough to cover child care and keep female households with young children out of poverty. The present welfare system (Aid to Families with Dependent Children), structured to support the "natural" family system, does not even provide

---

[4] Among the Rangiroa, adopted children were given equal status and rights as biological offspring, and considered "one belly" (from the same mother) with one another and with their other siblings (Sahlins 1976). In the New England and Southern colonies, mothering among the wealthy was essentially biological, producing one's husband's children, who were then nursed and cared for by poor white or slave women. Mead (1935) found societies where men and women shared the early care of children. Many societies see polygamy as the norm for marriage; others have allowed females to live as men and take wives after having cross-sex dreams (Blackwood 1984). Among the ancient Greeks, the highest form of love for an adult man was homosexual love for a younger man.

[5] In 1983, only 35% of mothers caring for their children with absent fathers received any child-support, and the average yearly payment was only $2,341; only 6% of separated or divorced women received any alimony (1987 Statistical Abstract).

headed families with poverty-level income. The result: the majority of black and Hispanic female-headed families (50 and 53%, respectively), and 27% of white female-headed families, are poor. Children are penalized the most: 54% of children in such families are poor (Current Population Reports 1985).

4. *"Natural" marriage creates inequality between the sexes.* Since wives are relegated to unpaid housework and low paid jobs, they are economically dependent upon their husbands. Fear of losing this financial support can force women into subservience to their husbands, and into staying in unsatisfying marriages. Indeed, some feminists see "natural" marriage as a struggle in which men have gained the upper hand by monopolizing the higher-paid jobs (Hartmann 1981). Whatever its origins, "natural" marriage is clearly unequal, making mutual love and respect difficult.

5. *"Natural" parenting is oppressive and unjust.* Along with financial responsibility, parents are given almost total power over children. Children have no rights, and no system through which they can complain about mistreatment or find alternative parents (Rodham 1976). In a society where most men are under the power of bosses, and women under that of their husbands, parenting provides an arena where adults have total power and authority. It is easy to forget one's children's needs and use or abuse them to fill one's own needs. What results is not only an epidemic of child physical and sexual abuse,[6] but also the training of each child to accept and participate in hierarchical and authoritarian systems, from schools to workplaces to politics (Miller 1981).

6. *The "natural" family perpetuates inequality between families* through the generations, because parents pass down their economic position to their children. Inheritance keeps ownership of the means of production in the hands of a few, mostly white, families.[7] Children born into higher-income families receive better nutrition, housing, health care, and schooling than their poor counterparts, have the "insurance" of wealthy relatives to back them up and encourage risk-taking, and can expect to inherit wealth. On the other hand, 11 million children (one in five) must live without even the most basic goods and services (Current Population Reports 1985). This

---

[6] The media have focussed on child abuse by strangers—on day care scandals and missing children—whereas the vast majority of children are abused by their parents or relatives (Eliasoph 1986).

[7] The wealthiest 2.4% of households owns 65% of the income-producing wealth (Edwards, Reich, Weisskopf 1986).

is not only unjust but also irrational: it is in society's interest to guarantee quality health care and education to its future workers and citizens.

7. *The "natural" family system discourages the formation of alternative families, while forcing many into unwanted "natural" families.* Its broad and virulent anti-gay discrimination from education, employment, housing, and marriage laws to media images—makes it very difficult for people to love and share their lives with people of the same sex. It discriminates against couples who are unable to have children biologically by treating adoption and artificial insemination as "unnatural" and undesirable options. On the other hand, the "natural" family's equation of sex, reproduction, and marriage creates unwanted children by creating opposition to sex education, birth control for unmarried teens, and abortion. Forty percent of all births are mistimed or unwanted—for those under 24, a disastrous 53%—forcing millions of women into premature or unwanted motherhood and/or marriages (1987 Statistical Abstract).

Conceptualizing a Social Family System

The "natural" family system is inadequate, oppressive, and is coming apart at the seams. At the same time, all need the love and warmth and sharing and parenting which family relationships provide.[8] Hence criticism is not enough; an *alternative* and better vision of family life needs to be delineated, along with a set of concrete policies to bring such a new family system into being.

The oppressiveness of the "natural" family system was accepted because its institutions were seen as natural and inevitable. Our new family system would be a *consciously* social one, its institutions developed through study, discussion, struggle and compromise, and continually criticized and improved so as to maximize freedom, equality, self-fulfillment, democracy, and justice. Here are some of the central principles of such a system; while it may appear utopian, many are living out parts of this vision now.

Social Marriage. Marriage would become a symmetrical relationship between whole, equal, and socially independent human

---

[8] Some feminists and gays have taken an "anti-family" position, as if the "natural" family is the only family form (Barrett and McIntosh 1982); however they usually advocate some alternative, family-like institutions.

beings, each participating in a similar range of familial, economic and political activities.[9] Its basis would be mutual love of the other, i.e., liking of, respect for, and sexual attraction to the person the other is, as providing the reason for intimate sharing of lives and living spaces and, if desired, parenting. Couples would not be expected to stay together "for better or for worse . . . as long as ye both shall live"; nor would they need to, since each would have earnings.

Social Parenting. Parenting would be recognized as a quintessentially *social* activity which, by shaping our unconsciousnesses, bodies, and minds, shapes the future of our society. Society would ensure that each child is well cared for and educated, since the upbringing of children as physically and psychologically healthy, creative, educated, and socially-conscious citizens is essential both to society's well-being, and to our belief in equal opportunity. This would include providing children and their parents with economic and institutional support, as well as seeking out optimal parenting practices and educating prospective parents in them.

Social Community. Cultural and economic differences between groups of people would be acknowledged to be social rather than natural products. All human beings would be recognized as equally human citizens of the world, and a concept of basic human rights, both political and economic, developed. Intercultural marriages would be encouraged to further social understanding.

Bringing the Social Family into Being: A Policy Checklist

Although the "natural" family system is in decline, the social family system cannot replace it unless there are many changes in our economic and social institutions. Here are some of the policies which will help bring about these changes; many are now in place in other countries.

1. *Policies which socialize parenting*   24

a. *Policies which establish the right of all adults to choose when and if they wish to parent.* Universal sex education and parenting training for adolescents, as well as access of all to free, safe, 100%

---

[9] If this seems far-fetched, an October 1977 CBS–*New York Times* National Survey found that 50% of 30–44 year olds, and 67% of 18–29 year olds, preferred a symmetrical marriage (of a man and woman who both had jobs, did housework, and cared for the children) over the traditional, complementary one.

effective birth control, abortions, and adoption placement, are needed to make every child a wanted child. At the same time, society must recognize the right of those who are infertile, gay, or single to parent, and support the development of alternative modes of obtaining children from adoption to artificial insemination and in-vitro fertilization.[10] The right to parent must also be protected by programs to help low-income parents with the costs of child-rearing (see 1b). Finally, the right to parent must be seen as socially established, rather than inhering in the genetic connection between a parent and a child; parenting rights must be revocable if a parent neglects or abuses a child, and society should seek to prevent child abuse through an effective system of child advocates and parenting support and training.

b. *Policies which ensure a basic, social inheritance for every child.* The best way to ensure healthy and provided-for children is to ensure this health and income to all families through a system of national health insurance and a combination of anti-poverty measures, from full employment, to comparable worth, to a guaranteed annual income. In addition, since having children does increase a family's poverty risk, family allowances should be provided to parents according to need.[11] Furthermore, all children need to have access to high quality, free or sliding-scale education, from preschool day care when their parents are at work, to elementary and secondary school and college. This "social inheritance" program would be paid for by high inheritance taxes and very progressive income and/or luxury taxes. Such taxes would, in themselves, help reduce the present gross inequalities of opportunity among children.[12]

c. *Policies which socialize child-care costs: government- and business-subsidized day care.* Making quality child care available and affordable to all should be the joint financial responsibility of business and government, since it benefits both employers and society at large.

---

[10] Most doctors refuse to artificially inseminate single or lesbian women. The developing practice of surrogate mothering is very controversial among feminists and radicals. Since eggs can be fertilized outside of a womb, and embryos can be raised in incubators from the age of a few months, there are many other possibilities, including impregnating men, or even producing infants entirely outside of human bodies, as Marge Piercy (1976) and Shulamith Firestone (1970) have envisioned.

[11] Sweden and France give housing allowances to parents (Kamerman and Kahn 1979); many European countries have national health insurance and family allowances. Swedish policy is to guarantee all citizens a minimum standard of living (Ibid.); in the U. S., the needy only receive support through "entitlement" programs, which require certain qualifications (such as being a female household head with children) other than being poor, and which do not, in any event, raise incomes up to the poverty level.

[12] See Chester (1982) for a review of Western thought on inheritance.

A few trend-setting employers now provide child-care benefits to their workers, having found that these more than pay for themselves by decreasing worker absenteeism, increasing productivity, and attracting top workers (Blau and Ferber 1986). Current federal funding through Title 20 is woefully inadequate; many states are serving less than 30% of their eligible populations (Select Committee on Children 1987). One survey found that ¼ of all full-time homemakers, and ½ of all single parents, were kept from employment and training programs by the unavailability of child care (Cal. Governor's Task Force on Child Care 1986). Again, Sweden provides the example to follow: the government pays 90% of the child-care costs of public day care centers, which are used by over half of children with employed mothers (Blau and Ferber 1986).

On the other hand, to permit parents with job commitments to spend more time with their children, especially their infants, a system of paid leaves from work without loss of one's job or seniority must be established. The U.S. does not even have laws guaranteeing prospective parents an *unpaid* leave when they have or adopt a child.[13] In a few states, women can use their temporary disability insurance to pay for 4 to 10 weeks of pregnancy/infant care leave (Kamerman et al. 1983). Again, Sweden is the model in this area, with 1) paid, year-long parental leaves, 2) up to 60 days a year paid leave to care for sick children, and 3) the right for all full-time employed parents with children under 8 to reduce their work weeks (with reduced pay) to 30 hours a week (Ginsberg 1983). Radicals have advocated a shorter work week without reduction in pay as a solution to unemployment and low productivity, for it would create more jobs, reduce unemployment, and increase output (Bowles, Gordon, and Weisskopf 1983); a consideration of the needs of parents makes such policies even more desirable. Other innovations which allow adults to combine work with parenting are flex-time and flex-place (working at home); the extension of health, pension, and other benefits to part-time workers; and the cafeteria benefit plan, which allows dual-career couples to eliminate doubly-covered benefits in favor of more of other benefits, such as leaves or child-care support (Farley 1983; Kamerman and Hayes 1982).

---

[13] Kamerman and Kingston (in Kamerman and Hayes 1982) found that paid maternity leave was available to fewer than one-third of all employed women in 1978, and averaged only about six weeks of benefits.

2. *Policies to support egalitarian, symmetrical marriages* in which partners participate equally in parenting, housework, the labor force, and political life.[14]

a. *Comparable worth, affirmative action, increased unionization.* Comparable worth would increase the pay of women's jobs to that of men's jobs requiring comparable skill, effort, and responsibility. Affirmative action encourages women to enter into traditionally masculine jobs. Women need to organize in unions to fight for the above, and for general wage increases; one platform is "solidarity wages," again practiced in Sweden, in which workers agree to take part of their wage increase to reduce inequalities among them. Together these policies would stop the segregation of women into low-paid, dead end, less-satisfying jobs, reduce women's economic dependence upon men, and encourage more similar work and family participation by the sexes.

b. *Socialization of parenting* (see #1 above) would support symmetrical marriage, for it would allow adults to combine parenting with labor force commitments, reducing the pressure to specialize as in "natural" marriage.

c. *Repeal of the laws that discourage formation of "unnatural" marriages and non-traditional households.* This includes repealing sodomy laws and advocating legislation prohibiting discrimination against gays in employment, housing, insurance, foster parenting, adoption, and other areas.[15] Gay relationships must be legitimized in marriage laws, to give spouses health insurance, pension, inheritance, and other benefits and rights enjoyed by heterosexual spouses.[16] The repeal of co-residence laws, which in many states prohibit the cohabitation of more than two unrelated adults, is needed to allow the formation of non-biologically–based extended families.

d. *Individual rather than joint taxation of married couples.* Our present income tax system is progressive and married couples are

---

[14] Cuba encourages such marriages through its "Family Code," adopted in 1975 (Randall 1981); however, it still discriminates against gay couples.

[15] Sodomy laws, which outlaw forms of "unnatural sex" (e.g., anal intercourse and oral/genital sex, either heterosexual or homosexual), still exist in many states, and were recently upheld by the Supreme Court, although they are seldom enforced. Many cities and a few states have passed gay rights legislation, and more and more employers have extended their non-discrimination policy to include sexual preference or orientation.

[16] In June 1987, the Swedish Parliament approved a bill which gave gay couples the same rights as heterosexuals married by common law; it will allow couples to sign housing leases as couples, regulate the division of property after a break-up, and grant lovers the right to inherit property in the absence of a will (*Gay Community News*, June 14–20, 1987).

from entering the labor force since, when a woman's earnings raise the household's tax bracket, much of her earnings are paid to the government in taxes.[17] Taxing adults individually (as is currently done in Sweden), rather than jointly, would instead encourage both members of a couple to participate in the labor force.

e. *Policies to aid the casualties of the "natural" marriage system.* Until the above changes are achieved, women and children will continue to face high poverty risks when they live in female-headed households. Many feminists advocate the strengthening of alimony and child-support laws; however, this both reinforces the "natural" marriage notion that husbands should be the main providers, and reproduces class and race inequality, because wives' and children's incomes depend on that of their husbands/fathers. Extensive welfare reform, combined with the policies above, is a better solution.

3. *Policies to create social community.* Labor market reforms (2a) must always aim at eliminating both race and sex segregation and discrimination. These, along with social inheritance policies, will go far in stopping the economic reproduction of racial inequality in the U.S. The decline of "natural" parenting views of children as "one's own flesh and blood" will foster, and in turn be fostered by, the decline of conceptions of race, as both are replaced by a view of a human community reproduced through social parenting.

Bibliography

Barrett, Michele, and McIntosh, Mary. 1982. *The Anti-Social Family*. London: New Left Books.

Blackwood, Evelyn. 1984. Sexuality and Gender in Certain Native Tribes: The Case of Cross-Gender Females. *Signs* 10(1):27–42.

Blau, Francine, and Ferber, Marianne. 1986. *The Economics of Women, Men, and Work*. Englewood Cliffs, N.J.: Prentice-Hall.

Bowles, Samuel, David M. Gordon, and Thomas E. Weisskopf. 1983. *Beyond the Wasteland: A Democratic Alternative to Economic Decline*. New York: Anchor Doubleday.

Chester, Ronald. 1982. *Inheritance, Wealth, and Society*. Bloomington: Indiana University Press.

Children's Defense Fund. 1987. Unpublished paper.

[17] Even though the recent tax reform reduced the progressivity of the tax system, and a 1983 reform exempted 10% of the income of the lower-earning partner from taxation, the "marriage penalty" persists (Blau and Ferber 1986).

Edwards, Richard, Reich, Michael, and Weisskopf, Thomas. 1986. *The Capitalist System*. Englewood Cliffs, N.J.: Prentice-Hall. Third Edition.

Eliasoph, Nina. 1986. Drive-In Mortality, Child Abuse, and the Media. *Socialist Review* #90, 16(6):7–31.

Farley, Jennie, ed. 1983. *The Woman in Management*. New York: ILR Press.

Firestone, Shulamith. 1970. *The Dialectic of Sex*. New York: Morrow.

Ginsberg, Helen. 1983. *Full Employment and Public Policy: The United States and Sweden*. Lexington, Mass.: D.C. Heath and Co.

Gould, Stephen J. 1981. *The Mismeasure of Man*. New York: Norton.

Hartmann, Heidi. 1981. The Unhappy Marriage of Marxism and Feminism. In *Women and Revolution: A Discussion of the Unhappy Marriage of Marxism and Feminism*, Lydia Sargent (ed.), pp. 1–41. Boston: South End Press.

Kamerman, Sheila, and Kahn, Alfred. 1979. *Family Policy: Government and Families in Fourteen Countries*. New York: Columbia University Press.

Kamerman, Sheila, and Hayes, Cheryl, eds. 1982. *Families that Work: Children in a Changing World*. Washington: National Academy Press.

Kamerman, Sheila, et al., eds. 1983. *Maternity Policies and Working Women*. New York: Columbia University Press.

Matthaei, Julie. 1982. *An Economic History of Women in America: Women's Work, the Sexual Division of Labor, and the Development of Capitalism*. New York: Schocken Books.

Mead, Margaret. 1935. *Sex and Temperament in Three Primitive Societies*. New York: William Morrow and Co.

Miller, Alice. 1981. *The Drama of the Gifted Child*. trans. by Ruth Ward. New York: Basic Books.

Piercy, Marge. 1976. *Woman on the Edge of Time*. New York: Fawcett.

Randall, Margaret. 1981. *Women in Cuba: Twenty Years Later*. New York: Smyrna Press.

Rodham, Hilary. 1976. Children under the Law. In *Rethinking Childhood* Arlene Skolnick (ed.). Boston: Little, Brown and Co.

Sahlins, Marshall. 1976. *The Use and Abuse of Biology: An Anthropological Critique of Sociobiology*. Ann Arbor: University of Michigan Press.

Select Committee on Children, Youth and Families, U.S. House of Representatives. 1987. Fact Sheet: Hearing on Child Care, Key to Employment in a Changing Economy. March 10.

Stack, Carol. 1974. *All Our Kin*. New York: Harper & Row.

U.S. Bureau of the Census, Current Population Reports. 1985. Household and Family Characteristics: March 1985.

——. 1985. Money Income and Poverty Status of Families and Persons in the United States.

——. 1986. 1987. Statistical Abstract of the United States.

Weeks, Jeffrey. 1979. *Coming Out: Homosexual Politics in Britain, from the Nineteenth Century to the Present*. London: Quartet Books.

Topics for Discussion and Writing

1. What, if anything, strikes you as "radical" in Matthaei's "radical analysis" of the "'natural' family" (paragraph 3)? Do any parts of this analysis strike you as unfair, misleading, or wrong? If so, which parts, and what do you find wrong with them?

2. In paragraph 7 Matthaei says that "adults are marrying later." Assuming this statement to be true, what do you think are the causes? What do you think may be the consequences, good and bad?

3. In paragraph 10 Matthaei denies that the "natural" family is natural. Do you think she proves her case? If not, in what way(s) does she fail?

4. Matthaei argues (paragraph 15) that the idea of the "natural" family can lead easily to child abuse. Can one argue in response that the "natural" family is better suited to assist children in growing into healthy, responsible, happy adults than is any conceivable alternative arrangement? If you think so, what arguments might you offer? (For an interesting argument that children should be granted legal rights to escape impossible families, see "Confessions of an Erstwhile Child," pages 143–48.)

5. In paragraph 17 Matthaei argues that the idea of the "natural" family "discriminates against couples who are unable to have children biologically." Is she saying that all adults—including the sterile, the infertile, and those who do not wish to engage in heterosexual sex—have a right to have children? If she is saying this, on what might she base this right? In her next paragraph she says, "All need the love and warmth and sharing and parenting which family relationships provide." Is this need perhaps the basis for a right—possessed by all adults—to have children? (See also the discussion in paragraph 24.)

6. Much of the essay is devoted to arguing on behalf of various kinds of equality. For example, in paragraph 20, in discussing "social marriage," Matthaei says that "marriage would become a symmetrical relationship between whole, equal, and socially independent human beings." The two persons involved would participate "in a similar range of familial, economic, and political activities." But what if both persons do not share an interest in, for example, political activities? Should they therefore not marry? (For an argument that it is better for a couple *not* to share their interests around the clock and seven days a week, see the essay by Perrin, pages 130–32.) Or suppose that one person enjoyed the world of paid work and the other preferred to engage, at least for a while, chiefly in the role of parenting and housekeeping. Do you think such a marriage would be inherently unstable?

7. In point 1b of paragraph 24, Matthaei argues for programs and policies that would redistribute wealth—for example, a guaranteed annual income. Suppose someone argued (or at least asserted) that he or she saw no reason to support the families of the poor. What reply might you make?

8. Matthaei apparently sees marriage as involving only two adults. Do you assume that she rejects polygamy (a practice not unknown in the United States and elsewhere)? And what about polyandry (one woman with two or more husbands)? If you accept Matthaei's arguments, or most of them, how do *you* feel about polygamy and polyandry? Arguments for polygamy can be found in the essay by Elizabeth Joseph (pages 127–29). What argument(s) for polyandry can you imagine?

Florence Trefethen

Florence Trefethen holds degrees from Bryn Mawr and the University of Cambridge. She has taught English at Tufts University and now is executive editor for books published by the Council on East Asian Studies at Harvard University. Her poems and short stories appear frequently.

This essay was originally published in the Washington Post.

Points of a Lifelong Triangle: Reflections of an Adoptive Mother

I have a friend who's a social worker. Her clients include a group of women who've given up a child for adoption. Their ages range widely, and the moment of surrender may have been long ago or last year. They form a birth mothers' support group.

My friend says their meetings are suffused with sorrow, sometimes bitterness. They describe their lost children and the new parents as ambling through life happily, selfishly, and with never a thought for the origins left behind. As an adoptive mother, I find that picture distorted.

I think of the biological father rarely, envisioning him as the dashing young fellow he must have been at the time he sired our daughter. But scarcely a day goes by when the birth mother is not in my thoughts, growing older as I do.

She's been with me from the start. When Gwyned was placed 4 with us on probation, there was always the threat that the birth mother might change her mind and snatch our baby back. She loomed as a fearsome adversary. I pictured her wild-eyed, manic, appearing in the courtroom a moment before the final decree, shouting, "She's mine, and her name is Monica!" Our papers were approved, however, without incident.

Those papers contain my signature and my husband's. The birth parents' signatures were folded under so that we never learned their names. The papers are dated Dec. 30, 1953, and are locked away in a Maryland court house, apparently inviolate. We received a "birth certificate" proclaiming that Gwyned was born to me and my husband on May 8, 1953, in Garfield Memorial Hospital, Washington D.C.

What is a birthday like for an adopted daughter who's 1 or 4 or 10 or 16 or all the years between and after? Just like birthdays for other children—parties, presents, friends and family gathered to celebrate. But for me there was always a special poignancy when lighting the candles on the cake. I, the mother in residence, would think of that first mother, wondering where she was, knowing she was remembering the day. I wanted to call out to her and say, "Look how delightful Gwyned is! Thank you." My hands always shook as I carried the cake to the table, trying not to quaver as I started singing "Happy Birthday."

Gwyned didn't seem to care. She grew up in a neighborhood and attended a school where there were several adopted children. No big deal, she said. In fact, she implied that there was a special cachet to being "selected." Though she knew better, I think she fantasized about our walking down an aisle lined with bassinets until we came to her and said, "That's the one!"

When Gwyned acquired a figure, it turned out to be more svelte 8 than the figures in my family; I imagined the birth mother trim in bikinis, mini skirts and other fashions I avoided. Gwyned took to singing in choruses, acting in plays; the birth mother became the repository of performing talents I'd never possessed. Gwyned liked skiing and running and in college elected "self defense" in gym; the birth mother assumed the dimensions of a sportswoman, perhaps Olympics material.

With the approach of Gwyned's wedding, I grew restless, then frantic. Ought we try to contact that birth mother, to assure her everything had turned out well, possibly to invite her to the marriage? I struggled with these questions through sleepless nights and finally consulted a psychiatrist. He offered a common-sense suggestion I wish I'd thought of in my anxiety: "Why don't you ask Gwyned?" I did. She said she'd just as soon leave things as they were. She spoke as though that issue was closed. But later in life she changed her mind. After giving birth to her own children, she began to wonder about physical traits and medical histories.

At the same time, large-scale changes were in motion. Mothers were locating long-lost children; adult adoptees were searching for parents, combing registers, placing ads; associations were established to facilitate these investigations and, it was hoped, ultimate reunions. Some agencies and some states offered help to the searchers. Others clung to the conditions in force at the time of adoption—usually an unbreachable barrier between birth parents and adoptive parents.

"Can't I get the name of at least one of my parents?" Gwyned asked. "With a name, I could search." She presented herself at the adoption agency; they declined to reveal that information. She petitioned the court and had a hearing before the judge; he said he did not want "to disturb the birth mother." In the hope that our support might be useful, my husband and I wrote to both agency and judge, to no avail.

It's difficult to sort out the rights and wrongs in a case like this. 12 Gwyned feels compelled to close a loop that's been open all her life. She gets encouragement from support groups but also pain, since they usually include happy birth mothers and adult adoptees who have found each other. My heart aches as I observe her thus far futile efforts to pinpoint anyone who can help her, any clue that might lead to success. Sometimes I feel guilty for having failed, in the initial wonder of acquiring a marvelous child, to anticipate that the secrecy then imposed might one day frustrate us all.

Yet we can understand the adamance of the adoption agency and the court. They are simply adhering to the rules in force nearly four decades ago when the decree became final. They were parties to a contract and are loath to break it. Perhaps they may even feel they are sparing us grief. Indeed, the birth mother, if located, might not wish to be disturbed, might reject Gwyned. Or she could prove to be a disappointment.

I doubt it, though. She's been in my mind and my mind's eye for 37 years, and I'm convinced she's a sad but lovely lady. Whatever her name, and whether or not we ever find her, she, Gwyned and I are the points of a triangle that will endure all our lives.

Topics for Discussion and Writing

1. Do you agree with the decisions made by the adoption agency and the judge? Why or why not? Do you know of any instances of reunions

between the birth parent and a child? If so, how do they influence your opinion about the advisability of agencies and courts facilitating such reunions?

2. The father is mentioned only briefly, in the first sentence of the third paragraph, and to our knowledge is rarely the parent sought by adopted children. Nor do we hear or read of adopted sons seeking their birth parents. What do you make of this phenomenon? Or do you know of exceptions to our generalizations?

3. The essay is about a controversial point—should agencies and courts reveal the names of birth parents to the children whom they surrendered?—but it is also about Gwyned, about the birth mother, and about the author. How would you characterize the author? What do you think the author's purposes in writing the essay were?

4. Consider the title (including the subtitle) and the opening and the concluding paragraphs. What does the title lead you to expect? What does the first paragraph suggest about birth mothers and the author's attitude toward them? How does the concluding paragraph change or enrich your reading (or rereading) of the title and the first paragraph?

5. Imagine that you are one of Gwyned's birth parents—since you are imagining, you can choose either gender—and you have happened on this article. What do you imagine you would feel or would do? Write a letter (but don't, of course, mail it) to Florence or to Gwyned Trefethen, or to the editor of *The Washington Post* (you can ask to have your name withheld), explaining what you feel and what you plan or do not plan to do.

Letty Cottin Pogrebin

Letty Cottin Pogrebin (b. 1939) is the author of Growing Up Free, *a book about the need to resist the sexist cultural programming of television, books, and schools. The essay that we reprint originally appeared in* The New York Times.

Consequences

In 1958, I had an illegal abortion. I was 19, a senior in college, an English major. Marriage was not an option: the boyfriend was my age but he was a sophomore majoring in basketball. When I met him after practice and told him I was pregnant, the panic in his eyes infuriated me. I assured him I didn't want to get married. The panic remainded. The poor guy was terified for my sake but he didn't know what to say or do. He started to cry, then caught himself and punched the cinder-block wall of the gym, breaking his hand and getting himself benched for the season.

I didn't know what to do, either. In all honesty, I wasn't even sure how I'd gotten into this fix. Many women of my generation believed you could get pregnant from a toilet seat but were never quite clear about how you got pregnant from a man. Our sexual gospel was full of axioms like "you can't get pregnant if you do it standing up" and "no one gets pregnant the first time." I needed two missed periods to believe that it had happened to me.

Finally I told my roommate. She was as innocent as I was of such matters, but she persuaded me to confide in our dorm counselor, a kindly woman who coached girls' field hockey. The coach hugged me as I sobbed, but didn't lecture me; she let me vent my misery, answered my questions and made sure I understood my options and their repercussions. In biology texts, I'd seen that at this stage a pregnancy is a mass of cells, not a "child." I told her I had decided to have an abortion, an early, immediate abortion.

She was nonjudgmental, but given the criminal penalties at the   4 time was afraid to get involved in my search for a doctor. She convinced me to have a pregnancy test, at least, to confirm my suspicions. The test came back positive. For about 48 hours, I thought about killing myself.

For those who didn't live through the 50's, it's hard to believe the suffocating terror of sexual shame and the coercive power of social propriety. In those years, etiquette demanded that women not wear white before Memorial Day or after Labor Day, so you can imagine the moral absolutes. For a well-bred middle-class girl, pregnancy "out of wedlock" was the ultimate disgrace, and in the Jewish community in which I grew up, it was a *shonda*, a scandal discussed in contemptuous whispers behind closed doors.

The category "single mothers" did not exist then. A woman could be a married mother, a widow with children or a "divorcee" with children, but unless her body was legitimized by marriage, the fruit of her womb was "illegitimate," and she herself forfeited the right to travel in polite company or win a respectable husband in the future. As a result, young pregnant women were quickly pressed into "shotgun" marriages or else, under a canopy of lies—"she's caring for a sick aunt in Cleveland"—were spirited away to "homes for unwed mothers" where they disappeared from view, like lepers, until the pregnancy ran its course. Until they gave birth among strangers and left their babies to be adopted by strangers.

I could not tolerate that idea. It seemed wrong to make pregnancy the punishment for my sexual activity (especially when, for the same activity, the young man would get off with some angst and a broken hand). And it seemed crazy to consider adoption a "solution." I would not carry a child for a full nine months, feel it move inside my body, endure morning sickness, swollen legs and the pain of labor only to have my baby taken away from me. I could never live in a world where a child of mine was being raised by someone else.

I wanted to be a mother, someday. I wanted to create a new life and give it the same loving, well-fed childhood my mother gave me. But I would not be an accidental mother, an ashamed mother, an impoverished mother, a hostile mother or what today is termed a "birth mother"—one who brings a child into the world but cannot share its life.

Even in 1958, I did not confuse my capacity to breed with my capability to mother. One day, I thought, I will be a terrific parent, but at 19 I was still raising myself out of adolescence, four years after my own mother died. She was my model of sensitivity, understanding and patience. Because of her, I had great respect for what it takes to be a good parent. I wanted to be worthy of the job. I would not be a mother before I could be an adult.

With single parenthood and adoption out of the question, abortion was my choice, the only choice for me. But where could I turn for money and help?

My father, a lawyer, subscribed to traditional gender roles except when it came to me and money. Earning his own living at an early age had been the making of him, he said, and he insisted it would be character-building for me, even though I was a girl. He paid for college, but I had to earn my spending money, which I did by taking summer jobs, tutoring athletes and working for the Hillel rabbi on campus. For all my bootstrap efforts, $12 was what I had left in the bank after I paid for the pregnancy test. I had to ask my father for help; there was no one else.

He was the sort of man who could talk about French conjugations or the First Amendment but not about problems or emotions. Paralyzed with fear, I finally breathed out the words: "Daddy, I'm pregnant, and I can't afford an abortion." His expression never changed; there was no moralizing, no scolding, but also no comfort. Nurturing wasn't his style. He went straight for the practical issues: who, when and how much. He said he would take care of the arrangements and lend me the money.

Although I had been warned about kitchen-table hacks, my father found a real doctor who did abortions on the side. Late one night, I hurried into a darkened medical office, accompanied by my father and his new wife. I hated having her along, but he insisted we might need a woman in case there were complications.

There were no complications.

These memories came flooding back last December, when a friend stunned me with the news that she'd just heard from the child she gave up for adoption 32 years ago. I know this woman's 28-year-old son, but I never knew about the secret daughter, the one who got born because a bogus abortionist took an unsuspecting young woman's money and left her pregnant. Now the baby she last saw in the delivery room was coming for Christmas with *her* baby.

"I'm excited to be a grandmother," my friend told me, "but I feel   16
such regret, loss and guilt about my daughter that it overpowers all my other feelings."

I hope my friend's reunion story ends well. All I know is what it aroused in me. Relief. Waves of God-grateful relief. Had I not been able to terminate that pregnancy in 1958, I might now have a 32-year-old daughter (or son) looking for *me,* and surely I would be a very different me for having carried the misery that burdened my friend all these years.

It's never simple. That's why public policy on abortion and adoption must be filtered through the experiences of women like us. When adoption is heralded as the answer to unwanted pregnancy, the targets of concern are infertile parents, not the woman, her feelings, her body and her future — or the future feelings of the child she must give away.

I was grateful I never had to leave a child of mine with strangers or unwittingly pass a legacy of rejection to an infant at birth. If such a child existed today, no matter how happy our reunion, I would forever mourn the 32 lost years.

The fact that I was able to choose abortion made possible the   20
life that was and is. Above all, the child-who-wasn't made possible the three wanted children who are my family today.

Topics for Discussion and Writing

1. In paragraph 10, Pogrebin writes: "With single parenthood and adoption out of the question, abortion was my choice, my only choice." How has she attempted to persuade us, up to this point in the essay, that single parenthood and adoption were "out of the question"?

2. How does her account of her mother in paragraph 8, her father in paragraphs 11 and 12, and the abortion in paragraph 13, further attempt to persuade? What further issue begins to appear in paragraph 15?

3. Although the essay is largely a personal narrative, it is also an argument. Which arguments are stated and which are implied? Overall, which arguments do you find most persuasive and which least? Try to explain why.

4. What arguments for or against abortion has she not touched on in this essay? Should she have?

5. Paragraph 14 consists of a single sentence. What is the effect? Notice also the fragment that concludes paragraph 6. Can you justify the use of a fragment here?

6. Pogrebin seems to assume that an adopted child retains a "legacy of rejection" (paragraph 19). Do you find this a valid assumption? Why or why not?

7. To what does the essay's title refer? Write a paragraph in which you explain the title to someone who has not read the essay.

8. Compare Pogrebin and Trefethen (pages 120–22) on their characterization and depiction of "birth mothers" and their attitudes toward the search by adopted children for their birth parents.

Elizabeth Joseph

Elizabeth Joseph, a lawyer, lives in Utah. This essay appeared in The New York Times *in 1991.*

My Husband's Nine Wives

BIG WATER, Utah

I married a married man. In fact, he had six wives when I married him 17 years ago. Today, he has nine.

In March, the Utah Supreme Court struck down a trial court's ruling that a polygamist couple could not adopt a child because of their marital style. Last month, the national board of the American Civil Liberties Union, in response to a request from its Utah chapter, adopted a new policy calling for the legalization of polygamy.

Polygamy, or plural marriage, as practiced by my famliy is a paradox. At first blush, it sounds like the ideal situation for the man and an oppressive one for the women. For me, the opposite is true.   4

While polygamists believe that the Old Testament mandates the practice of plural marriage, compelling social reasons make the life style attractive to the modern career woman.

Pick up any women's magazine and you will find article after article about the problems of successfully juggling career, motherhood and marriage. It is a complex act that many women struggle to manage daily; their frustrations fill up the pages of those magazines and consume the hours of afternoon talk shows.

In a monogamous context, the only solutions are compromises. The kids need to learn to fix their own breakfast, your husband needs to get used to occasional microwave dinners, you need to divert more of your income to insure that your pre-schooler is in a good day care environment.

I am sure that in the challenge of working through these compromises, satisfaction and success can be realized. But why must women only embrace a marital arrangement that requires so many trade-offs?

When I leave for the 60-mile commute to court at 7 A.M., my two-year-old daughter, London, is happily asleep in the bed of my husband's wife, Diane. London adores Diane. When London awakes, about the time I'm arriving at the courthouse, she is surrounded by family members who are as familiar to her as the toys in her nursery. 8

My husband Alex, who writes at night, gets up much later. While most of his wives are already at work, pursuing their careers, he can almost always find one who's willing to chat over coffee.

I share a home with Delinda, another wife, who works in town government. Most nights, we agree we'll just have a simple dinner with our three kids. We'd rather relax and commiserate over the pressures of our work day than chew up our energy cooking and doing a ton of dishes.

Mondays, however, are different. That's the night Alex eats with us. The kids, excited that their father is coming to dinner, are on their best behavior. We often invite another wife or one of his children. It's a special event because it only happens once a week.

Tuesday night, it's back to simplicity for us. But for Alex and the household he's dining with that night, it's their special time. 12

The same system with some variation governs our private time with him. While spontaneity is by no means ruled out, we basically use an appointment system. If I want to spend Friday evening at his house, I make an appointment. If he's already "booked," I either request another night or if my schedule is inflexible, I talk to the other wife and we work out an arrangement. One thing we've all learned is that there's always another night.

Most evenings, with the demands of career and the literal chasing after the needs of a toddler, all I want to do is collapse into bed and sleep. But there is also the longing for intimacy and comfort that only he can provide, and when those feelings surface, I ask to be with him.

Plural marriage is not for everyone. But it is the life style for me. It offers men the chance to escape from the traditional, confining roles that often isolate them from the surrounding world. More important, it enables women, who live in a society full of obstacles, to fully meet their career, mothering and marriage obligations. Polygamy provides a whole solution. I believe American women would have invented it if it didn't already exist.

Topics for Discussion and Writing

1. In her fourth paragraph Joseph suggests that "compelling social reasons" make polygamy "the life style attractive to the modern career woman." How does she support this assertion? Do you think that she adequately supports it? Why, or why not?

2. Try to imagine advantages that Joseph does not discuss for women in polygamy, for example for women who are divorced or widowed. Whether or not you support polygamy, make the strongest arguments for these advantages that you can (and then, if you wish, answer them).

3. Joseph does not suggest or discuss any problems in polygamous marriages. What problems occur to you? Why should she or should she not have discussed them?

4. Many societies have practiced (and continue to practice) plural marriage, but it is illegal in the United States. Do you think that plural marriage should be a legal option? Why, or why not?

5. Does Joseph's article provide an answer to Brady's "Why I Want a Wife"? Read the article (104–06), imagine you are Brady, and answer this question. Or, imitating Joseph, write an article supporting polyandry (the practice of having more than one husband at a time).

Noel Perrin

Noel Perrin (b. 1927) was educated at Williams College, Duke University, and Cambridge University. He has written on a wide variety of subjects, for instance on Thomas Bowdler (the editor of an expurgated edition of Shakespeare, and hence the source of the word bowdlerize, *"to expurgate prudishly") and on the introduction of guns to Japan in the sixteenth century. Since 1959 he has taught English at Dartmouth College.*

A Part-time Marriage

When my wife told me she wanted a divorce, I responded like any normal college professor. I hurried to the college library. I wanted to get hold of some books on divorce and find out what was happening to me.

Over the next week (my wife meanwhile having left), I read or skimmed about 20. Nineteen of them were no help at all. They offered advice on financial settlements. They told me my wife and I should have been in counseling. A bit late for *that* advice.

What I sought was insight. I especially wanted to understand what was wrong with me that my wife had left, and not even for someone else, but just to be rid of *me.* College professors think they can learn that sort of thing from books.

As it turned out, I could. Or at least I got a start. The twentieth   4 book was a collection of essays by various sociologists, and one of the pieces took my breath away. It was like reading my own horoscope.

The two authors had studied a large group of divorced people much like my wife and me. That is, they focused on middle-class Americans of the straight-arrow persuasion. Serious types, believers in marriage for life. Likely to be parents—and, on the whole, good parents. Likely to have pillar-of-the-community potential. But, nevertheless, all divorced.

Naturally there were many different reasons why all these people had divorced, and many different ways they behaved after divorce. But there was a dominant pattern, and I instantly recognized myself in it. Recognized my wife, too. Reading the essay told me not only what was wrong with me, but also with her. It was the same flaw in both of us. It even gave me a hint as to what my postdivorce behavior was likely to be, and how I might find happiness in the future.

This is the story the essay told me. Or, rather, this is the story the essay hinted at, and that I have since pieced together with much observation, a number of embarrassingly personal questions put to divorced friends, and to some extent from my own life.

Somewhere in some suburb or town or small city, a middle-class couple separate. They are probably between 30 and 40 years old. They own a house and have children. The conscious or official reason for their separation is quite different from what it would have been in their parents' generation. Then, it would have been a man leaving his wife for another, and usually younger, woman. Now it's a woman leaving her husband in order to find herself.   8

When they separate, the wife normally stays in the house they occupied as a married couple. Neither wants to uproot the children. The husband moves to an apartment, which is nearly always going to be closer to his place of employment than the house was. The ex-wife will almost certainly never see that apartment. The husband, however, sees his former house all the time. Not only is he coming by to pick up the children for visits; if he and his ex-wife are on reasonably good terms, he is apt to visit them right there, while she makes use of the time to do errands or to see a friend.

Back when these two were married, they had an informal labor division. She did inside work, he did outside. Naturally there were exceptions: She gardened, and he did his share of the dishes, maybe even baked bread. But mostly he mowed the lawn and fixed the lawn mower; she put up any new curtains, often enough ones she had made herself.

One Saturday, six months or a year after they separated, he comes to see the kids. He plans also to mow the lawn. Before she leaves, she says, "That damn overhead garage door you got is off the track again. Do you think you'd have time to fix it?" Apartment life makes him restless. He jumps at the chance.

She, just as honorable and straight-arrow as he, has no idea of asking for this as a favor. She invites him to stay for an early dinner. She may put it indirectly—"Michael and Sally want their daddy to have supper with them"—but he is clear that the invitation also proceeds from her.   12

Provided neither of them has met a really attractive other person yet, they now move into a routine. He comes regularly to do the outside chores, and always stays for dinner. If the children are young enough, he may read to them before bedtime. She may wash his shirts.

One such evening, they both happen to be stirred not only by physical desire but by loneliness. "Oh, you might as well come upstairs," she says with a certain self-contempt. He needs no second invitation; they are upstairs in a flash. It is a delightful end to the evening. More delightful than anything they remember from their marriage, or at least from the later part of it.

That, too, now becomes part of the pattern. He never stays the full night, because, good parents that they are, they don't want the children to get any false hopes up—as they would, seeing their father at breakfast.

Such a relation may go on for several years, may even be inter- 16
rupted by a romance on one side or the other and then resume. It may even grow to the point where she's mending as well as washing his shirts, and he is advising her on her tax returns and fixing her car.

What they have achieved postdivorce is what their marriage should have been like in the first place. Part-time. Seven days a week of marriage was too much. One afternoon and two evenings is just right.

Although our society is even now witnessing de facto part-time arrangements, such as the couple who work in different cities and meet only on weekends, we have no theory of part-time marriage, at least no theory that has reached the general public. The romantic notion still dominates that if you love someone, you obviously want to be with them all the time.

To me it's clear we need such a theory. There are certainly people who thrive on seven-day-a-week marriages. They have a high level of intimacy and they may be better, warmer people than the rest of us. But there are millions and millions of us with medium or low levels of intimacy. We find full-time family membership a strain. If we could enter marriage with more realistic expectations of what closeness means for us, I suspect the divorce rate might permanently turn downward. It's too bad there isn't a sort of glucose tolerance test for intimacy.

As for me personally, I still do want to get married again. About 20
four days a week.

Topics for Discussion and Writing

1. In the model that Perrin discusses, what is the cause for divorce?
2. Judging from what you have seen around you, do you think many divorces proceed from the cause Perrin cites?
3. Does Perrin's behavior (and that of his wife) strike you as immoral? As bad for themselves, bad for the children, and bad for society? Or, on

the other hand, should this sort of arrangement be recognized as a type of satisfactory family arrangement?

4. In paragraph 19 Perrin argues that a need exists for part-time marriages. Does he persuade you, or do you think he is rationalizing his own shortcomings or sense of failure?

5. Did you enjoy reading the essay? Why, or why not? If some passages especially pleased you—perhaps because they were amusing, or notably insightful—examine them to see why they impressed you.

6. Perrin begins his essay as a first-person narrative: "When my wife told me she wanted a divorce . . . " Beginning with paragraph 8 he shifts into a third-person narrative: "Somewhere in some suburb or town or small city, a middle-class couple separate." Can you suggest reasons for this shift? Does it work—that is, does the shift retain or heighten your interest? If you have first-hand knowledge of divorce, try telling about it through a third-person narrative.

Laura Cunningham

Laura Cunningham was born in 1947. Orphaned at the age of eight, she was brought up by two unmarried uncles, both of whom were writers. She says that she became a writer because she didn't know that one could become anything else. Had she known of other possibilities, she says, she would have become a ballerina. The essay that we reprint appeared originally in The New York Times.

The Girls' Room

When I heard she was coming to stay with us I was pleased. At age eight I thought of "grandmother" as a generic brand. My friends had grandmothers who seemed permanently bent over cookie racks. They were a source of constant treats and sweets. They were pinchers of cheeks, huggers and kissers. My own grandmother had always lived in a distant state; I had no memory of her when she decided to join the household recently established for me by my two uncles.

But with the example of my friends' grandmothers before me, I could hardly wait to have a grandmother of my own—and the cookies would be nice too. For while my uncles provided a cuisine that ranged from tuna croquettes to Swedish meatballs, they showed no signs of baking anything more elegant than a potato.

My main concern on the day of my grandmother's arrival was: How soon would she start the cookies? I remember her arrival, my uncles flanking her as they walked down the apartment corridor. She wore a hat, a tailored navy blue suit, an ermine stole. She held, tucked under her arm, the purple leather folder that contained her work in progress, a manuscript entitled "Philosophy for Women." She was preceded by her custom-made white trunk packed with purses, necklaces, earrings, dresses and more purple-inked pages that stress "the spiritual above the material."

She was small—at five feet one inch not much taller than I was— thin and straight, with a pug nose, one brown eye (the good eye) and one blue eye (the bad eye, frosted by cataracts). Her name was "Esther in Hebrew, Edna in English, and Etka in Russian." She preferred the Russian, referring to herself as "Etka from Minsk." It was not at once apparent that she was deaf in her left ear (the bad ear) but could hear with the right (the good ear). Because her good ear happened to be on the opposite side from the good eye, anyone who spoke to her had to run around her in circles, or sway to and fro, if eye contact and audibility were to be achieved simultaneously. 4

Etka from Minsk had arrived not directly from Minsk, as the black-eyed ermine stole seemed to suggest, but after many moves. She entered with the draft of family scandal at her back, blown out of her daughter's home after assaults upon her dignity. She held the evidence: an empty-socketed peacock pin. My cousin, an eleven-year-old boy, had surgically plucked out the rhinestone eyes. She could not be expected to stay where such acts occurred. She had to be among "human beings," among "real people" who could understand. We seemed to understand. We—my two uncles and I— encircled her, studied her vandalized peacock pin and vowed that such things would never happen with "us."

She patted my head—a good sign—and asked me to sing the Israeli national anthem. I did, and she handed me a dollar. My uncles went off to their jobs, leaving me alone with my grandmother for the first time. I looked at her, expecting her to start rolling out the cookie dough. Instead she suggested: "Now maybe you could fix me some lunch?"

It wasn't supposed to be this way, I thought, as I took her order: "toasted cheese and a sliced orange." Neither was she supposed to share my pink and orange bedroom, but she did. The bedroom soon exhibited a dual character—stuffed animals on one side, a hospital bed on the other. Within the household this chamber was soon referred to as "the girls' room." The name, given by Uncle Abe, who saw no incongruity, only the affinity of sex, turned out to be apt, for what went on in the girls' room could easily have been labeled sibling rivalry if she had not been eighty and I eight. I soon found that I had acquired not a traditional grandmother but an aged kid sister.

The theft and rivalry began within days. My grandmother had 8 given me her most cherished possession, a violet beaded bag. In return I gave her my heart-shaped "ivory" pin and matching earrings. That night she stole back the purse but insisted on keeping the pin and earrings. I turned to my uncles for mediation and ran up against unforeseen resistance. They thought my grandmother should keep the beaded bag; they didn't want to upset her.

I burned at the injustice of it and felt the heat of an uncomfortable truth: where I once had my uncles' undivided indulgence, they were now split as my grandmother and I vied for their attention. The household, formerly geared to my little-girl needs, was rearranged to accommodate hers. I suffered serious affronts—my grandmother, in a fit of frugality, scissored all the household blankets, including what a psychiatrist would have dubbed my "security" blanket, in half. "Now," she said, her good eye gleaming, "we have twice as many." I lay under my narrow slice of blanket and stared hopelessly up at the ceiling. I thought evilly of ways of getting my grandmother out of the apartment.

Matters worsened, as more and more of my trinkets disappeared. One afternoon I came home from school to find her squeezed into my unbuttoned favorite blouse. Rouged and beribboned, she insisted that the size 3 blouse was hers. Meanwhile, I was forced to adapt to her idiosyncrasies: she covered everything black—from the dog to the telephone—with white doilies. She left saucers balanced on top of glasses. She sang nonstop. She tried to lock my dog out of the apartment.

The word that explained her behavior was "arteriosclerosis." She had forgotten so much that sometimes she would greet me with "You look familiar." At other times she'd ask, "What hotel is this?" My answer, shouted in her good ear, was: "We're not in a hotel! This is our apartment!" The response would be a hoot of laughter: "Then why are we in the ballroom?"

Finally we fought: arm-to-arm combat. I was shocked at her grip, 12 steely as the bars that locked her into bed at night. Her good eye burned into mine and she said, "I'll tell." And she did. For the first time I was scolded. She had turned their love to disapproval, I thought, and how it chafed. Eventually our rivalry mellowed into conspiracy. Within months we found we had uses for each other. I provided the lunches and secret, forbidden ice cream sundaes. She rewarded me with cold cash. She continued to take my clothes; I charged her competitive prices. I hated school; she paid me not to go. When I came home for lunch I usually stayed.

Our household endured the status quo for eight years: my uncles, my grandmother and I. Within the foursome rivalries and alliances shifted. I became my grandmother's friend and she became mine. We were the source of all the family comedy. When she said she wanted a college diploma we gave her one—with tinfoil stars and a "magna magna summa summa cum laude" inscription. We sang and performed skits. We talcum-powdered hair and wearing one of her old dresses, I would appear as her "long-lost friend." We had other themes, including a pen pal, "The Professor."

Of course, living with an elderly person had its raw aspects. When she was ill our girls' room took on the stark aura of a geriatrics ward. I imagined, to my shame, that neighbors could stare in through curtainless windows as I tended to my grandmother's most personal needs.

Yet, in these times of age segregation, with grandmothers sent 16 off to impersonal places, I wonder if the love and the comedy weren't worth the intermittent difficulties. Certainly I learned what it might be to become old. And I took as much comfort as my grandmother did in a nightly exchange of Russian endearments—"Ya tebya lyublyu," "Ya tebya tozhe lyublyu—"I love you," "I love you, too."

If I sold my grandmother blouses and baubles, maybe she gave me the truth in exchange. Once, when we were alone in the girls' room, she turned to me, suddenly lucid, her good eye as bright as it would ever be—a look I somehow recognized as her "real" gaze—and said, "My life passes like a dream."

Topics for Discussion and Writing

1. In the second sentence, what does Cunningham mean by "a generic brand"?
2. What is the title of Esther's manuscript? What is it about? Do you detect any irony in the way Cunningham conveys this information? Explain.

3. In the second sentence of paragraph 4, what is conveyed by putting the names within quotation marks?
4. Is paragraph 4—about Esther's physical disabilities—in bad taste? Explain.
5. In her last paragraph Cunningham says that perhaps her grandmother gave her "the truth." What does she mean?
6. "I burned at the injustice of it and felt the heat of an uncomfortable truth." Where in the narrative does Cunningham say this? What was the "truth"? If you remember a similar experience, write a narrative that discloses both the experience and the truth on which it was based. Or, write an essay of 500 words on your own most potent experience of living with or near an elderly person.

Black Elk

Black Elk, a wichasha wakon (holy man) of the Oglala Sioux, as a small boy witnessed the battle of the Little Bighorn (1876). He lived to see his people all but annihilated and his hopes for them extinguished. In 1931, toward the end of his life, he told his life story to the poet and scholar John G. Neihardt to preserve a sacred vision given him.

"High Horse's Courting" is a comic interlude in Black Elk Speaks, *a predominantly tragic memoir.*

High Horse's Courting

You know, in the old days, it was not very easy to get a girl when you wanted to be married. Sometimes it was hard work for a young man and he had to stand a great deal. Say I am a young man and I have seen a young girl who looks so beautiful to me that I feel all sick when I think about her. I cannot just go and tell her about it and then get married if she is willing. I have to be a very sneaky fellow to talk to her at all, and after I have managed to talk to her, that is only the beginning.

Probably for a long time I have been feeling sick about a certain girl because I love her so much, but she will not even look at me, and her parents keep a good watch over her. But I keep feeling worse and worse all the time; so maybe I sneak up to her tepee in the dark and wait until she comes out. Maybe I just wait there all night and don't get any sleep at all and she does not come out. Then I feel sicker than ever about her.

Maybe I hide in the brush by a spring where she sometimes goes to get water, and when she comes by, if nobody is looking, then I jump out and hold her and just make her listen to me. If she likes me too, I can tell that from the way she acts, for she is very bashful and maybe will not say a word or even look at me the first time. So I let her go, and then maybe I sneak around until I can see her father alone, and I tell him how many horses I can give him for his beautiful girl, and by now I am feeling so sick that maybe I would give him all the horses in the world if I had them.

Well, this young man I am telling about was called High Horse, 4 and there was a girl in the village who looked so beautiful to him that he was just sick all over from thinking about her so much and he was getting sicker all the time. The girl was very shy, and her parents thought a great deal of her because they were not young any more and this was the only child they had. So they watched her all day long, and they fixed it so that she would be safe at night too when they were asleep. They thought so much of her that they had made a rawhide bed for her to sleep in, and after they knew that High Horse was sneaking around after her, they took rawhide thongs and tied the girl in bed at night so that nobody could steal her when they were asleep, for they were not sure but that their girl might really want to be stolen.

Well, after High Horse had been sneaking around a good while and hiding and waiting for the girl and getting sicker all the time, he finally caught her alone and made her talk to him. Then he found out that she liked him maybe a little. Of course this did not make him feel well. It made him sicker than ever, but now he felt as brave as a bison bull, and so he went right to her father and said he loved the girl so much that he would give two good horses for her—one of them young and the other one not so very old.

But the old man just waved his hand, meaning for High Horse to go away and quit talking foolishness like that.

High Horse was feeling sicker than ever about it; but there was another young fellow who said he would loan High Horse two ponies and when he got some more horses, why, he could just give them back for the ones he had borrowed.

Then High Horse went back to the old man and said he would 8 give four horses for the girl—two of them young and the other two not hardly old at all. But the old man just waved his hand and would not say anything.

So High Horse sneaked around until he could talk to the girl again, and he asked her to run away with him. He told her he thought he would just fall over and die if she did not. But she said she would not do that; she wanted to be bought like a fine woman. You see she thought a great deal of herself too.

That made High Horse feel so very sick that he could not eat a bite, and he went around with his head hanging down as though he might just fall down and die any time.

Red Deer was another young fellow, and he and High Horse were great comrades, always doing things together. Red Deer saw how High Horse was acting, and he said: "Cousin, what is the matter? Are you sick in the belly? You look as though you were going to die."

Then High Horse told Red Deer how it was, and said he thought   12
he could not stay alive much longer if he could not marry the girl pretty quick.

Red Deer thought awhile about it, and then he said: "Cousin, I have a plan, and if you are man enough to do as I tell you, then everything will be all right. She will not run away with you; her old man will not take four horses; and four horses are all you can get. You must steal her and run away with her. Then after-while you can come back and the old man cannot do anything because she will be your woman. Probably she wants you to steal her anyway."

So they planned what High Horse had to do, and he said he loved the girl so much that he was man enough to do anything Red Deer or anybody else could think up. So this is what they did.

That night late they sneaked up to the girl's tepee and waited until it sounded inside as though the old man and the old woman and the girl were sound asleep. Then High Horse crawled under the tepee with a knife. He had to cut the rawhide thongs first, and then Red Deer, who was pulling up the stakes around that side of the tepee, was going to help drag the girl outside and gag her. After that, High Horse could put her across his pony in front of him and hurry out of there and be happy all the rest of his life.

When High Horse had crawled inside, he felt so nervous that he   16
could hear his heart drumming, and it seemed so loud he felt sure it would 'waken the old folks. But it did not, and afterwhile he began cutting the thongs. Every time he cut one it made a pop and nearly scared him to death. But he was getting along all right and all the thongs were cut down as far as the girl's thighs, when he became so nervous that his knife slipped and stuck the girl. She gave a big, loud yell. Then the old folks jumped up and yelled too. By this time High Horse was outside, and he and Red Deer were

running away like antelope. The old man and some other people chased the young men but they got away in the dark and nobody knew who it was.

Well, if you ever wanted a beautiful girl you will know how sick High Horse was now. It was very bad the way he felt, and it looked as though he would starve even if he did not drop over dead sometime.

Red Deer kept thinking about this, and after a few days he went to High Horse and said: "Cousin, take courage! I have another plan, and I am sure, if you are man enough, we can steal her this time." And High Horse said: "I am man enough to do anything anybody can think up, if I can only get that girl."

So this is what they did.

They went away from the village alone, and Red Deer made   20 High Horse strip naked. Then he painted High Horse solid white all over, and after that he painted black stripes all over the white and put black rings around High Horse's eyes. High Horse looked terrible. He looked so terrible that when Red Deer was through painting and took a good look at what he had done, he said it scared even him a little.

"Now," Red Deer said, "if you get caught again, everybody will be so scared they will think you are a bad spirit and will be afraid to chase you."

So when the night was getting old and everybody was sound asleep, they sneaked back to the girl's tepee. High Horse crawled in with his knife, as before, and Red Deer waited outside, ready to drag the girl out and gag her when High Horse had all the thongs cut.

High Horse crept up by the girl's bed and began cutting at the thongs. But he kept thinking, "If they see me they will shoot me because I look so terrible." The girl was restless and kept squirming around in bed, and when a thong was cut, it popped. So High Horse worked very slowly and carefully.

But he must have made some noise, for suddenly the old woman   24 awoke and said to her old man: "Old Man, wake up! There is somebody in this tepee!" But the old man was sleepy and didn't want to be bothered. He said: "Of course there is somebody in this tepee. Go to sleep and don't bother me." Then he snored some more.

But High Horse was so scared by now that he lay very still and as flat to the ground as he could. Now, you see, he had not been sleeping very well for a long time because he was so sick about the girl. And while he was lying there waiting for the old woman to snore, he just forgot everything, even how beautiful the girl was.

Red Deer who was lying outside ready to do his part, wondered and wondered what had happened in there, but he did not dare call out to High Horse.

Afterwhile the day began to break and Red Deer had to leave with the two ponies he had staked there for his comrade and girl, or somebody would see him.

So he left.

Now when it was getting light in the tepee, the girl awoke and the first thing she saw was a terrible animal, all white with black stripes on it, lying asleep beside her bed. So she screamed, and then the old woman screamed and the old man yelled. High Horse jumped up, scared almost to death, and he nearly knocked the tepee down getting out of there.

People were coming running from all over the village with guns and bows and axes, and everybody was yelling.

By now High Horse was running so fast that he hardly touched the ground at all, and he looked so terrible that the people fled from him and let him run. Some braves wanted to shoot at him, but the others said he might be some sacred being and it would bring bad trouble to kill him.

High Horse made for the river that was near, and in among the brush he found a hollow tree and dived into it. Afterwhile some braves came there and he could hear them saying that it was some bad spirit that had come out of the water and gone back in again.

That morning the people were ordered to break camp and move away from there. So they did, while High Horse was hiding in his hollow tree.

Now Red Deer had been watching all this from his own tepee and trying to look as though he were as much surprised and scared as all the others. So when the camp moved, he sneaked back to where he had seen his comrade disappear. When he was down there in the brush, he called, and High Horse answered, because he knew his friend's voice. They washed off the paint from High Horse and sat down on the river bank to talk about their troubles.

High Horse said he never would go back to the village as long as he lived and he did not care what happened to him now. He said he was going to go on the war-path all by himself. Red Deer said: "No, cousin, you are not going on the war-path alone, because I am going with you."

So Red Deer got everything ready, and at night they started out on the war-path all alone. After several days they came to a Crow camp just about sundown, and when it was dark they sneaked up to where the Crow horses were grazing, killed the horse guard, who was not thinking about enemies because he thought all the Lakotas were far away, and drove off about a hundred horses.

They got a big start because all the Crow horses stampeded and it was probably morning before the Crow warriors could catch any horses to ride. Red Deer and High Horse fled with their herd three days and nights before they reached the village of their people. Then they drove the whole herd right into the village and up in front of the girl's tepee. The old man was there, and High Horse called out to him and asked if he thought maybe that would be enough horses for his girl. The old man did not wave him away that time. It was not the horses that he wanted. What he wanted was a son who was a real man and good for something.

So High Horse got his girl after all, and I think he deserved her.

Topics for Discussion and Writing

Although High Horse's behavior is amusing and at times ridiculous, how does Black Elk make it clear that he is not ridiculing the young man, but is instead in sympathy with him? Consider the following questions:

1. What is the effect of the first three paragraphs? Think about the first two sentences, and then the passage beginning "Say I am a young man . . . " and ending " . . . I would give him all the horses in the world if I had them."
2. Describe the behavior of the young girl, and of her father and mother. How do they contribute to the comedy? How does their behavior affect your understanding of Black Elk's attitude toward High Horse?
3. What is the function of Red Deer?
4. The narrative consists of several episodes. List them in the order in which they occur, and then describe the narrative's structure. How does this structure affect the tone?

Anonymous

The anonymous author of this essay has revealed only that he was forty when he wrote it, is married, and is the father of three children. The essay originally appeared in The New Republic, *a magazine regarded by some as liberal.*

Confessions of an Erstwhile Child

Some years ago I attempted to introduce a class of Upward Bound students to political theory via More's *Utopia*. It was a mistake: I taught precious little theory and earned More a class full of undying enemies on account of two of his ideas. The first, that all members of a Utopian family were subject to the lifelong authority of its eldest male. The second, the Utopian provision that should a child wish to follow a profession different from that of his family, he could be transferred by adoption to a family that practiced the desired trade. My students were not impressed with my claim that the one provision softened the other and made for a fair compromise—for what causes most of our quarrels with our parents but our choice of life-patterns, of occupation? In objecting to the first provision my students were picturing themselves as children, subject to an unyielding authority. But on the second provision they surprised me by taking the parents' role and arguing that this form of ad lib adoption denied them a fundamental right of ownership over their children. It occurred to me that these reactions were two parts of the same pathology: having suffered the discipline of unreasonable parents, one has earned the right to be unreasonable in turn to one's children. The phenomenon has well-known parallels, such as frantic martinets who have risen from the ranks. Having served time as property, my Upward Bound students wanted theirs back as proprietors. I shuddered. It hardly takes an advanced course in Freudian psychology to realize that the perpetuation, generation after generation, of psychic lesions must go right to this source, the philosophically dubious notion that children are the property of their biological parents, compounded with the unphilosophic certitude so many parents harbor, that their children must serve an apprenticeship as like their own as they can manage.

The idea of the child as property has always bothered me, for personal reasons I shall outline. I lack the feeling that I own my

143

children and I have always scoffed at the idea that what they are and do is a continuation or a rejection of my being. I like them, I sympathize with them, I acknowledge the obligation to support them for a term of years—but I am not so fond or foolish as to regard a biological tie as a lien on their loyalty or respect, nor to imagine that I am equipped with preternatural powers of guidance as to their success and happiness. Beyond inculcating some of the obvious social protocols required in civilized life, who am I to pronounce on what makes for a happy or successful life? How many of us can say that we have successfully managed our own lives? Can we do better with our children? I am unimpressed, to say no more, with parents who have no great track record, presuming to oracular powers in regard to their children's lives.

The current debate over the Equal Rights Amendment frequently turns to custody questions. Opponents of ERA have made the horrifying discovery that ERA will spell the end of the mother's presumed rights of custody in divorce or separation cases, and that fathers may begin custody rights. Indeed a few odd cases have been so settled recently in anticipation of the ratification of ERA. If ratified, ERA would be an extremely blunt instrument for calling the whole idea of custody into question, but I for one will applaud anything that serves to begin debate. As important as equal rights between adults may be, I think that the rights of children are a far more serious and unattended need. To me, custody by natural parents, far from being a presumed right only re-examined in case of collapsing marriages, should be viewed as a privilege.

At this point I have to explain why I can so calmly contemplate the denial of so-called parental rights. 4

I am the only child of two harsh and combative personalities who married, seemingly, in order to have a sparring partner always at hand. My parents have had no other consistent or lasting aim in life but to win out over each other in a contest of wills. They still live, vigorous and angry septuagenarians, their ferocity little blunted by age or human respect. My earliest memories—almost my sole memories—are of unending combat, in which I was sometimes an appalled spectator, more often a hopeless negotiator in a war of no quarter, and most often a bystander accused of covert belligerency on behalf of one side or the other, and frequently of both! I grew up with two supposed adults who were absorbed in their hatreds and recriminations to the exclusion of almost all other reality. Not only did I pass by almost unnoticed in their struggle, the Depression and World War II passed them by equally unnoticed.

I figured mainly as a practice target for sarcasm and invective, and occasionally as the ultimate culprit responsible for their unhappiness. ("If it weren't for you," my mother would sometimes say, "I could leave that SOB," a remark belied by her refusal to leave the SOB during these 20 long years since I left their "shelter.")

The reader may ask, "How did you survive if your parents' house was all that bad?" I have three answers. First, I survived by the moral equivalent of running away to sea or the circus, i.e., by burying myself in books and study, especially in the history of faraway and (I thought) more idealistic times than our own, and by consciously shaping my life and tastes to be as different as possible from those of my parents (this was a reproach to them, they knew, and it formed the basis of a whole secondary area of conflict and misunderstanding). Second, I survived because statistically most people "survive" horrible families, but survival can be a qualified term, as it is in my case by a permanently impaired digestive system and an unnatural sensitivity to raised voices. And third, though I found solace in schooling and the rationality, cooperation and basic fairness in teachers that I missed in my parents, I must now question whether it is healthy for a child to count so heavily on schooling for the love and approval that he deserves from his home and family. Even if schooling can do this well, in later life it means that one is loyal and affectionate toward schooling, not toward parents, who may in some sense need affection even if they don't "deserve" it. I am not unaware that however fair and rational I may be in reaction to my parents' counter-examples, I am a very cold-hearted man. I might have done better transferred to a new family, not just by receiving love, but through learning to give it—a lack I mourn as much or more than my failure to receive.

It is little wonder then that I have an acquired immunity to the notion that parental custody is by and large a preferable thing. In my case, almost anything else would have been preferable, including even a rather callously run orphanage—anything for a little peace and quiet. Some people are simply unfit, under any conditions, to be parents, even if, indeed especially if, they maintain the charade of a viable marriage. My parents had no moral right to custody of children, and I cannot believe that my experience is unique or particularly isolated. There are all too many such marriages, in which some form of horror, congenial enough to adults too sick or crazed to recognize it, works its daily ruination on children. Surely thousands of children conclude at age 10 or 11, as I did, that marriage is simply an institution in which people are free to be as beastly as they have a mind to, which may lead either to a rejection of marriage or to a decision to reduplicate a sick marriage a second time, with another generation of victims. It is time to consider the rights of the victims.

How to implement a nascent theory of justice for children is difficult to say. One cannot imagine taking the word of a five-year-old against his parents, but what about a ten- or twelve-year-old? At *some* point, children should have the right to escape the dominance of impossible parents. The matter used to be easier than it has been since World War I. The time-honored solution—for boys—of running away from home has been made infeasible by economic conditions, fingerprints, social security and minimum wage laws. No apprenticeship system exists any more, much less its upper-class medieval version—with required exchange of boys at puberty among noble families to serve as pages and so forth. The adoption system contemplated in More's *Utopia* is a half-remembered echo of a medieval life, in which society, wiser than its theory, decreed a general exchange of children at or just before puberty, whether through apprenticeship or page-service, or more informal arrangements, like going to a university at 14 or running away with troubadors or gypsies. 8

Exchanging children is a wisely conceived safety valve against a too traumatic involvement between the biological parent and the child. Children need an alternative to living all their formative life in the same biological unit. They should have the right to petition for release from some sorts of families, to join other families, or to engage in other sorts of relationships that may provide equivalent service but may not be organized as a family. The nuclear family, after all, is not such an old or proven vehicle. Phillippe Aries' book, *Centuries of Childhood,* made the important point that the idea of helpless childhood is itself a notion of recent origin, that grew up simultaneously in the 16th and 17th centuries with the small and tight-knit nuclear family, sealed off from the world by another recent invention, "privacy." The older *extended* family (which is the kind More knew about) was probably more authoritarian on paper but much less productive of dependency in actual operation. There ought to be more than one way a youngster can enter adult society with more than half of his sanity left. At least no one should be forced to remain in a no-win game against a couple of crazy parents for 15–18 years. At 10 or 12, children in really messy situations should have the legal right to petition for removal from impossible families, and those rights should be reasonably easy to exercise. (This goes on de facto among the poor, of course, but it is not legal, and usually carries both stigma and danger.) The minimum wage laws should be modified to exempt such persons, especially if they wish to continue their education, working perhaps for public agencies, if they have no other means of support. If their parents can support them, then the equivalent of child support should be charged them to maintain their children, not in luxury, but adequately. Adoption of older children should be facilitated by easing of legal procedures (designed mainly to govern the adoption of *infants*) plus tax advantages for those willing to adopt older children on grounds of goodwill. Indeed children wishing to escape impossible family situations should be allowed a fair degree of initiative in finding and negotiating with possible future families.

Obviously the risk of rackets would be very high unless the exact terms of such provisions were framed very carefully, but the possibility of rackets is less frightening to anyone who thinks about it for long than the dangers of the present situation, which are evident and unrelieved by any signs of improvement. In barely a century this country has changed from a relatively loose society in which Huckleberry Finns were not uncommon, to a society of tense, airless nuclear families in which unhealthy and neurotic tendencies, once spawned in a family, tend to repeat themselves at a magnifying and accelerating rate. We may soon gain the distinction of being the only nation on earth to need not just medicare but "psychi-care." We have invested far too heavily in the unproved "equity" called the nuclear family; that stock is about to crash and we ought to begin finding escape options. In colonial days many New England colonies passed laws imposing fines or extra taxes on parents who kept their children under their own roofs after age 15 or 16, on the sensible notion that a person of that age ought to be out and doing on his own, whether going to Yale or apprenticing in a foundry. Even without the benefit of Freud, the colonial fathers had a good sense of what was wrong with a closely bound and centripetal family structure—it concentrates craziness like compound interest, and so they hit it with monetary penalties, a proper Protestant response, intolerant at once of both mystery and excuses. But this was the last gasp of a medieval and fundamentally Catholic idea that children, God help them, while they may be the children of *these* particular parents biologically, spiritually are the children of God, and more appositely are the children of the entire community, for which the entire community takes responsibility. The unguessed secret of the middle ages was not that monasteries relieved parents of unwanted children; more frequently, they relieved children of unwanted parents!

Topics for Discussion and Writing

1. What is the author's thesis? (Quote the thesis sentence.) Apart from his own experience, what evidence or other means does he offer to persuade you to accept his thesis?

2. What part does the *tone* of his article play in persuading you to agree with him, or in alienating you? Does his tone strike you, perhaps, as vigorous or belligerent, as ironic or bitter, as reasonable or hysterical?

3. The author admits (paragraph 6) that he is "a very cold-hearted man." Do you remember your initial reaction to that sentence? What was it? Overall, does the author strengthen or jeopardize his argument by this admission? Explain.

4. If you did not find the article persuasive, did you find it interesting? Can you explain why?

Garrison Keillor

This short essay, which we have entitled "Something from the Sixties," comes from "The Talk of the Town," a heading used over several short, anonymous essays published weekly in The New Yorker. *The essay purports to be a letter from a friend, except for the first line ("A friend writes"), but one may conjecture that the piece was composed by Garrison Keillor, who, following a convention used in "The Talk of the Town," does not use the first person singular pronoun. Keillor is the author of several books including* Lake Wobegon Days, *and was the host of a popular radio show, "A Prairie Home Companion."*

Something from the Sixties

A friend writes:

About five o'clock last Sunday evening, my son burst into the kitchen and said, "I didn't know it was so late!" He was due at a party immediately—a sixties party, he said—and he needed something from the sixties to wear. My son is almost fifteen years old, the size of a grown man, and when he bursts into a room glassware rattles and the cat on your lap grabs on to your knees and leaps from the starting block. I used to think the phrase "burst into the room" was only for detective fiction, until my son got his growth. He can burst in a way that, done by an older fellow, would mean that angels had descended into the front yard and were eating apples off the tree, and he does it whenever he's late — as being my son, he often is. I have so little sense of time that when he said he needed something from the sixties it took me a moment to place that decade. It's the one he was born toward the end of.

I asked, "What sort of stuff you want to wear?"

He said, "I don't know. Whatever they wore then."   4

We went up to the attic, into a long, low room under the eaves where I've squirrelled away some boxes of old stuff; I dug into one box, and the first thing I hauled out was the very thing he wanted. A thigh-length leather vest covered with fringe and studded with silver, it dates from around 1967, a fanciful time in college-boy fashions. Like many boys, I grew up in nice clothes my mother bought, but was meanwhile admiring Roy Rogers, Sergeant Rock, the Cisco Kid, and other sharp dressers, so when I left home I was ready to step out and be somebody. Military Surplus was the basic style then — olive drab, and navy-blue pea jackets — with a touch of Common Man in the work boots and blue work shirts, but if you showed up in Riverboat Gambler or Spanish Peasant or Rodeo King nobody blinked, nobody laughed. I haven't worn the vest in ten years, but a few weeks ago, seeing a picture of Michael Jackson wearing a fancy band jacket like the ones the Beatles wore on the cover of "Sgt. Pepper," I missed the fun I used to have getting dressed in the morning. Pull on the jeans, a shirt with brilliant-red roses, a pair of Red Wing boots. A denim jacket. Rose-tinted glasses. A cowboy hat. Or an engineer's cap. Or, instead of jeans, bib overalls. Or white trousers with blue stripes. Take off the denim jacket, take off the rose shirt, try the neon-green bowling shirt with "Moose" stitched on the pocket, the black dinner jacket. Now the dark-green Chinese Army cap. And an orange tie with hula dancers and palm trees.

Then — presto! — I pulled the rose shirt out. He put it on, and the vest, which weighs about fifteen pounds, and by then I had found him a hat — a broad-brimmed panama that ought to make you think of a cotton planter enjoying a Sazerac[1] on a veranda in New Orleans. I followed him down to his bedroom, where he admired himself in a full-length mirror.

"Who wore this?" he asked.

---

[1] A bourbon cocktail flavored with a bitter liqueur. (Editors' note)

I said that I did.   8

"Did you really? This? You?"

Yes, I really did. After he was born, in 1969, I wore it less and less, finally settling down with what I think of as the Dad look, and now I would no sooner wear my old fringed vest in public than walk around in a taffeta tutu. I loved the fact that it fitted him so well, though, and his pleasure at the heft and extravagance of the thing, the poses he struck in front of the mirror. Later, when he got home and reported that his costume was a big hit and that all his friends had tried on the vest, it made me happy again. You squirrel away old stuff on the principle of its being useful and interesting someday; it's wonderful when the day finally arrives. That vest was waiting for a boy to come along — a boy who has a flair for the dramatic, who bursts into rooms — and to jump right into the part. I'm happy to be the audience.

Topics for Discussion and Writing

1. In the second line of this essay we are told that the action begins "About five o'clock last Sunday evening." Does it matter that we know what time it was, or what day of the week? Explain.

2. Much of paragraph 1 is used to describe the way the son enters the room. How does the description characterize the son? How does it relate to the point of the narrative?

3. Toward the end of paragraph 5 Keillor writes a string of fragments. Try to describe the effect of this rhetorical device.

4. In the next-to-last paragraph, what feelings toward his father does the son communicate in "Did you really? This? You?" What feelings does the father have for his son, and how do you know?

5. In the last paragraph Keillor says he settled down with "what I think of as the Dad look." When you read that, what picture of him comes to mind? Try to describe the clothes, the body stance, the expression of a man wearing "the Dad look." Be as specific as you can.

6. The conclusion to the piece is: "I'm happy to be the audience." What details in the account make the word "audience" especially fitting? And what other details persuade you that "happy" is the precise word to summarize the tone of the essay?

7. In the last paragraph the writer says: "You squirrel away old stuff on the principle of its being useful and interesting some day." What do you (or members of your family) "squirrel away"? Why? Explain, in two or three paragraphs.

Celia E. Rothenberg

Celia E. Rothenberg graduated from Wellesley College in 1991. A history major with a special interest in the lives of Middle Eastern women, she was awarded a Marshall fellowship and is now studying modern Middle Eastern history at Oxford. She has served as an intern in an Israeli-Palestinian women's peace group in Jerusalem, and she plans to continue working for understanding between these two groups.

Rothenberg wrote the following essay while she was an undergraduate.

Child of Divorce

Over this past winter vacation my parents, brother, and I spent a few days together—a rare event now that the four of us live in four different states. As I watched my parents and brother engage in our usual laughter and reminiscing, accompanied by an occasional tear at a past both bitter and sweet, I listened more closely than ever before to what is a frequent topic of discussion, our relationship as a family.

Perhaps because my parents divorced when I was a small child, it seems to surprise my friends that my family's recollections of those years are filled with many pleasant memories. After all, those who don't know my family have reason to assume that the memories of growing up with divorced parents in some tough economic times might be rather dreary. In fact, however, my memories center on the results of the thoughtfulness and conscious effort exerted by both my parents to create a sense of love and protection for my brother and me. I have always felt that my family was a team, a team that sometimes fumbled, and sometimes seemed to have two, three, or even four captains, and a team that underwent a change in plan mid-game, but a team nevertheless. It is only recently, however, that I have realized how much patience and understanding went into achieving that sense of belonging and love, and how achieving it was part of the long and often painful process for us of divorce and healing.

My parents divorced, after fifteen years of marriage, when I was six. I have nearly no memories of living in a two-parent household. From the time of my earliest memories, my mother has always studied or worked full time. Immediately after the divorce, she, like many women who find themselves single after many years as a "housewife," went back to school. My brother at the time was twelve. Although I remember my Cinderella-shaped cake for my

151

seventh birthday, a few of my favorite pets, and a well-loved school teacher, I remember very little of my mom's return to school, or my own or brother's adjustment to our new surroundings. Perhaps the gaps in my memory serve as some kind of mental defense mechanism to protect me from the reality of the harder times; no matter the reason for my memory voids, however, my brother's recollections are so vivid, and my mom and dad so open about those years, that my scattered memories have been augmented by their storytelling—to the point that I often confuse my memories with theirs.

It is only recently, in fact, that I have realized how difficult the   4 initial years following the divorce were for my mother, brother and father. Over this past winter vacation, my mom told me for the first time how taxing even the simplest tasks seemed to be. For example, locking the doors to our new, small house conjured up all the difficulties and sadnesses of this new beginning. Because my dad had customarily locked up, she had rarely been the one to lock each lock and turn off each light. Doing these tasks in a new house in a new city was a constant reminder of her changed circumstances. Late in the evening she would carefully plot the order in which to turn off the lights, so as not to be alone in the dark. She would lock a door, and then a window, pausing in between the locks to distract her mind from the task at hand—and the frightening and lonely feelings these new responsibilities brought with them.

My family now openly recalls that those years were a difficult time of adjustment to new schools, a new city, and a new life. We had moved from a small suburb of St. Louis to Champaign-Urbana, a community largely centered on the life of the University of Illinois. Our first house in Champaign and my mom's tuition for the Master's degree in Library and Information Science were largely financed by the sale of the lovely Steinway baby grand piano that had graced my parents' living room since before I was born. Before the divorce, my father was an attorney until he found himself in legal difficulties, which ultimately led him to give up the practice of law. His reduced income and my mom's tuition bills placed us under a great financial strain.

My brother, who was twelve at the time of the divorce, particularly recalls how difficult communication was between the three of us and my father, and at times even among the three of us. To help ease the tension of my dad's monthly visits and maintain a relationship which included some fun, my brother and dad played checkers through the mail. They carefully conceived of a plan of multiple paper copies of the checker board and colored pencils for their game. One of my few early memories of those years focusses on the checker board we set up on the dining room table to represent the game my brother and dad played on paper. One evening, the cat we brought with us from (as my mother often said) our "other life," jumped on the board, knocking the pieces all over the table. Steve was inconsolable, and only a prolonged long-distance phone call to figure out where each piece belonged resolved the situation.

That first year my brother escaped into a world of books, often reading fiction and plays when he should have been doing homework, a coping behavior he practiced until he was nearly through high school.

But even the deepest hurts can heal over time. With encouragement and support from both my parents, Steve channeled his considerable energy and anger into planning for an early graduation from high school and a year in Israel between high school and college. The only conditions set were that he had to earn enough money to buy his own plane ticket and he had to have a college acceptance letter in hand before he left. These goals gave him something to work for at a time when he felt that he had lost friends and status in coming to a new, very different, and less comfortable environment than had been part of his early days.

As for me, perhaps because I was six years younger, I appeared to go blithely along, oblivious to most of the tensions and strains that Steve seemed to feel. With my mother studying for her classes and Steve spending almost all his time reading, I became an avid reader myself, almost in self defense. I found new friends and reveled in my new elementary school, a magnet school where we studied French every day. I wrote long, detailed stories of a young girl who lived on a farm with both parents and a dozen brothers and sisters and a beautiful horse. Perhaps I, too, was seeking some consolation in an imaginary life far removed from our little house.

It can take years for wounds to heal, and I am happy to say that my family healed more quickly than most. Perhaps we got past that initial phase early on because my parents did not make too many mistakes. They avoided some common pitfalls of divorcing families. The divorce was quick—the process was completed a few months after my parents sold their house and moved to their new homes—there were no court battles, no screaming fights, no wrenching decisions that we children were required to make. Steve and

I were never asked—or allowed—to choose sides or express a preference for one parent over the other. Although my own memories
are blurry, the few recollections I have of those first five years focus
on my dad's regular monthly visits (he lived a few hours away by
car). By the time I was ten, he was spending nearly every weekend
with us at the house, a pattern which continued for the next decade, until I was out of high school and off to Wellesley.

Nothing worthwhile, my mother has always told me, is ever
easy. It could not have always been easy for either of my parents
to spend so much of their free time together when they had chosen
to create separate lives, but at the time Steve and I rarely saw anything but civility and fondness. As parents they were determined
not to let their children suffer for mistakes they may have made in
their marriage. It is one of their greatest gifts to Steve and me, for
it was the ultimate lesson in learning about the commitment and
cost of love and the lifelong responsibilities of family.

The stories we have accumulated over the years have become   12
more hilarious as I have grown older. My dad, determined not to
be a "Disneyland daddy," showing up on the weekends for shopping and dinners out, was not uncomfortable in our new home. In
fact, he helped us figure out how to do various home improvement
projects. Under his direction, we rewired our house (and nearly elec-
trocuted Steve in the process), insulated our attic (the family story
lingers that we nearly blew off the roof), and painted the house (and,
of course, ourselves). Our projects probably didn't save us very
much money, since we seemed to spend as much money on fixing
the mistakes we made as on the project itself, yet we were not merely
building the house, or growing gardens, or mowing the lawn. We
were rebuilding our lives, making memories, and creating a sense
of togetherness.

My own clear and more complete memories begin at the age
of eleven, when my mother, brother, and I began a new lifestyle, which reflected a newly achieved flexibility and confidence
in our ability to manage our lives. When my brother entered the
University of Illinois, we moved into a big old house and I began
high school. The house was what a real estate broker fondly
calls a "fixer-upper," and was perfect for my mom's income (she
worked for the University after she finished her Master's degree)
and our need for space for friends of mine and Steve's. Steve, in
particular, brought home countless Jewish college students whom
he knew from his involvement in the campus Jewish student

organization. They often needed a good meal, a shoulder to lean on, an opinion on a paper, or a good night's sleep.

I remember our dining room on Shabbos, furnished with a dining room set probably beautiful in my grandmother's day but battered after three generations of use, packed with college students eating dinner. I remember vividly the talk and the laughter, the jesting and the endless debates. My mom was not only an intellectual support for those students but also an inspiration, someone who had experienced a marriage gone bad, the trials and tribulations of parenting alone (at least during the week), and the tough economics of a single-parent household. Conversations stretched from the abstract to the concrete, from the politics of the Eastern bloc to the intricacies of love and sex.

Over the years it has become clear that the divorce, although traumatic, opened our minds, enriched our relationships with each other, and loosened restraints we did not know we were subject to. I vividly remember my high school years as a busy time full of my friends and my brothers' who simply enjoyed being around the house. The slightly chaotic, easy-going atmosphere of the house was fostered in large part by our mom; she had disliked the isolated feeling of life in suburbia when she was married. She wanted to create a different atmosphere for Steve and me, a place where young people were comfortable to come and go.

My friends in high school were fascinated by my home, and I 16 enjoyed it as much as they did. My dad was able to watch us grow and change from weekend to weekend, his place secure and comfortable at the head of the Shabbos table surrounded by students. He helped us with science projects, participated in countless carpools, and, most of all, was there when we needed him. Although from the point of view of the Census Bureau we were a "single parent household," in actuality we were a *family* that happened to have divorced parents. Perhaps our experience was not typical of some families in which there has been a divorce, but the labels obscure our understanding of the needs and hopes of all families, which I think are probably the same, divorced or not. My parent's expectations for Steve and me were not altered by their marital status, nor do I think that Steve and I let them get away with very much on the excuse that they were divorced!

I have always loved my family, but I find that I admire each of them increasingly as time goes on. Now, when we gather from different corners of the country and world during vacations a few times a year, we admit that the best and the worst, but always the most precious times, were when we were together on the weekends in that big old house, sometimes with the students and sometimes with only each other. On special occasions, we have a (very patient) long-distance operator connect the four of us on the same phone line, and we talk as if there is no tomorrow. We are fiercely proud of one another; I often have to restrain myself from blurting out the merits of my exceptional family to my unsuspecting friends.

At times I wonder how different we would be if we had not gone through the divorce, but for that question I can conjure up no really meaningful speculation. I know that we immensely value our time together, freely share our money (or, I should say, our student loans, as my brother is now in law school, my mom is a full-time doctoral student and my father shoulders the Wellesley burden), and exorbitantly rejoice in each other's company. What more could any of us want from family? So often, it seems to me, I see families that do not realize they possess a great wealth—time. They are together all the time. They don't miss the moments of their mother/father/brother/sister's lives that are irreplaceable.

There is no question that it is often difficult to be a family. My own family's life took a path with an unexpected curve. We weathered times of tough adjustments, economic difficulties, and typical adolescent rebellion. Through it all, though, there was a guiding (if unspoken until many years later) principle of life: family is family forever, and there is no escaping either the trials or the rewards. My parents expect my brother and me to extend ourselves and do work that in some way will bring more light into the world. I have parents who, on modest incomes and budgets, have endowed me with dreams and a sense that the impossible is possible. I have parents for whom I am extremely grateful.

When I told my family that Wellesley asked me to write an article on growing up in a single parent household, they responded in their typical chaotic fashion. My brother forced each of us to sit and write a page about the "Single-Parent Thing" before he let us eat dinner. My mother began plotting a book made up of chapters written from the different perspectives of mother, father, son, and daughter in the single-parent household. My dad insisted we discuss it over dinner (and promised to write his page immediately after dessert). In the end, I took their contributions with me back to Wellesley and wrote down my own feelings, late at night in Munger Hall.

Topics for Discussion and Writing

1. What are your earliest memories of your family? How would you account for the fact that Rothenberg has "nearly no memories of living in a two-parent household"?
2. Rothenberg calls her family "exceptional." What do you find to be her strongest evidence for this claim?
3. In paragraph 2 Rothenberg refers to assumptions that her friends make about a child who grew up with divorced parents. What are or were your assumptions? On what are (or were) they based?
4. A highly personal essay runs the risk of being of little interest to persons other than the author. If you found this essay interesting, try to account for its appeal.

Jamaica Kincaid

Jamaica Kincaid was born in 1949 in St. Johns, Antigua, in the West Indies. She was educated at the Princess Margaret School in Antigua and, briefly, at Westchester Community College and Franconia College. Since 1974 she has been a contributor to The New Yorker, *where "Girl" first was published. "Girl" was later included in the first of Kincaids four books,* At the Bottom of the River. *Her most recent book is a short novel about a young black woman who comes to the United States from the West Indies.*

Ms. Kincaid informs us that "benna," mentioned early in "Girl," refers to "songs of the sort your parents didnt want you to sing, at first calypso and later rock and roll."

Girl

Wash the white clothes on Monday and put them on the stone heap; wash the color clothes on Tuesday and put them on the clothesline to dry; don't walk barehead in the hot sun; cook pumpkin fritters in very hot sweet oil; soak your little clothes right after you take them off; when buying cotton to make yourself a nice blouse, be sure that it doesn't have gum on it, because that way it won't hold up well after a wash; soak salt fish overnight before you cook it; is it true that you sing benna in Sunday school?; always eat your food in such a way that it won't turn someone else's stomach; on Sundays try to walk like a lady and not like the slut you are so bent on becoming; don't sing benna in Sunday school; you mustn't speak to wharf-rat boys, not even to give directions;

don't eat fruits on the street—flies will follow you; *but I don't sing benna on Sundays at all and never in Sunday school;* this is how to sew on a button; this is how to make a buttonhole for the button you have just sewed on; this is how to hem a dress when you see the hem coming down and so to prevent yourself from looking like the slut I know you are so bent on becoming; this is how you iron your father's khaki shirt so that it doesn't have a crease; this is how you iron your father's khaki pants so that they don't have a crease; this is how you grow okra—far from the house, because okra tree harbors red ants; when you are growing dasheen, make sure it gets plenty of water or else it makes your throat itch when you are eating it; this is how you sweep a corner; this is how you sweep a whole house; this is how you sweep a yard; this is how you smile to someone you don't like too much; this is how you smile to someone you don't like at all; this is how you smile to someone you like completely; this is how you set a table for tea; this is how you set a table for dinner; this is how you set a table for dinner with an important guest; this is how you set a table for lunch; this is how you set a table for breakfast; this is how to behave in the presence of men who don't know you very well, and this way they won't recognize immediately the slut I have warned you against becoming; be sure to wash every day, even if it is with your own spit; don't squat down to play marbles—you are not a boy, you know; don't pick people's flowers—you might catch something; don't throw stones at blackbirds, because it might not be a blackbird at all; this is how to make a bread pudding; this is how to make doukona; this is how to make pepper pot; this is how to make a good medicine for a cold; this is how to make a good medicine to throw away a child before it even becomes a child; this is how to catch a fish; this is how to throw back a fish you don't like, and that way something bad won't fall on you; this is how to bully a man; this is how a man bullies you; this is how to love a man, and if this doesn't work there are other ways, and if they don't work don't feel too bad about giving up; this is how to spit up in the air if you feel like it, and this is how to move quick so that it doesn't fall on you; this is how to make ends meet; always squeeze bread to make sure it's fresh; *but what if the baker won't let me feel the bread?;* you mean to say that after all you are really going to be the kind of woman who the baker won't let near the bread?

Topic for Discussion and Writing

In a paragraph, identify the two characters whose voices we hear in this story. Explain what we know about them (their circumstances and their relationship). Cite specific evidence from the text. For example, what is the effect of the frequent repetition of "this is how"? Are there other words or phrases frequently repeated?

Sharon Olds

Sharon Olds was born in San Francisco in 1942 and was educated at Stanford University and Columbia University. She has published several volumes of poetry and has received major awards.

I Go Back to May 1937

I see them standing at the formal gates of their colleges,
I see my father strolling out
under the ochre sandstone arch, the
red tiles glinting like bent
plates of blood behind his head, I   5
see my mother with a few light books at her hip
standing at the pillar made of tiny bricks with the
wrought-iron gate still open behind her, its
sword-tips black in the May air,
they are about to graduate, they are about to get married,   10
they are kids, they are dumb, all they know is they are
innocent, they would never hurt anybody.
I want to go up to them and say Stop,
don't do it—she's the wrong woman,
he's the wrong man, you are going to do things   15
you cannot imagine you would ever do,
you are going to do bad things to children,
you are going to suffer in ways you never heard of,
you are going to want to die. I want to go
up to them there in the late May sunlight and say it,   20
her hungry pretty blank face turning to me,

his pitiful beautiful untouched body,
his arrogant handsome blind face turning to me,
his pitiful beautiful untouched body,
but I don't do it. I want to live. I   25
take them up like the male and female
paper dolls and bang them together
at the hips like chips of flint as if to
strike sparks from them, I say
Do what you are going to do, and I will tell about it.   30

[1987]

Topics for Discussion and Writing

1. Having read the poem, how do you understand its title? How does Olds
   seem to define "I"? What does she mean by "Go Back to"? And why
   "May 1937"?

2. In the first line Olds says, "I see them." *How* does she see them? Actually? In imagination? In photographs? Or can't we know?

3. Consider the comparisons, such as the simile in lines 4–5 ("red tiles
   glinting like bent / plates of blood") and the metaphor in lines 8–9 (the
   uprights of the wrought-iron fence are "sword-tips"). What do they tell
   us about the speaker's view of things?

4. Observe where the sentences of the poem begin and end. Can you explain these sentence boundaries? What shifts of meaning or mood accompany the end of one sentence and the beginning of the next?

5. How are the mother and father characterized when young? Are these
   characterizations consistent or inconsistent with the violent emotions
   of lines 13–19?

6. How do you read the last line? Do you feel that the speaker is, for
   example, angry, or vengeful, or sympathetic, or resigned? How do you
   interpret "and I will tell about it."? To whom will she "tell about it," and
   how?

6
TEACHING AND LEARNING

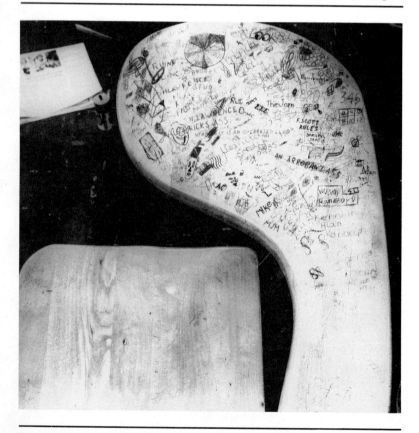

The Target Collection of American Photography, museum purchase with funds provided by Target Stores, Museum of Fine Arts, Houston, © Catherine Wagner

The Lesson—Planning a Career
Ron James, 1963

Short Views

Knowledge is power.
Francis Bacon

Hard students are commonly troubled with gouts, catarrahs, rheums, cachexia, bradypepsia, bad eyes, stone, and collick, crudities, oppilations, vertigo, winds, consumptions, and all such diseases as come by over-much sitting: they are most part lean, dry, ill-colored . . . and all through immoderate pains and extraordinary studies.
Robert Burton

In my opinion, the only justification for high schools is as therapeutic halfway houses for the deranged. Normal adolescents can find themselves and grow further only by coping with the jobs, sex, and chances of the real world—it is useless to feed them curricular imitations. I would simply abolish the high schools, substituting apprenticeships and other alternatives and protecting the young from gross exploitation by putting the school money directly in their pockets. The very few who have authentic scholarly interests will gravitate to their own libraries, teachers, and academies, as they always did in the past, when they could afford it. In organic communities, adolescents cluster together in their own youth houses, for their fun and games and loud music, without bothering sober folk. I see no reason whatsoever for adults to set up or direct such nests or to be there at all unless invited.
Paul Goodman

I can judge one of the main effects of personal grading by the attitudes of students who land in my remedial course in college. They hate and fear writing more than anything else they have had to do in school. If they see a blank sheet of paper on which they are expected to write something, they look as though they want to scream. Apparently they have never written anything that anyone thought was good. At least, no one ever told them that anything in their writing was good. All their teachers looked for were mistakes, and there are so many kinds of mistakes in writing that their students despair of ever learning to avoid them.

The attitude toward writing that these students have developed is well illustrated by a story told by the Russian writer Chekhov about a kitten that was given to his uncle. The uncle wanted to make the kitten a champion killer of mice, so while it was still very young, he showed it a live mouse in a cage. Since the kitten's hunting instinct had not yet developed, it examined the mouse curiously but without any hostility. The uncle wanted to teach it that such fraternizing with the enemy was wrong, so he slapped the kitten, scolded it, and sent it away in disgrace. The next day the same mouse was shown to the kitten again. This time the kitten regarded it rather fearfully but without any aggressive intent. Again the uncle slapped it, scolded it, and sent it away. This treatment went on day after day. After some time, as soon as the kitten saw or smelled that mouse, it screamed and tried to climb up the walls. At that point the uncle lost patience and gave the kitten away, saying that it was stupid and would never learn. Of course the kitten had learned perfectly, and had learned exactly what it had been taught, but unfortunately not what the uncle intended to teach. "I can sympathize with that kitten," says Chekhov, "because that same uncle tried to teach me Latin."

Paul B. Diederich

A woman came to Rabbi Israel, the great maggid or teacher in Koznitz, and told him, with many tears, that she had been married a dozen years and still had not borne a son. "What are you willing to do about it?" he asked her. She did not know what to say. "My mother," so the maggid told her, "was aging and still had no child. Then she heard that the holy Baal Shem was stopping over in Apt in the course of a journey. She hurried to his inn and begged him to pray she might bear a son. 'What are you willing to do about it?' he asked. 'My husband is a poor book-binder,' she replied, 'but I do have one fine thing that I shall give to the rabbi.' She went home as fast as she could and fetched her good cape, her 'Katinka,' which was carefully stowed away in a chest. But when she returned to the inn with it, she heard that the Baal Shem had already left for Mezbizh. She immediately set out after him and since she had no money to ride, she walked from town to town with her 'Katinka' until she came to Mezbizh. The Baal Shem took the cape and hung it on the wall. 'It is well,' he said. My mother walked all the way back, from town to town, until she reached Apt. A year later, I was born."

"I, too," cried the woman, "will bring you a cape of mine so that I may get a son."

"That won't work," said the maggid. "You heard the story. My mother had no story to go by."

Hasidic Tale

You go to a great school not for knowledge so much as for arts and habits; for the habit of attention, for the art of expression, for the art of assuming at a moment's notice a new intellectual posture, for the art of entering quickly into another person's thought, for the habit of submitting to censure and refutation, for the art of indicating assent or dissent in graduated terms, for the habit of regarding minute points of accuracy, for the habit of working out what is possible in a given time, for taste, for discrimination, for mental courage and mental soberness. Above all, you go to a great school for self-knowledge.

William Cory

How people keep correcting us when we are young! There's always some bad habit or other they tell us we ought to get over. Yet most bad habits are tools to help us through life.

Johann Wolfgang von Goethe

Supposing anyone were to suggest that the best results for the individual and society could be derived through compulsory feeding, would not the most ignorant rebel against such a stupid procedure? And yet the stomach has far greater adaptability to almost any situation than the brain. With all that, we find it quite natural to have compulsory mental feeding.

Indeed, we actually consider ourselves superior to other nations, because we have evolved a compulsory brain tube through which, for a certain number of hours every day, and for so many years, we can force into the child's mind a large quantity of mental nutrition.

. . . The great harm done by our system of education is not so much that it teaches nothing worth knowing, that it helps to perpetuate privileged classes, that it assists them in the criminal procedure of robbing and exploiting the masses; the harm of the system lies in its boastful proclamation that it stands for true education, thereby enslaving the masses a great deal more than could an absolute ruler.

Emma Goldman

The education of women should always be relative to that of men. To please, to be useful to us, to make us love and esteem them, to educate us when young, to take care of us when grown up; to advise, to console us, to render our lives easy and agreeable. These are the duties of women at all times, and what they should be taught in their infancy.

Jean Jacques Rousseau, *Emile*

If Johnny can't learn because he is hungry, that's the fault of poverty. But if Johnny can't pay attention because he is sleepy, that's the fault of parents.

What does it matter if we have a new book or an old book, if we open neither?

Jesse Jackson

Universities are, of course, hostile to geniuses.

Ralph Waldo Emerson

The man who can make hard things easy is the educator.

Ralph Waldo Emerson

It is perhaps idle to wonder what, from my present point of view, would have been an ideal education. If I could provide such a curriculum for my own children they, in their turn, might find it all a bore. But the fantasy of what I would have liked to learn as a child may be revealing, since I feel unequipped by education for problems that lie outside the cloistered, literary domain in which I am competent and at home. Looking back, then, I would have arranged for myself to be taught survival techniques for both natural and urban wildernesses. I would want to have been instructed in self-hypnosis, in *aikido* (the esoteric and purely self-defensive style of judo), in elementary medicine, in sexual hygiene, in vegetable gardening, in astronomy, navigation, and sailing; in cookery and clothesmaking, in metalwork and carpentry, in drawing and painting, in printing and typography, in botany and biology, in optics and acoustics, in semantics and psychology, in mysticism and yoga, in electronics and mathematical fantasy, in drama and dancing, in singing and in playing an instrument by ear; in wandering, in advanced daydreaming, in prestidigitation, in techniques of escape from bondage, in disguise, in conversation with birds and beasts, in ventriloquism, in French and German conversation, in planetary history, in morphology, and in classical Chinese. Actually, the main

thing left out of my education was a proper love for my own body, because one feared to cherish anything so obviously mortal and prone to sickness.
Alan Watts

Education! Which of the various me's do you propose to educate, and which do you propose to suppress?
D. H. Lawrence

Think about the kind of world you want to live and work in. What do you need to know to build the world? Demand that your teachers teach you that.
Prince Kropotkin

The entire object of true education is to make people not merely *do* the right things, but *enjoy* the right things.
John Ruskin

Learning without thought is labor lost; thought without learning is dangerous.
Confucius

Nan-in, a Japanese master during the Meiji era (1868–1912), received a university professor who came to inquire about Zen.

Nan-in served tea. He poured his visitor's cup full, and then kept on pouring.

The professor watched the overflow until he no longer could restrain himself. "It is overfull. No more will go in!"

"Like this cup," Nan-in said, "you are full of your own opinions and speculations. How can I show you Zen unless you first empty your cup?"
Anonymous Zen Anecdote

I think [Raymond Weaver] first attracted my attention as someone worth watching when, while we were both new instructors, I heard from a bewildered freshman about the quiz he had just given. The first question written on the blackboard was, "Which of the required readings in this course did you find least interesting?" Then, after members of the class had had ten minutes in which to expatiate on what was certainly to many a congenial topic, he wrote the second question: "To what defect in yourself do you attribute this lack of interest?"
Joseph Wood Krutch

Plato

Plato (427–347 B.C.), born in Athens, the son of an aristocratic family, wrote thirty dia-
logues in which Socrates is the chief speaker. Socrates, about twenty-five years older
than Plato, was a philosopher who called himself a gadfly to Athenians. For his efforts
at stinging them into thought, the Athenians executed him in 399 B.C. "The Myth of the
Cave" is the beginning of Book VII of Plato's dialogue entitled The Republic. *Socrates*
is talking with Glaucon.

For Plato, true knowledge is philosophic insight or awareness of the Good, not mere
opinion or the knack of getting along in this world by remembering how things have
usually worked in the past. To illustrate his idea that awareness of the Good is different
from the ability to recognize the things of this shabby world, Plato (through his spokes-
man Socrates) resorts to an allegory: men imprisoned in a cave see on a wall in front
of them the shadows or images of objects that are really behind them, and they hear
echoes, not real voices. (The shadows are caused by the light from a fire behind the
objects, and the echoes by the cave's acoustical properties.) The prisoners, unable to
perceive the real objects and the real voices, mistakenly think that the shadows and
the echoes are real, and some of them grow highly adept at dealing with this illusory
world. Were Plato writing today, he might have made the cave a movie theater: we see
on the screen in front of us images caused by an object (film, passing in front of light)
that is behind us. Moreover, the film itself is an illusory image, for it bears only the traces
of a yet more real world — the world that was photographed — outside of the movie theater.
And when we leave the theater to go into the real world, our eyes have become so ac-
customed to the illusory world that we at first blink with discomfort — just as Plato's freed
prisoners do when they move out of the cave — at the real world of bright day, and we
long for the familiar darkness. So too, Plato suggests, dwellers in ignorance may prefer
the familiar shadows of their unenlightened world ("the world of becoming") to the bright
world of the eternal Good ("the world of being") that education reveals.

We have just used the word "education." You will notice that the first sentence in
the translation (by Benjamin Jowett) says that the myth will show "how far our nature
is enlightened or unenlightened" In the original Greek the words here translated "enlight-
ened" and "unenlightened" are paideia *and* apaideusia. *No translation can fully catch*
the exact meanings of these elusive words. Depending on the context, paideia *may be*
translated as "enlightenment," education," "civilization," "culture," "knowledge of the good."

The Myth of the Cave

And now, I said, let me show in a figure how far our
nature is enlightened or unenlightened—Behold! human beings living in an underground den, which has a mouth open toward the
light and reaching all along the den; here they have been from their
childhood, and have their legs and necks chained so that they cannot move, and can only see before them, being prevented by the
chains from turning round their heads. Above and behind them a
fire is blazing at a distance, and between the fire and the prisoners

there is a raised way; and you will see, if you look, a low wall built along the way, like the screen which marionette players have in front of them, over which they show the puppets.

I see.

And do you see, I said, men passing along the wall carrying all sorts of vessels, and statues and figures of animals made of wood and stone and various materials, which appear over the wall? Some of them are talking, others silent.

You have shown me a strange image, and they are strange 4 prisoners.

Like ourselves, I replied; and they see only their own shadows, or the shadows of one another, which the fire throws on the opposite wall of the cave?

True, he said; how could they see anything but the shadows if they were never allowed to move their heads?

And of the objects which are being carried in like manner they would only see the shadows?

Yes, he said. 8

And if they were able to converse with one another, would they not suppose that they were naming what was actually before them?

Very true.

And suppose further that the prison had an echo which came from the other side, would they not be sure when one of the passersby spoke that the voice which they heard came from the passing shadow?

No question, he replied. 12

To them, I said, the truth would be literally nothing but the shadows of the images.

That is certain.

And now look again, and see what will naturally follow if the prisoners are released and disabused of their error. At first, when any of them is liberated and compelled suddenly to stand up and turn his neck round and walk and look toward the light, he will suffer sharp pains; the glare will distress him, and he will be unable to see the realities of which in his former state he had seen the shadows; and then conceive some one saying to him, that what he saw before was an illusion, but that now, when he is approaching nearer to being and his eye is turned toward more real existence, he has a clearer vision—what will be his reply? And you may further imagine that his instructor is pointing to the objects as they pass and requiring him to name them—will he not be perplexed? Will he not fancy that the shadows which he formerly saw are truer than the objects which are now shown to him?

Far truer.   16

And if he is compelled to look straight at the light, will he not have a pain in his eyes which will make him turn away to take refuge in the objects of vision which he can see, and which he will conceive to be in reality clearer than the things which are now being shown to him?

True, he said.

And suppose once more, that he is reluctantly dragged up a steep and rugged ascent, and held fast until he is forced into the presence of the sun himself, is he not likely to be pained and irritated? When he approaches the light his eyes will be dazzled, and he will not be able to see anything at all of what are now called realities.

Not all in a moment, he said.   20

He will require to grow accustomed to the sight of the upper world. And first he will see the shadows best, next the reflections of men and other objects in the water, and then the objects themselves; then he will gaze upon the light of the moon and the stars and the spangled heaven; and he will see the sky and the stars by night better than the sun or the light of the sun by day?

Certainly.

Last of all he will be able to see the sun, and not mere reflections of him in the water, but he will see him in his own proper place, and not in another; and he will contemplate him as he is.

Certainly.   24

He will then proceed to argue that this is he who gives the season and the years, and is the guardian of all that is in the visible world, and in a certain way the cause of all things which he and his fellows have been accustomed to behold?

Clearly, he said, he would first see the sun and then reason about him.

And when he remembered his old habitation, and the wisdom of the den and his fellow-prisoners, do you not suppose that he would felicitate himself on the change, and pity them?

Certainly, he would.   28

And if they were in the habit of conferring honors among themselves on those who were quickest to observe the passing shadows and to remark which of them went before, and which followed after, and which were together; and who were therefore best able to draw conclusions as to the future, do you think that he would care for such honors and glories, or envy the possessors of them? Would he not say with Homer,

Better to be the poor servant of a poor master,

and to endure anything, rather than think as they do and live after their manner?

Yes, he said, I think that he would rather suffer anything than entertain these false notions and live in this miserable manner.

Imagine once more, I said, such an one coming suddenly out of the sun to be replaced in his old situation; would he not be certain to have his eyes full of darkness?

To be sure, he said.

And if there were a contest, and he had to compete in measuring the shadows with the prisoners who had never moved out of the den, while his sight was still weak, and before his eyes had become steady (and the time which would be needed to acquire this new habit of sight might be very considerable), would he not be ridiculous? Men would say of him that up he went and down he came without his eyes; and that it was better not even to think of ascending; and if any one tried to loose another and lead him up to the light, let them only catch the offender, and they would put him to death.

No question, he said.

This entire allegory, I said, you may now append, dear Glaucon, to the previous argument; the prison-house is the world of sight, the light of the fire is the sun, and you will not misapprehend me if you interpret the journey upwards to be the ascent of the soul into the intellectual world according to my poor belief, which, at your desire, I have expressed — whether rightly or wrongly God knows. But, whether true or false, my opinion is that in the world of knowledge the idea of good appears last of all, and is seen only with an effort; and, when seen, is also inferred to be the universal author of all things beautiful and right, parent of light and of the lord of light in this visible world, and the immediate source of reason and truth in the intellectual; and that this is the power upon which he who would act rationally either in public or private life must have his eye fixed.

I agree, he said, as far as I am able to understand you.

Moreover, I said, you must not wonder that those who attain to this beatific vision are unwilling to descend to human affairs; for their souls are ever hastening into the upper world where they desire to dwell; which desire of theirs is very natural, if our allegory may be trusted.

Yes, very natural.

And is there anything surprising in one who passes from divine contemplations to the evil state of man, misbehaving himself in a ridiculous manner; if, while his eyes are blinking and before he has become accustomed to the surrounding darkness, he is compelled to fight in courts of law, or in other places, about the images or the shadows of images of justice, and is endeavoring to meet the conceptions of those who have never yet seen absolute justice?

Anything but surprising, he replied.   40

Any one who has common sense will remember that the bewilderments of the eyes are of two kinds, and arise from two causes, either from coming out of the light or from going into the light, which is true of the mind's eye, quite as much as of the bodily eye; and he who remembers this when he sees any one whose vision is perplexed and weak, will not be too ready to laugh; he will first ask whether that soul of man has come out of the brighter life, and is unable to see because unaccustomed to the dark, or having turned from darkness to the day is dazzled by excess of light. And he will count the one happy in his condition and state of being, and he will pity the other; or, if he have a mind to laugh at the soul which comes from below into the light, there will be more reason in this than in the laugh which greets him who returns from above out of the light into the den.

That, he said, is a very just distinction.

But then, if I am right, certain professors of education must be wrong when they say that they can put a knowledge into the soul which was not there before, like sight into blind eyes.

They undoubtedly say this, he replied.   44

Whereas, our argument shows that the power and capacity of learning exists in the soul already; and that just as the eye was unable to turn from darkness to light without the whole body, so too the instrument of knowledge can only by the movement of the whole soul be turned from the world of becoming into that of being, and learn by degrees to endure the sight of being, and of the brightest and best of being, or in other words, of the good.

Very true.

And must there not be some art which will effect conversion in the easiest and quickest manner; not implanting the faculty of sight, for that exists already, but has been turned in the wrong direction, and is looking away from the truth?

Yes, he said, such an art may be presumed.   48

And whereas the other so-called virtues of the soul seem to be akin to bodily qualities, for even when they are not originally innate they can be implanted later by habit and exercise, the virtue of wisdom more than anything else contains a divine element which always remains, and by this conversion is rendered useful and profitable; or, on the other hand, hurtful and useless. Did you never observe the narrow intelligence flashing from the keen eye of a clever rogue—how eager he is, how clearly his paltry soul sees the way to his end; he is the reverse of blind, but his keen eyesight is forced into the service of evil, and he is mischievous in proportion to his cleverness?

Very true, he said.

But what if there had been a circumcision of such natures in the days of their youth; and they had been severed from those sensual pleasures, such as eating and drinking, which, like leaden weights, were attached to them at their birth, and which drag them down and turn the vision of their souls upon the things that are below—if, I say, they had been released from these impediments and turned in the opposite direction, the very same faculty in them would have seen the truth as keenly as they see what their eyes are turned to now.

Very likely.   52

Yes, I said; and there is another thing which is likely, or rather a necessary inference from what has preceded, that neither the uneducated and uninformed of the truth, nor yet those who never make an end of their education, will be able ministers of State; not the former, because they have no single aim of duty which is the rule of all their actions, private as well as public; nor the latter, because they will not act at all except upon compulsion, fancying that they are already dwelling apart in the islands of the blest.

Very true, he replied.

Then, I said, the business of us who are the founders of the State will be to compel the best minds to attain that knowledge which we have already shown to be the greatest of all—they must continue to ascend until they arrive at the good; but when they have ascended and seen enough we must not allow them to do as they do now.

What do you mean?   56

I mean that they remain in the upper world: but this must not be allowed; they must be made to descend again among the prisoners in the den, and partake of their labors and honors, whether they are worth having or not.

But is not this unjust? he said; ought we to give them a worse life, when they might have a better?

You have again forgotten, my friend, I said, the intention of the legislator, who did not aim at making any one class in the State happy above the rest; the happiness was to be in the whole State, and he held the citizens together by persuasion and necessity, making them benefactors of the State, and therefore benefactors of one another; to this end he created them, not to please themselves, but to be his instruments in binding up the State.

True, he said, I had forgotten.   60

Observe, Glaucon, that there will be no justice in compelling our philosophers to have a care and providence of others; we shall explain to them that in other States, men of their class are not obliged to share in the toils of politics: and this is reasonable, for they grow up at their own sweet will, and the government would rather not have them. Being self-taught, they cannot be expected to show any gratitude for a culture which they have never received. But we have brought you into the world to be rulers of the hive, kings of yourselves and of the other citizens, and have educated you far better and more perfectly than they have been educated, and you are better able to share in the double duty. Wherefore each of you, when his turn comes, must go down to the general underground abode, and get the habit of seeing in the dark. When you have acquired the habit, you will see ten thousand times better than the inhabitants of the den, and you will know what the several images are, and what they represent, because you have seen the beautiful and just and good in their truth. And thus our State which is also yours will be a reality, and not a dream only, and will be administered in a spirit unlike that of other States, in which men fight with one another about shadows only and are distracted in the struggle for power, which in their eyes is a great good. Whereas the truth is that the State in which the rulers are most reluctant to govern is always the best and most quietly governed, and the State in which they are most eager, the worst.

Quite true, he replied.

And will our pupils, when they hear this, refuse to take their turn at the toils of State, when they are allowed to spend the greater part of their time with one another in the heavenly light?

Impossible, he answered; for they are just men, and the com- 64
mands which we impose upon them are just; there can be no doubt
that every one of them will take office as a stern necessity, and not
after the fashion of our present rulers of State.

Yes, my friend, I said; and there lies the point. You must contrive for your future rulers another and a better life than that of a
ruler, and then you may have a well-ordered State; for only in the
State which offers this, will they rule who are truly rich, not in silver and gold, but in virtue and wisdom, which are the true bless-
ings of life. Whereas if they go to the administration of public affairs, poor and hungering after their own private advantage, thinking
that hence they are to snatch the chief good, order there can never
be; for they will be fighting about office, and the civil and domestic
broils which thus arise will be the ruin of the rulers themselves and
of the whole State.

Most true, he replied.

And the only life which looks down upon the life of political
ambition is that of true philosophy. Do you know of any other?

Indeed, I do not, he said.   68

And those who govern ought not to be lovers of the task? For,
if they are, there will be rival lovers, and they will fight.

No question.

Who then are those whom we shall compel to be guardians?
Surely they will be the men who are wisest about affairs of State,
and by whom the State is best administered, and who at the same
time have other honors and another and a better life than that of
politics?

They are the men, and I will choose them, he replied.   72

And now shall we consider in what way such guardians will
be produced, and how they are to be brought from darkness to
light—as some are said to have ascended from the world below to
the gods?

By all means, he replied.

The process, I said, is not the turning over of an oyster-shell,[1]
but the turning round of a soul passing from a day which is little
better than night to the true day of being, that is, the ascent from
below which we affirm to be true philosophy?

Quite so.

---

[1] An allusion to a game in which two parties fled or pursued according as an oyster shell that
was thrown into the air fell with the dark or light side uppermost. (Translator's note)

Topics for Discussion and Writing

1. Plato is not merely reporting one of Socrates' conversations; he is teaching. What advantages does a dialogue have over a narrative or an essay as a way of teaching philosophy? How is the form of a dialogue especially suited to solving a problem?

2. If you don't know the etymology of the word "conversion," look it up in a dictionary. How is the etymology appropriate to Plato's idea about education?

3. In paragraph 19, describing the prisoner as "reluctantly dragged" upward and "forced" to look at the sun, Socrates asks: "Is he not likely to be pained and irritated?" Can you recall experiencing pain and irritation while learning something you later were glad to have learned? Can you recall learning something new *without* experiencing pain and irritation?

4. "The State in which rulers are most reluctant to govern is always the best and most quietly governed, and the State in which they are most eager, the worst" (paragraph 61). What does Socrates mean? Using examples from contemporary politics, defend this proposition, or argue against it.

5. Can you account for the power of this myth or fable? In our introductory comment (page 171) we tried to clarify the message by saying that a movie theater might serve as well as a cave, but in fact if the story were recast using a movie theater, would the emotional power be the same? Why or why not?

6. The metaphors of education as conversion and ascent are linked by the metaphor of light. Consider such expressions as "I see" (meaning "I understand") and "Let me give an illustration" (from the Latin *in* = in, and *lustrare* = to make bright). What other expressions about light are used metaphorically to describe intellectual comprehension?

Diane Ravitch

Diane Ravitch (b. 1938) has taught history and education at Teachers College; Colum-bia University. In 1991 she was appointed an Assistant Secretary of Education in the George Bush administration. The essay that we print here appeared in 1991 in The Key Reporter, *a newsletter published by Phi Beta Kappa, a national academic society.*

Multiculturalism: E Pluribus Plures[1]

Questions of race, ethnicity, and religion have been a perennial source of conflict in American education. The schools have often attracted the zealous attention of those who wish to influence the future, as well as those who wish to change the way we view the past. In our history, the schools have been not only an institu-tion in which to teach young people skills and knowledge, but an arena where interest groups fight to preserve their values, or to re-vise the judgments of history, or to bring about fundamental social change.

Given the diversity of American society, it has been impossible to insulate the schools from pressures that result from differences and tensions among groups. When people differ about basic values, sooner or later those disagreements turn up in battles about how schools are organized or what the schools should teach. Sometimes these battles remove a terrible injustice, like racial segregation. Some-times, however, interest groups politicize the curriculum and at-tempt to impose their views on teachers, school officials, and text-book publishers. When groups cross the line into extremism, advancing their own agendas without regard to reason or to others, they threaten public education itself, making it difficult to teach any issues honestly and making the entire curriculum vulnerable to po-litical campaigns.

For many years, the public schools attempted to neutralize con-troversies over race, religion, and ethnicity by ignoring them. The textbooks minimized problems among groups and taught a sanitized version of history. Race, religion, and ethnicity were presented as minor elements in the American saga; slavery was treated as an

---

[1] **E Pluribus Plures** Latin for "Out of Many, Many" (a variant on a motto of the United States, E Pluribus Unum, "Out of Many, One"). All notes are the editors'.

episode, immigration as a sidebar, and women were largely absent. The textbooks concentrated on presidents, wars, national politics, and issues of state. An occasional "great black" or "great woman" received mention, but the main narrative paid little attention to minority groups and women.

With the ethnic revival of the 1960s, this approach to the teaching of history came under fire, because the history of national leaders — virtually all of whom were white, Anglo-Saxon, and male — ignored the place in American history of those who were none of the above. The traditional history of elites had been complemented by an assimilationist view of American society, which presumed that everyone in the American melting pot would eventually lose or abandon those ethnic characteristics that distinguished each from mainstream Americans. The ethnic revival demonstrated that many groups did not want to be assimilated or melted. Ethnic studies programs popped up on campuses to teach not only that "black is beautiful," but also that every other variety of ethnicity is "beautiful" as well; everyone who had "roots" began to look for them so that they, too, could recover that ancestral part of themselves that had not been homogenized.

As ethnicity became an accepted subject for study in the late 1960s, textbooks were assailed for their failure to portray blacks accurately; within a few years, the textbooks in wide use were carefully screened to eliminate bias against minority groups and women. At the same time, new scholarship about the history of women, blacks, and various ethnic minorities found its way into the textbooks. Today's history textbooks routinely incorporate the experiences of women, blacks, American Indians, and various immigrant groups.

As a result of the political and social changes of recent decades, cultural pluralism is now generally recognized as an organizing principle of this society. In contrast to the idea of the melting pot, which promised to erase ethnic and group differences, children now learn that variety is the spice of life. They learn that America has provided a haven for many different groups and has allowed them to maintain their cultural heritage or to assimilate, or — as is often the case — to do both; the choice is theirs, not the state's. They learn that cultural pluralism is one of the norms of a free society; that differences among groups are a national resource rather than a problem to be solved. Indeed, the unique feature of the United States is that its common culture has been formed by the interaction of its subsidiary cultures.

It is a culture that has been influenced over time by immigrants, American Indians, Africans (slave and free) and by their descendants. American music, art, literature, language, food, clothing, sports, holidays, and customs all show the effects of the commingling of diverse cultures in one nation. Paradoxical though it may seem, the United States has a common culture that is multicultural.

This understanding of the pluralistic nature of American culture has taken a long time to forge. It is based on sound scholarship and has led to major revisions in what children are taught and what they read in school. The new history is—indeed, must be—a warts-and-all history; it demands an unflinching examination of racism and discrimination in our history. Making these changes is difficult, raises tempers, and ignites controversies, but gives a more interesting and accurate account of American history. Accomplishing these changes is valuable, because there is also a useful lesson for the rest of the world in America's relatively successful experience as a pluralistic society. Throughout human history, the clash of different cultures, races, ethnic groups, and religions has often been the cause of bitter hatred, civil conflict, and international war. The ethnic tensions that now are tearing apart Lebanon, Sri Lanka, Kashmir, and various republics of the Soviet Union remind us of the costs of unfettered group rivalry. Thus, it is a matter of more than domestic importance that we closely examine and try to understand that part of our national history in which different groups competed, fought, suffered, but ultimately learned to live together in relative peace and even achieved a sense of common nationhood.

Particularism

Alas, these painstaking efforts to expand the understanding of American culture into a richer and more varied tapestry have taken a new turn, and not for the better. Almost any idea, carried to its extreme, can be made pernicious, and this is what is happening now to multiculturalism. Today, pluralistic multiculturalism must contend with a new, particularistic multiculturalism. The pluralists seek a richer common culture; the particularists insist that no common culture is possible or desirable. 8

The new particularism is entering the curriculum in a number of school systems across the country. Advocates of particularism propose an ethnocentric curriculum to raise the self-esteem and academic achievement of children from racial and ethnic minority backgrounds. Without any evidence, they claim that children from minority backgrounds will do well in school *only* if they are immersed in a positive, prideful version of their ancestral culture. If children are of, for example, Fredonian ancestry, they must hear that Fredonians were important in mathematics, science, history, and literature. If they learn about great Fredonians and if their studies use Fredonian examples and Fredonian concepts, they will do well in school. If they do not, they will have low self-esteem and will do badly.

The particularistic version of multi-culturalism is unabashedly filiopietistic[2] and deterministic. It teaches children that their identity is determined by their "cultural genes"—that something in their blood or their racial memory or their cultural DNA defines who they are and what they may achieve; that the culture in which they live is not their own culture, even though they were born here; that American culture is "Eurocentric," and therefore hostile to anyone whose ancestors are not European. Perhaps the most insidious implication of particularism is that racial and ethnic minorities are not and should not try to be part of American culture; it implies that American culture belongs only to those who are white and European; it implies that those who are neither white nor European are alienated from American culture by virtue of their race or ethnicity; it implies that the only culture they do belong to or can ever belong to is the culture of their ancestors, even if their families have lived in this country for generations.

The pluralist approach to multiculturalism promotes a broader interpretation of the common American culture and seeks due recognition for the ways that the nation's many racial, ethnic, and cultural groups have transformed the national culture. The pluralists say, in effect, "American culture belongs to us, all of us; the United States is us, and we remake it in every generation." But particularists have no interest in extending or revising American culture; indeed, they deny that a common culture exists. Particularists reject any accommodation among groups, any interactions that blur the distinct lines between them. The brand of history that they espouse is one in which everyone is a descendant of victims or oppressors. By taking this approach, they fan and re-create ancient hatreds in each new generation.

Particularism has its intellectual roots in the ideology of ethnic separatism and in the black nationalist movement. In the particularist analysis, the nation has five cultures: African American, Asian

12

[2] **filiopietistic** excessively reverential of ancestors

American, European American, Latino/Hispanic, and American Indian. The huge cultural, historical, religious, and linguistic differences within these categories are ignored, as is the considerable intermarriage among these groups, as are the linkages (like gender, class, sexual orientation, and religion) that cut across these five groups. No serious scholar would claim that all Europeans and white Americans are part of the same culture, or that all Asians are part of the same culture, or that all people of Latin American descent are of the same culture, or that all people of African descent are of the same culture. Any categorization this broad is essentially meaningless and useless.

Particularism is a bad idea whose time has come. It is also a fashion spreading like wildfire through the education system, actively promoted by organizations and individuals with a political and professional interest in strengthening ethnic power bases in the university, in the education profession, and in society itself. One can scarcely pick up an educational journal without learning about a school district that is converting to an ethnocentric curriculum in an attempt to give "self-esteem" to children from racial minorities. A state-funded project in a Sacramento high school is teaching young black males to think like Africans and to develop the "African Mind Model Technique," in order to free themselves of the racism of American culture. A popular black rap singer, KRS-One, complained in an op-ed article in the *New York Times* that the schools should be teaching blacks about their cultural heritage, instead of trying to make everyone Americans. "It's like trying to teach a dog to be a cat," he wrote. KRS-One railed about having to learn about Thomas Jefferson and the Civil War, which had nothing to do (he said) with black history.

Ethnomathematics

Pluralism can easily be transformed into particularism, as may be seen in the potential uses in the classroom of the Mayan contribution to mathematics. The Mayan example was popularized in a movie called *Stand and Deliver*, about a charismatic Bolivian-born mathematics teacher in Los Angeles who inspired his students (who are Hispanic) to learn calculus. He told them that their ancestors invented the concept of zero; but that wasn't all he did. He used imagination to put across mathematical concepts. He required students to do homework and to go to school on Saturdays and during the Christmas holidays, so that they might pass the advanced placement mathematics examination. The teacher's reference to the Mayans' mathematical genius was a valid instructional device: It was an attention-getter and would have interested even students who were not Hispanic. But the Mayan example would have had little effect without the teacher's insistence that the class study hard for a difficult examination.

Ethnic educators have seized on the Mayan contribution to mathematics as the key to simultaneously boosting the ethnic pride of Hispanic children and attacking Eurocentrism. One proposal claims that Mexican-American children will be attracted to science and mathematics if they study Mayan mathematics, the Mayan calendar, and Mayan astronomy. Children in primary grades are to be taught that the Mayans were first to discover the zero and that Europeans learned it long afterward from the Arabs, who had learned it in India. This will help students see that Europeans were latecomers in the discovery of great ideas. Botany is to be learned by study of the agricultural techniques of the Aztecs, a subject of somewhat limited relevance to children in urban areas. Furthermore, "ethnobotanical" classifications of plants are to be substituted for the Eurocentric Linnaean system. At first glance, it may seem curious that Hispanic children are deemed to have no cultural affinity with Spain; but to acknowledge the cultural tie would confuse the ideological assault on Eurocentrism.

This proposal suggests some questions: Is there any evidence 16 that the teaching of "culturally relevant" science and mathematics will draw Mexican-American children to the study of these subjects? Will Mexican-American children lose interest or self-esteem if they discover that their ancestors were Aztecs or Spaniards, rather than Mayans? Are children who learn in this way prepared to study the science and mathematics that are taught in American colleges and universities and that are needed for advanced study in these fields? Are they even prepared to study the science and mathematics taught in *Mexican* universities? If the class is half Mexican-American and half something else, will only the Mexican-American children study in a Mayan and Aztec mode or will all the children? But shouldn't all children study what is culturally relevant for them? How will we train teachers who have command of so many different systems of mathematics and science?

The interesting proposal to teach ethnomathematics comes at a time when American mathematics educators are trying to overhaul present practices, because of the poor performance of American children on national and international assessments. Mathematics educators are attempting to change the teaching of their subject so that children can see its uses in everyday life. There would seem to be an incipient conflict between those who want to introduce real-life applications of mathematics and those who want to teach the mathematical systems used by ancient cultures. I suspect that most mathematics teachers would enjoy doing a bit of both, if there were time or student interest. But any widespread movement to replace modern mathematics with ancient ethnic mathematics runs the risk of disaster in a field that is struggling to up-date existing curricula. If, as seems likely, ancient mathematics is taught mainly to minority children, the gap between them and middle-class white children is apt to grow. It is worth noting that children in Korea, who score highest in mathematics on international assessments, do not study ancient Korean mathematics.

Particularism is akin to cultural Lysenkoism[3] for it takes as its premise the spurious notion that cultural traits are inherited. It implies a dubious, dangerous form of cultural predestination. Children are taught that if their ancestors could do it, so could they. But what happens if a child is from a cultural group that made no significant contribution to science or mathematics? Must children find a culturally appropriate field in which to strive? How does a teacher find the right cultural buttons for children of mixed heritage? And how in the world will teachers use this technique when the children in their classes are drawn from many different cultures, as is usually the case? By the time that every culture gets its due, there may be no time left to teach the subject itself. This explosion of filiopietism (which, we should remember, comes from adults, not from students) is reminiscent of the period some years ago when the Russians claimed that they had invented everything first; as we now know, this nationalistic braggadocio did little for their self-esteem and nothing for their economic development. We might reflect, too, on how little social prestige has been accorded in this country to immigrants from Greece and Italy, even though the achievements of their ancestors were at the heart of the classical curriculum.

In school districts where most children are black and Hispanic, there has been a growing tendency to embrace particularism rather than pluralism. Many of the chidren in these districts perform poorly in academic classes and leave school without graduating. They

---

[3] **Lysenkoism**   named for T. F. Lysenko (1898–1976), a Soviet geneticist who claimed that acquired characteristics can be inherited

would fare better in school if they had well-educated and well-paid teachers, small classes, good materials, encouragement at home and school, summer academic programs, protection from the drugs and crime that ravage their neighborhoods, and higher expectations of satisfying careers upon graduation. These are expensive and time-consuming remedies that must also engage the large society beyond the school. The lure of particularism is that it offers a less compli-cated anodyne, one in which the children's academic deficiencies may be addressed—or set aside—by inflating their racial pride. The danger of this remedy is that it will detract attention from the real needs of schools and the real interests of children, while simultane-ously arousing distorted race pride in the children of all races, in-creasing racial antagonism and producing fresh recruits for white and black racist groups.

The Effects of Particularism

The rising tide of particularism encourages the politicization of all curricula in the schools. If education bureaucrats bend to the politi-cal and ideological winds, as is their wont, we can anticipate a gener-ation of struggle over the content of the curriculum in mathematics, science, literature, and history. Demands for "culturally relevant" studies, for ethnostudies of all kinds, will open the classroom to un-ending battles over whose version is taught, who gets credit for what, and which ethno-interpretation is appropriate.

The spread of particularism throws into question the very idea of American public education. Public schools exist to teach children the general skills and knowledge that they need to succeed in Ameri-can society, and the specific skills and knowledge that they need in order to function as American citizens. They receive public sup-port because they have a public function. Historically, the public schools were known as "common schools" because they were schools for all, even if the children of all the people did not attend them. Over the years, the courts have found that it was unconstitu-tional to teach religion in the common schools, or to separate children on the basis of their race in the common schools. In their curricu-lum, their hiring practices, and their general philosophy, the pub-lic schools must not discriminate against or give preference to any racial or ethnic group. Yet they are permitted to accommodate cul-tural diversity by, for example, serving food that is culturally ap-propriate or providing library collections that emphasize the interests of the local community. They should not, however, be expected to teach children to view the world through an ethnocentric perspective that rejects or ignores the common culture.

For generations, those groups that wanted to inculcate their religion or their ethnic heritage have instituted private schools—after school, on weekends, or on a full-time basis. There, children learn with others of the same group—Greeks, Poles, Germans, Japanese, Chinese, Jews, Lutherans, Catholics, and so on—and are taught by people from the same group. Valuable as this exclusive experience has been for those who choose it, this has not been the role of public education. One of the primary purposes of public education has been to create a national community, a definition of citizenship and culture that is both expansive and *inclusive.*

The multicultural controversy may do wonders for the study of history, which has been neglected for years in American schools. At this time, only half of our high school graduates ever study any world history. Any serious attempt to broaden students' knowledge of Africa, Europe, Asia, and Latin America will require at least two, and possibly three, years of world history (a requirement thus far only in California). American history, too, will need more time than the one-year high-school survey course. Those of us who have insisted for years on the importance of history in the curriculum may not be ready to assent to its redemptive power, but hope that our new allies will ultimately join a constructive dialogue that strengthens the place of history in the schools.

Some Solutions

As cultural controversies arise, educators must adhere to the principle of "E Pluribus Unum." That is, they must maintain a balance   24 between the demands of the one—the nation of which we are common citizens—and the many—the varied histories of the American people. It is not necessary to denigrate either the one or the many. Pluralism is a positive value, but it is also important that we preserve a sense of an American community—a society and a culture to which we all belong. If there is no overall community with an agreed upon vision of liberty and justice, if all we have is a collection of racial and ethnic cultures, lacking any common bonds, then we have no means to mobilize public opinion on behalf of people who are not members of our particular group. We have, for example, no reason to support public education. If there is no larger community, then each group will want to teach its own children in its own way, and public education ceases to exist.

History should not be confused with filiopietism. History gives no grounds for race pride. No race has a monopoly on virtue. If anything, a study of history should inspire humility, rather than pride. People of every racial group have committed terrible crimes, often against others of the same group. Whether one looks at the history or Europe or Africa or Latin America or Asia, every continent offers examples of inhumanity. Slavery has existed in civilizations around the world for centuries. Examples of genocide can be found around the world, throughout history, from ancient times right through to our own day. Governments and cultures, sometimes by edict, sometimes simply following tradition, have practiced not only slavery, but human sacrifice, infanticide, cliterodectomy, and mass murder. If we teach children this, they might recognize how absurd both racial hatred and racial chauvinism are.

What must be preserved in the study of history is the spirit of inquiry, the readiness to open new questions and to pursue new understandings. History, at its best, is a search for truth. The best way to portray this search is through debate and controversy, rather than through imposition of fixed beliefs and immutable facts. Perhaps the most dangerous aspect of school history is its tendency to become Official History, a sanctified version of the Truth taught by the state to captive audiences and embedded in beautiful mass-market textbooks as holy writ. When Official History is written by committees responding to political pressures, rather than by scholars synthesizing the best available research, the errors of the past are replaced by the politically fashionable errors of the present. It may be difficult to teach children that history is both important and uncertain, and that even the best historians never have all the pieces of the jigsaw puzzle, but it is necessary to do so. If state education departments permit the revision of their history courses and textbooks to become an exercise in power politics, the entire process of state-level curriculum-making becomes suspect, as does public education itself.

The question of self-esteem is extraordinarily complex, and it goes well beyond the content of the curriculum. Most of what we call self-esteem is formed in the home and in a variety of life experiences, not only in school. Nonetheless, it has been important for blacks—and for other racial groups—to learn about the history of slavery and of the civil rights movement; it has been important for blacks to know that their ancestors actively resisted enslavement and actively pursued equality; and it has been important for blacks and others to learn about black men and women who fought courageously against racism and who provide models of courage, persistence, and intellect. These are instances where the content of the curriculum reflects sound scholarship, and at the same time probably lessens racial prejudice and provides inspiration for those who are descendants of slaves. But knowing about the travails and triumphs of one's forebears does not necessarily translate into either self-esteem or personal accomplishment. For most children, self-esteem — the self-confidence that grows out of having reached a goal — comes not from hearing about the monuments of their ancestors but as a consequence of what they are able to do and accomplish through their own efforts.

As I reflected on these issues, I recalled reading an interview   28
a few years ago with a talented black runner. She said that her model is Mikhail Baryshnikov. She admires him because he is a magnificent athlete. He is not black; he is not female; he is not American-born; he is not even a runner. But he inspires her because of the way he trained and used his body. When I read this, I thought how narrow-minded it is to believe that people can be inspired *only* by those who are exactly like them in race and ethnicity.

Topics for Discussion and Writing

1. How does Ravitch define ethnicity? How does it differ from race?
2. In paragraph 4 Ravitch writes of the "ethnic revival of the 1960s." To what does she refer? What is Ravitch's attitude toward the changes in schools produced by the ethnic revival?
3. What does Ravitch mean by "particularism"? How does it differ from "pluralism"?
4. In paragraph 17 Ravitch cites an example from Korean education. What point is she trying to establish through this example? How might a "particularist" dispute this point? Do you find the example relevant?
5. In paragraph 18 Ravitch argues that in the classroom "by the time that every culture gets its due there may be no time to teach the subject itself." What is "the subject itself"? How might a "particularist" answer this argument?
6. What dangers does Ravitch ascribe to particularism? Have you been a witness to these dangers yourself? Or does your experience suggest that she exaggerates the dangers?
7. In paragraph 26, what does Ravitch imply by capitalizing "Official History" and "Truth"?
8. In the schools you attended, what history courses were offered? Were race, religion, and ethnicity prominent topics? Were the lives and works

of women studied? Compare your experience of learning history with Ravitch's description of how history was taught before the "ethnic revival of the 60's." If the emphasis was what Ravitch calls "particularist" rather than "pluralistic," describe that too and try to assesss its effect on both your understanding of history and on your self-esteem.

Maya Angelou

Maya Angelou, born in St. Louis, Missouri, in 1938, grew up in Arkansas and California. She studied music, dance, and drama (she had a role in the televised version of Alex Haley's Roots*), and she is now a professor of American studies at Wake Forest University. She has also worked as a cook, streetcar conductor, and waitress. In addition to writing books of poetry, she has written five autobiographical volumes.*

"Graduation" (editors' title) comes from her first autobiography, I Know Why the Caged Bird Sings *(1969).*

Graduation

The children in Stamps trembled visibly with anticipation. Some adults were excited too, but to be certain the whole young population had come down with graduation epidemic. Large classes were graduating from both the grammar school and the high school. Even those who were years removed from their own day of glorious release were anxious to help with preparations as a kind of dry run. The junior students who were moving into the vacating classes' chairs were tradition-bound to show their talents for leadership and management. They strutted through the school and around the campus exerting pressure on the lower grades. Their authority was so new that occasionally if they pressed a little too hard it had to be overlooked. After all, next term was coming, and it never hurt a sixth grader to have a play sister in the eighth grade, or a tenth-year student to be able to call a twelfth grader Bubba. So all was endured in a spirit of shared understanding. But the graduating classes themselves were the nobility. Like travelers with exotic destinations on their minds, the graduates were remarkably forgetful. They came to school without their books, or tablets or even pencils. Volunteers fell over themselves to secure replacements for the missing equipment. When accepted, the willing workers might or might not be thanked, and it was of no importance to the pregraduation rites. Even teachers were respectful of the now quiet and aging seniors, and tended to speak to them, if not as equals, as beings only slightly lower than themselves. After tests were returned and grades given, the student body, which acted like an extended family, knew who did well, who excelled, and what piteous ones had failed.

Unlike the white high school, Lafayette County Training School distinguished itself by having neither lawn, nor hedges, nor tennis court, nor climbing ivy. Its two buildings (main classrooms, the grade school and home economics) were set on a dirt hill with no fence to limit either its boundaries or those of bordering farms. There was a large expanse to the left of the school which was used alternately as a baseball diamond or a basketball court. Rusty hoops on the swaying poles represented the permanent recreational equipment, although bats and balls could be borrowed from the P.E. teacher if the borrower was qualified and if the diamond wasn't occupied.

Over this rocky area relieved by a few shady tall persimmon trees the graduating class walked. The girls often held hands and no longer bothered to speak to the lower students. There was a sadness about them, as if this old world was not their home and they were bound for higher ground. The boys, on the other hand, had become more friendly, more outgoing. A decided change from the closed attitude they projected while studying for finals. Now they seemed not ready to give up the old school, the familiar paths and classrooms. Only a small percentage would be continuing on to college—one of the South's A & M (agricultural and mechanical) schools, which trained Negro youths to be carpenters, farmers, handymen, masons, maids, cooks and baby nurses. Their future rode heavily on their shoulders, and blinded them to the collective joy that had pervaded the lives of the boys and girls in the grammar school graduating class.

Parents who could afford it had ordered new shoes and ready-made clothes for themselves from Sears and Roebuck or Montgomery Ward. They also engaged the best seamstresses to make the floating graduating dresses and to cut down secondhand pants which would be pressed to a military slickness for the important event. 4

Oh, it was important, all right. Whitefolks would attend the ceremony, and two or three would speak of God and home, and the Southern way of life, and Mrs. Parsons, the principal's wife, would play the graduation march while the lower-grade graduates paraded down the aisles and took their seats below the platform. The high school seniors would wait in empty classrooms to make their dramatic entrance.

In the Store I was the person of the moment. The birthday girl. The center. Bailey had graduated the year before, although to do so he had had to forfeit all pleasures to make up for his time lost in Baton Rouge.

My class was wearing butter-yellow piqué dresses, and Momma launched out on mine. She smocked the yoke into tiny crisscrossing puckers, then shirred the rest of the bodice. Her dark fingers ducked in and out of the lemony cloth as she embroidered raised daisies around the hem. Before she considered herself finished she had added a crocheted cuff on the puff sleeves, and a pointy crocheted collar.

I was going to be lovely. A walking model of all the various styles of fine hand sewing and it didn't worry me that I was only twelve years old and merely graduating from the eighth grade. Besides, many teachers in Arkansas Negro schools had only that diploma and were licensed to impart wisdom.

The days had become longer and more noticeable. The faded beige of former times had been replaced with strong and sure colors. I began to see my classmates' clothes, their skin tones, and the dust that waved off pussy willows. Clouds that lazed across the sky were objects of great concern to me. Their shiftier shapes might have held a message that in my new happiness and with a little bit of time I'd soon decipher. During that period I looked at the arch of heaven so religiously my neck kept a steady ache. I had taken to smiling more often, and my jaws hurt from the unaccustomed activity. Between the two physical sore spots, I suppose I could have been uncomfortable, but that was not the case. As a member of the winning team (the graduating class of 1940) I had outdistanced unpleasant sensations by miles. I was headed for the freedom of open fields.

Youth and social approval allied themselves with me and we trammeled memories of slights and insults. The wind of our swift passage remodeled my features. Lost tears were pounded to mud and then to dust. Years of withdrawal were brushed aside and left behind, as hanging ropes of parasitic moss.

My work alone had awarded me a top place and I was going to be one of the first called in the graduating ceremonies. On the classroom blackboard, as well as on the bulletin board in the auditorium, there were blue stars and white stars and red stars. No absences, no tardinesses, and my academic work was among the best of the year. I could say the preamble to the Constitution even faster than Bailey. We timed ourselves often: "WethepeopleoftheUnitedStatesinorder-toformamoreperfectunion . . ." I had memorized the Presidents of the United States from Washington to Roosevelt in chronological as well as alphabetical order.

My hair pleased me too. Gradually the black mass had length- 12 ened and thickened, so that it kept at last to its braided pattern, and I didn't have to yank my scalp off when I tried to comb it.

Louise and I had rehearsed the exercises until we tired out ourselves. Henry Reed was class valedictorian. He was a small, very black boy with hooded eyes, a long, broad nose and an oddly shaped head. I had admired him for years because each term he and I vied for the best grades in our class. Most often he bested me, but instead of being disappointed I was pleased that we shared top places between us. Like many Southern Black children, he lived with his grandmother, who was as strict as Momma and as kind as she knew how to be. He was courteous, respectful and soft-spoken to elders, but on the playground he chose to play the roughest games. I admired him. Anyone, I reckoned, sufficiently afraid or sufficiently dull could be polite. But to be able to operate at a top level with both adults and children was admirable.

His valedictory speech was entitled "To Be or Not To Be." The rigid tenth-grade teacher had helped him to write it. He'd been working on the dramatic stresses for months.

The weeks until graduation were filled with heady activities. A group of small children were to be presented in a play about buttercups and daisies and bunny rabbits. They could be heard throughout the building practicing their hops and their little songs that sounded like silver bells. The older girls (non-graduates, of course) were assigned the task of making refreshments for the night's festivities. A tangy scent of ginger, cinnamon, nutmeg and chocolate wafted around the home economics building as the budding cooks made samples for themselves and their teachers.

In every corner of the workshop, axes and saws split fresh timber 16 as the woodshop boys made sets and stage scenery. Only the graduates were left out of the general bustle. We were free to sit in the library at the back of the building or look in quite detachedly, naturally, on the measures being taken for our event.

Even the minister preached on graduation the Sunday before. His subject was, "Let your light so shine that men will see your good works and praise your Father, Who is in Heaven." Although the sermon was purported to be addressed to us, he used the occasion to speak to backsliders, gamblers, and general ne'er-do-wells. But since he had called our names at the beginning of the service we were mollified.

Among Negroes the tradition was to give presents to children going only from one grade to another. How much more important this was when the person was graduating at the top of the class. Uncle Willie and Momma had sent away for a Mickey Mouse watch like Bailey's. Louise gave me four embroidered handkerchiefs. (I gave her three crocheted doilies.) Mrs. Sneed, the minister's wife, made me an underskirt to wear for graduation, and nearly every customer gave me a nickel or maybe even a dime with the instruction "Keep on moving to higher ground," or some such encouragement.

Amazingly the great day finally dawned and I was out of bed before I knew it. I threw open the back door to see it more clearly, but Momma said, "Sister, come away from that door and put your robe on."

I hoped the memory of that morning would never leave me. Sunlight was itself still young, and the day had none of the insistence maturity would bring it in a few hours. In my robe and barefoot in the backyard, under cover of going to see about my new beans, I gave myself up to the gentle warmth and thanked God that no matter what evil I had done in my life He had allowed me to live to see this day. Somewhere in my fatalism I had expected to die, accidentally, and never have the chance to walk up the stairs in the auditorium and gracefully receive my hard-earned diploma. Out of God's merciful bosom I had won reprieve. 20

Bailey came out in his robe and gave me a box wrapped in Christmas paper. He said he had saved his money for months to pay for it. It felt like a box of chocolates, but I knew Bailey wouldn't save money to buy candy when we had all we could want under our noses.

He was as proud of the gift as I. It was a soft-leather-bound copy of a collection of poems by Edgar Allan Poe, or, as Bailey and I called him, "Eap." I turned to "Annabel Lee" and we walked up and down the garden rows, the cool dirt between our toes, reciting the beautifully sad lines.

Momma made a Sunday breakfast although it was only Friday. After we finished the blessing, I opened my eyes to find the watch on my plate. It was a dream of a day. Everything went smoothly

and to my credit. I didn't have to be reminded or scolded for anything. Near evening I was too jittery to attend to chores, so Bailey
volunteered to do all before his bath.

Days before, we had made a sign for the Store and as we turned   24
out the lights Momma hung the cardboard over the doorknob. It
read clearly: CLOSED. GRADUATION.

My dress fitted perfectly and everyone said that I looked like
a sunbeam in it. On the hill, going toward the school, Bailey walked
behind with Uncle Willie, who muttered, "Go on, Ju." He wanted
him to walk ahead with us because it embarrassed him to have to
walk so slowly. Bailey said he'd let the ladies walk together, and
the men would bring up the rear. We all laughed, nicely.

Little children dashed by out of the dark like fireflies. Their
crepe-paper dresses and butterfly wings were not made for running
and we heard more than one rip, dryly, and the regretful "uh uh"
that followed.

The school blazed without gaiety. The windows seemed cold
and unfriendly from the lower hill. A sense of ill-fated timing crept
over me, and if Momma hadn't reached for my hand I would have
drifted back to Bailey and Uncle Willie, and possibly beyond. She
made a few slow jokes about my feet getting cold, and tugged me
along to the now-strange building.

Around the front steps, assurance came back. There were my fel-   28
low "greats," the graduating class. Hair brushed back, legs oiled,
new dresses and pressed pleats, fresh pocket handkerchiefs and little
handbags, all homesewn. Oh, we were up to snuff, all right. I joined
my comrades and didn't even see my family go in to find seats in
the crowded auditorium.

The school band struck up a march and all classes filed in as
had been rehearsed. We stood in front of our seats, as assigned,
and on a signal from the choir director, we sat. No sooner had this
been accomplished than the band started to play the national anthem. We rose again and sang the song, after which we recited the
pledge of allegiance. We remained standing for a brief minute before the choir director and the principal signaled to us, rather desperately I thought, to take our seats. The command was so unusual
that our carefully rehearsed and smooth-running machine was
thrown off. For a full minute we fumbled for our chairs and bumped
into each other awkwardly. Habits change or solidify under pressure, so in our state of nervous tension we had been ready to follow our usual assembly pattern: the American National Anthem,
then the pledge of allegiance, then the song every Black person I

knew called the Negro National Anthem. All done in the same key, with the same passion and most often standing on the same foot.

Finding my seat at last, I was overcome with a presentiment of worse things to come. Something unrehearsed, unplanned, was going to happen, and we were going to be made to look bad. I distinctly remember being explicit in the choice of pronoun. It was "we," the graduating class, the unit, that concerned me then.

The principal welcomed "parents and friends" and asked the Baptist minister to lead us in prayer. His invocation was brief and punchy, and for a second I thought we were getting back on the high road to right action. When the principal came back to the dais, however, his voice had changed. Sounds always affected me profoundly and the principal's voice was one of my favorites. During assembly it melted and lowed weakly into the audience. It had not been in my plan to listen to him, but my curiosity was piqued and I straightened up to give him my attention.

He was talking about Booker T. Washington, our "late great 32 leader," who said we can be as close as the fingers on the hand, etc. . . . Then he said a few vague things about friendship and the friendship of kindly people to those less fortunate than themselves. With that his voice nearly faded, thin, away. Like a river diminishing to a stream and then to a trickle. But he cleared his throat and said, "Our speaker tonight, who is also our friend, came from Texarkana to deliver the commencement address, but due to the irregularity of the train schedule, he's going to, as they say, 'speak and run.'" He said that we understood and wanted the man to know that we were most grateful for the time he was able to give us and then something about how we were willing always to adjust to another's program, and without more ado—"I give you Mr. Edward Donleavy."

Not one but two white men came through the door offstage. The shorter one walked to the speaker's platform, and the tall one moved over to the center seat and sat down. But that was our principal's seat, and already occupied. The dislodged gentleman bounced around for a long breath or two before the Baptist minister gave him his chair, then with more dignity than the situation deserved, the minister walked off the stage.

Donleavy looked at the audience once (on reflection, I'm sure that he wanted only to reassure himself that we were really there), adjusted his glasses and began to read from a sheaf of papers.

He was glad "to be here and to see the work going on just as it was in the other schools."

At the first "Amen" from the audience I willed the offender to   36
immediate death by choking on the word. But Amen's and Yes,
sir's began to fall around the room like rain through a ragged um-
brella.

He told us of the wonderful changes we children in Stamps had
in store. The Central School (naturally, the white school was Central) had already been granted improvements that would be in use
in the fall. A well-known artist was coming from Little Rock to teach
art to them. They were going to have the newest microscopes and
chemistry equipment for their laboratory. Mr. Donleavy didn't leave
us long in the dark over who made these improvements available
to Central High. Nor were we to be ignored in the general betterment scheme he had in mind.

He said that he had pointed out to people at a very high level
that one of the first-line football tacklers at Arkansas Agricultural and Mechanical College had graduated from good old Lafayette County Training School. Here fewer Amen's were heard. Those
few that did break through lay dully in the air with the heaviness
of habit.

He went on to praise us. He went on to say how he had bragged
that "one of the best basketball players at Fisk sank his first ball right
here at Lafayette County Training School."

The white kids were going to have a chance to become Galileos   40
and Madame Curies and Edisons and Gauguins, and our boys (the
girls weren't even in on it) would try to be Jesse Owenses and Joe
Louises.

Owens and the Brown Bomber were great heroes in our world,
but what school official in the white-goddom of Little Rock had the
right to decide that those two men must be our only heroes? Who
decided that for Henry Reed to become a scientist he had to work
like George Washington Carver, as a bootblack, to buy a lousy microscope? Bailey was obviously always going to be too small to be an
athlete, so which concrete angel glued to what country seat had
decided that if my brother wanted to become a lawyer he had to
first pay penance for his skin by picking cotton and hoeing corn and
studying correspondence books at night for twenty years?

The man's dead words fell like bricks around the auditorium and
too many settled in my belly. Constrained by hard-learned manners
I couldn't look behind me, but to my left and right the proud
graduating class of 1940 had dropped their heads. Every girl in my
row had found something new to do with her handkerchief. Some

folded the tiny squares into love knots, some into triangles, but most were wadding them, then pressing them flat on their yellow laps.

On the dais, the ancient tragedy was being replayed. Professor Parsons sat, a sculptor's reject, rigid. His large, heavy body seemed devoid of will or willingness, and his eyes said he was no longer with us. The other teachers examined the flag (which was draped stage right) or their notes, or the windows which opened on our now-famous playing diamond.

Graduation, the hush-hush magic time of frills and gifts and con- 44 gratulations and diplomas, was finished for me before my name was called. The accomplishment was nothing. The meticulous maps, drawn in three colors of ink, learning and spelling decasyllabic words, memorizing the whole of *The Rape of Lucrece*—it was noth- ing. Donleavy had exposed us.

We were maids and farmers, handymen and washerwomen, and anything higher that we aspired to was farcical and presump- tuous. Then I wished that Gabriel Prosser and Nat Turner had killed all whitefolks in their beds and that Abraham Lincoln had been as- sassinated before the signing of the Emancipation Proclamation, and that Harriet Tubman had been killed by that blow on her head and Christopher Columbus had drowned in the *Santa Maria*.

It was awful to be Negro and have no control over my life. It was brutal to be young and already trained to sit quietly and listen to charges brought against my color and no chance of defense. We should all be dead. I thought I should like to see us all dead, one on top of the other. A pyramid of flesh with the whitefolks on the bottom, as the broad base, then the Indians with their silly toma- hawks and teepees and wigwams and treaties, the Negroes with their mops and recipes and cotton sacks and spirituals sticking out of their mouths. The Dutch children should all stumble in their wooden shoes and break their necks. The French should choke to death on the Louisiana Purchase (1803) while silkworms ate all the Chinese with their stupid pigtails. As a species, we were an abomi- nation. All of us.

Donleavy was running for election, and assured our parents that if he won we could count on having the only colored paved playing field in that part of Arkansas. Also—he never looked up to acknowl- edge the grunts of acceptance—also, we were bound to get some new equipment for the home economics building and the workshop.

He finished, and since there was no need to give any more than 48 the most perfunctory thank-you's, he nodded to the men on the stage, and the tall white man who was never introduced joined him at the door. They left with the attitude that now they were off to something really important. (The graduation ceremonies at Lafayette County Training School had been a mere preliminary.)

The ugliness they left was palpable. An uninvited guest who wouldn't leave. The choir was summoned and sang a modern arrangement of "Onward, Christian Soldiers," with new words pertaining to graduates seeking their place in the world. But it didn't work. Elouise, the daughter of the Baptist minister, recited "Invictus," and I could have cried at the impertinence of "I am the master of my fate, I am the captain of my soul."

My name had lost its ring of familiarity and I had to be nudged to go and receive my diploma. All my preparations had fled. I neither marched up to the stage like a conquering Amazon, nor did I look in the audience for Bailey's nod of approval. Marguerite Johnson, I heard the name again, my honors were read, there were noises in the audience of appreciation, and I took my place on the stage as rehearsed.

I thought about colors I hated: ecru, puce, lavender, beige and black.

There was shuffling and rustling around me, then Henry Reed was giving his valedictory address, "To Be or Not to Be." Hadn't he heard the whitefolks? We couldn't *be*, so the question was a waste of time. Henry's voice came out clear and strong. I feared to look at him. Hadn't he got the message? There was no "nobler in the mind" for Negroes because the world didn't think we had minds, and they let us know it. "Outrageous fortune"? Now, that was a joke. When the ceremony was over I had to tell Henry Reed some things. That is, if I still cared. Not "rub," Henry, "erase." "Ah, there's the erase." Us.

Henry had been a good student in elocution. His voice rose on tides of promise and fell on waves of warnings. The English teacher had helped him to create a sermon winging through Hamlet's soliloquy. To be a man, a doer, a builder, a leader, or to be a tool, an unfunny joke, a crusher of funky toadstools. I marveled that Henry could go through with the speech as if we had a choice.

I had been listening and silently rebutting each sentence with my eyes closed; then there was a hush, which in an audience warns that something unplanned is happening. I looked up and saw Henry Reed, the conservative, the proper, the A student, turn his back to the audience and turn to us (the proud graduating class of 1940) and sing, nearly speaking,

Lift ev'ry voice and sing
Till earth and heaven ring
Ring with the harmonies of Liberty . . .

It was the poem written by James Weldon Johnson. It was the music composed by J. Rosamond Johnson. It was the Negro National Anthem. Out of habit we were singing it.

Our mothers and fathers stood in the dark hall and joined the hymn of encouragement. A kindergarten teacher led the small children onto the stage and the buttercups and daisies and bunny rabbits marked time and tried to follow:

Stony the road we trod
Bitter the chastening rod
Felt in the days when hope, unborn, had died.
Yet with a steady beat
Have not our weary feet
Come to the place for which our fathers sighed?

Every child I knew had learned that song with his ABC's and 56
along with "Jesus Loves Me This I Know." But I personally had never heard it before. Never heard the words, despite the thousands of times I had sung them. Never thought they had anything to do with me.

On the other hand, the words of Patrick Henry had made such an impression on me that I had been able to stretch myself tall and trembling and say, "I know not what course others may take, but as for me, give me liberty or give me death."

And now I heard, really for the first time:

We have come over a way that with tears has been watered,
We have come, treading our path through the blood of the slaughtered.

While echoes of the song shivered in the air, Henry Reed bowed his head, said "Thank you," and returned to his place in the line. The tears that slipped down many faces were not wiped away in shame.

We were on top again. As always, again. We survived. The 60
depths had been icy and dark, but now a bright sun spoke to our souls. I was no longer simply a member of the proud graduating class of 1940; I was a proud member of the wonderful, beautiful Negro race.

Oh, Black known and unknown poets, how often have your auctioned pains sustained us? Who will compute the lonely nights made less lonely by your songs, or the empty pots made less tragic by your tales?

If we were a people much given to revealing secrets, we might raise monuments and sacrifice to the memories of our poets, but slavery cured us of that weakness. It may be enough, however, to have it said that we survive in exact relationship to the dedication of our poets (include preachers, musicians and blues singers).

Topics for Discussion and Writing

1. In paragraph 1 notice such overstatements as "glorious release," "the graduating classes themselves were the nobility," and "exotic destinations." Find further examples in the next few pages. What do you think is the function of this diction?
2. Characterize the writer as you perceive her through paragraph 28. Support your characterization with references to specific passages. Next, characterize her in paragraph 46, which begins "It was awful to be Negro." Next, characterize her on the basis of the entire essay. Finally, in a sentence, try to describe the change, telling the main attitudes or moods that she goes through.
3. How would you define "poets" as Angelou uses the word in the last sentence?

Pauline Kael

Pauline Kael, born in 1919 in Petaluma, California, grew up in San Francisco and attended the University of California at Berkeley. She regularly wrote film criticism for The New Yorker, *where this review originally appeared.*

High School and Other Forms of Madness

Many of us grow to hate documentaries in school, because the use of movies to teach us something seems a cheat—a pill disguised as candy—and documentaries always seem to be about something we're not interested in. But Wiseman's documentaries show what is left out of both fictional movies and standard documentaries that simplify for a purpose, and his films deal with the primary institutions of our lives: *Titicut Follies* (Bridgewater, an institution in which we lock away the criminally insane), *High School* (a high school in a large Eastern city), and *Law and Order* (the Kansas City police force). Television has been accustoming us to a horrible false kind of "involvement"; sometimes it seems that the only thing the news shows can think of is to get close to emotion. They shove a camera and a microphone in front of people in moments of stress and disaster and grief, and ram their equipment into any pores and cavities they can reach. Wiseman made comparable mistakes in *Titicut Follies*, but he learned better fast.

High School is so familiar and so extraordinarily evocative that a feeling of empathy with the students floods over us. How did we live through it? How did we keep any spirit? When you see a kid trying to make a phone call and being interrupted with "Do you have a pass to use the phone?" it all floods back—the low ceilings and pale-green walls of the basement where the lockers were, the constant defensiveness, that sense of always being in danger of breaking some pointless, petty rule. When since that time has one ever needed a pass to make a phone call? This movie takes one back to where, one discovers, time has stood still. Here is the girl humiliated for having worn a short dress to the Senior Prom, being told it was "offensive" to the whole class. Here it is all over again— the insistence that you be "respectful"; and the teachers' incredible instinct for "disrespect," their antennae always extended for that little bit of reservation or irony in your tone, the tiny spark that you desperately need to preserve your self-respect. One can barely hear it in the way a boy says "Yes, sir" to the dean, but the dean, ever on the alert, snaps, "Don't give me that 'Yes, sir' business!. . . . There's no sincereness behind it." Here, all over again, is the dullness of high-school education:

Teacher: What on the horizon or what existed that forced labor to turn to collective bargaining? What was there a lack of?
Girl: Communications?
Teacher: Security, yes, communications, lack of security, concern for the job. The important thing is this, let's get to the beginning. First of all, there was the lack of security; second of all, there was a lack of communication. . . .

The same old pseudo-knowledge is used to support what the schools think is moral. The visiting gynecologist in a sex-education class lectures the boys:

> The more a fellow gets into bed with more different girls, the more insecure he is, and this shows up actually later in all the divorce statistics in America. . . . You can graph right on a graph, the more girls fellows got into bed with or vice-versa the higher the divorce rate, the greater the sexual inadequacy. . . .

And there's the beautiful military doubletalk when it's a question of a teacher's incompetence or unfairness. A boy protests a disciplinary action against him by a teacher, and after he has explained his innocence, the dean talks him into accepting the punishment "to establish that you can be a man and that you can take orders." The teachers are masters here; they're in a superior position for the only time in their lives, probably, and most of the petty tyrannies—like laying on the homework—aren't fully conscious. They justify each other's actions as a matter of course, and put the students in the wrong in the same indifferent way. They put a student down with "It's nice to be individualistic, but there are certain places to be individualistic," yet they never tell you where. How can one stand up against such bland authoritarianism? The teachers, crushing and processing, are the most insidious kind of enemy, the enemy with corrupt values who means well. The counsellor advising on college plans who says "You can have all your dream schools, but at the bottom you ought to have some college of last resort where you could be sure that you would go, if none of your dreams came through" certainly means to be realistic and helpful. But one can imagine what it must feel like to be a kid trudging off to the bottom college of last resort. There's a jolly good Joe of a teacher staging a fashion show who tells the girls, "Your legs are all too heavy. . . . Don't wear it too short; it looks miserable." And she's not wrong. But, given the beauty norms set up in this society, what are they to do? Cut off their legs? Emigrate? They're defeated from the legs up. Mediocrity and defeat sit in the offices and classrooms, and in those oppressive monitored halls.

We went through it all in order to graduate and be rid of passes forever, and once it was over we put it out of our minds, and here are the students still serving time until graduation, still sitting in class staring out the windows or watching the crawling hands of those ugly school clocks. So much of this education is part of an obsolete system of authority that broke down long ago, yet the teachers and administrators are still out there, persevering, "building character." *High School* seems an obvious kind of film to make, but as far as I know no one before has gone into an ordinary, middle-class, "good" (most of the students go to college) high school with a camera and looked around to see what it's like. The students are even more apathetic than we were. Probably the conflicts over the restrictions come earlier now—in junior high—and by high school the kids either are trying to cool it and get through to college or are just beaten down and sitting it out. We may have had a few teachers who really got us interested in something—it was one of the disappointments of the movie *Up the Down Staircase* that, treating this theme, it failed to be convincing—and, remembering our good luck, we could always say that even if a school was rotten, there were bound to be a few great teachers in it. This movie shows competent teachers and teachers who are trying their best but not one teacher who really makes contact in the way that means a difference in your life. The students are as apathetic toward the young English teacher playing and analyzing a Simon & Garfunkel record as toward the English teacher reciting "Casey at the Bat," and, even granted that as poetry there might not be much to choose between them—and perhaps Casey has the edge—still, one might think the students would, just as a *courtesy*, respond to the young teacher's attempt, the way one always gave the ingénue in the stock company a special round of applause. But it's very likely that high schools no longer *are* saved by live teachers, if hostility and cynicism and apathy set in right after children learn their basic skills. The students here sit on their hands even when a teacher tries. That's the only visible difference between this school and mine. I think we would have responded appreciatively to obvious effort, even if we thought the teacher was a jerk; these kids are beyond that. So the teachers are trapped, too. The teachers come off much worse than the police do in *Law and Order*. *High School* is a revelation because now that we see school from the outside, the teachers seem to give themselves away every time they open their mouths—and to be unaware of it.

At the end, the principal—a fine-looking woman—holds up a letter from a former student, on stationery marked "U.S.S. Okinawa," and reads it to the faculty:

> I have only a few hours before I go. Today I will take a plane trip from this ship. I pray that I'll make it back but it's all in God's hands now. You see, I am going with three other men. We are going to be dropped

behind the D.M.Z. (the Demilitarized Zone). The reason for telling you this is that all my insurance money will be given for that scholarship I once started but never finished, if I don't make it back. I am only insured for $10,000. Maybe it could help someone. I have been trying to become a Big Brother in Vietnam, but it is very hard to do. I have to write back and forth to San Diego, California, and that takes time. I only hope that I am good enough to become one. God only knows. My personal family usually doesn't understand me. . . . They say: "Don't you value life? Are you crazy?" My answer is: "Yes. But I value all the lives of South Vietnam and the free world so that they and all of us can live in peace." Am I wrong? If I do my best and believe in what I do, believe that what I do is right—that is all I can do. . . . Please don't say anything to Mrs. C. She would only worry over me. I am not worth it. I am only a body doing a job. In closing I thank everyone for what they all have done for me.

And the principal comments, "Now, when you get a letter like this, to me it means that we are very successful at [this] high school. I think you will agree with me."

It's a great scene—a consummation of the educational process we've been watching: They are successful at turning out bodies to do a job. Yet it's also painfully clear that the school must have given this soldier more kindness and affection than he'd ever had before. There must be other students who respond to the genuine benevolence behind the cant and who are grateful to those who labor to turn them into men. For those students, this schooling in conformity is successful.

Wiseman extends our understanding of our common life the 8 way novelists used to—a way largely abandoned by the modern novel and left to the journalists but not often picked up by them. What he's doing is so simple and so basic that it's like a rediscovery of what we knew, or should know. We often want more information about the people and their predicaments than he gives, but this is perhaps less a criticism of Wiseman's method than it is a testimonial to his success in making us care about his subjects. With fictional movies using so little of our shared experience, and the big TV news "specials" increasingly using that idiot "McLuhanite" fragmentation technique that scrambles all experience—as if the deliberate purpose were to make us indifferent to the life around us—it's a good sign when a movie sends us out wanting to know more and feeling that there is more to know. Wiseman is probably the most sophisticated intelligence to enter the documentary field in recent years.

Topics for Discussion and Writing

1. In paragraph 2 Kael assumes that her readers share with her the view, based on experience, that high school is dull, dispiriting, and even humiliating. In your experience, is the assumption warranted?
2. At the end of paragraph 2 Kael quotes a bit of dialogue. Pinpoint examples of dullness in the dialogue.
3. The language of paragraph 4 suggests that high school is a battleground between teachers and students. Are the hostilities Kael cites familiar? If not, do you find them nevertheless convincing? With what weapons is each side armed?
4. In paragraph 1 Kael writes: "Many of us grow to hate documentaries in school." Did you? If so, why? What reasons might you offer to argue that the documentary films you saw in school were educational or anti-educational?

Nathan Glazer

Nathan Glazer, born in 1923 in New York City, is a professor of education and sociology at Harvard University. He is co-editor of The Public Interest *magazine and the co-author of* The Lonely Crowd *and* Beyond the Melting Pot. *This essay was first published in 1984.*

Some Very Modest Proposals for the Improvement of American Education

That we can do a great deal for the sorry state of American education with more money is generally accepted. Even apparently modest proposals will, however, cost a great deal of money. Consider something as simple as increasing the average compensation of American teachers—who are generally considered underpaid—by $2,000 a year each. The bill would come to five billion dollars a year. A similar figure is reached by the report of the highly qualified Twentieth Century Fund Task Force on Federal, Elementary, and Secondary Educational Policy, which proposes fellowships and additional compensation for master teachers. Reducing class size 10 percent, or increasing the number of teachers by the same percentage, would cost another five billion dollars: With present-day federal deficits, these look like small sums, but since education is paid for almost entirely by states and local government, these modest proposals would lead to substantial and painful tax increases. (I leave aside for the moment the views of skeptics who believe that none of these changes would matter.)

But the occasional visitor to American schools will note some changes that would cost much less, nothing at all, or even save money—and yet would improve at least the educational *environment* in American schools (once again, we ignore those skeptics who would insist that even a better educational environment cannot be guaranteed to improve educational achievement). In the spirit of evoking further cheap proposals, here is a small list of suggestions that, to my mind at least—and the mind I believe of any adult who visits American public schools—would mean a clear plus for American education:

1. *Disconnect all loudspeaker systems in American schools—or at least reserve them, like the hotline between Moscow and Washington, for only the gravest emergencies.* The American classroom—and the American teacher and his or her charges—is continually interrupted by announcements from central headquarters over the loudspeaker system. These remind teachers to bring in some form or other; or students to bring in some form or other; or students engaged in some activity to remember to come to practice or rehearsal; or they announce a change of time for some activity. There is nothing so unnerving to a teacher engaged in trying to explain something, or a student engaged in trying to understand something, as the crackle of the loudspeaker prepared to issue an announcement, and the harsh and gravelly voice (the systems are not obviously of the highest grade) of the announcement itself.

Aside from questions of personal taste, why would this be a good idea? As I have suggested, one reason is that the loudspeaker interrupts efforts to communicate complicated material that requires undivided attention. Second, it demeans the teacher as professional: every announcement tells her whatever she is doing is not very important and can be interrupted at any time. Third, it accentuates the notion of hierarchy in education—the principal and assistant principal are the important people, and command time and attention even in the midst of instruction. Perhaps I have been softened by too many years as a college teacher, but it would be unimaginable that a loudspeaker, if one existed, would ever interrupt a college class except under conditions of the gravest and most immediate threat to life and limb. One way of showing students that education is important is not to interrupt it for band-rehearsal announcements.

2. *Disarm the school.* One of the most depressing aspects of the urban school in the United States is the degree of security manifest within it, and that seems to me quite contradictory to what a school should be. Outer doors are locked. Security guards are present in the corridors. Internal doors are locked. Passes are necessary to enter the school or move within it, for outsiders and for students. Students are marched in groups from classroom to classroom, under the eye of the teachers. It is understandable that given the conditions in lower-class areas in our large cities—and not only lower-class areas—some degree of security-mindedness is necessary. There is valuable equipment—typewriters, computers, audio-visual equipment—that can be stolen; vandalism is a serious concern; marauders can enter the school in search for equipment, or teachers' pocketbooks, or to threaten directly personal safety in search of money or sex, and so on. School integration and busing, at least in their initial stages, have contributed to increased interracial tensions in schools and have in part severed the link between community and school. The difference in ethnic and racial composition of faculty, other staff, administrators, and students contributes to the same end.

Having acknowledged all this, I still believe the school should feel less like a prison than it does. One should examine to what extent outside doors must be closed; to what extent the security guard cannot be replaced by local parents, volunteer or paid; the degree to which the endless bells indicating "stop" and "go" are really necessary. I suspect that now that the most difficult period of school integration has passed, now that teachers and administrators and staff more closely parallel in race and ethnic background students and community owing to the increase in black and Hispanic teachers and administrators, we may be saddled with more security than we need. Here we come to the sticky problem of *removing* security measures whose need has decreased. What school board will open itself to suit or to public criticism by deliberately providing *less* security? And yet one must consider the atmosphere of the school and a school's primary objective as a teaching agent: can this be reconciled with a condition of maximum security? Perhaps there are lessons to be learned from colleges and community colleges in older urban areas, which in my experience do seem to manage with less security. One reason is that there are more adults around in such institutions. Is that a hint as to how we could manage better in our public schools?

3. *Enlist the children in keeping the school clean.* Occasionally we see a practice abroad that suggests possible transfer to the American scene. In Japan, the children clean the school. There is a time of day when mops and pails and brooms come out, and the children sweep up and wash up. This does, I am sure, suggest to the children that this is *their* school, that it is not simply a matter of being forced to go to a foreign institution that imposes alien demands upon them. I can imagine some obstacles in the way of instituting regular student clean-up in American schools—custodians' unions, for example, might object. But they can be reassured that children don't do that good a job, and they will still be needed. Once again, as in the case of the security problem, one wants to create in the school, if at all possible, a common enterprise of teachers and students, without the latter being bored and resistant, the former, in response, becoming equally indifferent. The school should be seen as everyone's workplace—and participation in cleaning the school will help.

4. *Save old schools.* Build fewer new ones. It has often surprised me that while in schools such as Eton and Oxford—and indeed well-known private schools and colleges in the United States—old buildings are prized, in so many communities older public schools are torn down when to the naked eye they have many virtues that would warrant their maintenance and use. Only a few blocks from where I live, an excellent example of late nineteenth-century fine brickwork and carved stonework that served as the Cambridge Latin School came down for a remodeling. The carved elements are still displayed about the remodeled school, but why a building of such character should have deserved demolition escaped my understanding, particularly since one can take it almost as a given that a school building put up before the 1940s will be built of heavier and sturdier materials than one constructed today. Even the inconveniences of the old can possess a charm that makes them worthwhile. And indeed many of the reforms that seemed to require new buildings (for example, classrooms without walls, concentrated around activities centers in large open rooms) have turned out, on use, to be not so desirable. Our aim should be to give each school a history, a character, something that at least some students respond to. The pressures for new buildings are enormous, and sometimes perfectly legitimate (as when communities expand), but often

illegitimate, as when builders and building-trades workers and contract-givers seek an opportunity or when state aid makes it appear as if a new building won't cost anything.

5. *Look on new hardware with a skeptical eye.* I think it likely that the passion for the new in the way of teaching-hardware not only does not contribute to higher educational achievement but may well serve as a temporary means to evade the real and hard tasks of teaching—which really require almost no hardware at all, besides textbooks, blackboard, and chalk. Admittedly, when one comes to high-school science, something more is called for. And yet our tendency is to always find cover behind new hardware. It's *fun* to get new audio-visual equipment, new rooms equipped with them in which all kinds of things can be done by flicking a switch or twisting a dial, or, as is now the case, to decide what kind of personal computers and software are necessary for a good educational program. Once again, foreign experience can be enlightening. When Japanese education was already well ahead of American, most Japanese schools were in prewar wooden buildings. (They are now as up-to-date as ours, but neither their age nor up-to-dateness has much to do with their good record of achievement.) Resisting the appeal of new hardware not only saves money, and provides less in the way of saleable goods to burglarize, but it also prevents distraction from the principal tasks of reading, writing, and calculating. When it turns out that computers and new software are shown to do a better job at these key tasks—I am skeptical as to whether this will ever be the case—there will be time enough to splurge on new equipment. The teacher, alone, up front, explaining, encouraging, guiding, is the heart of the matter—the rest is fun, and very helpful to corporate income, and gives an inflated headquarters staff something new to do. But students will have time enough to learn about computers when they get to college, and getting there will depend almost not at all on what they can do with computers, but how well they understand words and sentences, and how well they do at simple mathematics.

There is nothing wrong with old textbooks, too. Recently, reviewing some recent high-school American history texts, I was astonished to discover they come out in new editions every two years or so, and not because the main body of the text is improved, but because the textbook wants to be able to claim it covers the very last presidential campaign, and the events of the last few years. This is a waste of time and energy and money. There is enough to teach in American history up to 1950 or 1960 not to worry about whether the text includes Reagan's tax cuts. I suspect many new texts in other areas also offer little advantage over the older ones. There is also a virtue in a teacher becoming acquainted with a particular textbook. When I read that a school is disadvantaged because its textbooks are old, I am always mystified. Even the newest advances in physics and biology might well be reserved for college.

6. *Expand the pool from which we draw good teachers.* This general heading covers a number of simple and concrete things, such as: if a teacher is considered qualified to teach at a good private school, that teacher should be considered qualified to teach at a public school. It has always seemed to me ridiculous that teachers accepted at the best private schools in New York City or top preparatory schools in the country would not be allowed to teach in the public school system of New York or Boston. Often, they are willing—after all, the pay is better in public schools and there are greater fringe benefits. They might, it is true, be driven out of those schools by the challenge of lower- and working-class children. But when they are willing, it seems unbelievable that the teacher qualified (or so Brearley thinks) for Brearley will not be allowed to teach at P.S. 122. Greater use of part-time teachers might also be able to draw upon people with qualities that we are told the average teacher unfortunately doesn't possess—such as a higher level of competence in writing and mathematics.

Our recurrent concern with foreign-language teaching should lead us to recruit foreign-born teachers. There are problems in getting teaching jobs today in Germany and France—yet teachers there are typically drawn from pools of students with higher academic skills than is the case in this country. Paradoxically, we make it easy for teachers of Spanish-language background to get jobs owing to the expansion of bilingual programs—but then their teaching is confined to children whose Spanish accent doesn't need improvement. It would make more sense to expose children of foreign-language background more to teachers with native English—and children from English-speaking families to teachers who speak French, German, Spanish, and, why not, Japanese, and Chinese natively. This would mean that rules requiring that a teacher must be a citizen, or must speak English without an accent, should be lifted for special teachers with special tasks. Perhaps we could make the most of the oversupply of teachers in some foreign countries by using them to teach mathematics—a subject where accent doesn't count. The school system in Georgia is already recruiting from Germany. Colleges often use teaching assistants whose English is not native and far from perfect, including Asians from Korea and China, to assist in science and mathematics courses. (There are many state laws which would not permit them to teach in elementary and secondary schools.)

All the suggestions above eschew any involvement with some great issues of education—tradition or reform, the teaching of values, the role of religion in the schools—that have in the past dominated arguments over education and still do today. But I add one more proposal that is still, I am afraid, somewhat controversial:

7. *Let students, within reason, pick their schools, or let parents choose them for them.* All those informed on school issues will sense the heaving depths of controversy under this apparently modest proposal. Does this mean they might choose parochial schools, without being required to pay tuition out of their own pockets? Or does this mean black children would be allowed to attend schools in black areas, and whites in white areas, or the reverse if each is so inclined? As we all know, the two great issues of religion and race stand in the way of any such simple and commonsensical arrangement. Students are regularly bused from one section of a city to another because of their race, and students cannot without financial penalty attend that substantial sector of schools—30 percent or so in most Northern and Midwestern cities—that are called "private." I ignore the question of whether, holding all factors constant, students do "better" in private or public schools, in racially well-mixed or hardly mixed schools. The evidence will always be uncertain. What is perhaps less arguable is that students will do better in a school that forms a community, in which teachers, parents, and students all agree that *that* is the school they want to teach in, to attend, to send their children to. I would guess that this is the kind of school most of the readers of this article have attended; it is the kind of school, alas, that our complex racial and religious history makes it harder and harder for those of minority race or of lower- and working-class status to attend.

I have eschewed the grand proposals—for curriculum change, for improving the quality of entering teachers, for checking on the competence of teachers in service, for establishing national standards for achievement in different levels of education—all of which now form the agenda for many state commissions of educational reform and all of which seem reasonable to me. Rather, I have concentrated on a variety of other things that serve to remove distraction, to open the school to those of quality who would be willing to enter it to improve it, to concentrate on the essentials of teaching and learning as I (and many others) have experienced it. It would be possible to propose larger changes in the same direction: for example, reduce the size of the bureaucracies in urban school systems. Some of my modest proposals are insidiously intended to do this—if there were less effort devoted to building new schools, buying new equipment, evaluating new textbooks, or busing children, there would be no need to maintain quite so many people at headquarters. Or so I would hope.

In the meantime, why not disconnect the loudspeakers?   16

Topics for Discussion and Writing

1. What does "modest" mean in Glazer's second sentence?
2. Glazer's third proposal is to have children clean their schools. How do you imagine high school students would respond to this proposal? How would you and your friends have responded?
3. Analyze the arrangement of Glazer's proposals. Do you discern any order or pattern in them?
4. If you disagree with one of Glazer's proposals, set forth your disagreement in a paragraph or two.
5. What proposals can you add to Glazer's list of "modest proposals"? Take one of your proposals and argue for it in a paragraph or two.

Neil Postman

Neil Postman, born in New York City in 1931, has taught in elementary and secondary schools and is now a professor of communication arts and sciences at New York University.

Order in the Classroom

William O'Connor, who is unknown to me in a personal way, was once a member of the Boston School Committee, in which capacity he made the following remark: "We have no inferior education in our schools. What we have been getting is an inferior type of student."

The remark is easy to ridicule, and I have had some fun with it in the past. But there are a couple of senses in which it is perfectly sound.

In the first place, a classroom is a technique for the achievement of certain kinds of learning. It is a workable technique provided that both the teacher and the student have the skill and, particularly, the attitudes that are fundamental to it. Among these, from the student's point of view, are tolerance for delayed gratification, a certain measure of respect for and fear of authority, and a willingness to accommodate one's individual desires to the interests of group cohesion and purpose. These attitudes cannot be taught easily in school because they are a necessary component of the teaching situation itself. The problem is not unlike trying to find out how to spell a word by looking it up in the dictionary. If you do not know how a word is spelled, it is hard to look it up. In the same way, little can be taught in school unless these attitudes are present. And if they are not, to teach them is difficult.

Obviously, such attitudes must be learned during the years 4 before a child starts school; that is, in the home. This is the real meaning of the phrase "preschool education." If a child is not made ready at home for the classroom experience, he or she usually cannot benefit from any normal school program. Just as important, the school is defenseless against such a child, who, typically, is a source of disorder in a situation that requires order. I raise this issue because education reform is impossible without order in the classroom. Without the attitudes that lead to order, the classroom is an entirely impotent technique. Therefore, one possible translation of Mr. O'Connor's remark is, "We have a useful technique for educating youth but too many of them have not been provided at home with the attitudes necessary for the technique to work."

In still another way Mr. O'Connor's remark makes plain sense. The electronic media, with their emphasis on visual imagery, immediacy, non-linearity, and fragmentation, do not give support to the attitudes that are fundamental to the classroom; that is, Mr. O'Connor's remark can be translated as, "We would not have an inferior education if it were the nineteenth century. Our problem is that we have been getting students who are products of the twentieth century." But there is nothing nonsensical about this, either. The nineteenth century had much to recommend it, and we certainly may be permitted to allow it to exert an influence on the twentieth. The classroom is a nineteenth-century invention, and we ought to prize what it has to offer. It is one of the few social organizations left to us in which sequence, social order, hierarchy, continuity, and deferred pleasure are important.

The problem of disorder in the classroom is created largely by two factors: a dissolving family structure, out of which come youngsters who are "unfit" for the presuppositions of a classroom; and a radically altered information environment, which undermines the foundation of school. The question, then, is, What should be done about the increasing tendency toward disorder in the classroom?

Liberal reformers, such as Kenneth Keniston, have answers, of a sort. Keniston argues that economic reforms should be made so that the integrity and authority of the family can be restored. He believes that poverty is the main cause of family dissolution, and that by improving the economic situation of families, we may kindle a sense of order and aspiration in the lives of children. Some of the reforms he suggests in his book *All Our Children* seem practical, although they are long-range and offer no immediate response to the problem of present disorder. Some Utopians, such as Ivan Illich, have offered other solutions; for example, dissolving the schools altogether, or so completely restructuring the school environment that its traditional assumptions are rendered irrelevant. To paraphrase Karl Kraus's epigram about psychoanalysis, these proposals are the Utopian disease of which they consider themselves the cure.

One of the best answers comes from Dr. Howard Hurwitz, who 8 is neither a liberal reformer nor a Utopian. It is a good solution, I believe, because it tries to respond to the needs not only of children who are unprepared for school because of parental failure but of children of all backgrounds who are being made strangers to the assumptions of school by the biases of the electronic media.

During the eleven years Dr. Hurwitz was principal at Long Island City High School, the average number of suspensions each year was three, while in many New York City high schools the average runs close to one hundred. Also, during his tenure, not one instance of an assault on a teacher was reported, and daily student attendance averaged better than 90 percent, which in the context of the New York City school scene represents a riot of devotion.

Although I consider some of Dr. Hurwitz's curriculum ideas uninspired and even wrong-headed, he understands a few things of overriding importance that many educators of more expansive imagination do not. The first is that educators must devote at least as much attention to the immediate consequences of disorder as to its abstract causes. Whatever the causes of disorder and alienation, the consequences are severe and, if not curbed, result in making the school impotent. At the risk of becoming a symbol of reaction, Hurwitz ran "a tight ship." He holds to the belief, for example, that a child's right to an education is terminated at the point where the child interferes with the right of other children to have one.

Dr. Hurwitz also understands that disorder expands proportionately to the tolerance for it, and that children of all kinds of home backgrounds can learn, in varying degrees, to function in situations where disorder is not tolerated at all. He does not believe that it is inevitably or only the children of the poor who are disorderly. In spite of what the "revisionist" education historians may say, poor people still regard school as an avenue of social and economic advancement for their children, and do not object in the least to its being an orderly and structured experience.

All this adds up to the common sense view that the school ought 12 not to accommodate itself to disorder, or to the biases of other communication systems. The children of the poor are likely to continue to be with us. Some parents will fail to assume competent responsibility for the preschool education of their children. The media will increase the intensity of their fragmenting influence. Educators must live with these facts. But Dr. Hurwitz believes that as a technique for learning, the classroom can work if students are oriented toward its assumptions, not the other way around. William O'Connor, wherever he is, would probably agree. And so do I. The school is not an extension of the street, the movie theater, a rock concert, or a playground. And it is certainly not an extension of the psychiatric clinic. It is a special environment that requires the enforcement of certain traditional rules of controlled group interaction. The school may be the only remaining public situation in which such rules have any meaning, and it would be a grave mistake to change those rules because some children find them hard or cannot function within them. Children who cannot ought to be removed from the environment in the interests of those who can.

Wholesale suspensions, however, are a symptom of disorder, not a cure for it. And what makes Hurwitz's school noteworthy is the small number of suspensions that have been necessary. This is not the result of his having "good" students or "bad" students. It is the result of his having created an unambiguous, rigorous, and serious attitude—a nineteenth-century attitude, if you will—toward what constitutes acceptable school behavior. In other words, Dr.

Hurwitz's school turns out to be a place where children of all backgrounds—fit and unfit—can function, or can learn to function, and where the biases of our information environment are emphatically opposed.

At this point I should like to leave the particulars of Dr. Hurwitz's solution and, retaining their spirit, indicate some particulars of my own.

Let us start, for instance, with the idea of a dress code. A dress code signifies that school is a special place in which special kinds of behavior are required. The way one dresses is an indication of an attitude toward a situation. And the way one is *expected* to dress indicates what that attitude ought to be. You would not wear dungarees and a T-shirt that says "Feel Me" when attending a church wedding. That would be considered an outrage against the tone and meaning of the situation. The school has every right and reason, I believe, to expect the same sort of consideration.

Those who are inclined to think this is a superficial point are   16 probably forgetting that symbols not only reflect our feelings but to some extent create them. One's kneeling in church, for example, reflects a sense of reverence but also engenders reverence. If we want school to *feel* like a special place, we can find no better way to begin than by requiring students to dress in a manner befitting the seriousness of the enterprise and the institution. I should include teachers in this requirement. I know of one high school in which the principal has put forward a dress code of sorts for teachers. (He has not, apparently, had the courage to propose one for the students.) For males the requirement is merely a jacket and tie. One of his teachers bitterly complained to me that such a regulation infringed upon his civil rights. And yet, this teacher will accept without complaint the same regulation when it is enforced by an elegant restaurant. His complaint and his acquiescence tell a great deal about how he values schools and how he values restaurants.

I do not have in mind, for students, uniforms of the type sometimes worn in parochial schools. I am referring here to some reasonable standard of dress which would mark school as a place of dignity and seriousness. And I might add that I do not believe for one moment the argument that poor people would be unable to clothe their children properly if such a code were in force. Furthermore, I do not believe that poor people have advanced that argument. It is an argument that middle-class education critics have made on behalf of the poor.

Another argument advanced in behalf of the poor and oppressed is the students' right to their own language. I have never heard this argument come from parents whose children are not competent to use Standard English. It is an argument, once again, put forward by "liberal" education critics whose children *are* competent in Standard English but who in some curious way wish to express their solidarity with and charity for those who are less capable. It is a case of pure condescension, and I do not think teachers should be taken in by it. Like the mode of dress, the mode of language in school ought to be relatively formal and exemplary, and therefore markedly different from the custom in less rigorous places. It is particularly important that teachers should avoid trying to win their students' affection by adopting the language of youth. Such teachers frequently win only the contempt of their students, who sense that the language of teachers and the language of students ought to be different; that is to say, the world of adults is different from the world of children.

In this connection, it is worth saying that the modern conception of childhood is a product of the sixteenth century, as Philippe Aries has documented in his *The Centuries of Childhood.* Prior to that century, children as young as six and seven were treated in all important respects as if they were adults. Their language, their dress, their legal status, their responsibilities, their labor, were much the same as those of adults. The concept of childhood as an identifiable stage in human growth began to develop in the sixteenth century and has continued into our own times. However, with the emergence of electronic media of communication, a reversal of this trend seems to be taking place. In a culture in which the distribution of information is almost wholly undifferentiated, age categories begin to disappear. Television, in itself, may bring an end to childhood. In truth, there is no such thing as "children's programming," at least not for children over the age of eight or nine. Everyone sees and hears the same things. We have already reached a point where crimes of youth are indistinguishable from those of adults, and we may soon reach a point where the punishments will be the same.

I raise this point because the school is one of our few remaining [20] institutions based on firm distinctions between childhood and adulthood, and on the assumption that adults have something of value to teach the young. That is why teachers must avoid emulating in dress and speech the style of the young. It is also why the school ought to be a place for what we might call "manners education": the adults in school ought to be concerned with teaching youth a standard of civilized interaction.

Again those who are inclined to regard this as superficial may be underestimating the power of media such as television and radio to teach how one is to conduct oneself in public. In a general sense, the media "unprepare" the young for behavior in groups. A young man who goes through the day with a radio affixed to his ear is learning to be indifferent to any shared sound. A young woman who can turn off a television program that does not suit her needs at the moment is learning impatience with any stimulus that is not responsive to her interests.

But school is not a radio station or a television program. It is a social situation requiring the subordination of one's own impulses and interests to those of the group. In a word, manners. As a rule, elementary school teachers will exert considerable effort in teaching manners. I believe they refer to this effort as "socializing the child." But it is astonishing how precipitously this effort is diminished at higher levels. It is certainly neglected in the high schools, and where it is not, there is usually an excessive concern for "bad habits," such as smoking, drinking, and in some nineteenth-century schools, swearing. But, as William James noted, our virtues are as habitual as our vices. Where is the attention given to the "Good morning" habit, to the "I beg your pardon" habit, to the "Please forgive the interruption" habit?

The most civilized high school class I have ever seen was one in which students and teacher said "Good morning" to each other and in which the students stood up when they had something to say. The teacher, moreover, thanked each student for any contribution made to the class, did not sit with his feet on the desk, and did not interrupt a student unless he had asked permission to do so. The students, in turn, did not interrupt each other, or chew gum, or read comic books when they were bored. To avoid being a burden to others when one is bored is the essence of civilized behavior.

Of this teacher, I might also say that he made no attempt to 24 entertain his students or model his classroom along the lines of a TV program. He was concerned not only to teach his students manners but to teach them how to attend in a classroom, which is partly a matter of manners but also necessary to their intellectual development. One of the more serious difficulties teachers now face in the classroom results from the fact that their students suffer media-shortened attention spans and have become accustomed, also through intense media exposure, to novelty, variety, and entertainment. Some teachers have made desperate attempts to keep their students "tuned in" by fashioning their classes along the lines of

Sesame Street or the *Tonight* show. They tell jokes. They change the pace. They show films, play records, and avoid *anything* that would take more than eight minutes. Although their motivation is understandable, this is what their students least need. However difficult it may be, the teacher must try to achieve student attention and even enthusiasm through the attraction of ideas, not razzmatazz. Those who think I am speaking here in favor of "dull" classes may themselves, through media exposure, have lost an understanding of the potential for excitement contained in an idea. The media (one prays) are not so powerful that they can obliterate in the young, particularly in the adolescent, what William James referred to as a "theoretic instinct," a need to know reasons, causes, abstract conceptions. Such an "instinct" can be seen in its earliest stages in what he calls the "sporadic metaphysical inquiries of children as to who made God, and why they have five fingers. . . ."

I trust that the reader is not misled by what I have been saying. As I see it, nothing in any of the above leads to the conclusion that I favor a classroom that is authoritarian or coldhearted, or dominated by a teacher insensitive to students and how they learn. I merely want to affirm the importance of the classroom as a special place, aloof from the biases of the media; a place in which the uses of the intellect are given prominence in a setting of elevated language, civilized manners, and respect for social symbols.

Topics for Discussion and Writing

1. In paragraph 3 what does Postman mean by "tolerance for delayed gratification"? By the way, two paragraphs later Postman uses an expression that is approximately synonymous with "delayed gratification." What is this expression?

2. Postman in part blames "the electronic media," because (he says in paragraph 5) they emphasize "fragmentation." Does he give any examples in his essay? Do you think you know what he means? And do you think he is right?

3. Who is Postman's audience? High school students? Parents and teachers? Professors of education? And who is Postman—that is, putting aside the biographical note on page 214, what sort of person does the author of the essay reveal himself to be? A frustrated high school teacher? A professor of education? An intelligent layperson? Does he seem to know what he is talking about?

4. In paragraph 10 we are told, with approval, that a principal named Dr. Howard Hurwitz "ran 'a tight ship.'" First, make sure that you know what

the phrase means, and then write an essay of 500 words evaluating the degree of success of some instructor or administrator who ran a tight ship in your school. Your essay will, of course, have to give us a sense of what the instructor or administrator did, as well as your evaluation of the results of his or her teaching or administrating.

5. If you disagree with Postman on the value of a dress code, set forth your disagreement in a persuasive essay of 500 words.

6. Write an editorial—as an alumnus or alumna—for your high school newspaper, summarizing Postman's essay in a paragraph, and then comparing your school with Postman's idea of a good school, and, finally, evaluating your school and Postman's essay. You may, for example, conclude that, thank heavens, your school was nothing like Postman's ideal school.

Merry White

Merry White is the author of The Japanese Educational Challenge *(1987). She is also the author of a book on noodles. White, who has served as an administrator of Harvard's East Asian Studies Program, now teaches sociology at Boston University. This essay was originally published in 1984, hence the average salaries specified in paragraph 19 must be adjusted upward.*

Japanese Education
How Do They Do It?

Japan has become the new reference point for the developing nations and the West, and comparisons with Japan cause increasing wonder and sometimes envy. Travel agents continue to profit from the curiosity of Americans, particularly businessmen, who take regular tours of Japan seeking the secrets of Japanese industry. They come back with photographs and full notebooks, convinced they have learned secrets that can be transplanted to their own companies.

Even the Japanese have entered the pop-sociological search for the secrets of their own success; their journalists suggest that they emphasize problem *prevention* while Americans make up for their lack of prescience and care through *remediation* (in the case of cars, recalls for flawed models). The explanation given by a European Economic Community report—that the Japanese are workaholics willing, masochistically, to live in "rabbit hutches" without complaint—

was met with amused derision in Japan. But it seems that those who do not look for transportable "secrets" are nonetheless willing to believe that the source of Japanese success is genetic, and thus completely untransferable. There are alternatives to these positions, and an examination of Japanese education provides us with a backdrop for considering them.

The Social Consensus

The attention given to the decline of both American industry and American education has not yet led to an awareness here of the close relationship between the development of people and the development of society, an awareness we see everywhere in Japanese thought and institutions, and whose effects we can see in the individual achievements of Japanese children. If Americans realized how powerful the relationship is between Japanese school achievement and social and economic successes we might see the same kind of protectionist language aimed at the Japanese educational system that we see directed at their automobile industry. ("The Japanese must stop producing such able and committed students because *it isn't fair.*")

The Japanese understand how important it is to have not just a 4 high level of literacy (which they have had since well before modernization), but also a high level of education in the whole population. It has been said that the Japanese high school graduate is as well educated as an American college graduate, and indeed it is impressive that any worker on the factory floor can be expected to understand statistical material, work from complex graphs and charts, and perform sophisticated mathematical operations. This consensus that education is important, however simple it may sound, is the single most important contributor to the success of Japanese schools. Across the population, among parents, at all institutional and bureaucratic levels, and highest on the list of national priorities, is the stress on excellence in education. This is not just rhetoric. If the consensus, societal mobilization, and personal commitment—all focused on education—are not available to Americans, the reason is not genetic, nor are we locked in an immutable cultural pattern. We simply have not mobilized around our children.

There are clear advantages to being a Japanese child: a homogeneous population focused on perpetuating its cultural identity; an occupational system where selection and promotion are based on educational credentials; a relatively equal distribution of educational opportunities; a universal core curriculum; highly trained and re-warded teachers; and families, especially mothers, devoted to en-hancing the life chances of children and working cooperatively with the educational system. Finally, there are high standards for per-formance in every sector, and a carefully graded series of perfor-mance expectations in the school curriculum.

It is clear from these assertions that the measurable cognitive achievements of Japanese education represent only part of the pic-ture. The American press stresses these achievements and accounts for them in terms of government expenditures, longer school years, and early use of homework. While the International Association for the Evaluation of Educational Achievement (IEA) test scores certainly indicate that Japanese children are testing higher than any children in the world (especially in math and science), and while some researchers have even claimed that Japanese children on average score 11 points more than American children on IQ tests, the social and psychological dimensions of Japanese education are similarly impressive and are primary contributors to cognitive achievement. The support given by family and teachers to the emotional and be-havioral development of the child provides a base for the child's ac-quisition of knowledge and problem-solving skills. But beyond this, the Japanese think a major function of education is the development of a happy, engaged, and secure child, able to work hard and cooper-ate with others.

Inside the Japanese School

In order to understand the context of the Japanese educational sys-tem, some basic information is necessary:

1. Education is compulsory for ages six to 15, or through lower secondary school. (Age is almost always correlated with grade level, by the way, because only rarely is a child "kept back" and almost never "put ahead.") Non-compulsory high school attendance (both public and private) is nearly universal, at 98 percent.

2. There is extensive "non-official" private education. Increas-ing numbers of children attend pre-schools. Currently, about 95 per-cent of the five-year olds are in kindergarten or nursery school, 70 percent of the four-year olds and 10 percent of three-year olds. Many older children attend *juku* (after school classes) as well. These are private classes in a great variety of subjects, but most enhance and reinforce the material to be learned for high school or college

entrance examinations. There are also *yobiko* (cram schools) for those taking an extra year between high school and college to prepare for the exams.

3. While competition for entrance to the most prestigious universities is very stiff, nearly 40 percent of the college-age group attend college or university. (The rates are slightly higher for women, since many attend two-year junior colleges.)

4. Japanese children attend school 240 days a year, compared to 180 in the U.S. Many children spend Sundays in study or tutoring, and vacation classes are also available. Children do not necessarily see this as oppressive, and younger children often ask their parents to send them to *juku* as a way of being with their friends after school. Homework starts in first grade, and children in Japan spend more time in home study than children in any other country except Taiwan. In Japan, 8 percent of the high school seniors spend less than five hours per week on homework, compared to 65 percent of American seniors.[1]

5. Primary and lower secondary schools provide what we would call a core curriculum: a required and comprehensive course of study progressing along a logical path, with attention given to children's developmental levels. In elementary and lower secondary school, language learning dominates the school curriculum, and takes up the greatest number of classroom hours, particularly from second to fourth grade. The large number of characters to be learned requires an emphasis on memorization and drill that is not exhibited in the rest of the curriculum. Arithmetic and math are next in number of class hours, followed by social studies. The curriculum includes regular physical education and morning exercise as part of a "whole-child" program. In high school all students take Japanese, English, math, science, and social studies each year, and all students have had courses in chemistry, biology, physics, and earth sciences. All high school students take calculus.

6. Computers and other technology do not play a large role in schools. The calculator is used, but has not replaced mental calculations or, for that matter, the abacus. There is no national program to develop high technology skills in children. Americans spend much more money on science and technology in the schools; the Japanese spend more on teacher training and salaries.

---

[1] Thomas Rohlen, *Japan's High Schools* (Berkeley: University of California Press, 1983), p. 277.

These features should be seen in the context of a history of emphasis on education in Japan. To begin with, an interest in mass (or at least widespread) education greatly antedated the introduction of Western schools to Japan. Literacy, numeracy, and a moral education were considered important for people of all classes. When Western style universal compulsory schooling was introduced in 1872, it was after a deliberate and wide-ranging search throughout the world that resulted in a selection of features from German, French, and American educational systems that would advance Japan's modernization and complement her culture. While uniform, centralized schooling was an import, it eventually brought out Japan's already refined powers of adaptation—not the ability to adapt to a new mode as much as *the ability to adapt the foreign mode to Japanese needs and conditions.*

Also striking was the rapidity with which Japan developed a modern educational system and made it truly universal. In 1873, one year after the Education Act, there was 28 percent enrollment in primary schools, but by 1904 enrollment had already reached 98 percent—one percent less than the current rate. The rush to educate children was buttressed both by the wish to catch up with the West and by a cultural interest in schooling.

A Truly National System

Tradition, ideology, and international competition are not, however, 16 the only motive forces in Japanese education: other factors are as significant. First, Japan has a relatively homogeneous population. Racially and economically there is little variety. Minority groups, such as Koreans and the former out-castes, exist and do suffer some discrimination, but all children have equal access to good schooling. Income is more evenly distributed in Japan than in America and most people (96 percent in a recent Prime Minister's Office poll) consider themselves middle class. There are few remaining regional differences that affect the educational system, except perhaps local accents.

Second, educational financing and planning are centralized. While American educational policy sees the responsibility for schooling as a local matter, Japanese planners can rely on a centralized source of funding, curriculum guidance, and textbook selection. In terms of educational spending as a percentage of total GNP, the U.S. and Japan are not so far apart: The U.S. devotes 6.8 percent of its GNP to education, and Japan devotes 8.6 percent. But in Japan about

50 percent of this is national funding, while in the U.S. the federal government provides only 8 percent of the total expenditure on education, most of which is applied to special education, not to core schooling. Moreover, in the U.S. there exist no national institutions to build a consensus on what and how our children are taught. The most significant outcome of centralization in Japan is the even distribution of resources and quality instruction across the country. National planners and policymakers can mobilize a highly qualified teaching force and offer incentives that make even the most remote areas attractive to good teachers.

Third (but perhaps most important in the comparison with the United States), teachers enjoy respect and high status, job security, and good pay. More than in any other country, teachers in Japan are highly qualified: Their mastery of their fields is the major job qualification, and all have at least a bachelor's degree in their specialty. Moreover, they have a high degree of professional involvement as teachers: 74 percent are said to belong to some professional teachers' association in which teaching methods and curriculum are actively discussed.[2]

Teachers are hired for life, at starting salaries equivalent to starting salaries for college graduates in the corporate world. Elementary and junior high school teachers earn $18,200 per year on the average, high school teachers $19,000. Compared to other Japanese public sector workers, who earn an average of $16,800, this is a high salary, but it is less than that of managers in large companies or bureaucrats in prestigious ministries. In comparison with American teachers, whose salaries average $17,600, it is an absolutely higher wage. The difference is especially striking when one considers that over all professions, salaries are lower in Japan than in the U.S. In fact, American teachers' salaries are near the bottom of the scale of jobs requiring a college degree. Relative status and prestige correlate with salary in both countries. Japanese teachers' pay increases, as elsewhere in Japan, are tied to a seniority ladder, and older "master teachers" are given extra pay as teacher supervisors in each subject.[3]

Japanese teachers see their work as permanent: Teaching is not 20 a waystation on a path to other careers. Teachers work hard at

---

[2] William Cummings, *Education and Equality in Japan* (Princeton: Princeton University Press, 1980), p. 159.

[3] There is a debate in Japan today concerning rewarding good teachers with higher pay: Professor Sumiko Iwao, of Keio University, reports that when quality is measured in yen, the commitment of teachers to good teaching declines.

improving their skills and knowledge of their subject, and attend refresher courses and upgrading programs provided by the Ministry of Education. While there are tendencies, encouraged by the Teachers' Union, to downplay the traditional image of the "devoted, selfless teacher" (since this is seen as exploitative), and to redefine the teacher as a wage laborer with regular hours, rather than as a member of a "sacred" profession, teachers still regularly work overtime and see their job's sphere extending beyond classroom instruction. Classes are large: The average is about 40 students to one teacher. Teachers feel responsible for their students' discipline, behavior, morality, and for their general social adjustment as well as for their cognitive development. They are "on duty" after school hours and during vacations, and supervise vacation play and study. They visit their students' families at home, and are available to parents with questions and anxieties about their children. The Teachers' Union protests strongly against this extensive role, but both teachers and parents reinforce this role, tied as it is to the high status of the teacher.

Fourth, there is strong ideological and institutional support for education because the occupational system relies on schools to select the right person for the right organization. Note that this is not the same as the "right job" or "slot": A new company recruit, almost always a recent graduate, is not expected to have a skill or special identity, but to be appropriate in general educational background and character for a company. The company then trains recruits in the skills they will need, as well as in the company style. Of course, the basic skill level of the population of high school and college graduates is extremely high. But the important fact is that the social consensus supports an educational system that creates a committed, productive labor force. And although the emphasis seems to be on educational credentials, the quality of graduates possessing these credentials is indisputably high.

Mom

The background I have presented—of national consensus, institutional centralization, and fiscal support—alone does not explain the successes of Japanese education. There are other, less tangible factors that derive from cultural conceptions of development and learning, the valued role of maternal support, and psychological factors in Japanese pedagogy, and which distinguish it from American schooling.

The role of mothers is especially important. The average Japanese mother feels her child has the potential for success: Children are believed to be born with no distinguishing abilities (or disabilities) and can be mobilized to achieve and perform at high levels. Effort and commitment are required, and, at least at the beginning, it is the mother's job to engage the child. One way of looking at Japanese child development is to look at the words and concepts related to parental goals for their children. A "good child" has the following, frequently invoked characteristics: He is *otonashii* (mild or gentle), *sunao* (compliant, obedient, and cooperative), *akarui* (bright, alert), and *genki* (energetic and spirited). *Sunao* has frequently been translated as "obedient," but it would be more appropriate to use "open minded," "nonresistant," or "authentic in intent and cooperative in spirit." The English word "obedience" implies subordination and lack of self-determination, but *sunao* assumes that what we call compliance (with a negative connotation) is really cooperation, an act of affirmation of the self. A child who is *sunao* has not yielded his personal autonomy for the sake of cooperation; cooperation does not imply giving up the self, but in fact implies that working with others is the appropriate setting for expressing and enhancing the self.

One encourages a *sunao* child through the technique, especially used by mothers and elementary school teachers, of *wakaraseru,* or "getting the child to understand." The basic principle of child rearing seems to be: Never go against the child. *Wakaraseru* is often a long-term process that ultimately engages the child in the mother's goals, and makes her goals the child's own, thus producing an authentic cooperation, as in *sunao.* The distinction between external, social expectations and the child's own personal goals becomes blurred from this point on. An American might see this manipulation of the child through what we would call "indulgence" as preventing him from havlng a strong will of his own, but the Japanese mother sees long term benefits of self-motivated cooperation and real commitment.

Japanese mothers are active teachers as well, and have a real curriculum for their pre-school children: Games, teaching aids, ordinary activities are all focused on the child's development. There are counting games for very small babies, songs to help children learn new words, devices to focus the child's concentration. Parents buy an average of two or three new books every month for their preschoolers, and there are about 40 monthly activity magazines for preschoolers, very highly subscribed. The result is that most, at least most urban children, can read and write the phonetic syllabary before they enter school, and can do simple computations.

Maternal involvement becomes much more extensive and "serious" once she and the child enter the elementary school community. In addition to formal involvement in frequent ceremonies and school events, PTA meetings and visiting days, the mother spends much time each day helping the child with homework (sometimes to the point at which the teachers joke that they are really grading the mothers by proxy). There are classes for mothers, called *mamajuku*, that prepare mothers in subjects their children are studying. Homework is considered above all a means for developing a sense of responsibility in the child, and like much in early childhood education, it is seen as a device to train character.

The Japanese phenomenon of maternal involvement recently surfaced in Riverdale, New York, where many Japanese families have settled. School teachers and principals there noted that each Japanese family was purchasing two sets of textbooks. On inquiring, they found that the second set was for the mother, who could better coach her child if she worked during the day to keep up with his lessons. These teachers said that children entering in September with no English ability finished in June at the top of their classes in every subject.

The effort mothers put into their children's examinations has been given a high profile by the press. This is called the *kyoiku mama* syndrome — the mother invested in her children's progress. In contrast to Western theories of achievement, which emphasize individual effort and ability, the Japanese consider academic achievement to be an outgrowth of an interdependent network of cooperative effort and planning. The caricature of the mother's overinvestment, however, portrays a woman who has totally identified with her child's success or failure, and who has no separate identity of her own. The press emphasizes the negative aspects of this involvement with accounts of maternal nervous breakdowns, reporting a murder by a mother of the child next-door, who made too much noise while her child was studying. But the press also feeds the mother's investment by exhorting her to prepare a good work environment for the studying child, to subscribe to special exam-preparation magazines, to hire tutors, and to prepare a nutritious and exam-appropriate diet.

High-schoolers from outlying areas taking entrance exams in Tokyo come with their mothers to stay in special rooms put aside by hotels. They are provided with special food, study rooms, counselors, and tension-release rooms, all meant to supply home-care away from home. The home study-desk bought by most parents for their smaller children symbolizes the hovering care and intensity of the mother's involvement: All models have a high front and half-sides, cutting out distractions and enclosing the workspace in womb-like protection. There is a built-in study light, shelves, a clock, electric pencil sharpener, and built-in calculator. The most popular model includes a push-button connecting to a buzzer in the kitchen to summon mother for help or for a snack.

How Do You Feel About Cubing?

Not much work has been done yet to analyze the relationship between the strongly supportive learning atmosphere and high achievement in Japan. In the home, mothers train small children in a disciplined, committed use of energy through what Takeo Doi has called the encouragement of "positive dependency"; in the schools as well there is a recognition that attention to the child's emotional relationship to his work, peers, and teachers is necessary for learning.

A look at a Japanese classroom yields some concrete examples of this. Many Westerners believe that Japanese educational successes are due to an emphasis on rote learning and memorization, that the classroom is rigidly disciplined. This is far from reality. An American teacher walking into a fourth grade science class in Japan would be horrified: children all talking at once, leaping and calling for the teacher's attention. The typical American's response is to wonder, "who's in control of this room?" But if one understands the content of the lively chatter, it is clear that all the noise and movement is focused on the work itself—children are shouting out answers, suggesting other methods, exclaiming in excitement over results, and not gossiping, teasing, or planning games for recess. As long as it is the result of this engagement, the teacher is not concerned over the noise, which may measure a teacher's success. (It has been estimated that American teachers spend about 60 percent of class time on organizing, controlling, and disciplining the class, while Japanese teachers spend only 10 percent.)

A fifth grade math class I observed reveals some elements of this pedagogy. The day I visited, the class was presented with a general statement about cubing. Before any concrete facts, formulae, or even 32 drawings were displayed, the teacher asked the class to take out their math diaries and spend a few minutes writing down their feelings and anticipations over this new concept. It is hard for me to imagine an American math teacher beginning a lesson with an exhortation to examine one's emotional predispositions about cubing (but that may be only because my own math training was antediluvian).

After that, the teacher asked for conjectures from the children about the surface and volume of a cube and asked for some ideas about formulae for calculation. The teacher asked the class to cluster into its component *han* (working groups) of four or five children each, and gave out materials for measurement and construction. One group left the room with large pieces of cardboard, to construct a model of a cubic meter. The groups worked internally on solutions to problems set by the teacher and competed with each other to finish first. After a while, the cubic meter group returned, groaning under the bulk of its model, and everyone gasped over its size. (There were many comments and guesses as to how many children could fit inside.) The teacher then set the whole class a very challenging problem, well over their heads, and gave them the rest of the class time to work on it. The class ended without a solution, but the teacher made no particular effort to get or give an answer, although she exhorted them to be energetic. (It was several days before the class got the answer—there was no deadline but the excitement did not flag.)

Several characteristics of this class deserve highlighting. First, there was attention to feelings and predispositions, provision of facts, and opportunities for discovery. The teacher preferred to focus on process, engagement, commitment, and performance rather than on discipline (in our sense) and production. Second, the *han*: Assignments are made to groups, not to individuals (this is also true at the workplace) although individual progress and achievement are closely monitored. Children are supported, praised, and allowed to make mistakes through trial and error within the group. The group is also pitted against other groups, and the group's success is each person's triumph, and vice versa. Groups are made up by the teacher and are designed to include a mixture of skill levels— there is a *hancho* (leader) whose job it is to choreograph the group's work, to encourage the slower members, and to act as a reporter to the class at large.

Japanese teachers seem to recognize the emotional as well as the intellectual aspects of engagement. Japanese pedagogy (and maternal socialization) are based on the belief that effort is the most important factor in achievement, and that the teacher's job is to get the child to commit himself positively and energetically to hard work. This emphasis is most explicit in elementary school, but persists later as a prerequisite for the self-discipline and effort children exhibit in high school.

American educational rhetoric does invoke "the whole child," does seek "self-expression," and does promote emotional engagement in "discovery learning." But Japanese teaching style, at least in primary schools, effectively employs an engaging, challenging teaching style that surpasses most American attempts. In the cubing class, I was struck by the spontaneity, excitement, and (to American eyes) "unruly" dedication of the children to the new idea, and impressed with the teacher's ability to create this positive mood. It could be a cultural difference: We usually separate cognition and emotional affect, and then devise artificial means of reintroducing "feeling" into learning. It is rather like the way canned fruit juices are produced—first denatured by the preserving process and then topped up with chemical vitamins to replace what was lost.

The Role of Competition

The frequent accusation that Japanese education involves children in hellish competition must also be examined. In the elementary school classroom, competition is negotiated by means of the *han*. The educational system tries to accommodate both the ideology of harmony and the interest in hierarchy and ranking. The introduction of graded, competitive Western modes of education into societies where minimizing differences between people is valued has often produced severe social and psychological dislocation (as in Africa and other parts of the Third World). In Japan, the importance of the modern educational system as a talent selector and the need to preserve harmony and homogeneity have produced complementary rather than conflicting forces. The regular classroom is a place where the individual does not stick out, but where individual needs are met and goals are set. Children are not held back nor advanced by ability: the cohesion of the age group is said to be more important. Teachers focus on pulling up the slower learners, rather than tracking the class to suit different abilities. For the most part, teachers and the school system refuse to engage in examination preparation hysteria. Part of the reason for this is pressure from the Teachers' Union, a very large and powerful labor union which consistently resists any moves away from the egalitarian and undifferentiating mode of learning. Turning teachers into drill instructors is said to be dehumanizing, and the process of cramming a poor substitute for education.

So where is the competitive selection principle served? In the *juku*. *Juku* are tough competitive classes, often with up to 500 in one lecture hall. The most prestigious are themselves very selective and there are examinations (and preparation courses for these) to enter the *juku*. Some *juku* specialize in particular universities' entrance exams, and they will boast of their rate of admission into their universities. It is estimated that one third of all primary school students and one half of all secondary school students attend *juku*, but in Tokyo the rate rises to 86 percent of junior high school students. The "king of *juku*," Furukawa Noboru, the creator of a vast chain of such classes, says that *juku* are necessary to bridge the gap of present realities in Japan. He says that public schools do not face the fact of competition, and that ignoring the reality does not help children. The Ministry of Education usually ignores this non-accredited alternative and complementary system, and permits this functional division to take the pressure off the public schools. While there is considerable grumbling by parents, and while it is clear that the *juku* introduce an inegalitarian element into the process of schooling (since they do cost money), they do, by their separation from the regular school, permit the persistence of more traditional modes of learning, while allowing for a fast track in the examinations.

It is important to note that in Japan there really is only one moment of critical importance to one's career chances—the entrance examination to college. There are few opportunities to change paths or retool. Americans' belief that one can be recreated at any time in life, that the self-made person can get ahead, simply is not possible in Japan—thus the intense focus on examinations.

The Problems—in Context

This rapid tour through the Japanese educational system cannot 40 neglect the problems. However, two things must be kept in mind when considering these well-publicized difficulties: One is that although problems do exist, the statistical reality is that, compared to the West, Japan still looks very good indeed. The other is that the Japanese themselves tend to be quite critical, and educational problems are given attention. But this attention should be seen in context: Not that people are not truly concerned about real problems, but that the anxiety seems related to a sense of national insecurity. The Japanese focus on educational issues may emanate from a sense of the importance of intellectual development in a society where there are few other resources. Any educational problem seems to put the nation truly at risk.

Japanese parents are critical and watchful of the schools and are not complacent about their children's successes. There was a telling example of this in a recent comparative study of American and Japanese education. Mothers in Minneapolis and in Sendai, roughly comparable cities, were asked to evaluate their children's school experiences. The Minneapolis mothers consistently answered that the schools were fine and that their children were doing well, while the Sendai mothers were very critical of their schools and worried that their children were not performing up to potential. Whose children were, in objective tests, doing better? The Sendai group—in fact so much better that the poorest performer in the Japanese group was well ahead of the best in the American group. Mothers in Japan and the U.S. have very different perspectives on performance: Japanese mothers attribute failure to lack of effort while American mothers explain it as lack of ability. Japanese children have an external standard of excellence to which they can aspire, while an American child normally can only say he will "do his best."

Problems have surfaced, of course. Psychotherapists report a syndrome among children related to school and examination pressure. School phobia, psychosomatic symptoms, and juvenile suicide are most frequently reported. Japan does lead the world in school-related suicides for the 15- to 19-year old age group, at about 300 per year. Recently, the "battered teacher" and "battered parent" syndromes have received much attention. There are cases where teenagers have attacked or killed parents and teachers, and these have been related to examination pressure. The numbers involved in these cases are very small—at least in comparison with American delinquency patterns and other juvenile pathologies. Dropouts, drug use, and violent juvenile crimes are almost nonexistent in Japan. The crimes reported in one year among school-age children in Osaka, for example, are equal to those reported in one day in New York.

Criticism leveled at Japanese education by Western observers focuses on what they regard as a suppression of genius and individuality, and a lack of attention to the development of creativity in children. The first may indeed be a problem—for the geniuses—because there is little provision for tracking them to their best advantage. There has been discussion of introducing tracking so that individual ability can be better served, but this has not been implemented. The superbright may indeed be disadvantaged.

On the other hand, creativity and innovation *are* encouraged, but   44
their manifestations may be different from those an American observer would expect. We must look at our own assumptions, to see if they are too limited. Americans see creativity in children as a fragile blossom that is stifled by rigid educational systems or adult standards. Creativity involves a necessary break with traditional content and methods, and implies the creation of a new idea or artifact. Whether creativity is in the child or in the teaching, and how it is to be measured, are questions no one has answered satisfactorily. Why we emphasize it is another question, probably related to our theories of progress and the importance we attach to unique accomplishments that push society forward. The fact is that, if anything, our schools do less to encourage creativity than do the Japanese, especially in the arts. All children in Japan learn two instruments and how to read music in elementary school, have regular drawing and painting classes, and work in small groups to create projects they themselves devise. It is true, though, that if everyone must be a soloist or composer to be considered creative, then most Japanese are not encouraged to be creative.

It is not enough to claim that the Japanese have been successful in training children to take exams at the expense of a broader education. And it is not at all appropriate to say that they are unable to develop children's individuality and create the geniuses who make scientific breakthroughs. The first is untrue and the second remains to be shown as false by the Japanese themselves, who are now mobilizing to produce more scientists and technologists. In fact, the scales are tipped in favor of Japan, and to represent it otherwise would be a distortion.

The success of the Japanese model has led to its use in other rapidly developing countries, including South Korea, Taiwan, and Singapore. There, education is seen as the linchpin for development, and attention to children has meant the allocation of considerable resources to schools. The results are similar to those seen in Japanese schools: highly motivated, hard-working students who like school and who have achieved very high scores on international achievement tests.

Seeing Ourselves through Japanese Eyes

What *America* can learn from Japan is rather an open question. We can, to begin with, learn more *about* Japan, and in doing so, learn more about ourselves. Japanese advancements of the past 20 years were based on American principles of productivity (such as "quality control"), not on samurai management skills and zen austerities. Looking for Japanese secrets, or worse, protesting that they are inhuman or unfair, will not get us very far. They have shown they can adjust programs and policies to the needs and resources of the times; we must do the same. We need to regain the scientific literacy we lost and reacquire the concrete skills and participatory techniques we need. We should see Japan as establishing a new standard, not as a model to be emulated. To match that standard we have to aim at general excellence, develop a long-term view, and act consistently over time with regard to our children's education.

Topics for Discussion and Writing

1. In paragraph 4 White contrasts Japanese commitment to education with our own. Where in our society might one look for evidence of commitment or lack of commitment to education?

2. In paragraph 5 White lists many "clear advantages to being a Japanese child." Considering your education, or any other grounds you choose, which of these "advantages" would you like to have? Are there any you would gladly do without? Can you explain why? How many of the Japanese advantages appear to be dependent on the first that White lists, "a homogeneous population"? Are you aware of advantages to growing up in a heterogeneous population? (For an explanation of Japanese homogeneity, see paragraph 16.)

3. At the end of paragraph 6 White says that "the Japanese think a major function of education is the development of a happy, engaged, and secure child, able to work hard and cooperate with others." Complete the following sentence: "Americans think a major function of education is . . ."

4. In paragraph 11 White discusses the amount of time Japanese students spend on homework. What were your own experiences with homework? Did homework contribute significantly to your education? Were there assignments you now regard as counterproductive?

5. In paragraph 13 White says that computers do not play a large role in Japanese schools. If computers played a fairly large role in your education, what do you think you learned from them, aside from how to operate them?

6. In paragraph 18 White reports that Japanese teachers are highly qualified. Do you think that, on the whole, your high school teachers were highly qualified? If you were able to do so, what measures would you take to insure well-qualified teachers in *all* American high schools? (White's paragraph 19 may provide some ideas.)

7. In paragraph 32 White briefly describes a math class about to study cubing. Does the procedure followed in the class strike you as being of any value? Why, or why not? And what about the procedure described in the next paragraph? (In thinking about this, consider also White's comments in paragraphs 34–35.) Looking back at a class in which you learned a good deal, what "elements of pedagogy" (White's words, paragraph 32) made the class successful?

8. In paragraph 37 White says that children in Japanese schools are almost never held back or advanced because of ability, and there is no tracking system. What do you think of this system? (Consider also paragraphs 43 and 44.)

9. In paragraph 39 White writes of the belief of Americans that "one can be recreated at any time in life, that the self-made person can get ahead." To what extent do you share these beliefs? To what extent did the schools you attended promote them?

10. Japan has produced relatively few winners of the Nobel Prize. Did White's essay help you to understand why this might be so? Do you take the lack of Nobel Prize winners to be a significant criticism of the Japanese educational system?

11. Given the great differences between our societies, what, if anything, do you think our educational system can learn from the Japanese system? (For example, we are far less homogeneous. And the mothers in our society often hold paying jobs, whereas few Japanese mothers do. Further, two thirds of our teenagers hold part-time jobs, whereas almost no Japanese teenagers hold jobs.)

Theodore Sizer

Theodore Sizer, born in New Haven in 1937, was educated at Yale and Harvard. After serving from 1964 to 1972 as dean of the Harvard Graduate School of Education, he served as headmaster of Phillips Academy, Andover. In 1981 and 1982 he visited some fifty secondary schools, preparing to write Horace's Compromise, *the book from which our selection is taken. (The title refers to an imaginary or composite teacher named Horace, who finds that he must compromise on his job.)*

Principals' Questions

As I traveled among schools, their principals pressed me with questions, many of which were practical, specific.

What's your curriculum . . . What subjects should be offered? they asked.

I replied: Let's not start with subjects; that usually leads us into the swamp called "coverage." What counts are positive answers to three questions: Can graduates of this high school teach themselves? Are they decent people? Can they effectively use the principal ways of looking at the world, ways represented by the major and tradition acacademic disciplines?

What do you mean, "teach themselves"?   4

Learning how to observe and analyze a situation or problem and being able to make sense of it, use it, criticize it, reject or accept it. This is more than simple "problem-solving," since many of the enriching things in life are not, in fact, problems. "Teaching oneself" is nothing more than knowing how to inform and enrich oneself. Ideally a school would like not only to equip a student with those skills, but also to inspire him or her to use them.

How is this done?

By directly giving students the task of teaching themselves and helping them with it. It means providing fewer answers and insisting that students find the right (or at least defensible) answers themselves. It means that teachers must focus more on *how* kids think than on what they think.

This will take lots of time.   8

Yes, indeed. There will be far less opportunity for teachers to tell things, and, as a result, less coverage, of fewer subject areas. Of course, ultimately it means more coverage because the student is able to learn on his or her own.

Which fewer areas? Be specific.

I will, but with the clear understanding that there is no One Best Curriculum for all schools. While we all have to agree on some general outcomes that give meaning to the high school diploma, the means to these outcomes must be kept flexible. No two schools will or should have precisely the same characteristics; wise diversity is *essential* for quality. Furthermore, top-down edicts about "what" and "how" demonstrably do not work. Each school must find its own way, and in so doing gain the energy that such a search provides.

Let me give you the beginnings of one model. I would organize   12
a high school into four areas or large departments:

1. Inquiry and Expression
2. Mathematics and Science
3. Literature and the Arts
4. Philosophy and History

You will immediately note that "English," that pivotally important but often misconstrued or even unconstrued "subject," would disappear. By "expression," I mean all kinds of communication, but above all writing, the litmus paper of thought. Some of "communication" is brute skill, such as the use of a keyboard (that sine qua non for the modern citizen) and clear, if rudimentary handwriting. Visual communication is included, as are gesture and physical nuance and tone, those tools used so powerfully by such masters as Winston Churchill and Ronald Reagan. A teacher cannot ascertain a student's thought processes unless they are expressed.

Mathematics is the language of science, the language of certainties. Science, of course, is full of uncertainty, as is much of higher mathematics, but for beginners it is the certainties that dominate. Number systems work in certain ways. Axioms hold. The pituitary gland secretes certain hormones; if it fails to do so, predictable consequences ensue. The world around us has its share of certainties, and we should learn about them, learn to be masters of them. Basic arithmetic, algebra, some geometry and statistics, physics and biology, are the keys. I would merge the traditional departments of mathematics and science, thus forcing coordination of the real and abstract worlds of certainty. The fresh, modern necessity for study in computer science can be the first bit of glue in this process of collaboration; that subject nicely straddles both areas.

Human expression cuts across written and spoken languages, theater, song, and visual art. There is much common ground in these attempts of man and woman to explain their predicament, yet

English, music, and art usually proceed in as much splendid isolation as do mathematics and science. This is wasteful, as aesthetic expression and learning from others' attempts to find meaning are of a piece. All need representation and benefit from an alliance.

History, if it is responsibly taught, is perhaps the most difficult subject for most high school students, because it involves the abstraction of time past. One often can engage it well first through autobiography and then through biography, proceeding finally to the "biographies" of communities, which make up most conventional history. Things were as they were for reasons, and from these incidents evolve concepts in geography, economics, and sociology. For most students at this stage, these disciplines should remain the handmaidens of history. The exception is philosophy, particularly moral and political philosophy. A political philosophy, essentially that associated with American constitutionalism, is the bedrock of enlightened democratic citizenship, and adolescence, more than any other stage of life, is filled with a search for values. The study of elementary ethics, for example, not only provides excellent opportunities for learning intellectual skills, but also powerfully engages students' interest.

Why so few subjects?   16

There are several reasons. One is to lessen the splintered view of knowledge that usually confronts high school students. Their world rarely uses the fine distinctions between academic disciplines; insisting on them confuses young scholars. A second serves teachers: strict specialization hobbles much skill training. Good coaching cuts across academic specializations. The current organization is very wasteful. A third reason: a few areas, taught in large time blocks, greatly reduce both the scheduling problems and the frenetic quality of the school day. Finally, more broadly and sensibly construed subject areas allow greater scope for teachers.

Won't students want electives?

Yes, in that they will want opportunities to study what interests them and what helps them. However, this personalization can be well accommodated *within* each broad area, rather than through a smorgasbord of unrelated courses.

This sounds deadly, very academic and removed from kids' lives.   20

It sounds deadly because it has often been taught in deadly ways. I am regularly assaulted for being an "elitist" for proposing this program, yet no critic will argue, when I press him, that any of the objectives I put forward is inappropriate for every adolescent. A teacher must start where the students are—and this may *not* be chapter one in the textbook. One works to engage each student, to get him or her to experience some aspect of an area, and to feel that experience to be successful. It takes time, ingenuity, patience. Most difficult to reach will be the demoralized youngsters, the ones who see school as a hostile place. Many of these students come from low-income families. They will need special attention and classes that use extensive coaching—not only to help them gain the skills they often lack but also to promote some fresh self-assurance in them. Vast classes heavy with lecturing must be avoided.

You've left out physical education and vocational education.

Let's start with physical education. Much of what happens in schools today under that rubric is neither education (or at best is disconnected applied biology) nor very physical (thirty minutes once a week playing volleyball does not mean much, except perhaps as a useful vent for built-up adolescent steam). Citizens should know about their bodies and be taught that the need for exercise is a good thing. These are worthy topics for a good science-mathematics area to present.

The same kind of argument can be made for vocational edu- 24 cation. Specific job training is a good thing, but not at the expense of a school's core. The best place to learn most jobs is on site. The common exception is business education, most prominently training for secretarial positions. The important points are ability to type and, beyond that, being well informed, literate, and able to handle numbers. If typing is a schoolwide requirement, and the other skills the inevitable consequence of the student's taking the core topics, the exception is moot.

Two more points about vocational education: tomorrow's economy will be volatile and dependent on flexible workers with a high level of intellectual skills. Thus, the best vocational education will be one in general education in the use of one's mind. Second, we must remember that most of today's high school students are or wish to be in the labor market. As the age cohort shrinks, the demand for its labor in most communities will grow. Educators are not going to reverse this trend; it will be better if they seize it, and adapt schools in demanding, sensible ways to the reality of adolescent employment. Working per se can be good for adolescents.

All that may be true in the abstract. But the fact remains that you'll lose a lot of kids if you cut out voc ed and athletics.

No, not necessarily. Remember that but a small minority of high school students are significantly involved in vocational education and interscholastic athletics. Furthermore, to the extent that these activities form a bridge to the central subjects, I'm for them. Unfortunately, today in many schools they have a life of their own, at the expense of an education in mind and character.

What of foreign language?   28

The cry for its requirement in schooling is abroad in the land as a cure for American isolation and chauvinism. For many adolescents, such study has merit; for others, little sense. If you cannot master your own language, it is inefficient to start another. If you have little immediate need to use a second language, the time spent in learning it is largely wasted—unless that "foreign" language is English. An absolute requirement for study of a foreign tongue can divert from other topics time that is crucial for a particularly needy student. The issue of ethnocentrism is more important than language study and must be addressed through the history courses.

What of bilingual education?

Ideally, all Americans should enjoy it—but the real problem is that of non-English speaking students. They should be immersed in English intensively. Their nonlinguistic studies should continue—for no longer than necessary—in their mother tongues. Their self-confidence, often associated with their facility in language, should be reinforced. Empathy and patience are crucial here; rigid formulae passed down from central authorities *guarantee* inefficiency and frustration. The goal is confident youngsters, adept and effectively fluent in two languages.

I'm still skeptical about your overall plan. You can pull this off only if   32
you had none but highly motivated students in your school. What of tracking and the turned-off student?

Just as now, some kids won't hook in; I know that. If they've shown themselves competent in the minima of literacy, numeracy, and civic understanding, let them leave high school—with the promise that they can come back in the future. The community college system in many regions makes this an easy alternative.

In addition, there are the troublemakers, the kids who don't want necessarily to leave school, but want just to stay there because it's fun, where their friends are. Of course, good teachers can work with them to try to change their attitudes. However, if they disrupt, they should be expelled, with the same opportunities to return later as all dropouts have. As long as they have met the state's requirements, no one should force them into school. Ideally, too, they should have a variety of programs from which to choose. Highly personalized alternative programs have frequently worked for this sort of student.

As to tracking: there would be none and there would be a great deal. Every student would be enrolled in each subject area all the time.There would therefore be none of the current tracks, usually called honors, college preparatory, general, technical, and so forth. But within each subject area, the students would progress at their own pace. This would create multiple tracks, ones that are flexible and that put no child in any dead end.

That will be very messy.   36

Yes, it will. Learning is messy. It can be handled if the units (separate high schools, or "houses" within high schools) are kept small enough to allow a particular group of teachers to know particular students well and develop a track for each. Class patterns will vary by need, some larger for telling, some smaller for coaching and questioning. Students will be working much more on their own than they do now; there will be no strict age grading. One learns how to learn by experience, not by being told things.

Won't this add financial cost?

Some, perhaps. It need not, as long as schools retreat from the objective of "comprehensiveness" and concentrate on classroom teaching. There are models of "zero-based budgets" which demonstrate that schools, if simply organized, can have well-paid faculty and fewer than eighty students per teacher, without increasing current per-pupil expenditure.

You haven't mentioned guidance counselors.   40

Counselors today act either as administrators, arranging schedules and job and college interviews and the like, or as teachers, coaching and questioning young people about their personal concerns. Good teachers *are* good counselors, in that second sense; students turn to them for help, whether or not their titles identify them as "guidance" people. Most high school guidance departments are overloaded with obligations, many of which are contradictory—for example, serving both as a place where students can obtain confidential personal counsel and as a disciplinary arm of the school (perhaps running the "inschool suspension" program for students who have repeatedly broken rules).

A decentralized school with small academic units has less need for specialized counseling offices; improved faculty-student ratios make this possible. The administrative obligations now traditionally handled by such offices can be placed directly under the principal. Staff members who are well trained in counseling and testing skills can support the teachers in each small academic unit.

We are being asked often these days about "computer literacy" and the needs of a "new technological society." How does your plan address these areas?

Computers, like calculators, books, and other familiar products 44 of technology, should be welcomed by schools. Well used, they might significantly extend teachers' coaching efforts as well as help students learn. While we should learn to employ the products of the new technologies, we should keep in mind two critical points: it is up to us to select the data to be put into them, and we must choose with care the uses we put them to.

Should public schools formally provide time for voluntary prayer?

No. There is ample time and opportunity outside school for religious observances. Furthermore, the fact that public schools would not set time aside for prayer does not imply rejection of its importance. Schools should not claim to be comprehensive, arrogating to their routines every consequential aspect of an adolescent's life. High schools are limited to helping adolescents use their minds well—and this includes becoming thoughtful and decent people.

What of standards?

The existence of final "exhibitions" by students as a condition to 48 receiving their diplomas will give teachers a much greater control of standards than they currently have. These standards, combined with a variety of external examinations, such as the Advanced Placement Examinations of the College Board, Regents' Examinations in some states, and, it is hoped, a growing list of other instruments that a school or an individual student could adopt or take voluntarily, would give outside authorities, like regional accrediting agencies, a good sense of the quality of work being done.

A lot turns on those teachers. Are they good enough?

They've got to be.

Remedies like all these are neat, but abstractions, castles in the air. Seeing adolescents in classrooms reminds one that, in substantial measure, school is *their* castle, that they have to want to build it.

I arrived by car at the school at 7:15 A.M., thirty minutes before 52 the first bell. It was a cool day, and the first arrivals to the large high school I was visiting were gathered in clots in the sun outside, around the low, meandering structures that housed their classrooms. Parking lots and hard-used lawns encircled the buildings. There were no sidewalks in this neighborhood, even though it was quite built up; the school property was ringed by small houses and business establishments. Everyone came to school by bus or by private car.

I turned into one of the driveways leading toward what appeared to be the school's central building and was immediately bounced out of the seat of my rented Datsun by the first of a series of asphalt bumps in the road. These barriers, it was painfully obvious, were there to slow down the dozens of vehicles that used the driveway and were already lined up in the lots next to the school, row on row of loyal steel beasts tethered by this pedagogical water hole. I found a place and parked.

It was immediately clear from the stares I received from nearby students that I picked a student lot, not one for staff or for visitors. Since it seemed to me large enough to accommodate one more little car, I left the Datsun where it was. It was ridiculously out of place, surrounded by pickup trucks, high on their springs and mud spattered, and by jalopies, late sixties' Chevrolets, old Ford Mustangs, Plymouth Satellites, each cumbrously settled upon great oversize rear tires. While all appeared poised, snouts down, to roar purposefully off to God knows where, for the moment they simply cowered here, submissive. Their masters and mistresses leaned against them or sat on them, chatting. Many drank coffee out of paper cups. Some smoked furtively as I drew near; though unfamiliar to them, I was wearing the drab coat-tie-slacks uniform of the school administrator who might admonish them.

My first instinct was to snicker at the parking lot scene. It was an eighties' version of an *American Graffiti* strip, indeed an overdrawn one, because the dusty trucks and drag-equipped cars were grotesquely numerous. My condescension disappeared, however, when I paid more attention to the students gathered around these vehicles, kids observing the visitor who had taken a space on their turf. Their attitude was in no way menacing, but it was freighted with an absence of interest. I was an object to be observed and, if they were smoking, to be mildly reacted to. Beyond that, I might have been a bird in the vast aviary of a boring zoo; I was a piece of the scenery, glimpsed as part of hanging out before school. None of these kids was playing principal's pet by coming up and asking me whether I needed help or directions to the office, but no one hassled me, either. The human confrontation was neutral, nearly nonexistent.

These were older students, drivers. In their easy chatting among themselves, in their self-absorption and nonchalance, they showed self-assurance bordering on truculence. They had their own world. 56

My reaction was nervousness. I tried to smile a sorry-fellas-but-I-didn't-know-where-the-visitors'-parking-lot-was message, but it did not come off. I felt the awkward outsider, at distance from these composed young people. Even as I knew that at the bell they would enter the buildings and engage in the rituals of dutiful school-going and that they would get more boisterous and engaging as the early morning mist over their spirits parted, I also knew that these were considerable people, ones who would play the game adult educators asked them to play only when and how they wanted to. The fact that many of them, for a host of reasons, chose to go along with the structures of the school did not lessen the force of the observation: they possessed the autonomous power not to.

In this sense, kids run schools. Their apparent acquiescence to what their elders want them to do is always provisional. Their ability to undermine even the illusions of certain adult authority and of an expectation of deference was admirably if benignly displayed by the students on the parking lot. A less benign challenge can be made by students in any classroom when, for whatever reason, they collectively, quietly, but assuredly decide to say no. The fact that most go along with the system masks the nascent power that students hold. Few adults outside the teaching profession understand this.

The evening before, I had met the superintendent of this school district. He was a man of great force and national reputation. His administration ran the district with efficiency and closely centralized authority. In talking of his work, we had both used the ready metaphors of schoolkeeping, most turning around an image of old folk (the teachers) passing something of self-evident importance to young folk (the students). This morning all of these metaphors seemed naïve. All assumed the young student to be a passive receptacle or, at the least, a supplicant for knowledge. The adolescents in that parking lot were neither passive nor suppliant. However much we adults may want them to be eagerly receptive and respectful of our agenda for their schooling, the choice to be that or something else—neutral, hostile, inattentive—was unequivocally theirs. If we want our well-intentioned plans to succeed, we'll have to *inspire* the adolescents to join in them—inspire even the sullen, uninterested kids one sees in parking lots at the start of a school day.

The vision of school as an uncomplicated place where teachers 60 pass along the torch of knowledge to eager students is sadly innocent.

Topics for Discussion and Writing

1. Sizer's essay seems to be divided into two parts, the second part beginning with paragraph 51. What is the connection between the second part and the first? Why do you think Sizer included the second part?

2. In paragraph 5, Sizer asserts that a good high school education teaches students "to observe and analyze a situation or problem" and "to make sense of it, use it, criticize it, reject or accept it." Do you think that your high school had such goals? Did some or all of your courses seek to produce such students? If at least one course or one instructor had such goals, discuss the methods of the course or of the instructor, or both. Sizer himself gives his ideas about how these skills can be taught. Does his formula apply to your experience?

3. Sizer says in paragraph 11 that "there is no One Best Curriculum for all schools." Why can't it be argued that since all students will face the responsibility of being informed citizens, a single curriculum (for instance, so many years of American history, so many years of other history, so many years of science, or literature, and so forth) makes sense for all—for males and females, farmers and city dwellers—in short, at least for all who speak English and who are not mentally handicapped?

4. Sizer, in paragraph 12, characterizes writing as "the litmus paper of thought." What does this mean?

5. In paragraph 13 Sizer proposes merging "the traditional departments of mathematics and science, thus forcing coordination of the real and abstract worlds of certainty." Drawing on your experience of science and mathematics in high school, write an essay of 750–1000 words imagining and evaluating the results of such a merger in your high school. Or, thinking of Sizer's remark (paragraph 14) that "English, music, and art usually proceed in . . . splendid isolation," imagine and evaluate a course in which two or perhaps all three of these were combined.

6. Taking into account Sizer's remarks on history (paragraph 15), evaluate the study of history in your high school.

Mary Field Belenky,
Blythe McVicker Clinchy,
Nancy Rule Goldberger,
and Jill Mattuck Tarule

Mary Belenky is an assistant research professor at the University of Vermont, Blythe Clinchy is a professor of psychology at Wellesley College, Nancy Goldberger is a visiting scholar in psychology at New York University, and Jill Tarule is an associate professor at Lesley College Graduate School. The essay printed here is part of Chapter 9 of their book, Women's Ways of Knowing, *a study of how women's intellectual abilities develop. (The title of the extract is the editors'.)*

How Women Learn

We begin with the reminiscences of two ordinary women, each recalling an hour during her first year at college. One of them, now middle-aged, remembered the first meeting of an introductory science course. The professor marched into the lecture hall, placed upon his desk a large jar filled with dried beans, and invited the students to guess how many beans the jar contained. After listening to an enthusiastic chorus of wildly inaccurate estimates the professor smiled a thin, dry smile, revealed the correct answer, and announced, "You have just learned an important lesson about science. Never trust the evidence of your own senses."

Thirty years later, the woman could guess what the professor had in mind. He saw himself, perhaps, as inviting his students to embark upon an exciting voyage into a mysterious underworld invisible to the naked eye, accessible only through scientific method and scientific instruments. But the seventeen-year-old girl could not accept or even hear the invitation. Her sense of herself as a knower was shaky, and it was based on the belief that she could use her own firsthand experience as a source of truth. This man was saying that this belief was fallacious. He was taking away her only tool for knowing and providing her with no substitute. "I remember feeling small and scared," the woman says, "and I did the only thing I could do. I dropped the course that afternoon, and I haven't gone near science since."

The second woman, in her first year at college, told a superficially similar but profoundly different story about a philosophy class she had attended just a month or two before the interview. The teacher came into class carrying a large cardboard cube. She placed it on the desk in front of her and asked the class what it was. They said it was a cube. She asked what a cube was, and they said a cube contained six equal square sides. She asked how they knew that this object contained six equal square sides. By looking at it, they said. "But how do you know?" the teacher asked again. She pointed to the side facing her and, therefore, invisible to the students; then she lifted the cube and pointed to the side that had been face down on the desk, and, therefore, also invisible. "We can't look at all six sides of a cube at once, can we? So we can't exactly *see* a cube. And yet, you're right. You know it's a cube. But you know it not just because you have eyes but because you have intelligence. You invent the sides you cannot see. You use your intelligence to create the 'truth' about cubes."

The student said to the interviewer,   4

> It blew my mind. You'll think I'm nuts, but I ran back to the dorm and I called my boyfriend and I said, "Listen, this is just incredible," and I told him all about it. I'm not sure he could see why I was so excited. I'm not sure I understand it myself. But I really felt, for the first time, like I was really in college, like I was—I don't know—sort of *grown up.*

Both stories are about the limitations of firsthand experience as a source of knowledge—we cannot simply see the truth about either the jar of beans or the cube—but there is a difference. We can know the truth about cubes. Indeed, the students did know it. As the science professor pointed out, the students were wrong about the beans; their senses had deceived them. But, as the philosophy teacher pointed out, the students were right about the cube; their minds had served them well.

The science professor was the only person in the room who knew how many beans were in that jar. Theoretically, the knowledge was available to the students; they could have counted the beans. But faced with that tedious prospect, most would doubtless take the professor's word for it. He is authority. They had to rely upon his knowledge rather than their own. On the other hand, every member of the philosophy class knew that the cube had six sides. They were all colleagues.

The science professor exercised his authority in a benign fashion, promising the students that he would provide them with the tools they needed to excavate invisible truths. Similarly, the philosophy teacher planned to teach her students the skills of philosophical analysis, but she was at pains to assure them that they already possessed the tools to construct some powerful truths. They had built cubes on their own, using only their own powers of inference, without the aid of elaborate procedures or fancy apparatus or even a teacher. Although a teacher might have told them once that a cube contained six equal square sides, they did not have to take the teacher's word for it; they could have easily verified it for themselves.

The lesson the science professor wanted to teach is that experience is a source of error. Taught in isolation, this lesson diminished the student, rendering her dumb and dependent. The philosophy teacher's lesson was that although raw experience is insufficient, by reflecting upon it the student could arrive at truth. It was a lesson that made the student feel more powerful ("sort of grown up"). 8

No doubt it is true that, as the professor in May Sarton's novel *The Small Room* says, the "art" of being a student requires humility. But the woman we interviewed did not find the science lesson humbling; she found it humiliating. Arrogance was not then and is not now her natural habitat. Like most of the women in our sample she lacked confidence in herself as a thinker; and the kind of learning the science teacher demanded was not only painful but crippling.

In thinking about the education of women, Adrienne Rich writes, "Suppose we were to ask ourselves, simply: What does a woman need to know?" A woman, like any other human being, does need to know that the mind makes mistakes; but our interviews have convinced us that every woman, regardless of age, social class, ethnicity, and academic achievement, needs to know that she is capable of intelligent thought, and she needs to know it right away. Perhaps men learn this lesson before going to college, or perhaps they can wait until they have proved themselves to hear it; we do not know. We do know that many of the women we interviewed had not yet learned it.

Topics for Discussion and Writing

1. How is the professor in the first anecdote characterized? Look particularly at the words used in paragraphs 1 and 2 to describe him. How is the student characterized? Look back at the first sentence: Why do the writers use the word "ordinary" to describe both students? Why did they not simply say, "We begin with the reminiscences of two women"?

2. In paragraph 5 the writers say, "Both stories are about the limitations of firsthand experience as a source of knowledge." What else do the stories have in common? What are the important differences? What particular difference is most relevant to the main point of the essay?

3. Look again at paragraph 6. The science teacher is described as being "authority." The students "had to rely upon his knowledge rather than their own." Is this relationship between teacher and students more likely in science courses than in philosophy or literature courses? Is it inevitable in sciences courses? If so, why?

4. What is the main point of the concluding paragraph? Do the two anecdotes support this point? To what extent does your own experience confirm it, or not confirm it?

John Holt

John Holt (1923–85) taught in schools and colleges and wrote numerous books on education. This essay is from Escape from Childhood.

The Right to Control One's Learning

Young people should have the right to control and direct their own learning, that is, to decide what they want to learn, and when, where, how, how much, how fast, and with what help they want to learn it. To be still more specific, I want them to have the right to decide if, when, how much, and by whom they want to be *taught* and the right to decide whether they want to learn in a school and if so which one and for how much of the time.

No human right, except the right to life itself, is more fundamental than this. A person's freedom of learning is part of his freedom of thought, even more basic than his freedom of speech. If we take from someone his right to decide what he will be curious about, we destroy his freedom of thought. We say, in effect, you must think not about what interests and concerns *you*, but about what interests and concerns *us*.

We might call this the right of curiosity, the right to ask whatever questions are most important to us. As adults, we assume that we have the right to decide what does or does not interest us, what we will look into and what we will leave alone. We take this right for granted, cannot imagine that it might be taken away from us. Indeed, as far as I know, it has never been written into any body of law. Even the writers of our Constitution did not mention it. They thought it was enough to guarantee citizens the freedom of speech and the freedom to spread their ideas as widely as they wished and could. It did not occur to them that even the most tyrannical government would try to control people's minds, what they thought and knew. That idea was to come later, under the benevolent guise of compulsory universal education.

This right of each of us to control our own learning is now in danger. When we put into our laws the highly authoritarian notion that someone should and could decide what all young people were to learn and beyond that, could do whatever might seem necessary (which now includes dosing them with drugs) to compel them to learn it, we took a long step down a very steep and dangerous path. The requirement that a child go to school, for about six hours a day, 180 days a year, for about ten years, whether or not he learns anything there, whether or not he already knows it or could learn it faster or better somewhere else, is such a gross violation of civil liberties that few adults would stand for it. But the child who resists is treated as a criminal. With this requirement we created an industry, an army of people whose whole work was to tell young people what they had to learn and to try to make them learn it. Some of these people, wanting to exercise even more power over others, to be even more "helpful," or simply because the industry is not growing fast enough to hold all the people who want to get into it, are now beginning to say, "If it is good for children for us to decide what they shall learn and to make them learn it, why wouldn't it be good for everyone? If compulsory education is a good thing, how can there be too much of it? Why should we allow anyone, of any age, to decide that he has had enough of it? Why should we allow older people, any more than young, not to know what we know when their ignorance may have bad consequences for all of us? Why should we not *make* them know what they *ought* to know?"

They are beginning to talk, as one man did on a nationwide TV show, about "womb-to-tomb" schooling. If hours of homework every night are good for the young, why wouldn't they be good for us all—they would keep us away from the TV set and other frivolous pursuits. Some group of experts, somewhere, would be glad to decide what we all ought to know and then every so often check up on us to make sure we knew it—with, of course, appropriate penalties if we did not.

I am very serious in saying that I think this is coming unless we prepare against it and take steps to prevent it. The right I ask

4

for the young is a right that I want to preserve for the rest of us, the right *to decide what goes into our minds.* This is much more than the right to decide whether or when or how much to go to school or what school you want to go to. That right is important, but it is only part of a much larger and more fundamental right, which I might call the right to Learn, as opposed to being Educated, *i.e.,* made to learn what someone else thinks would be good for you. It is not just compulsory schooling but compulsory Education that I oppose and want to do away with.

That children might have the control of their own learning, including the right to decide if, when, how much, and where they wanted to go to school, frightens and angers many people. They ask me, "Are you saying that if the parents wanted the child to go to school, and the child didn't want to go, that he wouldn't have to go? Are you saying that if the parents wanted the child to go to one school, and the child wanted to go to another, that the child would have the right to decide?" Yes, that is what I say. Some people ask, "If school wasn't compulsory, wouldn't many parents take their children out of school to exploit their labor in one way or another?" Such questions are often both snobbish and hypocritical. The questioner assumes and implies (though rarely says) that these bad parents are people poorer and less schooled than he. Also, though he appears to be defending the right of children to go to school, what he really is defending is the right of the state to compel them to go whether they want to or not. What he wants, in short, is that children should be in school, not that they should have any choice about going.

But saying that children should have the right to choose to go or 8 not to go to school does not mean that the ideas and wishes of the parents would have no weight. Unless he is estranged from his parents and rebelling against them, a child cares very much about what they think and want. Most of the time, he doesn't want to anger or worry or disappoint them. Right now, in families where the parents feel that they have some choice about their children's schooling, there is much bargaining about schools. Such parents, when their children are little, often ask them whether they want to go to nursery school or kindergarten. Or they may take them to school for a while to try it out. Or, if they have a choice of schools, they may take them to several to see which they think they will like the best. Later, they care whether the child likes his school. If he does not, they try to do something about it, get him out of it, find a school he will like.

I know some parents who for years had a running bargain with their children, "If on a given day you just can't stand the thought of school, you don't feel well, you are afraid of something that may happen, you have something of your own that you very much want to do—well, you can stay home." Needless to say, the schools, with their supporting experts, fight it with all their might—Don't Give in to Your Child, Make Him Go to School, He's Got to Learn. Some parents, when their own plans make it possible for them to take an interesting trip, take their children with them. They don't ask the school's permission, they just go. If the child doesn't want to make the trip and would rather stay in school, they work out a way for him to do that. Some parents, when their child is frightened, unhappy, and suffering in school, as many children are, just take him out. Hal Bennett, in his excellent book *No More Public School*, talks about ways to do this.

A friend of mine told me that when her boy was in third grade, he had a bad teacher, bullying, contemptuous, sarcastic, cruel. Many of the class switched to another section, but this eight-year-old, being tough, defiant, and stubborn, hung on. One day—his parents did not learn this until about two years later—having had enough of the teacher's meanness, he just got up from his desk and without saying a word, walked out of the room and went home. But for all his toughness and resiliency of spirit, the experience was hard on him. He grew more timid and quarrelsome, less outgoing and confident. He lost his ordinary good humor. Even his handwriting began to go to pieces—was much worse in the spring of the school year than in the previous fall. One spring day he sat at breakfast, eating his cereal. After a while he stopped eating and sat silently thinking about the day ahead. His eyes filled up with tears, and two big ones slowly rolled down his cheeks. His mother, who ordinarily stays out of the school life of her children, saw this and knew what it was about. "Listen," she said to him, "we don't have to go on with this. If you've had enough of that teacher, if she's making school so bad for you that you don't want to go any more, I'll be perfectly happy just to pull you right out. We can manage it. Just say the word." He was horrified and indignant. "No!" he said, "I couldn't do that." "Okay," she said, "whatever you want is fine. Just let me know." And so they left it. He had decided that he was going to tough it out, and he did. But I am sure knowing that he had the support of his mother and the chance to give it up if it got too much for him gave him the strength he needed to go on.

To say that children should have the right to control and direct their own learning, to go to school or not as they chose, does not mean that the law would forbid the parents to express an opinion or wish or strong desire on the matter. It only means that if their natural authority is not strong enough the parents can't call in the cops to make the child do what they are not able to persuade him to do. And the law may say that there is a limit to the amount of pressure or coercion the parents can apply to the child to deny him a choice that he has a legal right to make.

When I urge that children should control their learning there is   12 one argument that people bring up so often that I feel I must antici- pate and meet it here. It says that schools are a place where chil- dren can for a while be protected against the bad influences of the world outside, particularly from its greed, dishonesty, and commer- cialism. It says that in school children may have a glimpse of a higher way of life, of people acting from other and better motives than greed and fear. People say, "We know that society is bad enough as it is and that children will be exposed to it and corrupted by it soon enough. But if we let children go out into the larger world as soon as they wanted, they would be tempted and corrupted just that much sooner."

They seem to believe that schools are better, more honorable places than the world outside—what a friend of mine at Harvard once called "museums of virtue." Or that people in school, both chil- dren and adults, act from higher and better motives than people outside. In this they are mistaken. There are, of course, some good schools. But on the whole, far from being the opposite of, or an an- tidote to, the world outside, with all its envy, fear, greed, and ob- sessive competitiveness, the schools are very much like it. If any- thing, they are worse, a terrible, abstract, simplified caricature of it. In the world outside the school, some work, at least, is done honestly and well, for its own sake, not just to get ahead of others; people are not everywhere and always being set in competition against each other; people are not (or not yet) in every minute of their lives subject to the arbitrary, irrevocable orders and judgment of others. But in most schools, a student is every minute doing what others tell him, subject to their judgment, in situations in which he can only win at the expense of other students.

This is a harsh judgment. Let me say again, as I have before, that schools are worse than most of the people in them and that many of these people do many harmful things they would rather not do, and a great many other harmful things that they do not even see as harmful. The whole of school is much worse than the sum of its parts. There are very few people in the U.S. today (or perhaps anywhere, any time) in any occupation, who could be trusted with the kind of power that schools give most teachers over their students. Schools seem to me among the most anti-democratic, most authoritarian, most destructive, and most dangerous institutions of modern society. No other institution does more harm or more lasting harm to more people or destroys so much of their curiosity, independence, trust, dignity, and sense of identity and worth. Even quite kindly schools are inhibited and corrupted by the knowledge of children and teachers alike that they are *performing* for the judgment and approval of others—the children for the teachers; the teachers for the parents, supervisors, school board, or the state. No one is ever free from feeling that he is being judged all the time, or soon may be. Even after the best class experiences teachers must ask themselves, "Were we right to do that? Can we prove we were right? Will it get us in trouble?"

What corrupts the school, and makes it so much worse than most of the people in it, or than they would like it to be, is its power—just as their powerlessness corrupts the students. The school is corrupted by the endless anxious demand of the parents to know how their child is doing—meaning is he ahead of the other kids—and their demand that he be kept ahead. Schools do not protect children from the badness of the world outside. They are at least as bad as the world outside, and the harm they do to the children in their power creates much of the badness of the world outside. The sickness of the modern world is in many ways a school-induced sickness. It is in school that most people learn to expect and accept that some expert can always place them in some sort of rank or hierarchy. It is in school that we meet, become used to, and learn to believe in the totally controlled society. We do not learn much science, but we learn to worship "scientists" and to believe that anything we might conceivably need or want can only come, and someday will come, from them. The school is the closest we have yet been able to come to Huxley's *Brave New World*, with its alphas and betas, deltas and epsilons—and now it even has its soma. Everyone, including children, should have the right to say "No!" to it.[1]

---

[1] Aldous Huxley's *Brave New World* (1932) depicts a totalitarian society that scientifically controls the populace. Babies are created in laboratories and are conditioned; adults are given *soma* pills to prevent depression. John Holt, following Huxley, plays on the Greek letters for A, B, D, and E, suggesting that the grading system of our schools turns into a doping system. (Editors' note)

Topics for Discussion and Writing

1. Holt's opening sentence pretty much dismisses the idea of compulsory education. What arguments can be offered on behalf of compulsory education? How can you defend the requirement that children be schooled—even if the children and their parents don't wish them to go to school?
2. In paragraph 4, Holt refers to "an industry, an army of people." To whom does he refer? What is the effect of describing them as an "industry" and an "army"?
3. Read paragraphs 12 and 13, and then write an essay of 500 words evaluating your high school in the light of Holt's comment that most schools encourage morally destructive competition.
4. If you have read Postman's essay (pages 214–21), write an essay of 500–750 words comparing and evaluating the two essays as examples of persuasive writing. Note: your topic is not "Which of the Two Essays I Subscribe to"; rather, it is an analysis and an evaluation of the essays as *persuasion*.
5. If you have read Anonymous, "Confessions of an Erstwhile Child" (pages 143–48), what ideas do you find there that are similar to Holt's? In a paragraph or two, point out the similarities, citing specific passages in each essay.

Paul Goodman

Paul Goodman (1911–72) received his bachelor's degree from City College in New York and his Ph.D. from the University of Chicago. He taught in several colleges and universities, and he wrote prolifically on literature, politics, and education. Goodman's view that students were victims of a corrupt society made him especially popular on campuses, even in the 1960s when students tended to distrust anyone over thirty. "A Proposal to Abolish Grading" (editors' title) is an extract from Compulsory Miseducation and the Community of Scholars *(1966).*

A Proposal to Abolish Grading

Let half a dozen of the prestigious Universities—Chicago, Stanford, the Ivy League—abolish grading, and use testing only and entirely for pedagogic purposes as teachers see fit.

Anyone who knows the frantic temper of the present schools will understand the transvaluation of values that would be effected by this modest innovation. For most of the students, the competitive grade has come to be the essence. The naïve teacher points to the beauty of the subject and the ingenuity of the research; the shrewd student asks if he is responsible for that on the final exam.

Let me at once dispose of an objection whose unanimity is quite fascinating. I think that the great majority of professors agree that grading hinders teaching and creates a bad spirit, going as far as cheating and plagiarizing. I have before me the collection of essays, *Examining in Harvard College,* and this is the consensus. It is uniformly asserted, however, that the grading is inevitable; for how else will the graduate schools, the foundations the corporations *know* whom to accept, reward, hire? How will the talent scouts know whom to tap?

By testing the applicants, of course, according to the specific 4 task-requirements of the inducting institution, just as applicants for the Civil Service or for licenses in medicine, law, and architecture are tested. Why should Harvard professors do the testing *for* corporations and graduate-schools?

The objection is ludicrous. Dean Whitla, of the Harvard Office of Tests, points out that the scholastic-aptitude and achievement tests used for *admission* to Harvard are a super-excellent index for all-around Harvard performance, better than high-school grades or particular Harvard course-grades. Presumably, these college-entrance tests are tailored for what Harvard and similar institutions want. By the same logic, would not an employer do far better to apply his own job-aptitude test rather than to rely on the vagaries of Harvard sectionmen. Indeed, I doubt that many employers bother to look at such grades; they are more likely to be interested merely in the fact of a Harvard diploma, whatever that connotes to them. The grades have most of their weight with the graduate schools — here, as elsewhere, the system runs mainly for its own sake.

It is really necessary to remind our academics of the ancient history of Examination. In the medieval university, the whole point of the gruelling trial of the candidate was whether or not to accept him as a peer. His disputation and lecture for the Master's was just that, a master-piece to enter the guild. It was not to make comparative evaluations. It was not to weed out and select for an extra-mural licensor or employer. It was certainly not to pit one young fellow against another in an ugly competition. My philosophic impression is that the medievals thought they knew what a good job of work was and that we are competitive because we do not know. But the more status is achieved by largely irrelevant competitive evaluation, the less will we ever know.

(Of course, our American examinations never did have this purely guild orientation, just as our faculties have rarely had absolute autonomy; the examining was to satisfy Overseers, Elders, distant Regents—and they as paternal superiors have always doted on giving grades, rather than accepting peers. But I submit that this set-up itself makes it impossible for the student to *become* a master, to *have* grown up, and to commence on his own. He will always be making A or B for some overseer. And in the present atmosphere, he will always be climbing on his friend's neck.)

Perhaps the chief objectors to abolishing grading would be the 8 students and their parents. The parents should be simply disregarded; their anxiety has done enough damage already. For the students, it seems to me that a primary duty of the university is to deprive them of their props, their dependence on extrinsic valuation and motivation, and to force them to confront the difficult enterprise itself and finally lose themselves in it.

A miserable effect of grading is to nullify the various uses of testing. Testing, for both student and teacher, is a means of structuring, and also of finding out what is blank or wrong and what has been assimilated and can be taken for granted. Review—including high-pressure review—is a means of bringing together the fragments, so that there are flashes of synoptic insight.

There are several good reasons for testing, and kinds of test. But if the aim is to discover weakness, what is the point of downgrading and punishing it, and thereby inviting the student to conceal his weakness, by faking and bulling, if not cheating? The natural conclusion of synthesis is the insight itself, not a grade for having had it. For the important purpose of placement, if one can establish in the student the belief that one is testing *not* to grade and make invidious comparisons but for his own advantage, the student should normally seek his own level, where he is challenged and yet capable, rather than trying to get by. If the student dares to accept himself as he is, a teacher's grade is a crude instrument compared with a student's self-awareness. But it is rare in our universities that students are encouraged to notice objectively their vast confusion. Unlike Socrates, our teachers rely on power-drives rather than shame and ingenuous idealism.

Many students are lazy, so teachers try to goad or threaten them by grading. In the long run this must do more harm than good. Laziness is a character-defense. It may be a way of avoiding learning, in order to protect the conceit that one is already perfect (deeper, the despair that one *never* can). It may be a way of avoiding just the risk of failing and being down-graded. Sometimes it is a way of politely saying, "I won't." But since it is the authoritarian grown-up demands that have created such attitudes in the first place, why repeat the trauma? There comes a time when we must treat people as adult, laziness and all. It is one thing courageously to fire a do-nothing out of your class; it is quite another thing to evaluate him with a lordly F.

Most important of all, it is often obvious that balking in doing the   12
work, especially among bright young people who get to great universities, means exactly what it says: The work does not suit me, not this subject, or not at this time, or not in this school, or not in school altogether. The student might not be bookish; he might be school-tired; perhaps his development ought now to take another direction. Yet unfortunately, if such a student is intelligent and is not sure of himself, he *can* be bullied into passing, and this obscures everything. My hunch is that I am describing a common situation. What a grim waste of young life and teacherly effort! Such a student will retain nothing of what he has "passed" in. Sometimes he must get mononucleosis to tell his story and be believed.

And ironically, the converse is also probably commonly true. A student flunks and is mechanically weeded out, who is really ready and eager to learn in a scholastic setting, but he has not quite caught on. A good teacher can recognize the situation, but the computer wreaks its will.

Topics for Discussion and Writing

1. In his opening paragraph Goodman limits his suggestion about grading and testing to "half a dozen of the prestigious Universities." Does he offer any reason for this limitation? Can you?
2. In paragraph 3 Goodman says that "the great majority of professors agree that grading hinders teaching." What evidence does he offer to support this claim? What arguments might be made that grading assists teaching? Should Goodman have made them?
3. As a student, have grades helped you to learn, or have grades hindered you? Explain.
4. If you have been a student in an ungraded course, describe the course and evaluate the experience.

Adrienne Rich

Adrienne Rich was born in Baltimore in 1929 and was educated at Radcliffe College. Her first book of poetry, published in the year she graduated from college, won the Yale Series of Younger Poets award, and her ninth book of poetry, Diving into the Wreck *(1973), won the National Book Award. When she accepted the award she did so not as an individual but on behalf of all women.*

The essay that we print was originally a talk delivered in 1977 at Douglass College, The Women's College of Rutgers University. It was first published in The Common Woman, *a feminist magazine.*

Claiming an Education

For this convocation, I planned to separate my remarks into two parts: some thoughts about you, the women students here, and some thoughts about us who teach in a women's college. But ultimately, those two parts are indivisible. If university education means anything beyond the processing of human beings into expected roles, through credit hours, tests, and grades (and I believe that in a women's colleged especially it *might* mean much more), it implies an ethical and intellectual contract between teacher and student. This contract must remain intuitive, dynamic, unwritten; but we must turn to it again and again if learning is to be reclaimed from the depersonalizing and cheapening pressures of the present-day academic scene.

The first thing I want to say to you who are students, is that you cannot afford to think of being here to *receive* an education; you will do much better to think of yourselves as being here to *claim* one. One of the dictionary definitions of the verb "to claim" is *to take as the rightful owner; to assert in the face of possible contradiction.* "To receive" is *to come into possession of; to act as receptacle or container for; to accept as authoritative or true.* The difference is that between acting and being acted-upon, and for women it can literally mean the difference between life and death.

One of the devastating weaknesses of university learning, of the store of knowledge and opinion that has been handed down through academic training, has been its almost total erasure of women's experience and thought from the curriculum, and its exclusion of women as members of the academic community. Today, with increasing numbers of women students in nearly every branch of higher learning, we still see very few women in the upper levels of faculty and administration in most institutions. Douglass College itself is a women's college in a university administered overwhelmingly by men, who in turn are answerable to the state legislature, again composed predominantly of men. But the most significant fact for you is that what you learn here, the very texts you read, the lectures you hear, the way your studies are divided into categories and fragmented one from the other—all this reflects, to a very large degree, neither objective reality, nor an accurate picture of the past, nor a group of rigorously tested observations about human behavior. What you can learn here (and I mean not only at Douglass but any college in any university) is how *men* have perceived and organized their experience, their history, their ideas of social relationships, good and evil, sickness and health, etc. When you read or hear about "great issues," "major texts," "the mainstream of Western thought," you are hearing about what men, above all white men, in their male subjectivity, have decided is important.

Black and other minority peoples have for some time recognized   4 that their racial and ethnic experience was not accounted for in the studies broadly labeled human; and that even the sciences can be racist. For many reasons, it has been more difficult for women to comprehend our exclusion, and to realize that even the sciences can be sexist. For one thing, it is only within the last hundred years that higher education has grudgingly been opened up to women at all, even to white, middle-class women. And many of us have found ourselves poring eagerly over books with titles like: *The Descent of Man; Man and His Symbols; Irrational Man; The Phenomenon of Man; The Future of Man; Man and the Machine; From Man to Man; May Man Prevail?; Man, Science and Society;* or *One-Dimensional Man*—books pretending to describe a "human" reality that does not include one-half the human species.

Less than a decade ago, with the rebirth of a feminist movement in this country, women students and teachers in a number of universities began to demand and set up women's studies courses—to *claim* a woman-directed education. And, despite the inevitable accusations of "unscholarly," "group therapy," "faddism," etc., despite backlash and budget cuts, women's studies are still growing, offering to more and more women a new intellectual grasp on their lives, new understanding of our history, a fresh vision of the human experience, and also a critical basis for evaluating what they hear and read in other courses, and in the society at large.

But my talk is not really about women's studies, much as I believe in their scholarly, scientific, and human necessity. While I think that any Douglass student has everything to gain by investigating and enrolling in women's studies courses, I want to suggest that there is a more essential experience that you owe yourselves, one which courses in women's studies can greatly enrich, but which finally depends on you, in all your interactions with yourself and your world. This is the experience of *taking responsibility toward yourselves.* Our upbringing as women has so often told us that this should come second to our relationships and responsibilities to other people. We have been offered ethical models of the self-denying wife and mother; intellectual models of the brilliant but slapdash dilettante who never commits herself to anything the whole way, or the intelligent woman who denies her intelligence in order to seem more "feminine," or who sits in passive silence even when she disagrees inwardly with everything that is being said around her.

Responsibility to yourself means refusing to let others do your thinking, talking, and naming for you; it means learning to respect and use your brains and instincts; hence, grappling with hard work. It means that you do not treat your body as a commodity with which to purchase superficial intimacy or economic security; for our bodies and minds are inseparable in this life, and when we allow our bodies to be treated as objects, our minds are in mortal danger. It means insisting that those to whom you give your friendship and love are able to respect your mind. It means being able to say, with Charlotte Brontë's *Jane Eyre:* "I have an inward treasure born with me, which can keep me alive if all the extraneous delights should be withheld or offered only at a price I cannot afford to give."

Responsibility to yourself means that you don't fall for shallow 8 and easy solutions—predigested books and ideas, weekend encounters guaranteed to change your life, taking "gut" courses instead of ones you know will challenge you, bluffing at school and life instead of doing solid work, marrying early as an escape from real decisions, getting pregnant as an evasion of already existing problems. It means that you refuse to sell your talents and aspirations short, simply to avoid conflict and confrontation. And this, in turn, means resisting the forces in society which say that women should be nice, play safe, have low professional expectations, drown in love and forget about work, live through others, and stay in the places assigned to us. It means that we insist on a life of meaningful work, insist that work be as meaningful as love and friendship in our lives. It means, therefore, the courage to be "different"; not to be continuously available to others when we need time for ourselves and our work; to be able to demand of other—parents, friends, roommates, teachers, lovers, husbands, children—that they respect our sense of purpose and our integrity as persons. Women everywhere are finding the courage to do this, more and more, and we are finding that courage both in our study of women in the past who possessed it, and in each other as we look to other women for comradeship, community, and challenge. The difference betwen a life lived actively, and life of passive drifting are dispersal of energies, is an immense difference. Once we begin to feel committed to our lives, responsible to ourselves, we can never again be satisfied with the old, passive way.

Now comes the second part of the contract. I believe that in a women's college you have the right to expect your faculty to take you seriously. The education of women has been a matter of debate for centuries, and old, negative attitudes about women's role, women's ability to think and take leadership, are still rife both in and outside the university. Many male professors (and I don't mean only at Douglass) still feel that teaching in a women's college is a second-rate career. Many tend to eroticize their women students—to treat them a sexual objects—instead of demanding the best of their minds. (At Yale a legal suit [*Alexander* v. *Yale*] has been brought against the university by a group of women students demanding a stated policy against sexual advances toward female students by male professors.) Many teachers, both men and women, trained in the male-centered tradition, are still handing the ideas and texts of that tradition on to students without teaching them to criticize its antiwoman attitudes, its omission of women as part of the species. Too often, all of us fail to teach the most important thing, which is that clear thinking, active discussion, and excellent writing are all necessary for intellectual freedom, and that these require *hard work*. Sometimes, perhaps in discouragement with a culture which is both antiintellectual and antiwoman, we may resign ourselves to low expectations for our students before we have given them half a chance to become more thoughtful, expressive human beings. We need to take to heart the words of Elizabeth Barrett Browning, a poet, a thinking woman, and a feminist, who wrote in 1845 of her impatience with studies which cultivate a "passive recipiency" in the mind, and asserted that "women want to be made to *think actively*: their apprehension is quicker than that of men, but their defect lies for the most part in the logical faculty and in the higher mental activities." Note that she implies a defect which can be remedied by intellectual training; *not* an inborn lack of ability.

I have said that the contract on the student's part involves that you demand to be taken seriously so that you can also go on taking yourself seriously. This means seeking out criticism, recognizing that the most affirming thing anyone can do for you is demand that you push yourself further, show you the range of what you *can* do. It means rejecting attitudes of "take-it-easy," "why-be-so-serious," "why-worry-you'll-probably-get-married-anyway." It means assuming your share of responsibility for what happens in the classroom, because that affects the quality of your daily life here. It means that the student sees herself engaged *with* her teachers in an active, ongoing struggle for a real education. But for her to do this, her teachers must be committed to the belief that women's minds and experience are intrinsically valuable and indispensable to any civilization worthy the name; that there is no more exhilarating and intellectually fertile place in the academic world today that a women's college—*if* both students and teachers in large enough numbers are trying to fulfill this contract. The contract is really a pledge of mutual seriousness about women, about language, ideas, methods, and values. It is our shared commitment toward a world in which the inborn potentialities of so many women's minds will no longer be wasted, raveled away, paralyzed, or denied.

Topics for Discussion and Writing

1. In the first paragraph Rich speaks of the "processing of human beings," which, she implies, passes for but is not education. What does she mean by "processing," and how does it become confused with education?

2. Again in paragraph 1, Rich says that university education implies an unwritten contract between students and teachers. What does the body of the essay suggest that the contract requires of both parties? Would Rich say—would *you* say—that all education implies such a contract? Or is the idea meaningful only in the context of the talk?

3. Rich was speaking to women at a women's college. To what extent, in your opinion, are her comments valid for men? Or do they now seem dated (they were delivered in 1977) for both men and women students?

4. In paragraph 9 Rich refers to sexual relationships between male professors and female students. What does she appear to assume about those relationships? (For example, who initiates them? Are they ever consensual?) What effect does she assume that they have on women's education? Do you agree?

5. Writing in the '70s, Rich notes (in paragraph 3) that "with increasing numbers of women students in nearly every branch of higher learning, we still see very few women in the upper levels of faculty and administration in most institutions." Looking at the institution you attend in the '90s, what changes do you see?
6. In paragraph 10 Rich says that taking yourself seriously means "seeking out criticism." Reread this paragraph and then examine and evaluate your own response to criticism. At this stage in your education do you agree with Rich about the effect of criticism? Why, or why not?

Patricia Nelson Limerick

Patricia Nelson Limerick was born in Banning, California, in 1951 and was educated at the Universities of California at Santa Cruz and Yale. She has taught history at Yale, Harvard, and the University of Colorado (her special interests are Western history, American Indian history, and environmental history), but she is also interested in the teaching of writing and in (as this essay reveals) students. "The Phenomenon of Phantom Students" was originally published in the Harvard Gazette, *a weekly publication for the university community.*

The Phenomenon of Phantom Students
Diagnosis and Treatment

On any number of occasions, students have told me that I am the first and only professor they have spoken to. This was, at first, flattering. Then curiosity began to replace vanity. How had conversation between teacher and student become, for many students, a novelty? These students conducted themselves as if the University were a museum: the professors on display, the students at a distance, directing any questions to the museum's guides and guards—the graduate students.

The museum model is not University policy. No "guide for instructors" tells professors to cultivate aloofness and keep students in their place. No "guide for undergraduates" tells them to speak to graduate students and only approach professors on extremely solemn and serious business.

This is not University policy, and it is by no means the experience of all Harvard students. Many confidently talk to their professors; in occasional cases, introducing a measure of shyness and humility would not be altogether unfortunate. I have no notion what the actual statistics are, but it is my impression that the disengaged are no insignificant minority. Harvard has an abundance of factors creating phantoms—my term for the radically disengaged, those staying resolutely on the academic periphery, taking large lecture classes, writing survivalist papers and exams. Phantomhood—even in its milder versions—is a significant problem and deserves the University's attention.

What creates phantoms? They tell remarkably similar stories. In   4
the basic narrative, the freshman arrives with the familiar doubt: did Admissions make a mistake? Paradoxically, the doubt coexists with vanity; high school was easy, and Harvard won't be much worse for an individual of such certified achievement. Then, in the basic phantom story, a paper comes back with a devastating grade. Since a direct nerve connects the student's prose to his self-respect and dignity, and since the Expository Writing Program stands as the Ellis Island of Harvard, many of these initial injuries involve Expos.

Crucial Fork

The crucial fork in the road comes here: the paper, more than likely produced in good faith, is a disaster; the student has been judged by standards he doesn't understand. The split outcome really cannot be overdramatized: one route goes direct to defeat, resignation, and cynicism; the other offers a struggle, rewriting, and very probably, the learning of new skills.

Some of those new skills involve writing, but for this subject, the significant skill involves conversation—direct, productive—in which the grader of the paper says precisely and clearly how the paper went wrong, and how the author can make it better. (On the instructor's side, if there is any more intellectually demanding exercise in the academic world than this, I don't know what it is.) One successful round of this kind of dialogue has, I think, an immunizing effect; on the occasion of the next disastrous paper, the precedent set makes another collapse unlikely.

For the representative phantom, though, any number of things go wrong. Even if the instructor clearly explains the paper's problems, panic keeps the phantom from hearing. Conversation with instructors becomes an unhappy experience, avoided by anyone with any sense, in which papers are picked on to no particular result.

The essential groundwork completed, the phantom can become   8
a part of a community in which groups of the radically disengaged
make their unfortunate academic status a matter of pride or, alternatively, the phantom can think of himself as uniquely and distinctively cut off from the University. In either case, the crucial transition is complete: from thinking, "I *may* be the fluke in Admissions,"
the student has moved on to certainty: "I *am* the fluke." From here
on, the prospect for positive student/faculty contact meets the un-
passable obstacle: the student's own fatalism.

I draw here a portrait of extreme cases — with academic under-
performance part of the package. There are a substantial number
of individuals doing perfectly competent academic work who still
would choose a visit to the dentist over a visit to a professor. Usually,
no particular unhappy event explains their shyness, and one could
certainly argue that their situation is not particularly unfortunate.
They are doing the reading, and writing their papers, and getting
solid educations. But they are missing something. Recently, my
course assistant arranged for me to have lunch with a recently graduated student who had been in my class; four years of a good academic performance, and she had never spoken to a professor. She
was a remarkable person, involved over a long time in volunteer
work for the homeless. I think both she and Harvard would have
profited had she been comfortable talking with professors.

Student/Faculty Contact

I address myself here to the problem of student faculty contact in
the case of students both with and without academic problems.
Reading and writing with both ease and intensity are fundamental
goals; speaking with ease and intensity should be in the package.

How are students to be persuaded to talk to professors? This
encouragement should not offer false advertising. One simply cannot say that all professors are at heart accessible and friendly. Some
of them are certifiably grumpy, and many of them are shy. They
are still worth talking to.

With a major interest in Indian/White relations, I cannot resist   12
thinking anthropologically. White people and Indian people still confront each other through a fog of stereotypes (all Indians are noble
and in touch with nature, or, alternatively, all Indians are demoralized and in touch with alcohol), and the impulse to provide a comparable analysis for student/professor relations is irresistible. Images
have equal powers in both situations.

Commonly Held Student Myths
about Professors

1a. *Professors Must Be Asked Specific, Better Yet, Bibliographic Questions.* Professors do not converse like ordinary people. To speak their language, you must address them in this fashion: "Professor X, I was very interested in your remarks about the unification of the Northwest Company and the Hudson's Bay Company in 1821, and I wondered if you might direct me to further reading." If you do not have a specific question like this, then you have no business troubling a professor.

1b. *Professors Only Like to Talk about Senior Theses.* This proposition was brought home to me at a Quincy House gathering. A number of students and I were speaking on a general, humane topic (sports?) when they discovered my hidden identity. The truth out, they began to tell me about their senior theses. The evening, I felt, became something of a busman's holiday.

2. *Professors Only Want to Talk with Other Elegant, Learned and Brilliant Conversationalists.* (Numbers 1 and 2 may appear to be contradictory, but they often coexist.) Living in the intellectual equivalent of Mt. McKinley or Mt. Whitney, professors do not like to descend the mountain to talk to the lowlanders. They are used to sophisticated, erudite conversation, in contrast to which normal speech sounds embarrassingly flat and pedestrian. Even if they seem to tolerate the speech of mortals, professors are inwardly thinking how stupid it sounds. They have, in their distinguished careers, heard nearly every insight there is. If a new idea seems to occur to a student in 1983, it can be assumed that the professor first heard that idea sometime in the 1950s. Having a memory built on the order of a steel trap, the professor does not need to hear it again.

3. *If I Speak to a Professor, He Will Probably (and Maybe Rightly)* 16 *Assume That I Am a Grade-grubbing Toady.* (The students, of course, use a more vivid term.) This belief actually concerns attitudes to other students: dependent, hypocritical drudges hang around professors, asking insincere questions, and seeking recommendation letters; students with integrity keep their distance and avoid the dishonor of visibly trying to make an impression.

Countering these three assumptions does not require a debasing of professional status; respect for achievement and authority, and excessive deference and fear are two different matters.

Number 1 and #2 are both extremely widespread, and #3 has, I think, the greatest power over phantoms. In the further reaches of phantomhood, these assumptions rest on considerable hostility toward the institution, a basic act of self-defense in which the individual reasons (if that's the word): "Harvard has ignored and injured me; well, Harvard is stupid anyway." We are dealing here, in other words, with wounded dignity, a condition not known for bringing out the finest in human behavior.

In the last eight years, I have seen many phantoms emerge from hiding; I have enormous faith in their potential for recovery. Nothing encouraged me more than the Committee on College Life meeting last spring. I had promised to bring expert witnesses—verifiable phantoms. Having made the promise, I began to regret it. If these individuals barely had the courage to talk to me, how would they face a panel of five professors, two deans and five students? Would any consent to appear? The first five I called said yes—without reluctance. At the committee, they spoke with frankness and energy. To be equally frank, that amazed me—I evidently expected that I would have to act as their interpreter. They were, instead, perfectly capable of speaking for themselves.

There is a fairly reliable personal solution to the problem of phantomhood for faculty to follow:

1. *Discover the phantoms* (midterm grade sheets locate the ones   20
with academic problems; reports from course assistants and from professorial visits to sections identify the others).

2. *Contact them.*

3. *Get an acknowledgment of the condition of phantomhood, directly and briefly.* (Don't milk it for its misery, which is often at a pretty high level.)

4. *Engage them in a specific project—ideally, rewriting a paper.* Here, the instructor is most productive when she uses her own enthusiasm for the subject to launch a discussion of the ideas in the paper, so that the student slides, without perceiving it, into what was hitherto unimaginable—"an intellectual conversation with a professor."

5. *Keep a careful eye out for achievement on the part of the student,*   24
during the conversation, and comment on it. This is only in part "encouragement"—the primary goal is to help the individual penetrate the mysterious standards of what constitutes "insight" or a "a solid point."

6. *Hold out for concrete evidence of recovery—a successfully rewritten paper, for instance.* These second drafts are almost without exception

much better papers—primarily because the student now has what was wholly lacking before—faith in a living, actual audience.

7. *Encourage a wide application of the new principles.* The student's logical next step is to say to the instructor, "I can work with you because you are different from the others." Resist this. The sports analogy is the best: you may need a coach at the start of learning a sport, but you do not need a coach at your elbow for the rest of your career in that sport. Professors, like most other individuals, like snowflakes, are all different. That, surely, is part of their charm.

Phantoms are not beyond understanding, and certainly not beyond recovery. But there is another, equally complex party to the basic transactions of student/faculty contact. We might now take up the question of the genesis of shyness, harriedness and grumpiness in professors.

How nice to lead a leisured life in a book-lined office, I used to think, chatting, reading and (if *real* work meant actually teaching classes) working only a few hours a week. Cross the line into professorhood, and the plot thickens considerably. Those few minutes a week in class rest on hours of preparation. Reading exams and papers closely eats up time. Then, of course, there is "one's own work"—research and writing for promised articles and books. Add to this, participation in professional organizations and department and University committees, and one's leisured time in the book-lined office often comes down to checking the datebook to see where one is due next. 28

That is in part why professors can seem grumpy and aloof, even when they are genuinely committed to teaching. Phantoms, and prospective phantoms, should be advised not to take personal injury when cut short by an individual who will have to stay up most of the night revising the next day's lecture and writing recommendation letters. Schedule a meeting for a time when the universe at least gives the illusion of being a bit more in the professor's control, and try not to resent any accidental rudeness.

More important, phantoms should be encouraged to use empathy in understanding the professors. Phantoms are, after all, experts in shyness; shyness, while not universal in the professorial population, is no stranger. Consider the pattern: the individual is initially drawn to the world of books and private contemplation, communicating more often through writing than through speech. How nice, the susceptible individual thinks, that there is a profession that encourages and supports this retreat to private intellectual exertion. And that promise seems to hold for the initial years of graduate school, and then, abruptly, the treachery stands exposed. One has to walk into a classroom, cause everyone else to fall silent, and become the center of attention. It is a shy person's nightmare, and individuals evolve the best mechanisms for dealing with it that they can. Once the mechanisms are in place, the individual holds on to them. It is undeniably more dignified to seem aloof and uncaring than to seem scared and shy.

I write as a reformed phantom myself—one, happily, in the category in which academic problems did not play a part. My papers carried me through college and graduate school; I was a veritable sphinx in classes. Occupying—initially to my horror—the teacher's chair, phantomhood became a luxury I could not afford.

A few years ago, when I had just started teaching, an old 32 professor of mine from Santa Cruz came to Yale for the year. "We're so fragmented at Santa Cruz," he said, "I am really looking forward to having hard-hitting intellectual conversations again."

"Hard-hitting intellectual conversations?" I didn't seem to have ever had one. It was a concept beyond the reach of an only partially recovered phantom.

Seven or eight years later, I am thoroughly addicted to the kind of conversations I thought I would never have. They provide the core of vitality for the university, the only real cement that makes such a collection of disparate individuals into a community. I want the phantoms included in the community.

Topics for Discussion and Writing

1. Limerick mentions that after receiving an essay with a "devastating grade," a student finds that "conversation with instructors becomes an unhappy experience, avoided by anyone with any sense." If on some occasion your good sense deserted you and you therefore engaged in conversation with an instructor, was the conversation profitable? Why, or why not?

2. Let's assume that you find this essay interesting, and not simply because of the subject matter. *Why* is it interesting? What are some of the rhetorical devices that the author uses to engage your attention?

3. In paragraph 4 Limerick refers to the Expository Writing Program as "the Ellis Island of Harvard." Explain the metaphor. In the same paragraph she says: "A direct nerve connects the student's prose to his self-respect." Again, explain the metaphor and then try to explain why, for most of us, it rings true.

4. In paragraph 3 Limerick mentions, but does not define or explain, something she labels "survivalist papers and exams." In a paragraph invent a definition for this term, using both Limerick's essay and your own experience as sources.
5. Without naming or in any other way clearly identifying the instructor, write an essay of 500 words in which you explain why—at least for that instructor—you are a phantom student. Or, on the other hand, write an essay explaining why you have enjoyed conversing with an instructor. Hint: a few bits of dialogue will probably be effective.
6. Write a dialogue of an imaginary conference between a composition teacher and a phantom. (Even though this is an exercise in writing pure fiction, you may use one of your own essays as a prop.)

E. B. White

E[lwyn] B[rooks] White (1899–85) wrote poetry and fiction, but he is most widely known as an essayist and as the coauthor (with William Strunk, Jr.) of Elements of Style. *After a long career at* The New Yorker *he retired to Maine, but he continued to write until the year before his death at the age of 86.*

Education

I have an increasing admiration for the teacher in the country school where we have a third-grade scholar in attendance. She not only undertakes to instruct her charges in all the subjects of the first three grades, but she manages to function quietly and effectively as a guardian of their health, their clothes, their habits, their mothers, and their snowball engagements. She has been doing this sort of Augean task for twenty years, and is both kind and wise. She cooks for the children on the stove that heats the room, and she can cool their passions or warm their soup with equal competence. She conceives their costumes, cleans up their messes, and shares their confidences. My boy already regards his teacher as his great friend, and I think tells her a great deal more than he tells us.

The shift from city school to country school was something we worried about quietly all last summer. I have always rather favored public school over private school, if only because in public school you meet a greater variety of children. This bias of mine, I suspect, is partly an attempt to justify my own past (I never knew anything but public schools) and partly an involuntary defense against getting kicked in the shins by a young ceramist on his way to the kiln. My wife was unacquainted with public schools, never having been exposed (in her early life) to anything more public than the washroom of Miss Winsor's. Regardless of our backgrounds, we both knew that the change in schools was something that concerned not us but the scholar himself. We hoped it would work out all right. In New York our son went to a medium-priced private institution with semi-progressive ideas of education, and modern plumbing. He learned fast, kept well, and we were satisfied. It was an electric, colorful, regimented existence with moments of pleasurable pause and giddy incident. The day the Christmas angel fainted and had to be carried out by one of the Wise Men was educational in the highest sense of the term. Our scholar gave imitations of it around the house for weeks afterward, and I doubt if it ever goes completely out of his mind.

His days were rich in formal experience. Wearing overalls and an old sweater (the accepted uniform of the private seminary), he sallied forth at morn accompanied by a nurse or a parent and walked (or was pulled) two blocks to a corner where the school bus made a flag stop. This flashy vehicle was as punctual as death: seeing us waiting at the cold curb, it would sweep to a halt, open its mouth, suck the boy in, and spring away with an angry growl. It was a good deal like a train picking up a bag of mail. At school the scholar was worked on for six or seven hours by half a dozen teachers and a nurse, and was revived on orange juice in mid-morning. In a cinder court he played games supervised by an athletic instructor, and in a cafeteria he ate lunch worked out by a dietitian. He soon learned to read with gratifying facility and discernment and to make Indian weapons of a semi-deadly nature. Whenever one of his classmates fell low of a fever the news was put on the wires and there were breathless phone calls to physicians, discussing periods of incubation and allied magic.

In the country all one can say is that the situation is different, and 4 somehow more casual. Dressed in corduroys, sweatshirt, and short rubber boots, and carrying a tin dinner-pail pail, our scholar departs at the crack of dawn for the village school, two and a half miles down the road, next to the cemetery. When the road is open and the car will start, he makes the journey by motor, courtesy of his old man. When the snow is deep or the motor is dead or both, he makes it on the hoof. In the afternoons he walks or hitches all or part of the way home in fair weather, gets transported in foul. The schoolhouse is a two-room frame building, bungalow type, shingles stained a burnt brown with weather-resistant stain. It has a chemical toilet in the basement and two teachers above the stairs. One takes the first three grades, the other the fourth, fifth, and sixth. They have little or no time for individual instruction, and no time at all for the esoteric. They teach what they know themselves, just as fast and as hard as they can manage. The pupils sit still at their desks in class, and do their milling around outdoors during recess.

There is no supervised play. They play cops and robbers (only they call it "Jail") and throw things at one another—snowballs in winter, rose hips in fall. It seems to satisfy them. They also construct darts, pinwheels, and "pick-up sticks" (jackstraws), and the school itself does a brisk trade in penny candy, which is for sale right in the classroom and which contains "surprises." The most highly prized surprise is a fake cigarette, made of cardboard, fiendishly lifelike.

The memory of how apprehensive we were at the beginning is still strong. The boy was nervous about the change too. The tension, on that first fair morning in September when we drove him to school, almost blew the windows out of the sedan. And when later we picked him up on the road, wandering along with his little blue lunch-pail, and got his laconic report "All right" in answer to our inquiry about how the day had gone, our relief was vast. Now, after almost a year of it, the only difference we can discover in the two school experiences is that in the country he sleeps better at night—and *that* probably is more the air than the education. When grilled on the subject of school-in-country vs. school-in-city, he replied that the chief difference is that the day seems to go so much quicker in the country. "Just like lightning," he reported.

Topics for Discussion and Writing

1. Which school, public or private, does White prefer? Since White doesn't state his preference outright, from what evidence were you able to infer it?

2. In the first half of paragraph 2 White admits to a bias in favor of public schools, and he speculates, half-seriously, about the origins of his bias. If his intention here is not simply to amuse us, what is it?

3. What is White's strongest argument in favor of the school he prefers? Where in the essay do you find it?

Toni Cade Bambara

Toni Cade Bambara, born in New York City in 1939, received her B.A. from Queens College in 1959 and her M.A. from City College in 1964. Both schools are part of the City University of New York. She has studied mime and dance, has taught at Livingston College of Rutgers University, and has worked for the New York State Department of Welfare.

The Lesson

Back in the days when everyone was old and stupid or young and foolish and me and Sugar were the only ones just right, this lady moved on our block with nappy hair and proper speech and no makeup. And quite naturally we laughed at her, laughed the way we did at the junk man who went about his business like he was some big-time president and his sorry-ass horse his secretary. And we kinda hated her too, hated the way we did the winos who cluttered up our parks and pissed on our handball walls and stank up our hallways and stairs so you couldn't half-way play hide-and-seek without a goddamn gas mask. Miss Moore was her name. The only woman on the block with no first name. And she was black as hell, cept for her feet, which were fish-white and spooky. And she was always planning these boring-ass things for us to do, us being my cousin, mostly, who lived on the block cause we all moved North the same time and to the same apartment then spread out gradual to breathe. And our parents would yank our heads into some kinda shape and crisp up our clothes so we'd be presentable for travel with Miss Moore, who always looked like she was going to church, though she never did. Which is just one of the things the grownups talked about when they talked behind her back like a dog. But when she came calling with some sachet she'd sewed up or some gingerbread she'd made or some book, why then they'd all be too embarrassed to turn her down and we'd get handed over all spruced up. She'd been to college and said it was only right that she should take responsibility for the young ones' education, and she not even related by marriage or blood. So they'd go for it. Specially Aunt Gretchen. She was the main gofer in the family. You got some ole dumb shit foolishness you want somebody to go for, you send for Aunt Gretchen. She been screwed into the go-along for so long, it's a blood-deep natural thing with her. Which is how she got saddled with me and Sugar and Junior in the first place while our mothers were in a la-de-da apartment up the block having a good ole time.

So this one day Miss Moore rounds us all up at the mailbox and it's puredee hot and she's knockin herself out about arithmetic. And school suppose to let up in summer I heard, but she don't never let up. And the starch in my pinafore scratching the shit outta me and I'm really hating this nappy-head bitch and her goddamn college degree. I'd much rather go to the pool or to the show where it's cool. So me and Sugar leaning on the mailbox being surly, which is a Miss Moore word. And Flyboy checking out what everybody brought for lunch. And Fat Butt already wasting his peanut-butter-and-jelly sandwich like the pig he is. And Junebug punchin on Q.T.'s arm for potato chips. And Rosie Giraffe shifting from one hip to the other waiting for somebody to step on her foot or ask her if she from Georgia so she can kick ass, preferably Mercedes'. And Miss Moore asking us do we know what money is, like we a bunch of retards. I mean real money, she say, like it's only poker chips or monopoly papers we lay on the grocer. So right away I'm tired of this and say so. And would much rather snatch Sugar and go to the Sunset and terrorize the West Indian kids and take their hair ribbons and their money too. And Miss Moore files that remark away for next week's lesson on brotherhood, I can tell. And finally I say we oughta get to the subway cause it's cooler and besides we might meet some cute boys. Sugar done swiped her mama's lipstick, so we ready.

So we heading down the street and she's boring us silly about what things cost and what our parents make and how much goes for rent and how money ain't divided up right in this country. And then she gets to the part about we all poor and live in the slums, which I don't feature. And I'm ready to speak on that, but she steps out in the street and hails two cabs just like that. Then she hustles half the crew in with her and hands me a five-dollar bill and tells me to calculate 10 percent tip for the driver. And we're off. Me and Sugar and Junebug and Flyboy hangin out the window and hollering to everybody, putting lipstick on each other cause Flyboy a faggot anyway, and making farts with our sweaty armpits. But I'm mostly trying to figure how to spend this money. But they all fascinated with the meter ticking and Junebug starts laying bets to how much it'll read when Flyboy can't hold his breath no more. Then Sugar lays bets as to how much it'll be when we get there. So I'm stuck. Don't nobody want to go for my plan, which is to jump out at the next light and run off to the first bar-b-que we can find. Then the driver tells us to get the hell out cause we there already. And the meter reads eighty-five cents. And I'm stalling to figure out the tip and Sugar say give him a dime. And I decide he don't need it as bad as I do, so later for him. But then he tries to take off with Junebug's foot still in the door so we talk about his mama something ferocious. Then we check out that we on Fifth Avenue and everybody dressed up in stockings. One lady in a fur coat, hot as it is. White folks crazy.

"This is the place," Miss Moore say, presenting it to us in the voice she uses at the museum. "Let's look in the windows before we go in." 4

"Can we steal?" Sugar asks very serious like she's getting the ground rules squared away before she plays. "I beg your pardon," say Miss Moore, and we fall out. So she leads us around the windows of the toy store and me and Sugar screamin, "This is mine, that's mine, I gotta have that, that was made for me, I was born for that," till Big Butt drowns us out.

"Hey, I'm goin to buy that there."

"That there? You don't even know what it is, stupid."

"I do so," he say punchin on Rosie Giraffe. "It's a microscope." 8

"Whatcha gonna do with a microscope, fool?"

"Look at things."

"Like what, Ronald?" ask Miss Moore. And Big Butt ain't got the first notion. So here go Miss Moore gabbing about the thousands of bacteria in a drop of water and the somethinorother in a speck of blood and the million and one living things in the air around us is invisible to the naked eye. And what she say that for? Junebug go to town on that "naked" and we rolling. Then Miss Moore ask what it cost. So we all jam into the window smudgin it up and the price tag say $300. So then she ask how long'd take for Big Butt and Junebug to save up their allowances. "Too long," I say. "Yeh," adds Sugar, "outgrown it by that time." And Miss Moore say no, you never outgrow learning instruments. "Why, even medical students and interns and," blah, blah, blah. And we ready to choke Big Butt for bringing it up in the first damn place.

"This here costs four hundred eighty dollars," say Rosie Giraffe. 12 So we pile up all over her to see what she pointin out. My eyes tell me it's a chunk of glass cracked with something heavy, and different-color inks dripped into the splits, then the whole thing put into a oven or something. But for $480 it don't make sense.

"That's a paperweight made of semi-precious stones fused together under tremendous pressure," she explains slowly, and her hands doing the mining and all the factory work.

"So what's a paperweight?" asks Rosie Giraffe.

"To weigh paper with, dumbbell," say Flyboy, the wise man from the East.

"Not exactly," say Miss Moore, which is what she say when you 16 warm or way off too. "It's to weigh paper down so it won't scatter and make your desk untidy." So right away me and Sugar curtsy to each other and then to Mercedes who is more the tidy type.

"We don't keep paper on top of the desk in my class," say Junebug, figuring Miss Moore crazy or lyin one.

"At home, then," she say. "Don't you have a calendar and a pencil case and a blotter and a letter-opener on your desk at home where you do your homework?" And she know damn well what our homes look like cause she nosys around in them every chance she gets.

"I don't even have a desk," say Junebug. "Do we?"

"No. And I don't get no homework neither," says Big Butt. 20

"And I don't even have a home," say Flyboy like he do at school to keep the white folks off his back and sorry for him. Send this poor kid to camp posters, is his specialty.

"I do," says Mercedes. "I have a box of stationery on my desk and a picture of my cat. My godmother bought the stationery and the desk. There's a big rose on each sheet and the envelopes smell like roses."

"Who wants to know about your smelly-ass stationery," say Rosie Giraffe fore I can get my two cents in.

"It's important to have a work area all your own so that . . ." 24

"Will you look at this sailboat, please," say Flyboy, cuttin her off and pointin to the thing like it was his. So once again we tumble all over each other to gaze at this magnificent thing in the toy store which is just big enough to maybe sail two kittens across the pond if you strap them to the posts tight. We all start reciting the price tag like we in assembly. "Hand-crafted sailboat of fiberglass at one thousand one hundred ninety-five dollars."

"Unbelievable," I hear myself say and am really stunned. I read it again for myself just in case the group recitation put me in a trance. Same thing. For some reason this pisses me off. We look at Miss Moore and she lookin at us, waiting for I dunno what.

"Who'd pay all that when you can buy a sailboat set for a quarter at Pop's, a tube of glue for a dime, and a ball of string for eight

cents? It must have a motor and a whole lot else besides," I say.
"My sailboat cost me about fifty cents."

"But will it take water?" say Mercedes with her smart ass.   28

"Took mine to Alley Pond Park once," say Flyboy. "String broke.
Lost it. Pity."

"Sailed mine in Central Park and it keeled over and sank. Had
to ask my father for another dollar."

"And you got the strap," laugh Big Butt. "The jerk didn't even
have a string on it. My old man wailed on his behind."

Little Q.T. was staring hard at the sailboat and you could see he   32
wanted it bad. But he too little and somebody'd just take it from
him. So what the hell. "This boat for kids, Miss Moore?"

"Parents silly to buy something like that just to get all broke up,"
say Rosie Giraffe.

"That much money it should last forever," I figure.

"My father'd buy it for me if I wanted it."

"Your father, my ass," say Rosie Giraffe getting a chance to   36
finally push Mercedes.

"Must be rich people shop here," say Q.T.

"You are a very bright boy," say Flyboy. "What was your first
clue?" And he rap him on the head with the back of his knuckles,
since Q.T. the only one he could get away with. Though Q.T. liable
to come up behind you years later and get his licks in when you
half expect it.

"What I want to know is," I says to Miss Moore though I never
talk to her, I wouldn't give the bitch that satisfaction, "is how much
a real boat costs? I figure a thousand'd get you a yacht any day."

"Why don't you check that out," she says, "and report back to   40
the group?" Which really pains my ass. If you gonna mess up a perfectly good swim day least you could do is have some answers. "Let's
go in," she say like she got something up her sleeve. Only she don't
lead the way. So me and Sugar turn the corner to where the entrance is, but when we get there I kinda hang back. Not that I'm
scared, what's there to be afraid of, just a toy store. But I feel funny,
shame. But what I got to be shamed about? Got as much right to
go in as anybody. But somehow I can't seem to get hold of the door,
so I step away for Sugar to lead. But she hangs back too. And I look
at her and she looks at me and this is ridiculous. I mean, damn,
I have never ever been shy about doing nothing or going nowhere.
But then Mercedes steps up and then Rosie Giraffe and Big Butt
crowd in behind and shove, and next thing we all stuffed into the
doorway with only Mercedes squeezing past us, smoothing out her

jumper and walking right down the aisle. Then the rest of us tumble in like a glued-together jigsaw done all wrong. And people lookin at us. And it's like the time me and Sugar crashed into the Catholic church on a dare. But once we got in there and everything so hushed and holy and the candles and the bowin and the handkerchiefs on all the drooping heads, I just couldn't go through with the plan. Which was for me to run up to the altar and do a tap dance while Sugar played the nose flute and messed around in the holy water. And Sugar kept givin me the elbow. Then later teased me so bad I tied her up in the shower and turned it on and locked her in. And she'd be there till this day if Aunt Gretchen hadn't finally figured I was lyin about the boarder takin a shower.

Same thing in the store. We all walkin on tiptoe and hardly touchin the games and puzzles and things. And I watched Miss Moore who is steady watchin us like she waitin for a sign. Like Mama Drewery watches the sky and sniffs the air and takes note of just how much slant is in the bird formation. Then me and Sugar bump smack into each other, so busy gazing at the toys, 'specially the sailboat. But we don't laugh and go into our fat-lady bump-stomach routine. We just stare at that price tag. Then Sugar run a finger over the whole boat. And I'm jealous and want to hit her. Maybe not her, but I sure want to punch somebody in the mouth.

"Whatcha bring us here for, Miss Moore?"

"You sound angry, Sylvia. Are you mad about something?" Givin me one of them grins like she tellin a grown-up joke that never turns out to be funny. And she's lookin very closely at me like maybe she plannin to do my portrait from memory. I'm mad, but I won't give her that satisfaction. So I slouch around the store bein very bored and say, "Let's go."

Me and Sugar at the back of the train watchin the tracks whizzin 44 by large then small then gettin gobbled up in the dark. I'm thinkin about this tricky toy I saw in the store. A clown that somersaults on a bar then does chin-ups just cause you yank lightly at his leg. Cost $35. I could see me askin my mother for a $35 birthday clown. "You wanna who that costs what?" she'd say, cocking her head to the side to get a better view of the hole in my head. Thirty-five dollars and the whole household could go visit Granddaddy Nelson in the country. Thirty-five dollars would pay for the rent and the piano bill too. Who are these people that spend that much for performing clowns and $1000 for toy sailboats? What kinda work they do and how they live and how come we ain't in on it? Where we are is who we are, Miss Moore always pointin out. But it don't necessarily have to be that way, she always adds then waits for somebody to say that poor people have to wake up and demand their share of the pie and don't none of us know what kind of pie she talkin about in the first damn place. But she ain't so smart cause I still got her four dollars from the taxi and she sure ain't gettin it. Messin up my day with this shit. Sugar nudges me in my pocket and winks.

Miss Moore lines us up in front of the mailbox where we started from, seem like years ago, and I got a headache for thinkin so hard. And we lean all over each other so we can hold up under the draggy-ass lecture she always finishes us off with at the end before we thank her for borin us to tears. But she just looks at us like she readin tea leaves. Finally she say, "Well, what do you think of F. A. O. Schwartz?"

Rosie Giraffe mumbles, "White folks crazy."

"I'd like to go there again when I get my birthday money," says Mercedes, and we shove her out the pack so she has to lean on the mailbox by herself.

"I'd like a shower. Tiring day," say Flyboy.   48

Then Sugar surprises me by sayin, "You know, Miss Moore, I don't think all of us here put together eat in a year what that sail-boat costs." And Miss Moore lights up like somebody goosed her. "And?" she say, urging Sugar on. Only I'm standin on her foot so she don't continue.

"Imagine for a minute what kind of society it is in which some people can spend on a toy what it would cost to feed a family of six or seven. What do you think?"

"I think," say Sugar pushing me off her feet like she never done before, cause I whip her ass in a minute, "that this is not much of a democracy if you ask me. Equal chance to pursue happiness means an equal crack at the dough, don't it?" Miss Moore is besides her-self and I am disgusted with Sugar's treachery. So I stand on her foot one more time to see if she'll shove me. She shuts up, and Miss Moore looks at me, sorrowfully I'm thinkin. And somethin weird is goin on, I can feel it in my chest.

"Anybody else learn anything today?" lookin dead at me. I walk   52 away and Sugar has to run to catch up and don't even seem to no-tice when I shrug her arm off my shoulder.

"Well, we got four dollars anyway," she says.

"Uh hunh."

"We could go to Hascombs and get half a chocolate layer and then go to the Sunset and still have plenty money for potato chips and ice cream sodas."

"Uh hunh."

"Race you to Hascombs," she say.

We start down the block and she gets ahead which is O.K. by me cause I'm going to the West End and then over to the Drive to think this day through. She can run if she want to and even run faster. But ain't nobody gonna beat me at nuthin.

Topics for Discussion and Writing

1. What is the point of Miss Moore's lesson? Why does Sylvia resist it?
2. Describe the relationship between Sugar and Sylvia. What is Sugar's function in the story?
3. What does the last line of the story suggest?

Wu-tsu Fa-yen

Wu-tsu Fa-yen (1025–1104) was a Chinese Zen Buddhist priest. More exactly, he was a Ch'an priest; Zen is Japanese for the Chinese Ch'an.

The practitioner of Zen (to use the more common name) seeks satori, "enlightenment" or "awakening." The awakening is from a world of blind strivings (including those of reason and of morality). The awakened being, free from a sense of the self in opposition to all other things, perceives the unity of all things. Wu-tsu belonged to the branch of Zen that uses "shock therapy, the purpose of which is to jolt the student out of his analytical and conceptual way of thinking and lead him back to his natural and spontaneous faculty" (Kenneth Ch'en, Buddhism in China [1964, rptd. 1972], p. 359).

The title of this story, from The Sayings of Goso Hōyen, is the editors'.

Zen and the Art of Burglary

If people ask me what Zen is like, I will say that it is like learning the art of burglary. The son of a burglar saw his father growing older and thought, "If he is unable to carry on his profession, who will be the breadwinner of the family, except myself? I must learn the trade." He intimated the idea to his father, who approved of it.

One night the father took the son to a big house, broke through the fence, entered the house, and, opening one of the large chests, told the son to go in and pick out the clothing. As soon as the son got into it, the father dropped the lid and securely applied the lock. The father now came out to the courtyard and loudly knocked at the door, waking up the whole family; then he quietly slipped away by the hole in the fence. The residents got excited and lighted candles, but they found that the burglar had already gone.

The son, who remained all the time securely confined in the chest, thought of his cruel father. He was greatly mortified, then a fine idea flashed upon him. He made a noise like the gnawing of a rat. The family told the maid to take a candle and examine the chest. When the lid was unlocked, out came the prisoner, who blew out the light, pushed away the maid, and fled. The people ran after him. Noticing a well by the road, he picked up a large stone and threw it into the water. The pursuers all gathered around the well trying to find the burglar drowning himself in the dark hole.

In the meantime he went safely back to his father's house. He 4 blamed his father deeply for his narrow escape. Said the father, "Be not offended, my son. Just tell me how you got out of it." When the son told him all about his adventures, the father remarked, "There you are, you have learned the art."

Topics for Discussion and Writing

1. What assumptions about knowledge did the father make? Can you think of any of your own experiences that substantiate these assumptions?
2. Is there anything you have studied or are studying to which Zen pedagogical methods would be applicable? If so, explain by setting forth a sample lesson.

7
WORK AND PLAY

Lettuce Cutters, Salinas Valley
Dorothea Lange, 1935

Canal Street, Chinatown, Manhattan, 1983
Paul Calhoun

Photo courtesy of the Center for Community Studies. In New York Chinatown History Project.

Short Views

Work and play are words used to describe the same thing under differing conditions.

Mark Twain

The Battle of Waterloo was won on the playing fields of Eton.

Attributed to the Duke of Wellington

The competitive spirit goes by many names. Most simply and directly, it is called "the work ethic." As the name implies, the work ethic holds that labor is good in itself; that a man or woman at work not only makes a contribution to his fellow man, but becomes a better person by virtue of the act of working. That work ethic is ingrained in the American character. That is why most of us consider it immoral to be lazy or slothful—even if a person is well off enough not to have to work or deliberately avoids work by going on welfare.

Richard Milhous Nixon

In the laws of political economy, the alienation of the worker from his product is expressed as follows: the more the worker produces, the less he has to consume; the more value he creates, the more valueless, the more unworthy he becomes; the better formed is his product, the more deformed becomes the worker; the more civilized his product, the more brutalized becomes the worker; the mightier the work, the more powerless the worker; the more ingenious the work, the duller becomes the worker and the more he becomes nature's bondsman.

Political economy conceals the alienation inherent in labor by avoiding any mention of the evil effects of work on those who work. Thus, whereas labor produces miracles for the rich, for the worker it produces destitution. Labor produces palaces, but for the worker, hovels. It produces beauty, but it cripples the worker. It replaces labor by machines, but how does it treat the worker? By throwing some workers back into a barbarous kind of work, and by turning the rest into machines. It produces intelligence, but for the worker, stupidity and cretinism.

Karl Marx

My young men shall never work. Men who work cannot dream, and wisdom comes in dreams.

Smohalla, of the Nez Perce

Everyone who is prosperous or successful must have dreamed of something. It is not because he is a good worker that he is prosperous, but because he dreamed.

Lost Star, of the Maricopa

The possible quantity of play depends on the possible quantity of pay.

John Ruskin

It can't be just a job. It's not worth playing just for money. It's a way of life. When we were kids there was the release in playing, the sweetness in being able to move and control your body. This is what play is. Beating somebody is secondary. When I was a kid, to really *move* was my delight. I felt released because I could move around anybody. I was free.

Eric Nesterenko, Professional Hockey Player

Winning is not the most important thing; it's everything.

Vince Lombardi

The games don't matter to me. I have no interest in the games. The only things that interested me in sports were the issues. I was interested in Muhammad Ali, in Jackie Roosevelt Robinson, in Curtis Flood. That's the kind of thing that mattered to me. Curtis Flood's assault on baseball, the reserve clause. I remember going to see Flood, who was tending bar in a place called The Rustic Inn. . . . He told me, "There's something in my heart and in my mind that says,

'No, you can't trade me. You can't sell me. This is the United States of America, and I will not be traded as a slave.' "I was fulfilled by his attitude and his behavior. That mattered to me. I was never interested in these silly games. I can't think of anything less important in life that who wins or loses a game. There are certain causes in sports that transcend sport, that have to do with constitutional law, that have to do with the nature of society.
                    Howard Cosell

Serious sport has nothing to do with fair play. It is bound up with hatred, jealousy, boastfulness, disregard of all rules and sadistic pleasure in witnessing violence: in other words, it is war minus the shooting.
                    George Orwell

The maturity of man—that means to have reacquired the seriousness that one has as a child at play.
                    Friedrich Nietzsche

The boys throw stones at the frogs in sport, but the frogs die not in sport but in earnest.
                    Bion

Bertrand Russell

Bertrand Russell (1872–1970) was educated at Trinity College, Cambridge. He published his first book, The Study of German Social Democracy, *in 1896; subsequent books on mathematics and on philosophy quickly established his international reputation. His pacifist opposition to World War I cost him his appointment at Trinity College and won him a prison sentence of six months. While serving this sentence he wrote his* Introduction to Mathematical Philosophy. *In 1940 an appointment to teach at the College of the City of New York was withdrawn because of Russell's unorthodox moral views. But he was not always treated shabbily; he won numerous awards, including (in 1950) a Nobel Prize. After World War II he devoted most of his energy to warning the world about the dangers of nuclear war.*

In reading the first sentence of the essay that we reprint, you should know that the essay comes from a book called The Conquest of Happiness, *published in 1930.*

Work

Whether work should be placed among the causes of happiness or among the causes of unhappiness may perhaps be regarded as a doubtful question. There is certainly much work which is exceedingly irksome, and an excess of work is always very painful. I think, however, that, provided work is not excessive in amount, even the dullest work is to most people less painful than idleness. There are in work all grades, from mere relief of tedium up to the profoundest delights, according to the nature of the work and the abilities of the worker. Most of the work that most people have to do is not in itself interesting, but even such work has certain great advantages. To begin with, it fills a good many hours of the day without the need of deciding what one shall do. Most people, when they are left free to fill their own time according to their own choice, are at a loss to think of anything sufficiently pleasant to be worth doing. And whatever they decide on, they are troubled by the feeling that something else would have been pleasanter. To be able to fill leisure intelligently is the last product of civilization, and at present very few people have reached this level. Moreover the exercise of choice is in itself tiresome. Except to people with unusual initiative it is positively agreeable to be told what to do at each hour of the day, provided the orders are not too unpleasant. Most of the idle rich suffer unspeakable boredom as the price of their freedom from drudgery. At times, they may find relief by hunting big game in Africa, or by flying round the world, but the number of such sensations is limited, especially after youth is past. Accordingly the more intelligent rich men work nearly as hard as if they were poor, while rich women for the most part keep themselves busy with innumerable trifles of whose earth-shaking importance they are firmly persuaded.

Work therefore is desirable, first and foremost, as a preventive of boredom, for the boredom that a man feels when he is doing necessary though uninteresting work is as nothing in comparison with the boredom that he feels when he has nothing to do with his days. With this advantage of work another is associated, namely that it makes holidays much more delicious when they come. Provided a man does not have to work so hard as to impair his vigor, he is likely to find far more zest in his free time than an idle man could possibly find.

The second advantage of most paid work and of some unpaid work is that it gives chances of success and opportunities for ambition. In most work success is measured by income, and while our capitalistic society continues, this is inevitable. It is only where the best work is concerned that this measure ceases to be the natural one to apply. The desire that men feel to increase their income is quite as much a desire for success as for the extra comforts that a higher income can procure. However dull work may be, it becomes bearable if it is a means of building up a reputation, whether in the world at large or only in one's own circle. Continuity of purpose is one of the most essential ingredients of happiness in the long run, and for most men this comes chiefly through their work. In this respect those women whose lives are occupied with housework are much less fortunate than men, or than women who work outside the home. The domesticated wife does not receive wages, has no means of bettering herself, is taken for granted by her husband (who sees practically nothing of what she does), and is valued by him not for her housework but for quite other qualities. Of course this does not apply to those women who are sufficiently well-to-do to make beautiful houses and beautiful gardens and become the envy of their neighbors; but such women are comparatively few, and for the great majority housework cannot bring as much satisfaction as work of other kinds brings to men and to professional women.

The satisfaction of killing time and of affording some outlet, 4 however modest, for ambition, belongs to most work, and is sufficient to make even a man whose work is dull happier on the average than a man who has no work at all. But when work is interesting, it is capable of giving satisfaction of a far higher order than mere relief from tedium. The kinds of work in which there is some interest may be arranged in a hierarchy. I shall begin with those which are only mildly interesting and end with those that are worthy to absorb the whole energies of a great man.

Two chief elements make work interesting; first, the exercise of skill, and second, construction.

Every man who has acquired some unusual skill enjoys exercising it until it has become a matter of course, or until he can no longer improve himself. This motive to activity begins in early childhood: a boy who can stand on his head becomes reluctant to stand on his feet. A great deal of work gives the same pleasure that is to be derived from games of skill. The work of a lawyer or a politician must contain in a more delectable form a great deal of the same pleasure that is to be derived from playing bridge. Here of course there is not only the exercise of skill but the outwitting of a skilled opponent. Even where this competitive element is absent, however, the performance of difficult feats is agreeable. A man who can do stunts in an aeroplane finds the pleasure so great that for the sake of it he is willing to risk his life. I imagine that an able surgeon, in spite of the painful circumstances in which his work is done, derives satisfaction from the exquisite precision of his operations. The same kind of pleasure, though in a less intense form, is to be derived from a great deal of work of a humbler kind. All skilled work can be pleasurable, provided the skill required is either variable or capable of indefinite improvement. If these conditions are absent, it will cease to be interesting when a man has acquired his maximum skill. A man who runs three-mile races will cease to find pleasure in this occupation when he passes the age at which he can beat his own previous record. Fortunately there is a very considerable amount of work in which new circumstances call for new skill and a man can go on improving, at any rate until he has reached middle age. In some kinds of skilled work, such as politics, for example, it seems that men are at their best between sixty and seventy, the reason being that in such occupations a wide experience of other men is essential. For this reason successful politicians are apt to be happier at the age of seventy than any other men of equal age. Their only competitors in this respect are the men who are the heads of big businesses.

There is, however, another element possessed by the best work, which is even more important as a source of happiness than is the exercise of skill. This is the element of constructiveness. In some work, though by no means in most, something is built up which remains as a monument when the work is completed. We may distinguish construction from destruction by the following criterion. In construction the initial state of affairs is comparatively haphazard, while the final state of affairs embodies a purpose: in destruction the reverse is the case; the initial state of affairs embodies a purpose, while the final state of affairs is haphazard, that is to say, all that is intended by the destroyer is to produce a state of affairs which does not embody a certain purpose. This criterion applies in the most literal and obvious case, namely the construction and destruction of buildings. In constructing a building a previously made plan is carried out, whereas in destroying it no one decides exactly how the materials are to lie when the demolition is complete. Destruction is of course necessary very often as a preliminary to subsequent construction; in that case it is part of a whole which is constructive. But not infrequently a man will engage in activities of which the purpose is destructive without regard to any construction that may come after. Frequently he will conceal this from himself by the belief that he is only sweeping away in order to build afresh, but it is generally possible to unmask this pretense, when it is a pretense, by asking him what the subsequent construction is to be. On this subject it will be found that he will speak vaguely and without enthusiasm, whereas on the preliminary destruction he has spoken precisely and with zest. This applies to not a few revolutionaries and militarists and other apostles of violence. They are actuated, usually without their own knowledge, by hatred: the destruction of what they hate is their real purpose, and they are comparatively indifferent to the question what is to come after it. Now I cannot deny that in the work of destruction as in the work of construction there may be joy. It is a fiercer joy, perhaps at moments more intense, but it is less profoundly satisfying, since the result is one in which little satisfaction is to be found. You kill your enemy, and when he is dead your occupation is gone, and the satisfaction that you derive from victory quickly fades. The work of construction, on the other hand, when completed is delightful to contemplate, and moreover is never so fully completed that there is nothing further to do about it. The most satisfactory purposes are those that lead on indefinitely from one success to another without ever coming to a dead end; and in this respect it will be found that construction is a greater source of happiness than destruction. Perhaps it would be more correct to say that those who find satisfaction in construction find in it greater satisfaction than the lovers of destruction can find in destruction, for if once you have become filled with hate you will not easily derive from construction the pleasure which another man would derive from it.

At the same time few things are so likely to cure the habit of   8 hatred as the opportunity to do constructive work of an important kind.

The satisfaction to be derived from success in a great constructive enterprise is one of the most massive that life has to offer, although unfortunately in its highest forms it is open only to men of exceptional ability. Nothing can rob a man of the happiness of successful achievement in an important piece of work, unless it be the proof that after all his work was bad. There are many forms of such satisfaction. The man who by a scheme of irrigation has caused the wilderness to blossom like the rose enjoys it in one of its most tangible forms. The creation of an organization may be a work of supreme importance. So is the work of those few statesmen who have devoted their lives to producing order out of chaos, of whom Lenin is the supreme type in our day. The most obvious examples are artists and men of science. Shakespeare says of his verse: "So long as men can breathe, or eyes can see, so long lives this." And it cannot be doubted that the thought consoled him for misfortune. In his sonnets he maintains that the thought of his friend reconciled him to life, but I cannot help suspecting that the sonnets he wrote to his friend were even more effective for this purpose than the friend himself. Great artists and great men of science do work which is in itself delightful; while they are doing it, it secures them the respect of those whose respect is worth having, which gives them the most fundamental kind of power, namely power over men's thoughts and feelings. They have also the most solid reasons for thinking well of themselves. This combination of fortunate circumstances ought, one would think, to be enough to make any man happy. Nevertheless it is not so. Michael Angelo, for example, was a profoundly unhappy man, and maintained (not, I am sure, with truth) that he would not have troubled to produce works of art if he had not had to pay the debts of his impecunious relations. The power to produce great art is very often, though by no means always, associated with a temperamental unhappiness, so great that but for the joy which the artist derives from his work, he would be driven to suicide. We cannot, therefore, maintain that even the greatest work must make a man happy; we can only maintain that it must make him less unhappy. Men of science, however, are far less often temperamentally unhappy than artists are, and in the main the men who do great work in science are happy men, whose happiness is derived primarily from their work.

One of the causes of unhappiness among intellectuals in the present day is that so many of them, especially those whose skill is literary, find no opportunity for the independent exercise of their talents, but have to hire themselves out to rich corporations directed by Philistines, who insist upon their producing what they themselves regard as pernicious nonsense. If you were to inquire among journalists in either England or America whether they believed in the policy of the newspaper for which they worked, you would find, I believe, that only a small minority do so; the rest, for the sake of a livelihood, prostitute their skill to purposes which they believe to be harmful. Such work cannot bring any real satisfaction, and in the course of reconciling himself to the doing of it, a man has to make himself so cynical that he can no longer derive whole-hearted satisfaction from anything whatever. I cannot condemn men who undertake work of this sort, since starvation is too serious an alternative, but I think that where it is possible to do work that is satisfactory to a man's constructive impulses without entirely starving, he will be well advised from the point of view of his own happiness if he chooses it in preference to work much more highly paid but not seeming to him worth doing on its own account. Without self-respect genuine happiness is scarcely possible. And the man who is ashamed of his work can hardly achieve self-respect.

The satisfaction of constructive work, though it may, as things are, be the privilege of a minority, can nevertheless be the privilege of a quite large minority. Any man who is his own master in his work can feel it; so can any man whose work appears to him useful and requires considerable skill. The production of satisfactory children is a difficult constructive work capable of affording profound satisfaction. Any woman who has achieved this can feel that as a result of her labor the world contains something of value which it would not otherwise contain.

Human beings differ profoundly in regard to the tendency to 12 regard their lives as a whole. To some men it is natural to do so, and essential to happiness to be able to do so with some satisfaction. To others life is a series of detached incidents without directed movement and without unity. I think the former sort are more likely to achieve happiness than the latter, since they will gradually build up those circumstances from which they can derive contentment and self-respect, whereas the others will be blown about by the winds of circumstances now this way, now that, without ever arriving at any haven. The habit of viewing life as a whole is an essential part both of wisdom and of true morality, and is one of the things which ought to be encouraged in education. Consistent purpose is not enough to make life happy, but it is an almost indispensable condition of a happy life. And consistent purpose embodies itself mainly in work.

Topics for Discussion and Writing

1. Russell says (paragraph 3): "The desire that men feel to increase their income is quite as much a desire for success as for the extra comforts that a higher income can procure." In its context, what does "success" mean? In your experience, do Russell's words ring true? Why, or why not?

2. In paragraphs 7–11 Russell develops a contrast between what he calls "destructive" and "constructive" work. Is the contrast clarified by the examples he offers? What examples from your own experience or knowledge can you add?

3. In paragraph 10 Russell speaks of workers who "prostitute their skills to purposes which they believe to be harmful." What work does he use as an example here? What other examples can you offer? Imagine yourself doing work that you do not respect or that you even find "harmful." Then imagine being offered work you do respect but at a much lower salary. How helpful would you find Russell's advice? What would you do? (Specific examples of work that you respect and work that you don't respect will help you to form a clear idea of the choice and a clear argument to support it.)

4. What new point does Russell introduce in his last paragraph? How well does this last paragraph work as a conclusion?

5. Russell is generally admired for his exceptionally clear prose. List some of the devices that make for clarity in this essay.

6. Through most of his essay, Russell writes as if only men were engaged in work. What references to women working do you find? From these references and from the predominant references to men, would you describe Russell as sexist? Why or why not?

7. Compare Russell with Steinem (page 334) on the value of work.

W. H. Auden

W[ystan] H[ugh] Auden (1907–73) was born and educated in England. In 1939 he came to the United States and he became an American citizen, but in 1972 he returned to England to live. Although Auden established his reputation chiefly with his poetry, he also wrote plays, libretti, and essays, all of high quality.

One of Auden's most unusual books is A Certain World: A Commonplace Book. *It is an anthology of some of his favorite passages from other people's books, along with brief reflections on his reading. The passage we print here begins with a reference to Hannah Arendt's* The Human Condition.

Work, Labor, and Play

So far as I know, Miss Hannah Arendt was the first person to define the essential difference between work and labor. To be happy, a man must feel, firstly, free and, secondly, important. He cannot be really happy if he is compelled by society to do what he does not enjoy doing, or if what he enjoys doing is ignored by society as of no value or importance. In a society where slavery in the strict sense has been abolished, the sign that what a man does is of social value is that he is paid money to do it, but a laborer to-day can rightly be called a wage slave. A man is a laborer if the job society offers him is of no interest to himself but he is compelled to take it by the necessity of earning a living and supporting his family.

The antithesis to labor is play. When we play a game, we enjoy what we are doing, otherwise we should not play it, but it is a purely private activity; society could not care less whether we play it or not.

Between labor and play stands work. A man is a worker if he is personally interested in the job which society pays him to do; what from the point of view of society is necessary labor is from his own point of view voluntary play. Whether a job is to be classified as labor or work depends, not on the job itself, but on the tastes of the individual who undertakes it. The difference does not, for example, coincide with the difference between a manual and a mental job; a gardener or a cobbler may be a worker, a bank clerk a laborer. Which a man is can be seen from his attitude toward leisure. To a worker, leisure means simply the hours he needs to relax and rest in order to work efficiently. He is therefore more likely to take too little leisure than too much; workers die of coronaries and forget their wives' birthdays. To the laborer, on the other hand, leisure means freedom from compulsion, so that it is natural for him to imagine that the fewer hours he has to spend laboring, and the more hours he is free to play, the better.

What percentage of the population in a modern technological 4 society are, like myself, in the fortunate position of being workers? At a guess I would say sixteen per cent, and I do not think that figure is likely to get bigger in the future.

Technology and the division of labor have done two things: by eliminating in many fields the need for special strength or skill; they have made a very large number of paid occupations which formerly were enjoyable work into boring labor, and by increasing productivity they have reduced the number of necessary laboring hours. It is already possible to imagine a society in which the majority of the population, that is to say, its laborers, will have almost as much leisure as in earlier times was enjoyed by the aristocracy. When one recalls how aristocracies in the past actually behaved, the prospect is not cheerful. Indeed, the problem of dealing with boredom may be even more difficult for such a future mass society than it was for aristocracies. The latter, for example, ritualized their time; there was a season to shoot grouse, a season to spend in town, etc. The masses are more likely to replace an unchanging ritual by fashion which it will be in the economic interest of certain people to change as often as possible. Again, the masses cannot go in for hunting, for very soon there would be no animals left to hunt. For other aristocratic amusements like gambling, dueling, and warfare, it may be only too easy to find equivalents in dangerous driving, drug-taking, and senseless acts of violence. Workers seldom commit acts of violence, because they can put their aggression into their work, be it physical like the work of a smith, or mental like the work of a scientist or an artist. The role of aggression in mental work is aptly expressed by the phrase "getting one's teeth into a problem."

Topics for Discussion and Writing

1. Some readers have had trouble following Auden in his first three paragraphs, although by the end of the third paragraph the difficulties have disappeared. Can you summarize the first paragraph in a sentence? If you think that the development of the idea in these first three paragraphs could be clearer, insert the necessary phrases or sentences, or with arrows indicate the places to which sentences should be moved.
2. Compare Auden with Russell (page 295) on the relationship between work and happiness.

Malcolm X

Malcolm X, born Malcolm Little in Nebraska in 1925, was the son of a Baptist minister. He completed the eighth grade, but then he got into trouble and was sent to a reformatory. After his release he became a thief, dope peddler, and pimp. In 1944 he was sent to jail, where he spent six-and-a-half years. During his years in jail he became a convert to the Black Muslim faith. Paroled in 1950, he served as a minister and founded Muslim temples throughout the United States. In 1964, however, he broke with Elijah Muhammad, leader of the Black Muslims and a powerful advocate of separation of whites and blacks. Malcolm X formed a new group, the Organization of Afro-American Unity, but a year later he was assassinated in New York. His Autobiography, *written with Alex Haley, was published in 1964. Haley (1921–92) is also the author of* Roots, *a study tracing a black family back through seven generations.*

"The Shoeshine Boy" (editors' title) is from The Autobiography of Malcolm X, *chapter 3.*

The Shoeshine Boy

When I got home, Ella said there had been a telephone call from somebody named Shorty. He had left a message that over at the Roseland State Ballroom, the shoeshine boy was quitting that night, and Shorty had told him to hold the job for me.

"Malcolm, you haven't had any experience shining shoes," Ella said. Her expression and tone of voice told me she wasn't happy about my taking that job. I didn't particularly care, because I was already speechless thinking about being somewhere close to the greatest bands in the world. I didn't even wait to eat any dinner.

The ballroom was all lighted when I got there. A man at the front door was letting in members of Benny Goodman's band. I told him I wanted to see the shoeshine boy, Freddie.

"You're going to be the new one?" he asked. I said I thought I 4 was, and he laughed, "Well, maybe you'll hit the numbers and get a Cadillac, too." He told me that I'd find Freddie upstairs in the men's room on the second floor.

But downstairs before I went up, I stepped over and snatched a glimpse inside the ballroom. I just couldn't believe the size of that waxed floor! At the far end, under the soft, rose-colored lights, was the bandstand with the Benny Goodman musicians moving around, laughing and talking, arranging their horns and stands.

A wiry, brown-skinned, conked fellow upstairs in the men's room greeted me. "You Shorty's homeboy?" I said I was, and he said he was Freddie. "Good old boy," he said. "He called me, he just heard I hit the big number, and he figured right I'd be quitting." I told Freddie what the man at the front door had said about a Cadillac. He laughed and said, "Burns them white cats up when you get yourself something. Yeah, I told them I was going to get me one—just to bug them."

Freddie then said for me to pay close attention, that he was going to be busy and for me to watch but not get in the way, and he'd try to get me ready to take over at the next dance, a couple of nights later.

As Freddie busied himself setting up the shoeshine stand, he 8 told me, "Get here early . . . your shoeshine rags and brushes by this footstand . . . your polish bottles, paste wax, suede brushes over here . . . everything in place, you get rushed, you never need to waste motion . . ."

While you shined shoes, I learned, you also kept watch on customers inside, leaving the urinals. You darted over and offered a
small white hand towel. "A lot of cats who ain't planning to wash
their hands, sometimes you can run up with a towel and shame
them. Your towels are really your best hustle in here. Cost you a
penny apiece to launder—you always get at least a nickel tip."

The shoeshine customers, and any from the inside rest room
who took a towel, you whiskbroomed a couple of licks. "A nickel
or a dime tip, just give 'em that," Freddie said. "But for two bits,
Uncle Tom a little—white cats especially like that. I've had them to
come back two, three times a dance."

From down below, the sound of the music had begun floating
up. I guess I stood transfixed. "You never seen a big dance?" asked
Freddie. "Run on awhile, and watch."

There were a few couples already dancing under the rose-   12
covered lights. But even more exciting to me was the crowd throng-
ing in. The most glamorous-looking white women I'd ever
seen—young ones, old ones, white cats buying tickets at the window, sticking big wads of green bills back into their pockets, checking the women's coats, and taking their arms and squiring them
inside.

Freddie had some early customers when I got back upstairs. Between the shoeshine stand and thrusting towels to me just as they
approached the wash basin, Freddie seemed to be doing four things
at once. "Here, you can take over the whiskbroom," he said, "just
two or three licks—but let 'em feel it."

When things slowed a little, he said, "You ain't seen nothing
tonight. You wait until you see a spooks' dance! Man, our own people carry *on!*" Whenever he had a moment, he kept schooling me.
"Shoelaces, this drawer here. You just starting out, I'm going to
make these to you as a present. Buy them for a nickel a pair, tell
cats they need laces if they do, and charge two bits."

Every Benny Goodman record I'd ever heard in my life, it
seemed, was filtering faintly into where we were. During another
customer lull, Freddie let me slip back outside again to listen. Peggy
Lee was at the mike singing. Beautiful! She had just joined the band
and she was from North Dakota and had been singing with a group
in Chicago when Mrs. Benny Goodman discovered her, we had
heard some customers say. She finished the song and the crowd
burst into applause. She was a big hit.

"It knocked me out, too, when I first broke in here," Freddie   16
said, grinning, when I went back in there. "But, look, you ever

shined any shoes?" He laughed when I said I hadn't, excepting my own. "Well, let's get to work. I never had neither." Freddie got on the stand and went to work on his own shoes. Brush, liquid polish, brush, paste wax, shine rag, lacquer sole dressing . . . step by step, Freddie showed me what to do.

"But you got to get a whole lot faster. You can't waste time!" Freddie showed me how fast on my own shoes. Then, because business was tapering off, he had time to give me a demonstration of how to make the shine rag pop like a firecracker. "Dig the action?" he asked. He did it in slow motion. I got down and tried it on his shoes. I had the principle of it. "Just got to do it faster," Freddie said. "It's a jive noise, that's all. Cats tip better, they figure you're knocking yourself out!"

Topics for Discussion and Writing

1. In this selection Malcolm X is more concerned with Benny Goodman than with learning about shining shoes. Freddie is concerned with teaching Malcolm the trade. What are we concerned with in this selection?
2. How would you characterize Freddie's attitude toward his job? Compare it with Maggie Holmes's attitude (pages 326–33) toward her job.
3. In paragraph 17 Freddie demonstrates a "jive noise." Using evidence from this selection, the library, mother wit, or what you will, define "jive."
4. On what date did Malcolm begin his apprenticeship as a shoeshine boy? How did you arrive at that date?

Studs Terkel

Studs Terkel was born Louis Terkel in New York City in 1912. He was brought up in Chicago and graduated from the University of Chicago. Terkel has been an actor, playwright, columnist, and disc jockey, but he is best known as the man who makes books out of tape recordings of people he gets to talk. Among these oral histories are Division Street: America *(1966),* Hard Times *(1970), and* Working *(1974).*

"Three Workers" (editors' title) is from the last of these books.

Three Workers

I. Terry Mason, Airline Stewardess

She has been an airline stewardess for six years. She is twenty-six-years old, recently married. "The majority of airline stewardesses are from small towns. I myself am from Nebraska. It's supposed to be one of the nicest professions for a woman—if she can't be a model or in the movies. All the great benefits: flying around the world, meeting all those people. It is a nice status symbol.

"I have five older sisters and they were all married before they were twenty. The minute they got out of high school, they would end up getting married. That was the thing everybody did, was get married. When I told my parents I was going to the airlines, they got excited. They were so happy that one of the girls could go out and see the world and spend some time being single. I didn't get married until I was almost twenty-five. My mother especially thought it would be great that I could have the ambition, the nerve to go to the big city on my own and try to accomplish being a stewardess."

When people ask you what you're doing and you say stewardess, you're really proud, you think it's great. It's like a stepping stone. The first two months I started flying I had already been to London, Paris, and Rome. And me from Broken Bow, Nebraska. But after you start working, it's not as glamorous as you thought it was going to be.

They like girls that have a nice personality and that are pleasant 4 to look at. If a woman has a problem with blemishes, they take her off. Until the appearance counselor thinks she's ready to go back on. One day this girl showed up, she had a very slight black eye. They took her off. Little things like that.

We had to go to stew school for five weeks. We'd go through a whole week of makeup and poise. I didn't like this. They make you feel like you've never been out in public. They showed you how to smoke a cigarette, when to smoke a cigarette, how to look at a man's eyes. Our teacher, she had this idea we had to be sexy. One day in class she was showing us how to accept a light for a cigarette from a man and never blow it out. When he lights it, just look in his eyes. It was really funny, all the girls laughed.

It's never proper for a woman to light her own cigarette. You hold it up and of course you're out with a guy who knows the right way to light the cigarette. You look into their eyes as they're lighting your cigarette and you're cupping his hand, but holding it just very light, so that he can feel your touch and your warmth. (Laughs.) You do not blow the match out. It used to be really great for a woman to blow the match out when she looked in his eyes, but she said now the man blows the match out.

The idea is not to be too obvious about it. They don't want you to look too forward. That's the whole thing, being a lady but still giving out that womanly appeal, like the body movement and the lips and the eyes. The guy's supposed to look in your eyes. You could be a real mean woman. You're a lady and doing all these evil things with your eyes.

She did try to promote people smoking. She said smoking can be   8 part of your conversation. If you don't know what to say, you can always pull out a cigarette. She says it makes you more comfortable. I started smoking when I was on the airlines.

Our airline picks the girl-next-door type. At one time they wouldn't let us wear false eyelashes and false fingernails. Now it's required that you wear false eyelashes, and if you do not have the right length nails, you wear false nails. Everything is supposed to be becoming to the passenger.

That's the whole thing: meeting all these great men that either have great business backgrounds or are good looking or different. You do meet a lot of movie stars and a lot of political people, but you don't get to really visit with them that much. You never really get to go out with these men. Stewardesses are impressed only by name people. But a normal millionaire that you don't know you're not impressed about. The only thing that really thrills a stewardess is a passenger like Kennedy or movie stars or somebody political. Celebrities.

I think our average age is twenty-six. But our supervisors tell us what kind of make-up to wear, what kind of lipstick to wear, if our hair is not the right style for us, if we're not smiling enough. They even tell us how to act when you're on a pass. Like last night I met my husband. I was in plain clothes. I wanted to kiss him. But I'm not supposed to kiss anybody at the terminal. You're not supposed to walk off with a passenger, hand in hand. After you get out of the terminal, that's all yours.

The majority of passengers do make passes. The ones that do   12 make passes are married and are business people. When I tell them I'm married, they say, "I'm married and you're married and you're away from home and so am I and nobody's gonna find out." The majority of those who make passes at you, you wouldn't accept a date if they were friends of yours at home.

After I was a stewardess for a year, and I was single, I came down to the near North Side of Chicago, which is the swinging place for singles. Stewardess, that was a dirty name. In a big city, it's an easy woman. I didn't like this at all. All these books—*Coffee, Tea and Me.*

I lived in an apartment complex where the majority there were stewardesses.[1] The other women were secretaries and teachers. They would go to our parties and they would end up being among the worst. They never had stories about these secretaries and nurses, but they sure had good ones about stewardesses.

I meet a lot of other wives or single women. The first minute they start talking to me, they're really cold. They think the majority of stewardesses are snobs or they may be jealous. These women think we have a great time, that we are playgirls, that we have the advantage to go out with every type of man we want. So when they first meet us, they really turn off on us.

When you first start flying, the majority of girls do live in apartment complexes by the airport. The men they meet are airport employees: ramp rats, cleaning airplanes and things like that, mechanics, and young pilots, not married, ones just coming in fresh.

After a year we get tired of that, so we move into the city to get involved with men that are usually young executives, like at Xerox or something. Young businessmen in the early thirties and late twenties, they really think stewardesses are the gals to go out with if they want to get so far. They wear their hats and their suits and in the winter their black gloves. The women are getting older, they're getting twenty-four, twenty-five. They get involved with bartenders too. Stewardesses and bartenders are a pair. (Laughs.)

One time I went down into the area of swinging bars with two other girls. We just didn't want anybody to know that we were stewardesses, so we had this story made up that we were going to a women's college in Colorado. That went over. We had people that were talking to us, being nice to us, being polite. Down there, they wouldn't even be polite. They'd buy you drinks but then they'd steal your stool if you got up to go to the restroom. But when they knew you weren't stewardesses, just young ladies that were going to a women's college, they were really nice to us.

They say you can spot a stewardess by the way she wears her makeup. At that time we all had short hair and everybody had it cut in stew school exactly alike. If there's two blondes they have their hair cut very short, wearing the same shade of makeup, and they get into uniform, people say, "Oh, you look like sisters." Wonder why? (Laughs.)

[1] "In New York, stewardesses live five or six girls to one apartment. They think they can get by because they're in and out so much. But there's gonna be a few nights they're all gonna be home at once and a couple of 'em will have to sleep on the floor."

The majority of us were against it because they wouldn't let you 20 say how *you'd* like your hair cut, they wouldn't let you have your own personality, *your* makeup, *your* clothes. They'd tell you what length skirts to wear. At one time they told us we couldn't wear anything one inch above the knees. And no pants at that time. It's different now.

Wigs used to be forbidden. Now it's the style. Now it's permissible for nice women to wear wigs, eyelashes, and false fingernails. Before it was the harder looking women that wore them. Women showing up in pants, it wasn't ladylike. Hot pants are in now. Most airlines change styles every year.

She describes stewardess schools in the past as being like college dorms: it was forbidden to go out during the week; signing in and out on Friday and Saturday nights. "They've cut down stewardess school quite a bit. Cut down on how-to-serve meal classes and paperwork. A lot of girls get on aircraft these days and don't know where a magazine is, where the tray tables are for passengers. . . . Every day we used to have an examination. If you missed over two questions, that was a failure. They'd ask us ten questions. If you failed two tests out of the whole five weeks, you would have to leave. Now they don't have any exams at all. Usually we get a raise every year. We haven't been getting that lately."

We have long duty hours. We can be on duty for thirteen hours. But we're not supposed to fly over eight hours. This is in a twenty-four-hour period. During the eight hours, you could be flying from Chicago to Flint, to Moline, short runs. You stop twenty minutes. So you get to New York finally, after five stops, let's say. You have an hour on your own. But you have to be on the plane thirty minutes before departure time. How many restaurants can serve you food in thirty minutes? So you've gone thirteen hours, off and on duty, having half-hours and no time to eat. This is the normal thing. If we have only thirty minutes and we don't have time to eat, it's our hard luck.

Pilots have the same thing too. They end up grabbing a sand- 24 wich and eating in the cockpit. When I first started flying we were not supposed to eat at all on the aircraft, even though there was an extra meal left over. Now we can eat in the buffet. We have to stand there with all those dirty dishes and eat our meals — if there's one left over. We cannot eat in the public eye. We cannot bring it out if there's an extra seat. You can smoke in the cockpit, in the restrooms, but not in the public's eye.

"We have a union. It's a division of the pilot's union. It helps us out on duty time and working privileges. It makes sure that if we're in Cleveland and stuck because of weather and thirteen hours have gone by, we can go to bed. Before we had a union the stew office would call and say, 'You're working another seven.' I worked one time thirty-six hours straight."

The other day I had fifty-five minutes to serve 101 coach passengers, a cocktail and full-meal service. You do it fast and terrible. You're very rude. You don't mean to be rude, you just don't have time to answer questions. You smile and you just ignore it. You get three drink orders in a hurry. There's been many times when you miss the glass, pouring, and you pour it in the man's lap. You just don't say I'm sorry. You give him a cloth and you keep going. That's the bad part of the job.

Sometimes I get tired of working first class. These people think they're great, paying for more, and want more. Also I get tired of coach passengers asking for something that he thinks he's a first-class passenger. We get this attitude of difference from our airlines. They're just dividing the class of people. If we're on a first-class pass, the women are to wear a dress or a nice pants suit that has a matching jacket, and the men are to dress with suit jacket and tie and white shirt. And yet so many types of first-class passengers: some have grubby clothes, jeans and moccasins and everything. They can afford to dress the way they feel. . . .

If I want to fly first class, I pay the five dollars difference. I like the idea of getting free drinks, free champagne, free wine. In a coach, you don't. A coach passenger might say, "Could I have a pillow?" So you give him a pillow. Then he'll say, "Could you bring me a glass of water?" A step behind him there's the water fountain. In first class, if the guy says, "I want a glass of water," even if the water fountain is right by his arm, you'd bring it for him. We give him all this extra because he's first class. Which isn't fair. . . .

When you're in a coach, you feel like there's just heads and heads and heads of people. That's all you can see. In first class, being less people, you're more relaxed, you have more time. When you get on a 727, we have one coatroom. Our airline tells us you hang up first class coats only. When a coach passenger says, "Could you hang up my coat?" most of the time I'll hang it up. Why should I hang up first class and not coach?

One girl is for first class only and there's two girls for coach. The senior girl will be first class. That first-class girl gets used to working first class. If she happens to walk through the coach, if someone asks her for something, she'll make the other girls do it. The first stew always stays at the door and welcomes everybody aboard and says good-by to everybody when they leave. That's why a lot of girls don't like to be first class.

There's an old story on the airline. The stewardess asks if he'd like something to drink, him and his wife. He says, "I'd like a martini." The stewardess asks the wife, "Would you like a drink?" She doesn't say anything, and the husband says, "I'm sorry, she's not used to talking to the help." (Laughs.) When I started flying, that was the first story I heard.

I've never had the nerve to speak up to anybody that's pinched me or said something dirty. Because I've always been afraid of these onion letters. These are bad letters. If you get a certain amount of bad letters, you're fired. When you get a bad letter you have to go in and talk to the supervisor. Other girls now, there are many of 'em that are coming around and telling them what they feel. The passenger reacts: She's telling me off! He doesn't believe it. Sometimes the passenger needs it. 32

One guy got his steak and he said, "This is too medium, I want mine rarer." The girl said, "I'm sorry, I don't cook the food, it's precooked." He picked up the meal and threw it on the floor. She says, "If you don't pick the meal up right now, I'll make sure the crew members come back here and make you pick it up." (With awe) She's talking right back at him and loud, right in front of everybody. He really didn't think she would yell at him. Man, he picked up the meal. . . . The younger girls don't take that guff any more, like we used to. When the passenger is giving you a bad time, you talk back to him.

It's always: the passenger is right. When a passenger says something mean, we're supposed to smile and say, "I understand." We're supposed to *really* smile because stewardesses' supervisors have been getting reports that the girls have been back-talking passengers. Even when they pinch us or say dirty things, we're supposed to smile at them. That's one thing they taught us at stew school. Like he's rubbing your body somewhere, you're supposed to just put his hand down and not say anything and smile at him. That's the main thing, smile.

When I first went to class, they told me I had a crooked smile. She showed me how to smile. She said, "Kinda press a little smile on"—which I did. "Oh, that's great," she said, "that's a *good* smile."

But I couldn't do it. I didn't feel like I was doing it on my own. Even if we're sad, we're supposed to have a smile on our face.

I came in after a flight one day, my grandfather had died. 36 Usually they call you up or meet you at the flight and say, "We have some bad news for you." I pick up this piece of paper in my mailbox and it says, "Mother called in. Your grandfather died today." It was written like, say, two cups of sugar. Was I mad! They wouldn't give me time off for the funeral. You can only have time off for your parents or somebody you have lived with. I have never lived with my grandparents. I went anyway.

A lot of our girls are teachers, nurses, everything. They do this part-time, 'cause you have enough time off for another kind of job. I personally work for conventions. I work electronic and auto shows. Companies hire me to stay in their booth and talk about products. I have this speech to tell. At others, all I do is pass out matches or candy. Nowadays every booth has a young girl in it.

People just love to drink on airplanes. They feel adventurous. So you're serving drinks and meals and there's very few times that you can sit down. If she does sit down, she's forgotten how to sit down and talk to passengers. I used to play bridge with passengers. But that doesn't happen any more. We're not supposed to be sitting down, or have a magazine or read a newspaper. If it's a flight from Boston to Los Angeles, you're supposed to have a half an hour talking to passengers. But the only time we can sit down is when we go to the cockpit. You're not supposed to spend any more than five minutes up there for a cigarette.

We could be sitting down on our jump seat and if you had a supervisor on board, she would write you up—for not mixing with the crowd. We're supposed to be told when she walks on board. Many times you don't know. They do have personnel that ride the flights that don't give their names—checking, and they don't tell you about it. Sometimes a girl gets caught smoking in the cabin. Say it's a long flight, maybe a night flight. You're playing cards with a passenger and you say, "Would it bother you if I smoke?" And he says no. She would write you up and get you fired for smoking in the airplane.

They have a limit on how far you can mix. They want you to be 40 sociable, but if he offers you a cigarette, not to take it. When you're outside, they encourage you to take cigarettes.

You give your time to everybody, you share it, not too much with one passenger. Everybody else may be snoring away and there's three guys, maybe military, and they're awake 'cause they're going home and excited. So you're playing cards with 'em. If you have a supervisor on, that would be a no-no. They call a lot of things no-no's.

They call us professional people but they talk to us as very young, childishly. They check us all the time on appearance. They check our weight every month. Even though you've been flying twenty years, they check you and say that's a no-no. If you're not spreading yourself around passengers enough, that's a no-no. Not hanging up first-class passenger's coats, that's a no-no, even though there's no room in the coatroom. You're supposed to somehow make room. If you're a pound over, they can take you off flight until you get under.

Accidents? I've never yet been so scared that I didn't want to get in the airplane. But there've been times at take-offs, there's been something funny. Here I am thinking, What if I die today? I've got too much to do. I can't die today. I use it as a joke.

I've had emergencies where I've had to evacuate the aircraft. 44 I was coming back from Las Vegas and being a lively steward-ess I stayed up all night, gambled. We had a load full of passengers. The captain tells me we're going to have an emergency landing in Chicago because we lost a pin out of the nose gear. When we land, the nose gear is gonna collapse. He wants me to prepare the whole cabin for the landing, but not for two more hours. And not to tell the other stewardesses, because they were new girls and would get all excited. So I had to keep this in me for two more hours, wondering, Am I gonna die today? And this is Easter Sun-day. And I was serving the passengers drinks and food and this guy got mad at me because his omelet was too cold. And I was gonna say, "You just wait, buddy, you're not gonna worry about that omelet." But I was nice about it, because I didn't want to have trouble with a passenger, especially when I have to prepare him for an emergency.

I told the passengers over the intercom: "The captain says it's just a precaution, there's nothing to worry about." I'm just gonna explain how to get out of the airplane fast, how to be in a braced position. They can't wear glasses or high heels, purses, things out of aisles, under the seats. And make sure everybody's pretty quiet. We had a blind woman on with a dog. We had to get people to help her off and all this stuff.

They were fantastic. Nobody screamed, cried, or hollered. When we got on the ground, everything was fine. The captain landed

perfect. But there was a little jolt, and the passengers started screaming and hollering: They held it all back and all of a sudden we got
on the ground, blah.

I was great. (Laughs.) That's what was funny. I thought, I have
a husband now. I don't know how he would take it, my dying on
an airplane. So I thought, I can't die. When I got on the intercom,
I was so calm. Also we're supposed to keep a smile on our face.
Even during an emergency, you're supposed to walk through the
cabin and make everybody feel comfortable with a smile. When
you're on the jump seat everybody's looking at you. You're supposed to sit there, holding your ankles, in a position to get out of
that airplane fast with a big fat smile on your face.

Doctors tell stewardesses two bad things about them. They're   48
gonna get wrinkles all over their face because they smile with their
mouth and their eyes. And also with the pressurization on the airplane, we're not supposed to get up while we're climbing because
it causes varicose veins in our legs. So they say being a stewardess
ruins your looks.

A lot of stewardesses wanted to be models. The Tanya girl used
to be a stewardess on our airline. A stewardess is what they could
get and a model is what they couldn't get. They weren't the type
of person, they weren't that beautiful, they weren't that thin. So
their second choice would be stewardess.

What did you want to be? I wanted to get out of Broken Bow, Nebraska.
(Laughs.)

POSTSCRIPT: *"Everytime I go home, they all meet me at the airplane. Not
one of my sisters has been on an airplane. All their children think that Terry
is just fantastic, because their mom and dad—my sisters and their
husbands—feel so stupid. 'Look at us. I wish I could have done that.' I know
they feel bad, that they never had the chance. But they're happy I can come
home and tell them about things. I send them things from Europe. They
get to tell all their friends that their sister's a stewardess. They get real
excited about that. The first thing they come out and say, 'One of my sisters is a stewardess.'*

"My father got a promotion with his company and they wrote   52
*in their business news that he had a family of seven, six girls and a boy,
and one girl is a stewardess in Chicago. And went on to say what I did,
and didn't say a word about anything else."*[2]

---

[2] Questions on this selection appear on page 333.

II. Roberta Victor, Hooker

She had been a prostitute, starting at the age of fifteen. During the first five or six years, she worked as a high-priced call girl in Manhattan. Later she was a streetwalker. . . .

You never used your own name in hustling. I used a different name practically every week. If you got busted, it was more difficult for them to find out who you really were. The role one plays when hustling had nothing to do with who you are. It's only fitting and proper you take another name.

There were certain names that were in great demand. Every second hustler had the name Kim or Tracy or Stacy and a couple others that were in vogue. These were all young women from seventeen to twenty-five, and we picked these very non-ethnic-oriented WASP names, rich names.

A hustler is any woman in American society. I was the kind of hustler who received money for favors granted rather than the type of hustler who signs a lifetime contract for her trick. Or the kind of hustler who carefully reads women's magazines and learns what it is proper to give for each date, depending on how much money her date or trick spends on her.

The favors I granted were not always sexual. When I was a call girl, men were not paying for sex. They were paying for something else. They were either paying to act out a fantasy or they were paying for companionship or they were paying to be seen with a well-dressed young woman. Or they were paying for somebody to listen to them. They were paying for a *lot* of things. Some men were paying for sex that *they* felt was deviant. They were paying so that nobody would accuse them of being perverted or dirty or nasty. A large proportion of these guys asked things that were not at all deviant. Many of them wanted oral sex. They felt they couldn't ask their wives or girl friends because they'd be repulsed. Many of them wanted somebody to talk dirty to them. Every good call girl in New York used to share her book and we all knew the same tricks.

We know a guy who used to lie in a coffin in the middle of his bedroom and he would see the girl only once. He got his kicks when the door would be open, the lights would be out, and there would be candles in the living room, and all you could see was his coffin on wheels. As you walked into the living room, he'd suddenly sit up. Of course, you screamed. He got his kicks when you screamed.

Or the guy who set a table like the Last Supper and sat in a robe and sandals and wanted you to play Mary Magdalene. (Laughs.)

I was about fifteen, going on sixteen. I was sitting in a coffee shop in the Village, and a friend of mine came by. She said: "I've got a cab waiting. Hurry up. You can make fifty dollars in twenty minutes." Looking back, I wonder why I was so willing to run out of the coffee shop, get in a cab, and turn a trick. It wasn't traumatic because my training had been in how to be a hustler anyway.

I learned it from the society around me, just as a woman. We're taught how to hustle, how to attract, hold a man, and give sexual favors in return. The language that you hear all the time, "Don't sell yourself cheap." "Hold out for the highest bidder." "Is it proper to kiss a man good night on the first date?" The implication is it may not be proper on the first date, but if he takes you out to dinner on the second date, it's proper. If he brings you a bottle of perfume on the third date, you should let him touch you above the waist. And go on from here. It's a market place transaction.

Somehow I managed to absorb that when I was quite young. So it wasn't even a moment of truth when this woman came into the coffee shop and said; "Come on." I was back in twenty-five minutes and I felt no guilt.

She was a virgin until she was fourteen. A jazz musician, with whom she had fallen in love, avoided her. "So I went out to have sex with somebody to present him with an accomplished fact. I found it nonpleasurable. I did a lot of sleeping around before I ever took money."

A precocious child, she was already attending a high school of demanding academic standards. "I was very lonely. I didn't experience myself as being attractive. I had always felt I was too big, too fat, too awkward, didn't look like a Pepsi-Cola ad, was not anywhere near the American Dream. Guys were mostly scared of me. I was athletic, I was bright, and I didn't know how to keep my mouth shut. I didn't know how to play the games right.

"I understood very clearly they were not attracted to me for what I was, but as a sexual object. I was attractive. The year before I started hustling there were a lot of guys that wanted to go to bed with me. They didn't want to get involved emotionally, but they did want to ball. For a while I was willing to accept that. It was feeling intimacy, feeling close, feeling warm.

"The time spent in bed wasn't unpleasant. It just wasn't terribly pleasant. It was a way of feeling somebody cared about me, at least for a

moment. And it mattered that I was there, that I was important. I disco-vered that in bed it was possible. It was one skill that I had and I was proud of my reputation as an amateur.

"I viewed all girls as being threats. That's what we were all taught. You can't be friends with another woman, she might take your man. If you tell her anything about how you really feel, she'll use it against you. You smile at other girls and you spend time with them when there's nothing better to do, but you'd leave any girl sitting anywhere if you had an oppor-tunity to go somewhere with a man. Because the most important thing in life is the way men feel about you."

How could you forget your first trick? (Laughs.) We took a cab to midtown Manhattan, we went to a penthouse. The guy up there was quite well known. What he really wanted to do was watch two women make love, and then he wanted to have sex with me. It was barely sex. He was almost finished by the time we started. He barely touched me and we were finished.

Of course, we faked it, the woman and me. The ethic was: You don't participate in a sexual act with another woman if a trick is watching. You always fake it. You're putting something over on him and he's paying for something he didn't really get. That's the only way you can keep any sense of self-respect. 68

The call girl ethic is very strong. You were the lowest of the low if you allowed yourself to feel anything with a trick. The bed puts you on their level. The way you maintain your integrity is by acting all the way through. It's not too far removed from what most Ameri-can women do—which is to put on a big smile and act.

It was a tremendous kick. Here I was doing absolutely noth-ing, *feeling* nothing, and in twenty minutes I was going to walk out with fifty dollars in my pocket. That just made me feel absolutely marvelous. I came downtown. I can't believe this! I'm not changed, I'm the same as I was twenty minutes ago, except that now I have fifty dollars in my pocket. It really was tremendous status. How many people could make fifty dollars for twenty minutes' work? Folks work for eighty dollars take-home pay. I worked twenty minutes for fifty dollars clear, no taxes, nothing! I was still in school, I was smoking grass, I was shooting heroin, I wasn't hooked yet, and I had money. It was terrific.

After that, I made it my business to let my friend know that I was available for more of these situations. (Laughs.) She had good connections. Very shortly I linked up with a couple of others who had a good call book.

Books of phone numbers are passed around from call girl to call   72
girl. They're numbers of folks who are quite respectable and with
whom there is little risk. They're not liable to pull a knife on you,
they're not going to cheat you out of money. Businessmen and society figures. There's three or four groups. The wealthy executive,
who makes periodic trips into the city and is known to several girls.
There's the social figure, whose name appears quite regularly in the
society pages and who's a regular once-a-week John. Or there's the
quiet, independently wealthy type. Nobody knows how they got
their money. I know one of them made his money off munitions
in World War II. Then there's the entertainer. There's another crowd
that runs around the night spots, the 21 Club. . . .

These were the people whose names you saw in the paper
almost every day. But I knew what they were really like. Any John
who was obnoxious or aggressive was just crossed out of your book.
You passed the word around that this person was not somebody
other people should call.

We used to share numbers—standard procedure. The book I had
I got from a guy who got it from a very good call girl. We kept a
copy of that book in a safe deposit box. The standard procedure was
that somebody new gave half of what they got the first time for each
number. You'd tell them: "Call so-and-so, that's a fifty-dollar trick."
They would give you twenty-five dollars. Then the number was
theirs. My first book, I paid half of each trick to the person who
gave it to me. After that, it was my book.

The book had the name and phone number coded, the price,
what the person wants, and the contact name. For four years I didn't
turn a trick for less than fifty dollars. They were all fifty to one
hundred dollars and up for twenty minutes, an hour. The understanding is: it doesn't get conducted as a business transaction. The
myth is that it's a social occasion.

You're expected to be well dressed, well made up, appear glad   76
to see the man. I would get a book from somebody and I would
call and say, "I'm a friend of so-and-so's, and she thought it would
be nice if we got together." The next move was his. Invariably he'd
say, "Why don't we do that? Tonight or tomorrow night. Why don't
you come over for a drink?" I would get very carefully dressed and
made up. . . .

There's a given way of dressing in that league—that's to dress
well but not ostentatiously. You have to pass doormen, cabdrivers.
You have to look as if you belong in those buildings on Park Avenue
or Central Park West. You're expected not to look cheap, not to look

hard. Youth is the premium. I was quite young, but I looked older, so I had to work very hard at looking my age. Most men want girls who are eighteen. They really want girls who are younger, but they're afraid of trouble.

Preparations are very elaborate. It has to do with beauty parlors and shopping for clothes and taking long baths and spending money on preserving the kind of front that gives you a respectable address and telephone and being seen at the right clubs and drinking at the right bars. And being able to read the newspapers faithfully, so that not only can you talk about current events, you can talk about the society columns as well.

It's a social ritual. Being able to talk about what is happening and learn from this great master, and be properly respectful and know the names that he mentions. They always drop names of their friends, their contacts, and their clients. You should recognize these. Playing a role. . . .

At the beginning I was very excited. But in order to continue I 80 had to turn myself off. I had to disassociate who I was from what I was doing.

It's a process of numbing yourself. I couldn't associate with people who were not in the life—either the drug life or the hustling life. I found I couldn't turn myself back on when I finished working. When I turned myself off, I was numb—emotionally, sexually numb.

At first I felt like I was putting one over on all the other poor slobs that would go to work at eight-thirty in the morning and come home at five. I was coming home at four in the morning and I could sleep all day. I really thought a lot of people would change places with me because of the romantic image: being able to spend two hours out, riding cabs, and coming home with a hundred dollars. I could spend my mornings doing my nails, going to the beauty parlor, taking long baths, going shopping. . . .

It was usually two tricks a night. That was easily a hundred, a hundred and a quarter. I always had money in my pocket. I didn't know what the inside of a subway smelled like. Nobody traveled any other way except by cab. I ate in all the best restaurants and I drank in all the best clubs. A lot of people wanted you to go out to dinner with them. All you had to do was be an ornament.

Almost all the call girls I knew were involved in drugs. The fast 84 life, the night hours. At after-hours clubs, if you're not a big drinker, you usually find somebody who has cocaine, 'cause that's the big drug in those places. You wake up at noon, there's not very much to do till nine or ten that night. Everybody else is at work, so you shoot heroin. After a while the work became a means of supplying drugs, rather than drugs being something we took when we were bored.

The work becomes boring because you're not part of the life. You're the part that's always hidden. The doormen smirk when you come in, 'cause they know what's going on. The cabdriver, when you give him a certain address—he knows exactly where you're going when you're riding up Park Avenue at ten o'clock at night, for Christ sake. You leave there and go back to what? Really, to what? To an emptiness. You've got all this money in your pocket and nobody you care about.

When I was a call girl I looked down on streetwalkers. I couldn't understand why anybody would put themselves in that position. It seemed to me to be hard work and very dangerous. What I was doing was basically riskless. You never had to worry about disease. These were folks who you know took care of themselves and saw the doctor regularly. Their apartments were always immaculate and the liquor was always good. They were always polite. You didn't have to ask them for money first. It was always implicit: when you were ready to leave, there would be an envelope under the lamp or there'd be something in your pocketbook. It never had to be discussed.

I had to work an awful lot harder for the same money when I was a streetwalker. I remember having knives pulled on me, broken bottles held over my head, being raped, having my money stolen back from me, having to jump out of a second-story window, having a gun pointed at me.

As a call girl, I had lunch at the same places society women had 88 lunch. There was no way of telling me apart from anybody else in the upper tax bracket. I made my own hours, no more than three or so hours of work an evening. I didn't have to accept calls. All I had to do was play a role.

As a streetwalker, I didn't have to act. I let myself show the contempt I felt for the tricks. They weren't paying enough to make it worth performing for them. As a call girl, I pretended I enjoyed it sexually. You have to act as if you had an orgasm. As a streetwalker, I didn't. I used to lie there with my hands behind my head and do mathematics equations in my head or memorize the keyboard typewriter.

It was strictly a transaction. No conversation, no acting, no myth around it, no romanticism. It was purely a business transaction. You always asked for your money in front. If you could get away without undressing totally, you did that.

It's not too different than the distinction between an executive secretary and somebody in the typing pool. As an executive secretary you really identify with your boss. When you're part of the typing pool, you're a body, you're hired labor, a set of hands on the typewriter. You have nothing to do with whoever is passing the work down to you. You do it as quickly as you can.

What led you to the streets?   92

My drug habit. It got a lot larger. I started looking bad. All my money was going for drugs. I didn't have any money to spend on keeping myself up and going to beauty parlors and having a decent address and telephone.

If you can't keep yourself up, you can't call on your old tricks. You drop out of circulation. As a call girl, you have to maintain a whole image. The trick wants to know he can call you at a certain number and you have to have a stable address. You must look presentable, not like death on a soda cracker.

I looked terrible. When I hit the streets, I tried to stick to at least twenty dollars and folks would laugh. I needed a hundred dollars a night to maintain a drug habit and keep a room somewhere. It meant turning seven or eight tricks a night. I was out on the street from nine o'clock at night till four in the morning. I was taking subways and eating in hamburger stands.

For the first time I ran the risk of being busted. I was never   96 arrested as a call girl. Every once in a while a cop would get hold of somebody's book. They would call one of the girls and say, "I'm a friend of so-and-so's." They would try to trap them. I never took calls from people I didn't know. But on the streets, how do you know who you're gonna pick up?

As a call girl, some of my tricks were upper echelon cops, not patrolmen. Priests, financiers, garment industry folks, bigtimers. On the street, they ranged from *junior* executive types, blue-collar workers, upwardly striving postal workers, college kids, suburban white collars who were in the city for the big night, restaurant workers. . . .

You walk a certain area, usually five or six blocks. It has a couple of restaurants, a couple of bars. There's the step in-between: hanging out in a given bar, where people come to you. I did that briefly.

You'd walk very slowly, you'd stop and look in the window. Somebody would come up to you. There was a ritual here too. The law says in order to arrest a woman for prostitution, she has to mention money and she has to tell you what she'll do for the money. We would keep within the letter of the law, even though the cops never did.

Somebody would come up and say, "It's a nice night, isn't it?"   100 "Yes." They'd say, "Are you busy?" I'd say, "Not particularly." "Would you like to come with me and have a drink?" You start walking and they say, "I have fifteen dollars or twelve dollars and I'm very lonely." Something to preserve the myth. Then they want you to spell out exactly what you're willing to do for the money.

I never approached anybody on the street. That was the ultimate risk. Even if he weren't a cop, he could be some kind of supersquare, who would call a cop. I was trapped by cops several times.

The first one didn't even trap me as a trick. It was three in the morning. I was in Chinatown. I ran into a trick I knew. We made contact in a restaurant. He went home and I followed him a few minutes later. I knew the address. I remember passing a banana truck. It didn't dawn on me that it was strange for somebody to be selling bananas at three in the morning. I spent about twenty minutes with my friend. He paid me. I put the money in my shoe. I opened the door and got thrown back against the wall. The banana salesman was a vice squad cop. He'd stood on the garbage can to peer in the window. I got three years for that one.

I was under age. I was four months short of twenty-one. They sent me to what was then called Girls' Term Court. They wouldn't allow me a lawyer because I wasn't an adult, so it wasn't really a criminal charge. The judge said I was rehabilitable. Instead of giving me thirty days, he gave me three years in the reformatory. It was very friendly of him. I was out on parole a couple of times before I'd get caught and sent back.

I once really got trapped. It was about midnight and a guy came   104 down the street. He said he was a postal worker who just got off the shift. He told me how much money he had and what he wanted. I took him to my room. The cop isn't supposed to undress. If you can describe the color of his shorts, it's an invalid arrest. Not only did he show me the color of his shorts, he went to bed with me. Then he pulled a badge and a gun and busted me.

He lied to me. He told me he was a narc and didn't want to bust me for hustling. If I would tell him who was dealing in the neighborhood, he'd cut me loose. I lied to him, but he won. He got me to walk out of the building past all my friends and when we got to the car, he threw me in. (Laughs.) It was great fun. I did time for that—close to four years.

What's the status of the streetwalker in prison?

It's fine. Everybody there has been hustling. It's status in reverse. Anybody who comes in saying things like they could never hustle is looked down on as being somewhat crazy.

She speaks of a profound love she had for a woman who she's met in prison; 108 *of her nursing her lover after the woman had become blind.*

"I was out of the country for a couple of years. I worked a house in Mexico. It had heavy velour curtains—a Mexican version of a French whorehouse. There was a reception area, where the men would come and we'd parade in front of them.

"The Mexicans wanted American girls. The Americans wanted Mexican girls. So I didn't get any American tricks. I had to give a certain amount to the house for each trick I turned and anything I negotiated over that amount was mine. It was far less than anything I had taken in the States.

"I was in great demand even though I wasn't a blonde. A girl friend of mine worked there two nights. She was Norwegian and very blonde. Every trick who came in wanted her. Her head couldn't handle it all. She quit after two nights. So I was the only American.

"That was really hard work. The Mexicans would play macho. Ameri- 112 can tricks will come as quickly as they can. Mexicans will hold back and make me work for my money. I swear to God they were doing multiplication tables in their heads to keep from having an orgasm. I would use every trick I knew to get them to finish. It was crazy!

"I was teaching school at the same time. I used Alice in Wonderland as the text in my English class. During the day I tutored English for fifth-and sixth-grade kids. In the evening, I worked in the call house.

"The junk down there was quite cheap and quite good. My habit was quite large. I loved dope more than anything else around. After a while I couldn't differentiate between working and not working. All men were tricks, all relationships were acting. I was completely turned off."

She quit shooting dope the moment she was slugged, brutally beaten by a dealer who wanted her. This was her revelatory experience. "It was the final indignity. I'd had tricks pulling broken bottles on me, I'd been in

razor fights, but nobody had ever hit me." *It was a threat to her status.*
"*I was strong. I could handle myself. A tough broad. This was threatened,*
so . . ."

I can't talk for women who were involved with pimps. That was   116
where I always drew the line. I always thought pimps were lower
than pregnant cockroaches. I didn't want anything to do with them.
I was involved from time to time with some men. They were either
selling dope or stealing, but they were not depending on my income. Nor were they telling me to get my ass out on the street. I
never supported a man.

As a call girl I got satisfaction, an unbelievable joy—perhaps
perverted—in knowing what these reputable folks were really like.
Being able to open a newspaper every morning, read about this pillar of society, and know what a pig he really was. The tremendous
kick in knowing that I didn't feel anything, that I was acting and
they weren't. It's sick, but no sicker than what every woman is
taught, all right?

I was in *control* with every one of those relationships. You're
vulnerable if you allow yourself to be involved sexually. I wasn't.
They were. I called it. Being able to manipulate somebody sexually,
I could determine when I wanted that particular transaction to end.
'Cause I could make the guy come. I could play all kinds of games.
See? It was a tremendous sense of power.

What I did was no different from what ninety-nine percent of
American women are taught to do. I took the money from under
the lamp instead of in Arpege. What would I do with 150 bottles
of Arpege a week?

You become your job. I became what I did. I became a hustler. I   120
became cold, I became hard, I became turned off, I became numb.
Even when I wasn't hustling, I was a hustler. I don't think it's terribly different from somebody who works on the assembly line forty
hours a week and comes home cut off, numb, dehumanized. People aren't built to switch on and off like water faucets.

What was really horrifying about jail is that it really isn't horrifying. You adjust very easily. The same thing with hustling. It became my life. It was too much of an effort to try to make contact
with another human being, to force myself to care, to feel.

I didn't care about me. It didn't matter whether I got up or didn't
get up. I got high as soon as I awoke. The first thing I'd reach for,
with my eyes half-closed, was my dope. I didn't like my work. It

was messy. That was the biggest feeling about it. Here's all these guys slobbering over you all night long. I'm lying there, doing math or conjugations or Spanish poetry in my head. (Laughs.) And they're slobbering. God! God! What enabled me to do it was being high— high and numb.

The overt hustling society is the microcosm of the rest of the society. The power relationships are the same and the games are the same. Only this one I was in control of. The greater one I wasn't. In the outside society, if I tried to be me, I wasn't in control of any-thing. As a bright, assertive woman, I had no power. As a cold, manipulative hustler, I had a lot. I knew I was playing a role. Most women are taught to become what they act. All I did was act out the reality of American womanhood.[3]

III. Maggie Holmes, Domestic

What bugs me now, since I'm on welfare, is people saying they give you the money for nothin'. When I think back what we had to come through, up from the South, comin' here. The hard work we had to do. It really gets me, when I hear people . . . It do somethin' to me. I think violence.

I think what we had to work for. I used to work for $1.50 a week. This is five days a week, sometimes six. If you live in the servant quarter, your time is never off, because if they decide to have a party at night, you gotta come out. My grandmother, I remember when she used to work, we'd get milk and a pound of butter. I mean this was pay. I'm thinkin' about what my poor parents worked for, get-tin' nothing. What do the white think about when they think? Do they ever think about what *they* would do?

She had worked as a domestic, hotel chambermaid, and as "kitchen help in cafés" for the past twenty-five years, Up North and down South. She lives with her four children.

When it come to housework, I can't do it now. I can't stand it, cause it do somethin' to my mind. They want you to clean the house, want you to wash, even the windows, want you to iron. You not supposed to wash no dishes. You ain't supposed to make no beds up. Lots of 'em try to sneak it in on you, think you don't know that. So the doorbell rings and I didn't answer to. The bell's ringin' and

[3] Questions on this selection appear on page 333.

I'm still doin' my work. She ask me why I don't answer the bell, I say; "Do I come here to be a butler?" And I don't see myself to be no doormaid. I came to do some work, and I'm gonna do my work. When you end up, you's nursemaid, you's cook. They puts all this on you. If you want a job to cleanin', you ask for just cleanin'. She wants you to do in one day what she hasn't did all year.

Now this bug me: the first thing she gonna do is pull out this damn rubber thing—just fittin' for your knees. Knee pads—like you're workin' in the fields, like people pickin' cotton. No mop or nothin'. That's why you find so many black women here got rheumatism in their legs, knees. When you get on that cold floor, I don't care how warm the house is, you can feel the cold on the floor, the water and stuff. I never see nobody on their knees until I come North. In the South, they had mops. Most times, if they had real heavy work, they always had a man to come in. Washin' windows, that's a man's job. They don't think nothin' about askin' you to do that here. They don't have no feeling that that's what bothers you. I think to myself; My God, if I had somebody come and do my floors, clean up for me, I'd appreciate it. They don't say nothin' about it. Act like you haven't even done anything. They has no feelin's.

I worked for one old hen on Lake Shore Drive. You remember that big snow they had there?[4] Remember when you couldn't get there? When I gets to work she says: "Call the office." She complained to the lady where I got the job, said I was late to work. So I called. So I said, in the phone (Shouts), *"What do you want with me?* I got home four black, beautiful kids. Before I go to anybody's job in the morning I see that my kids are at school. I gonna see that they have warm clothes on and they fed." I'm lookin' right at the woman I'm workin' for. (Laughs.) When I get through the phone I tell this employer: "That goes for you too. The only thing I live for is my kids. There's nothin', you and nobody else." The expression on her face: What is this? (Laughs.) She thought I was gonna be like (mimics "Aunt Jemima"): "Yes ma'am, I'll try to get here a little early." But it wasn't like that. (Laughs.)

When I come in the door that day she told me pull my shoes off. I said, "For what? I can wipe my feet at the door here, but I'm not gettin' out of my shoes, it's cold." She look at me like she said: Oh my God, what I got here? (Laughs.) I'm knowin' I ain't gonna make no eight hours here. I can't take it.

---

[4] It was the week of Chicago's Big Snow-In, beginning January 25, 1967. Traffic was hopelessly snarled. Scores of thousands couldn't get to work.

She had everything in there snow white. And that means work, believe me. In the dining room she had a blue set, she had sky-blue chairs. They had a bedroom with pink and blue. I look and say, "I know what this means." It means sho' 'nough—knees. I said, "I'm gonna try and make it today, *if* I can make it." Usually when they're so bad, you have to leave.

I ask her where the mop is. She say she don't have no mop. I said, "Don't tell me you mop the floor on your knees. I know you don't." They usually hid these mops in the clothes closet. I go out behind all these clothes and get the mop out. (Laughs.) They don't get on their knees, but they don't think nothin' about askin' a black woman. She says, "All you—you girls . . ." She stop. I say, "All you *niggers,* is that what you want to say?" She give me this stupid look. I say, "I'm glad you tellin' me that there's more like me." (Laughs.) I told her, "You better give me my money and let me go, 'cause I'm gettin' angry. So I made her give me my carfare and what I had worked that day.

Most when you find decent work is when you find one that work themselves. They know what it's like to get up in the morning and go to work. In the suburbs they ain't got nothin' to do. They has nothin' else to think about. Their mind's just about blowed.

It's just like they're talkin' about mental health. Poor people's mental health is different than the rich white. Mine could come from a job or not havin' enough money for my kids. Mine is from me being poor. That don't mean you're sick. His sickness is from money, graftin' where he want more. I don't have *any.* You live like that day to day, penny to penny.

I worked for a woman, her husband's a judge. I cleaned the whole house. When it was time for me to go home, she decided she wants some ironing. She goes in the basement, she turn on the air conditioner. She said, "I think you can go down in the basement and finish your day out. It's air conditioned." I said, "I don't care what you got down there, I'm not ironing. You look at that slip, it says cleanin'. Don't say no ironin'. She wanted me to wash the walls in the bathroom. I said, "If you look at that telephone book they got all kinds of ads there under house cleanin'." She said the same thing as the other one, "All you girls—" I said same thing I said to the other one; "You mean niggers." (Laughs.)

They ever call you by your last name?

Oh God, they wouldn't do that. (Laughs.)

Do you call her by her last name?

Most time I don't call her, period. I don't say anything to her. I don't talk nasty to nobody, but when I go to work I don't talk to people. Most time they don't like what you're gonna say. So I keeps quiet.

Most of her jobs were "way out in the suburbs. You get a bus and you ride til 140 *you get a subway. After you gets to Howard,[5] you gets the El. If you get to the end of the line and there's no bus, they pick you up. I don't like to work in the city, 'cause they don't pay you nothin.' And these old buildings are so nasty. It takes so much time to clean 'em. They are not kept up so good, like suburbs. Most of the new homes out there, it's easier to clean."*

A commonly observed phenomenon: during the early evening hour, trains, crowded, predominantly by young white men carrying attaché cases, pass trains headed in the opposite direction, crowded, predominantly by middle-aged black women carrying brown paper bags. Neither group, it appears, glances at the other.

"We spend most of the time ridin'. You get caught goin' out from the suburbs at nighttime, man, you're really sittin' there for hours. There's nothin' movin'. You got a certain hour to meet trains. You get a transfer, you have to get that train. It's a shuffle to get in and out of the job. If you miss that train at five o'clock, what time you gonna get out that end? Sometime you don't get home till eight o'clock. . . ."

You don't feel like washin' your own window when you come from out there, scrubbin'. If you work in one of them houses eight hours, you gotta come home do the same thing over . . . you don't feel like . . . (sighs softly) . . . tired. You gotta come home, take care of your kids, you gotta cook, you gotta wash. Most of the time, you gotta wash for the kids for somethin' to wear to school. You gotta clean up, 'cause you didn't have time in the morning. You gotta wash and iron and whatever you do, nights. You be so tired, until you don't feel like even doin' nothin'.

You get up at six, you fix breakfast for the kids, you get them 144 ready to go on to school. Leave home about eight. Most of the time I make biscuits for my kids, cornbread you gotta make. I don't mean

---

[5] The boundary line separating Chicago from the North Shore suburb, Evanston.

the canned kind. This I don't call cookin', when you go in that refrigerator and get some beans and drop 'em in a pot. And TV dinners, they go stick 'em in the stove and she say she cooked. This is not cookin'.

And *she's* tired. Tired from doin' what? You got a washing dryer, you got an electric sweeper, anything at fingertips. All she gotta do is unfroze 'em, dump 'em in the pot, and she's tired! I go to the store, I get my vegetables, greens, I wash 'em. I gotta pick 'em first. I don't eat none of that stuff, like in the cans. She don't do that, and she says she's tired.

When you work for them, when you get in that house in the morning, boy, they got one arm in their coat and a scarf on their head. And when you open that door, she shoots by you, she's gone. Know what I mean? They want you to come there and keep the kids and let them get out. What she think about how am I gonna do? Like I gets tired of my kids too. I'd like to go out too. It bugs you to think that they don't have no feelin's about that.

Most of the time I work for them and they be out. I don't like to work for 'em when they be in the house so much. They don't have no work to do. All they do is get on the telephone and talk about one another. Make you sick. I'll go and close the door. They're all the same, everybody's house is the same. You think they rehearse it. . . .

When I work, only thing I be worryin' about is my kids. I just don't like to leave 'em too long. When they get out of school, you wonder if they out on the street. The only thing I worry is if they had a place to play in easy. I always call two, three times. When she don't like you to call, I'm in a hurry to get out of there. (Laughs.) My mind is gettin' home, what are you gonna find to cook before the stores close. 148

This Nixon was sayin' he don't see nothin' wrong with people doin' scrubbin'. For generations that's all we done. He should know we wants to be doctors and teachers and lawyers like him. I don't want my kids to come up and do domestic work. It's degrading. You can't see no tomorrow there. We done this for generation and generation cooks and butlers all your life. They want their kids to be lawyers, doctors, and things. You don't want 'em in no cafes workin'. . . .

When they say about the neighborhood we live in is dirty, why do they ask me to come and clean their house? We, the people in the slums, the same nasty women they have come to their house in the suburbs every day. If these women are so filthy, why you want them to clean for you? They don't go and clean for us. We go and clean for them.

I worked one day where this white person did some housework. I'm lookin' at the difference how she with me and her. She had a guilt feeling towards that lady. They feel they shouldn't ask them to do this type of work, but they don't mind askin' me.

They want you to get in a uniform. You take me and my mother, she work in what she wear. She tells you, "If that place so dirty where I can't wear my dress, I won't do the job." You can't go to work dressed like they do, 'cause they think you're not working—like you should get dirty, at least. They don't say what kind of uniform, just say uniform. This is in case anybody come in, the black be workin'. They don't want you walkin' around dressed up, lookin' like them. They asks you sometimes, "Don't you have somethin' else to put on?" I say, "No, 'cause I'm not gettin' on my knees."

They move with caution now, believe me. They want to know, "What should I call you?" I say, "Don't call me a Negro, I'm black." So they say, "Okay, I don't want to make you angry with me." (Laughs.) The old-timers, a lot of 'em was real religious. "Lord'll make a way." I say, "I'm makin' my own way." I'm not anti-Bible or anti-God, but I just let 'em know I don't think thataway.

The younger women, they don't pay you too much attention. Most of 'em work. The older women, they behind you, wiping. I don't like nobody checkin' behind me. When you go to work, they want to show you how to clean. That really gets me, somebody showin' me how to clean. I been doin' it all my life. They come and get the rag and show you how to do it. (Laughs.) I stand there, look at 'em. Lotta times I ask her, "You finished?" I say, "If there's anything you gotta go and do, I wish you'd go." I don't need nobody to show me how to clean.

I had them put money down and pretend they can't find it and have me look for it. I worked for one, she had dropped ten dollars on the floor, and I was sweepin' and I'm glad I seen it, because if I had put that sweeper on it, she coulda said I got it. I had to push the couch back and the ten dollars was there. Oh, I had 'em, when you go to dust, they put something . . . to test you.

I worked at a hotel. A hotel's the same thing. You makin' beds, scrubbin' toilets, and things. You gotta put in linens and towels. You still cleanin'. When people come in the room—that's what bugs me—they give you that look: You just a maid. It do some-thin' to me. It really gets into me.

Some of the guests are nice. The only thing you try to do is to hurry up and get this bed made and get outa here, 'cause they'll get you to do somethin' else. If they take that room, they want every-thing they paid for. (Laughs.) They get so many towels, they can't use 'em all. But you gotta put up all those towels. They want that pillow, they want that blanket. You gotta be trottin' back and forth and gettin' all those things.

In the meantime, when they have the hotel full, we put in extra beds—the little foldin' things. They say they didn't order the bed. They stand and look at you like you crazy. Now you gotta take this bed back all the way from the twelfth floor to the second. The guy at the desk, he got the wrong room. He don't say, "I made a mis-take." You take the blame.

And you get some guys . . . you can't work with afightin' 'em. He'll call down and say he wants some towels. When you knock, he says, "Come in." He's standing there without a stitch of clothes on, buck naked. You're not goin' in there. You only throw those towels and go back. Most of the time you wait till he got out of there.

When somethin's missin', it's always the maid took it. If we find one of those type people, we tell the house lady, "You have to go in there and clean it yourself." If I crack that door, and nobody's in, I wouldn't go in there. If a girl had been in there, they would call and tell you, "Did you see something?" They won't say you got it. It's the same thing. You say no. They say, "It *musta* been in there."

Last summer I worked at a place and she missed a purse. I didn't work on that floor that day. She called the office, "Did you see that lady's purse?" I said, "No, I haven't been in the room." He asked me again, Did I . . .? I had to stay till twelve o'clock. She found it. It was under some papers. I quit, 'cause they end up sayin' you stole somethin'.

You know what I wanted to do all my life? I wanted to play piano. And I'd want to write songs and things, that's what I really wanted to do. If I could just get myself enough to buy a piano. . . . And I'd like to write about my life, if I could sit long enough: How I growed up in the South and my grandparents and my father—I'd like to do that. I would like to dig up more of black history, too. I would love to for my kids.

Lotta times I'm tellin' 'em about things, they'll be sayin', "Mom, that's olden days." (Laughs.) They don't understand, because it's so far from what happening now. Mighty few young black women

160

are doin' domestic work. And I'm glad. That's why I want my kids to go to school. This one lady told me, "All you people are gettin' like that." I said, "I'm glad." There's no more gettin' on their knees.

Topics for Discussion and Writing

Terry Mason, Airline Stewardess

1. How satisfied is Terry Mason with her job? What are the sources of her satisfactions? Her dissatisfactions? Try to sketch her values, and to characterize her.
2. Using Mason's remarks as evidence, evaluate the training program for stewardesses (now called flight attendants). Is it intelligent? Is it immoral? Do you think that after stew school the airlines deal fairly with the stewardesses?
3. Has this selection changed your idea of the job of a stewardess? If so, in what ways?

Roberta Victor, Hooker

1. In paragraph 55 Victor lists some desirable ("very non-ethnic-oriented WASP") names: Kim, Tracy, Stacy. Why are such names considered desirable?
2. In the first paragraph of her interview Victor says: "The role one plays when hustling had nothing to do with who you are." Judging from the interview as a whole, is she deceiving herself? In paragraph 56 she says that all women in America are hustlers, and she returns to this notion, especially in the final paragraph. Again, is she deceiving herself, or has she put her finger on a truth, or at least a partial truth? Terkel tells us (paragraph 63) that she was a bright child. During the interview does Victor say anything that strikes you as especially perceptive? Does her language occasionally show unusual vitality? Are there touches of wit?

Maggie Holmes, Domestic

1. How do you account for the difference in treatment (paragraph 128) of domestic help in the North and the South?
2. What evidences is there that Holmes is witty? resourceful? insightful?
3. How would you describe Holme's attitude toward suburban housewives? Dos it make sense?

Gloria Steinem

Gloria Steinem was born in Toledo in 1934 and educated at Smith College. An active figure in politics, civil rights affairs, and feminist issues, she was a cofounder of the Women's Action Alliance and a co-founder and editor of Ms. *magazine. We reprint an essay from one of her books,* Outrageous Acts and Everyday Rebellions *(1983).*

The Importance of Work

Toward the end of the 1970s, *The Wall Street Journal* devoted an eight-part, front-page series to "the working woman"—that is, the influx of women into the paid-labor force—as the greatest change in American life since the Industrial Revolution.

Many women readers greeted both the news and the definition with cynicism. After all, women have always worked. If all the productive work of human maintenance that women do in the home were valued at its replacement cost, the gross national product of the United States would go up by 26 percent. It's just that we are now more likely than ever before to leave our poorly rewarded, low-security, high-risk job of homemaking (though we're still trying to explain that it's a perfectly good one and that the problem is male society's refusal both to do it and to give it an economic value) for more secure, independent, and better-paid jobs outside the home.

Obviously, the real work revolution won't come until all productive work is rewarded—including child rearing and other jobs done in the home—and men are integrated into so-called women's work as well as vice versa. But the radical change being touted by the *Journal* and other media is one part of that long integration process: the unprecedented flood of women into salaried jobs, that is, into the labor force as it has been male-defined and previously occupied by men. We are already more than 41 percent of it—the highest proportion in history. Given the fact that women also make up a whopping 69 percent of the "discouraged labor force" (that is, people who need jobs but don't get counted in the unemployment statistics because they've given up looking), plus an official female unemployment rate that is substantially higher than men's, it's clear that we could expand to become fully half of the national work force by 1990.

Faced with this determination of women to find a little independence and to be paid and honored for our work, experts have rushed to ask: "Why?" It's a question rarely directed at male workers. Their basic motivations of survival and personal satisfaction are taken for granted. Indeed, men are regarded as "odd" and therefore subjects for sociological study and journalistic reports only when they *don't* have work, even if they are rich and don't need jobs or are poor and can't find them. Nonetheless, pollsters and sociologists have gone to great expense to prove that women work outside the home because of dire financial need, or if we persist despite the presence of a wage-earning male, out of some desire to buy "little extras" for our families, or even out of good old-fashioned penis envy.

Job interviewers and even our own families may still ask salaried women the big "Why?" If we have small children at home or are in some job regarded as "men's work," the incidence of such questions increases. Condescending or accusatory versions of "What's a nice girl like you doing in a place like this?" have not disappeared from the workplace.

How do we answer these assumptions that we are "working" out of some pressing or peculiar need? Do we feel okay about arguing that it's as natural for us to have salaried jobs as for our husbands—whether or not we have young children at home? Can we enjoy strong career ambitions without worrying about being thought "unfeminine"? When we confront men's growing resentment of women competing in the work force (often in the form of such guilt-producing accusations as "You're taking men's jobs away" or "You're damaging your children"), do we simply state that a decent job is a basic human right for everybody?

I'm afraid the answer is often no. As individuals and as a movement, we tend to retreat into some version of a tactically questionable defense: "Womenworkbecausewehaveto." The phrase has become one word, one key on the typewriter—an economic form of the socially "feminine" stance of passivity and self-sacrifice. Under attack, we still tend to present ourselves as creatures of economic necessity and familial devotion. "Womenworkbecausewehaveto" has become the easiest thing to say.

Like most truisms, this one is easy to prove with statistics. Economic need *is* the most consistent work motive—for women as well as men. In 1976, for instance, 43 percent of all women in the paid-labor force were single, widowed, separated, or divorced, and working to support themselves and their dependents. An additional 21 percent were married to men who had earned less than ten thousand dollars in the previous year, the minimum then required to support a family of four. In fact, if you take men's pensions, stocks, real estate, and various forms of accumulated wealth into account, a good statistical case can be made that there are more women who "have" to work (that is, who have neither the accumulated wealth, nor husbands whose work or wealth can support them for the rest of their lives) than there are men with the same need. If we were going to ask one group "Do you really need this job?" we should ask men.

But the first weakness of the whole "have to work" defense is its deceptiveness. Anyone who has ever experienced dehumanized life on welfare or any other confidence-shaking dependency knows that a paid job may be preferable to the dole, even when the hand-out is coming from a family member. Yet the will and self-confidence to work on one's own can diminish as dependency and fear increase. That may explain why – contrary to the "have to" rationale – wives of men who earn less than three thousand dollars a year are actually *less* likely to be employed than wives whose husbands make ten thousand dollars a year or more.

Furthermore, the greatest proportion of employed wives is found among families with a total household income of twenty-five to fifty thousand dollars a year. This is the statistical underpinning used by some sociologists to prove that women's work is mainly important for boosting families into the middle or upper middle class. Thus, women's incomes are largely used for buying "luxuries" and "little extras": a neat double-whammy that renders us secondary within our families, and makes our jobs expendable in hard times. We may even go along with this interpretation (at least, up to the point of getting fired so a male can have our job). It preserves a husbandly ego-need to be seen as the primary bread-winner, and still allows us a safe "feminine" excuse for working.

But there are often rewards that we're not confessing. As noted in *The Two-Career Couple*, by Francine and Douglas Hall: "Women who hold jobs by choice, even blue-collar routine jobs, are more satisfied with their lives than are the full-time housewives."

In addition to personal satisfaction, there is also society's need 12 for all its members' talents. Suppose that jobs were given out on only a "have to work" basis to both women and men – one job per household. It would be unthinkable to lose the unique abilities of, for instance, Eleanor Holmes Norton, the distinguished chair of the Equal Employment Opportunity Commission. But would we then be forced to question the important work of her husband, Edward Norton, who is also a distinguished lawyer? Since men earn more than twice as much as women on the average, the wife in most households would be more likely to give up her job. Does that mean the nation could do as well without millions of its nurses, teachers, and secretaries? Or that the rare man who earns less than his wife should give up his job?

It was this kind of waste of human talents on a society-wide scale that traumatized millions of unemployed or underemployed Americans during the Depression. Then, a one-job-per-household rule seemed somewhat justified, yet the concept was used to displace women workers only, create intolerable dependencies, and waste female talent that the country needed. That Depression experience, plus the energy and example of women who were finally allowed to work during the manpower shortage created by World War II, led Congress to reinterpret the meaning of the country's full-employment goal in its Economic Act of 1946. Full employment was officially defined as "the employment of those who want to work, without regard to whether their employment is, by some definition, necessary. This goal applies equally to men and to women." Since bad economic times are again creating a resentment of employed women—as well as creating more need for women to be employed—we need such a goal more than ever. Women are again being caught in a tragic double bind: We are required to be strong and then punished for our strength.

Clearly, anything less than government and popular commitment to this 1946 definition of full employment will leave the less powerful groups, whoever they may be, in danger. Almost as important as the financial penalty paid by the powerless is the suffering that comes from being shut out of paid and recognized work. Without it, we lose much of our self-respect and our ability to prove that we are alive by making some difference in the world. That's just as true for the suburban woman as it is for the unemployed steel worker.

But it won't be easy to give up the passive defense of "wework-becausewehaveto."

When a woman who is struggling to support her children 16 and grandchildren on welfare sees her neighbor working as a waitress, even though that neighbor's husband has a job, she may feel resentful; and the waitress (of course, not the waitress's husband) may feel guilty. Yet unless we establish the obligation to provide a job for everyone who is willing and able to work, that welfare woman may herself be penalized by policies that give out only one public-service job per household. She and her daughter will have to make a painful and divisive decision about which of them gets that precious job, and the whole household will have to survive on only one salary.

A job as a human right is a principle that applies to men as well as women. But women have more cause to fight for it. The phenomenon of the "working woman" has been held responsible for everything from an increase in male impotence (which turned out, incidentally, to be attributable to medication for high blood pressure) to the rising cost of steak (which was due to high energy costs and beef import restrictions, not women's refusal to prepare the cheaper, slower-cooking cuts). Unless we see a job as part of every citizen's right to autonomy and personal fulfillment, we will continue to be vulnerable to someone else's idea of what "need" is, and whose "need" counts the most.

In many ways, women who do not have to work for simple survival, but who choose to do so nonetheless, are on the frontier of asserting this right for all women. Those with well-to-do husbands are dangerously easy for us to resent and put down. It's easier still to resent women from families of inherited wealth, even though men generally control and benefit from that wealth. (There is no Rockefeller Sisters Fund, no J. P. Morgan & Daughters, and sons-in-law may be the ones who really sleep their way to power.) But to prevent a woman whose husband or father is wealthy from earning her own living, and from gaining the self-confidence that comes with that ability, is to keep her needful of that unearned power and less willing to disperse it. Moreover, it is to lose forever her unique talents.

Perhaps modern feminists have been guilty of a kind of reverse snobbism that keeps us from reaching out to the wives and daughters of wealthy men; yet it was exactly such women who refused the restrictions of class and financed the first wave of feminist revolution.

For most of us, however, "womenworkbecausewehaveto" is just [20] true enough to be seductive as a personal defense.

If we use it without also staking out the larger human right to a job, however, we will never achieve that right. And we will always be subject to the false argument that independence for women is a luxury affordable only in good economic times. Alternatives to layoffs will not be explored, acceptable unemployment will always be used to frighten those with jobs into accepting low wages, and we will never remedy the real cost, both to families and to the country, of dependent women and a massive loss of talent.

Worst of all, we may never learn to find productive, honored work as a natural part of ourselves and as one of life's basic pleasures.

Topics for Discussion and Writing

1. In paragraph 2 Steinem characterizes homemaking as a "poorly rewarded, low-security, high-risk job." How might she justify each of these descriptions of homemaking? Do you agree that homemaking is rightly classified as a job? If so, do you agree with her description of it?

2. Restate in your own words Steinem's explanation (paragraph 9) of why "wives of men who earn *less* than three thousand dollars a year are actually *less* likely to be employed than wives whose husbands make ten thousand dollars a year or more." The salary figures are, of course, out of date. Is the point nevertheless still valid? Explain.

3. To whom does Steinem appear to address her remarks? Cite evidence for your answer. In your opinion, is this audience likely to find her argument persuasive? Would a different audience find it more or less persuasive? Explain.

4. In addition to arguments, what persuasive devices does Steinem use? How, for example, does she persuade you that she speaks with authority? What other authorities does she cite? How would you characterize her diction and tone, for instance in paragraph 18? (On diction, see page 877; on tone, see page 886.)

5. Steinem suggests two reasons for working: "personal satisfaction" and "society's need for all its members' talents." Suppose that you had no financial need to work. Do you imagine that you would choose to work in order to gain "personal satisfaction"? Or, again if you had no need to work, would you assume that you are morally obligated to contribute to society by engaging in paid work?

6. Summarize, in a paragraph of about 100–150 words, Steinem's argument that it is entirely proper for wealthy women to work for pay. In the course of your paragraph you may quote briefly from the essay.

7. Compare Steinem with Russell (page 295) on the value of work.

Barbara Ehrenreich

Barbara Ehrenreich, born in Butte, Montana, in 1941, and educated at Reed College and at Rockefeller University, has taught at the State University of New York in Old Westbury. The author of several books, since 1982 she has been a fellow of the Institute of Policy Studies in Washington, D.C. This essay was originally published in Ms.

A Step Back to the Workhouse?

The commentators are calling it a "remarkable consensus." Workfare, as programs to force welfare recipients to work are known, was once abhorred by liberals as a step back toward the 17th-century workhouse or—worse—slavery. But today no political candidate dares step outdoors without some plan for curing "welfare dependency" by putting its hapless victims to work—if necessary, at the nearest Burger King. It is as if the men who run things, or who aspire to run things (and we are, unfortunately, talking mostly about men when we talk about candidates), had gone off and caucused for a while and decided on the one constituency that could be safely sacrificed in the name of political expediency and "new ideas," and that constituency is poor women.

Most of the arguments for workfare are simply the same indestructible stereotypes that have been around, in one form or another, since the first public relief program in England 400 years ago: that the poor are poor because they are lazy and dissolute, and that they are lazy and dissolute because they are suffering from "welfare dependency." Add a touch of modern race and gender stereotypes and you have the image that haunts the workfare advocates: a slovenly, over-weight, black woman who produces a baby a year in order to augment her welfare checks.

But there is a new twist to this season's spurt of welfare-bashing: workfare is being presented as a kind of *feminist* alternative to welfare. As Senator Daniel Patrick Moynihan (D.-N.Y.) has put it, "A program that was designed to pay mothers to stay at home with their children [i.e., welfare, or Aid to Families with Dependent Children] cannot succeed when we now observe most mothers going out to work." Never mind the startling illogic of this argument, which is on a par with saying that no woman should stay home with her children because other women do not, or that a laid-off male worker should not receive unemployment compensation because most men have been observed holding jobs. We are being asked to believe that pushing destitute mothers into the work force (in some versions of workfare, for no other compensation than the welfare payments they would have received anyway) is consistent with women's strivings toward self-determination.

Now I will acknowledge that most women on welfare—like most unemployed women in general—would rather have jobs. And I will further acknowledge that many of the proponents of workfare, possibly including Senator Moynihan and the Democratic Presidential candidates, have mounted the bandwagon with the best of intentions. Welfare surely needs reform. But workfare is not the solution, because "dependency"—with all its implications of laziness and depravity—is not the problem. The problem is poverty, which most women enter in a uniquely devastating way—with their children in tow.

Let me introduce a real person, if only because real people, as opposed to imaginative stereotypes, never seem to make an appearance in the current rhetoric on welfare. "Lynn," as I will call her, is a friend and onetime neighbor who has been on welfare for two years. She is also about as unlike the stereotypical "welfare mother" as one can get—which is to say that she is a fairly typical welfare recipient. She has only one child, which puts her among the 74 percent of welfare recipients who have only one or two children. She is white (not that that should matter), as are almost half of welfare recipients. Like most welfare recipients, she is not herself the daughter of a welfare recipient, and hence not part of anything that could be called an "intergenerational cycle of dependency." And like every woman on welfare I have ever talked to, she resents the bureaucratic hassles that are the psychic price of welfare. But, for now, there are no alternatives.

When I first met Lynn, she seemed withdrawn and disoriented. She had just taken the biggest step of her 25 years; she had left an abusive husband and she was scared: scared about whether she could survive on her own and scared of her estranged husband. He owned a small restaurant; she was a high school dropout who had been a waitress when she met him. During their three years of marriage he had beaten her repeatedly. Only after he threw her down a flight of stairs had she realized that her life was in danger and moved out. I don't think I fully grasped the terror she had lived in until one summer day when he chased Lynn to the door of my house with a drawn gun.

Gradually Lynn began to put her life together. She got a divorce and went on welfare; she found a pediatrician who would accept Medicaid and a supermarket that would take food stamps. She fixed up her apartment with second-hand furniture and flea market curtains. She was, by my admittedly low standards, a compulsive housekeeper and an overprotective mother; and when she wasn't waxing her floors or ironing her two-year-old's playsuits, she was studying the help-wanted ads. She spent a lot of her time struggling with details that most of us barely notice—the price of cigarettes, mittens, or of a bus ticket to the welfare office—yet, somehow, she regained her sense of humor. In fact, most of the time we spent together was probably spent laughing—over the foibles of the neighbors, the conceits of men, and the snares of welfare and the rest of "the system."

Yet for all its inadequacies, Lynn was grateful for welfare. Maybe 8 if she had been more intellectually inclined she would have found out that she was suffering from "welfare dependency," a condition that is supposed to sap the will and demolish the work ethic. But "dependency" is not an issue when it is a choice between an abusive husband and an impersonal government. Welfare had given Lynn a brief shelter in a hostile world, and as far as she was concerned, it was her ticket to *independence*.

Suppose there had been no welfare at the time when Lynn finally summoned the courage to leave her husband. Suppose she had gone for help and been told she would have to "work off" her benefits in some menial government job (restocking the toilet paper in rest rooms is one such "job" assigned to New York women in a current workfare program). Or suppose, as in some versions of workfare, she had been told she would have to take the first available private sector job, which (for a non-high school graduate like Lynn) would have paid near the minimum wage, or $3.35 an hour. How would she have been able to afford child care? What would she have done for health insurance (as a welfare recipient she had Medicaid, but most low-paying jobs offer little or no coverage)? Would she have ever made the decision to leave her husband in the first place?

As Ruth Sidel points out in *Women and Children Last* (Viking), most women who are or have been on welfare have stories like Lynn's. They go onto welfare in response to a crisis—divorce, illness, loss of a job, the birth of an additional child to feed—and they remain on welfare for two years or less. They are not victims of any "welfare culture," but of a society that increasingly expects women to both raise and support children—and often on wages that would barely support a woman alone. In fact, even some of the most vociferous advocates of replacing welfare with workfare admit that, in their own estimation, only about 15 percent of welfare recipients fit the stereotype associated with "welfare dependency": demoralization, long-term welfare use, lack of drive, and so on.

But workfare will not help anyone, not even the presumed 15 percent of "bad apples" for whose sake the majority will be penalized. First, it will not help because it does not solve the problem that drives most women into poverty in the first place: how to hold a job *and* care for children. Child care in a licensed, professionally run center can easily cost as much as $100 a week per child—more than most states now pay in welfare benefits and (for two children) more than most welfare recipients could expect to earn in the work force. Any serious effort to get welfare recipients into the work force would require childcare provisions at a price that would probably end up higher than the current budget for AFDC. But none of the workfare advocates are proposing that sort of massive public commitment to child care.

Then there is the problem of jobs. So far, studies show that exist- 12 ing state workfare programs have had virtually no success in improving their participants' incomes or employment rates. Small wonder: nearly half the new jobs generated in recent years pay poverty-level wages; and most welfare recipients will enter jobs that pay near the minimum wage, which is $6,900 a year—26 percent less than the poverty level for a family of three. A menial, low-wage job may be character-building (from a middle-class vantage point), but it will not lift anyone out of poverty.

Some of my feminist activist friends argue that it is too late to stop the workfare juggernaut. The best we can do, they say, is to try to defeat the more pernicious proposals: those that are over-coercive, that do not offer funds for child care, or that would relegate workfare clients to a "subemployee" status unprotected by federal labor and civil rights legislation. Our goal, the pragmatists argue, should be to harness the current enthusiasm for workfare to push for services welfare recipients genuinely need, such as child care and job training and counseling.

I wish the pragmatists well, but for me, it would be a betrayal of women like Lynn to encourage the workfare bandwagon in any way. Most women, like Lynn, do not take up welfare as a career, but as an emergency measure in a time of personal trauma and dire need. At such times, the last thing they need is to be hustled into a low-wage job, and left to piece together child care, health insurance, transportation, and all the other ingredients of survival. In fact, the main effect of workfare may be to discourage needy women from seeking any help at all—a disastrous result in a nation already suffering from a child poverty rate of nearly 25 percent. Public policy should be aimed at giving impoverished mothers (and, I would add, fathers) the help they so urgently need—not only in the form of job opportunities, but sufficient income support to live on until a job worth taking comes along.

Besides, there is an ancient feminist principle at stake. The premise of all the workfare proposals—the more humane as well as the nasty—is that single mothers on welfare are *not working.* But, to quote the old feminist bumper sticker, EVERY MOTHER IS A WORK-ING MOTHER. And those who labor to raise their children in poverty—to feed and clothe them on meager budgets and to nurture them in an uncaring world—are working the hardest. The feminist position has never been that all women must pack off their children and enter the work force, but that all women's work—in the home or on the job—should be valued and respected.

Barbara Ehrenreich's essay stimulated a lively response from Ms. *readers. The following letters were published in the February 1988 issue.*

I was absolutely thrilled when I read Barbara Ehrenreich's article on   16
workfare ("A Step Back to the Workhouse?" November 1987). As a single mother who received welfare for several years (with no child support) I'm against everything that workfare stands for. I belong to an organization called Women, Work, and Welfare, a group of current and former welfare recipients trying to empower ourselves and become a part of the decisions that affect our lives as poor women. It seems as if everybody but the welfare recipient herself has a hand in the decisions that are made.

CHERI HONKALA
Minneapolis, Minn.

I arrived in Chicago in 1952 with a husband and two children from a camp in Europe. I had another child in 1953, lost a newborn in 1954, had a miscarriage, a hysterectomy, and a divorce in 1955. I *never* received child support. My ex-husband was remarried within two months.

I *never* received welfare. I worked in another culture, while in very bad health. I found a two-room flat, had no furniture and slept for years on the floor. I even went back to school at night and had to contend with companies like Gulf Oil Corp., which did not believe in promoting women. But I just slugged on.

By the end of the sixties, I had two daughters in college, and I had bought a house. My total earnings for 1970 from three jobs came to a whopping $8,000.

A full-time minimum wage job *can* support one adult and one   20 child. One just has to learn how to do it.

URSULA SCHRAMM
Hurley, Wis.

I found myself agreeing with the problems that Barbara Ehrenreich outlines in the present workfare program.

Yet deep inside a protesting rumbling exploded when I read that impoverished mothers should receive sufficient income support to live on "until a job worth taking comes along." *Bullshit!* Sure, we all should have the right to only work a job we love, but how many of us can afford to wait for it? That we are often forced to work at jobs that are not fulfilling says a lot about our society in which more needs to be changed than just the welfare system!

My mother was forced to go to work when I was nine years old. Our family was in dire financial straits and at the age of 50 she took a job in a factory. Was that job "worth taking"? Did it utilize her unique talents? *No!* Did it bring her personal fulfillment? *No!* Did it prevent the bank from foreclosing on our home? *Yes!* Did it give my mother the power to overcome our financial crisis and maintain her autonomy? *Yes!* You tell me if it was "worth taking." That depends on what your self-respect is worth to you.

GAIL FREI
Newtown Square, Pa.

Barbara Ehrenreich omitted a major element in her discussion of the   24 victimization of welfare families: the inability or unwillingness of the legal system to award *and enforce* realistic child support. Until it stops being easier to abandon your children than to default on that car loan, women and those who depend on them will be welfare/workfare victims.

SUSAN MARTIN RYNARD
Durham, N.C.

I went on welfare when my daughter was three, when I left my husband. I had a high school education, but had always wanted to go to college. I was 25.

So, with the help of the government, I got my B.S. in nursing. I worked for several years as an R.N. and then returned to school for my master's degree. For graduate school, I lived on savings, loans, and grants. The loans ($19,000 for undergrad and graduate in all) will be paid off in less than a year, in time for my daughter to begin college!

KATHRYN REID
Silverado, Calif.

Although I share Barbara Ehrenreich's concerns about workfare and the plight of her friend Lynn, the conclusions she draws strike me as misguided. We live in a society where the myths of the work ethic and self-help are deeply embedded in the popular culture; where resort to the dole is frowned upon unless the need is temporary or arises from disability; where the middle-class majority feels inequitably taxed, as compared to the wealthy, to support a system that directly benefits few of its members.

Feminists and other liberals should acknowledge the swelling 28 demand for welfare reform. Our support should be conditional upon the incorporation in any welfare reform plan of provision for *quality* childcare facilities; upon the minimization of coercion; and upon further efforts to compel ex-spouses to pay their fair share of support. Nothing in this approach rules out our going ahead simultaneously with other, parallel efforts to question the mystique of work or to expose the links between welfare and poverty, on the one hand, and capitalism and the subordination of women, on the other.

DAVID G. BECKER
Hanover, N.H.

California *is* serious about workfare, but we call it GAIN (Greater Avenues for Independence). It offers welfare recipients vocational counseling, up to two years of vocational training, and workshops in how to get and hold a job.

GAIN also pays for child care and transportation. No job need be accepted by the recipient unless she/he will net at least as much as their AFCD grant, *including* child care, transportation, and medical insurance. And even then, they will receive funds to cover these costs for three months after they begin working to help them make the transition to the work force.

JANE KIRCHMAN
Guerneville, Calif.

Topics for Discussion and Writing

1. List the objections Ehrenreich makes to workfare, and pose an answer for each. Your answers may attempt to rebut her objections, on grounds either of their logic or of information she neglects to consider (for example, provisions in workfare programs you know of). Where her objections seem reasonable, propose improvements to workfare that you would like to see embodied in a program in your community. The letters answering Ehrenreich may provide some assistance. If so, quote, summarize, or paraphrase useful parts of the letters, giving appropriate acknowledgment to the writers.

2. Gloria Steinem in "The Importance of Work" (page 334) does not address the issue of welfare versus workfare, but a careful reading of her essay will suggest ideas and arguments on both sides of the question. Read her essay and report on the two or three ideas that struck you as interesting contributions to a discussion of workfare.

Sir Thomas More

Sir Thomas More (1478–1535) was an extremely able English administrator and diplomat who rose to high rank in the government of King Henry VIII, but when he opposed the King's break with Roman Catholicism (Henry demanded that his subjects recognize him as Supreme Head of the Church), More was beheaded. Four hundred years later, in 1935, he was canonized.

More wrote Utopia *in Latin (the international language of the Renaissance) in 1516. The word is Greek for "no place," but the Greek-sounding names for officials in this imaginary land — a syphogrant is elected by a group of thirty households, and a tranibor governs a group of ten syphogrants — have no meaning. Though the book is fictional, setting forth a playful vision of an ideal society, there is no story; it is not a novel but a sort of essay.*

"Work and Play" (editors' title) is about a tenth of the book.

Work and Play in Utopia

Their Occupations

Agriculture is the one occupation at which everyone works, men and women alike, with no exceptions. They are trained in it from childhood, partly in the schools where they learn theory, and partly through field trips to nearby farms, which make something like a game of practical instruction. On these trips they not only watch the work being done, but frequently pitch in and get a workout by doing the jobs themselves.

Besides farm work (which, as I said, everybody performs), each person is taught a particular trade of his own, such as wool-working, linen-making, masonry, metal-work, or carpentry. There is no other craft that is practiced by any considerable number of them. Throughout the island people wear, and down through the centuries they have always worn, the same style of clothing, except for the distinction between the sexes, and between married and unmarried persons. Their clothing is attractive, does not hamper bodily movement, and serves for warm as well as cold weather; what is more, each household can make its own.

Every person (and this includes women as well as men) learns a second trade, besides agriculture. As the weaker sex, women practice the lighter crafts, such as working in wool or linen; the heavier crafts are assigned to the men. As a rule, the son is trained to his father's craft; for which most feel a natural inclination. But if anyone is attracted to another occupation, he is transferred by adoption into a family practicing the trade he prefers. When anyone makes such a change, both his father and the authorities make sure that he is assigned to a grave and responsible householder. After a man has learned one trade, if he wants to learn another, he gets the same permission. When he has learned both, he pursues whichever he likes better, unless the city needs one more than the other.

The chief and almost the only business of the syphogrants is to manage matters so that no one sits around in idleness, and assure that everyone works hard at his trade. But no one has to exhaust himself with endless toil from early morning to late at night, as if he were a beast of burden. Such wretchedness, really worse than slavery, is the common lot of workmen in all countries, except Utopia. Of the day's twenty-four hours, the Utopians devote only six to work. They work three hours before noon, when they go to dinner. After dinner they rest for a couple of hours, then go to work for another three hours. Then they have supper, and at eight o'clock (counting the first hour after noon as one), they go to bed and sleep eight hours.

The other hours of the day, when they are not working, eating, or sleeping, are left to each man's individual discretion, provided he does not waste them in roistering or sloth, but uses them busily in some occupation that pleases him. Generally these periods are devoted to intellectual activity. For they have an established custom of giving public lectures before daybreak; attendance at these lectures is required only of those who have been specially chosen to devote themselves to learning, but a great many other people, both men and women, choose voluntarily to attend. Depending on their interests, some go to one lecture, some to another. But if anyone would rather devote his spare time to his trade, as many do who don't care for the intellectual life, this is not discouraged; in fact, such persons are commended as especially useful to the commonwealth.

After supper, they devote an hour to recreation, in their gardens when the weather is fine, or during winter weather in the common halls where they have their meals. There they either play music or amuse themselves with conversation. They know nothing about gambling with dice, or other such foolish and ruinous games. They do play two games not unlike our own chess. One is a battle of numbers, in which one number captures another. The other is a game in which the vices fight a battle against the virtues. The game is set up to show how the vices oppose one another, yet readily combine against the virtues; then, what vices oppose what virtues, how they try to assault them openly or undermine them in secret; how the virtues can break the strength of the vices or turn their purposes to good; and finally, by what means one side or the other gains the victory.

But in all this, you may get a wrong impression, if we don't go back and consider one point more carefully. Because they allot only six hours to work, you might think the necessities of life would be in scant supply. This is far from the case. Their working hours are ample to provide not only enough but more than enough of the necessities and even the conveniences of life. You will easily appreciate this if you consider how large a part of the population in other countries exists without doing any work at all. In the first place, hardly any of the women, who are a full half of the population, work; or, if they do, then as a rule their husbands lie snoring in the bed. Then there is a great lazy gang of priests and so-called religious men. Add to them all the rich, especially the landlords, who are commonly called gentlemen and nobility. Include with them their retainers, that mob of swaggering bullies. Finally, reckon in with these the sturdy and lusty beggars, who go about feigning some disease as an excuse for their idleness. You will certainly find that the things which satisfy our needs are produced by far fewer hands than you had supposed.

And now consider how few of those who do work are doing 8 really essential things. For where money is the standard of everything, many superfluous trades are bound to be carried on simply to satisfy luxury and licentiousness. Suppose the multitude of those who now work were limited to a few trades, and set to producing more and more of those conveniences and commodities that nature really requires. They would be bound to produce so much that the prices would drop, and the workmen would be unable to gain a living. But suppose again that all the workers in useless trades were put to useful ones, and that all the idlers (who now guzzle twice as much as the workingmen who make what they consume) were assigned to productive tasks—well, you can easily see how little time each man would have to spend working, in order to produce all the goods that human needs and conveniences require—yes, and human pleasure too, as long as it's true and natural pleasure.

The experience of Utopia makes this perfectly apparent. In each city and its surrounding countryside barely five hundred of those men and women whose age and strength make them fit for work are exempted from it. Among these are the syphogrants, who by law are free not to work; yet they don't take advantage of the privilege, preferring to set a good example to their fellow-citizens. Some others are permanently exempted from work so that they may devote themselves to study, but only on the recommendation of the priests and through a secret vote of the syphogrants. If any of these scholars disappoints their hopes, he becomes a workman again. On the other hand, it happens from time to time that a craftsman devotes his leisure so earnestly to study, and makes such progress as a result, that he is relieved of manual labor, and promoted to the class of learned men. From this class of scholars are chosen ambassadors, priests, tranibors, and the prince himself, who used to be called Barzanes, but in their modern tongue is known as Ademus.

Since all the rest of the population is neither idle nor occupied in useless trades, it is easy to see why they produce so much in so short a working day.

Apart from all this, in severai of the necessary crafts their way of life requires less total labor than does that of people elsewhere. In other countries, building and repairing houses requires the constant work of many men, because what a father has built, his thriftless heirs lets fall into ruin; and then his successor has to repair, at great expense, what could easily have been maintained at a very small charge. Further, even when a man has built a splendid house at large cost, someone else may think he has finer taste, let the first house fall to ruin, and then build another one somewhere else for just as much money. But among the Utopians, where everything has been established, and the commonwealth is carefully regulated, building a brand-new home on a new site is a rare event. They are not only quick to repair damage, but foresighted in preventing it. The result is that their buildings last for a very long time with minimum repairs; and the carpenters and masons sometimes have so little to do, that they are set to hewing timber and cutting stone in case some future need for it should arise.

Consider, too, how little labor their clothing requires. Their work clothes are loose garments made of leather which last as long as seven years. When they go out in public, they cover these rough working-clothes with a cloak. Throughout the entire island, everyone wears the same colored cloak, which is the color of natural wool. As a result, they not only need less wool than people in other countries, but what they do need is less expensive. They use linen cloth most, because it requires least labor. They like linen cloth to be white and wool cloth to be clean; but they put no price on fineness of texture. Elsewhere a man is not satisfied with four or five woolen cloaks of different colors and as many silk shirts, or if he's a show-off, even ten of each are not enough. But a Utopian is content with a single cloak, and generally wears it for two seasons. There is no reason at all why he should want any others, for if he had them, he would not be better protected against the cold, nor would he appear in any way better dressed.

When there is an abundance of everything, as a result of everyone working at useful trades, and nobody consuming to excess, then great numbers of the people often go out to work on the roads, if any of them need repairing. And when there is no need even for this sort of public work, then the officials very often proclaim a short work day, since they never force their citizens to perform useless labor. The chief aim of their constitution and government is that, whenever public needs permit, all citizens should be free, so far as possible, to withdraw their time and energy from the service of the body, and devote themselves to the freedom and culture of the mind. For that, they think, is the real happiness of life. . . .

Their Moral Philosophy

They conclude, after carefully considering and weighing the matter, that all our actions and the virtues exercised within them look toward pleasure and happiness at their ultimate end.

By pleasure they understand every state or movement of body or mind in which man naturally finds delight. They are right in considering man's appetites natural. By simply following his senses and his right reason a man may discover what is pleasant by nature—it is a delight which does not injure others, which does not preclude a greater pleasure, and which is not followed by pain. But a pleasure which is against nature, and which men call "delightful" only by the emptiest of fictions (as if one could change the real nature of things just by changing their names), does not really make for happiness; in fact they say, it destroys happiness. And the reason is that men whose minds are filled with false ideas of pleasure have no room left for true and genuine delight. As a matter of fact, there are a great many things which have no sweetness in them, but are mainly or entirely bitter—yet which through the perverse enticements of evil lusts are considered very great pleasures, and even the supreme goals of life.

Among those who pursue this false pleasure the Utopians include those whom I mentioned before, the men who think themselves finer fellows because they wear finer clothes. These people are twice mistaken: first in thinking their clothes better than anyone else's, and then in thinking themselves better because of their clothes. As far as a coat's usefulness goes, what does it matter if it was woven of thin thread or thick? Yet they act as if they were set apart by nature herself, rather than their own fantasies; they strut about, and put on airs. Because they have a fancy suit, they think themselves entitled to honors they would never have expected if they were poorly dressed, and they get very angry if someone passes them by without showing special respect.

It is the same kind of absurdity to be pleased by empty, cere- 16
monial honors. What true and natural pleasure can you get from someone's bent knee or bared head? Will the creaks in your own

knees be eased thereby, or the madness in your head? The phantom of false pleasure is illustrated by other men who run mad with delight over their own blue blood, plume themselves on their nobility, and applaud themselves for all their rich ancestors (the only ancestors worth having nowadays), and all their ancient family estates. Even if they don't have the shred of an estate themselves, or if they've squandered every penny of their inheritance, they don't consider themselves a bit less noble.

In the same class the Utopians put those people I described before, who are mad for jewelry and gems, and think themselves divinely happy if they find a good specimen, especially of the sort which happens to be fashionable in their country at the time—for stones vary in value from one market to another. The collector will not make an offer for the stone till it's taken out of its setting, and even then he will not buy unless the dealer guarantees and gives security that it is a true and genuine stone. What he fears is that his eyes will be deceived by a counterfeit. But if you consider the matter, why should a counterfeit give any less pleasure when your eyes cannot distinguish it from a real gem? Both should be of equal value to you, as they would be, in fact, to a blind man.

Speaking of false pleasure, what about those who pile up money, not because they want to do anything with the heap, but so they can sit and look at it? Is that true pleasure they experience, or aren't they simply cheated by a show of pleasure? Or what of those with the opposite vice, the men who hide away money they will never use and perhaps never even see again? In their anxiety to hold onto their money, they actually lose it. For what else happens when you deprive yourself, and perhaps other people too, of a chance to use money, by burying it in the ground? And yet when the miser has hidden his treasure, he exults over it as if his mind were now free to rejoice. Suppose someone stole it, and the miser died ten years later, knowing nothing of the theft. During all those ten years, what did it matter whether the money was stolen or not? In either case, it was equally useless to the owner.

To these false and foolish pleasures they add gambling, which they have heard about, though they've never tried it, as well as hunting and hawking. What pleasure can there be, they wonder, in throwing dice on a table? If there were any pleasure in the action, wouldn't doing it over and over again quickly make one tired of it? What pleasure can there be in listening to the barking and yelping of dogs—isn't that rather a disgusting noise? Is there any more real pleasure when a dog chases a rabbit than there is when a dog chases a dog? If what you like is fast running, there's plenty of that in both cases; they're just about the same. But if what you really want is slaughter, if you want to see a living creature torn apart under your eyes, then the whole thing is wrong. You ought to feel nothing but pity when you see the hare fleeing from the hound, the weak creature tormented by the stronger, the fearful and timid beast brutalized by the savage one, the harmless hare killed by the cruel dog. The Utopians, who regard this whole activity of hunting as unworthy of free men, have assigned it, accordingly, to their butchers, who as I said before, are all slaves. In their eyes, hunting is the lowest thing even butchers can do. In the slaughterhouse, their work is more useful and honest—besides which, they kill animals only from necessity; but in hunting they seek merely their own pleasure from the killing and mutilating of some poor little creature. Taking such relish in the sight of death, even if it's only beasts, reveals, in the opinion of the Utopians, a cruel disposition. Or if he isn't cruel to start with, the hunter quickly becomes so through the constant practice of such brutal pleasures.

Most men consider these activities, and countless others like them, to be pleasures; but the Utopians say flatly they have nothing at all to do with real pleasure since there's nothing naturally pleasant about them. They often please the senses, and in this they are like pleasure, but that does not alter their basic nature. The enjoyment doesn't arise from the experience itself, but only from the perverse mind of the individual, as a result of which he mistakes the bitter for the sweet, just as pregnant women, whose taste has been turned awry, sometimes think pitch and tallow taste sweeter than honey. A man's taste may be similarly depraved, by disease or by custom, but that does not change the nature of pleasure, or of anything else.

Topics for Discussion and Writing

1. What does More assume are the only functions of clothing? Do you agree with More, or do you find other important reasons why people wear the clothes that they wear?

2. The "work ethic" assumes that labor is good in itself—that there is some sort of virtue in work. (See Nixon's remark on page 292.) Further, many people assume that work, at least certain kinds of work done under certain conditions, affords happiness to the worker. What does More's attitude seem to be on these two related points?

3. What is More's opinion of hunting? What arguments in support of hunting are commonly offered? In your opinion, does More successfully counter those arguments?
4. In approximately 500 words set forth More's assumptions about the sources of happiness.
5. More says that each Utopian is free to do what he wishes with leisure hours, "provided he does not waste them in roistering or sloth." (By the way, since the Utopians work six hours a day, if they sleep eight hours they have ten hours of free time.) In 500 words develop an argument for or against this proviso concerning the pursuit of happiness. (You may want to recall that our own government to some degree regulates our pleasure, for instance by outlawing bullfights.)
6. Note the passage (paragraph 6) in which More describes two games enjoyed by Utopians. Imitating More's style in describing the second game, write a paragraph describing a video game as a Utopian, or anti-Utopian, recreation.

Marie Winn

Marie Winn, born in Czechoslovakia in 1936, came to New York when she was still a child. She later graduated from Radcliffe College and then did further academic work at Columbia University. Our selection comes from Childhood Without Children *(1983), a book based in part on interviews with hundreds of children and parents.*

The End of Play

Of all the changes that have altered the topography of childhood, the most dramatic has been the disappearance of childhood play. Whereas a decade or two ago children were easily distinguished from the adult world by the very nature of their play, today children's occupations do not differ greatly from adult diversions.

Infants and toddlers, to be sure, continue to follow certain timeless patterns of manipulation and exploration; adolescents, too, have not changed their free-time habits so very much, turning as they ever have towards adult pastimes and amusements in their drive for autonomy, self-mastery, and sexual discovery. It is among the ranks of school-age children, those six-to-twelve-year-olds who once avidly filled their free moments with childhood play, that the greatest change is evident. In the place of traditional, sometimes ancient childhood games that were still popular a generation ago, in the place of fantasy and make-believe play—"You be the mommy and I'll be the daddy"—doll play or toy-soldier play, jump-rope play, ball-bouncing play, today's children have substituted television viewing and, most recently, video games.

Many parents have misgivings about the influence of television. They sense that a steady and time-consuming exposure to passive entertainment might damage the ability to play imaginatively and resourcefully, or prevent this ability from developing in the first place. A mother of two school-age children recalls: "When I was growing up, we used to go out into the vacant lots and make up week-long dramas and sagas. This was during third, fourth, fifth grades. But my own kids have never done that sort of thing, and somehow it bothers me. I wish we had cut down on the TV years ago, and maybe the kids would have learned how to play."

The testimony of parents who eliminate television for periods of   4 time strengthens the connection between children's television watching and changed play patterns. Many parents discover that when their children don't have television to fill their free time, they resort to the old kinds of imaginative, traditional "children's play." Moreover, these parents often observe that under such circumstances "they begin to seem more like children" or "they act more childlike." Clearly, a part of the definition of childhood, in adults' minds, resides in the nature of children's play.

Children themselves sometimes recognize the link between play and their own special definition as children. In an interview about children's books with four ten-year-old girls, one of them said: "I read this story about a girl my age growing up twenty years ago— you know, in 1960 or so,—and she seemed so much younger than me in her behavior. Like she might be playing with dolls, or playing all sorts of children's games, or jump-roping or something." The other girls all agreed that they had noticed a similar discrepancy between themselves and fictional children in books of the past: those children seemed more like children. "So what do *you* do in your spare time, if you don't play with dolls or play make-believe games or jump rope or do things kids did twenty years ago?" they were asked. They laughed and answered, "We watch TV."

But perhaps other societal factors have caused children to give up play. Children's greater exposure to adult realities, their knowledge of adult sexuality, for instance, might make them more sophisticated, less likely to play like children. Evidence from the counterculture communes of the sixties and seventies adds weight to the argument that it is television above all that has eliminated children's play. Studies of children raised in a variety of such communes, all television-free, showed the little communards continuing to fill their time with those forms of play that have all but vanished from the lives of conventionally reared American children. And yet these counterculture kids were casually exposed to all sorts of adult matters—drug taking, sexual intercourse. Indeed, they sometimes incorporated these matters into their play: "We're mating," a pair of six-year-olds told a reporter to explain their curious bumps and grinds. Nevertheless, to all observers the commune children preserved a distinctly childlike and even innocent demeanor, an impression that was produced mainly by the fact that they spent most of their time playing. Their play defined them as belonging to a special world of childhood.

Not all children have lost the desire to engage in the old-style childhood play. But so long as the most popular, most dominant members of the peer group, who are often the most socially precocious, are "beyond" playing, then a common desire to conform makes it harder for those children who still have the drive to play to go ahead and do so. Parents often report that their children seem ashamed of previously common forms of play and hide their involvement with such play from their peers. "My fifth-grader still plays with dolls," a mother tells, "but she keeps them hidden in the basement where nobody will see them." This social check on the play instinct serves to hasten the end of childhood for even the least advanced children.

What seems to have replaced play in the lives of great numbers 8 of preadolescents these days, starting as early as fourth grade, is a burgeoning interest in boy-girl interactions—"going out" or "going together." These activities do not necessarily involve going anywhere or doing anything sexual, but nevertheless are the first stage of a sexual process that used to commence at puberty or even later. Those more sophisticated children who are already involved in such manifestly unchildlike interest make plain their low opinion of their peers who still *play.* "Some of the kids in the class are real weird," a fifth-grade boy states. "They're not interested in going out, just in trucks and stuff, or games pretending they're monsters. Some of them don't even *try* to be cool."

Video Games Versus Marbles

Is there really any great difference, one might ask, between that gang of kids playing video games by the hour at their local candy store these days and those small fry who used to hang around together spending equal amounts of time playing marbles? It is easy to see a similarity between the two activities: each requires a certain amount of manual dexterity, each is almost as much fun to watch as to play, each is simple and yet challenging enough for that middle-childhood age group for whom time can be so oppressive if unfilled.

One significant difference between the modern pre-teen fad of video games and the once popular but now almost extinct pastime of marbles is economic: playing video games costs twenty-five cents for approximately three minutes of play; playing marbles, after a small initial investment, is free. The children who frequent video-game machines require a considerable outlay of quarters to subsidize their fun; two, three, or four dollars is not an unusual expenditure for an eight-or nine-year-old spending an hour or two with his friends play-ing Asteroids or Pac-Man or Space Invaders. For most of the children the money comes from their weekly allowance. Some augment this amount by enterprising commercial ventures—trading and selling comic books, or doing chores around the house for extra money.

But what difference does it make *where* the money comes from? Why should that make video games any less satisfactory as an amuse-ment for children? In fact, having to pay for the entertain-ment, whatever the source of the money, and having its duration limited by one's financial resources changes the nature of the game, in a subtle way diminishing the satisfactions it offers. Money and time become intertwined, as they so often are in the adult world and as, in the past, they almost never were in the child's world. For the child playing marbles, meanwhile, time has a far more carefree quality, bounded only by the requirements to be home by suppertime or by dark.

But the video-game-playing child has an additional burden—a   12
burden of choice, of knowing that the money used for playing Pac-Man could have been saved for Christmas, could have been used to buy something tangible, perhaps something "worthwhile," as his parents might say, rather than being "wasted" on video games. There is a certain sense of adultness that spending money imparts, a feeling of being a consumer, which distinguishes a game with a price from its counterparts among the traditional childhood games children once played at no cost.

There are other differences as well. Unlike child-initiated and child-organized games such as marbles, video games are adult-created mechanisms not entirely within the child's control, and thus less likely to impart a sense of mastery and fulfillment: the coin may get jammed, the machine may go haywire, the little blobs may stop eating the funny little dots. Then the child must go to the storekeeper to complain, to get his money back. He may be "ripped off" and simply lose his quarter, much as his parents are when they buy a faulty appliance. This possibility of disaster gives the child's play a certain weight that marbles never imposed on its light-hearted players.

Even if a child has a video game at home requiring no coin outlay, the play it provides is less than optimal. The noise level of the machine is high—too high, usually, for the child to conduct a conversation easily with another child. And yet, according to its enthusiasts, this very noisiness is a part of the game's attraction. The loud whizzes, crashes, and whirrs of the video-game machine "blow the mind" and create an excitement that is quite apart from the excitement generated simply by trying to win a game. A traditional childhood game such as marbles, on the other hand, has little built-in stimulation; the excitement of playing is generated entirely by the players' own actions. And while the pace of a game of marbles is close to the child's natural physiological rhythms, the frenzied activities of video games serve to "rev up" the child in an artificial way, almost in the way a stimulant or an amphetamine might. Meanwhile the perceptual impact of a video game is similar to that of watching television—the action, after all, takes place on a television screen—causing the eye to defocus slightly and creating a certain alteration in the child's natural state of consciousness.

Parents' instinctive reaction to their children's involvement with video games provides another clue to the difference between this contemporary form of play and the more traditional pastimes such as marbles. While parents, indeed most adults, derive open pleasure from watching children at play, most parents today are not delighted to watch their kids flicking away at the Pac-Man machine. This does not seem to them to be real play. As a mother of two school-age children anxiously explains, "We used to do real childhood sorts of things when I was a kid. We'd build forts and put on crazy plays and make up new languages, and just generally we *played*. But today my kids don't play that way at all. They like video games and of course they still go in for sports outdoors. They go roller skating and ice skating and skiing and all. But they don't seem to really *play*."

Some of this feeling may represent a certain nostalgia for the past   16
and the old generation's resistance to the different ways of the new.
But it is more likely that most adults have an instinctive understanding of the importance of play in their own childhood. This feeling
stokes their fears that their children are being deprived of something irreplaceable when they flip the levers on the video machines
to manipulate the electronic images rather than flick their fingers
to send a marble shooting towards another marble.

Play Deprivation

In addition to television's influence, some parents and teachers
ascribe children's diminished drive to play to recent changes in the
school curriculum, especially in the early grades.

"Kindergarten, traditionally a playful port of entry into formal
school, is becoming more academic, with children being taught
specific skills, taking tests, and occasionally even having homework," begins a report on new directions in early childhood education. Since 1970, according to the United States census, the proportion of three- and four-year-olds enrolled in school has risen
dramatically, from 20.5 percent to 36.7 percent in 1980, and these
nursery schools have largely joined the push towards academic ac-
celeration in the early grades. Moreover, middle-class nursery
schools in recent years have introduced substantial doses of academic
material into their daily programs, often using those particular
devices originally intended to help culturally deprived preschoolers
in compensatory programs such as Headstart to catch up with their
middle-class peers. Indeed, some of the increased focus on academic
skills in nursery schools and kindergartens is related to the
widespread popularity among young children and their parents of
Sesame Street, a program originally intended to help deprived children attain academic skills, but universally watched by middle-class
toddlers as well.

Parents of the *Sesame Street* generation often demand a "serious," skill-centered program for their preschoolers in school, afraid
that the old-fashioned, play-centered curriculum will bore their
alphabet-spouting, number-chanting four- and five-year-olds. A few
parents, especially those whose children have not attended television classes or nursery school, complain of the high-powered pace
of kindergarten these days. A father whose five-year-old daughter
attends a public kindergarten declares: "There's a lot more pressure
put on little kids these days than when we were kids, that's for sure.

My daughter never went to nursery school and never watched *Sesame*, and she had a lot of trouble when she entered kindergarten this fall. By October, just a month and a half into the program, she was already flunking. The teacher told us our daughter couldn't keep up with the other kids. And believe me, she's a bright kid! All the other kids were getting gold stars and smiley faces for their work, and every day Emily would come home in tears because she didn't get a gold star. Remember when we were in kindergarten? We were *children* then. We were allowed just to play!"

A kindergarten teacher confirms the trend towards early academic pressure. "We're expected by the dictates of the school system to push a lot of curriculum," she explains. "Kids in our kindergarten can't sit around playing with blocks any more. We've just managed to squeeze in one hour of free play a week, on Fridays."

The diminished emphasis on fantasy and play and imaginative activities in early childhood education and the increased focus on early academic-skill acquisition have helped to change childhood from a play-centered time of life to one more closely resembling the style of adulthood: purposeful, success-centered, competitive. The likelihood is that these preschool "workers" will not metamorphose back into players when they move on to grade school. This decline in play is surely one of the reasons why so many teachers today comment that their third- or fourth-graders act like tired businessmen instead of like children.

What might be the consequences of this change in children's play? Children's propensity to engage in that extraordinary series of behaviors characterized as "play" is perhaps the single great dividing line between childhood and adulthood, and has probably been so throughout history. The make-believe games anthropologists have recorded of children in primitive societies around the world attest to the universality of play and to the uniqueness of this activity to the immature members of each society. But in those societies, and probably in Western society before the middle or late eighteenth century, there was always a certain similarity between children's play and adult work. The child's imaginative play took the form of imitation of various aspects of adult life, culminating in the gradual transformation of the child's play from make-believe work to *real* work. At this point, in primitive societies or in our own society of the past, the child took her or his place in the adult work world and the distinctions between adulthood and childhood virtually vanished. But in today's technologically advanced society there is no place for the child in the adult work world. There are not enough jobs, even of the most menial kind, to go around for adults, much less for children. The child must continue to be dependent on adults for many years while gaining the knowledge and skills necessary to become a working member of society.

This is not a new situation for children. For centuries children have endured a prolonged period of dependence long after the help-lessness of early childhood is over. But until recent years children remained childlike and playful far longer than they do today. Kept isolated from the adult world as a result of deliberate secrecy and protectiveness, they continued to find pleasure in socially sanctioned childish activities until the imperatives of adolescence led them to strike out for independence and self-sufficiency.

Today, however, with children's inclusion in the adult world 24 both through the instrument of television and as a result of a deliber-ately preparatory, integrative style of child rearing, the old forms of play no longer seem to provide children with enough excitement and stimulation. What then are these so-called children to do for fulfillment if their desire to play has been vitiated and yet their entry into the working world of adulthood must be delayed for many years? The answer is precisely to get involved in those areas that cause contemporary parents so much distress: addictive television viewing during the school years followed, in adolescence or even before, by a search for similar oblivion via alcohol and drugs; ex-ploration of the world of sensuality and sexuality before achieving the emotional maturity necessary for altruistic relationships.

Psychiatrists have observed among children in recent years a marked increase in the occurrence of depression, a state long consi-dered antithetical to the nature of childhood. Perhaps this phenome-non is at least somewhat connected with the current sense of use-lessness and alienation that children feel, a sense that play may once upon a time have kept in abeyance.

Topics for Discussion and Writing

1. In a sentence or two sum up Winn's thesis.
2. When you were a child, what did you do in your "spare time"? Judging from your own experience, is Winn's first paragraph true, or at least roughly true?
3. Assuming that children today do indeed spend many hours watching television and playing video games, is it true that these activities "do not differ greatly from adult diversions"? To test Winn's assertion, list

the diversions of adults and of children that you know of from your own experience. Are the two lists indeed strikingly similar? Or do the lists reveal important differences? Explain.

4. Winn's argument is largely composed of a series of comparisons between the play of children before access to TV and after; between traditional and contemporary kindergarten; between childhood in "primitive" (and our own pre-industrial) society and in technologically advanced societies. List the points she makes to develop each of these comparisons. How well does each comparison support her thesis?

5. Winn obviously prefers that children in play make up stories rather than watch television. What reasons can be given to prefer making up stories, or reading stories in a book, to watching stories on television? Winn does not mention being read to by an adult as an activity of childhood. Draw your own comparison between traditional bedtime story-reading and nighttime TV-watching. Would such a comparison have strengthened or weakened Winn's argument?

6. Speaking of video games (paragraph 11), Winn argues that "having to pay for the entertainment . . . changes the nature of the game, in a subtle way diminishing the satisfactions it offers." Can one reply that having to pay helps a child to appreciate the value of money? In short, can it be argued that paying for one's pleasure is a way of becoming mature?

Black Elk

Black Elk, a wichasha wakon (holy man) of the Oglala Sioux, as a small boy witnessed the battle of the Little Bighorn (1876). He lived to see his people all but annihilated and his hopes for them extinguished. In 1931, toward the end of his life, he told his life story to the poet and scholar John G. Neihardt to preserve a sacred vision given him.
"War Games" (editors' title) is from Black Elk Speaks.

War Games

When it was summer again we were camping on the Rosebud, and I did not feel so much afraid, because the Wasichus seemed farther away and there was peace there in the valley and there was plenty of meat. But all the boys from five or six years up were playing war. The little boys would gather together from the different bands of the tribe and fight each other with mud balls that they threw with willow sticks. And the big boys played the game

called Throwing-Them-Off-Their-Horses, which is a battle all but
the killing; and sometimes they got hurt. The horsebacks from the
different bands would line up and charge upon each other, yelling;
and when the ponies came together on the run, they would rear
and flounder and scream in a big dust, and the riders would seize
each other, wrestling until one side had lost all its men, for those
who fell upon the ground were counted dead.

When I was older, I, too, often played this game. We were always naked when we played it, just as warriors are when they go
into battle if it is not too cold, because they are swifter without
clothes. Once I fell off on my back right in the middle of a bed of
prickly pears, and it took my mother a long while to pick all the
stickers out of me. I was still too little to play war that summer, but
I can remember watching the other boys, and I thought that when
we all grew up and were big together, maybe we could kill all the
Wasichus or drive them far away from our country. . . .

There was a war game that we little boys played after a big hunt.
We went out a little way from the village and built some grass tepees,
playing we were enemies and this was our village. We had an adviser, and when it got dark he would order us to go and steal some
dried meat from the big people. He would hold a stick up to us and
we had to bite off a piece of it. If we bit a big piece we had to get
a big piece of meat, and if we bit a little piece, we did not have to
get so much. Then we started for the big people's village, crawling
on our bellies, and when we got back without getting caught, we
would have a big feast and a dance and make kill talks, telling of
our brave deeds like warriors. Once, I remember, I had no brave
deed to tell. I crawled up to a leaning tree beside a tepee and there
was meat hanging on the limbs. I wanted a tongue I saw up there
in the moonlight, so I climbed up. But just as I was about to reach
it, the man in the tepee yelled "Ye-a-a!" He was saying this to his
dog, who was stealing some meat too, but I thought the man had
seen me, and I was so scared I fell out of the tree and ran away
crying.

Then we used to have what we called a chapped breast dance.   4
Our adviser would look us over to see whose breast was burned
most from not having it covered with the robe we wore; and the
boy chosen would lead the dance while we all sang like this:

I have a chapped breast.
My breast is red.
My breast is yellow.

And we practiced endurance too. Our adviser would put dry sun-
flower seeds on our wrists. These were lit at the top, and we had
to let them burn clear down to the skin. They hurt and made sores,
but if we knocked them off or cried Owh!, we would be called
women.

Topics for Discussion and Writing

1. Notice the subjective passages in Black Elk's descriptions of the games
   he played as a child. What do they reveal about Black Elk as a child
   and as an adult? How appropriate are these revelations to his topic?
2. The Duke of Wellington is reported to have said that the battle of Waterloo was won on the playing fields of Eton. Try to describe a game that
   is a small version of an adult activity and that teaches adult habits, good
   or bad. As an experiment, write the description as objectively as you
   can. Then rewrite it, allowing your description to reveal your attitudes,
   as a child and now, to the game, to other children, and to the adult world.

Joseph Epstein

*Joseph Epstein was born in Chicago in 1937. He is the author of several books on Ameri-
can culture, the editor of* American Scholar *(a quarterly review published by Phi Beta
Kappa), and an occasional teacher of English at Northwestern University. This essay
first appeared in* Harper's Magazine.

Obsessed with Sport

I cannot remember when I was not surrounded by sports,
when talk of sports was not in the air, when I did not care passionately about sports. As a boy in Chicago in the late Forties, I lived
in the same building as the sister and brother-in-law of Barney Ross,
the welterweight champion. Half a block away, down near the lake,
the Sullivan High School football team worked out in the spring
and autumn. Summers the same field was given over to baseball
and men's softball on Sundays. A few blocks to the north was the
Touhy Avenue Fieldhouse, where basketball was played, and
lifeguards trained, and behind which, in a softball field frozen over

in winter, crack-the-whip, hockey, and speed skating took over. To the west, a block or so up Morse Avenue, was the Morse Avenue "L" Recreations, a combined pool hall and bowling alley. Life, in short, was games.

My father had no interest in sports. He had grown up, one of the ten children of Russian Jewish immigrant parents, on tough Notre Dame Street in Montreal, where the major sports were craps, poker, and petty larceny. He left Montreal at seventeen to come to Chicago, where he worked hard and successfully so that his sons might play. Two of his boyhood friends from Notre Dame Street, who had the comic-book names of Sammy and Danny Spunt, had also come to Chicago, where they bought the Ringside Gym on Dearborn Street in the Loop. All the big names worked out at Ringside for their Chicago fights: Willie Pep, Tony Zale, Joe Louis. At eight or nine I would take the El downtown to the Ringside, be introduced around by Danny Spunt ("Tony Zale, I'd like you to meet the son of an old friend of mine. Kid, I'd like you to meet the middleweight champion of the world"), and return home with an envelope filled with autographed 8-by-10 glossies of Gus Lesnevich, Tammy Maurielo, Kid Gavilan, and the wondrous Sugar Ray.

I lived on, off, and in sports. *Sport* magazine had recently begun publication, and I gobbled up its issues cover to cover, soon becoming knowledgeable not only about the major sports—baseball, football, and basketball—but about golf, hockey, tennis, and horse racing, so that I scored reputably on the Sport Quiz, a regular department at the front of the magazine. Another regular department was the Sport Classic, which featured longish profiles of the legendary figures in the history of sports: Ty Cobb, Jim Thorpe, Bobby Jones, Big Bill Tilden, Red Grange, Man o' War. I next moved on to the sports novels of John R. Tunis—*All-American, The Iron Duke, The Kid from Tomkinsville, The Kid Comes Back, World Series*, the lot—which I read with as much excitement as any books I have read since.

The time was, as is now apparent, a splendid era in sports. Ted [4] Williams, Joe DiMaggio, and Stan Musial were afield; first Jack Kramer, then Pancho Gonzales, dominated tennis; George Mikan led the Minneapolis Lakers, and the Harlem Globetrotters could still be taken seriously; Doc Blanchard and Glen Davis, Mr. Inside and Mr. Outside, were playing for Army, Johnny Lujack was at Notre Dame; in the pros Sammy Baugh, Bob Waterfield, and Sid Luckman were the major T-formation quarterbacks; Joe Louis and Sugar Ray Robinson fought frequently; the two Willies, Mosconi and

Hoppe, put in regular appearances at Bensinger's in the Loop; Eddie Arcaro seemed to ride three, four winners a day. Giants, it truly seemed, walked the earth.

All learning of craft—which sport, like writing, most assuredly is—involves imitation, especially in the early stages; and I was an excellent mimic. By the time I was ten years old I had mastery over all the big-time moves: the spit in the mitt, the fluid infield chatter, the knocking of dirt from the spikes; the rhythmic barking out of signals, hands high under the center's crotch to take the ball; the three bounces and deep breath before shooting the free throw (on this last, I regretted not being a Catholic, so that I might be able to make the sign of the cross before shooting, as was then the fashion among Catholic high-school and college players). I went in for athletic haberdashery in a big way, often going beyond mimicry to the point of flat-out phoniness—wearing, for example, a knee pad while playing basketball, though my knees were always, exasperatingly, intact.

I always looked good, which was important, because form is intrinsic to sports; but in my case it was doubly important, because the truth is that I wasn't really very good. Or at any rate not good enough. Two factors accounted for this. The first was that, without being shy about body contact, I lacked a certain indispensable aggressiveness; the second, connected closely to the first, was that, when it came right down to it, I did not care enough about winning. I would rather lose a point attempting a slashing cross-court backhand than play for an easier winner down the side; the long jump shot always had more allure for me than the safer drive to the basket. Given a choice between the two vanities of winning and looking good, I almost always preferred looking good.

I shall never forget the afternoon, sometime along about my thirteenth year, when, shooting baskets alone, I came upon the technique for shooting the hook. Although today it has nowhere near the consequence of the jump shot—an innovation that has been to basketball what the jet has been to air travel—the hook is still the single most beautiful shot in the game. The rhythm and grace of it, the sway of the body off the pivot, the release of the ball behind the head and off the fingertips, the touch and instinct involved in its execution, make the hook altogether a balletic thing, and to achieve it is to feel one of the most delectable sensations in sports. That afternoon, on a deserted side street, shooting on a rickety wooden backboard and a black rim without a net, I felt it and grew nearly drunk on the feeling. Rain came down, dirt washed in the gutters, flecks of it spattering my clothes and arms and face, but, soaked and cold though I was, I do not think I would have left that basket on that afternoon for anything. I threw up hook after hook, from every angle, from farther and farther out, off the board, without the board, and hook after hook went in. Only pitch darkness drove me home.

I do not say that not to have shot the hook is never to have lived, 8 but only that, once having done so, the pleasure it gives is not so easily forgotten. Every sport offers similar pleasures, the pleasures taken differing by temperament: the canter into the end zone to meet a floating touchdown pass, or the clean, crisp feel of a perfect block or tackle; the long straight drive or the precisely played approach shot to the green; the solid overhead; the pickup on the tricky short hop or the long ball down one of the power alleys. Different sports, different pleasures. But so keen are these pleasures—pleasures of execution, of craft completed—that, along with being unforgettable, they are also worth recapturing in any available way, and the most available way, when reflexes have slowed, when muscle no longer responds so readily to brain, is from the grandstand or, perhaps more often nowadays, from the chair before the television.

Pleasures of the Spectator

I have put in days on the bench, but years in my chair before the television set. Recently it has occurred to me that over the years I have heard more hours of talk from the announcer Curt Gowdy than from my own father, who is not a reticent man. I have been thoroughly Schenkeled, Mussbergered, Summeralled, Cosselled, DeRogotissed, and Garagiolaed. How many hundreds—thousands— of hours have I spent watching sports of all sorts, either at parks or stadiums or over television? I am glad I shall never have a precise answer. Yet neither apparently can I get enough. What is the fascination? Why is it that, with the prospect of a game to watch in the evening or on the weekend, the day seems lighter and brighter? What do I get out of it?

What I get out of it, according to one fairly prominent view, is an outlet for my violent emotions. Knee-wrenching, rib-cracking, head-busting, this view has it, is what sports are really about, with sports fans being essentially sadists, and cowardly sadists at that, for they take their violence not at firsthand but at second remove. Enthusiasm for sports among Americans is little more than a reflection of the national penchant for violence. Military men talk about game plans; the long touchdown pass is called the bomb. The average pro-football fan, seeing a quarterback writhing on the ground at midfield as a result of the ministrations of Joe Green, Carl Eller, or Lyle Alzado, twitters with glee, finds his ultimate reward, and declares a little holiday in the blackest corner of his heart.

But this is a criticism that comes at sports by way of politics. To believe it one has to believe that the history of the United States is chiefly one of rape, expropriation, and aggressive imperialism. To dismiss it, however, one need only know something about sports. Violence is indubitably a part of some sports; in some—hockey is an example—it sometimes comes close to being featured. But in no sport—not even boxing, that most rudimentary of sports—is it the main item, and in many other sports it plays no part at all. A distinction worth insisting on is that between violence and roughness. Roughness, a willingness to mix it up, to take if need be an elbow in the jaw, is part of rebounding in basketball, yet violence is not. Even in pro football, most maligned of modern American sports, more of roughness than of violence is involved. Roughness raises the stakes, provides the pressure, behind execution. A splendid because true phrase has come about in pro football to cover the situation in which a pass receiver, certain that he will be tackled upon the instant he makes his reception, drops a ball he should otherwise have caught easily—the phrase, best delivered in a Southern accent such as Don Meredith's, is "He heard footsteps on that one, Howard." Although a part of the attraction, it is not so much those footsteps that fill the stands and the den chairs on Sunday afternoons as it is those men who elude them: the Lynn Swanns, the Fran Tarkentons, the O. J. Simpsons. The American love of violence theory really will not wash. Dick Butkus did not get us into Vietnam.

Many who would not argue that sports reflect American violence   12
nevertheless claim that they imbue one with the competitive spirit. In some who are already amply endowed with it, sports doubtless do tend to refine (or possibly brutalize) the desire to win. Yet sports also teach a serious respect for craft. Competition, though it flourishes as always, is in bad odor nowadays; but craft, officially respected, does not flourish greatly outside the boutique.

If the love of violence or the competitive urge does not put me in my chair for the countless games I watch, is it, then, nostalgia, a yearning to regain the more glowing moments of adolescence? Many argue that this is precisely so, that American men exist in a state of perpetual immaturity, suspended between boy- and man-hood. "The difference between men and boys," says Liberace, "is the price of their toys." (I have paid more than $300 for two half-season tickets to the Chicago Bulls games, parking fees not included.) Such unending enthusiasm for games may have something to do with adolescence, but little, I suspect, with regaining anything whatever. Instead, it has more to do with watching men do regularly and surpassingly what, as an adolescent, one did often bumblingly though with an occasional flash of genius. To have played these games oneself as a boy or a young man helps immeasurably the appreciation that in watching a sport played at professional caliber one is witnessing the extraordinary made to look ordinary. That a game may have no consequence outside itself—no effect on history, on one's own life, on anything really—does not make it trivial but only makes the enjoyment of it all the purer.

The notion that men watch sports to regain their adolescence pictures them sitting in the stands or at home watching a game and, within their psyches, muttering, "There, but for the lack of grace of God, go I." And it is true that a number of contemporary authors who are taken seriously have indeed written about sports with a strong overlay of yearning. In the men's softball games described in the fiction of Philip Roth, center field is a place akin to Arcady. Arcadian, too, is the outfield in Willie Morris's memoir of growing up in the South, *North Toward Home.* In the first half of *Rabbit Run* John Updike takes up the life of a man whose days are downhill all the way after hitting his peak as a high-school basketball star—and in the writing Updike himself evinces a nice soft touch of undisguised longing. In *A Fan's Notes,* a book combining yearning and self-disgust in roughly equal measure, Frederick Exley makes plain that he would much prefer to have been born into the skin of Frank Gifford rather than into his own.

But most men who are enraptured by sports do not think any such thing. I should like to have Kareem Abdul-Jabbar's sky hook, but not, especially for civilian life, the excessive height that is necessary to its execution. I should like to have Jimmy Connors's ground strokes, but no part of his mind. These are men born with certain gifts, gifts honed by practice and determination, that I, and millions along with me, enjoy seeing on display. But the reality principle is too deeply ingrained, at least in a man of my years, for me to even imagine exchanging places with them. One might as well imagine oneself in the winner's circle at Churchill Downs as the horse.

Fantasy is an element in sports when they are played in adoles- 16
cence—an alley basket becomes the glass backboard at Madison
Square Garden, a concrete park district tennis court with grass creeping out of the service line becomes center court at Wimbledon—but
fantasy of this kind is hard to come by. Part of this has to do with
age; but as large a part has to do with the age in which we live.
Sport has always been a business but never more so than currently,
and nothing lends itself less to fantasy than business. Reading the
sports section has become rather like reading the business section—
mergers, trades, salary negotiations, contract disputes, options, and
strikes fill the columns. Along with the details of business, those
of the psychological and social problems of athletes have come to
the fore. The old *Sport* magazine concentrated on play on the field,
with only an occasional digressive reference to personal life. ("Yogi
likes plenty of pizza in the off-season and spends a lot of his time
at his teammate Phil Rizzuto's bowling alley" is a rough facsimile
of a sentence from its pages that I recall.) But the magazine in its
current version, as well as the now more popular *Sports Illustrated*,
expends much space on the private lives of athletes—their divorces,
hang-ups, race relations, need for approval, concern for security,
potted philosophies—with the result that the grand is made to seem
small.

On the other side of the ledger, there is a view that finds a shim-
mering significance in everything having to do with sports. Literary men in general are notoriously to be distrusted on the subject.
They dig around everywhere, and can be depended upon to find
much treasure where none is buried. Norman Mailer mining
metaphysical ore in every jab of Muhammad Ali, an existential nug-
get in each of his various and profuse utterances, is a particularly
horrendous example. Even the sensible William Carlos Williams was
not above this sort of temptation. In a poem entitled "At the Ball
Game," we find the lines "It is the Inquisition, the Revolution." Dr.
Williams could not have been much fun at the ball park.

The Real Thing

If enthusiasm for sports has little to do with providing an outlet for
violent emotions, regaining adolescence, discovering metaphysical truths, the Inquisition or the Revolution, then what, I ask myself, am I doing past midnight, when I have to be up at 5:30 the
next morning, watching on television what will turn out to be a

seventeen-inning game between the New York Mets and the St. Louis Cardinals? The conversation coming out of my television set is of a very low grade, even for sports announcing. But even the dreary talk cannot put me off—the rehash of statistics, the advice to youngsters to keep their gloves low when in the field, the thin jokes. Neither the Mets nor the Cards figure to be contenders this year. The only possible effect that this game can have on my life is to make me dog-tired the next day. Yet I cannot pull myself away. I want to know how it is going to end. True, the score will be available in the morning paper. But that is not the same thing. What is going on here?

One thing that is going on is the practice of craft of a very high order, which is intrinsically interesting. But something as important is involved, something rarer in contemporary life, the spectacle of which gives enormous satisfaction. To define this satisfaction negatively, it is the absence of fraudulence and fakery. No small item, this, when one stops to think that in nearly every realm of contemporary life fraud and fakery have an established—some would say a preponderant—place. Advertising, politics, business, and journalism are only the most obvious examples. Fraud seems similarly pervasive in modern art: in painters whose reputations rest on press agentry; in writers who write one way and live quite another; in composers who are taken seriously but whose work cannot be seriously listened to. At a time when *image* is one of the most frequently used words in American speech and writing, one does not too often come upon the real thing.

Sport may be the toy department of life, but one of its abiding 20 compensations is that, at least on the field, it is the real thing. Much has been done in recent years in the attempt to ruin sport—the ruthlessness of owners, the greed of players, the general exploitation of fans. But even all this cannot destroy it. On the court, down on the field, sport is fraud-free and fakeproof. With a full count, two men on, his team down by one run in the last of the eighth, a batter (as well as a pitcher) is beyond the aid of public relations. At match point at Forest Hills a player's press clippings are of no help. Last year's earnings will not sink a twelve-foot putt on the eighteenth at Augusta. Alan Page, galloping up along a quarterback's blind side, figures to be neglectful of that quarterback's image as a swinger. In all these situations, and hundreds of others, a man either comes through or he doesn't. He is alone out there, naked but for his ability, which counts for everything. Something there is that is elemental about this, and something greatly satisfying.

Another part of the satisfaction to be got from sports—from playing them, but also from watching them being played—derives from
their special clarity. Sports offer clarity of a kind sufficient to engage the most serious minds. That the Cambridge mathematician
G. H. Hardy closely followed cricket and avidly read cricket scores
is not altogether surprising. Numbers in sports are ubiquitous.
Scores, standings, averages, times, records—comfort is found in such
numbers. ERA, RBI, FGP, pass completions, turnovers, category
upon category of statistics are kept for nearly every aspect of athletic activity. (Why, I recently heard someone ask, are records not
kept for catchers throwing out runners attempting to steal? Because,
the answer is, often runners steal on pitchers, and so it would be
unfair to charge these stolen bases against catchers.) As perhaps in
no other sphere, numbers in sports tell one where things stand. No
loopholes here, where figures, for once, do not lie. Nowhere else
is such specificity of result available.

Clarity about character is also available in sports. "You Americans hold to the proposition that it is self-evident that all men are
created equal," I not long ago heard an Englishman say, adding,
"it had better be self-evident, for no other evidence for it exists."
Sport coldly demonstrates physical inequalities—there are the larger,
the faster, the stronger, the more graceful athletes—but it also throws
up human types who have devised ways to redress these inequalities. One such type is the hustler. In every realm but that of sports
the word *hustle* is pejorative, whereas in sports it is approbative.
Two of the hustler breed, Pete Rose of the Cincinnati Reds and Jerry
Sloan of the Chicago Bulls, are men who supplement reasonably
high levels of ability with unreasonably high levels of courage and
desire. Other athletes—Joe Morgan and Oscar Robertson come to
mind—bring superior athletic intelligence to bear upon their play.
And Bill Russell, late of the Boston Celtics, who if the truth be known
was not an inherently superior athlete, blended hustle and intelligence with what abilities he did have and through force of character established supremacy.

Whence do hustle, intelligence, and character in sports derive,
especially since they apparently do not necessarily carry over into
life? Joe DiMaggio and Sugar Ray Robinson, two of the most instinctively intelligent and physically elegant athletes, brought little of
either of these qualities over into their business or personal activities. Some athletes can do all but one important thing well: Wilt
Chamberlain at the free-throw line, for those who recall his misery
there, leaves a permanent picture of a mental block in action. Other

athletes—Connie Hawkins, Ilie Nastase, Dick Allen—have all the physical gifts in superabundance, yet, because of some insufficiency of character, some searing flaw, never come near to fulfilling their promise. Coaches supply yet another gallery of human types, from the fanatical Vince Lombardi to the comical Casey Stengel to the measured and aptly named John Wooden. The cast of characters in sport, the variety of situations, the complexity of behavior it puts on display, the overall human exhibit it offers—together these supply an enjoyment akin to that once provided by reading interminably long but inexhaustibly rich nineteenth-century novels.

In a wider sense, sport is culture. For many American men it 24 represents a common background, a shared interest. It has a binding power that transcends social class and education. Some years ago I found myself working in the South among men with whom I shared nothing in the way of region, religion, education, politics, or general views; we shared nothing, in fact, but sports, which was enough for us to get along and grow to become friends, in the process showing how superficial all the things that might have kept us apart in fact were. More recently, in Chicago, at a time when race relations were in a particularly jagged state, I recall emerging from an NBA game, in which the Chicago Bulls in overtime beat the Milwaukee Bucks, into a snowy night and an aura of common good feeling that, for a time, submerged the enmity between races; laughing, throwing snowballs, exuberant generally, the crowd leaving the Chicago Stadium that night was not divided by being black and white but unified by being Bull fans. Last year's Boston-Cincinnati World Series, one of the most gratifying in memory, coming hard upon a year of extreme political divisiveness, performed, however briefly, something of the same function. How much better it felt to agree about the mastery of Luis Tiant than to argue about the wretchedness of Richard Nixon.

In sports as in life, character does not much change. I have recently begun to play a game called racquet ball, and I find I would still rather look good than win, which is what I usually do: look good and lose. I beat the rum-dums but go down before quality players. I get compliments in defeat. Men who beat me admire the whip of my strokes, my wrist action, my anticipation, the power I get behind the ball. When this occurs I feel like a woman who is complimented for the shape of her bottom when it is her mind she craves admiration for, though of course she will take what praise she can get.

R. H. Tawney, the great historian of religion and capitalism, once remarked that the only progress he could note during the course of his lifetime was in the deportment of dogs. For myself, I would say that the chief progress in the course of my lifetime has been in the quality and variety of athletic gear. Racquets made of metal, aluminum, wood, and fiberglass, balls of different colors, sneakers of all materials and designs, posh warm-up suits, tube socks, sweatbands for the head and wrist in various colors and pipings; only the athletic supporter, the old jockstrap, remains unornamented, but perhaps even now Vera or Peter Max is at the drawing board. In any event, with all this elegant plumage available, it is a nice time to be playing ball again.

Sports can be impervious to age. My father-in-law, a man of style, seriousness, and great good humor who died a year ago in his late sixties, was born in South Bend, Indiana, and in his early manhood left the Catholic Church—two facts that conjoined to give him an intense interest in the fortunes of the teams from Notre Dame. He loved to see them lose. The torch has been passed on. I now love to see Notre Dame lose, and when it does I think of him and remember his smile.

When I was a boy I had a neighbor, a man who, after retirement, had a number of strokes. An old man and a young boy, we had in common a love of sports, which, when we met on the street, was our only topic of conversation. He once inspected a new glove of mine, and instructed me to rub it down with neat's-foot-oil, place a ball firmly in the pocket, wrap string tightly around the glove, and leave it like that for the winter. I did, and it worked. After his last stroke but one, he seldom left his house. Afternoons he spent in a chair in his bedroom, a blanket over his lap, listening to Cub games over the radio. It was while listening to a ball game that he quietly died. I cannot imagine a better way.

Topics for Discussion and Writing

1. In his first two paragraphs Epstein writes of the opportunities he had when growing up in Chicago in the 1940s to live "on, off, and in sports." Compare or contrast those opportunities with your own. How do you account for the differences? (Were there some similarities?)

2. In paragraph 4 Epstein writes of the 1940s: "The time was, as is now apparent, a splendid era in sports." Looking back at the decade in your life (which can be the current decade) in which you have been most engaged as a sports fan, would you characterize it also as "a splendid

era"? If not, how would you characterize it—disillusioning, mediocre, uneven? Try to support your characterization concretely, as Epstein does in paragraph 4.

3. In paragraph 5 Epstein writes: "All learning of craft—which sport, like writing, most assuredly is—involves imitation, especially in the early stages." Did you learn sports by imitation? Explain. What about writing? Why, or why not?

4. In paragraph 13 Epstein points out that having played a game as a boy or young man (presumably also as a girl or young woman) helps one to appreciate the performance of professionals. Do you think the same principle holds true for literature, music, dance, art? Should all children have a chance to learn to play musical instruments, to paint, and to write, not in the expectation that they will all practice those arts as adults, but to enhance their later enjoyment and support of concerts, museums, books, and theater?

5. What makes spectator sports appealing? After dismissing violence and the spectator's nostalgia for adolescence as the source of their appeal, Epstein cites three or four reasons why spectator sports appeal to him. Why does your favorite spectator sport appeal to you?

6. If you are not a sports fan, is there an area of your experience in which you feel close to being obsessed? Music? food? clothes? dogs? sex? If you were to write about this obsession, how might outlining Epstein's essay help you to find ideas?

Pete Hamill

Pete Hamill, born in Brooklyn in 1935, attended Pratt Institute and Mexico City College, worked as a reporter in Vietnam in the 1960s, and now works as a freelance writer. His essays have appeared in such magazines as Cosmopolitan, Playboy, *and (the source of the piece that we reprint)* Gentlemen's Quarterly.

Winning Isn't Everything

One of the more widely accepted maxims of modern American life was uttered on a frozen winter afternoon during the early sixties. The late Vince Lombardi, who coached the Green Bay Packers when they were the greatest team in football, said it. "Winning isn't everything," he declared, "It's the only thing."

Vince Lombardi's notion was immediately appropriated by an extraordinary variety of American males: presidents and lesser politicians, generals, broadcasters, political columnists, Little League coaches, heads of corporations, and probably millions of others. In fact, it sometimes seems that Lombardi's words have had greater impact than any sentence uttered by an American since Stephen Decatur's "our country, right or wrong."

That's surprising on many levels, beginning with the obvious: It's a deceptively simple premise. Winning *isn't* "the only thing." Such an idea muddles the idea of competition, not simply in sports, but in all aspects of our lives. We've learned the hard way in this century that the world is a complex place; it's certainly not the National Football League. Winning isn't the only thing in love, art, marriage, commerce, or politics; it's not even the only thing in sports.

In sports, as in so many other areas of our national life, we've 4 always cherished gallant losers. I remember one afternoon in the fall of 1956 when Sal Maglie was pitching for the Brooklyn Dodgers against the hated Yankees. Maglie was an old man that year, as age is measured in sports. But this was the World Series, and he hauled his thirty-nine-year-old body to the mound, inning after inning, gave everything he had, held the Yankees to a few scattered hits and two runs – and lost. That day Don Larsen pitched his perfect game: no runs, no hits, no errors. Yet, to me, the afternoon belonged to Maglie – tough, gallant, and a loser.

There was an evening in Manila when Joe Frazier went up against Muhammad Ali for the third and final time. That night, Frazier brought his workman's skills into combat against the magic of the artist, called on his vast reservoir of courage and will, and came up empty at the end of fourteen rounds. Frazier was the loser, but that evening, nobody really lost. Because of that fight, Joe Frazier can always boast with honor that he made Muhammad Ali a great fighter. He was the test, the implacable force who made Ali summon all of his own considerable reserves of skill, heart, and endurance for a final effort. The contest consumed them both. Neither was ever again a good fighter. But during their violent confrontation, winning or losing was, in the end, a marginal concern; that all-consuming effort was everything.

There are hundreds of similar examples of losers who showed us how to be more human, and their performances make the wide acceptance of Lombardi's notions even more mystifying. Lombardi's thesis, in fact, represented something of a shift in the nation's popular thought. Americans had been the people who remembered the Alamo or Pearl Harbor; we blew taps over the graves of those who lost at the Battle of the Bulge or Anzio or the Yalu Basin. Those soldiers had all been defeated, but we honored them for their display of a critical human quality: courage.

Ernest Hemingway once defined courage as grace under pressure, and that's always struck me as an eminently useful definition. The best professional athletes not only possess that kind of courage but, more important, are willing to display it to strangers. Baseball's Reggie Jackson or Richard ("Goose") Gossage, for instance, function most completely as athletes and as men when appearing before gigantic crowds under pressure: bases loaded, late innings, a big game. They come to their tasks with gladness and absolute focus, neither whimpering, complaining, nor shirking when doing their job; they just try their best to get that job done. And, of course, sometimes they fail. Gossage gives up a single and his team loses. Jackson strikes out. No matter. The important thing is that such men keep their appointments with confidence and grace. Courage has become so deep a part of their character that they don't even think about it. (They certainly *want* to win. Sometimes they absolutely lust for victory. But they know that winning isn't everything. All a man can do is his best.)

Competition isn't really a problem for Americans. All sports, in   8
one way or another, are competitive. But an individual's primary competition is with himself and all his attendant weaknesses. That's obviously true of boxing, where fear must be dominated and made to work to the fighter's benefit. Yet it's also true for team sports, as well as such solitary endeavors as golf, where a player must learn control before anything else. The problem isn't competition, which is a part of life; it's in the notion of the necessity of triumph. A man can lose but still win. And the point of competition in sports is an old and not very fashionable one: It builds character.

That's especially true of prizefighters, the athletes I've known best. Outside the ring, almost all fighters are the gentlest of men. They carry themselves with the dignity of those who have little to prove, either to others or themselves. They're not bullies, rarely use their dangerous skills against ordinary citizens and avoid pointless confrontations. When a fighter hears that a colleague has been involved in a bar brawl or a swingout with a cop, he dismisses that fighter as a cowardly bum. Most of the boxers I know are honest, generous, funny. Yet they also know that as good as they are, there might be someone down the line who has their number. Again, they would prefer to be winners. But they're aware that losing, if a courageous effort is made, is never a disgrace. The highest compliment one fighter can pay another is to say that he has "heart."

There are lessons to be learned from such athletes that can be applied to how we live our lives. In the long run, we'll all come up losers because there's no greater loss than death. And since primitive man first began to think, we humans have devised strategies to deal with dying. Religion is the most obvious one, usually demanding that we adhere to a moral code on earth in exchange for a serene existence after death. Ideologies offer secular versions of the same instinct, insisting that we sacrifice now, directing our lives toward the ideal of a better future, with each man becoming an architect of his own utopia. Patriotism and nationalism carry some of the same fearful baggage.

An athlete's goals are less cosmic, his field of struggle less gandiose and therefore more applicable to ordinary citizens. Great athletes teach us that life is a series of struggles, not one giant effort. Just when we appear to have triumphed, we must stop like Sisyphus and again begin rolling the boulder up that mountain. The true athlete teaches us that winning isn't everything, but struggle is—the stuggle to simply get up in the morning or to see hope through the minefields of despair.

Viewed that way, a marriage, or any relationship with another human being, is an ongoing struggle. The mastering of a skill or craft doesn't end with the granting of a diploma; it goes on for life. The relationship between parents and children doesn't end when the children turn eighteen. The running of a corporation isn't a one-shot affair, measured by a single year's statements of profits and losses; it's a continuing process, accomplished by human beings who learn from mistakes, plunge fearlessly into the struggle, take risks and prepare for the future.

It's probably no accident that American capitalism, with its often permanently infantile male executives, experienced a decline that coincided with the period when Vince Lombardi's values received their widest acceptance. The results are visible everywhere. Sit on a plane with American businessmen and they'll be chattering about the Pittsburgh Steelers. Join a group of Japanese businessmen and they'll be discussing twenty-first-century technology. One group is trapped in a philosophy that demands winning as its goal; the other cares more about patient, long-term growth—and for the moment at least, the latter is winning.

Another great maxim of the years of America's triumphs also came from the sports page via the writer Grantland Rice: "It matters not who won or lost," declared the esteemed chronicler of the prewar years, "but how they played the game." By the time Vince

Lombardi came along, such sentiments were sneered at. We had then become a superpower, capable of blowing up the world. The man of grace, courage, endurance, and compassion was replaced in the public imagination by the swaggering macho blowhard; Humphrey Bogart gave way to John Wayne. With such attitudes dominating the landscape, we were certain to get into trouble, and we did. Vietnam and Watergate underscored the idea of winning at all costs. Yet today we seem incapable of admitting that an obsession with winning often leads to the most squalid of defeats.

Solid marriages are often built upon the experience of disastrous one. Politicians who lose elections become tempered for the contests that follow, sometimes going on to solid, useful careers. Painters, playwrights, novelists,and other artists often learn as much from their failures as they do from those rare moments when vision, craft, and ambition come together to produce masterpieces. It's also that way in sports.

I remember a night when my friend José Torres, then a middle- 16 weight, was boxing Florentino Fernandez in Puerto Rico. I couldn't go to the fight, so I spent the night tuning in and out of the all-news radio stations, anxious about the result because Florentino was a great puncher. About three in the morning, Torres called.

"Oh, Pete," he said, close to tears. "I'm so sorry."

"What happened?"

"I got knocked out," Torres replies, his voice brimming with emotion, since he'd never lost as a professional. We started discussing what had happened. Emotions cooled; the talk became technical. Torres explained that he had learned some things about himself, about boxing. He now understood some of his flaws, and thought he could correct them. We talked for an hour. Then I asked what he was going to do next.

"Go to the gym," he said. "I'm going to be champion of the 20 world."

Two years later, Torres *was* the world's light-heavyweight champion. He didn't quit after his first defeat. That night in San Juan he didn't say winning was the only thing, that it was time to pack it in. He had learned something from defeat, and knew that one violent night, somewhere down the line, he would show the world what he had learned. And that was precisely what he did. But he was aware of something else too: Sooner or later, someone might come along who was better than he was, for at least one evening. After all, even champions are human. Even champions eventually lose. That happened to José Torres as well. But then it didn't really matter. José Torres, like the rest of us, had learned that winning wasn't everything. Living was all, and in life, defeat and victory are inseparable brothers.

Topics for Discussion and Writing

1. In paragraph 6 Hamill finds "The wide acceptance of Lombardi's notions . . . mystifying." Do you find it mystifying? If not, why not?
2. Hamill thinks (paragraph 6) that Lombardi's view represents "something of a shift in the nation's popular thought," and he gives some evidence. How convincing do you find this evidence? Why?
3. In paragraph 8 Hamill says that competition "builds character." Drawing on your experience—what you have witnessed as well as what you have actually undergone—can you offer evidence that supports or rebuts this assertion?
4. In paragraph 11 Hamill says that "great athletes teach us that life is a series of struggles, not one giant step." Had you ever thought that great athletes teach this lesson? In any case, now that Hamill has said it, do you think there is something to his claim? If so, try to provide an example; think of athletes whom you admire, and try to formulate the lessons they teach. Conversely, if there is an athlete whom you despise, what message is conveyed by his or her life or game?
5. On the basis of Hamill's essay and Epstein's (page 365), which writer would you invite to accompany you to a ball game, and why?

John Updike

John Updike was born in 1932 in Shillington, Pennsylvania. After graduating from college he studied art for a year in England, but he then returned to the United States and began working as a staff reporter for the New Yorker. *He soon published stories in the magazine, and he continues to do so. He has also written novels (including* Rabbit, Run *and* The Witches of Eastwick*), essays, and light verse. The story we print here, "A & P," was published in 1961, but many readers find that except for the prices mentioned there is nothing dated about it.*

A & P

In walks these three girls in nothing but bathing suits. I'm in the third checkout slot, with my back to the door, so I don't see them until they're over by the bread. The one that caught my eye first was the one in the plaid green two-piece. She was a chunky kid, with a good tan and a sweet broad soft-looking can with those two crescents of white just under it, where the sun never seems to hit, at the top of the backs of her legs. I stood there with my hand on a box of HiHo crackers trying to remember if I rang it up or not. I ring it up again and the customer starts giving me hell. She's one of these cash-register-watchers, a witch about fifty with rouge on her cheekbones and no eyebrows, and I know it made her day to trip me up. She'd been watching cash registers for fifty years and probably never seen a mistake before.

By the time I got her feathers smoothed and her goodies into a bag—she gives me a little snort in passing, if she'd been born at the right time they would have burned her over in Salem—by the time I get her on her way the girls had circled around the bread and were coming back, without a pushcart, back my way along the counters, in the aisle between the checkouts and the Special bins. They didn't even have shoes on. There was this chunky one, with the two-piece—it was bright green and the seams on the bra were still sharp and her belly was still pretty pale so I guessed she just got it (the suit)—there was this one, with one of those chubby berry-faces, the lips all bunched together under her nose, this one, and a tall one, with black hair that hadn't quite frizzed right, and one of these sunburns right across under the eyes, and a chin that was too long—you know, the kind of girl other girls think is very "striking" and "attractive" but never quite makes it, as they very well know, which is why they like her so much—and then the third one, that wasn't quite so tall. She was the queen. She kind of led them, the other two peeking around and making their shoulders round. She didn't look around, not this queen, she just walked straight on slowly, on these long white prima-donna legs. She came down a little hard on her heels, as if she didn't walk in her bare feet that much, putting down her heels and then letting the weight move along to her toes as if she was testing the floor with every step, putting a little deliberate extra action into it. You never know for sure how girls' minds work (do they really think it's a mind in there or just a little buzz like a bee in a glass jar?) but you got the idea she had talked the other two into coming in here with her, and now she was showing them how to do it, walk slow and hold yourself straight.

She had on a kind of dirty pink—beige maybe, I don't know—bathing suit with a little nubble all over it and, what got me, the straps were down. They were off her shoulders looped loose around the cool tops of her arms, and I guess as a result the suit had slipped on her, so all around the top of the cloth there was this shining rim. If it hadn't been there you wouldn't have known there could have been anything whiter than those shoulders. With the straps pushed off, there was nothing between the top of the suit and the top of her head except just *her*, this clean bare plane of the top of her chest down from the shoulder bones like a dented sheet of metal tilted in the light. I mean, it was more than pretty.

She had sort of oaky hair that the sun and salt had bleached, done up in a bun that was unravelling, and a kind of prim face. Walking into the A & P with your straps down, I suppose it's the only kind of face you *can* have. She held her head so high her neck, coming up out of those white shoulders, looked kind of stretched, but I didn't mind. The longer her neck was, the more of her there was.

She must have felt in the corner of her eye me and over my shoulder Stokesie in the second slot watching, but she didn't tip. Not this queen. She kept her eyes moving across the racks, and stopped, and turned so slow it made my stomach rub the inside of my apron, and buzzed to the other two, who kind of huddled against her for relief, and then they all three of them went up the cat and dog food-breakfast cereal-macaroni-rice-raisins-seasonings-spreads-spaghetti-soft drinks-crackers-and-cookies aisle. From the third slot I look straight up this aisle to the meat counter, and I watched them all the way. The fat one with the tan sort of fumbled with the cookies, but on second thought she put the package back. The sheep pushing their carts down the aisle—the girls were walking against the usual traffic (not that we have one-way signs or anything)—were pretty hilarious. You could see them, when Queenie's white shoulders dawned on them, kind of jerk, or hop, or hiccup, but their eyes snapped back to their own baskets and on they pushed. I bet you could set off dynamite in the A & P and the people would by and large keep reaching and checking oatmeal off their lists and muttering "Let me see, there was a third thing, began with A, asparagus, no, ah, yes, applesauce!" or whatever it is they do mutter. But there was no doubt, this jiggled them. A few house slaves in pin curlers even look around after pushing their carts past to make sure what they had seen was correct.

You know, it's one thing to have a girl in a bathing suit down on the beach, where what with the glare nobody can look at each other much anyway, and another thing in the cool of the A & P, under the fluorescent lights, against all those stacked packages, with her feet paddling along naked over our checker-board green-and-cream rubber-tile floor.

"Oh, Daddy," Stokesie said beside me. "I feel so faint."

"Darling," I said. "Hold me tight." Stokesie's married, with two babies chalked up on his fuselage already, but as far as I can tell that's the only difference. He's twenty-two, and I was nineteen this April.   8

"Is it done?" he asks, the responsible married man finding his voice. I forgot to say he thinks he's going to be a manager some sunny day, maybe in 1990 when it's called the Great Alexandrov and Petrooshki Tea Company or something.

What he meant was, our town is five miles from a beach, with a big summer colony out on the Point, but we're right in the middle of town, and the women generally put on a shirt or shorts or something before they get out of the car into the street. And anyway these are usually women with six children and varicose veins mapping their legs and nobody, including them, could care less. As I say, we're right in the middle of town, and if you stand at our front doors you can see two banks and the Congregational church and the newspaper store and three real estate offices and about twenty-seven old freeloaders tearing up Central Street because the sewer broke again. It's not as if we're on the Cape; we're north of Boston and there's people in this town haven't seen the ocean for twenty years.

The girls had reached the meat counter and were asking McMahon something. He pointed, they pointed, and they shuffled out of sight behind a pyramid of Diet Delight peaches. All that was left for us to see was old McMahon patting his mouth and looking after them sizing up their joints. Poor kids, I began to feel sorry for them, they couldn't help it.

Now here comes the sad part of the story, at least my family says it's sad, but I don't think it's so sad myself. The store's pretty empty, it being Thursday afternoon, so there was nothing much to do except lean on the register and wait for the girls to show up again. The whole store was like a pinball machine and I didn't know which tunnel they'd come out of. After a while they come around out of the far aisle, around the light bulbs, records at discount of the Caribbean Six or Tony Martin Sings or some such gunk you wonder they waste the wax on, sixpacks of candy bars, and plastic toys done up in cellophane that fall apart when a kid looks at them anyway. Around they come, Queenie still leading the way, and holding a little gray jar in her hand. Slots Three through Seven are unmanned and I could see her wondering between Stokes and me, but Stokesie   12 with his usual luck draws an old party in baggy gray pants who stumbles up with four giant cans of pineapple juice (what do these bums *do* with all that pineapple juice? I've often asked myself) so the girls come to me. Queenie puts down the jar and I take it into my fingers icy cold. Kingfish Fancy Herring Snacks in Pure Sour Cream: 49¢. Now her hands are empty, not a ring or a bracelet, bare as God made them, and I wonder where the money's coming from. Still with the prim look she lifts a folded dollar bill out of the hollow at the center of her nubbled pink top. The jar went heavy in my hand. Really, I thought that was so cute.

Then everybody's luck begins to run out. Lengel comes in from haggling with a truck full of cabbages on the lot and is about to scuttle into the door marked MANAGER behind which he hides all day when the girls touch his eye. Lengel's pretty dreary, teaches Sunday school and the rest, but he doesn't miss that much. He comes over and says, "Girls, this isn't the beach."

Queenie blushes, though maybe it's just a brush of sunburn I was noticing for the first time, now that she was so close. "My mother asked me to pick up a jar of herring snacks." Her voice kind of startled me, the way voices do when you see the people first, coming out so flat and dumb yet kind of tony, too, the way it ticked over "pick up" and "snacks." All of a sudden I slid right down her voice into her living room. Her father and the other men were standing around in ice-cream coats and bow ties and the women were in sandals picking up herring snacks on toothpicks off a big glass plate and they were all holding drinks the color of water with olives and sprigs of mint in them. When my parents have somebody over they get lemonade and if it's a real racy affair Schlitz in tall glasses with "They'll Do It Every Time" cartoons stencilled on.

"That's all right," Lengel said. "But this isn't the beach." His repeating this struck me as funny, as if it had just occurred to him, and he had been thinking all these years the A & P was a great big dune and he was the head lifeguard. He didn't like my smiling—as I say he doesn't miss much—but he concentrates on giving the girls that sad Sunday-school-superintendent stare.

Queenie's blush was no sunburn now, and the plump one in plaid, that I liked better from the back—a really sweet can—pipes up, "We weren't doing any shopping. We just came in for the one thing."

"That makes no difference," Lengel tells her, and I could see from the way his eyes went that he hadn't noticed she was wearing a two-piece before. "We want you decently dressed when you come in here."

16

"We *are* decent," Queenie says suddenly, her lower lip pushing, getting sore now that she remembers her place, a place from which the crowd that runs the A & P must look pretty crummy. Fancy Herring Snacks flashed in her very blue eyes.

"Girls, I don't want to argue with you. After this come in here with your shoulders covered. It's our policy." He turns his back. That's policy for you. Policy is what the kingpins want. What the others want is juvenile delinquency.

All this while, the customers had been showing up with their carts but, you know, sheep, seeing a scene, they had all bunched up on Stokesie, who shook open a paper bag as gently as peeling a peach, not wanting to miss a word. I could feel in the silence everybody getting nervous, most of all Lengel, who asks me, "Sammy, have you rung up this purchase?" 20

I thought and said "No" but it wasn't about that I was thinking. I go through the punches, 4, 9, GROC, TOT — it's more complicated than you think and after you do it often enough, it begins to make a little song, that you hear words to, in my case "Hello (*bing*) there, you (*gung*) hap-py *pee*pul (*splat*)!" — the *splat* being the drawer flying out. I uncrease the bill, tenderly as you may imagine, it just having come from between the two smoothest scoops of vanilla I had ever known were there, and pass a half and a penny into her narrow pink palm and nestle the herrings in a bag and twist its neck and hand it over, all the time thinking.

The girls, and who'd blame them, are in a hurry to get out, so I say "I quit" to Lengel quick enough for them to hear, hoping they'll stop and watch me, their unsuspected hero. They keep right on going, into the electric eye; the door flies open and they flicker across the lot to their car, Queenie and Plaid and Big Tall Goony-Goony (not that as raw material she was so bad), leaving me with Lengel and a kink in his eyebrow.

"Did you way something, Sammy?"

"I said I quit."   24

"I thought you did."

"You didn't have to embarrass them."

"It was they who were embarrassing us."

I started to say something that came out "Fiddle-de-doo." It's 28 a saying of my grandmother's, and I know she would have been pleased.

"I don't think you know what you're saying," Lengel said.

"I know you don't," I said. "But I do." I pull the bow at the back of my apron and start shrugging it off my shoulders. A couple customers that had been heading for my slot begin to knock against each other, like scared pigs in a chute.

Lengel sighs and begins to look very patient and old and gray. He's been a friend of my parents for years. "Sammy, you don't want to do this to your Mom and Dad," he tells me. It's true, I don't. But it seems to me that once you begin a gesture it's fatal not to go through with it. I fold the apron, "Sammy" stitched in red on the pocket, and put it on the counter, and drop the bow tie on top of it. The bow tie is theirs, if you've ever wondered. "You'll feel this for the rest of your life," Lengel says, and I know that's true, too, but remembering how he made that pretty girl blush makes me so scrunchy inside I punch the No Sale tab and the machine whirs "pee-pul" and the drawer splats out. One advantage to this scene taking place in summer, I can follow this up with a clean exit, there's no fumbling around getting your coat and galoshes, I just saunter into the electric eye in my white shirt that my mother ironed the night before, and the door heaves itself open, and outside the sunshine is skating around on the asphalt.

I look around for my girls, but they're gone, of course. There wasn't anybody but some young married screaming with her children about some candy they didn't get by the door of a powder-blue Falcon station wagon. Looking back in the big windows, over the bags of peat moss and aluminum lawn furniture stacked on the pavement, I could see Lengel in my place in the slot, checking the sheep through. His face was dark gray and his back stiff, as if he'd just had an injection of iron, and my stomach kind of fell as I felt how hard the world was going to be to me hereafter.   32

Topics for Discussion and Writing

1. Have you ever quit a job on a matter of principle? If so, explain the circumstances, and the short- and long-term consequences.
2. If you have ever thought of quitting a job on a matter of principle but then did not do so, explain the circumstances and your present analysis of your behavior.
3. Some students regard Sammy as a sexist, and say that the failure of the girls to notice his gesture is a fitting punishment for his sexism. Evaluate this view.

Robert Francis

Robert Francis (1901–87) was born in Upland, Pennsylvania, and was educated at Harvard. He taught occasionally, a term here or there or in the summer, but for the most part he devoted himself to reading and writing.

Pitcher

His art is eccentricity, his aim
How not to hit the mark he seems to aim at,

His passion how to avoid the obvious,
His technique how to vary the avoidance.   4

The others throw to be comprehended. He
Throws to be a moment misunderstood.

Yet not too much. Not errant, arrant, wild,
But every seeming aberration willed.   8

Not to, yet still, still to communicate
Making the batter understand too late.

Topics for Discussion and Writing

1. Why is the pitcher's art "eccentricity"? Consult a dictionary for the origin (etymology) of *eccentricity.* How is the origin of the word *eccentricity* apt for the meaning here? How is the origin of *errant* (and *arrant* and *aberration*) appropriate?

2. The first four stanzas do not rhyme, though the fourth uses a device close to rhyme (*wild, willed*). The last stanza, however, rhymes exactly. Why?

3. It has been said that pitching is "the art of instilling fear." Francis says that the pitcher's "art is eccentricity." Which view of pitching seems more accurate? Can the two views be reconciled? Who are some pitchers who instill fear? Who are some who practice the art of "eccentricity"?

8
OPEN FOR BUSINESS

John Pierpont Morgan
Edward Steichen, 1903

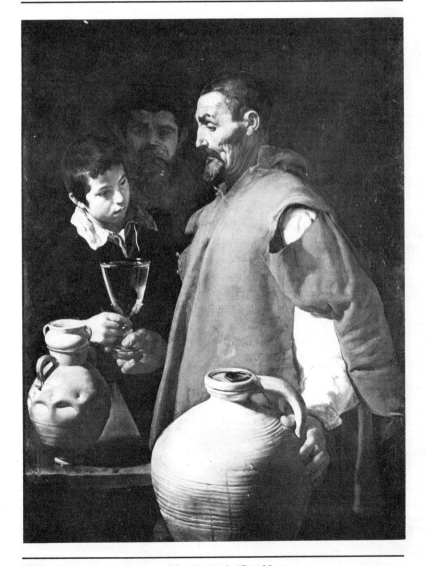

Wellington Museum, by courtesy of the Victoria & Albert Museum

A Graveyard and Steel Mill in Bethlehem, Pennsyslvania
Walker Evans, 1935

Dorothea Lange Collection/Collection of The Oakland Museum

Short Views

The chief business of the American people is business.
Calvin Coolidge

The business of business is business.
Anonymous

Business underlies everything in our national life, including our spiritual life. Witness the fact that in the Lord's Prayer the first petition is for daily bread. No one can worship God or love his neighbor on an empty stomach.
Woodrow Wilson

We demand that big business give the people a square deal; in return we must insist that when anyone engaged in big business honestly endeavors to do right he shall himself be given a square deal.
Theodore Roosevelt

Entrepreneurial profit . . . is the expression of the value of what the entrepreneur contributes to production in exactly the same sense that wages are the value expression of what the worker "produces." It is not a profit of exploitation any more than are wages.
Joseph Alois Schumpeter

Every individual necessarily labors to render the annual revenue of the society as great as he can. He generally indeed neither intends to promote the public interest, nor knows how much he is promoting it. . . . He intends only his own gain, and he is in this, as in many other cases, led by an invisible hand to promote an end which was no part of his intention. . . . By pursuing his own interest he frequently promotes that of the society more effectually than when he really intends to promote it. I have never known much good done by those who affected to trade for the public good.
Adam Smith

It's every man for herself.
Diane Sawyer

Don't gamble. Take all your savings and buy some good stock and
hold it till it goes up. If it don't go up, don't buy it.
> **Will Rogers**

Men of business must not break their word twice.
> **Thomas Fuller**

A corporation cannot blush.
> **attributed to Howel Walsh**

All business sagacity reduces itself in the last analysis to a judicious
use of sabotage.
> **Thorstein Veblen**

W. H. Auden

*W. H. Auden (1907–73) was born and educated in England, but in 1939 he emigrated
to the United States, and in 1946 he became a naturalized citizen. Although Auden is
known chiefly as a poet — indeed, as one of the chief poets of the period — he also wrote
plays, libretti, and essays.*

The Almighty Dollar

Political and technological developments are rapidly ob-
literating all cultural differences and it is possible that, in a not remote future, it will be impossible to distinguish human beings
living on one area of the earth's surface from those living on any
other, but our different pasts have not yet been completely erased
and cultural differences are still perceptible. The most striking difference between an American and a European is the difference in their
attitudes towards money. Every European knows, as a matter of
historical fact, that in Europe wealth could only be acquired at the
expense of other human beings, either by conquering them or by
exploiting their labor in factories. Further, even after the Industrial
Revolution began, the number of persons who could rise from
poverty to wealth was small; the vast majority took it for granted
that they would not be much richer nor poorer than their fathers.
In consequence, no European associates wealth with personal merit
or poverty with personal failure.

To a European, money means power, the freedom to do as he likes, which also means that, consciously or unconsciously, he says: "I want to have as much money as possible myself and others to have as little money as possible."

In the United States, wealth was also acquired by stealing, but the real exploited victim was not a human being but poor Mother Earth and her creatures who were ruthlessly plundered. It is true that the Indians were expropriated or exterminated, but this was not, as it had always been in Europe, a matter of the conquerer seizing the wealth of the conquered, for the Indian had never realized the potential riches of his country. It is also true that, in the Southern states, men lived on the labor of slaves, but slave labor did not make them fortunes; what made slavery in the South all the more inexcusable was that, in addition to being morally wicked, it didn't even pay off handsomely.

Thanks to the natural resources of the country, every American, 4 until quite recently, could reasonably look forward to making more money than his father, so that, if he made less, the fault must be his; he was either lazy or inefficient. What an American values, therefore, is not the possession of money as such, but his power to make it as proof of his manhood; once he has proved himself by making it, it has served its function and can be lost or given away. In no society in history have rich men given away so large a part of their fortunes. A poor American feels guilty at being poor, but less guilty than an American *rentier*[1] who had inherited wealth but is doing nothing to increase it; what can the latter do but take to drink and psychoanalysis?

In the Fifth Circle on the Mount of Purgatory,[2] I do not think that many Americans will be found among the Avaricious; but I suspect that the Prodigals may be almost an American colony. The great vice of Americans is not materialism but a lack of respect for matter.

Topics for Discussion and Writing

1. Do you think that Auden's generalizations (in the first three paragraphs) about European versus American attitudes toward wealth are fundamentally accurate? If not, what are your objections?

---

[1] A *rentier* (French) is one who derives income from property or investments. (Editors' note)
[2] A reference to Dante's *Divine Comedy,* part of which describes repentant souls being purged by suffering on various levels of a mountain. (Editors' note)

2. In paragraph 4, in the first sentence, how does Auden seem to define "American"? What assumptions does he appear to be making?
3. If you have some knowledge of an Asian, African, or Latin American country, what generalization can you offer about its citizens' attitude toward wealth?
4. Restate in your own words Auden's last paragraph. Do you agree with Auden's final sentence? Why, or why not?
5. Read the next essay, Ben Franklin's "Advice to a Young Tradesman." Then argue that Franklin is (or is not) a good example of the American whom Auden describes or characterizes.

Benjamin Franklin

Benjamin Franklin (1706–90), born in Boston, left school at the age of ten to help his father, a soapmaker, and then was apprenticed to his half-brother, a printer. They did not get along, and in 1723 Franklin went to Philadelphia to work as a printer. In time he acquired a part-ownership of The Pennsylvania Gazette, *for which he wrote regularly, and he went on to other publishing adventures, including* Poor Richard's Almanack *(1732–57). By 1748—the year of the essay we reprint—he had acquired enough wealth to devote himself largely to careers as a statesman and as an inventor. He continued to write, however, working (from 1771 to 1789) especially on his autobiography.*

Advice to a Young Tradesman, Written by an Old One. To My Friend A. B.

As *you have desired it of me, I write the following Hints, which have been of Service to me, and may, if observed, be so to you.*

Remember that TIME is Money. He that can earn Ten Shillings[1] a Day by his Labour, and goes abroad, or sits idle one half of that Day, tho' he spends but Sixpence during his Diversion or Idleness, ought not to reckon That the only Expence; he has really spent or rather thrown away Five Shillings besides.

[1] **Ten Shillings** A shilling is a monetary unit. Later in the essay Franklin speaks also of other units—pounds, crowns, pennies, and groats. A pound was worth 20 shillings; a crown was worth five shillings; a shilling was worth 12 pennies; a groat (fourpence) was virtually worthless.

Remember that CREDIT is Money. If a Man lets his Money lie in my Hands after it is due, he give me the Interest, or so much as I can make of it during that Time. This amounts to a considerable Sum where a Man has good and large Credit, and makes good Use of it.

Remember that Money is of a prolific generating Nature. Money can beget Money, and its Offspring can beget more, and so on. Five Shillings turn'd, is *Six:* Turn'd again, 'tis Seven and Three Pence; and so on 'til it becomes an Hundred Pound. The more there is of it, the more it produces every Turning, so that the Profits rise quicker and quicker. He that kills a breeding Sow, destroys all her Offspring to the thousandth Generation. He that murders a Crown, destroys all it might have produc'd, even Scores of Pounds.

Remember that Six Pounds a Year is but a Groat a Day. For this 4 little Sum (which may be daily wasted either in Time or Expence unperceiv'd) a Man of Credit may on his own Security have the constant Possession and Use of an Hundred Pounds. So much in Stock briskly turn'd by an industrious Man, produces great advantage.

Remember this Saying, *That the good Paymaster is Lord of another Man's Purse.* He that is known to pay punctually and exactly to the Time he promises, may at any Time, and on any Occasion, raise all the Money his Friends can spare. This is sometimes of great Use: Therefore never keep borrow'd Money an Hour beyond the Time you promis'd, lest a Disappointment shuts up your Friends Purse forever.

The most trifling Actions that affect a Man's Credit, are to be regarded. The Sound of your Hammer at Five in the Morning or Nine at Night, heard by a Creditor, makes him easy Six Months longer. But if he sees you at a Billiard Table, or hears your Voice in a Tavern, when you should be at Work, he sends for his Money the next Day. Finer Cloaths than he or his Wife wears, or greater Expence in any particular than he affords himself, shocks his Pride, and he duns you to humble you. Creditors are a kind of People, that have the sharpest Eyes and Ears, as well as the best Memories of any in the World.

Good-natur'd Creditors (and such one would always chuse to deal with if one could) feel Pain when they are oblig'd to ask for Money. Spare 'em that Pain, and they will love you. When you receive a Sum of Money, divide it among 'em in Proportion to your Debts. Don't be asham'd of paying a small Sum because you owe a greater. Money, more or less, is always welcome; and your

Creditor had rather be at the Trouble of receiving Ten Pounds voluntarily brought him, tho' at ten different Times or Payments, than be oblig'd to go ten Times to demand it before he can receive it in a Lump. It shews, besides, that you are mindful of what you owe; it makes you appear a careful as well as an honest Man; and that still encreases your Credit.

Beware of thinking all your own that you possess, and of living 8 accordingly. 'Tis a Mistake that many People who have Credit fall into. To prevent this, keep an exact Account for some Time of both your Expences and your Incomes. If you take the Pains at first to mention Particulars, it will have this good Effect; you will discover how wonderfully small trifling Expences mount up to large Sums, and will discern what might have been, and may for the future be saved, without occasioning any great Inconvenience.

In short, the Way to Wealth, if you desire it, is as plain as the Way to Market. It depends chiefly on two Words, INDUSTRY and FRUGALITY; i.e. Waste neither Time nor Money, but make the best Use of both. He that gets all he can honestly, and saves all he gets (necessary Expences excepted) will certainly become RICH; If that Being who governs the World, to whom all should look for a Blessing on their honest Endeavours, doth not in his wise Providence otherwise determine.

Topics for Discussion and Writing

1. Look at the first sentence of each of the first five paragraphs. Describe the pattern you find, and then describe the effect.

2. Look at the pattern of paragraph 6. What does the first sentence do? Describe the succeeding sentences.

3. What does Franklin mean in paragraph 3 by the words "turn'd" and "Turning"? What is his point in this paragraph? Paraphrase the last sentence. (See "paraphrase" in the glossary, page 882.)

4. If one or two of Franklin's maxims strike you as particularly sound or particularly repellent, specify which they are and explain why you admire or abhor them.

5. Would you agree that Franklin's advice is suitable only for a maniac whose life is devoted exclusively to making money? Or do you think that it has value for all of us?

6. What do you make of Franklin's last sentence?

Ellen Goodman

Ellen Goodman, born in Boston in 1941, was educated at Radcliffe College. After gradu-ating she worked as a reporter for Newsweek, *a feature writer for the* Detroit Free Press, *and (from 1967) a feature writer and columnist for* The Boston Globe. *Her column is now syndicated in some 400 newspapers. In 1980 she was awarded a Pulitzer Prize.*

The Company Man

He worked himself to death, finally and precisely, at 3:00 A.M. Sunday morning.

The obituary didn't say that, of course. It said that he died of a coronary thrombosis—I think that was it—but everyone among his friends and acquaintances knew it instantly. He was a perfect Type A, a workaholic, a classic, they said to each other and shook their heads—and thought for five or ten minutes about the way they lived.

This man who worked himself to death finally and precisely at 3:00 A.M. Sunday morning—on his day off—was fifty-one years old and a vice-president. He was, however, one of six vice-presidents, and one of three who might conceivably—if the president died or retired soon enough—have moved to the top spot. Phil knew that.

He worked six days a week, five of them until eight or nine at 4 night, during a time when his own company had begun the four-day week for everyone but the executives. He worked like the Im-portant People. He had no outside "extracurricular interests," un-less, of course, you think about a monthly golf game that way. To Phil, it was work. He always ate egg salad sandwiches at his desk. He was, of course, overweight, by 20 or 25 pounds. He thought it was okay, though, because he didn't smoke.

On Saturdays, Phil wore a sports jacket to the office instead of a suit, because it was the weekend.

He had a lot of people working for him, maybe sixty, and most of them liked him most of the time. Three of them will be seriously considered for his job. The obituary didn't mention that.

But it did list his "survivors" quite accurately. He is survived by his wife, Helen, forty-eight years old, a good woman of no par-ticular marketable skills, who worked in an office before marrying and mothering. She had, according to her daughter, given up try-ing to compete with his work years ago, when the children were small. A company friend said, "I know how much you will miss him." And she answered, "I already have."

"Missing him all these years," she must have given up part of 8
herself which had cared too much for the man. She would be "well
taken care of."

His "dearly beloved" eldest of the "dearly beloved" children is
a hard-working executive in a manufacturing firm down South. In
the day and a half before the funeral, he went around the neighborhood researching his father, asking the neighbors what he was
like. They were embarrassed.

His second child is a girl, who is twenty-four and newly married. She lives near her mother and they are close, but whenever
she was alone with her father, in a car driving somewhere, they had
nothing to say to each other.

The youngest is twenty, a boy, a high-school graduate who has
spent the last couple of years, like a lot of his friends, doing enough
odd jobs to stay in grass and food. He was the one who tried to
grab at his father, and tried to mean enough to him to keep the man
at home. He was his father's favorite. Over the last two years, Phil
stayed up nights worrying about the boy.

The boy once said, "My father and I only board here." 12

At the funeral, the sixty-year-old company president told the
forty-eight-year-old widow that the fifty-one-year-old deceased had
meant much to the company and would be missed and would be
hard to replace. The widow didn't look him in the eye. She was
afraid he would read her bitterness and, after all, she would need
him to straighten out the finances—the stock options and all that.

Phil was overweight and nervous and worked too hard. If he
wasn't at the office, he was worried about it. Phil was a Type A,
a heart-attack natural. You could have picked him out in a minute
from a lineup.

So when he finally worked himself to death, at precisely 3:00
A.M. Sunday morning, no one was really surprised.

By 5:00 P.M. the afternoon of the funeral, the company president 16
had begun, discreetly of course, with care and taste, to make inquiries about his replacement. One of three men. He asked around:
"Who's been working the hardest?"

Topics for Discussion and Writing

1. Do you assume that the man Goodman is writing about is a fairly typi-
    cal business man? Or a highly exceptional exception? Or a caricature?

2. What would you say Goodman's attitude toward the man is? Pity? Contempt? (Of course you don't have to settle for a single word.) How would you support your view of what you take to be her attitude?
3. Would you agree that Goodman is trying to teach a lesson? If so, what is the lesson? And do you agree with it?
4. Compare and contrast Goodman's "Company Man" with Auden's "Unknown Citizen" (page 454).

Felice N. Schwartz

Felice N. Schwartz is founder and president of Catalyst, a not-for-profit organization that works with corporations to foster the career development of women.

In 1989 Schwartz published in the Harvard Business Review *an article that was widely interpreted as advising women to limit their expectations of advancement if they entered the business world. The controversy was reported in the newspapers, and Schwartz took the opportunity to reach a mass audience by writing an essay—printed below—for* The New York Times.

The "Mommy Track" Isn't Anti-Woman

"The cost of employing women in business is greater than the cost of employing men."

This sentence, the first of my recent article in the *Harvard Business Review,* has provoked an extraordinary debate, now labeled by others "the Mommy track." The purpose of the article was to urge employers to create policies that help mothers balance career and family responsibilities, and to eliminate barriers to female productivity and advancement.

But two fears have emerged in the debate. One is that, by raising the issue that it costs more to employ women, we will not be hired and promoted. The other is the fear that if working mothers are offered a variety of career paths, including a part-time option, all women will be left with the primary responsibility for child care.

Acknowledging that there are costs associated with employing women will not lead companies to put women in dead-end jobs. Time taken from work for childbearing, recovery and child care, as well the counterproductive attitudes and practices women face in a male-dominated workplace, do take their toll on women's productivity. But in our competitive marketplace, the costs of employing women pale beside the payoffs.

Current "baby-bust" demographics compel companies to employ women at every level, no matter what the cost. Why? Women comprise half the talent and competence in the country. The idea that companies are looking for excuses to send women home again is untrue. Companies are looking for solutions, not excuses.

Over and over, corporate leaders tell me that their most pressing concern is not why but *how* to respond cost-effectively to the needs of women. Some take bold steps to provide women with the flexibility and family supports they need; others implement groundbreaking programs to remove barriers to women's leadership. The farsighted do both.

Their programs address the needs of women as individuals. There can be no one career "track" to which women, or men, can be expected to adhere throughout their lives. Few can know from the start to what degree they will be committed to career or to family. Raising the issue of the costs of employing women motives companies to find solutions that work for individuals with diverse and sometimes changing goals and needs.

The second fear voiced in this debate is that making alternative 8 career paths available to women may freeze them in the role of primary caretakers of children.

Today, men are more involved in their children's upbringing, from fixing breakfast to picking up kids at school—enriching our children's lives. But despite increased sharing of parental responsibilities, women remain at the center of family life. According to a recent study, 54 percent of married women who work full-time said child care was their responsibility—contrasted with two percent of surveyed men.

The danger of charting our direction on the basis of wishful thinking is clear. Whether or not men play a greater role in child rearing, companies must reduce the family-related stresses on working women. The flexibility companies provide for women now will be a model in the very near future for men—thus women will not be forced to continue to take primary responsibility for child care. Giving men flexibility will benefit companies in many ways, including greater women's productivity.

What I advocate is that companies create options that allow employees to set their own pace, strive for the top, find satisfaction at the midlevel or cut back for a period of time—not to be penalized for wanting to make a substantial commitment to family. Achievement should not be a function of whether an employee has children. Success is the reward of talent, hard work and commitment.

What benefits women benefits companies. In reducing the cost   12
of employing women—by clearing obstacles to their advancement and providing family benefits—companies create an environment in which all can succeed. But employers will not be motivated to reduce the costs if it remains taboo to discuss them. Only by putting the facts on the table will employers and women—and men—be able to form a partnership in addressing the issues.

Felice N. Schwartz's short essay stimulated responses. The following letters were published in *The New York Times,* on 2 April 1989.

To the Editor:

Felice N. Schwartz might have had the best of intentions when she wrote "Management Women and the New Facts of Life" for the *Harvard Business Review* and reiterated her thesis in "The 'Mommy Track' Isn't Anti-Woman" (Op-Ed, March 22). Her arguments, however, are hardly supported by her scholarship, which relies on unidentified studies at unnamed corporations about undefined "turnover" rates, assertions that begin with phrases like "we know" and "what we know to be true," and an undocumented assumption that women in business cost more.

The linchpin of Ms. Schwartz's thesis is an unidentified study at a single multinational corporation where the turnover rate for female managers was allegedly two and a half times that for male managers. Ms. Schwartz does not say whether the actual rates were an insignificant 1 percent for men and 2.5 percent for women, a significant 40 percent for men and 100 percent for women or something between. Moreover, she fails to explore the reasons for the difference. These might include poor personnel policies, like rigid relocation demands or a lack of parental leave, better job opportunities at other corporations or downturns in the company's fortunes that prompted more recently hired female managers to seek greener pastures.

Ms. Schwartz cites a second unidentified study (apparently of all female employees, not just managers) at another unnamed company, where "half of the women who take maternity leave return to their jobs late or not at all." That is, half returned as scheduled, and an unspecified number did not return, but for unexplained reasons.

Singling out turnover rates among female employees, whether clerks or managers, is a dubious approach. The days of an employee's spending 50 years with a single employer and retiring with a gold watch and a handshake are over. (Indeed, thanks to the buy-out, merger and acquisition mania of the 1980s, the days of a company's lasting even a few years under the same ownership, management or even the same name, are diminishing.)

A January 1983 Bureau of Labor Statistics job-tenure survey that represented 54 million male and 42 million female workers reported that fewer that 10 percent of workers of either sex had been with their current employers 25 years or more. Of the 14 million male and 9.5 million female managers and executives covered by the survey, the median tenure was 6.6 years for males and 4.7 years for females.

The survey also showed that 60 percent of the male managers and executives and 74 percent of their female counterparts had the same employer for 9 years or less. Only 11 percent of the males and 3 percent of the females had the same employer for 25 years or more.

In short, few men or women remain with one employer for their entire careers, and women's somewhat lower managerial tenures might be explained partly by women's having only recently entered the executive ranks in significant numbers.

If Ms. Schwartz's scholarship is suspect, her two-track career model (future mommies in this corner, future nonmommies in that corner) is quaint—indeed Victorian—in view of what businesses are doing for men and women.

Impelled by the changing American work force and striving to remain competitive, corporations like U S West, I.B.M., A.T.&T., Time Inc., Corning Glass, Quaker Oats and Merck have concluded that productivity and family obligations are not mutually exclusive, that the almighty dollar and the family are not enemies. To accommodate these new realities companies have instituted such employment practices as parental leave, flexible and part-time schedules, sabbaticals, child care, telecommuting and job sharing.

But workers are not the only beneficiaries of these new practices. Employers are finding that meeting the needs of employees makes companies more productive and more competitive.

PAT SCHROEDER
Member of Congress, 1st Dist., Colo.
Washington, March 27, 1989

To the Editor:

Corporations may welcome Felice Schwartz's discovery of the "career and family" woman and "her willingness to accept lower pay and little advancement in return for a flexible schedule" (news story, March 8), but such women should consider the recent history of divorce laws before agreeing to this definition.

Although the law says marriage is an economic partnership that values child rearing and other domestic contributions as well as earning power, the reality is that when a marriage ends, women are not adequately compensated for having devoted themselves to their families at the expense of pursuing their career development.

If young women are going to be doubly penalized this way for choosing "the mommy track," they would do well to look closely at the experience of a generation of middle-aged women who have been left divorced and financially derailed by that choice.

LOIS BRENNER
New York, March 19, 1989

The writer heads the family law department of a law firm and is co-author of not-yet-published book on divorce for women.

To the Editor:

Felice N. Schwartz, in her attempt to persuade us that "The 'Mommy Track' Isn't Anti-Woman" (Op-Ed, March 22), cites an intriguing statistic. According to a recent study, she says, 54 percent of married women working full-time regard child care as their responsibility, whereas only 2 percent of men say the same.

Does this mean that 46 percent of women in these circumstances see child care as a shared responsibility—presumably because men are sharing in the work? While not a majority, such a figure would be a significant enough minority to lend force to the argument for the importance of making businesses more responsive to the needs of both mothers and fathers—and, perhaps more compellingly, to the needs of the nation's children.

While Ms. Schwartz's assurance that "current 'baby-bust' demographics compel companies to employ women at every level" may be true, it is also true that few mothers have reached the top.

The idea of tracks has always had its limitations—whether in junior high school or in the corporate world. But if we must have such tracks in business, the chances of discrimination are surely much less for a "parent track" than for a "mommy track."

Corporations may or may not believe that they can get along without mothers in high places, but they must realize that they cannot function without parents.

HOPE DELLON
New York, March 24, 1989

To the Editor:
Another problem with Felice Schwartz's proposal to track working women according to the likelihood they will want to raise children is that it is impossible to tell ahead of time which women are which.

In interviewing highly successful career women in predominantly male fields, I found that some women who as late as age 34 said adamantly that they did not want children had, by 40, had them. One executive who had had her tubes tied at 29, with the idea that she wanted a career and no children was, at 35, about to be married; she wanted desperately to have the ligation reversed and was seriously contemplating a completely different line of work.

Women who in their 20's had expected to quit work to have families found themselves in their 30's still single or divorced and enjoying their careers. Most women, married or single, with or without children, expressed ambivalence both about children and about their careers.

The problem is not that women don't know what they want, but that women, like men, grow and change along the life cycle. Stereotyping women early on into mothers and nonmothers would hamper their ability to develop fully both as individuals and as productive employees.

Even worse, it would perpetuate a cycle in which generations of women have been depreciated, divided and weakened through a paradoxical message that says women are inferior if they—and unles they—compete in terms that are set by and for men.

ANITA M. HARRIS
Cambridge, Mass. March 13, 1989

The writer, an assistant professor of communications at Simmons College in Boston, is completing a book on professional women.

To the Editor:
While I mostly agree with your response to "Management Women and the New Facts of Life" (editorial, March 13), your

perspective does not include or explore the profoundly different attitudes men and women have toward money, which is, after all, why people work. There has been a spate of surveys highlighting these different attitudes.

Men see money as a means to power, heightening their visibility for selection for leadership within society. Looked at this way, the insatiable appetite for money, frequently bordering on greed, makes sense, albeit an insane sense. Capital accumulation is seen as primarily a male activity.

Women, on the other hand, see money as a means of power to purchase. Money purchases food, clothing, shelter or the means of nurturing. This idea too has its insane side, giving rise to gross materialism. Excessive spending is seen as a female trait.

Both these traits cross gender, but a greater number fall within a male-female perspective.

Women cannot satisfy their primary need, nurturing family and society, with the same single-minded directness that men can bring to their primary need of territory (capital accumulation). The marketplace, a male invention, reflects this bias, presenting women with unnatural choices, creating for them a practical as well as psychological disadvantage.

We must force the news media to include differing economic attitudes in covering the brave woman who daily deals with the multifaceted pressures of family life and living up to her potential as described by others.

PEG MCAULEY BYRD
Madison, N.J., March 20, 1989

Topics for Discussion and Writing

1. In paragraph 5 Schwartz says that "'baby-bust' demographics compel companies to employ women at every level, no matter what the cost." Exactly what does she mean?
2. In paragraph 9 Schwartz says that "Today, men are more involved in their children's upbringing. . . . " One often hears comparable statements, but are they true? How would one verify such a statement? In any case, if *you* have any reason to agree or disagree with the statement, express the grounds. To what extent do you think men *ought* to be involved in child-rearing?

3. Schwartz begins her final paragraph by asserting, "What benefits women benefits companies." What evidence or arguments does she offer to support this claim? Or do you think the point is self-evident and needs no support?
4. List the three most cogent arguments the letter-writers make against Schwartz's position.
5. Imagine that you are Schwartz. Write a letter to *The New York Times* in which you reply to one of the letters.

Alexandra Armstrong

Alexandra Armstrong, president of an independent financial planning firm, has appeared on such television programs as Good Morning America *and* Wall Street Week. *In 1987* Money *magazine called her one of the "most qualified Financial Planners in the U.S." The essay reprinted here appeared in* Ms. *magazine.*

Starting a Business

Marian Strong, a 33-year-old married woman with two children, ages six and eight, worked at a bank until her first child was born. Her husband, Edward, has worked for the same corporation for the past 10 years. Paid $50,000 annually, he feels that his job is stable. Their expenses are moderate, both mortgage on their home and the car loan payments are low. Although they live on Edward's salary, three years ago Marian went to work for H & R Block preparing tax returns. While there, she managed to save $5,000 of her earnings.

In addition to enjoying the work, Marian discovered that many of the company's clients needed to know how to set up and maintain financial records. A number were willing to pay a fee to have this done and some even wanted her to pay their monthly bills. As a result, Marian, who recently inherited $5,000 from an aunt, would like to use this windfall to start her own home-based business to organize and maintain financial records for clients.

I recommended Marian prepare a business plan describing the nature of her business, and why she believes there's a need for it. Estimates of her start-up costs, as well as projected expenses and income for the first year, must also be included. I also reminded her that people in home-based offices often find excuses not to work, and that a wise move would be to have a separate room devoted exclusively to business.

Having decided to give one room totally to her work, Marian needed a computer, a copying machine, some furniture and stationery. Her savings, which she estimates at $5,000, will cover these expenses. I told her not to expect to be profitable in the first year, but to plan for the worst case. Marian has her inheritance to fall back on, as well as an untapped $5,000 line of credit that she shares with her husband.

Marian wasn't sure whether her business should be a sole proprietorship, partnership, or a corporation. As a rule one should achieve $100,000 in revenues before incorporation is worthwhile. I recommended a sole proprietorship until her revenues become substantial, because it is less encumbering than a partnership.

We then discussed her marketing strategy. She needs to make sure that people find out about her business, while keeping her costs minimal. I suggested that she write letters introducing herself to estate planners and CPAs who don't want to be involved in record keeping; use personal contacts for referrals, like her former colleagues at H & R Block; and also make contact with organizations that cater to women over the age of 60, since they usually have little experience handling their own financial affairs.

It is important that Marian regularly review her situation to see how her sales and profits are progressing in line with projections and whether more marketing should be done or cost reduction techniques be employed.

Last, but not least, I stressed the importance when starting a business of getting good advisers: a lawyer to help determine potential liabilities that might be involved; an insurance agent to make sure of sufficient liability coverage; and a tax adviser who specializes in small businesses. This is not an area where one should try to save money, but on the other hand, one good initial conversation with a business lawyer or consultant at an hourly rate is often sufficient, and the same holds true for a tax adviser. Then one can continue to consult on a need-to-know basis.

There are also a number of organizations that Marian can turn to for advice and valuable information. The National Association of Women Business Owners, 600 South Federal Street, Suite 400, Chicago, Illinois 60605, is an excellent resource for women in sole proprietorships and has many local chapters. The National Alliance of Homebased Businesswomen, P. O. Box 306, Midland Park, New Jersey 07432, and the Small Business Administration are also useful.

Topics for Discussion and Writing

1. This essay is fundamentally an essay on a process—in this case, how to start a business. Reread it, and see whether (within the severe limitations of the space allowed) it covers all the main points. And does it waste space on irrelevant matters?
2. Do you think the essay is well organized? What *is* the organization?
3. What do you think of Marian Strong's idea for a business, and why?

Bill Totten

Bill Totten, an American, runs a company in Tokyo. His essay appeared in American newspapers as part of a paid advertising supplement about doing business in Japan.

Eigyoman

I am an "Eigyo-man"—a Salesman. My company, K.K. Ashisuto, neither creates nor manufactures, but sells computer software packages. I started Ashisuto with only $5,000 when I arrived from America in 1969. The company now boasts over 600 employees and more than $100 million in annual revenues. I owe my success in large measure to an understanding of the critical differences between Japanese "Eigyo" and American "Sales."

Ashisuto has only three goals. For our customers—to be the best supplier of software products. For creators of software—to be the best distributor of their products. For employees—to be the best employer of people who want to sell software products. Our customers come first, our suppliers second, and we, the employees, third. Our stockholders are all employees and are rewarded as employees, not as stockholders.

Does all this sound strange? Not to Japanese ears. This is how most Japanese companies operate. The most important Japanese business value is to serve customers, not to enrich stockholders or executives. Revenue, profit, and return-on-investment goals are measures of how well a company is doing for its stockholders, not for its customers.

Ashisuto and other Japanese companies are not against mak-   4
ing a profit. To the contrary. But we do not want profits that come at the expense of our customers. We believe that serving our customers best encourages our customers to continue buying from us and recommending us to their friends. As in baseball or tennis, the player who wants the higher score must concentrate on the ball, not the scoreboard.

Our salespersons do not have quotas—the hallmark of American sales—nor are they rewarded on how much they sell over short periods. We believe that such quotas merely stimulate to sell as much to each customer as fast as possible, and encourage practices that produce sales and revenues at the expense of customers.

"Eigyo" vs. "Sales"

At Ashisuto, we expect each of our salespersons to visit fifteen customers per week and to visit each customer at least once a month. We measure how many sales calls our salespersons make rather than the business they bring in. Why? Because the salespersons who visit their customers frequently, without being pressed to close sales quickly, build personal friendships, discover ways to satisfy customers' problems and needs. Over the long term, they bring in a lot of business, because most customers prefer to buy from people they know, and like, and trust.

Providing the best service to existing customers makes then excellent prospects for additional products. Seventy-five percent of our business is repeat business. Moreover, building a reputation for providing the best service to customers is the best way to convert new prospects into customers. The circle continues—prospect, customer, repeat customer, recommender, repeat customer. The key to this "Eigyo" approach is that it works best over the long term. Unlike Americans, Japanese are more interested in the long-term health of their businesses than in short-term profits.

Our second priority is to be the best distributor for the creators   8
and manufacturers of computer software products. Just as customers buy from us because we put them first, creators of software distribute through us because we put their needs above our own.

In Ashisuto as in most Japanese companies, employees are given higher priority than stockholders or executives. Executives, in fact, are merely the highest ranking employees. Their power and compensation are on the same scale as all other employees'. Although I am the president and majority stockholder of Ashisuto, my total income last year, after taxes, was only nine times that of a new employee and only six times that of our average employee. This ratio is typical of Japanese company presidents and much lower than in the United States where the average CEO makes ninety-three times as much as the average factory worker.

Trust Is a Product

Stockholders matter even less. Japanese companies sacrifice profits to maintain employment. They do not lay off employees to maintain profits. Only employees can produce high productivity and quality—the only impact executives have is through employees. So Japanese companies make sure that the benefits of prosperity go first to employees, then to executive as employees, and lastly to stockholders. Since employees know that they are the first to benefit from high productivity and higher quality, they are motivated to produce both. And they do!

The most important thing I have learned as an Eigyo-man is that trust is a product. Customers are looking for salespersons they can trust. Life is easy for a salesperson who earns a reputation for serving customers, for putting their interests first and ensuring they get the value they expect.

I am tempted to say I learned this in Japan, but I really learned 12 it from my father while growing up in the United States in the 1940s and '50s. It seems that the "Japanese secret" for success is that they have adopted the values that made America great at the same time we have abandoned them.

Topics for Discussion and Writing

1. How (and where) does Totten describe his job with K.K. Ashisuto? How would his job be described in the United States? In addition to providing information, what point is Totten making with his description?

2. Consider paragraphs 2–7, on relations with customers. Do you assume that Americans should use this approach, or do you assume that the approach would work only in Japan? Explain why you hold your view.

3. Totten says (paragraph 11) that he has learned that "trust is a product." What does he mean, and how is this idea important to his argument?
4. In so far as the essay explains Japanese ways of doing business, it is an expository essay. Is there also a thesis? If so, what is the thesis?
5. Do you think Benjamin Franklin (page 397) would invest in Bill Totten's company? Explain.

Robert W. Keidel

Robert W. Keidel, a graduate of Williams College and the Wharton School of the University of Pennsylvania, directs a consulting firm. He is the author of Game Plans: Sports Strategies for Business *(1985) and* Corporate Players: Designs for Working and Winning Together *(1988).*

A New Game for Managers to Play

As the football season gradually gives way to basketball, corporate managers would do well to consider the differences between these games. For just as football mirrors industrial structures of the past, basketball points the way to the corporate structure of the future.

It's the difference between the former chief executive officer of I. T. T., Harold Geneen, the master football coach who dictates his players' roles and actions, and Donald Burr, the People Express Airlines chief executive officer, who puts his players on the floor and lets them manage themselves.

Football is, metaphorically, a way of life in work today—the corporate sport. This is reflected in the language many managers use:

"It's taken my staff and me a sizable chunk of time, but we now have a solid game plan for the XYZ job. Jack, I want you to quarterback this thing all the way into the end zone. Of course, a lot of it will be making the proper assignments—getting the right people to run interference and the right ones to run with the ball. But my main concern is that we avoid mistakes. No fumbles, no interceptions, no sacks, no penalties. I don't want us to have to play catchup; no two-minute drills at the end. I want the game plan executed exactly the way it's drawn. When we're done we want to look back with pride at a win—and not have to Monday-morning-quarterback a loss."

Does this football language represent more than just a convenient shorthand? Almost certainly it does, because the metaphors we use routinely are the means by which we structure experience. Thus, football metaphors may well reflect—and reinforce—underlying organizational dynamics. But football, despite its pervasiveness, is the wrong model for most corporations.

Consider the scenario above. Planning has been neatly separated from implementation; those expected to carry out the game plan had no part in creating it. Also, the communication flow is one-way: from the head coach (speaker) to the quarterback (Jack)—and, presumably, from the quarterback to the other players. And the thrust of the message is risk-averse; the real name of the game is control—minimizing mistakes. But perhaps most significant is the assumption of stability, — that nothing will change to invalidate the corporate game plan. "No surprises!" as Mr. Geneen likes to say.

Stability is a realistic assumption in football, even given the sport's enormous complexity, because of the time available to coaches—between games and between plays. A pro football game can very nearly be programmed. Carl Peterson, formerly with the Philadelphia Eagles and now president of the United States Football League's champions, the Baltimore Stars, has estimated that managing a game is 75 percent preparation and only 25 percent adjustment.

Thus, football truly is the realm of the coach—the head coach, 8 he who calls the shots. (Most pro quarterbacks do not call their own plays.) As Bum Phillips has said in tribute to the head coach of the Miami Dolphins, Don Shula, "He can take his'n and beat your'n, or he can take your'n and beat his'n."

But football is not an appropriate model for most businesses precisely because instability is an overwhelming fact of life. Market competition grows ever more spastic, product life-cycles shrink unimaginably and technology courses on paths of its own.

In this milieu, corporate "players" simply cannot perform effectively if they must wait for each play to be called for them, and remain in fixed positions—or in narrowly defined roles—like football players; increasingly, they need to deploy themselves flexibly, in novel combinations.

Thirty years ago it may have been possible to regard core business functions—R&D, manufacturing and marketing as separate worlds, with little need for interaction. R&D would design the product and then lob it over the wall to manufacturing; manufacturing would make the product and lob it over another wall to the customer.

No need to worry about problems that do not fit neatly into the standard departments; these are inconsequential and infrequent. And when they do arise, they are simply bumped up the hierarchy to senior management—the head coach and his staff.   12

In effect, performance is roughly the sum of the functions—just as a football team's performance is the sum of the performances of its platoons—offense, defense and special teams. Clearly, this view of the corporation is anachronistic. Yet it remains all too common.

Business's "season" is changing, and a new metaphor is needed. While football will continue to be a useful model for pursuing machinelike efficiency and consistency—that is, for minimizing redundancies, bottlenecks and errors—this design favors stability at the expense of change. Since now more than ever businesses must continuously innovate and adapt, a more promising model is basketball.

To begin with, basketball is too dynamic a sport to permit the rigid separation of planning and execution that characterizes football. Unlike football teams, basketball teams do not pause and regroup after each play. As the former star player and coach Bill Russell has noted, "Your game plan may be wiped out by what happens in the first minute of play." Success in basketball depends on the ability of the coach and players to plan and adjust while in motion. Such behavior requires all-around communication—just as basketball demands all-around passing, as opposed to football's linear sequence of "forward," one-way passing.

Basketball also puts a premium on generalist skills. Although different players will assume somewhat different roles on the court, all must be able to dribble, pass, shoot, rebound and play defense. Everyone handles the ball—a far cry from what happens on the gridiron. Indeed, basketball is much more player-oriented than football—a sport in which players tend to be viewed as interchangeable parts.   16

If football is a risk-averse game, basketball is risk-accepting. In basketball, change is seen as normal, not exceptional; hence, change is regarded more as the source of opportunities than of threats. Mr. Geneen has claimed that "Ninety-nine percent of all surprises in business are negative."

Mr. Geneen's perspective is classic football and is tenable in stable, "controllable" environments. But such environments are becoming rare. The future increasingly belongs to managers like Mr. Burr or James Treybig, the founder of Tandem Computers, who thrive on change rather than flee from it.

We need fewer head coaches and more player-coaches, less scripted teamwork and more spontaneous teamwork. We need to integrate planning and doing—managing and working—far more than we have to date. Are you playing yesterday's game—or tomorrow's?

Topics for Discussion and Writing

1. In his first paragraph Keidel says that "football mirrors industrial structures of the past" whereas "basketball points the way to the corporate structure of the future." He several times makes similar assertions—for instance, in paragraph 5 he says "football . . . is the wrong model for most corporations." Does he support his view with evidence? If so, call attention to the evidence he offers. Are you convinced by his argument? Why, or why not?

2. Keidel says (paragraph 5) that "the metaphors we use routinely are the means by which we structure experience." Consider metaphors drawn from the world of business but used in the context of education. An administrator, for instance, may say, "Last year we *produced* 1,000 majors in business administration; next year we hope to *turn out* twelve hundred; the *bottom line* is, the *supply still falls short of the demand.*" What do such metaphors tell us about the ways in which the speaker sees education (or, to use Keidel's words, the ways in which he or she "structure[s] experience")?

3. As the preceding question indicates, business itself can provide metaphors, such as "producing" or "turning out" students. In the next few days jot down examples that you encounter in newspapers, television ads, political speeches, or whatever and analyze their implications. (You may even find businesses that use metaphors drawn from business.)

4. In paragraph 2 Keidel refers to People Express Airlines. What point does he hope to make? Is People Express still in business? (If you don't know, how would you go about finding out?) Does the current status of People Express affect the status of his argument?

Warren Bennis

*Warren Bennis, born in New York City in 1925, was educated at Antioch College
and the Massachusetts Institute of Technology. From 1971 to 1977 he served as the
president of the University of Cincinnati. The author of several important books on management, he now teaches at the School of Business in the University of Southern
California.*

Time to Hang Up the Old Sports Clichés

Americans are, on the whole, simple and direct people.
We do not incline toward nuances or subtleties, in either our lives
or our work. We opt inevitably for the concrete over the abstract.
We are also extremely competitive, relishing opponents' losses as
we boast of our own victories. For these reasons, sports are not only
our favorite form of entertainment but the principal model and
metaphor for our own lives.

At home and at work, we talk often of winning and losing, scor-
ing touchdowns, carrying the ball, close calls, going down to the
wire, batting a thousand, hitting paydirt and going into extra innings, and while we may like movie, TV and music stars, we admire sports stars. Every father wants his sons to shine on the
playing fields, which is why Little League games frequently have
all the carefree air of the London blitz.

Preachers and politicians, among others, see this national obsession as healthy, portray us as good people interested in good,
clean fun. Universities, including mine, celebrate and reward their
athletes as heroes. When the Super Bowl rolls around, the country
focuses on The Game.

I am admittedly as obsessed as anyone. I seem to remember for- 4
ever great plays, great players and even the scores of great games,
though I sometimes cannot recall whom I sat next to at dinner three
nights ago. But I am also convinced that it is time to find a new
model.

Life is not a baseball game. It's never called on account of darkness, much less canceled because of inclement weather. And while
major sports are big business now, business is not a sport, and never
was. Indeed, thinking of business as a kind of game or sport was
always simplistic. Now it's downright dangerous.

Games are of limited duration, take place on or in fixed and finite sites and are governed by openly promulgated rules that are enforced on the spot by neutral professionals. Moreover, they are performed by relatively evenly matched teams that are counseled and led through every move by seasoned hands. Scores are kept, and at the end of the game, a winner is declared.

Business is usually a little different. In fact, if there is anyone out there who can say that his business is of limited duration, takes place on a fixed site, is governed by openly promulgated rules that are enforced on the spot by neutral professionals, competes only on relatively even terms and performs in a way that can be measured in runs or points, then he is either extraordinarily lucky or seriously deluded.

The risks in thinking of business in sports terms are numerous. 8 First, to measure a business on the basis of wins and losses is to misunderstand both the purposes of a specific business and the nature of business itself. No business—whether it sells insurance or manufactures cars—can or should be designed to win. Rather, it should be designed to grow, both quantitatively and qualitatively. In this sense, it vies more with itself than with its competition. This is not to say there are never winners or losers—in head-to-head contests, as when two ad agencies are competing for the same account, someone will win and someone will lose. It is to say, to paraphrase Vince Lombardi's legendary dictum, winning isn't everything, it's one of many things a business must accomplish.

Thus, a company designed merely to win will probably lose in the long run. For example, the John Doe Insurance Company could win the auto market overnight by offering comprehensive coverage for $100 a year. However, the company would fail when the claims began coming in.

Second, it is perilous to think of limits, rules and absolutes in lo business. Athletes compete for a given number of hours in a given number of games over a given period of weeks or months. Businesses are in the arena for decades, sometimes centuries. Though the action may rise and subside, it never stops. It does not offer any timeouts, much less neatly defined beginnings and endings.

American business has traditionally been schizophrenic about rules. When it is flourishing, it wants no rules or regulations. When it failing, it wants a plethora of rules. For example, Detroit saw Washington as its nemesis until foreign cars flooded the market.

Then, Chrysler went to the Feds for a loan, and now Detroit begs Washington to regulate imports while lobbying against Federal safety and quality controls.

Athletes perform in a static environment—the size of the field, the length of the contest, even the wardrobes of the players remain the same, day after month after year. Businesses function in a volatile universe, which changes from moment to moment, and hardly ever repeats. It is affected by droughts half a world away, a new gizmo down the street, consumer attitudes and needs, a million things. Given this mercurial context, any business that is not at least as dynamic and flexible as the world in which it functions will soon be out of step or out of business.   12

Clearly, then, there are far more differences between sports and business than similarities. But the danger is that many people will continue to imagine that success in business is like success in sports—flat-out, total victory; a world championship. But the best-run and most successful companies in America do not think in terms of victories and defeats, coming from behind, last-minute saves or shining moments, and they do not count on regulations or referees. Instead, they think in terms of staying power, dedication to quality, and an endless effort to do better than they have done. They see change as the only constant, and they try to adapt to the world rather than expect the world to adapt to them. Indeed, it is a business's ability to adapt to an everchanging world that is the basis for both its success and progress.

I should emphasize that I am not criticizing the management of professional sports teams, which are themselves businesses. Some teams are poorly run, but others, like the Boston Celtics or Los Angeles Lakers, operate on the same principles that other successful businesses do. They change, they plan for the long-term, and they strive ceaselessly for quality. What I object to is comparing the playing field to the marketplace.

The truth is that there is no workable or appropriate metaphor for business except business itself, and that should be sufficient. Like a well-played game, a well-run business is something to see, but, unlike a well-played game, it is not a diversion. Rather, it is life itself—complex, difficult, susceptible to both success and failure, sometimes unruly, always challenging, and often joyful.

So let's leave the home runs to the Phillies' Mike Schmidt and the touchdowns to the Bears' Walter Payton, and get down to business.   16

Topics for Discussion and Writing

1. In paragraph 5 Bennis suggests that "it's downright dangerous" to see business in terms of metaphors drawn from the world of sports. On the other hand, presumably those who use metaphors believe that the metaphors help them see things freshly and clearly. If you have read Robert Keidel's essay (page 414), do you think that Keidel's use of metaphor clarifies your understanding of business or, on the contrary, does it lead to dangerous misapprehensions? Be as specific as possible.

2. In paragraph 8, when Bennis says that a business "should be designed to grow," he is using a metaphor, for he is comparing a business to a living organism. And in paragraph 11, when he says that American business is "schizophrenic," he uses a metaphor from psychiatry. Reread his essay closely and jot down a list of the metaphors he uses. Do you think his metaphors are useful, or are they (to quote paragraph 5) "dangerous"?

3. Evaluate Bennis's final paragraph as a final paragraph. What makes it effective or ineffective? Now look at Bennis's opening paragraph. Does his description of Americans largely exclude some groups? Are there readers his opening paragraph might unintentionally "exclude" or turn away?

Milton Friedman

Milton Friedman, born in Brooklyn in 1912, is a graduate of Rutgers University, the University of Chicago, and Columbia University. A leading conservative economist, Friedman has had considerable influence on economic thought in America through his popular writings (he wrote a regular column in Newsweek), *his numerous scholarly writings, and his presence on national committees.*

The Social Responsibility of Business Is to Increase Its Profits

When I hear businessmen speak eloquently about the "social responsibilities of business in a free-enterprise system," I am reminded of the wonderful line about the Frenchman who discovered at the age of 70 that he had been speaking prose all his life.

The businessmen believe that they are defending free enterprise when they declaim that business is not concerned "merely" with profit but also with promoting desirable "social" ends; that business has a "social conscience" and takes seriously its responsibilities for providing employment, eliminating discrimination, avoiding pollution and whatever else may be the catchwords of the contemporary crop of reformers. In fact they are—or would be if they or anyone else took them seriously—preaching pure and unadulterated socialism. Businessmen who talk this way are unwitting puppets of the intellectual forces that have been undermining the basis of a free society these past decades.

The discussions of the "social responsibilities of business" are notable for their analytical looseness and lack of rigor. What does it mean to say that "business" has responsibilities? Only people can have responsibilities. A corporation is an artificial person and in this sense may have artificial responsibilities, but "business" as a whole cannot be said to have responsibilities, even in this vague sense. The first step toward clarity in examining the doctrine of the social responsibility of business is to ask precisely what it implies for whom.

Presumably, the individuals who are to be responsible are businessmen, which means individual proprietors or corporate executives. Most of the discussion of social responsibility is directed at corporations, so in what follows I shall mostly neglect the individual proprietors and speak of corporate executives.

In a free-enterprise, private-property system, a corporate executive is an employee of the owners of the business. He has direct responsibility to his employers. That responsibility is to conduct the business in accordance with their desires, which generally will be to make as much money as possible while conforming to the basic rules of the society, both those embodied in law and those embodied in ethical custom. Of course, in some cases his employers may have a different objective. A group of persons might establish a corporation for an eleemosynary purpose—for example, a hospital or a school. The manager of such a corporation will not have money profit as his objectives but the rendering of certain services.

In either case, the key point is that, in his capacity as a corporate executive, the manager is the agent of the individuals who own the corporation or establish the eleemosynary institution, and his primary responsibility is to them.

Needless to say, this does not mean that it is easy to judge how well he is performing his task. But at least the criterion of performance is straightforward, and the persons among whom a voluntary contractual arrangement exists are clearly defined.

Of course, the corporate executive is also a person in his own right. As a person, he may have many other responsibilities that he recognizes or assumes voluntarily—to his family, his conscience, his feelings of charity, his church, his clubs, his city, his country. He may feel impelled by these responsibilities to devote part of his income to causes he regards as worthy, to refuse to work for particular corporations, even to leave his job, for example, to join his country's armed forces. If we wish, we may refer to some of these responsibilities as "social responsibilities." But in these respects he is acting as a principal, not an agent; he is spending his own money or time or energy, not the money of his employers or the time or energy he has contracted to devote to their purposes. If these are "social responsibilities," they are the social responsibilities of individuals, not of business.

What does it mean to say that the corporate executive has a "social responsibility" in his capacity as businessman? If this statement is not pure rhetoric, it must mean that he is to act in some way that is not in the interest of his employers. For example, that he is to refrain from increasing the price of the product in order to contribute to the social objective of preventing inflation, even though a price increase would be in the best interests of the corporation. Or that he is to make expenditures on reducing pollution beyond the amount that is in the best interests of the corporation or that is required by law in order to contribute to the social objective of improving the environment. Or that, at the expense of corporate profits, he is to hire "hardcore" unemployed instead of better qualified available workmen to contribute to the social objective of reducing poverty.

In each of these cases, the corporate executive would be spending someone else's money for a general social interest. Insofar as his actions in accord with his "social responsibility" reduce returns to stockholders, he is spending their money. Insofar as his actions raise the price to customers, he is spending the customers' money. Insofar as his actions lower the wages of some employees, he is spending their money.

The stockholders or the customers or the employees could separately spend their own money on the particular action if they wished to do so. The executive is exercising a distinct "social responsibility," rather than serving as an agent of the stockholders or the customers or the employees, only if he spends the money in a different way than they would have spent it.

But if he does this, he is in effect imposing taxes, on the one hand, and deciding how the tax proceeds shall be spent, on the other.

This process raises political questions on two levels: principle 12 and consequences. On the level of political principle, the imposition of taxes and the expenditure of tax proceeds are governmental functions. We have established elaborate constitutional, parliamentary and judicial provisions to control these functions, to assure that taxes are imposed so far as possible in accordance with the preferences and desires of the public—after all, "taxation without representation" was one of the battle cries of the American Revolution. We have a system of checks and balances to separate the legislative function of imposing taxes and enacting expenditures from the executive function of collecting taxes and administering expenditure programs and from the judicial function of mediating disputes and interpreting the law.

Here the businessman—self-selected or appointed directly or indirectly by stockholders—is to be simultaneously legislator, executive and jurist. He is to decide whom to tax by how much and for what purpose, and he is to spend the proceeds—all this guided only by general exhortations from on high to restrain inflation, improve the environment, fight poverty and so on and on.

The whole justification for permitting the corporate executive to be selected by the stockholders is that the executive is an agent serving the interests of his principal. This justification disappears when the corporate executive imposes taxes and spends the proceeds for "social" purposes. He becomes in effect a public employee, a civil servant, even though he remains in name an employee of a private enterprise. On grounds of political principle, it is intolerable that such civil servants— insofar as their actions in the name of social responsibility are real and not just window-dressing,—should be selected as they are now. If they are to be civil servants, then they must be elected through a political process. If they are to impose taxes and make expenditures to foster "social" objectives, then political machinery must be set up to make the assessment of taxes and to determine through a political process the objectives to be served.

This is the basic reason why the doctrine of "social responsibility" involves the acceptance of the socialist view that political mechanisms, not market mechanisms, are the appropriate way to determine the allocation of scarce resources to alternative uses.

On the grounds of consequences, can the corporate executive 16 in fact discharge his alleged "social responsibilities"? On the other hand, suppose he could get away with spending the stockholders' or customers' or employees' money. How is he to know how to spend it? He is told that he must contribute to fighting inflation. How is he to know what action of his will contribute to that end? He is presumably an expert in running his company—in producing a product or selling it or financing it. But nothing about his selection makes him an expert on inflation. Will his holding down the price of his product reduce inflationary pressure? Or, by leaving more spending power in the hands of his customers, simply divert it elsewhere? Or, by forcing him to produce less because of the lower price, will it simply contribute to shortages? Even if he could answer these questions, how much cost is he justified in imposing on his stockholders, customers and employees for this social purpose? What is his appropriate share and what is the appropriate share of others?

And, whether he wants to or not, can he get away with spending his stockholders', customers' or employees' money? Will not the stockholders fire him? (Either the present ones or those who take over when his actions in the name of social responsibility have reduced the corporation's profits and the price of its stock.) His customers and his employees can desert him for other producers and employers less scrupulous in exercising their social responsibilities.

This facet of "social responsibility" doctrine is brought into sharp relief when the doctrine is used to justify wage restraint by trade unions. The conflict of interest is naked and clear when union officials are asked to subordinate the interest of their members to some more general purpose. If the union officials try to enforce wage restraint, the consequence is likely to be wildcat strikes, rank-and-file revolts and the emergence of strong competitors for their jobs. We thus have the ironic phenomenon that union leaders—at least in the U.S.—have objected to Government interference with the market far more consistently and courageously than have business leaders.

The difficulty of exercising "social responsibility" illustrates, of course, the great virtue of private competitive enterprise—it forces people to be responsible for their own actions and makes it difficult for them to "exploit" other people for either selfish or unselfish purposes. They can do good—but only at their own expense.

Many a reader who has followed the argument this far may be 20 tempted to remonstrate that it is all well and good to speak of Government's having the responsibility to impose taxes and determine expenditures for such "social" purposes as controlling pollution or training the hard-core unemployed, but that the problems are too urgent to wait on the slow course of political processes, that the exercise of social responsibility by businessmen is a quicker and surer way to solve pressing current problems.

Aside from the question of fact—I share Adam Smith's skepticism about the benefits that can be expected from "those who affected to trade for the public good"—this argument must be rejected on grounds of principle. What it amounts to is an assertion that those who favor the taxes and expenditures in question have failed to persuade a majority of their fellow citizens to be of like mind and that they are seeking to attain by undemocratic procedures what they cannot attain by democratic procedures. In a free society, it is hard for "evil" people to do "evil," especially since one man's good is another's evil.

I have, for simplicity, concentrated on the special case of the corporate executive, except only for the brief digression on trade unions. But precisely the same argument applies to the newer phenomenon of calling upon stockholders to require corporations to exercise social responsibility (the recent G.M. crusade for example). In most of these cases, what is in effect involved is some stockholders trying to get other stockholders (or customers or employees) to contribute against their will to "social" causes favored by the activists. Insofar as they succeed, they are again imposing taxes and spending the proceeds.

The situation of the individual proprietor is somewhat different. If he acts to reduce the returns of his enterprise in order to exercise his "social responsibility," he is spending his own money, not someone else's. If he wishes to spend his money on such purposes, that is his right, and I cannot see that there is any objection to his doing so. In the process, he, too, may impose costs on employees and customers. However, because he is far less likely than a large corporation or union to have monopolistic power, any such side effects will tend to be minor.

Of course, in practice the doctrine of social responsibility is frequently a cloak for actions that are justified on other grounds rather than a reason for those actions. 24

To illustrate, it may well be in the long-run interest of a corporation that is a major employer in a small community to devote resources to providing amenities to that community or to improving its government. That may make it easier to attract desirable employees, it may reduce the wage bill or lessen losses from pilferage and sabotage or have other worthwhile effects. Or it may be that, given the laws about the deductibility of corporate charitable contributions, the stockholders can contribute more to charities they favor by having the corporation make the gift than by doing it themselves, since they can in that way contribute an amount that would otherwise have been paid as corporate taxes.

In each of these—and many similar—cases, there is a strong temptation to rationalize these actions as an exercise of "social responsibility." In the present climate of opinion, with its widepread aversion to "capitalism," "profits," the "soulless corporation" and so on, this is one way for a corporation to generate goodwill as a byproduct of expenditures that are entirely justified in its own self-interest.

It would be inconsistent of me to call on corporate executives to refrain from this hypocritical window-dressing because it harms the foundations of a free society. That would be to call on them to exercise a "social responsibility"! If our institutions and the attitudes of the public make it in their self-interest to cloak their actions in this way, I cannot summon much indignation to denounce them. At the same time, I can express admiration for those individual proprietors or owners of closely held corporations or stockholders of more broadly held corporations who disdain such tactics as approaching fraud.

Whether blameworthy or not, the use of the cloak of social responsibility, and the nonsense spoken in its name by influential and prestigious businessmen, does clearly harm the foundations of a free society. I have been impressed time and again by the schizophrenic character of many businessmen. They are capable of being extremely far-sighted and clear-headed in matters that are internal to their businesses. They are incredibly short-sighted and muddle-headed in matters that are outside their businesses but affect the possible survival of business in general. This short-sightedness is strikingly exemplified in the calls from many businessmen for wage and price guidelines or controls or income policies. There is nothing that could do more in a brief period to destroy a market system and replace it by a centrally controlled system than effective governmental control of prices and wages.

The short-sightedness is also exemplified in speeches by businessmen on social responsibility. This may gain them kudos in the short run. But it helps to strengthen the already too prevalent view that the pursuit of profits is wicked and immoral and must be curbed and controlled by external forces. Once this view is adopted, the external forces that curb the market will not be the social consciences, however highly developed, of the pontificating executives; it will be the iron fist of Government bureaucrats. Here, as with price and wage controls, businessmen seem to me to reveal a suicidal impulse.

The political principle that underlies the market mechanism is unanimity. In an ideal free market resting on private property, no individual can coerce any other, all cooperation is voluntary, all parties to such cooperation benefit or they need not participate. There are no values, no "social" responsibilities in any sense other than the shared values and responsibilities of individuals. Society is a collection of individuals and of the various groups they voluntarily form.

The political principle that underlies the political mechanism is conformity. The individual must serve a more general social interest—whether that be determined by a church or a dictator or a majority. The individual may have a vote and say in what is to be done, but if he is overruled, he must conform. It is appropriate for some to require others to contribute to a general social purpose whether they wish to or not.

Unfortunately, unanimity is not always feasible. There are some respects in which conformity appears unavoidable, so I do not see how one can avoid the use of the political mechanism altogether. 32

But the doctrine of "social responsibility" taken seriously would extend the scope of the political mechanism to every human activity. It does not differ in philosophy from the most explicitly collectivist doctrine. It differs only by professing to believe that collectivist ends can be attained without collectivist means. That is why, in my book "Capitalism and Freedom," I have called it a "fundamentally subversive doctrine" in a free society, and have said that in such a society, "there is one and only one social responsibility of business—to use its resources and engage in activities designed to increase its profits so long as it stays within the rules of the game, which is to say, engages in open and free competition without deception or fraud."

Topics for Discussion and Writing

1. Friedman says that corporate executives who spend the corporation's money "for a general social interest" are "in effect imposing taxes . . . and deciding how the tax proceeds shall be spent . . . " (paragraphs 9 and 11). Is the use of the word "tax" effective? Is it fair? (Notice that paragraphs 12, 13, and 14, as well as some later paragraphs, also speak of taxes.)

2. "The socialist view," Friedman says in paragraph 15, is "that political mechanisms, not market mechanisms, are the appropriate way to

determine the allocation of scarce resources to alternative uses." Suppose a fellow student told you that he or she found this passage puzzling. How would you clarify it?

3. Some persons in business have replied to Friedman by arguing that because the owners of today's corporations are rarely involved in running them, the corporations can properly be viewed not as private property but as social institutions able to formulate goals of their own. These people argue that the managers of a corporation are public trustees of a multipurpose organization, and their job is to use their power to promote the interests not only of stockholders but of employees and of the general public. What do you think are the strengths and the weaknesses of this reply?

4. Does Friedman argue that corporations have no responsibilities?

5. In *Religion and the Rise of Capitalism* R. H. Tawney said that "economic organization must allow for the fact that, unless industry is to be paralyzed by recurrent revolts on the part of outraged human nature, it must satisfy criteria which are not purely economic." Do you think Friedman would agree? Why, or why not?

Barbara Ehrenreich and Annette Fuentes

Barbara Ehrenreich writes regularly for the New York Times *and for* Ms. *magazine. Annette Fuentes, the editor of* Sisterhood Is Global, *has also written for* Ms., *where this article originally appeared.*

Life on the Global Assembly Line

In *Ciudad Juárez, Mexico, Anna M. rises at 5 A.M. to feed her son before starting on the two-hour bus trip to the maquiladora (factory). He will spend the day along with four other children in a neighbor's one-room home. Anna's husband, frustrated by being unable to find work for himself, left for the United States six months ago. She wonders, as she carefully applies her new lip gloss, whether she ought to consider herself still married. It might be good to take a night course, become a secretary. But she seldom gets home before eight at night, and the factory, where she stitches brassieres that will be sold in the United States through J. C. Penney, pays only $48 a week.*

In Penang, Malaysia, Julie K. is up before the three other young women with whom she shares a room, and starts heating the leftover rice from last night's supper. She looks good in the company's green-trimmed uniform, and she's proud to work in a modern, American-owned factory. Only not quite so proud as when she started working three years ago—she thinks as she squints out the door at a passing group of women. Her job involves peering all day through a microscope, bonding hair-thin gold wires to a silicon chip destined to end up inside a pocket calculator, and at 21, she is afraid she can no longer see very clearly.

Every morning, between four and seven, thousands of women like Anna and Julie head out for the day shift. In Ciudad Juárez, they crowd into *ruteras* (rundown vans) for the trip from the slum neighborhoods to the industrial parks on the outskirts of the city. In Penang they squeeze, 60 or more at a time, into buses for the trip from the village to the low, modern factory buildings of the Bayan Lepas free trade zone. In Taiwan, they walk from the dormitories—where the night shift is already asleep in the still-warm beds—through the checkpoints in the high fence surrounding the factory zone.

This is the world's new industrial proletariat: young, female, Third World. Viewed from the "first world," they are still faceless, genderless "cheap labor," signaling their existence only through a label or tiny imprint,—"made in Hong Kong," or Taiwan, Korea, the Dominican Republic, Mexico, the Philippines. But they may be one of the most strategic blocs of womanpower in the world of the 1980s. Conservatively, there are 2 million Third World female industrial workers employed now, millions more looking for work, and their numbers are rising every year. Anyone whose image of Third World women features picturesque peasants with babies slung on their backs should be prepared to update it. Just in the last decade, Third World women have become a critical element in the global economy and a key "resource" for expanding multinational corporations.

It doesn't take more than second-grade arithmetic to understand what's happening. In the United States, an assembly-line worker is likely to earn, depending on her length of employment, between $3.10 and $5 an hour. In many Third World countries, a woman doing the same work will earn $3 to $5 a *day*. According to the magazine *Business Asia*, in 1976 the average hourly wage for unskilled work (male or female) was 55 cents in Hong Kong, 52 cents in South Korea, 32 cents in the Philippines, and 17 cents in Indonesia. The logic of the situation is compelling: why pay someone in Massachusetts $5 an hour to do what someone in Manila will do for $2.50 a day? Or, as a corollary, why pay a male worker anywhere to do what a female worker will do for 40 to 60 percent less?

And so, almost everything that can be packed up is being moved out to the Third World; not heavy industry, but just about anything light enough to travel — garment manufacture, textiles, toys, footwear, pharmaceuticals, wigs, appliance parts, tape decks, computer components, plastic goods. In some industries, like garment and textile, American jobs are lost in the process, and the biggest losers are women, often black and Hispanic. But what's going on is much more than a matter of runaway shops. Economists are talking about a "new international division of labor," in which the process of production is broken down and the fragments are dispersed to different parts of the world. In general, the low-skilled jobs are farmed out to the Third World, where labor costs are minuscule, while control over the overall process and technology remains safely at company headquarters in "first world" countries like the United States and Japan.

The American electronics industry provides a classic example: circuits are printed on silicon wafers and tested in California; then the wafers are shipped to Asia for the labor-intensive process by which they are cut into tiny chips and bonded to circuit boards; final assembly into products such as calculators or military equipment usually takes place in the United States. Garment manufacture too is often broken into geographically separated steps, with the most repetitive, labor-intensive jobs going to the poor countries of the southern hemisphere. Most Third World countries welcome whatever jobs come their way in the new division of labor, and the major international development agencies — like the World Bank and the United States Agency for International Development (AID) — encourage them to take what they can get.

So much any economist could tell you. What is less often noted [8] is the *gender* breakdown of the emerging international division of labor. Eighty to 90 percent of the low-skilled assembly jobs that go to the Third World are performed by women — in a remarkable switch from earlier patterns of foreign-dominated industrialization. Until now, "development" under the aegis of foreign corporations has usually meant more jobs for men and — compared to traditional agricultural society — a diminished economic status for women. But multinational corporations and Third World governments alike consider assembly-line work — whether the product is Barbie dolls or missile parts — to be "women's work."

One reason is that women can, in many countries, still be legally paid less than men. But the sheer tedium of the jobs adds to the multinationals' preference for women workers—a preference made clear, for example, by this ad from a Mexican newspaper: *We need female workers; older than 17, younger than 30; single and without children; minimum education primary school, maximum education one year of preparatory school [high school]: available for all shifts.*

It's an article of faith with management that only women can do, or will do, the monotonous, painstaking work that American business is exporting to the Third World. Bill Mitchell, whose job is to attract United States businesses to the Bermudez Industrial Park in Ciudad Juárez told us with a certain macho pride: "A man just won't stay in this tedious kind of work. He'd walk out in a couple of hours." The personnel manager of a light assembly plant in Taiwan told anthropologist Linda Gail Arrigo: "Young male workers are too restless and impatient to do monotonous work with no career value. If displeased, they sabotage the machines and even threaten the foreman. But girls? At most, they cry a little."

In fact, the American businessmen we talked to claimed that Third World women genuinely enjoy doing the very things that would drive a man to assault and sabotage. "You should watch these kids going into work " Bill Mitchell told us. "You don't have any sullenness here. They smile." A top-level management consultant who specializes in advising American companies on where to relocate their factories gave us this global generalization: "The [factory] girls genuinely enjoy themselves. They're away from their families. They have spending money. They can buy motorbikes, whatever. Of course it's a regulated experience too—with dormitories to live in—so it's a healthful experience."

What is the real experience of the women in the emerging Third 12 World industrial work force? The conventional Western stereotypes leap to mind: You can't really compare, the standards are so different. . . . Everything's easier in warm countries. . . . They really don't have any alternatives. . . . Commenting on the low wages his company pays its women workers in Singapore, a Hewlett-Packard vice-president said, "They live much differently here than we do. . . ." But the differences are ultimately very simple. To start with, they have less money.

The great majority of the women in the new Third World work force live at or near the subsistence level for one person, whether they work for a multinational corporation or a locally owned factory. In the Philippines, for example, starting wages in U.S.-owned electronics plants are between $34 to $46 a month, compared to a cost of living of $37 a month; in Indonesia the starting wages are actually about $7 a month less than the cost of living. "Living," in these cases, should be interpreted minimally: a diet of rice, dried fish, and water—a Coke might cost a half-day's wages—lodging in a room occupied by four or more other people. Rachael Grossman, a researcher with the Southeast Asia Resource Center, found women employees of U.S. multinational firms in Malaysia and the Philippines living four to eight in a room in boardinghouses, or squeezing into tiny extensions built onto squatter huts near the factory. Where companies do provide dormitories for their employees, they are not of the "healthful," collegiate variety implied by our corporate informant. Staff from the American Friends Service Committee report that dormitory space is "likely to be crowded, with bed rotation paralleling shift rotation—while one shift works, another sleeps, as many as twenty to a room." In one case in Thailand, they found the dormitory "filthy," with workers forced to find their own place to sleep among "splintered floorboards, rusting sheets of metal, and scraps of dirty cloth."

Wages do increase with seniority, but the money does not go to pay for studio apartments or, very likely, motorbikes. A 1970 study of young women factory workers in Hong Kong found that 88 percent of them were turning more than half their earnings over to their parents. In areas that are still largely agricultural (such as parts of the Philippines and Malaysia), or places where male unemployment runs high (such as northern Mexico), a woman factory worker may be the sole source of cash income for an entire extended family.

But wages on a par with what an 11-year-old American could earn on a paper route, and living conditions resembling what Engels found in nineteenth-century Manchester are only part of the story. The rest begins at the factory gate. The work that multinational corporations export to the Third World is not only the most tedious, but often the most hazardous part of the production process. The countries they go to are, for the most part, those that will guarantee no interference from health and safety inspectors, trade unions, or even free-lance reformers. As a result, most Third World factory women work under conditions that already have broken or will break their health—or their nerves—within a few years, and often before they've worked long enough to earn any more than a subsistence wage.

Consider first the electronics industry, which is generally 16
thought to be the safest and cleanest of the exported industries. The
factory buildings are low and modern, like those one might find in
a suburban American industrial park. Inside, rows of young women,
neatly dressed in the company uniform or T-shirt, work quietly at
their stations. There is air conditioning (not for the women's comfort, but to protect the delicate semiconductor parts they work with),
and high-volume piped-in Bee Gees hits (not so much for entertainment, as to prevent talking).

For many Third World women, electronics is a prestige occupation, at least compared to other kinds of factory work. They are
unlikely to know that in the United States the National Institute on
Occupational Safety and Health (NIOSH) has placed electronics on
its select list of "high health-risk industries using the greatest number of toxic substances." If electronics assembly work is risky here,
it is doubly so in countries where there is no equivalent of NIOSH
to even issue warnings. In many plants toxic chemicals and solvents
sit in open containers, filling the work area with fumes that can literally knock you out. "We have been told of cases where ten to twelve
women passed out at once," an AFSC field worker in northern Mexico told us, "and the newspapers report this as 'mass hysteria.' "

In one stage of the electronics assembly process, the workers
have to dip the circuits into open vats of acid. According to Irene
Johnson and Carol Bragg, who toured the National Semiconductor
plant in Penang, Malaysia, the women who do the dipping "wear
rubber gloves and boots, but these sometimes leak, and burns are
common." Occasionally, whole fingers are lost. More commonly,
what electronics workers lose is the 20/20 vision they are required
to have when they are hired. Most electronics workers spend seven
to nine hours a day peering through microscopes, straining to meet
their quotas. One study in South Korea found that most electronics
assembly workers developed severe eye problems after only one year
of employment: 88 percent had chronic conjunctivitis; 44 percent
became nearsighted; and 19 percent developed astigmatism. A
manager for Hewlett-Packard's Malaysia plant, in an interview with
Rachael Grossman, denied that there were any eye problems: "These
girls are used to working with 'scopes.' We've found no eye
problems. But it sure makes me dizzy to look through those things."

Electronics, recall, is the "cleanest" of the exported industries. 20
Conditions in the garment and textile industry rival those of any
nineteenth-century sweatshop. The firms, generally local subcon-
tractors to large American chains such as J. C. Penney and Sears,

as well as smaller manufacturers, are usually even more indifferent to the health of their employees than the multinationals. Some of the worst conditions have been documented in South Korea, where the garment and textile industries have helped spark that country's "economic miracle." Workers are packed into poorly lit rooms, where summer temperatures rise above 100 degrees. Textile dust, which can cause permanent lung damage, fills the air. When there are rush orders, management may require forced overtime of as much as 48 hours at a stretch, and if that seems to go beyond the limits of human endurance, pep pills and amphetamine injections are thoughtfully provided. In her diary (originally published in a magazine now banned by the South Korean government) Min Chong Suk, 30, a sewing-machine operator, wrote of working from 7 A.M. to 11:30 P.M. in a garment factory: "When [the apprentices] shake the waste threads from the clothes, the whole room fills with dust, and it is hard to breathe. Since we've been working in such dusty air, there have been increasing numbers of people getting tuberculosis, bronchitis, and eye diseases. Since we are women, it makes us so sad when we have pale, unhealthy, wrinkled faces like dried-up spinach. . . . It seems to me that no one knows our blood dissolves into the threads and seams, with sighs and sorrow."

In all the exported industries, the most invidious, inescapable health hazard is stress. On their home ground United States corporations are not likely to sacrifice productivity for human comfort. On someone else's home ground, however, anything goes. Lunch breaks may be barely long enough for a woman to stand in line at the canteen or hawkers' stalls. Visits to the bathroom are treated as privilege; in some cases, workers must raise their hands for permission to use the toilet, and waits up to a half hour are common. Rotating shifts—the day shift one week, the night shift the next—wreak havoc with sleep patterns. Because inaccuracies or failure to meet production quotas can mean substantial pay losses, the pressures are quickly internalized; stomach ailments and nervous problems are not unusual in the multinationals' Third World female work force. In some situations, good work is as likely to be punished as slow or shoddy work. Correspondent Michael Flannery, writing for the AFL-CIO's *American Federationist,* tells the story of 23-year-old Basilia Altagracia, a seamstress who stitched collars onto ladies' blouses in the La Romana (Dominican Republic) free trade zone (a heavily guarded industrial zone owned by Gulf & Western Industries, Inc.):

"A nimble veteran seamstress, Miss Altagracia eventually began to earn as much as $5.75 a day. . . . 'I was exceeding my piecework quota by a lot.' . . . But then, Altagracia said, her plant supervisor, a Cuban emigré, called her into his office. 'He said I was doing a fine job, but that I and some other of the women were making too much money, and he was being forced to lower what we earned for each piece we sewed.' On the best days, she now can clear barely $3, she said. 'I was earning less, so I started working six and seven days a week. But I was tired and I could not work as fast as before.'"Within a few months, she was too ill to work at all.

As if poor health and the stress of factory life weren't enough to drive women into early retirement, management actually encourages a high turnover in many industries. "As you know, when seniority rises, wages rise," the management consultant to U.S. multinationals told us. He explained that it's cheaper to train a fresh supply of teenagers than to pay experienced women higher wages. "Older" women, aged 23 or 24, are likely to be laid off and not rehired.

We estimate, based on fragmentary data from several sources, that the multinational corporations may already have used up (cast off) as many as 6 million Third World workers—women who are too ill, too old (30 is over the hill in most industries), or too exhausted to be useful any more. Few "retire" with any transferable skills or savings. The lucky ones find husbands.   24

The unlucky ones find themselves at the margins of society—as bar girls, "hostesses," or prostitutes.

At 21, Julie's greatest fear is that she will never be able to find a husband. She knows that just being a "factory girl" is enough to give anyone a bad reputation. When she first started working at the electronics company, her father refused to speak to her for three months. Now every time she leaves Penang to go back to visit her home village she has to put up with a lecture on morality from her older brother—not to mention a barrage of lewd remarks from men outside her family. If they knew that she had actually gone out on a few dates, that she had been to a discotheque, that she had once kissed a young man who said he was a student. . . . Julie's stomach tightens as she imagines her family's reaction. She tries to concentrate on the kind of man she would like to marry: an engineer or technician of some sort, someone who had been to California, where the company headquarters are located and where even the grandmothers wear tight pants and lipstick—someone who had a good attitude about women. But if she ends up having to wear glasses, like her cousin who worked three years at the "scopes," she might as well forget about finding anyone to marry her.

One of the most serious occupational hazards that Julie and millions of women like her may face is the lifelong stigma of having been a "factory girl." Most of the cultures favored by multinational corporations in their search for cheap labor are patriarchal in the grand old style: any young woman who is not under the wing of a father, husband, or older brother must be "loose." High levels of unemployment among men, as in Mexico, contribute to male resentment of working women. (Ironically, in some places the multinationals have increased male unemployment—for example, by paving over fishing and farming villages to make way for industrial parks.) Add to all this the fact that certain companies—American electronics firms are in the lead—actively promote Western-style sexual objectification as a means of insuring employee loyalty: there are company-sponsored cosmetics classes, "guess whose legs these are" contests, and swim-suit-style beauty contests where the prize might be a free night *for two* in a fancy hotel. Corporate-promoted Westernization only heightens the hostility many men feel toward any independent working women—having a job is bad enough, wearing jeans and mascara to work is going too far.

Anthropologist Patricia Fernandez, who has worked in a *maqui- ladora* herself, believes that the stigmatization of working women serves, indirectly, to keep them in line. "You have to think of the kind of socialization that girls experience in a very Catholic—or, for that matter, Muslim—society. The fear of having a 'reputation' is enough to make a lot of women bend over backward to be 'respectable' and ladylike, which is just what management wants." She points out that in northern Mexico, the tabloids delight in playing up stories of alleged vice in the *maquiladoras*—indiscriminate sex on the job, epidemics of venereal disease, fetuses found in factory rest rooms. "I worry about this because there are those who treat you differently as soon as they know you have a job at a *maquiladora*," one woman told Fernandez. "Maybe they think that if you have to work, there is a chance you're a whore."

And there is always a chance you'll wind up as one. Probably only a small minority of Third World factory workers turn to prostitution when their working days come to an end. But it is, as for women everywhere, the employment of last resort, the only thing to do when the factories don't need you and traditional society won't—or, for economic reasons, can't—take you back. In the Philippines, the brothel business is expanding as fast as the factory system. If they can't use you one way, they can use you another.

Topics for Discussion and Writing

1. Consider the title of the essay. When you first saw it, what connotations did "global assembly line" immediately suggest? Now that you have finished reading the essay, evaluate the title.
2. Before you read this essay, what was your image of the multinational corporation? Was it mostly positive, or negative, or neutral? To what extent has the article affected the way you think about multinational corporations? If, for example, you were offered a managerial job in a multinational, would you be inclined to ask questions about their employment practices abroad that you might not have asked before reading this article?
3. Paragraph 1, which gives us a quick portrait of Anna, tells us that "Anna's husband, frustrated by being unable to find work for himself, left for the United States six months ago." Why do the authors bother to include this detail? Is it in any way relevant to their thesis, or is it simply for human interest?
4. According to paragraph 10, management believes "that only women can do, or will do, the monotonous, painstaking work that American business is exporting to the Third World." Do the authors of the essay believe this? Do you believe that women by nature,—or by training—are more suited than men "to do monotonous work with no career value"?
5. Paragraph 11 reports some statements businessmen offer as reasons why Third World women supposedly enjoy their jobs. Do you think these reasons (or some of them) have any merit? Do paragraphs 12–14 and 17–21 adequately refute these reasons?
6. In paragraph 14 we learn that 88 percent of the young female workers in Hong Kong turned more than half of their wages over to their parents. What conclusions can one reasonably draw from this assertion?
7. Why do you suppose that Julie (paragraphs 2 and 26) works in a factory?
8. In paragraph 27 the author tells us that "high levels of unemployment among men, as in Mexico, contribute to male resentment of working women." Does this analysis strike you as probably true? If so, what do you think American business can do about the Mexican economy?
9. What is the effect of using the second person pronoun ("you") in the final paragraph?
10. Given what you have read about the working conditions of women in Third World countries, when you buy your next sweater (or tennis racquet or calculator or whatever) will you reject products made in Third World countries?

John S. Fielden

John S. Fielden, formerly an associate editor of the Harvard Business Review *— the journal in which this essay first appeared — is now University Professor of Management at the University of Alabama.*

"What Do You Mean You Don't Like My Style"

In large corporations all over the country, people are playing a game of paddleball — with drafts of letters instead of balls. Volley after volley goes back and forth between those who sign the letters and those who actually write them. It's a game nobody likes, but it continues, and we pay for it. The workday has no extra time for such unproductiveness. What causes this round robin of revision?

Typos? Factual misstatements? Poor format? No. *Style* does. Ask yourself how often you hear statements like these:

"It takes new assistants about a year to learn my style. Until they do, I have no choice but to bounce letters back for revision. I won't sign a letter if it doesn't sound like me."

"I find it difficult, almost impossible, to write letters for my boss's signature. The boss's style is different from mine."

In companies where managers primarily write their own letters, confusion about style also reigns. Someone sends out a letter and hears later that the reaction was not at all the one desired. It is reported that the reader doesn't like the writer's "tone." A colleague looks over a copy of the letter and says, "No wonder the reader doesn't like this letter. You shouldn't have said things the way you did. You used the wrong style for a letter like this." "Style?" the writer says. "What's wrong with my style?" "I don't know" is the response. "I just don't like the way you said things."

Everybody talks about style, but almost nobody understands the meaning of the word in the business environment. And this lack of understanding hurts both those who write letters for another's signature and those who write for themselves. Neither knows where to turn for help. Strunk and White's marvelous book *The Elements* 4 *of Style* devotes only a few pages to a discussion of style, and that concerns only literary style.[1] Books like the Chicago *Manual of Style*[2] seem to define style as all the technical points they cover, from abbreviations and capitalizations to footnotes and bibliographies. And dictionary definitions are usually too vague to be helpful.

Even such a general definition as this offers scant help, although perhaps it comes closest to how business people use the word:

Style is "the way something is said or done, as distinguished from its substance."[3]

Managers signing drafts written by subordinates, and the subordinates themselves, already know that they have trouble agreeing on "the way things should be said." What, for instance, is meant by "way"? In trying to find that way, both managers and subordinates are chasing a will-o'-the-wisp. There is no magical way, no perfect, universal way of writing things that will fend off criticism of style. There *is* no one style of writing in business that is appropriate in all situations and for all readers, even though managers and subordinates usually talk and behave as if there were.

But why all the confusion? Isn't style really the way we say things? Certainly it is. Then writing style must be made up of the particular words we select to express our ideas and the types of sentences and paragraphs we put together to convey those ideas. What else could it be? Writing has no tone of voice or body gesture to impart additional meanings. In written communication, tone comes from what a reader reads into the words and sentences used.

Words express more than *denotations*, the definitions found in dictionaries. They also carry *connotations*. In the feelings and images associated with each word lies the capacity a writing style has for producing an emotional reaction in a reader. And in that capacity lies the tone of a piece of writing. Style is largely a matter of tone. The writer uses a style; the reader infers a communication's tone. Tone comes from what a reader reads into the words and sentences a writer uses.

In the business environment, tone is especially important. Business writing is not literary writing. Literary artists use unique styles

8

[1] William Strunk, Jr., and E. B. White, *The Elements of Style* (New York: Macmillan, 1979)
[2] *A Manual of Style* (Chicago: University of Chicago Press, 1969)
[3] *The American Heritage Dictionary of the English Language* (Boston: American Heritage and Houghton Mifflin, 1969)

to "express" themselves to a general audience. Business people write to particular persons in particular situations, not so much to express themselves as to accomplish particular purposes, "to get a job done." If a reader doesn't like a novelist's tone, nothing much can happen to the writer short of failing to sell some books. In the business situation, however, an offensive style may not only prevent a sale but may also turn away a customer, work against a promotion, or even cost you a job.

While style can be distinguished from substance, it cannot be divorced from substance. In business writing, style cannot be divorced from the circumstances under which something is written or from the likes, dislikes, position, and power of the reader.

A workable definition of style in business writing would be something like this:

> Style is that choice of words, sentences, and paragraph format which by virtue of being appropriate to the situation and to the power positions of both writer and reader produces the desired reaction and result.

Let's take a case and see what we can learn from it. Assume that you are an executive in a very large information-processing company. You receive the following letter: 12

Mr. (Ms.) Leslie J. Cash
XYZ Corporation
Main Street
Anytown, U.S.A.

Dear Leslie:
As you know, I respect your professional opinion highly. The advice your people have given us at ABC Corporation as we have moved into a comprehensive information system over the past three years has been very helpful. I'm writing to you now, however, in my role as chairman of the executive committee of the trustees of our hospital. We at Community General Hospital have decided to establish a skilled volunteer data processing evaluation team to assess proposals to automate our hospital's information flow.

I have suggested your name to my committee. I know you could get real satisfaction from helping your community as a member of this evaluation team. Please say yes. I look forward to being able to count on your advice. Let me hear from you soon.

Frank J. Scalpel
Chairman
Executive Committee
Community General Hospital
Anytown, U.S.A.

If you accepted the appointment mentioned in this letter, you would have a conflict of interest. You are an executive at XYZ, Inc. You know that XYZ will submit a proposal to install a comprehensive information system for the hospital. Mr. Scalpel is the vice president of finance at ABC Corp., a very good customer of yours. You know him well since you have worked with him on community programs as well as in the business world.

I can think of four typical responses to Scalpel's letter. Each says essentially the same thing, but each is written in a different business style:

Response 1

Mr. Frank J. Scalpel
Chairman, Executive Committee
Community General Hospital
Anytown, U.S.A.

Dear Frank,
As you realize, this litigious age often makes it necessary for large companies to take stringent measures not only to avoid conflicts of interest on the part of their employees but also to preclude even the very suggestion of conflict. And, since my company intends to submit a proposal with reference to automating the hospital's information flow, it would not appear seemly for me to be part of an evaluation team assessing competitors' proposals. Even if I were to excuse myself from consideration of the XYZ proposal, I would still be vulnerable to charges that I gave short shrift to competitors' offerings.

If there is any other way that I can serve the committee that will not raise this conflict-of-interest specter, you know that I would find it pleasurable to be of service, as always.

Sincerely,

Response 2

Dear Frank,

Your comments relative to your respect for my professional opinion are most appreciated. Moreover, your invitation to serve on the hospital's data processing evaluation team is received with gratitude, albeit with some concern.

The evaluation team must be composed of persons free of alliance with any of the vendors submitting proposals. For that reason, it is felt that my services on the team could be construed as a conflict of interest.

Perhaps help can be given in some other way. Again, please be assured that your invitation has been appreciated.

Sincerely,

Response 3

Dear Frank,

Thank you for suggesting my name as a possible member of your data processing evaluation team. I wish I could serve, but I cannot.

XYZ intends, naturally, to submit a proposal to automate the hospital's information flow. You can see the position of conflict I would be in if I were on the evaluation team.

Just let me know of any other way I can be of help. You know I would be more than willing. Thanks again for the invitation.

Cordially,

Response 4

Dear Frank,

Thanks for the kind words and the invitation. Sure wish I could say yes. Can't, though.

XYZ intends to submit a sure-fire proposal on automating the hospital's information. Shouldn't be judge and advocate at the same time!

Any other way I can help, Frank—just ask. Thanks again.

Cordially,

What Do You Think of These Letters?

Which letter has the style you like best? Check off the response you prefer.

Response   1   2   3   4
          ☐   ☐   ☐   ☐

Which letter has the style resembling the one you customarily use? 16
Again, check off your choice.

Response   1   2   3   4
            ☐   ☐   ☐   ☐

Which terms best describe the style of each letter? Check the appropriate boxes.

| Response 1 | ☐ Colorful | ☐ Passive | ☐ Personal |
| | ☐ Dull | ☐ Forceful | ☐ Impersonal |

| Response 2 | ☐ Colorful | ☐ Passive | ☐ Personal |
| | ☐ Dull | ☐ Forceful | ☐ Impersonal |

| Response 3 | ☐ Colorful | ☐ Passive | ☐ Personal |
| | ☐ Dull | ☐ Forceful | ☐ Impersonal |

| Response 4 | ☐ Colorful | ☐ Passive | ☐ Personal |
| | ☐ Dull | ☐ Forceful | ☐ Impersonal |

Let's Compare Reactions

Now that you've given your reactions, let's compare them with some of mine.

Response 1 seems cold, impersonal, complex. Most business people would, I think, react somewhat negatively to this style because it seems to push the reader away from the writer. Its word choice has a cerebral quality that, while flattering to the reader's intelligence, also parades the writer's.

Response 2 is fairly cool, quite impersonal, and somewhat 20 complex. Readers' reactions will probably be neither strongly positive nor strongly negative. This style of writing is "blah" because it is heavily passive. Instead of saying "I appreciate your comments," it says "Your comments are most appreciated"; instead of "I think that my service could be construed as a conflict of interest," it says "It is felt that my service could be construed. . . ." The use of the passive voice subordinates writers modestly to the back of sentences or causes them to disappear.

This is the impersonal, passive style of writing that many with engineering, mathematics, or scientific backgrounds feel most comfortable using. It is harmless, but it is certainly not colorful; nor is it forceful or interesting.

Response 3 illustrates the style of writing that most high-level executives use. It is simple; it is personal; it is warm without being syrupy; it is forceful, like a firm handshake. Almost everybody in business likes this style, although lower-level managers often find themselves afraid to write so forthrightly (and, as a result, often find themselves retreating into the styles of responses 1 and 2 – the style of 1 to make themselves look "smart" to superiors and the style of 2 to appear unbossy and fairly impersonal). Persons who find response 2 congenial may feel a bit dubious about the appropriateness of response 3. (Although I have no way of proving this judgment, I would guess that more readers in high positions – perhaps more owner-managers – would like response 3 than would readers who are still in lower positions.)

Response 4 goes beyond being forceful; it is annoyingly self-confident and breezy. It is colorful and conversational to an extreme, and it is so intensely personal and warm that many business people would be offended, even if they were very close acquaintances of Frank Scalpel's. "It sounds like an advertising person's chitchat," some would probably say.

As you compared your responses with mine, did you say, "What 24 difference does it make which style *I* like or which most resembles *my* customary style? What matters is which style will go over best with Mr. Scalpel in this situation"? If you did, we're getting somewhere.

Earlier, when we defined business writing style, some may have wanted to add, "And that style should sound like me." This was left out for a good reason. Circumstances not only alter cases; they alter the "you" that it is wise for your style to project. Sometimes it's wise to be forceful; at other times it's suicidal. Sometimes being sprightly and colorful is appropriate; at other times it's ludicrous. There are times to be personal and times to be impersonal.

Not understanding this matter of style and tone is why the big corporation game of paddleball between managers and subordinates goes on and on. The subordinate tries to imitate the boss's style, but in actuality – unless the boss is extremely insensitive – he or she has no single style for all circumstances and for all readers. What usually happens is that after several tries, the subordinate writes a letter that the boss signs. "Aha!" the subordinate says. "So that's what the boss wants!" And then the subordinate tries to use that style for all situations and readers. Later, the superior begins rejecting drafts written in the very style he or she professed liking before. Both parties throw up their hands.

This volleying is foolish and wasteful. Both superior and subordinate have to recognize that in business writing, style cannot be considered apart from the given situation or from the person to whom the writing is directed. Expert writers select the style that fits a particular reader and the type of writing situation with which they are faced. In business, people often face the following writing situations:

Positive situations.
Saying yes or conveying good news.

Situations where some action is asked of the reader.
Giving orders or persuading someone to do as requested.

Information-conveying situations.
Giving the price of ten widgets, for example.

Negative situations.
Saying no or relaying bad news.

In each of these situations, the choice of style is of strategic importance. 28

In positive situations, a writer can relax on all fronts. Readers are usually so pleased to hear the good news that they pay little attention to anything else. Yet it is possible for someone to communicate good news in such a cold, impersonal, roundabout, and almost begrudging way that the reader becomes upset.

Action-request situations involve a form of bargaining. In a situation where the writer holds all the power, he or she can use a forceful commanding style. When the writer holds no power over the reader, though, actions have to be asked for and the reader persuaded, not ordered. In such cases, a forceful style will not be suitable at all.

In information-conveying situations, getting the message across forcefully and straightforwardly is best. Such situations are not usually charged emotionally.

In negative situations, diplomacy becomes very important. The 32 right style depends on the relative positions of the person saying no and the person being told no.

For instance, if you were Leslie Cash, the person in the example at the beginning of the article whom Frank Scalpel was inviting to serve on a hospital's evaluation team, you would be in a situation of having to say no to a very important customer of your company. You would also be in a doubly sensitive situation because it is unlikely that Mr. Scalpel would fail to recognize that he is asking you to enter a conflict-of-interest situation. He is probably asking you *anyway*. Therefore, you would not only have to tell him no, but you would have to avoid telling him that he has asked you to do something that is highly unethical. In this instance, you would be faced with communicating two negative messages at once or else not giving Scalpel any sensible reason for refusing to serve.

Now that we've thought about the strategic implications of style, let's go back to look at each of the responses to Scalpel's request and ask ourselves which is best.

Do we *want* to be personal and warm? Usually yes. But in this situation? Do we want to communicate clearly and directly and forcefully? Usually yes. But here? Do we want to appear as if we're brushing aside the conflict, as the third response does? Or do we want to approach that issue long-windedly, as in the first response, or passively, as in the second? What is the strategically appropriate style?

In the abstract, we have no way of knowing which of these responses will go over best with Mr. Scalpel. The choice is a matter of judgment in a concrete situation. Judging the situation accurately is what separates successful from unsuccessful executive communicators.

Looking at the situation with strategy in mind, we note that in the first response, the writer draws back from being close, knowing that it is necessary to reject not only one but two of the reader's requests. By using legalistic phraseology and Latinate vocabulary, the writer lowers the personal nature of the communication and transforms it into a formal statement. It gives an abstract, textbook-like response that removes the tone of personal rejection.

The very fact that response 1 is difficult to read and dull in impact may be a strategic asset in this type of negative situation. But if in this situation a subordinate presented response 1 to you for your signature, would it be appropriate for you to reject it because it is not written in the style *you* happen to *like* best in the abstract— say, the style of response 3?

Now let's look at response 2. Again, we see that a lack of personal warmth may be quite appropriate to the situation at hand. Almost immediately, the letter draws back into impersonality. And by using the passive constantly, the writer avoids the need to say "I must say no." Furthermore, the term *construed* reinforces the passive in the second paragraph. This term is a very weak but possibly a strategically wise way of implying that *some* persons (*other* people, not the writer) could interpret Scalpel's request as an invitation to participate in an improper action. Now we can see that, instead of seeming dull and lacking in personal warmth as it did in the abstract, response 2 may be the type of letter we would be wise to send out, that is, when we have taken the whole situation into careful consideration and not just our personal likes and dislikes.

The third response, and to even greater extent the fourth, have styles that are strategically inappropriate for this situation. In fact, Scalpel might well regard the colorful style of the fourth response as highly offensive. Both responses directly and forcefully point out the obvious conflict, but by being so direct each runs the risk of subtly offending him. (The third response is "you can see the position of conflict I'd be in if I were on the evaluation team," and the fourth is "Shouldn't be judge and advocate at the same time!") We could make a pretty strong argument that the direct, forceful, candid style of the third response and the breezy, warm, colorful, intensely personal "advertising" style of the fourth response may both prove ineffectual in a delicate, negative situation such as this.

At this point, readers may say, "All right. I'm convinced. I need to adjust my style to what is appropriate in each situation. And I also need to give directions to others to let them know how to adjust their styles. But I haven't the foggiest notion of how to do either!" Some suggestions for varying your writing style follow. I am not implying that a communication must be written in one style only. A letter to be read aloud at a colleague's retirement party, for instance, may call not only for a warm, personal style but for colorfulness as well. A long analytic report may require a passive, impersonal style, but the persuasive cover letter may call for recommendations being presented in a very forceful style.

For a Forceful Style

This style is usually appropriate only in situations where the writer has the power, such as in action requests in the form of orders or when you are saying no firmly but politely to a subordinate.

Use the active voice. Have your sentences do something to people and to objects, not just lie there having things done to them; have them give orders: "Correct this error immediately" (you-understood is the subject) instead of "A correction should be made" (which leaves the reader wondering, made by whom).

Step up front and be counted: "I have decided not to recommend you for promotion" instead of "Unfortunately, a positive recommendation for your promotion is not forthcoming."

Do not beat around the bush or act like a politician. If something needs to be said, say it directly.

Write most of your sentences in subject-verb-object order. Do not weaken them by putting namby-pamby phrases before the subject: "I have decided to fund your project" instead of "After much deliberation and weighing of the pros and cons, I have decided to fund your project."

Do not weaken sentences by relegating the point or the action to a subordinate clause: If your point is that your company has won a contract, say "Acme won the contract, although the bidding was intense and highly competitive," not "Although Acme won the contract, the bidding was intense and highly competitive."

Adopt a tone of confidence and surety about what you say by avoiding weasel words like: "Possibly," "maybe," "perhaps," "It could be concluded that . . ." "Some might conclude that . . ."

For a Passive Style

This style is often appropriate in negative situations and in situations where the writer is in a lower position than the reader.

Avoid the imperative—never give an order: Say "A more effective and time-conserving presentation of ideas should be devised before our next meeting" as opposed to "Do a better job of presenting your ideas at our next meeting. Respect my time and get right to the point."

Use the passive voice heavily because it subordinates the subject to the end of the sentence or buries the subject entirely. The passive is especially handy when you are in a low-power position and need to convey negative information to a reader who is in a higher position (an important customer, for instance): Say "Valuable resources are being wasted" instead of "Valuable resources are being wasted by your company" or, even worse, "You are wasting valuable resources."

Avoid taking responsibility for negative statements by attributing them to faceless, impersonal "others": Say "It is more than possible that several objections to your proposed plans might be raised by some observers" or "Several objections might be raised by those hostile to your plans" instead of "I have several objections to your plans."

Use weasel words, especially if the reader is in a high-power position and will not like what you are saying.

Use long sentences and heavy paragraphs to slow down the reader's comprehension of sensitive or negative information.

For a Personal Style

This style is usually appropriate in good-news and persuasive action-request situations.

Use the active voice, which puts you, as the writer, at the front of sentences: "Thank you very much for your comments" or "I appreciated your comments" instead of "Your comments were very much appreciated by me" or the even more impersonal "Your comments were very much appreciated."

Use persons' names (first names, when appropriate) instead of referring to them by title: "Bill James attended the meeting" instead of "Acme's director attended the meeting."

Use personal pronouns — especially "you" and "I" — when you are saying positive things: "I so much appreciate the work you've done" as opposed to "The work you've done is appreciated."

Use short sentences that capture the rhythm of ordinary conversation: "I discussed your proposal with Frank. He's all for it!" as opposed to "This is to inform you that your proposal was taken up at Friday's meeting and that it was regarded with favor."

Use contractions ("can't," "won't," "shouldn't") to sound informal and conversational.

Direct questions to the reader: "Just ask yourself, how would your company like to save $10,000?"

Interject positive personal thoughts and references that will make the reader know that this letter is really to him or her and not some type of form letter sent to just anyone.

For an Impersonal Style

This style is usually appropriate in negative and information-conveying situations. It's always appropriate in technical and scientific writing and usually when you are writing to technical readers.

Avoid using persons' names, especially first names. Refer to people, if at all, by title or job description: "I would like to know what you think of this plan" instead of "What do you think of this, Herb?" "Our vice president of finance" or "the finance department," not "Ms. Jones."

Avoid using personal pronouns, especially "you" and "I" ("we" may be all right because the corporate we is faceless and impersonal): "The logistics are difficult, and the idea may not work" instead of "I think you have planned things so that the logistics are difficult and your idea may not work." "We wonder if the idea will work" rather than "I don't think the idea will work."

Use the passive voice to make yourself conveniently disappear when desirable: "An error in the calculations has been made" instead of "I think your calculations are wrong."

Make some of your sentences complex and some paragraphs long; avoid the brisk, direct, simple-sentence style of conversation.

For a Colorful Style

Sometimes a lively style is appropriate in good-news situations. It is most commonly found in the highly persuasive writing of advertisements and sales letters.

Insert some adjectives and adverbs: Instead of "This proposal will save corporate resources," write "This (hard-hitting) (productivity-building) (money-saving) proposal will (easily) (surely) (quickly) (immediately) save our (hard-earned) (increasingly scarce) (carefully guarded) corporate resources."

If appropriate, use a metaphor (A is B) or a simile (A is like B) to make a point: "Truly this program is a *miracle* of logical design." "Our solution strikes at the very *root* of Acme's problems." "This program is like *magic* in its ability to . . ."

For a Less Colorful Style

By avoiding adjectives, adverbs, metaphors, and figures of speech, you can make your style less colorful. Such a style is appropriate for ordinary business writing and also results from:

Blending the impersonal style with the passive style.

Employing words that remove any semblance of wit, liveliness, and vigor from the writing.

Please bear in mind that these six styles are not mutually exclu- 48
sive. There is some overlap. A passive style is usually far more impersonal than personal and also not very colorful. A forceful style is
likely to be more personal than impersonal, and a colorful style is
likely to be fairly forceful. Nevertheless, these styles are distinct
enough to justify talking about them. If we fail to make such distinctions, style becomes a catchall term that means nothing specific. Even
if not precise, these distinctions enable us to talk about style and its
elements and to learn to write appropriately for each situation.

What conclusions can we draw from this discussion? Simply
that, whether you write your own letters or have to manage the writing of subordinates, to be an effective communicator, you must realize that:

1.   Each style has an impact on the reader.
2.   Style communicates to readers almost as much as the content
     of a message.
3.   Style cannot be isolated from a situation.
4.   Generalizing about which style is the best in all situations is im-
     possible.
5.   Style must be altered to suit the circumstances.
6.   Style must be discussed sensibly in the work situation.

These conclusions will be of obvious help to managers who write
their own letters. But what help will these conclusions be to
managers who direct assistants in the writing of letters? In many
instances, writing assignments go directly to subordinates for handling. Often, manager and assistant have no chance to discuss style
strategy together. In such cases, rather than merely submitting a
response for a signature, the subordinate would be wise to append
a note: e.g., "This is a very sensitive situation, I think. Therefore,
I deliberately drew back into a largely impersonal and passive style."
At least, the boss will not jump to the conclusion that the assistant
has written a letter of low impact by accident.

When they do route writing assignments to assistants, superiors
could save much valuable time and prevent mutual distress if they
told the subordinates what style seemed strategically wise in each
situation. Playing guessing games also wastes money.

And if, as is often the case, neither superior nor subordinate has 52
a clear sense of what style is best, the two can agree to draft a
response in one style first, and if that doesn't sound right, to adjust
the style appropriately.

Those who write their own letters can try drafting several responses to tough but important situations, each in a different style. It's wise to sleep on them and then decide which sounds best.

Whether you write for yourself or for someone else, it is extremely unlikely that in difficult situations a first draft will be signed by you or anyone else. Only the amateur expects writing perfection on the first try. By learning to control your style and to engineer the tone of your communications, you can make your writing effective.

Topics for Discussion and Writing

1. Characterize the style of Fielden's first two paragraphs. (His essay, of course, says much about style, but for a brief additional discussion of style you may wish to consult page 884 in the glossary.)

2. In paragraph 11 Fielden offers what he calls a "workable definition of style in business writing." Do you find this definition workable for other forms of writing as well—for example, term papers, editorials in the school newspaper, love letters? Why, or why not?

3. If you disagree with Fielden's analysis of any of the four letters Leslie Cash drafts to send to Frank Scalpel, explain the basis of your disagreement.

4. Many textbooks urge students to avoid using the passive voice, but in paragraph 43 Fielden says that the passive "is often appropriate in negative situations and in situations where the writer is in a lower position than the reader." Look at his examples and then evaluate his advice.

5. This essay appeared in the *Harvard Business Review* and has been one of its most popular reprints. Explain why, in your opinion, it has been popular, or why you find its popularity surprising.

6. Let's assume that Cash sent Scalpel the third letter. You are Scalpel; write a letter to Cash acknowledging receipt of Cash's letter. In fact, write two letters, one a poor letter and one a good letter.

7. In discussing "strategy," Fielden writes in paragraph 25: "Sometimes it's wise to be forceful; at other times it's suicidal. Sometimes being sprightly and colorful is appropriate; at other times it's ludicrous. There are times to be personal and times to be impersonal." Try to recall examples from your own experience (whether writing or speaking) that illustrate one or more of these circumstances. Then write a paragraph combining Fielden's sentence (which you should feel free to modify) with your illustration of it.

W. H. Auden

W[ystan] H[ugh] Auden (1907–73) was born and educated in England. In 1939 he came to the United States and later became an American citizen; but in 1972 he returned to England to live. Auden established his reputation chiefly with his poetry, but he also wrote plays, libretti, and essays (we include two of his essays in this book), all bearing the stamp of his highly original mind.

The Unknown Citizen
(To JS/07/M/378
This Marble Monument
Is Erected by the State)

He was found by the Bureau of Statistics to be
One against whom there was no official complaint,
And all the reports on his conduct agree
That, in the modern sense of an old-fashioned word, he was
    a saint,
For in everything he did he served the Greater Community.   5
Except for the War till the day he retired
He worked in a factory and never got fired,
But satisfied his employers, Fudge Motors Inc.
Yet he wasn't a scab or odd in his views,
For his Union reports that he paid his dues,   10
(Our report on his Union shows it was sound)
And our Social Psychology workers found
That he was popular with his mates and liked a drink.
The press are convinced that he bought a paper every day
And that his reactions to advertisements were normal in
    every way.   15
Policies taken out in his name prove that he was fully
    insured,
And his Health-card shows he was once in hospital but left it
    cured.
Both Producers Research and High-Grade Living declare
He was fully sensible to the advantages of the Installment
    Plan
And had everything necessary to the Modern Man,   20
A phonograph, radio, a car and a frigidaire.
Our researchers into Public Opinion are content

That he held the proper opinions for the time of year;
When there was peace, he was for peace; when there was
     war, he went.
He was married and added five children to the population,   25
Which our Eugenist says was the right number for a parent of
     his generation,
And our teachers report that he never interfered with their
     education.
Was he free? Was he happy? The question is absurd:
Had anything been wrong, we should certainly have heard.

Topics for Discussion and Writing

1. Who is the speaker, and on what occasion is he supposed to be speaking?
2. What do the words "The Unknown Citizen" suggest to you?
3. How does Auden suggest that he doesn't share the attitudes of the speaker and is, in fact, satirizing them? What else does he satirize?
4. If Auden were writing the poem today, what might he substitute for "Installment Plan" in line 19 and the items listed in line 21?
5. Explicate the last two lines.
6. Write a tribute to The Unknown Student or The Unknown Professor or Politician or Professional Athlete or some other object of your well-deserved scorn.

9
NETWORKS

Restaurant—US 1 Leaving Columbia, South Carolina
Robert Frank, 1955

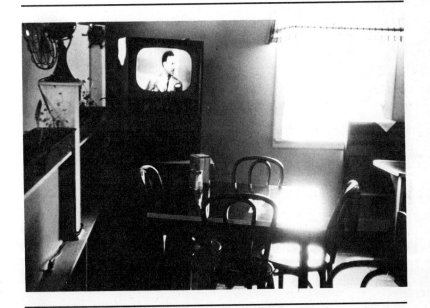

Courtesy Pace MacGill Gallery

Just what is it that makes today's homes so different, so appealing?
Richard Hamilton, 1956

Short Views

We must be as clear as our natural reticence allows us to be.
Marianne Moore

Darling Laura, sweet whiskers, do try to write me better letters. Your last, dated 19 December received today, so eagerly expected, was a bitter disappointment. Do realize that a letter need not be a bald chronicle of events; I know you lead a dull life now, my heart bleeds for it, though I believe you could make it more interesting if you had the will. But that is no reason to make your letters as dull as your life. I simply am not interested in Bridget's children. Do grasp that. A letter should be a form of conversation; write as though you were talking to me.
Evelyn Waugh

[From the dedication of Robert Louis Stevenson's *Travels with a Donkey*] Every book is, in an intimate sense, a circular letter to the friends of him who writes it. They alone take his meaning; they find private messages, assurances of love, and expressions of gratitude dropped for them in every corner. The public is but a generous patron who defrays the postage. Yet, though the letter is directed to all, we have an old and kindly custom of addressing it on the outside to one. Of what shall a man be proud, if he is not proud of his friends? And so, my dear Sidney Colvin, it is with pride that I sign myself affectionately yours,
Robert Louis Stevenson

While I am thinking about metaphor, a flock of purple finches arrives on the lawn. Since I haven't seen these birds for some years, I am only fairly sure of their being in fact purple finches, so I get down Peterson's *Field Guide* and read his description: "Male: About size of House Sparrow, rosy-red, brightest on head and rump." That checks quite well, but his next remark—"a sparrow dipped in raspberry juice," is decisive: it fits. I look out the window again, and now I know that I am seeing purple finches.
Howard Nemerov

We will understand the world, and preserve ourselves and our values in it, only insofar as we have a language that is alert and responsive to it, and careful of it. I mean that literally. When we give our plows such brand names as "Sod Blaster," we are imposing on their use conceptual limits which raise the likelihood that they will be used destructively. When we speak of man's "war against nature," or of a "peace offensive," we are accepting the limitations of a metaphor that suggests, and even proposes, violent solutions. When students ask for the right of "participatory input" at the meetings of a faculty organization, they are thinking of democratic process, but they are *speaking* of a convocation of robots, and are thus devaluing the very traditions that they invoke.

    Wendell Berry

A man is known by the books he reads, by the company he keeps, by the praise he gives, by his dress, by his tastes, by his distastes, by the stories he tells, by his gait, by the motion of his eye, by the look of his house, of his chamber; for nothing on earth is solitary, but everything hath affinities infinite. . . .

    Ralph Waldo Emerson

Gifts from parents to children always carry the most meaningful messages. The way parents think about presents goes one step beyond the objects themselves—the ties, dolls, sleds, record players, kerchiefs, bicycles and model airplanes that wait by the Christmas tree. The gifts are, in effect, one way of telling boys and girls, "We love you even though you have been a bad boy all month" or, "We love having a daughter" or, "We treat all our children alike" or, "It is all right for girls to have some toys made for boys" or, "This alarm clock will help you get started in the morning all by yourself." Throughout all the centuries since the invention of a Santa Claus figure who represented a special recognition of children's behavior, good and bad, presents have given parents a way of telling children about their love and hopes and expectations for them.

    Margaret Mead

A good painter is to paint two main things, namely, man and the working of man's mind. The first is easy, the second difficult, for it is to be represented through the gestures and movements of the limbs.

    Leonardo da Vinci

If you saw a bullet hit a bird, and he told you he wasn't shot, you might weep at his courtesy, but you would certainly doubt his word.
    Emily Dickinson

For a while everybody was laughing at Marvel because we were going after the college crowd. But I've always felt comics were a very valid form of entertainment. There's no reason to look down on telling a good story in the comic book medium. It's just dialogue and illustrations, after all, like film, except that it's a little harder than film because our action is frozen. If Ernest Hemingway had written comic books, they would have been just as good as his novels.
    Stan Lee, of *Marvel Comics*

If there is one consistently dishonest element in every situation comedy, no matter how realistic, how bold, how relevant or controversial it may be, it is that no one in a situation comedy is isolated, alone, atomized. In a country where broken marriages are increasing almost geometrically, and where the trend of living alone is becoming an important national fact of life, the world of the situation comedy depicts strong bonds between friends, coworkers, and family. No one sits home at night watching television: the most pervasive habit in American life today usually goes unrecorded in even the most "realistic" comedies because it is not funny.
    Jeff Greenfield

The medium is the message.
    Marshall McLuhan

I beheld the wretch—the miserable monster whom I had created.
    Mary Shelley, *Frankenstein*

The storyteller's own experience of people and things, whether for good or ill—not only what he has passed through himself, but even events which he has only witnessed or been told of—has moved the writer to an emotion so passionate that he can no longer keep it shut up in his heart. Again and again something in his own life or in that around him will seem to the writer so important that he cannot bear to let it pass into oblivion. There must never come a time, he feels, when people do not know about it.
    Lady Murasaki, *The Tale of Genji*

Ballads, *bon mots*, anecdotes, give us better insight into the depths of past centuries than grave and voluminous chronicles. "A Straw," says Selden, "thrown up into the air will show how the wind sits, which cannot be learned by casting up a stone."
Ralph Waldo Emerson

Watching television is a habit.
Martin Meyer

Abraham Lincoln

Abraham Lincoln (1809–65), sixteenth president of the United States, is not usually thought of as a writer, but his published speeches and writings comprise about 1,078,000 words, the equivalent of about 4,000 pages of double-spaced typing. They were all composed without the assistance of a speech writer.

    The Gettysburg campaign — a series of battles fought near Gettysburg in southeastern Pennsylvania — took place in June and July of 1863. Each side lost something like 23,000 men. The battle is regarded as a turning point in the war, but the Confederate army escaped and the war continued until April, 1865.

    On November 19, 1863 Lincoln delivered a short speech (printed below) at the dedication of a national cemetery on the battlefield at Gettysburg.

Address at the Dedication of the Gettysburg National Cemetery

Four score and seven years ago our fathers brought forth on this continent, a new nation, conceived in Liberty, and dedicated to the proposition that all men are created equal.

Now we are engaged in a great civil war; testing whether that nation, or any nation so conceived and so dedicated, can long endure. We are met on a great battlefield of that war. We have come to dedicate a portion of that field as a final resting-place for those who here gave their lives that that nation might live. It is altogether fitting and proper that we should do this.

But, in a larger sense, we cannot dedicate—we cannot conse-crate—we cannot hallow—this ground. The brave men, living and dead, who struggled here have consecrated it, far above our poor power to add or detract. The world will little note, nor long remem-ber, what we say here, but it can never forget what they did here. It is for us the living, rather, to be dedicated here to the unfinished work which they who fought here have thus far so nobly advanced. It is rather for us to be here dedicated to the great task remaining before us—that from these honored dead we take increased devo-tion to that cause for which they gave the last full measure of devo-tion; that we here highly resolve that these dead shall not have died in vain; that this nation, under God, shall have a new birth of free-dom; and that government of the people, by the people, for the peo-ple, shall not perish from the earth.

Gilbert Highet

Gilbert Highet (1906–78) was born in Glasgow, Scotland, and was educated at Glas-gow University and at Oxford University. In 1937 he came to the United States, and in 1951 he was naturalized. Until his retirement in 1972 he taught Latin, Greek, and com-parative literature at Columbia University. In addition to writing scholarly studies of clas-sical authors, he wrote several general and more popular books.

The Gettysburg Address

Fourscore and seven years ago. . . .

These five words stand at the entrance to the best-known monu-ment of American prose, one of the finest utterances in the entire language, and surely one of the greatest speeches in all history. Greatness is like granite: it is molded in fire, and it lasts for many centuries.

Fourscore and seven years ago. . . . It is strange to think that President Lincoln was looking back to the 4th of July 1776, and that he and his speech are now further removed from us than he himself was from George Washington and the Declaration of Independence. Fourscore and seven years before the Gettysburg Address, a small group of patriots signed the Declaration. Fourscore and seven years after the Gettysburg Address, it was the year 1950, and that date is already receding rapidly into our troubled, adventurous, and valiant past.

Inadequately prepared and at first scarcely realized in its full 4 importance, the dedication of the graveyard at Gettysburg was one of the supreme moments of American history. The battle itself had been a turning point of the war. On the 4th of July 1863, General Meade repelled Lee's invasion of Pennsylvania. Although he did not follow up his victory, he had broken one of the most formidable aggressive enterprises of the Confederate armies. Losses were heavy on both sides. Thousands of dead were left on the field, and thousands of wounded died in the hot days following the battle. At first, their burial was more or less haphazard; but thoughtful men gradually came to feel that an adequate burying place and memorial were required. These were established by an interstate commission that autumn, and the finest speaker in the North was invited to dedicate them. This was the scholar and statesman Edward Everett of Harvard. He made a good speech—which is still extant: not at all academic, it is full of close strategic analysis and deep historical understanding.

Lincoln was not invited to speak, at first. Although people knew him as an effective debater, they were not sure whether he was capable of making a serious speech on such a solemn occasion. But one of the impressive things about Lincoln's career is that he constantly strove to *grow.* He was anxious to appear on that occasion and to say something worthy of it. (Also, it has been suggested, he was anxious to remove the impression that he did not know how to behave properly—an impression which had been strengthened by a shocking story about his clowning on the battlefield of Antietam the previous year.) Therefore when he was invited he took considerable care with his speech. He drafted rather more than half of it in the White House before leaving, finished it in the hotel at Gettysburg the night before the ceremony (not in the train, as sometimes reported), and wrote a fair copy next morning.

There are many accounts of the day itself, 19 November 1863. There are many descriptions of Lincoln, all showing the same curious blend of grandeur and awkwardness, or lack of dignity, or—it would be best to call it humility. In the procession he rode horseback: a tall lean man in a high plug hat, straddling a short horse, with his feet too near the ground. He arrived before the chief speaker, and had to wait patiently for half an hour or more. His own speech came right at the end of a long and exhausting ceremony, lasted less than three minutes, and made little impression on the audience. In part this was because they were tired, in part because (as eyewitnesses said) he ended almost before they knew he had begun, and in part because he did not speak the Address, but read it, very slowly, in a thin high voice, with a marked Kentucky accent, pronouncing "to" as "toe" and dropping his final R's.

Some people of course were alert enough to be impressed. Everett congratulated him at once. But most of the newspapers paid little attention to the speech, and some sneered at it. The *Patriot and Union* of Harrisburg wrote, "We pass over the silly remarks of the President; for the credit of the nation we are willing . . . that they shall no more be repeated or thought of"; and the London *Times* said, "The ceremony was rendered ludicrous by some of the sallies of that poor President Lincoln," calling his remarks "dull and commonplace." The first commendation of the Address came in a single sentence of the Chicago *Tribune,* and the first discriminating and detailed praise of it appeared in the Springfield *Republican,* the Providence *Journal,* and the Philadelphia *Bulletin.* However, three weeks after the ceremony and then again the following spring, the editor of *Harper's Weekly* published a sincere and thorough eulogy of the Address, and soon it was attaining recognition as a masterpiece.

At the time, Lincoln could not care much about the reception of his words. He was exhausted and ill. In the train back to Washington, he lay down with a wet towel on his head. He had caught smallpox. At that moment he was incubating it, and he was stricken down soon after he re-entered the White House. Fortunately it was a mild attack, and it evoked one of his best jokes: he told his visitors, "At last I have something I can give to everybody."

He had more than that to give to everybody. He was a unique person, far greater than most people realize until they read his life with care. The wisdom of his policy, the sources of his statesmanship—these were things too complex to be discussed in a brief essay. But we can say something about the Gettysburg Address as a work of art.[1]

A work of art. Yes: for Lincoln was a literary artist, trained both by others and by himself. The textbooks he used as a boy were full

---

[1] For further reference, see W. E. Barton, *Lincoln at Gettysburg* (Bobbs-Merrill, 1930); R. P. Basler, "Abraham Lincoln's Rhetoric." *Amercan Literature* 11 (1939–40), 167–82; and L. E. Robinson, *Abraham Lincoln as a Man of Letters* (Chicago, 1918).

of difficult exercises and skillful devices in formal rhetoric, stressing the qualities he practiced in his own speaking: antithesis, parallelism, and verbal harmony. Then he read and reread many admirable models of thought and expression: the King James Bible, the essays of Bacon, the best plays of Shakespeare. His favorites were *Hamlet, Lear, Macbeth, Richard III*, and *Henry VIII*, which he had read dozens of times. He loved reading aloud, too, and spent hours reading poetry to his friends. (He told his partner Herndon that he preferred getting the sense of any document by reading it aloud.) Therefore his serious speeches are important parts of the long and noble classical tradition of oratory which begins in Greece, runs through Rome to the modern world, and is still capable (if we do not neglect it) of producing masterpieces.

The first proof of this is that the Gettysburg Address is full of quotations—or rather of adaptations—which give it strength. It is partly religious, partly (in the highest sense) political: therefore it is interwoven with memories of the Bible and memories of American history. The first and the last words are Biblical cadences. Normally Lincoln did not say "fourscore" when he meant eighty; but on this solemn occasion he recalled the important dates in the Bible—such as the age of Abraham when his first son was born to him, and he was "fourscore and six years old." Similarly, he did not say there was a chance that democracy might die out: he recalled the somber phrasing in the Book of Job—where Bildad speaks of the destruction of one who shall vanish without a trace, and says that "his branch shall be cut off; his remembrance shall perish from the earth." Then again, the famous description of our State as "government of the people, by the people, for the people" was adumbrated by Daniel Webster in 1830 (he spoke of "the people's government, made for the people, made by the people, and answerable to the people") and then elaborated in 1854 by the abolitionist Theodore Parker (as "government of all the people, by all the people, for all the people"). There is good reason to think that Lincoln took the important phrase "under God" (which he interpolated at the last moment) from Weems, the biographer of Washington; and we know that it had been used at least once by Washington himself.

Analyzing the Address further, we find that it is based on a highly imaginative theme, or group of themes. The subject is—how can we put it so as not to disfigure it?—the subject is the kinship of life and death, that mysterious linkage which we see sometimes as the physical succession of birth and death in our world, 12 sometimes as the contrast, which is perhaps a unity, between death and immortality. The first sentence is concerned with birth:

> Our *fathers brought forth a new* nation, *conceived* in liberty.

The final phrase but one expresses the hope that

> this nation, under God, shall have a *new birth* of freedom.

And that last phrase of all speaks of continuing life as the triumph over death. Again and again throughout the speech, this mystical contrast and kinship reappear: "those who *gave their lives* that that nation might *live*," "the brave men *living* and *dead*," and so in the central assertion that the dead have already consecrated their own burial place, while "it is for us, the *living*, rather to be dedicated . . . to the great task remaining." The Gettysburg Address is a prose poem; it belongs to the same world as the great elegies, and the adagios of Beethoven.

Its structure, however, is that of a skillfully contrived speech. The oratorical pattern is perfectly clear. Lincoln describes the occasion, dedicates the ground, and then draws a larger conclusion by calling on his hearers to dedicate themselves to the preservation of the Union. But within that, we can trace his constant use of at least two important rhetorical devices.

The first of these is *antithesis:* opposition, contrast. The speech is full of it. Listen:

	The world will little	*note*		
	nor long	*remember*	what	*we say* here
but	it can never	*forget*	what	*they did* here

And so in nearly every sentence: "brave men, *living* and *dead*"; "to *add* or *detract*." There is the antithesis of the Founding Fathers and men of Lincoln's own time:

> Our *fathers brought forth* a new nation . . .
> now *we* are testing whether that nation . . . can *long endure*.

And there is the more terrible antithesis of those who have already died and those who still live to do their duty. Now, antithesis is the figure of contrast and conflict. Lincoln was speaking in the midst of a great civil war.

The other important pattern is different. It is technically called *tricolon*—the division of an idea into three harmonious parts, usually of increasing power. The most famous phrase of the Address is a tricolon:

> government of the people
> by the people
> for the people.

The most solemn sentence is a tricolon:

> we cannot dedicate
> we cannot consecrate
> we cannot hallow   this ground.

And above all, the last sentence (which has sometimes been criticized as too complex) is essentially two parallel phrases, with a tricolon growing out of the second and then producing another tricolon: a trunk, three branches, and a cluster of flowers. Lincoln says that it is for his hearers to be dedicated to the great task remaining before them. Then he goes on.

> that from these honored dead

—apparently he means "in such a way that from these honored dead"—

> we take increased devotion to that cause.

Next, he restates this more briefly:

> that we here highly resolve. . . .

And now the actual resolution follows, in three parts of growing intensity:

> that these dead shall not have died in vain
> that this nation, under God, shall have a new birth
>   of freedom

and that (one more tricolon)

> government of the people
>   by the people
>   for the people
> shall not perish from the earth.

Now, the tricolon is the figure which, through division, emphasizes basic harmony and unity. Lincoln used antithesis because he was speaking to a people at war. He used the tricolon because he was hoping, planning, praying for peace.

No one thinks that when he was drafting the Gettysburg Address, Lincoln deliberately looked up these quotations and consciously chose these particular patterns of thought. No, he chose the theme. From its development and from the emotional tone of the entire occasion, all the rest followed, or grew—by that marvelous process of choice and rejection which is essential to artistic creation. It does not spoil such a work of art to analyze it as closely as we have done; it is altogether fitting and proper that we should do this: for it helps us to penetrate more deeply into the rich meaning of the Gettysburg Address, and it allows us the very rare privilege of watching the workings of a great man's mind. 16

Topics for Discussion and Writing

1. At the start of his essay, after quoting the opening words of Lincoln's speech, Highet uses a metaphor and a simile: he says that the words "stand at the entrance to the best-known monument," and that "greatness is like granite: it is molded in fire, and it lasts for many centuries." Are these figures of speech effective? Why or why not? How are the two figures related to each other?

2.   Analyze the structure of Highet's essay.
3.   This essay was a talk given on the radio, presumably to a large general public. Find passages in the essay that suggest oral delivery to an unspecialized audience. How would you describe Highet's tone?
4.   It has been suggested that "government of the people, by the people" is redundant; a government *of* the people, it is argued, must be the same as a government *by* the people. Did Lincoln repeat himself merely to get a triad: "of the people, by the people, for the people"? If so, is this a fault? Or can it be argued that "government of the people" really means "government over the people"? If so, what does the entire expression mean?
5.   Highet claims that Lincoln was not only a great statesman but also a literary artist. According to Highet, what was Lincoln's training as a literary artist? Highet implies that such training is still available. To what extent has it been available to you? Traditionally, studying "admirable models of thought and expession," including poetry, was an important part of writing instruction, but it is less common now. Should such study be included in writing courses? Why, or why not?
6.   In paragraph 11 Highet points out that "the Gettysburg Address is full of quotations — or rather of adaptations," and he analyzes several examples of Lincoln's adaptations of sources. How is such adaptation different from plagiarism? Or is it?

George Orwell

George Orwell (1903–50) was the pen name adopted by Eric Blair, an Englishman born in India. Orwell was educated at Eton, in England, but in 1921 he went back to the East and served for five years as a police officer in Burma. He then returned to Europe, doing odd jobs while writing novels and stories. In 1936 he fought in the Spanish Civil War on the side of the Republicans, an experience reported in Homage to Catalonia *(1938). His last years were spent writing in England.*

Politics and the English Language

Most people who bother with the matter at all would admit that the English language is in a bad way, but it is generally assumed that we cannot by conscious action do anything about it.

Our civilization is decadent and our language—so the argument runs—must inevitably share in the general collapse. It follows that any struggle against the abuse of language is a sentimental archaism, like preferring candles to electric light or hansom cabs to aeroplanes. Underneath this lies the half-conscious belief that language is a natural growth and not an instrument which we shape for our own purposes.

Now, it is clear that the decline of a language must ultimately have political and economic causes: it is not due simply to the bad influence of this or that individual writer. But an effect can become a cause, reinforcing the original cause and producing the same effect in an intensified form, and so on indefinitely. A man may take to drink because he feels himself to be a failure, and then fail all the more completely because he drinks. It is rather the same thing that is happening to the English language. It becomes ugly and inaccurate because our thoughts are foolish, but the slovenliness of our language makes it easier for us to have foolish thoughts. The point is that the process is reversible. Modern English, especially written English, is full of bad habits which spread by imitation and which can be avoided if one is willing to take the necessary trouble. If one gets rid of these habits one can think more clearly, and to think clearly is a necessary first step towards political regeneration: so that the fight against bad English is not frivolous and is not the exclusive concern of professional writers. I will come back to this presently, and I hope that by that time the meaning of what I have said here will have become clearer. Meanwhile, here are five specimens of the English language as it is now habitually written.

These five passages have not been picked out because they are especially bad—I could have quoted far worse if I had chosen—but because they illustrate various of the mental vices from which we now suffer. They are a little below the average, but are fairly representative samples. I number them so that I can refer back to them when necessary:

1.   I am not, indeed, sure whether it is not true to say that the Milton who once seemed not unlike a seventeenth-century Shelley had not become, out of an experience ever more bitter in each year, more alien [sic] to the founder of that Jesuit sect which nothing could induce him to tolerate.

    Professor Harold Laski (Essay in *Freedom of Expression*)

2. Above all, we cannot play ducks and drakes with a native battery of idioms which prescribes such egregious collocations of vocables as the Basic *put up with* for *tolerate* or *put at a loss* for *bewilder*.

    Professor Lancelot Hogben (*Interglossa*)

3. On the one side we have the free personality: by definition it is not neurotic, for it has neither conflict nor dream. Its desires, such as they are, are transparent, for they are just what institutional approval keeps in the forefront of consciousness; another institutional pattern would alter their number and intensity; there is little in them that is natural, irreducible, or culturally dangerous. But *on the other side*, the social bond itself is noticing but the mutual reflection of these self-secure integrities. Recall the definition of love. Is not this the very picture of a small academic? Where is there a place in this hall of mirrors for either personality or fraternity?

    Essay on Psychology in *Politics* (New York)

4. All the "best people" from the gentlemen's clubs, and all the frantic fascist captains, united in common hatred of Socialism and bestial horror of the rising tide of the mass revolutionary movement, have turned to acts of provocation, to foul incendiarism, to medieval legends of poisoned wells, to legalize their own destruction of proletarian organizations, and rouse the agitated petty-bourgeoisie to chauvinistic fervor on behalf of the fight against the revolutionary way out of the crisis.

    Communist Pamphlet

5. If a new spirit *is* to be infused into this old country, there is one thorny and contentious reform which must be tackled, and that is the humanization and galvanization of the B.B.C. Timidity here will bespeak canker and atrophy of the soul. The heart of Britain may be sound and of strong beat, for instance, but the British lion's roar at present is like that of Bottom in Shakespeare's *Midsummer Night's Dream*—as gentle as any sucking dove. A virile new Britain cannot continue indefinitely to be traduced in the eyes or rather ears, of the world by the effete languors of Langham Place, brazenly masquerading as "standard English." When the voice of Britain is heard at nine o'clock, better far and infinitely less ludicrous to hear aitches honestly dropped than the present priggish, inflated, inhibited, school-ma'amish arch braying of blameless bashful mewing maidens!

    Letter in *Tribune*

Each of these passages has faults of its own, but, quite apart   4
from avoidable ugliness, two qualities are common to all of them.
The first is staleness of imagery; the other is lack of precision. The
writer either has a meaning and cannot express it, or he inadver-
tently says something else, or he is almost indifferent as to whether
his words mean anything or not. This mixture of vagueness and
sheer incompetence is the most marked characteristic of modern English prose, and especially of any kind of political writing. As soon
as certain topics are raised, the concrete melts into the abstract and
no one seems able to think of turns of speech that are not hackneyed:
prose consists less and less of *words* chosen for the sake of their
meaning, and more and more of *phrases* tacked together like the sections of a prefabricated henhouse. I list below, with notes and examples, various of the tricks by means of which the work of prose-
construction is habitually dodged:

Dying Metaphors

A newly invented metaphor assists thought by evoking a visual
image, while on the other hand a metaphor which is technically
"dead" (e.g., *iron resolution*) has in effect reverted to being an
ordinary word and can generally be used without loss of vividness.
But in between these two classes there is a huge dump of worn-out
metaphors which have lost all evocative power and are merely used
because they save people the trouble of inventing phrases for
themselves. Examples are: *Ring the changes on, take up the cudgels for,
toe the line, ride roughshod over, stand shoulder to shoulder with, play
into the hands of, no axe to grind, grist to the mill, fishing in troubled
waters, on the order of the day, Achilles' heel, swan song, hotbed.* Many
of these are used without knowledge of their meaning (what is a
"rift," for instance?), and incompatible metaphors are frequently
mixed, a sure sign that the writer is not interested in what he is
saying. Some metaphors now current have been twisted out of
their original meaning without those who use them even being
aware of the fact. For example, *toe the line* is sometimes written *tow
the line.* Another example is *the hammer and the anvil,* now always
used with the implication that the anvil gets the worst of it. In
real life it is always the anvil that breaks the hammer, never the
other way about: a writer who stopped to think what he was saying would be aware of this, and would avoid perverting the original phrase.

Operators or Verbal False Limbs

These save the trouble of picking out appropriate verbs and nouns, and at the same time pad each sentence with extra syllables which give it an appearance of symmetry. Characteristic phrases are *render inoperative, militate against, make contact with, be subjected to, give rise to, give grounds for, have the effect of, play a leading part (role) in, make itself felt, take effect, exhibit a tendency to, serve the purpose of, etc., etc.* The keynote is the elimination of simple verbs. Instead of being a single word, such as *break, stop, spoil, mend, kill,* a verb becomes *a phrase,* made up of a noun or adjective tacked on to some general-purpose verb such as *prove, serve, form, play, render.* In addition, the passive voice is wherever possible used in preference to the active, and noun constructions are used instead of gerunds (*by examination of* instead of *by examining*). The range of verbs is further cut down by means of the *-ize* and *de-* formations, and the banal statements are given an appearance of profundity by means of the *not un-* formation. Simple conjunctions and prepositions are replaced by such phrases as *with respect to, having regard to, the fact that, by dint of, in view of, in the interests of, on the hypothesis that;* and the ends of sentences are saved from anticlimax by such resounding commonplaces as *greatly to be desired, cannot be left out of account, a development to be expected in the near future, deserving of serious consideration, brought to a satisfactory conclusion,* and so on and so forth.

Pretentious Diction

Words like *phenomenon, element, individual* (as noun), *objective, categorical, effective, virtual, basic, primary, promote, constitute, exhibit, exploit, utilize, eliminate, liquidate,* are used to dress up simple statements and give an air of scientific impartiality to biased judgments. Adjectives like *epoch-making, epic, historic, unforgettable, triumphant, age-old, inevitable, inexorable, veritable,* are used to dignify the sordid processes of international politics, while writing that aims at glorifying war usually takes on an archaic color, its characteristic words being: *realm, throne, chariot, mailed fist, trident, sword, shield, buckler, banner, jackboot, clarion.* Foreign words and expressions such as *cul de sac, ancien regime, deus ex machina, mutatis mutandis, status quo, gleichschaltung, weltanschauung,* are used to give an air of culture and elegance. Except for the useful abbreviations *i.e., e.g.,* and *etc.,* there is no real need for any of the hundreds of foreign phrases now current in English. Bad writers, and especially scientific, political and sociological writers, are nearly always haunted by the notion that Latin or Greek words are grander than Saxon ones, and unnecessary words like *expedite, ameliorate, predict, extraneous, deracinated, clandestine, subaqueous* and hundreds of others constantly gain ground from their Anglo-Saxon opposite numbers.[1] The jargon peculiar to Marxist writing (*hyena, hangman, cannibal, petty bourgeois, these gentry, lacquey, flunkey, mad dog, White Guard,* etc.) consists largely of words and phrases translated from Russian, German or French; but the normal way of coining a new word is to use a Latin or Greek root with the appropriate affix and, where necessary, the *-ize* formation. It is often easier to make up words of this kind (*deregionalize, impermissible, extramarital, nonfragmentary* and so forth) than to think up the English words that will cover one's meaning. The result, in general, is an increase in slovenliness and vagueness.

Meaningless Words

In certain kinds of writing, particularly in art criticism and literary criticism, it is normal to come across long passages which are almost completely lacking in meaning.[2] Words like *romantic, plastic, values, human, dead, sentimental, natural, vitality,* as used in art criticism, are strictly meaningless, in the sense that they not only do not point to any discoverable object, but are hardly ever expected to do so by the reader. When one critic writes, "The outstanding feature of Mr. X's work is its living quality," while another writes, "the immediately striking thing about Mr. X's work is its peculiar deadness," the reader accepts this as a simple difference of opinion. If words like *black* and *white* were involved, instead of the jargon words *dead* and *living,* he would see at once that language was being used in an improper way. Many political words are similarly abused. The

8

---

[1] An interesting illustration of this is the way in which the English flower names which were in use till very recently are being ousted by Greek ones, *snapdragon* becoming *antirrhinum, forget-me-not* becoming *myosotis,* etc. It is hard to see any practical reason for this change of fashion: it is probably due to an instinctive turning-away from the more homely word and a vague feeling that the Greek word is scientific.

[2] Example: "Comfort's catholicity of perception and image, strangely Whitmanesque in range, almost the exact opposite in aesthetic compulsion, continues to evoke that trembling atmospheric accumulative hinting at a cruel, an inexorably serene timelessness. . . . Wrey Gardiner scores by aiming at simple bull's-eyes with precision. Only they are not simple, and through this contented sadness runs more than the surface bitter-sweet of resignation." (*Poetry Quarterly*)

word *Facism* has now no meaning except in so far as it signifies "something not desirable." The words *democracy, socialism, freedom, patriotic, realistic, justice,* have each of them several different meanings which cannot be reconciled with one another. In the case of a word like *democracy,* not only is there no agreed definition, but the attempt to make one is resisted from all sides. It is almost universally felt that when we call a country democratic we are praising it: consequently the defenders of every kind of régime claim that it is a democracy, and fear that they might have to stop using the word if it were tied down to any one meaning. Words of this kind are often used in a consciously dishonest way. That is, the person who uses them has his own private definition, but allows his hearer to think he means something quite different. Statements like *Marshal Pétain was a true patriot, The Soviet Press is the freest in the world, The Catholic Church is opposed to persecution,* are almost always made with intent to deceive. Other words used in variable meanings, in most cases more or less dishonestly, are: *class, totalitarian, science, progressive, reactionary, bourgeois, equality.*

Now that I have made this catalogue of swindles and perversions, let me give another example of the kind of writing that they lead to. This time it must of its nature be an imaginary one. I am going to translate a passage of good English into modern English of the worst sort. Here is a well-known verse from *Ecclesiastes:*

> I returned and saw under the sun, that the race is not to the swift, nor the battle to the strong, neither yet bread to the wise, nor yet riches to men of understanding, nor yet favour to men of skill; but time and chance happeneth to them all.

Here it is in modern English:

> Objective consideration of contemporary phenomena compels the conclusion that success or failure in competitive activities exhibits no tendency to be commensurate with innate capacity, but that a considerable element of the unpredictable must invariably be taken into account.

This is a parody, but not a very gross one. Exhibit (3), above, for instance, contains several patches of the same kind of English. It will be seen that I have not made a full translation. The beginning and ending of the sentence follow the original meaning fairly closely, but in the middle the concrete illustrations — race, battle, bread — dissolve into the vague phrase "success or failure in competitive activities." This had to be so, because no modern writer of the kind I am discussing — no one capable of using phrases like "objective consideration of contemporary phenomena" — would ever tabulate his thoughts in that precise and detailed way. The whole tendency of modern prose is away from concreteness. Now analyze these two sentences a little more closely. The first contains forty-nine words but only sixty syllables, and all its words are those of everyday life. The second contains thirty-eight words of ninety syllables: eighteen of its words are from Latin roots, and one from Greek. The first sentence contains six vivid images, and only one phrase ("time and chance") that could be called vague. The second contains not a single fresh, arresting phrase, and in spite of its ninety syllables it gives only a shortened version of the meaning contained in the first. Yet without a doubt it is the second kind of sentence that is gaining ground in modern English. I do not want to exaggerate. This kind of writing is not yet universal, and outcrops of simplicity will occur here and there in the worst-written page. Still, if you or I were told to write a few lines on the uncertainty of human fortunes, we should probably come much nearer to my imaginary sentence than to the one from *Ecclesiastes*.

As I have tried to show, modern writing at its worst does not   12
consist in picking out words for the sake of their meaning and inventing images in order to make the meaning clearer. It consists in gumming together long strips of words which have already been set in order by someone else, and making the results presentable by sheer humbug. The attraction of this way of writing is that it is easy. It is easier — even quicker, once you have the habit — to say *In my opinion it is not an unjustifiable assumption that* than to say *I think.* If you use ready-made phrases, you not only don't have to hunt about for words; you also don't have to bother with the rhythms of your sentences, since these phrases are generally so arranged as to be more or less euphonious. When you are composing in a hurry — when you are dictating to a stenographer, for instance, or making a public speech — it is natural to fall into a pretentious, Latinized style. Tags like *a consideration which we should do well to bear in mind* or *a conclusion to which all of us would readily assent* will save many a sentence from coming down with a bump. By using stale metaphors, similes and idioms, you save much mental effort, at the cost of leaving your meaning vague, not only for your reader but for yourself. This is the significance of mixed metaphors. The

sole aim of a metaphor is to call up a visual image. When these images clash—as in *The Fascist octopus has sung its swan song, the jackboot is thrown into the melting pot*—it can be taken as certain that the writer is not seeing a mental image of the objects he is naming; in other words he is not really thinking. Look again at the examples I gave at the beginning of this essay. Professor Laski (1) uses five negatives in fifty-three words. One of these is superfluous, making nonsense of the whole passage, and in addition there is the slip *alien* for *akin*, making further nonsense, and several avoidable pieces of clumsiness which increase the general vagueness. Professor Hogben (2) plays ducks and drakes with a battery which is able to write prescriptions, and while, disapproving of the everyday phrase *put up with*, is unwilling to look *egregious* up in the dictionary and see what it means; (3), if one takes an uncharitable attitude towards it, is simply meaningless: probably one could work out its intended meaning by reading the whole of the article in which it occurs. In (4), the writer knows more or less what he wants to say, but an accumulation of stale phrases chokes him like tea leaves blocking a sink. In (5), words and meaning have almost parted company. People who write in this manner usually have a general emotional meaning—they dislike one thing and want to express solidarity with another—but they are not interested in the detail of what they are saying. A scrupulous writer, in every sentence that he writes, will ask himself at least four queshons, thus: What am I trying to say? What words will express it? What image or idiom will make it clearer? Is this image fresh enough to have an effect? And he will probably ask himself two more: Could I put it more shortly? Have I said anything that is avoidably ugly? But you are not obliged to go to all this trouble. You can shirk it by simply throwing your mind open and letting the ready-made phrases come crowding in. They will construct your sentences for you—even think your thoughts for you, to a certain extent—and at need they will perform the important service of partially concealing your meaning even from yourself. It is at this point that the special connection between politics and the debasement of language becomes clear.

In our time it is broadly true that political writing is bad writing. Where it is not true, it will generally be found that the writer is some kind of rebel, expressing his private opinions and not a "party line." Orthodoxy, of whatever color, seems to demand a lifeless, imitative style. The political dialects to be found in pamphlets, leading articles, manifestos, White Papers and the speeches of undersecretaries do, of course, vary from party to party, but they are all alike in that one almost never finds in them a fresh, vivid, home-made turn of speech. When one watches some tired hack on the platform mechanically repeating the familiar phrases — *bestial atrocities, iron heel, bloodstained tyranny, free peoples of the world, stand shoulder to shoulder* — one often has a curious feeling that one is not watching a live human being but some kind of dummy: a feeling which suddenly becomes stronger at moments when the light catches the speaker's spectacles and turns them into blank discs which seem to have no eyes behind them. And this is not altogether fanciful. A speaker who uses that kind of phraseology has gone some distance towards turning himself into a machine. The appropriate noises are coming out of his larynx, but his brain is not involved as it would be if he were choosing his words for himself. If the speech he is making is one that he is accustomed to make over and over again, he may be almost unconscious of what he is saying, as one is when one utters the responses in church. And this reduced state of consciousness, if not indispensable, is at any rate favorable to political conformity.

In our time, political speech and writing are largely the defense of the indefensible. Things like the continuance of British rule in India, the Russian purges and deportations, the dropping of the atom bombs on Japan, can indeed be defended, but only by arguments which are too brutal for most people to face, and which do not square with the professed aims of political parties. Thus political language has to consist largely of euphemism, question-begging and sheer cloudy vagueness. Defenseless villages are bombarded from the air, the inhabitants driven out into the countryside, the cattle machine-gunned, the huts set on fire with incendiary bullets: this is called *pacification*. Millions of peasants are robbed of their farms and sent trudging along the roads with no more than they can carry: this is called *transfer of population* or *rectification of frontiers*. People are imprisoned for years without trial, or shot in the back of the neck or sent to die of scurvy in Arctic lumber camps: this is called *elimination of unreliable elements*. Such phraseology is needed if one wants to name things without calling up mental pictures of them. Consider for instance some comfortable English professor defending Russian totalitarianism. He cannot say outright, "I believe in killing off your opponents when you can get good results by doing so." Probably, therefore, he will say something like this:

> While freely conceding that the Soviet regime exhibits certain features which the humanitarian may be inclined to deplore, we must, I think,

agree that a certain curtailment of the right to political opposition is an unavoidable concomitant of transitional periods, and that the rigors which the Russian people have been called upon to undergo have been amply justified in the sphere of concrete achievement.

The inflated style is itself a kind of euphemism. A mass of Latin words falls upon the facts like soft snow, blurring the outlines and covering up all the details. The great enemy of clear language is insincerity. When there is a gap between one's real and one's declared aims, one turns as it were instinctively to long words and exhausted idioms, like a cuttlefish squirting out ink. In our age there is no such thing as "keeping out of politics." All issues are political issues, and politics itself is a mass of lies, evasions, folly, hatred and schizophrenia. When the general atmosphere is bad, language must suffer. I should expect to find—this is a guess which I have not sufficient knowledge to verify—that the German, Russian and Italian languages have all deteriorated in the last ten to fifteen years, as a result of dictatorship.

But if thought corrupts language, language can also corrupt 16 thought. A bad usage can spread by tradition and imitation, even among people who should and do know better. The debased language that I have been discussing is in some ways very convenient. Phrases like *a not unjustifiable assumption, leaves much to be desired, would serve no good purpose, a consideration which we should do well to bear in mind,* are a continuous temptation, a packet of aspirins always at one's elbow. Look back through this essay, and for certain you will find that I have again and again committed the very faults I am protesting against. By this morning's post I have received a pamphlet dealing with conditions in Germany. The author tells me that he "felt impelled" to write it. I open it at random, and here is almost the first sentence that I see: "[The Allies] have an opportunity not only of achieving a radical transformation of Germany's social and political structure in such a way as to avoid a nationalistic reaction in Germany itself, but at the same time of laying the foundations of cooperative and unified Europe." You see, he "feels impelled" to write—feels, presumably, that he has something new to say—and yet his words, like cavalry horses answering the bugle, group themselves automatically into the familiar dreary pattern. This invasion of one's mind by ready-made phrases (*lay the foundations, achieve a radical transformation*) can only be prevented if one is constantly on guard against them, and every such phrase anaesthetizes a portion of one's brain.

I said earlier that the decadence of our language is probably curable. Those who deny this would argue, if they produced an argument at all, that language merely reflects existing social conditions, and that we cannot influence its development by any direct tinkering with words and constructions. So far as the general tone or spirit of a language goes, this may be true, but it is not true in detail. Silly words and expressions have often disappeared, not through any evolutionary process but owing to the conscious action of a minority. Two recent examples were *explore every avenue* and *leave no stone unturned*, which were killed by the jeers of a few journalists. There is a long list of flyblown metaphors which could similarly be got rid of if enough people would interest themselves in the job; and it should also be possible to laugh the *not un-* formation out of existence,[3] to reduce the amount of Latin and Greek in the average sentence, to drive out foreign phrases and strayed scientific words, and, in general, to make pretentiousness unfashionable. But all these are minor points. The defense of the English language implies more than this, and perhaps it is best to start by saying what it does *not* imply.

To begin with it has nothing to do with archaism, with the salvaging of obsolete words and turns of speech, or with the setting up of a "standard English" which must never be departed from. On the contrary, it is especially concerned with the scrapping of every word or idiom which has outworn its usefulness. It has nothing to do with correct grammar and syntax, which are of no importance so long as one makes one's meaning clear, or with the avoidance of Americanisms, or with having what is called a "good prose style." On the other hand it is not concerned with fake simplicity and the attempt to make written English colloquial. Nor does it even imply in every case preferring the Saxon word to the Latin one, though it does imply using the fewest and shortest words that will cover one's meaning. What is above all needed is to let the meaning choose the word, and not the other way about. In prose, the worst thing one can do with words is to surrender to them. When you think of a concrete object, you think wordlessly, and then, if you want to describe the thing you have been visualizing you probably hunt about till you find the exact words that seem to fit in. When you think of something abstract you are more inclined to use words from the start, and unless you make a conscious effort to prevent it, the

---

[3] One can cure oneself of the *not un-* formation by memorizing this sentence: *A not unblack dog was chasing a not unsmall rabbit across a not ungreen field.*

existing dialect will come rushing in and do the job for you, at the expense of blurring or even changing your meaning. Probably it is better to put off using words as long as possible and get one's meaning as clear as one can through pictures or sensations. Afterwards one can choose—not simply accept—the phrases that will best cover the meaning, and then switch round and decide what impression one's words are likely to make on another person. This last effort of the mind cuts out all stale or mixed images, all prefabricated phrases, needless repetitions, and humbug and vagueness generally. But one can often be in doubt about the effect of a word or a phrase, and one needs rules that one can rely on when instinct fails. I think the following rules will cover most cases:

  (i) Never use a metaphor, simile or other figure of speech which you are used to seeing in print.
 (ii) Never use a long word where a short one will do.
(iii) If it is possible to cut a word out, always cut it out.
 (iv) Never use the passive where you can use the active.
  (v) Never use a foreign phrase, a scientific word or a jargon word if you can think of an everyday English equivalent.
 (vi) Break any of these rules sooner than say anything outright barbarous.

These rules sound elementary, and so they are, but they demand a deep change of attitude in anyone who has grown used to writing in the style now fashionable. One could keep all of them and still write bad English, but one could not write the kind of stuff that I quoted in those five specimens at the beginning of this article.

I have not here been considering the literary use of language, but merely language as an instrument for expressing and not for concealing or preventing thought. Stuart Chase and others have come near to claiming that all abstract words are meaningless, and have used this as a pretext for advocating a kind of political quietism. Since you don't know what Fascism is, how can you struggle against Fascism? One need not swallow such absurdities as this, but one ought to recognize that the present political chaos is connected with the decay of language, and that one can probably bring about some improvement by starting at the verbal end. If you simplify your English, you are freed from the worst follies of orthodoxy. You cannot speak any of the necessary dialects, and when you make a stupid remark its stupidity will be obvious, even to yourself. Political language—and with variations this is true of all political parties, from

Conservatives to Anarchists—is designed to make lies sound truthful and murder respectable, and to give an appearance of solidity to pure wind. One cannot change this all in a moment, but one can at least change one's own habits, and from time to time, one can even, if one jeers loudly enough, send some worn-out and useless phrase—some *jackboot, Achilles' heel, hotbed, melting pot, acid test, veritable inferno* or other lump of verbal refuse—into the dustbin where it belongs.

Topics for Discussion and Writing

1. Revise one or two of Orwell's examples of bad writing.
2. Examine Orwell's metaphors. Do they fulfill his requirements for good writing?
3. Look again Orwell's grotesque revision (paragraph 10) of a passage from the Bible. Write a similar version of another passage from the Bible.
4. Can you recall any occasion when you have used words, in writing or speaking, in a consciously dishonest way? If so, can you explain why, or go further and justify your behavior?
5. In paragraph 2 Orwell says, "Written English is full of bad habits which spread by imitation." Are you aware of having acquired any bad writing habits by imitation? If so, imitation of what or whom?

Robin Lakoff

Robin Lakoff was born in 1943 and was educated at Radcliffe College and Harvard University. A professor of linguistics at the University of California at Berkeley, she has been especially interested in the language that women use. The essay that we give here was first published in Ms. *magazine in 1974.*

You Are What You Say

Women's language is that pleasant (dainty?), euphemistic never-aggressive way of talking we learned as little girls. Cultural bias was built into the language we were allowed to speak, the subjects we were allowed to speak about, and the ways we were spoken of. Having learned our linguistic lesson well, we go out in the world, only to discover that we are communicative cripples—damned if we do, and damned if we don't.

If we refuse to talk "like a lady," we are ridiculed and criticized for being unfeminine. ("She thinks like a man" is, at best, a left-handed compliment.) If we do learn all the fuzzy-headed, unassertive language of our sex, we are ridiculed for being unable to think clearly, unable to take part in a serious discussion, and therefore unfit to hold a position of power.

It doesn't take much of this for a woman to begin feeling she deserves such treatment because of inadequacies in her own intelligence and education.

"Women's language" shows up in all levels of English. For example, women are encouraged and allowed to make far more precise discriminations in naming colors than men do. Words like *mauve, beige, ecru, aquamarine, lavender,* and so on, are unremarkable in a woman's active vocabulary, but largely absent from that of most men. I know of no evidence suggesting that women actually *see* a wider range of colors than men do. It is simply that fine discriminations of this sort are relevant to women's vocabularies, but not to men's; to men, who control most of the interesting affairs of the world, such distinctions are trivial—irrelevant.

In the area of syntax, we find similar gender-related peculiarities of speech. There is one construction, in particular, that women use conversationally far more than men: the tag question. A tag is midwaybetween an outright statement and a yes-no question; it is less assertive than the former, but more confident than the latter.

A *flat statement* indicates confidence in the speaker's knowledge and is fairly certain to be believed; a *question* indicates a lack of knowledge on some point and implies that the gap in the speaker's knowledge can and will be remedied by an answer. For example, if, at a Little League game, I have had my glasses off, I can legitimately ask someone else: "Was the player out at third?" A *tag question*, being intermediate between statement and question, is used when the speaker is stating a claim, but lacks full confidence in the truth of that claim. So if I say, "Is Joan here?" I will probably not be surprised if my respondent answers "no"; but if I say, "Joan is here, isn't she?" instead, chances are I am already biased in favor of a positive answer, wanting only confirmation. I still want a response, but I have enough knowledge (or think I have) to predict that response. A tag question, then, might be thought of as a statement that doesn't demand to be believed by anyone but the speaker, a way of giving leeway, of not forcing the addressee to go along with the views of the speaker.

Another common use of the tag question is in small talk when the speaker is trying to elicit conversation: "Sure is hot here, isn't it?"

But in discussing personal feelings or opinions, only the speaker   8
normally has any way of knowing the correct answer. Sentences such as "I have a headache, don't I?" are clearly ridiculous. But there are other examples where it is the speaker's opinions, rather than perceptions, for which corroboration is sought, as in "The situation in Southeast Asia is terrible, isn't it?"

While there are, of course, other possible interpretations of a sentence like this, one possibility is that the speaker has a particular answer in mind "yes" or "no"—but is reluctant to state it baldly. This sort of tag question is much more apt to be used by women than by men in conversation. Why is this the case?

The tag question allows a speaker to avoid commitment, and thereby avoid conflict with the addressee. The problem is that, by so doing, speakers may also give the impression of not really being sure of themselves, or looking to the addressee for confirmation of their views. This uncertainty is reinforced in more subliminal ways, too. There is a peculiar sentence-intonation pattern, used almost exclusively by women, as far as I know, which changes a declarative answer into a question. The effect of using the rising inflection typical of a yes-no question is to imply that the speaker is seeking confirmation, even though the speaker is clearly the only one who has the requisite information, which is why the question was put to her in the first place:

(Q) When will dinner be ready?
(A) Oh . . . around six o'clock . . . ?

It is as though the second speaker was saying, "Six o'clock—if that's okay with you, if you agree." The person being addressed is put in the position of having to provide confirmation. One likely consequence of this sort of speech pattern in a woman is that, often unbeknownst to herself, the speaker builds a reputation of tentativeness, and others will refrain from taking her seriously or trusting her with any real responsibilities, since she "can't make up her mind," and "isn't sure of herself."

Such idiosyncrasies may explain why women's language sounds much more "polite" than men's. It is polite to leave a decision open, not impose your mind, or views, or claims, or anyone else. So a tag question is a kind of polite statement, in that it does not force agreement or belief on the addressee. In the same way a request is a polite command, in that it does not force obedience on the addressee, but rather suggests something be done as a favor to the speaker. A clearly stated order implies a threat of certain consequences if it is not followed, and—even more impolite—implies that the speaker is in a superior position and able to enforce the order. By couching wishes in the form of a request, on the other hand, a speaker implies that if the request is not carried out, only the speaker will suffer; noncompliance cannot harm the addressee. So the decision is really left up to the addressee. The distinction becomes clear in these examples:

Close the door.
Please close the door.
Will you close the door?
Will you please close the door?
Won't you close the door?

In the same ways as words and speech patterns used *by* women 12
undermine her image, those used to *describe* women make matters even worse. Often a word may be used of both men and women (and perhaps of things as well); but when it is applied to women, it assumes a special meaning that, by implication rather than outright assertion, is derogatory to women as a group.

The use of euphemisms has this effect. A euphemism is a substitute for a word that has acquired a bad connotation by association with something unpleasant or embarrassing. But almost as soon as the new word comes into common usage, it takes on the same old bad connotations, since feelings about the things or people referred to are not altered by a change of name; thus new euphemisms must be constantly found.

There is one euphemism for *woman* still very much alive. The word, of course, is *lady*. *Lady* has a masculine counterpart, namely *gentleman*, occasionally shortened to *gent*. But for some reason *lady* is very much commoner than *gent(leman)*.

The decision to use *lady* rather than *woman*, or vice versa, may considerably alter the sense of a sentence, as the following examples show:

(a) A woman (lady) I know is a dean at Berkeley.
(b) A woman (lady) I know makes amazing things out of shoelaces and old boxes.

The use of *lady* in (a) imparts a frivolous, or nonserious, tone to   16
the sentence: the matter under discussion is not one of great moment. Similarly, in (b), using *lady* here would suggest that the speaker considered the "amazing things" not to be serious art, but merely a hobby or an aberration. If *woman* is used, she might be a serious sculptor. To say *lady doctor* is very condescending, since no one ever says *gentleman doctor* or even *man doctor*. For example, mention in the San Francisco *Chronicle* of January 31, 1972, of Madalyn Murray O'Hair as the *lady atheist* reduces her position to that of scatterbrained eccentric. Even *woman atheist* is scarcely defensible: sex is irrelevant to her philosophical position.

Many women argue that, on the other hand, *lady* carries with it overtones recalling the age of chivalry: conferring exalted stature on the person so referred to. This makes the term seem polite at first, but we must also remember that these implications are perilous: they suggest that a "lady" is helpless, and cannot do things by herself.

Lady can also be used to infer frivolousness, as in titles of organizations. Those that have a serious purpose (not merely that of enabling "the ladies" to spend time with one another) cannot use the word *lady* in their titles, but less serious ones may. Compare the *Ladies' Auxiliary* of a men's group, or the *Thursday Evening Ladies' Browning and Garden Society* with *Ladies' Liberation* or *Ladies' Strike for Peace*.

What is curious about this split is that *lady* is in origin a euphemism—a substitute that puts a better face on something people find uncomfortable—for *woman*. What kind of euphemism is it that subtly denigrates the people to whom it refers? Perhaps *lady* functions as a euphemism for *woman* because it does not contain the sexual implications present in *woman*: it is not "embarrassing" in that way. If this is so, we may expect that, in the future, *lady* will replace woman as the primary word for the human female, since *woman* will have become too blatantly sexual. That this distinction is already made in some contexts at least is shown in the following examples, where you can try replacing *woman* with *lady*:

(a) She's only twelve, but she's already a woman.
(b) After ten years in jail, Harry wanted to find a woman.
(c) She's my woman, see, so don't mess around with her.

Another common substitute for *woman* is *girl*. One seldom   20
hears a man past the age of adolescence referred to as a boy, save in expressions like "going out with the boys," which are meant to suggest an air of adolescent frivolity and irresponsibility. But women

of all ages are "girls": one can have a man—not a boy—Friday, but only a girl—never a woman or even a lady—Friday; women have girlfriends, but men do not—in a nonsexual sense—have boyfriends. It may be that this use of *girl* is euphemistic in the same way the use of *lady* is: in stressing the idea of immaturity, it removes the sexual connotations lurking in *woman*. *Girl* brings to mind irresponsibility: you don't send a girl to do a woman's errand (or even, for that matter, a boy's errand). She is a person who is both too immature and too far from real life to be entrusted with responsibilities or with decisions of any serious or important nature.

Now let's take a pair of words which, in terms of the possible relationships in an earlier society, were simple male-female equivalents, analogous to *bull: cow*. Suppose we find that, for independent reasons, society has changed in such a way that the original meanings now are irrelevant. Yet the words have not been discarded, but have acquired new meanings, metaphorically related to their original senses. But suppose these new metaphorical uses are no longer parallel to each other. By seeing where the parallelism breaks down, we discover something about the different roles played by men and women in this culture. One good example of such a divergence through time is found in the pair, *master: mistress*. Once used with reference to one's power over servants, these words have become unusable today in their original master-servant sense as the relationship has become less prevalent in our society. But the words are still common.

Unless used with reference to animals, *master* now generally refers to a man who has acquired consummate ability in some field, normally nonsexual. But its feminine counterpart cannot be used this way. It is practically restricted to its sexual sense of "paramour." We start out with two terms, both roughly paraphrasable as "one who has power over another." But the masculine form, once one person is no longer able to have absolute power over another, becomes usable metaphorically in the sense of "having power over *something*." *Master* requires as its object only the name of some activity, something inanimate and abstract. But *mistress* requires a masculine noun in the possessive to precede it. One cannot say: "Rhonda is a mistress." One must be *someone's* mistress. A man is defined by what he does, a woman by her sexuality, that is, in terms of one particular aspect of her relationship to men. It is one thing to be an *old master* like Hans Holbein,[1] and another to be an *old mistress*.

---

[1] A German painter of the sixteenth century. (Editors' note)

The same is true of the words *spinster* and *bachelor*—gender words for "one who is not married." The resemblance ends with the definition. While *bachelor* is a neuter term, often used as a compliment, *spinster* normally is used pejoratively, with connotations of prissiness, fussiness, and so on. To be a bachelor implies that one has a choice of marrying or not, and this is what makes the idea of a bachelor existence attractive, in the popular literature. He has been pursued and has successfully eluded his pursuers. But a spinster is one who has not been pursued, or at least not seriously. She is old, unwanted goods. The metaphorical connotations of *bachelor* generally suggest sexual freedom; of *spinster*, puritanism or celibacy.

These examples could be multiplied. It is generally considered a 24 *faux pas*, in society, to congratulate a woman on her engagement, while it is correct to congratulate her fiancé. Why is this? The reason seems to be that it is impolite to remind people of things that may be uncomfortable to them. To congratulate a woman on her engagement is really to say, "Thank goodness! You had a close call!" For the man, on the other hand, there was no such danger. His choosing to marry is viewed as a good thing, but not something essential.

The linguistic double standards holds throughout the life of the relationship. After marriage, bachelor and spinster become man and wife, not man and woman. The woman whose husband dies remains "John's widow"; John, however, is never "Mary's widower."

Finally, why is it that salesclerks and others are so quick to call women customers "dear," "honey," and other terms of endearment they really have no business using? A male customer would never put up with it. But women, like children, are supposed to enjoy these endearments, rather than being offended by them.

In more ways than one, it's time to speak up.

Topics for Discussion and Writing

1. Lakoff's first example of "women's language" (paragraph 4) has to do with colors. She says that women are more likely than men to use such words as *mauve, beige,* and *lavender* not because women see a wider range of colors but because men, "who control most of the interesting affairs of the world," regard distinctions of color as trivial and presumably leave them to the women. How adequate does this explanation seem to you?

2. For a day or so try to notice if Lakoff is correct in suggesting that women are more inclined than men to use "tag questions" and to use a "rising

inflection" with a declarative sentence. Jot down examples you hear, and write an essay of about 500 words, either supporting or refuting Lakoff.

3. While you are eavesdropping, you might notice, too, whether or not in mixed company women talk more than men. Many men assume that "women talk a lot," but is it true? If, for instance, you spend an evening with an adult couple, try to form an impression about which of the two does more of the talking. Of course this is too small a sample to allow for a generalization; still, it is worth thinking about. If you are at a meeting—perhaps a meeting of a committee with men and women— again try to see whether the males or the females do most of the talking. Try also to see whether one sex interrupts the other more often than the other way around. And try to make some sense out of your findings.

4. In paragraph 11 Lakoff says, "Women's language sounds much more 'polite' than men's," and she implies that this politeness is a way of seeming weak. Do you associate politeness with weakness?

5. The essay originally appeared in *Ms.*, a feminist magazine, rather than in an academic journal devoted to language or to sociology. Why do you suppose she chose *Ms.*? What would you say Lakoff's purpose was in writing and publishing the essay?

6. This essay was first published in 1974. Do you think it is dated? You might begin by asking yourself if women today use "women's language."

Barbara Lawrence

Barbara Lawrence was born in Hanover, New Hampshire, and she was educated at Connecticut College and at New York University. She teaches at the State University of New York, at Old Westbury. This essay first appeared in The New York Times.

Four-Letter Words Can Hurt You

Why should any words be called obscene? Don't they all describe natural human functions? Am I trying to tell them, my students demand, that the "strong, earthy, gut-honest"—or, if they are fans of Norman Mailer, the "rich, liberating, existential"— language they use to describe sexual activity isn't preferable to "phony-sounding, middle-class words like 'intercourse' and 'copulate'?" "Cop You Late!" they say with fancy inflections and gagging grimaces. "Now, what is *that* supposed to mean?"

Well, what is it supposed to mean? And why indeed should one group of words describing human functions and human organs be acceptable in ordinary conversation and another, describing presumably the same organs and functions, be tabooed—so much so, in fact, that some of these words still cannot appear in print in many parts of the English-speaking world?

The argument that these taboos exist only because of "sexual hangups" (middle-class, middle-age, feminist), or even that they are a result of class oppression (the contempt of the Norman conquerors for the language of their Anglo-Saxon serfs), ignores a much more likely explanation, it seems to me, and that is the sources and functions of the words themselves.

The best known of the tabooed sexual verbs, for example, comes 4 from the German *ficken*, meaning "to strike"; combined, according to Partridge's etymological dictionary *Origins*, with the Latin sexual verb *futuere*; associated in turn with the Latin *fustis*, "a staff or cudgel"; the Celtic *buc*, "a point, hence to pierce"; the Irish *bot*, "the male member"; the Latin *battuere*, "to beat"; the Gaelic *batair*, "a cudgeller"; the Early Irish *bualaim*, "I strike"; and so forth. It is one of what etymologists sometimes call "the sadistic group of words for the man's part in copulation."

The brutality of this word, then, and its equivalents ("screw," "bang," etc.), is not an illusion of the middle class or a crotchet of Women's Liberation. In their origins and imagery these words carry undeniably painful, if not sadistic, implications, the object of which is almost always female. Consider, for example, what a "screw" actually does to the wood it penetrates; what a painful, even mutilating, activity this kind of analogy suggests. "Screw" is particularly interesting in this context, since the noun, according to Partridge, comes from words meaning "groove," "nut," "ditch," "breeding sow," "scrofula" and "swelling," while the verb, besides its explicit imagery, has antecedent associations to "write on," "scratch," "scarify," and so forth—a revealing fusion of a mechanical or painful action with an obviously denigrated object.

Not all obscene words, of course, are as implicitly sadistic or denigrating to women as these, but all that I know seem to serve a similar purpose: to reduce the human organism (especially the female organism) and human functions (especially sexual and procreative) to their least organic, most mechanical dimension; to substitute a trivializing or deforming resemblance for the complex human reality of what is being described.

Tabooed male descriptives, when they are not openly denigrating to women, often serve to divorce a male organ or function from any significant interaction with the female. Take the word "testes," for example, suggesting "witnesses" (from the Latin *testis*) to the sexual and procreative strengths of the male organ; and the obscene counterpart of this word, which suggests little more than a mechanical shape. Or compare almost any of the "rich," "liberating" sexual verbs, so fashionable today among male writers, with that much-derided Latin word "copulate" ("to bind or join together") or even that AngloSaxon phrase (which seems to have had no trouble surviving the Norman Conquest) "make love."

How arrogantly self-involved the tabooed words seem in comparison to either of the other terms, and how contemptuous of the female partner. Understandably so, of course, if she is only a "skirt," a "broad," a "chick," a "pussycat" or a "piece." If she is, in other words, no more than her skirt, or what her skirt conceals; no more than a breeder, or the broadest part of her; no more than a piece of a human being or a "piece of tail." 8

The most severely tabooed of all the female descriptives, incidentally, are those like a "piece of tail," which suggest (either explicitly or through antecedents) that there is no significant difference between the female channel through which we are all conceived and born and the anal outlet common to both sexes—a distinction that pornographers have always enjoyed obscuring.

This effort to deny women their biological identity, their individuality, their humanness, is such an important aspect of obscene language that one can only marvel at how seldom, in an era preoccupied with definitions of obscenity, this fact is brought to our attention. One problem, of course, is that many of the people in the best position to do this (critics, teachers, writers) are so reluctant today to admit that they are angered or shocked by obscenity. Bored, maybe, unimpressed, aesthetically, displeased, but—no matter how brutal or denigrating the material—never angered, never shocked.

And yet how eloquently angered, how piously shocked many of these same people become if denigrating language is used about any minority group other than women; if the obscenities are racial or ethnic, that is, rather than sexual. Words like "coon," "kike," "spic," "wop," after all, deform identity, deny individuality and humanness in almost exactly the same way that sexual vulgarisms and obscenities do.

No one that I know, least of all my students, would fail to ques- 12
tion the values of a society whose literature and entertainment rested
heavily on racial or ethnic pejoratives. Are the values of a society
whose literature and entertainment rest as heavily as ours on sexual pejoratives any less questionable?

Topics for Discussion and Writing

1. In addition to giving evidence to support her view, what persuasive
   devices (such as irony, analogy) does Lawrence use? (On irony, see
   page 880; on analogy, see page 875.)
2. Examine your own use or non-use of four-letter words. How and when
   did you learn to use them, or to avoid using them? If you have reasons
   to avoid them other than the ones Lawrence provides, what are they?
   If you do use such words, under what circumstances are you likely to
   use them? Will Lawrence's analysis persuade you to avoid them altogether? Why, or why not?

Edward T. Hall

*Edward T. Hall, was born in Missouri in 1914, was for many years a professor of anthro-
pology at Northwestern University.*

*Hall is especially concerned with "proxemics," a word derived from the Latin proxi-
mus, "nearest." Proxemics is the study of people's responses to spatial relationships —
for example, their ways of marking out their territory in public places, and their responses
to what they consider to be crowding. In these pages from his book* The Hidden Dimension *(1966), Hall suggests that Arabs and Westerners must understand the proxemic
customs of each other's culture; without such understanding, other communications between them are likely to be misunderstood.*

Proxemics in the
Arab World

In spite of over two thousand years of contact, Westerners and Arabs still do not understand each other. Proxemic
research reveals some insights into this difficulty. Americans in the
Middle East are immediately struck by two conflicting sensations.

In public they are compressed and overwhelmed by smells, crowding, and high noise levels; in Arab homes Americans are apt to rattle around, feeling exposed and often somewhat inadequate because of too much space! (The Arab houses and apartments of the middle and upper classes which Americans stationed abroad commonly occupy are much larger than the dwellings such Americans usually inhabit.) Both the high sensory stimulation which is experienced in public places and the basic insecurity which comes from being in a dwelling that is too large provide Americans with an introduction to the sensory world of the Arab.

Behavior in Public

Pushing and shoving in public places is characteristic of Middle Eastern culture. Yet it is not entirely what Americans think it is (being pushy and rude) but stems from a different set of assumptions concerning not only the relations between people but how one experiences the body as well. Paradoxically, Arabs consider northern Europeans and Americans pushy, too. This was very puzzling to me when I started investigating these two views. How could Americans who stand aside and avoid touching be considered pushy? I used to ask Arabs to explain this paradox. None of my subjects was able to tell me specifically what particulars of American behavior were responsible, yet they all agreed that the impression was widespread among Arabs. After repeated unsuccessful attempts to gain insight into the cognitive world of the Arab on this particular point, I filed it away as a question that only time would answer. When the answer came, it was because of a seemingly inconsequential annoyance.

While waiting for a friend in a Washington, D.C., hotel lobby and wanting to be both visible and alone, I had seated myself in a solitary chair outside the normal stream of traffic. In such a setting most Americans follow a rule, which is all the more binding because we seldom think about it, that can be stated as follows: as soon as a person stops or is seated in a public place, there balloons around him a small sphere of privacy which is considered inviolate. The size of the sphere varies with the degree of crowding, the age, sex, and the importance of the person, as well as the general surroundings Anyone who enters this zone and stays there is intruding. In fact, a stranger who intrudes, even for a specific purpose, acknowledges the fact that he has intruded by beginning his request with "Pardon me, but can you tell me . . . ?"

To continue, as I waited in the deserted lobby, a stranger walked   4
up to where I was sitting and stood close enough so that not only
could I easily touch him but I could even hear him breathing. In
addition, the dark mass of his body filled the peripheral field of vision on my left side. If the lobby had been crowded with people,
I would have understood his behavior, but in an empty lobby his
presence made me exceedingly uncomfortable. Feeling annoyed by
this intrusion, I moved my body in such a way as to communicate
annoyance. Strangely enough, instead of moving away, my actions
seemed only to encourage him, because he moved even closer. In
spite of the temptation to escape the annoyance, I put aside thoughts
of abandoning my post, thinking, "To hell with it. Why should I
move? I was here first and I'm not going to let this fellow drive me
out even if he is a boor." Fortunately, a group of people soon arrived whom my tormentor immediately joined. Their mannerisms
explained his behavior, for I knew from both speech and gestures
that they were Arabs. I had not been able to make this crucial identification by looking at my subject when he was alone because he
wasn't talking and he was wearing American clothes.

In describing the scene later to an Arab colleague, two contrasting patterns emerged. My concept and my feelings about my own
circle of privacy in a "public" place immediately struck my Arab
friend as strange and puzzling. He said, "After all, it's a public place,
isn't it?" Pursuing this line of inquiry, I found that an Arab thought
I had no rights whatsoever by virtue of occupying a given spot;
neither my place nor my body was inviolate! For the Arab, there
is no such thing as an intrusion in public. Public means public. With
this insight, a great range of Arab behavior that had been puzzling,
annoying, and sometimes even frightening began to make sense.
I learned, for example, that if A is standing on a street corner and
B wants his spot, B is within his rights if he does what he can to
make A uncomfortable enough to move. In Beirut only the hardy
sit in the last row in a movie theater, because there are usually stan-
dees who want seats and who push and shove and make such a
nuisance that most people give up and leave. Seen in this light, the
Arab who "intruded" on my space in the hotel lobby had apparently selected it for the very reason I had: it was a good place to
watch two doors and the elevator. My show of annoyance, instead
of driving him away, had only encouraged him. He thought he was
about to get me to move.

Another silent source of friction between Americans and Arabs
is in an area that Americans treat very informally — the manners and

rights of the road. In general, in the United States we tend to defer to the vehicle that is bigger, more powerful, faster, and heavily laden. While a pedestrian walking along a road may feel annoyed he will not think it unusual to step aside for a fast-moving automobile. He knows that because he is moving he does not have the right to the space around him that he has when he is standing still (as I was in the hotel lobby). It appears that the reverse is true with the Arabs who apparently *take on rights to space as they move.* For someone else to move into a space an Arab is also moving into is a violation of his rights. It is infuriating to an Arab to have someone else cut in front of him on the highway. It is the American's cavalier treatment of moving space that makes the Arab call him aggressive and pushy.

Concepts of Privacy

The experience described above and many others suggested to me that Arabs might actually have a wholly contrasting set of assumptions concerning the body and the rights associated with it. Certainly the Arab tendency to shove and push each other in public and to feel and pinch women in public conveyances would not be tolerated by Westerners. It appeared to me that they must not have any concept of a private zone outside the body. This proved to be precisely the case.

In the Western world, the person is synonymous with an individual inside a skin. And in northern Europe generally, the skin and even the clothes may be inviolate. You need permission to touch either if you are a stranger. This rule applies in some parts of France, where the mere touching of another person during an argument used to be legally defined as assault. For the Arab the location of the person in relation to the body is quite different. The person exists somewhere down inside the body. The ego is not completely hidden, however, because it can be reached very easily with an insult. It is protected from touch but not from words. The dissociation of the body and the ego may explain why the public amputation of a thief's hand is tolerated as standard punishment in Saudi Arabia. It also sheds light on why an Arab employer living in a modern apartment can provide his servant with a room that is a box-like cubicle approximately 5 by 10 by 4 feet in size that is not only hung from the ceiling to conserve floor space but has an opening so that the servant can be spied on.

As one might suspect, deep orientations toward the self such as the one just described are also reflected in the language. This was brought to my attention one afternoon when an Arab colleague who is the author of an Arab-English dictionary arrived in my office and threw himself into a chair in a state of obvious exhaustion. When I asked him what had been going on, he said: "I have spent the entire afternoon trying to find the Arab equivalent of the English word 'rape.' There is no such word in Arabic. All my sources, both written and spoken, can come up with no more than an approximation, such as 'He took her against her will.' There is nothing in Arabic approaching your meaning as it is expressed in that one word."

Differing concepts of the placement of the ego in relation to the body are not easily grasped. Once an idea like this is accepted, however, it is possible to understand many other facets of Arab life that would otherwise be difficult to explain. One of these is the high population density of Arab cities like Cairo, Beirut, and Damascus. According to the animal studies described [elsewhere], the Arabs should be living in a perpetual behavioral sink. While it is probable that Arabs are suffering from population pressures, it is also just as possible that continued pressure from the desert has resulted in a cultural adaptation to high density which takes the form described above. Tucking the ego down inside the body shell not only would permit higher population densities but would explain why it is that Arab communications are stepped up as much as they are when compared to northern European communication patterns. Not only is the sheer noise level much higher, but the piercing look of the eyes, the touch of the hands, and the mutual bathing in the warm moist breath during conversation represent stepped-up sensory inputs to a level which many Europeans find unbearably intense.

The Arab dream is for lots of space in the home, which unfortunately many Arabs cannot afford. Yet when he has space, it is very different from what one finds in most American homes. Arab spaces inside their upper middle-class homes are tremendous by our standards. They avoid partitions because Arabs *do not like to be alone.* The form of the home is such as to hold the family together inside a single protective shell, because Arabs are deeply involved with each other. Their personalities are intermingled and take nourishment from each other like the roots and soil. If one is not with people and actively involved in some way, one is deprived of life. An old Arab saying reflects this value: "Paradise without people should not be entered because it is Hell." Therefore, Arabs in the United States often feel socially and sensorially deprived and long to be back where there is human warmth and contact.

Since there is no physical privacy as we know it in the Arab 12
family, not even a word for privacy, one could expect that the Arabs
might use some other means to be alone. Their way to be alone is
to stop talking. Like the English, an Arab who shuts himself off in
this way is not indicating that anything is wrong or that he is with-
drawing, only that he wants to be alone with his own thoughts or
does not want to be intruded upon. One subject said that her father
would come and go for days at a time without saying a word, and
no one in the family thought anything of it. Yet for this very reason, an Arab exchange student visiting a Kansas farm failed to pick
up the cue that his American hosts were mad at him when they gave
him the "silent treatment." He only discovered something was
wrong when they took him to town and tried forcibly to put him
on a bus to Washington, D.C., the headquarters of the exchange
program responsible for his presence in the U.S.

Arab Personal Distances

Like everyone else in the world, Arabs are unable to formulate
specific rules for their informal behavior patterns. In fact, they often
deny that there are any rules, and they are made anxious by suggestions that such is the case. Therefore, in order to determine how
the Arab sets distances, I investigated the use of each sense
separately. Gradually, definite and distinctive behavioral patterns
began to emerge.

Olfaction occupies a prominent place in the Arab life. Not only
is it one of the distance-setting mechanisms, but it is a vital part of
a complex system of behavior. Arabs consistently breathe on people when they talk. However, this habit is more than a matter of
different manners. To the Arab good smells are pleasing and a way
of being involved with each other. To smell one's friend is not only
nice but desirable, for to deny him your breath is to act ashamed.
Americans, on the other hand, trained as they are not to breathe
in people's faces, automatically communicate shame in trying to be
polite. Who would expect that when our highest diplomats are putting on their best manners they are also communicating shame? Yet
this is what occurs constantly, because diplomacy is not only "eyeball to eyeball" but breath to breath.

By stressing olfaction, Arabs do not try to eliminate all the body's
odors, only to enhance them and use them in building human relationships. Nor are they self-conscious about telling others when
they don't like the way they smell. A man leaving his house in the

morning may be told by his uncle, "Habib, your stomach is sour and your breath doesn't smell too good. Better not talk too close to people today." Smell is even considered in the choice of a mate. When couples are being matched for marriage, the man's go-between will sometimes ask to smell the girl, who may be turned down if she doesn't "smell nice." Arabs recognize that smell and disposition may be linked.

In a word, the olfactory boundary performs two roles in Arab life. It enfolds those who want to relate and separates those who don't. The Arab finds it essential to stay inside the olfactory zone as a means of keeping tab on changes in emotion. What is more, he may feel crowded as soon as he smells something unpleasant. While not much is known about "olfactory crowding," this may prove to be as significant as any other variable in the crowding complex because it is tied directly to the body chemistry and hence to the state of health and emotions. It is not surprising, therefore, that the olfactory boundary constitutes for the Arabs an informal distance-setting mechanism in contrast to the visual mechanisms of the Westerner.

Facing and Not Facing

One of my earliest discoveries in the field of intercultural communication was that the position of the bodies of people in conversation varies with the culture. Even so, it is used to puzzle me that a special Arab friend seemed unable to walk and talk at the same time. After years in the United States, he could not bring himself to stroll along, facing forward while talking. Our progress would be arrested while he edged ahead, cutting slightly in front of me and turning sideways so we could see each other. Once in this position, he would stop. His behavior was explained when I learned that for the Arabs to view the other person peripherally is regarded as impolite, and to sit or stand back-to-back is considered very rude. You must be involved when interacting with Arabs who are friends.

One mistaken American notion is that Arabs conduct all conversations at close distances. This is not the case at all. On social occasions, they may sit on opposite sides of the room and talk across the room to each other. They are, however, apt to take offense when Americans use what are to them ambiguous distances, such as the four- to seven-foot social-consultative distance. They frequently complain that Americans are cold or aloof or "don't care." This was what an elderly Arab diplomat in an American hospital thought when the American nurses used "professional" distance. He had the feeling that he was being ignored, that they might not take good care of him. Another Arab subject remarked, referring to American behavior, "What's the matter? Do I smell bad? Or are they afraid of me?"

Arabs who interact with Americans report experiencing a certain flatness traceable in part to a very different use of the eyes in private and in public as well as between friends and strangers. Even though it is rude for a guest to walk around the Arab home eying things, Arabs look at each other in ways which seem hostile or challenging to the American. One Arab informant said that he was in constant hot water with Americans because of the way he looked at them without the slightest intention of offending. In fact, he had on several occasions barely avoided fights with American men who apparently thought their masculinity was being challenged because of the way he was looking at them. As noted earlier, Arabs look each other in the eye when talking with an intensity that makes most Americans highly uncomfortable.

Involvement

As the reader must gather by now, Arabs are involved with each other on many different levels simultaneously. Privacy in a public place is foreign to them. Business transactions in the bazaar, for example, are not just between buyer and seller, but are participated in by everyone. Anyone who is standing around may join in. If a grownup sees a boy breaking a window, he must stop him even if he doesn't know him. Involvement and participation are expressed in other ways as well. If two men are fighting, the crowd must intervene. On the political level, *to fail to intervene* when trouble is brewing is to take sides, which is what our State Department always seems to be doing. Given the fact that few people in the world today are even remotely aware of the cultural mold that forms their thoughts, it is normal for Arabs to view *our* behavior as though it stemmed from *their* own hidden set of assumptions.

Feelings about Enclosed Spaces

In the course of my interviews with Arabs the term "tomb" kept cropping up in conjunction with enclosed space. In a word, Arabs don't mind being crowded by people but hate to be hemmed in by walls. They show a much greater overt sensitivity to architectural crowding than we do. Enclosed space must meet at least three requirements that I know of if it is to satisfy the Arabs: there must be plenty of unobstructed space in which to move around (possibly as much as a thousand square feet); very high ceilings—so high in fact that they do not normally impinge on the visual field; and, in addition, there must be an unobstructed view. It was spaces such as these in which the Americans referred to earlier felt so uncomfortable. One sees the Arab's need for a view expressed in many ways, even negatively, for to cut off a neighbor's view is one of the most effective ways of spiting him. In Beirut one can see what is known locally as the "spite house." It is nothing more than a thick, four-story wall, built at the end of a long fight between neighbors, on a narrow strip of land, for the express purpose of denying a view of the Mediterranean to any house built on the land behind. According to one of my informants, there is also a house on a small plot of land between Beirut and Damascus which is completely surrounded by a neighbor's wall built high enough to cut off the view from all windows!

Boundaries

Proxemic patterns tell us other things about Arab culture. For example, the whole concept of the boundary as an abstraction is almost impossible to pin down. In one sense, there are no boundaries. "Edges" of towns, yes, but permanent boundaries out in the country (hidden lines), no. In the course of my work with Arab subjects I had a difficult time translating our concept of a boundary into terms which could be equated with theirs. In order to clarify the distinctions between the two very different definitions, I thought it might be helpful to pinpoint acts which constituted trespass. To date, I have been unable to discover anything even remotely resembling our own legal concept of trespass.

Arab behavior in regard to their own real estate is apparently an extension of, and therefore consistent with, their approach to the body. My subjects simply failed to respond whenever trespass was mentioned. They didn't seem to understand what I meant by this term. This may be explained by the fact that they organize relationships with each other according to closed social systems rather than spatially. For thousands of years Moslems, Marinites, Druses,

and Jews have lived in their own villages, each with strong kin af-
filiations. Their hierarchy of loyalties is: first to one's self, then to
kinsman, townsman, or tribesman, co-religionist and/or countryman. Anyone not in these categories is a stranger. Strangers and
enemies are very closely linked, if not synonymous, in Arab thought.
Trespass in this context is a matter of who you are, rather than a
piece of land or a space with a boundary that can be denied to anyone and everyone, friend and foe alike.

In summary, proxemic patterns differ. By examining them it is 24
possible to reveal hidden cultural frames that determine the structure of a given people's perceptual world. Perceiving the world
differently leads to differential definitions of what constitutes
crowded living, different interpersonal relations, and a different approach to both local and international politics.

Topics for Discussion and Writing

1. According to Hall, why do Arabs think Americans are pushy? And, again
   according to Hall, why do Arabs not consider themselves pushy?
2. Explain what Hall means by "cognitive world" (paragraph 2); by "ego"
   (paragraph 10); by "behavioral sink" (in the same paragraph). Then explain, for the benefit of someone who did not understand the terms,
   how you know what Hall means by each.
3. In paragraph 9 Hall points out that there is no Arabic equivalent of the
   English word "rape." Can you provide an example of a similar gap in
   English or in another language? Does a cultural difference account for
   the linguistic difference?
4. In paragraph 3 Hall says of a rule that it "is all the more binding because we seldom think about it." Is this generally true of rules? What
   examples or counter-examples support your view?

Deborah Tannen

Deborah Tannen holds a Ph.D. in linguistics from the University of California, Berkeley, and is an associate professor of linguistics at Georgetown University. She is the author of scholarly articles and books as well as of popular articles in such magazines as New York *and* Vogue. *We reprint a chapter from one of her books,* That's Not What I Meant!

The Workings of Conversational Style

The Meaning Is the Metamessage

You're sitting at a bar—or in a coffee shop or at a party—and suddenly you feel lonely. You wonder, "What do all these people find to talk about that's so important?" Usually the answer is, Nothing. Nothing that's so important. But people don't wait until they have something important to say in order to talk.

Very little of what is said is important for the information expressed in the words. But that doesn't mean that the talk isn't important. It's crucially important, as a way of showing that we are involved with each other, and how we feel about being involved. Our talk is saying something about our relationship.

Information conveyed by the meanings of words is the message. What is communicated about relationships—attitudes toward each other, the occasion, and what we are saying—is the metamessage. And it's metamessages that we react to most strongly. If someone says, "I'm not angry," and his jaw is set hard and his words seem to be squeezed out in a hiss, you won't believe the message that he's not angry; you'll believe the metamessage conveyed by the way he said it—that he is. Comments like "It's not what you said but the way you said it" or "Why did you say it like that?" or "Obviously it's not nothing; something's wrong" are responses to metamessages of talk.

Many of us dismiss talk that does not convey important information as worthless—meaningless small talk if it's a social setting or "empty rhetoric" if it's public. Such admonitions as "Skip the small talk," "Get to the point," or "Why don't you say what you mean?" may seem to be reasonable. But they are reasonable only if information is all that counts. This attitude toward talk ignores the fact that people are emotionally involved with each other and that talking is the major way we establish, maintain, monitor, and adjust our relationships. 4

506

Whereas words convey information, how we speak those words—how loud, how fast, with what intonation and emphasis—communicates what we think we're doing when we speak: teasing, flirting, explaining, or chastising; whether we're feeling friendly, angry, or quizzical; whether we want to get closer or back off. In other words, how we say what we say communicates social meanings.

Although we continually respond to social meaning in conversation, we have a hard time talking about it because it does not reside in the dicitonary definitions of words, and most of us have unwavering faith in the gospel according to the dictionary. It is always difficult to talk about—even to see or think about—forces and processes for which we have no names, even if we feel their impact. Linguistics provides terms that describe the processes of communication and therefore make it possible to see, talk, and think about them.

This chapter introduces some of the linguistic terms that give names to concepts that are crucial for understanding communication—and therefore relationships. In addition to the concept of metamessages—underlying it, in a sense—there are universal human needs that motivate communication: the needs to be connected to others and to be left alone. Trying to honor these conflicting needs puts us in a double bind. The linguistic concept of politeness accounts for the way we serve these needs and react to the double bind—through metamessages in our talk.

Involvement and Independence

The philosopher Schopenhauer gave an often-quoted example of 8 porcupines trying to get through a cold winter. They huddle together for warmth, but their sharp quills prick each other, so they pull away. But then they get cold. They have to keep adjusting their closeness and distance to keep from freezing and from getting pricked by their fellow porcupines—the source of both comfort and pain.

We need to get close to each other to have a sense of community, to feel we're not alone in the world. But we need to keep our distance from each other to preserve our independence, so others don't impose on or engulf us. This duality reflects the human condition. We are individual and social creatures. We need other people to survive, but we want to survive as individuals.

Another way to look at this duality is that we are all the same—and all different. There is comfort in being understood and pain in the impossibility of being understood completely. But there is also comfort in being different—special and unique—and pain in being the same as everyone else, just another cog on the wheel.

Valuing Involvement and Independence

We all keep balancing the needs for involvement and independence, but individuals as well as cultures place different relative values on these needs and have different ways of expressing those values. America as a nation has glorified individuality, especially for men. This is in stark contrast to people in many parts of the world outside Western Europe, who more often glorify involvement in family and clan, for women and men.

The independent pioneers—and later our image of them—have served us well. The glorification of independence served the general progress of the nation as (traditionally male) individuals have been willing to leave their hometowns—the comfort of the familiar and familial—to find opportunity, get the best education, travel, work wherever they could find the best jobs or wherever their jobs sent them. The yearning for involvement enticed (traditionally female) individuals to join them. 12

The values of the group are reflected in personal values. Many Americans, especially (but not only) American men, place more emphasis on their need for independence and less on their need for social involvement. This often entails paying less attention to the metamessage level of talk—the level that comments on relationships—focusing instead on the information level. The attitude may go as far as the conviction that only the information level really counts—or is really there. It is then a logical conclusion that talk not rich in information should be dispensed with. Thus, many daughters and sons of all ages, calling their parents, find that their fathers want to exchange whatever information is needed and then hang up, but their mothers want to chat, to "keep in touch."

American men's information-focused approach to talk has shaped the American way of doing business. Most Americans think it's best to "get down to brass tacks" as soon as possible, and not "waste time" in small talk (social talk) or "beating around the bush." But this doesn't work very well in business dealings with Greek, Japanese, or Arab counterparts for whom "small talk" is necessary to establish the social realtionship that must provide the foundation for conducting business.

Another expression of this difference—one that costs American tourists huge amounts of money—is our inability to understand the logic behind bargaining. If the African, Indian, Arab, South American, or Mediterranean seller wants to sell a product, and the tourist wants to buy it, why not set a fair price and let the sale proceed? Because the sale is only one part of the interaction. Just as important, if not more so, is the interaction that goes on during the bargaining: an artful way for buyer and seller to reaffirm their recognition that they're dealing with—and that they are—humans, not machines.

Believing that only the information level of communication 16
is important and real also lets men down when it comes to maintaining personal relationships. From day to day, there often isn't any significant news to talk about. Women are negatively stereotyped as frivolously talking at length without conveying significant information. Yet their ability to keep talking to each other makes it possible for them to maintain close friendships. *Washington Post* columnist Richard Cohen observed that he and the other men he knows don't really have friends in the sense that women have them. This may be at least partly because they don't talk to each other if they can't think of some substantive topic to talk about. As a result, many men find themselves without personal contacts when they retire.

The Double Bind

No matter what relative value we place on involvement and independence, and how we express these values, people, like porcupines, are always balancing the conflicting needs for both. But the porcupine metapor is a little misleading because it suggests a sequence: alternately drawing close and pulling back. Our needs for involvement and independence—to be connected and to be separate—are not sequential but simultaneous. We must serve both needs at once in all we say.

And that is why we find ourselves in a double bind. Anything we say to show we're involved with others is in itself a threat to our (and their) individuality. And anything we say to show we're keeping our distance from others is in itself a threat to our (and their) need for involvement. It's not just a conflict—feeling torn between two alternatives—or ambivalence—feeling two ways about one thing. It's a double bind because whatever we do to serve one need necessarily violates the other. And we can't step out of the cirlce. If we try to withdraw by not communicating, we hit the force field of our need for involvement and are hurled back in.

Because of this double bind, communication will never be perfect; we cannot reach stasis. We have no choice but to keep trying to balance independence and involvement, freedom and safety, the familiar and the strange—continually making adjustments as we list to one side or the other. The way we make these adjustments in our talk can be understood as politeness phenomena.

Information and Politeness in Talk

A language philosopher, H. P. Grice, codified the rules by which   20
conversation would be constructed if information were its only point:

> Say as much as necessary and no more.
> Tell the truth.
> Be relevant.
> Be clear.

These make perfect sense—until we start to listen to and think about real conversations. For one thing, all the seeming absolutes underlying these injunctions are really relative. How much is necessary? Which truth? What is relevant? What is clear?

But even if we could agree on these values, we wouldn't want simply to blurt out what we mean, because we're juggling the needs for involvement and independence. If what we mean shows involvement, we want to temper it to show we're not imposing. If what we mean shows distance, we want to temper it with involvement to show we're not rejecting. If we state what we want to believe, others may not agree or may not want the same thing, so our statement could introduce disharmony; therefore we prefer to get an idea of what others want or think, or how they feel about what we want or think, before we commit ourselves to—maybe even before we make up our minds about—what we mean.

This broad concept of the social goals we serve when we talk is called "politeness" by linguists and anthropologists—not the pinky-in-the-air idea of politeness, but a deeper sense of trying to take into account the effect of what we say on other people.

Linguist Robin Lakoff devised another set of rules that describe the motivations behind politeness—that is, how we adjust what we say to take into account its effects on others. Here they are as Lakoff presents them:

1. Don't impose; keep your distance.
2. Give options; let the other person have a say.
3. Be friendly; maintain camaraderie.

Following Rule 3, Be friendly, makes others comfortable by serving their need for involvement. Following Rule 1, Don't impose, makes others comfortable by serving their need for independence. Rule 2, Give options, falls between Rules 1 and 3. People differ with respect to which rules they tend to apply, and when, and how.

To see how these rules work, let's consider a fairly trivial but common conversation. If you offer me something to drink, I may say, "No, thanks," even though I am thirsty. In some societies this is expected; you insist, and I give in after about the third offer. This is polite in the sense of Rule 1, Don't impose. If you expect this form of politeness and I accept on the first offer, you will think I'm too forward—or dying of thirst. If you don't expect this form of politeness, and I use it, you will take my refusal at face value—and I might indeed die of thirst while waiting for you to ask again.

I may also say, in response to your offer, "I'll have whatever you're having." This is polite in the sense of Rule 2, Give options: I'm letting you decide what to give me. If I do this, but you expect me to refuse the first offer, you may still think I'm pushy. But if you expect Rule 3, Be friendly, you may think me wishy-washy. Don't I know what I want?

Exercising Rule 3-style politeness, Be friendly, I might respond to your offer of something to drink by saying, "Yes, thanks, some apple juice, please." In fact, if this is my style of politeness, I might not wait for you to offer at all, but ask right off, "Have you got anything to drink?," or even head straight for your kitchen, throw open the refrigerator door, and call out, "Got any juice?"

If you and I both feel this is appropriate, my doing it will reinforce our rapport because we both subscribe to the rule of breaking rules; not having to follow the more formal rule sends a metamessage: "We are such good friends, we don't have to stand on ceremony." But if you don't subscribe to this brand of politeness, or don't want to get that chummy with me, you will be offended by my way of being friendly. If we have only recently met, that could be the beginning of the end of our friendship.

Of course, these aren't actually rules, but senses we have of the "natural" way to speak. We don't think of ourselves as following rules, or even (except in formal situations) of being polite. We simply talk in ways that seem obviously appropriate at the time they pop out of our mouths—seemingly self-evident ways of being a good person.

Yet our use of these "rules" is not unconscious. If asked about why we said one thing or another in this way or that, we are likely to explain that we spoke the way we did "to be nice" or "friendly" or "considerate." These are commonsense terms for what linguists refer to, collectively, as politeness—ways of taking into account the effect on others of what we say.

The rules, or senses, of politeness are not mutually exclusive. We don't choose one and ignore the others. Rather we balance them all to be appropriately friendly without imposing, to keep appropriate distance without appearing aloof.

Negotiating the offer of a drink is a fairly trivial matter, though the importance of such fleeting conversations should not be underestimated. The way we talk in countless such daily encounters is part of what constitutes our image of ourselves, and it is on the basis of such encounters that we form our impressions of each other. They have a powerful cumulative effect on our personal and interactive lives.

Furthermore, the process of balancing these conflicting senses of politeness—serving involvement and independence—is the basis for the most consequential of interactions as well as the most trivial. Let's consider the linguistic means we have of serving these needs—and their inherent indeterminacy, which means they can easily let us down. 32

The Two-Edged Sword of Politeness

Sue was planning to visit Amy in a distant city, but shortly before she was supposed to arrive, Sue called and canceled. Although Amy felt disappointed, she tried to be understanding. Being polite by not imposing, and respecting Sue's need for independence, Amy said it was really okay if Sue didn't come. Sue was very depressed at that time, and she got more depressed. She took Amy's considerateness—a sign of caring, respecting Sue's independence—as indifference—not caring at all, a lack of involvement. Amy later felt partly responsible for Sue's depression because she hadn't insisted that Sue visit. This confusion was easy to fall into and hard to climb out of because ways of showing caring and indifference are inherently ambiguous.

You can be nice to some one either by showing your involvement or by not imposing. And you can be mean by refusing to show involvement—cutting her off—or by imposing—being "inconsiderate." You can show someone you're angry by shouting at her—imposing—or refusing to talk to her at all: the silent activity called snubbing.

You can be kind by saying something or by saying nothing. For example, if someone has suffered a misfortune—failed an exam, lost a job, or contracted a disease—you may show sympathy by expressing your concern in words or by deliberately not mentioning it to avoid causing pain by bringing it up. If everyone takes the latter approach, silence becomes a chamber in which the ill, the bereaved, and the unemployed are isolated.

If you choose to avoid mentioning a misfortune, you run the risk of seeming to have forgotten, or of not caring. You may try to circumvent that interpretation by casting a knowing glance, making an indirect reference, or softening the impact with euphemisms ("your situation"), hedges and hesitations ("your . . . um . . . well . . . er . . . you know"), or apologies ("I hope you don't mind my mentioning this"). But meaningful glances and verbal hedging can themselves offend by sending the metamessage "This is too terrible to mention" or "Your condition is shameful." A person thus shielded may feel like shouting, "Why don't you just say it!?" 36

An American couple visited the husband's brother in Germany, where he was living with a German girlfriend. One evening during dinner, the girlfriend asked the brother where he had taken his American guests that day. Upon hearing that we had taken them to the concentration camp at Dachau, she exclaimed in revulsion that that was an awful place to take them; why would he do such a stupid thing? The brother cut off her exclamations by whispering to her while glancing at the American woman. His girlfriend immediately stopped complaining and nodded in understanding, also casting glances at the American, who was not appreciative of their discretion. Instead, she was offended by the assumption that being Jewish is cause for whispering and furtive glances.

Any attempt to soften the impact of what is said can have the opposite effect. For example, a writer recalled the impression that a colleague had written something extremely critical about the manuscript of her book. Preparing to revise the manuscript, she returned to his comments and was surprised to see that the criticism was very mild indeed. The guilty word was the one that preceded the comment, not the comment itself. By beginning the sentence with "Frankly," her colleague sent a metamessage: "Steel yourself. This is going to hurt a lot."

Such layers of meaning are always at work in conversation; anything you say or don't say sends metamessages that become part of the meaning of the conversation.

Mixed Metamessages at Home

Parental love puts relative emphasis on involvement, but as children grow up, most parents give more and more signs of love by respecting their independence. Usually this comes too late for the children's tastes. The teenager who resents being told to put on a sweater or eat breakfast interprets the parent's sign of involvement as an imposition. Although this isn't in the message, the teenager hears a metamessage to the effect "You're still a child who needs to be told how to take care of yourself."

Partners in intimate relationships often differ about how they   40
balance involvement and independence. There are those who show love by making sure the other eats right, dresses warmly, or doesn't drive alone at night. There are others who feel this is imposing and treating them like children. And there are those who feel that their partners don't care about them because they aren't concerned with what they eat, wear, or do. What may be meant as a show of respect for their independence is taken as lack of involvement—which it also might be.

Maxwell wants to be left alone, and Samantha wants attention. So she gives him attention, and he leaves her alone. The adage "Do unto others as you would have others do unto you" may be the source of a lot of anguish and misunderstanding if the doer and the done unto have different styles.

Samantha and Maxwell might feel differently if the other acted differently. He may want to be left alone precisely because she gives him so much attention, and she may want attention precisely because he leaves her alone. With a doting spouse she might find herself craving to be left alone, and with an independent spouse, he might find himself craving attention. It's important to remember that others' ways of talking to you are partly a reaction to your style, just as your style with them is partly a reaction to their style—with you.

The ways we show our involvement and considerateness in talk seem self-evidently appropriate. And in interpreting what others say, we assume they mean what we would mean if we said the same thing in the same way. If we don't think about differences in conversational style, we see no reason to question this. Nor do we question whether what we perceive as considerate or inconsiderate, loving or not, was *intended* to be so.

In trying to come to an understanding with someone who has 44 misinterpreted our intentions, we often end up in a deadlock, reduced to childlike insistence:

> "You said so."
> "I said no such thing!"
> "You did! I heard you!"
> "Don't tell me what I said."

In fact, both parties may be sincere—and both may be right. He recalls what he meant, and she recalls what she heard. But what he intended was not what she understood—which was what she would have meant if she had said what he said in the way he said it.

These paradoxical metamessages are recursive and potentially confusing in all conversations. In a series of conversations between the same people, each encounter bears the burdens as well as the fruits of earlier ones. The fruits of ongoing relationships are an ever-increasing sense of understanding based on less and less talk. This is one of the great joys of intimate conversations. But the burdens include the incremental confusion and disappointment of past misunderstandings, and hardening conviction of the other's irrationality or ill will.

The benefits of repeated communication need no explanation; all our conventional wisdom about "getting to know each other," "working it out," and "speaking the same language" gives us ways to talk about and understand that happy situation. But we need some help—and some terms and concepts—to understand why communicating over time doesn't always result in understanding each other better, and why some times it begins to seem that one or the other is speaking in tongues.

Mixed Metamessages across Cultures

The danger of misinterpretation is greatest, of course, among speakers who actually speak different native tongues, or come from different cultural backgrounds, because cultural difference necessarily implies different assumptions about natural and obvious ways to be polite.

Anthropologist Thomas Kochman gives the example of a white   48
office worker who appeared with a bandaged arm and felt rejected
because her black fellow worker didn't mention it. The (doubly)
wounded worker assumed that her silent colleague didn't notice or
didn't care. But the co-worker was purposely not calling attention
to something her colleague might not want to talk about. She let
her decide whether or not to mention it: being considerate by not
imposing. Kochman says, based on his research, that these differences reflect recognizable black and white styles.

An American woman visiting England was repeatedly
offended—even, on bad days, enraged—when Britishers ignored her
in settings in which she thought they should pay attention. For example, she was sitting at a booth in a railroad-station cafeteria. A
couple began to settle into the opposite seat in the same booth. They
unloaded their luggage; they laid their coats on the seat; he asked
what she would like to eat and went off to get it; she slid into the
booth facing the American. And throughout all this, they showed
no sign of having noticed that someone was already sitting in the
booth.

When the British woman lit up a cigarette, the American had
a concrete object for her anger. She began ostentatiously looking
around for another table to move to. Of course there was none; that's
why the British couple had sat in her booth in the first place. The
smoker immediately crushed out her cigarette and apologized. This
showed that she had noticed that someone else was sitting in the
booth, and that she was not inclined to disturb her. But then she
went back to pretending the American wasn't there, a ruse in which
her husband collaborated when he returned with their food and they
ate it.

To the American, politeness requires talk between strangers
forced to share a booth in a cafeteria, if only a fleeting "Do you mind
if I sit down?" or a conventional "Is anyone sitting here?" even if
it's obvious no one is. The omission of such talk seemed to her like
dreadful rudeness. The American couldn't see that another system
of politeness was at work. (She could see nothing but red.) By not
acknowledging her presence, the British couple freed her from the
obligation to acknowledge theirs. The American expected a show
of involvement; they were being polite by not imposing.

An American man who had lived for years in Japan explained   52
a similar politeness ethic. He lived, as many Japanese do, in fright-
fully close quarters—a tiny room separated from neighboring rooms
by paper-thin walls. In this case the walls were literally made of

paper. In order to preserve privacy in this most unprivate situation, his Japanese neighbors simply acted as if no one else lived there. They never showed signs of having overheard conversations, and if, while walking down the hall, they caught a neighbor with the door open, they steadfastly glued their gaze ahead as if they were alone in a desert. The American confessed to feeling what I believe most Americans would feel if a next-door neighbor passed within a few feet without acknowledging their presence—snubbed. But he realized that the intention was not rudeness by omitting to show involvement, but politeness by not imposing.

The fate of the earth depends on cross-cultural communication. Nations must reach agreements, and agreements are made by individual representatives of nations sitting down and talking to each other—public analogues of private conversations. The processes are the same, and so are the pitfalls. Only the possible consequences are more extreme.

We Need the Eggs

Despite the fact that talking to each other frequently fails to yield the understanding we seek, we keep at it, just as nations keep trying to negotiate and reach agreement. Woody Allen knows why, and tells, in his film *Annie Hall*, which ends with a joke that is heard voice over:

> This guy goes to a psychiatrist and says, "Doc my brother's crazy. He thinks he's a chicken." And the doctor says, "Well, why don't you turn him in?" And the guy says, "I would, but I need the eggs." Well, I guess that's pretty much how I feel about relationships.

Even though intimate as well as fleeting conversations don't yield the perfect communication we crave—and we can see from past experience and from the analysis presented here that they can't—we still keep hoping and trying because we need the eggs of involvement and independence. The communication chicken can't give us these golden eggs because of the double bind: Closeness threatens our lives as individuals, and our real differences as individuals threaten our needs to be connected to other people.

But because we can't step out of the situation—the human situation—we keep trying to balance these needs. We do it by not saying exactly what we mean in our messages, while at the same time negotiating what we mean in metamessages. Metamessages depend for their meaning on subtle linguistic signals and devices. These signals and devices, and how they work (or fail to), are presented and explained in the next chapter.

Notes

[The page references have been changed to accord with pages in *The Little, Brown Reader*, 6th ed., and the bibliographic citations have been amplified where necessary.]

pp. 506, 509. The terms *metamessage* and *double bind* are found in Gregory Bateson, *Steps to an Ecology of Mind* (1972). For Bateson, a double bind entailed contradictory orders at different levels: the message and metamessage conflict. I use the term, as do other linguists (for example, Scollon, "The Rythmic Integration of Ordinary Talk," in *Analyzing Discourse: Text and Talk,* Deborah Tannen, ed. [1981]), simply to describe the state of receiving contradictory orders without being able to step out of the situation.

p. 507. I am grateful to Pamela Gerloff for bringing to my attention Bettelheim's reference (in *Surviving* [1979]) to Schopenhauer's porcupine metaphor.

p. 509–10. Mary Catherine Bateson, *With a Daughter's Eye: A Memoir of Margaret Mead and Gregory Bateson* (1984), discusses G. Bateson's idea that living systems (biological processes as well as human interaction) never achieve a static state of balance, but achieve balance only as a series of adjustments within a range.

p. 510. For his conversational maxims see H. P. Grice, "Logic and Conservation," rptd. in *Syntax and Semantics,* vol. 3, *Speech Acts,* eds. Peter Cole and Jerry Morgan (1975).

p. 511. Lakeoff's original statement of the rules of politeness is in Lakoff, "The Logic of Politeness, or Minding Your P's and Q's," *Papers from the Ninth Regional Meeting of the Chicago Linguistics Society* (1973). She also presents this system in the context of discussing male/female differences (Lakeoff, *Language and Woman's Place* [1975]). Penelope Brown and Stephen Levinson, "Universals in Language Usage: Politeness Phenomena," in *Questions and Politeness,* ed. Esther Goody (1978), provide an extended and formalized discussion of politeness phenomena.

p. 516. Thomas Kochman presents an extended analysis of *Black and White Styles in Conflict* (1981).

p. 517. The quotation from *Annie Hall* is taken from the screenplay by Woody Allen and Marshall Brickman in *Four Films of Woody Allen* (NY: Random House, 1982).

Topics for Discussion and Writing

1. Tannen begins this chapter using the second person ("You're sitting at a bar—or in a coffee shop or at a party—and suddenly you feel lonely. You wonder . . ."), a usage often prohibited in high school English classes and textbooks. How well do you think it works here? Try to make the same point without using the second person. *Have* you made the same point? What has been left out?
2. How does Tannen define "metamessages"? The word will not appear in most dictionaries, but we can probably guess what it means, even without Tannen's explanation. What does *meta* usually mean as a prefix to a word? (Most dictionaries do define *meta* as a prefix.)
3. Why, according to Tannen, has the word metamessages been invented? What other linguistic terms does she introduce, and what do they mean?
4. What is the example of porcupines introduced to explain? Why do you suppose it is easier to remember the example than to remember what it explains?
5. In paragraph 11, Tannen says "individuals as well as cultures place different relative values" on the "needs for involvement and independence." In the same paragraph and in the next several paragraphs, she says that Americans glorify independence and she offers an historical explanation of the glorification of independence and other values that flow from it. What does she assume here about "Americans," American culture, and American history?
6. In paragraph 16, Tannen contrasts women talking to women and men talking to men. What does she *assume* here, in addition to what she *says*, about the differences? On the whole, do you agree with her about women's talk and men's talk?
7. In paragraphs 48–54 Tannen talks about misinterpretations between persons of different cultural backgrounds. If possible, provide an example from your own experience.
8. Write an essay or a journal entry analyzing an encounter which illustrates the "double bind," a "politeness phenomenon," or "mixed metamessages," as Tannen defines these terms and situations. Or summarize this chapter in 750 words.

Richard A. Hawley

Richard Hawley was born in Chicago in 1945 and was educated at Middlebury College, Cambridge University, and Case Western Reserve University. Since 1968 he has taught at University School, Hunting Valley, Ohio, where he is now the headmaster. In addition to writing books on adolescence and issues in teaching, Hawley has written half-a-dozen works of fiction and nonfiction, two volumes of poetry, and an opera libretto.

Television and Adolescents
A Teacher's View

Ever since its novelty wore off in the fifties, we have all known, really, that television in its commercial form wasn't up to much good. This isn't to say that millions of people don't still depend on it, but dependency is hardly a sign of virtue. Except for Marshall McLuhan's grab-bag theoretics, few claims have been advanced for the improving effects of television. In fact, recently there has been a flurry of publishing activity, most notably Marie Winn's *The Plug-in Drug*, about television as a cause of downright mental erosion. But what I think Marie Winn and others need is a concrete, closely observed, and intensely felt illustration of the larger thesis. That's what I offer here.

Television has a way of intruding into our lives, and last year it intruded into my life and into the life of the school where I work in a way that many of us there will never forget. We had all taken our seats for morning assembly. The usual announcements were read, after which the morning's senior speaker was introduced. Like many independent schools, ours requires each senior to address the student body in some manner before he graduates. Since public speaking is not a widely distributed gift these days, the senior speeches are infrequently a source of much interest or intentional amusement.

As the curtains parted, we could see that the speaker had opted for a skit. On the stage were a covered table and a number of cooking implements. Out stepped the speaker wearing an apron and chef's hat, which very quickly established that he was going to satirize one of my colleagues who has a national reputation as a gourmet chef. Since this colleague is also a man who can take a joke, the prospects for the skit seemed bright. But not for long.

At first, I think almost all of us pretended that we didn't hear,   4
that we were making too much of certain, possibly accidental, double entendres. But then came the direct statements and a few blatant physical gestures. Then it was clear! This boy was standing before five hundred of us making fun of what he suggested at some
length was the deviant sexual nature of one of his teachers. The
response to this was at first stupefaction, then some outbursts of
laughter (the groaning kind of laughter that says, "I don't believe
you said that"), then a quieting, as the speech progressed, to periodic oohs (the kind that say, "You *did* say that, and you're in for it").

When he had finished, there was a nearly nauseating level of
tension afloat. As the students filed off to class, I made my way back-
stage to find the speaker. It had by now dawned on him that he
had done something wrong, even seriously wrong. We met in my
office.

He expressed remorse at having offended a teacher whom he
said he particularly liked. (Before the conference I had checked briefly with the teacher and found him badly flustered and deeply hurt.)
The remorse was, I felt, genuine. But something was decidedly missing in the boy's explanation of how he came to think that such a
presentation might, under any circumstances, have been appropriate. He hadn't, he admitted, really thought about it, and some of
his friends thought the idea was funny, and, well, he didn't know.
When it occurred to him that serious school action was in the off-
ing, he protested that in no way had he intended the sexual references to be taken seriously—they were, you know, a joke.

I pointed out to him that the objects of such jokes have no way
to respond: To ignore the insinuation might affirm its validity; on
the other hand, to object vigorously would draw additional attention to the offense and sustain the embarrassment connected with
it. I pointed out further that sometimes innocent parties *never* regain
their stature after being offended in this manner, and that the injured party was, at the very least, in for a terrible day of school.

The boy became reflective and said, "Was it *that* bad? You can   8
see worse on 'Saturday Night Live'." I told him I doubted this, but
if it were true, and were I in a position to judge, I would be in favor
of expelling "Saturday Night Live" from the air. He left the office,
and subsequently endured the appropriate consequences.

For my part, I resolved to turn on "Saturday Night Live," and
when I did, I realized the student had spoken truly. The show's
quick-succession, absurdist comedy spots depended for their appeal

on establishing an almost dangerous sense of inappropriateness: exactly that sense created by our senior speaker. To me, for some years a lapsed viewer, it seemed that both the variety and specificity of sexual innuendo had developed considerably since, say, the once daring Smothers Brothers show of the sixties. What struck me more, however, was how many punch lines and visual gags depended on suddenly introducing the idea of injury or violent death.

I happened to tune in the night a funny caption was put over the documentary shot of Middle Eastern political partisans being dragged to death behind an automobile. Was this funny? I asked my students. They said it was "sick" and laughed. Does this kind of fun trivialize crisis? Trivialize cruelty? Inure us to both? Or is it, you know, a joke?

The right things were said, I think, to our students about the boy's speech. But I can't say the situation improved. Not more than a couple of weeks later, a speaker garbed in a woman's tennis dress took the podium and began to talk humorously about the transsexual tennis player Renee Richards. I can't think of a subject harder for an adolescent to discuss before an adolescent audience. Rarely noted for their confidence and breadth of vision in matters of human sexuality, adolescents are unlikely to be objective, sympathetic, or (let me tell you) funny about so disturbing a phenomenon as sex change. This particular boy, whose inflection is very flat and whose normal countenance is especially stony, managed to convey almost a sense of bitterness in making his string of insulting and, in his reference to genitals and to menstruation, awfully tasteless cracks.

So there it was again: the inappropriateness, the tension. This time the injured party was remote from our particular world, so the hastily arranged conference with the boy turned on general considerations of taste and judgment. This time, however, the speaker was recalcitrant: We could disapprove of his speech and discipline him if we chose, but we ought to know that we could hear the same thing on television.

At that moment something clicked for me. Not only did my brief exposure to "Saturday Night Live" convince me that, yes, I would hear the same thing on television, but I was suddenly struck with the realization that he was using television as an arbiter of taste—that is, *as an arbiter of good taste*. I began to see in this premise a common ground upon which he and I could at least argue. Both of us were in agreement that what is broadcast over television ought to be acceptable; our point of disagreement was his feeling that broadcasting something over television *made* it acceptable. Alarming as such a feeling is to me, it is not hard to see how it has developed over the past few decades.

Until the middle sixties, with the exception of the very earthiest plays and novels, the values of home and school and the values of the popular culture were fairly continuous; if anything, radio, television, and motion pictures were more staid than real life. Of course, all this would change very quickly—not because change was requested or even consented to, but because it wasn't, perhaps couldn't be, resisted. And suddenly there it all was at once: the most embarrassing expletives as common speech; every imaginable kind of sexual coupling depicted in ever-increasing candor; obsessively specific wounds, mutilations.

These formerly unacceptable kinds of stimulation made their way more easily into the relatively insulated world of print and film than they did into the more communal world of the television set. Television is typically viewed in homes, and what is communally seen and heard must be communally integrated, or there will be friction. Since American households—set-holds?—share this communal experience for an estimated two to seven hours per day, the potential for friction is considerable. This is why, on grounds of taste, criticism of television programming tends to be more bitter and more relentless than criticism of books and films.

Television foes and partisans alike continue to advise, with some reason, that those who object to certain programs ought not to watch them. But given the impossibility of monitoring the set at all hours, control over the amount and quality of viewing is difficult to maintain even in principled, surveillant households. Too, some viewers will insist on being their brother's keeper. Not everyone who is convinced that what is beaming over the national airwaves is inhumane, unscrupulous, or scurrilous is going to fight to the death for the networks' right to be so.   16

For many people, television is no longer on the polite side of real life. This is an obvious observation about a novel development, one whose consequences are only just dawning on us. A realist or an existentialist may argue that the unflappably suburban world of "Father Knows Best" revealed none of the complex, ambivalent, and often irrational forces at work in real families: But it is hard to argue that "Father Knows Best" in any way *contributed* to those dark forces. On the contrary, it is possible to argue—although one hesitates to carry it too far—that the theme of Father Knowing Best serves as a psychologically soothing backdrop to the prickly dynamics of real family life. And while today's most highly rated shows suggest that the prevailing seventies' theme is Nobody Knows Anything, there are still apparently enough viewers who like Father Knowing Best to support series like "The Waltons" and "Little House on the Prairie."

Sometimes the theme is compromised in a typical seventies' manner, of which "James at 16" provides a good example: The parents are cast very much in the Robert Young-Jane Wyatt mold, but their son James is, to borrow a phrase, kind of now. By far the most interesting thing he did was to lose his virginity on prime time. The fifteen-going-on-sixteen-year-old boys I work with, many of them at least as sophisticated as James, typically hold on to their virginity a bit longer, until the disposition of their sexual feelings is under surer control. The best clinical evidence maintains that the process of bringing newly emergent sexuality under control is *inherently* delicate and troublesome. James' television plunge planted the anxiety-provoking notion in the mind of the adolescent viewer that he was sexually lagging behind not only the precocious kid down the block, but the Average American Boy character of James. (One was allowed to be less anxious when Father Knew Best.)

Why shouldn't television make people anxious? say the producers of programs that make people anxious. After all, the *world* is anxious. (An awfully self-serving position: Programs that arouse anxiety are relevant; those that don't are enjoyable.) Before long, this line of argument begins to lay claim that programs which bring up irritating subjects in an irritating manner are performing a valuable social mission. Norman Lear, the producer of comedies such as "All in the Family" and "Maude," makes such a claim. According to the Lear formula, a controversial topic will be raised, tossed around for laughs, then either discarded or resolved. Resolution occurs when one of the characters tolerates or forgives the controversial person or practice, while some other character, usually a combination of lovable old coot and ass, does not.

As many critics have pointed out, this is only apparent resolu-   20
tion. Nothing much really happens to a racial or sexual conflict when it is laughed at (a device that is supposed to soften outright slurring and stereotyping), discarded, tolerated, or forgiven. The idea that "if we can joke about it this way, we have taken a humanitarian stride" is mistaken. There is plenty of evidence, particularly among the student population, that, for one thing, race relations are more strained today than they were a decade ago. No one would want

to claim that racism among youth disappeared during the politically active sixties; however, a claim can be made that when a student was confronted then with having made a racial slur, he seemed to be aware of having violated a standard.

Who is to say that Archie Bunker hath no sting? More and more television comedians, in the manner of Don Rickles, seek *only* to sting. It is really an empirical question, not a matter of taste, whether or not it is harmless, much less healing, to denigrate everybody, including oneself. A hit song by Randy Newman insults small people: this is no parody of unkindness or bigotry, but the real thing. My students understand it perfectly and parrot it enthusiastically. Rebuked, they grimace in exasperation. Nothing in their youthful experience tells them that bigotry is a sign of cultural regression ("It isn't bigotry; it's, you know, a joke"). They prefer to see whatever wicked delights crop up in the media as a progressive casting off of prudish inhibitions. According to such a view, progress is whatever happens next.

Toleration of the intolerable is always worrying, but it is especially so when it takes place among the young, in whom we want to invest so much hope. Tolerating the intolerable is part of a dynamic, not a static, process; the intolerable, when it is nurtured, grows.

Which brings me back to the senior speeches. Two so thoroughly inappropriate presentations in a single year represented a high count for us, so we were not ready, at least I wasn't, for the third.

This time the talk was about a summer spent working on a 24 ranch, and the format was that of a commentary with slides. No apparent harm in this, but there were a number of factors working against the speech's success. The first was that the speaker was renowned for being a card, a reputation the welcoming ovation insisted he live up to. Second, he had not adequately rehearsed the projection of the slides, so that they tended to appear out of order and askew, the effect of which was to provide a subtextual comedy of visual non sequiturs. Third, he chose to capitalize on the audience's nearly unrestrained hilarity by playing up certain questionable references.

The speaker made a fairly good, not too inappropriate crack about a slide which depicted a bull mounting a cow—"Sometimes the corrals get so crowded we have to stack the cattle on top of one another." But he chose to exploit his references to the gelding of bulls. There were, in all, four jokey and brutal evocations of this process which served to keep the image of bull genitalia before our minds for quite a few minutes. Since laughter had already been spent, the castration jokes were met with a kind of nervous applause. Bolstered by this, the speaker closed with a coda to the effect that he would be available after assembly to anybody who wanted tips on "cutting meat."

Since I happened to be in charge that day, I sent him home. It seemed to me, in light of the various reprisals and forewarnings connected with the previous speeches, that this particular performance, though perhaps less offensive in its specific references than the other two, ought to be the last straw. The speaker had clearly exceeded anything required by either schoolboy or cowboy saltiness. He had created an anything-goes atmosphere, and then he had let it go—for which he was applauded. "That was great!" said the boy next to me on the way out of the auditorium.

That morning and afterward scores of students, most, but not all, of them civil, hastened to let me know that they felt it was unfair to have sent the speaker home. Not one of them failed to remind me that I could see worse on television. Had I never seen "Saturday Night Live"? That afternoon an opinion poll went up requesting signatures from those who disapproved of the action I had taken and, in an opposing column, those who approved. Within the hour, hundreds expressed disapproval, only one approved.

For a day or two at school there was an animated atmosphere of martyrdom (the speaker's, not mine), but it dissipated rapidly, possibly because the right to make castration jokes from the stage was not, as a cause, very catalytic. The banished speaker, a very likable boy, returned, was received warmly, and apologized not at all cringingly.

In the calm that has followed, my colleagues and I have taken pains to stress to our students, especially at the commencement of the new school year, that whenever somebody addresses an assembly, it is a special occasion. Speakers are expected to observe definite standards when they speak or perform; audiences are expected to be courteous and restrained. Humor at someone else's expense is out, unless it is prearranged with the party lampooned, and even then it ought not to be inhumane. Excretory and copulatory humor is out; it's too easy. Preparation is important. Being persuasive is important. Being controversial is important. Being funny is a delight to all, though it is harder than it looks.

Perhaps these expectations are high. However, schools, especially parochial and independent schools, are gloriously unencumbered in setting such standards: Schools are often *chosen* for the standards they set, the difference they represent. One of the things schools have an opportunity to be different from is television, for although we are all wired into it and it feels public, like the law, it is actually private, like a door-to-door salesman. We don't have to buy the goods.

Since children who watch a fair amount of television will quite naturally assume they are being told and shown the truth, it seems to me crucial that they are exposed to models who view it selectively and critically, who judge it by criteria other than its potential to engage. My own experience has been that students are surprised, but not hostile, when television programming is harshly judged. I think they may even come to like the idea that they themselves, at their discriminating best, are in the process of becoming people television ought to measure up to.

Topics for Discussion and Writing

1. In paragraph 10 Hawley refers to a "comedy spot" on *Saturday Night Live,* which his students labeled "sick" humor. He then asks "Does this kind of fun trivialize crisis? Trivialize cruelty? Inure us to both?" Reread the paragraph and explain how you might respond to Hawley's questions. If you can think of a recent example of similar humor, explain your response to it as well. (Or, use the example Stephen King provides, p. 548.)

2. In paragraph 14 Hawley refers to a sudden change in what became acceptable on television and film. All at once, he says, there were "the most embarrassing expletives as common speech; every imaginable kind of sexual coupling depicted in ever-increasing candor; obsessively specific wounds, mutilations." Are these forms of "unacceptable kinds of stimulation" (paragraph 15) available in the films and television shows of the '90s? If so, how do you feel about them? Are there actions (including speech) that you also find unacceptable?

4. Why, according to Hawley, is criticism of television programming "more bitter and more relentless than criticism of books and films"? Try to recall the last public controversy over taste. Was it over a television show, or some other form of popular entertainment?

5. In paragraph 16, what does Hawley seem to suggest that viewers can do about objectionable television programs? What does he mean by "some viewers will insist on being their brother's keeper"?

6. In paragraph 17 Hawley comments on the family values represented in shows popular in the '60s and '70s, such as "Father Knows Best," "The Waltons," and "Little House on the Prairie." What generalizations

can you make about families in shows of the '90s? If you have seen
reruns of the earlier shows, have you been struck by any differences
in representations of family life then and now?

7. In paragraphs 20–22, Hawley implies that popular culture (his exam-
    ples include a popular singer, a television show, and a comedian seen
    primarily on television) promotes the "toleration of the intolerable," par-
    ticularly of racial and sexual bigotry. Using some current examples in
    which racial and sexual conflicts are represented, would you argue that
    they tend to reinforce bigotry, or reduce it, or leave the audience's bi-
    ases unaffected?

8. Hawley argues for restrictions in the behavior and speech of students.
    How does he defend such restrictions on freedom? How would you feel
    about attending a school with such restrictions? How does the school
    you currently attend deal with speech or behavior containing racial, eth-
    nic, or sexual slurs? What is your attitude toward current policy?

9. Hawley reveals that his school is "independent." What else can we infer
    about the school, its student body, teachers, parents, administration?
    How do these inferences affect your willingness to accept Hawley's ar-
    gument?

Marya Mannes

Marya Mannes served as an editor for Vogue *and* Mademoiselle, *and wrote for many
magazines, including* TV Guide *and* The New Republic. *The essay that we reprint originally appeared in* The Saturday Review, *a magazine devoted to the arts and to social
issues.*

Television Advertising
The Splitting Image

A bride who looks scarcely fourteen whispers, "Oh,
Mom, I'm so *happy!*" while a doting family adjust her gown and veil
and a male voice croons softly, "A woman is a harder thing to be than
a man. She has more feelings to feel." The mitigation of these ex-
cesses, it appears, is a feminine deodorant called Secret, which allows our bride to approach the altar with security as well as emotion.

Eddie Albert, a successful actor turned pitchman, bestows his
attention on a lady with two suitcases, which prompt him to ask
her whether she has been on a journey. "No," she says, or words
to that effect, as she opens the suitcases. "My two boys bring back

their soiled clothes every weekend from college for me to wash." And she goes into the familiar litany of grease, chocolate, mud, coffee, and fruitjuice stains, which presumably record the life of the average American male from two to fifty. Mr. Albert compliments her on this happy device to bring her boys home every week and hands her a box of Biz, because "Biz *is* better."

Two women with stony faces meet cart to cart in a supermarket as one takes a jar of peanut butter off a shelf. When the other asks her in a voice of nitric acid why she takes that brand, the first snaps, "Because I'm choosy for my family!" The two then break into delighted smiles as Number Two makes Number One taste Jif for "mothers who are choosy."

If you have not come across these dramatic interludes, it is because you are not home during the day and do not watch daytime television. It also means that your intestinal tract is spared from severe assaults, your credibility unstrained. Or, for that matter, you may look at commercials like these every day and manage either to ignore them or find nothing—given the fact of advertising—wrong with them. In that case, you are either so brainwashed or so innocent that you remain unaware of what this daily infusion may have done and is doing to an entire people as the long-accepted adjunct of free enterprise and support of "free" television.

"Given the fact" and "long-accepted" are the key words here. Only socialists, communists, idealists (or the BBC) fail to realize that a mass television system cannot exist without the support of sponsors, that the massive cost of maintaining it as a free service cannot be met without the massive income from selling products. You have only to read of the unending struggle to provide financial support for public, noncommercial television for further evidence.

Besides, aren't commercials in the public interest? Don't they help you choose what to buy? Don't they provide needed breaks from programming? Aren't many of them brilliantly done, and some of them funny? And now, with the new sexual freedom, all those gorgeous chicks with their shining hair and gleaming smiles? And if you didn't have commercials taking up a good part of each hour, how on earth would you find enough program material to fill the endless space/time void?

Tick off the yesses and what have you left? You have, I venture to submit, these intangible but possibly high costs: the diminution of human worth, the infusion and hardening of social attitudes no longer valid or desirable, pervasive discontent, and psychic fragmentation.

Should anyone wonder why deception is not an included 8
detriment, I suggest that our public is so conditioned to promotion
as a way of life, whether in art or politics or products, that elements
of exaggeration or distortion are taken for granted. Nobody really
believes that a certain shampoo will get a certain swain, or that an
unclogged sinus can make a man a swinger. People are merely prepared to hope it will.

But the diminution of human worth is much more subtle and
just as pervasive. In the guise of what they consider comedy, the
producers of television commercials have created a loathsome gallery
of men and women patterned, presumably, on Mr. and Mrs.
America. Women liberationists have a major target in the commercial image of woman flashed hourly and daily to the vast majority.
There are, indeed, only four kinds of females in this relentless sales
procession: the gorgeous teen-age swinger with bouncing locks; the
young mother teaching her baby girl the right soap for skin care;
the middle-aged housewife with a voice like a power saw; and the
old lady with dentures and irregularity. All these women, to be sure,
exist. But between the swinging sex object and the constipated
granny there are millions of females never shown in commercials.
These are—married or single—intelligent, sensitive women who
bring charm to their homes, who work at jobs as well as lend grace
to their marriage, who support themselves, who have talents or hobbies or commitments, or who are skilled at their professions.

To my knowledge, as a frequent if reluctant observer, I know
of only one woman on a commercial who has a job; a comic plumb-
er pushing Comet. Funny, heh? Think of a dame with a plunger.

With this one representative of our labor force, which is well
over thirty million women, we are left with nothing but the full-
time housewife in all her whining glory: obsessed with whiter wash,
moister cakes, shinier floors, cleaner children, softer diapers, and
greaseless fried chicken. In the rare instances when these ladies are
not in the kitchen, at the washing machine, or waiting on hubby,
they are buying beauty soaps (fantasy, see?) to take home so that
their hair will have more body. Or out at the supermarket being
choosy.

If they were attractive in their obsessions, they might be bear- 12
able. But they are not. They are pushy, loud-mouthed, stupid,
and—of all things now—bereft of sexuality. Presumably, the argument in the tenets of advertising is that once a woman marries she
changes overnight from plaything to floor-waxer.

To be fair, men make an equivalent transition in commercials. The swinging male with the mod hair and the beautiful chick turns inevitably into the paunchy slob who chokes on his wife's cake. You will notice, however, that the voice urging the viewer to buy the product is nearly always male: gentle, wise, helpful, seductive. And the visible presence telling the housewife how to get shinier floors and whiter wash and lovelier hair is almost invariably a man: the Svengali in modern dress, the Trilby (if only she were!), his willing object.[1]

Woman, in short, is consumer first and human being fourth. A wife and mother who stays home all day buys a lot more than a woman who lives alone or who—married or single—has a job. The young girl hell-bent on marriage is the next most susceptible consumer. It is entirely understandable, then, that the potential buyers of detergents, foods, polishes, toothpastes, pills, and housewares are the housewives, and that the sex object spends more of *her* money on cosmetics, hair lotions, soaps, mouthwashes, and soft drinks.

Here we come, of course, to the youngest class of consumers, the swinging teen-agers so beloved by advertisers keen on telling them (and us) that they've "got a lot to live, and Pepsi's got a lot to give." This affords a chance to show a squirming, leaping, jiggling group of beautiful kids having a very loud high on rock and—of all things—soda pop. One of commercial TV's most dubious achievements, in fact, is the reinforcement of the self-adulation characteristic of the young as a group.

As for the aging female citizen, the less shown of her the better. She is useful for ailments, but since she buys very little of anything, not having a husband or any children to feed or house to keep, nor—of course—sex appeal to burnish, society and commercials have little place for her. The same is true, to be sure, of older men, who are handy for Bosses with Bad Breath or Doctors with Remedies. Yet, on the whole, men hold up better than women at any age—in life or on television. Lines on their faces are marks of distinction, while on women they are signatures of decay. 16

There is no question, in any case, that television commercials (and many of the entertainment programs, notably the soap serials that are part of the selling package) reinforce, like an insistent drill,

---

[1] In George Du Maurier's novel, *Trilby* (1894), Svengali mesmerizes Trilby and causes her to become a famous singer; when Svengali dies, Trilby loses her voice, dwindles, and soon dies. (Editors' note)

the assumption that a woman's only valid function is that of wife, mother, and servant of men: the inevitable sequel to her earlier function as sex object and swinger.

At a time when more and more women are at long last learning to reject these assumptions as archaic and demeaning, and to grow into individual human beings with a wide option of lives to live, the sellers of the nation are bent upon reinforcing the ancient pattern. They know only too well that by beaming their message to the Consumer Queen they can justify her existence as the housebound Mrs. America: dumber than dumb, whiter than white.

The conditioning starts very early: with the girl child who wants the skin Ivory soap has reputedly given her mother, with the nine-year-old who brings back a cake of Camay instead of the male deodorant her father wanted. (When she confesses that she bought it so she could be "feminine," her father hugs her, and, with the voice of a child-molester, whispers, "My little girl is growing up on me, huh.") And then, before long, comes the teen-aged bride who "has feelings to feel." It is the little boys who dream of wings, in an airplane commercial; who grow up (with fewer cavities) into the doers. Their little sisters turn into *Cosmopolitan* girls, who in turn become housewives furious that their neighbors' wash is cleaner than theirs.

There is good reason to suspect that this manic obsession with cleanliness, fostered, quite naturally, by the giant soap and detergent interests, may bear some responsibility for the cultivated sloppiness of so many of the young in their clothing as well as in their chosen hideouts. The compulsive housewife who spends more time washing and vacuuming and polishing her possessions than communicating to, or stimulating her children creates a kind of sterility that the young would instinctively reject. The impeccably tidy home, the impeccably tidy lawn are — in a very real sense — unnatural and confining. Yet the commercials confront us with broods of happy children, some of whom — believe it or not — notice the new fresh smell their clean, white sweatshirts exhale thanks to Mom's new "softener."

Some major advertisers, for that matter, can even cast a benign eye on the population explosion. In another Biz commercial, the genial Eddie Albert surveys with surprise a long row of dirty clothes heaped before him by a young matron. She answers his natural query by telling him gaily they are the products of her brood of eleven "with one more to come!" she adds as the twelfth turns up. "That's great!" says Mr. Albert, curdling the soul of Planned Parenthood and the future of this planet.

Who are, one cannot help but ask, the writers who manage to combine the sales of products with the selling-out of human dreams and dignity? Who people this cosmos of commercials with dolts and fools and shrews and narcissists? Who know so much about quirks and mannerisms and ailments and so little about life? So much about presumed wants and so little about crying needs?

Can women advertisers so demean their own sex? Or are there no women in positions of decision high enough to see that their real selves stand up? Do they not know, these extremely clever creators of commercials, what they could do for their audience even while they exploit and entertain them? How they could raise the levels of manners and attitudes while they sell their wares? Or do they really share the worm's-eye view of mass communication that sees, and addresses, only the lowest common denominator?

It can be argued that commercials are taken too seriously, that their function is merely to amuse, engage, and sell, and that they do this brilliantly. If that were all to this wheedling of millions, well and good. But it is not. There are two more fallouts from this chronic sales explosion that cannot be measured but that at least can be expected. One has to do with the continual celebration of youth at the expense of maturity. In commercials only the young have access to beauty, sex, and joy in life. What do older women feel, day after day, when love is the exclusive possession of a teen-age girl with a bobbing mantle of hair? What older man would not covet her in restless impotence? 24

The constant reminder of what is inaccessible must inevitably produce a subterranean but real discontent, just as the continual sight of things and places beyond reach has eaten deeply into the ghetto soul. If we are constantly presented with what we are not or cannot have, the dislocation deepens, contentment vanishes, and frustration reigns. Even for the substantially secure, there is always a better thing, a better way, to buy. That none of these things makes a better life may be consciously acknowledged, but still the desire lodges in the spirit, nagging and pulling.

This kind of fragmentation works in potent ways above and beyond the mere fact of program interruption, which is much of the time more of a blessing than a curse, especially in those rare instances when the commercial is deft and funny: the soft and subtle sell. Its overall curse, due to the large number of commercials in each hour, is that it reduces the attention span of a people already so conditioned to constant change and distraction that they cannot tolerate continuity in print or on the air.

Specifically, commercial interruption is most damaging during that 10 per cent of programing (a charitable estimate) most important to the mind and spirit of a people: news and public affairs, and drama. To many (and among these are network news producers), commercials have no place or business during the vital process of informing the public. There is something obscene about a newscaster pausing to introduce a deodorant or shampoo commercial between an airplane crash and a body count. It is more than an interruption; it tends to reduce news to a form of running entertainment, to smudge the edges of reality by treating death or disaster or diplomacy on the same level as household appliances or a new gasoline.

The answer to this would presumably be to lump the commer- 28
cials before and after the news or public affairs broadcasts—an answer unpalatable, needless to say, to the sponsors who support them.

The same is doubly true of that most unprofitable sector of television, the original play. Essential to any creative composition, whether drama, music or dance, are mood and continuity, both inseparable from form and meaning. They are shattered by the periodic intrusion of commercials, which have become intolerable to the serious artists who have deserted commercial television in droves because the system allows them no real freedom or autonomy. The selling comes first, the creation must accommodate itself. It is the rare and admirable sponsor who restricts or fashions his commercials so as to provide a minimum of intrusion or damaging inappropriateness.

If all these assumptions and imponderables are true, as many suspect, what is the answer or alleviation?

One is in the course of difficult emergence: the establishment of a public television system sufficiently funded so that it can give a maximum number of people an alternate diet of pleasure, enlightenment, and stimulation free from commercial fragmentation. So far, for lack of funds to buy talent and equipment, this effort has been in terms of public attention a distinctly minor operation. Even if public television should greatly increase its scope and impact, it cannot in the nature of things and through long public conditioning equal the impact and reach the size of audience now tuned to commercial television.

Enormous amounts of time, money, and talent go into commer- 32
cials. Technically they are often brilliant and innovative—the product

not only of the new skills and devices but of imaginative minds. A few of them are both funny and endearing. Who, for instance, will forget the miserable young man with the appalling cold, or the kids taught to use—as an initiation into manhood—a fork instead of a spoon with a certain spaghetti? Among the enlightened sponsors, moreover, are some who manage to combine an image of their corporation and their products with accuracy and restraint.

What has to happen to mass medium advertisers as a whole, and especially on TV, is a totally new approach to their function not only as sellers but as social influencers. They have the same obligation as the broadcast medium itself: not only to entertain but to reflect, not only to reflect but to enlarge public consciousness and human stature.

This may be a tall order, but it is a vital one at a time when Americans have ceased to know who they are and where they are going, and when all the multiple forces acting upon them are daily diminishing their sense of their own value and purpose in life, when social upheaval and social fragmentation have destroyed old patterns, and when survival depends on new ones.

If we continue to see ourselves as the advertisers see us, we have no place to go. Nor, I might add, has commercial broadcasting itself.

Topics for Discussion and Writing

1. What does "The Splitting Image" in the title mean? How does it begin to communicate Mannes's attitude toward television ads?
2. In the first three paragraphs, Mannes describes three commercials. How does she indicate her contempt for them?
3. In paragraph 9 Mannes lists "four kinds of females" pictured in daytime television commercials. She wrote the essay in 1970. If you tune in on daytime television today, what kinds of females do you see depicted? Are there still four kinds? The same four?
4. Mannes says (paragraph 17) that advertisements assume that "a woman's only valid function is that of wife, mother, and servant of men." What do television advertisers assume about a man's "valid function"?
5. In paragraph 20 Mannes suggests: "There is good reason to suspect that this manic obsession with cleanliness, fostered, quite naturally, by the giant soap and detergent interests, may bear some responsibility for the cultivated sloppiness of so many of the young in their clothing

as well as in their chosen hideouts." Is there really good reason to suspect this connection? Does Mannes sometimes make doubtful assumptions? If so, point them out.
6. Examine some of Mannes's metaphors, such as "There are two more fallouts from this chronic sales explosion" (paragraph 24), and evaluate them. Are they effective or strained?
7. Mannes writes about daytime television commercials; Richard Hawley (page 520) is primarily concerned with evening television shows. What concerns do they share about the effects of television?

Dolores Hayden

Dolores Hayden was born in New York City in 1945. She did her undergraduate work at Mount Holyoke, and she earned a master's degree in architecture at Harvard. Hayden has taught architecture at the University of California (Berkeley) and at Massachusetts Institute of Technology. She is especially concerned with the political and social implications of public spaces.

Advertisements, Pornography, and Public Space

Americans need to look more consciously at the ways in which the public domain is misused for spatial displays of gender stereotypes: These appear in outdoor advertising, and to a lesser extent in commercial displays, architectural decoration, and public sculpture. While the commercial tone and violence of the American city is often criticized, there is little analysis of the routine way that crude stereotypes appear in public, urban spaces as the staple themes of commercial art. Most Americans are accustomed to seeing giant females in various states of undress smiling and carressing products such as whiskey, food, and records. Male models also sell goods, but they are usually active and clothed—recent ad campaigns aimed at gay men seem to be the first major exception. Several geographers have established that men are most often shown doing active things, posed in the great outdoors; women are shown in reflective postures responding to male demands in interior spaces.

As the nineteenth-century sexual double standard is preserved by the urban advertising, many twentieth-century urban men behave as if good women are at home while bad ones adorn the billboards and travel on their own in urban space; at the same time, many urban women are encouraged to think of emotionlessness, war-mongering, and sexual inexhaustibility as natural to the Marlboro cowboy, war heroes' statues, and every other male adult.

This double standard is the result of advertising practices, graphic design, and urban design. Sanctioned by the zoning laws, billboards are approved by the same urban planning boards who will not permit child care centers or mother-in-law apartments in many residential districts. But the problem with billboards is not only aesthetic degradation. By presenting gender stereotypes in the form of nonverbal body language, fifty feet long and thirty feet high, billboards turn the public space of the city into a stage set for a drama starring enticing women and stern men.

Let us observe outdoor advertising and other urban design phenomena with similar effects, as they are experienced by two women on an urban commuting trip along the Sunset Strip in Los Angeles in June 1981. Standing on a street corner, the two women are waiting for a bus to go to work. The bus arrives, bearing a placard on the side advertising a local night club. It shows strippers doing their act, their headless bodies naked from neck to crotch except for a few blue sequins. The two women get on the bus and find seats for the ride along Sunset Boulevard. They look out the windows. As the bus pulls away, their heads appear incongruously above the voluptuous cardboard female bodies displayed on the side. They ride through a district of record company headquarters and film offices, one of the most prosperous in L.A.

Their first views reveal rows of billboards. Silent Marlboro man 4 rides the range; husky, khaki-clad Camel man stares at green hills; gigantic, uniformed professional athletes catch passes and hit home runs on behalf of booze. These are the male images. Then, on a billboard for whiskey, a horizontal blonde in a backless black velvet dress, slit to the thigh, invites men to "Try on a little Black Velvet." Next, a billboard shows a well-known actress, reclining with legs spread, who notes that avocadoes are only sixteen calories a slice. "Would this body lie to you?" she asks coyly, emphasizing that the body language which communicates blatant sexual availability is only meant to bring attention to her thin figure. Bo Derek offers a pastoral contrast garbed in nothing but a few bits of fur and leather, as she swings on a vine of green leaves, promoting *Tarzan, the Ape Man.*

Next the bus riders pass a club called the Body Shop that advertises "live, nude girls." Two reclining, realistic nudes, one in blue tones in front of a moonlight cityscape, one in orange sunshine tones, stretch their thirty-foot bodies along the sidewalk. This is the same neighborhood where a billboard advertising a Rolling Stones' record album called "Black and Blue" made news ten years ago. A manacled, spread-legged woman with torn clothes proclaimed "I'm Black and Blue from the Rolling Stones—and I love it!" Members of a group called Women Against Violence Against Women (WAVAW) arrived with cans of spray paint and climbed the scaffolding to make small, uneven letters of protest: "This is a crime against women." Demonstrations and boycotts eventually succeeded in achieving the removal of that image, but not in eliminating the graphic design problem. "Black and Blue" has been replaced by James Bond in a tuxedo, pistol in hand, viewed through the spread legs and buttocks of a giant woman in a bathing suit and improbably high heels, captioned "For Your Eyes Only."

When the two women get off the bus in Hollywood, they experience more gender stereotypes as pedestrians. First, they walk past a department store. In the windows mannequins suggest the prevailing ideals of sartorial elegance. The male torsos lean forward, as if they are about to clinch a deal. The female torsos, pin-headed, tip backward and sideways, at odd angles, as if they are about to be pushed over onto a bed. The themes of gender advertisements are trumpeted here in the mannequins' body language as well as on billboards. Next, the women pass an apartment building. Two neoclassical caryatids support the entablature over the front door. Their breasts are bared, their heads carry the load. They recall the architecture of the Erechtheum on the Acropolis in Athens, dating from the 5th century B.C., where the sculptured stone forms of female slaves were used as support for a porch in place of traditional columns and capitals. This is an ancient image of servitude.

After the neo-classical apartment house, the commuters approach a construction site. Here they are subject to an activity traditionally called "running the gauntlet," but referred to as "girl watching" by urban sociologist William H. Whyte. Twelve workers stop whatever they are doing, whistle, and yell: "Hey, baby!" The women put their heads down, and walk faster, tense with anger. The construction workers take delight in causing exactly this response: "You're cute when you're mad!" Whyte regards this type of behavior as charming, pedestrian fun in "Street Life," where he even takes pleasure in tracing its historic antecedents, but he has never been whistled at, hooted at, and had the dimensions of his body parts analyzed out loud on a public street.[1]

Finally, these women get to the office building where they work. It has two statues out front of women. Their bronze breasts culminate in erect nipples. After they pass this last erotic public display of women's flesh, sanctioned as fine art, they walk in the door to begin the day's work. Their journey has taken them through an urban landscape filled with images of men as sexual aggressors and women as submissive sexual objects.

The transient quality of male and female interaction in public streets makes the behavior provoked by billboards and their public design images particularly difficult to attack. Psychologist Erving Goffman has analyzed both print ads and billboards as *Gender Advertisements* because art directors use exaggerated body language to suggest that consumers buy not products but images of masculinity or femininity.[2] If passers-by are driving at fifty miles per hour, these gender cues cannot be subtle. In *Ways of Seeing,* art historian John Berger describes the cumulative problem that gender stereotypes in advertising create for woman as "split consciousness."[3] While many women guard themselves, some men assume that ogling is part of normal public life. Women are always wary, watching men watch them, and wondering if and when something is going to happen to them.

Urban residents also encounter even more explicit sexual images in urban space. Tawdry strip clubs, X-rated films, "adult" bookstores and sex shops are not uncommon sights. Pornographic video arcades are the next wave to come. Pornography is a bigger, more profitable industry in the United States than all legitimate film and record business combined.[4] It spills over into soft-porn, quasi-porn, and tasteless public imagery everywhere. In the midst of this sex-exploitation, if one sees a real prostitute, there is mild surprise. Yet soliciting is still a crime. Of course, the male customer of an adult

---

[1] William H. Whyte, "Street Life," *Urban Open Spaces* (Summer 1980), 2. For a more detailed critique of hassling: Lindsy Van Gelder, "The International Language of Street Hassling," *Ms.* 9 (May 1981),15–20, and letters about this article, *Ms.* (Sept. 1981); and Cheryl Benard and Edith Schlaffer, "The Man in the Street: Why He Harasses," *Ms.* 9 (May 1981), 18–19.
[2] Erving Goffman, *Gender Advertisements* (New York: Harper Colphon, 1976), 24–27; Nancy Henley, *Body Politics: Power, Sex, and Nonverbal Communication* (Englewood Cliffs, N.J.: Prentice-Hall, 1977), 30, Marianne Wex, *Let's Take Back Our Space* (Berlin: Movimento Druck, 1979).
[3] John Berger, et al., *Ways of Seeing* (Harmondsworth, England: BBC and Penguin, 1972), 45–64.
[4] Tom Hayden, *The American Future: New Visions Beyond Old Frontiers* (Boston: South End Press, 1980), 15.

prostitute is almost never arrested, but the graphic designer, the urban designer, and the urban planner never come under suspicion for their contributions to a commercial public landscape that preserves the sexual double standard in a brutal and vulgar way.

Feminist Laura Shapiro calls our society a "rape culture."[5] Adrienne Rich has written of "a world masculinity made unfit for women or men."[6] But surely most Americans do not consciously, deliberately accept public space given over to commercial exploitation, violence and harassment of women. Indeed, the success of the "Moral Majority" displays how a few activists were able to tap public concern effectively about commercialized sexuality, albeit in a narrow, antihumanist way. In contrast, the example of the Women's Christian Temperance Union under Frances Willard's leadership, and the parks movement under Olmsted's,[7] show religious idealism, love of nature, and concern for female safety can be activated into dynamic urban reform movements that enlarge domestic values into urban values, instead of diminishing them into domestic pieties.

Topics for Discussion and Writing

1. How does Hayden organize her material? Note, in particular, the narrative of two women traveling to work. What does this device add to the essay?

2. How does Hayden suggest that displays of gender stereotypes contribute to violence against women? What evidence supports this assumption?

3. In a paragraph or two, describe and analyze a magazine advertisement that promotes gender stereotypes or one that is aimed at gay men. (See Hayden's first paragraph.)

4. If you are familiar with a sculpture of a female figure in a public space in your neighborhood (perhaps in a plaza or in a public building), in a paragraph set forth what the image "says." Or, compare two sculptures, one of a female and one of a male, and explain what each says.

[5] Laura Shapiro, "Violence: The Most Obscene Fantasy," in Freeman, ed., *Women: A Feminist Perspective*, 469–73.

[6] *Ibid.*, 469.

[7] Frederick Law Olmsted (1822–1903) was an American landscape architect. Among his noble works are Central Park in Manhattan and Prospect Park in Brooklyn.

5. In an essay of two or three pages, describe and analyze two billboards, one featuring a man and one featuring a woman. How do they present the "gender stereotypes" that Hayden talks about? Your essay should respond to this question with a clearly formulated thesis sentence (see page 886).

Tipper Gore

Tipper Gore, co-founder of the Parents' Music Resource Center, is the author of a book about violence and obscenity in the arts. Her husband is a United States senator from Tennessee.

Curbing the Sexploitation Industry

I can't even count the times in the last three years, since I began to express my concern about violence and sexuality in rock music, that I have been called a prude, a censor, a music hater, even a book burner. So let me be perfectly clear: I detest censorship. I'm not advocating censorship but rather a candid and vigorous debate about the dangers posed for our children by what I call the "sexploitation industry."

We don't need to put a childproof cap on the world, but we do need to remind the nation that children live in it, too, and deserve respect and sensitive treatment.

When I launched this campaign in 1985 . . . I went to the source of the problem, sharing my concerns and proposals with the entertainment industry. Many producers were sympathetic. Some cooperated with my efforts. But others have been overtly hostile, accusing me of censorship and suggesting, unfairly, that my motives are political. This resistance and hostility has convinced me of the need for a two-pronged campaign, with equal effort from the entertainment industry and concerned parents. Entertainment producers must take the first step, by labeling sexually explicit material.

But the industry cannot be expected to solve the problem on its own. Parents should encourage producers to cooperate and praise   4 them when they do. Producers need to know that parents are aware of the issue and are reading their advisory labels. Above all, they need to know that somebody out there cares, that the community at large is not apathetic about the deep and lasting damage being done to our children.

What's at issue is not the occasional sexy rock lyric. What troubles—indeed, outrages—me is far more vicious: a celebration of the most gruesome violence, coupled with the explicit message that sado-masochism is the essence of sex. We're surrounded by examples—in rock lyrics, on television, at the movies and in rental videos. One major TV network recently aired a preview of a soap opera rape scene during a morning game show.

The newest craze in horror movies is something called the "teen slasher" film, and it typically depicts the killing, torture and sexual mutilation of women in sickening detail. Several rock groups now simulate sexual torture and murder during live performances. Others titillate youthful audiences with strippers confined in cages on stage and with half-naked dancers, who often act out sex with band members. Sexual brutality has become the common currency of America's youth culture and with it the pervasive degradation of women.

Why is this graphic violence dangerous? It's especially damaging for young children because they lack the moral judgment of adults. Many children are only dimly aware of the consequences of their actions, and, as parents know, they are excellent mimics. They often imitate violence they see on TV, without necessarily understanding what they are doing or what the consequences might be. One 5-year-old boy from Boston recently got up from watching a teen-slasher film and stabbed a 2-year-old girl with a butcher knife. He didn't mean to kill her (and luckily he did not). He was just imitating the man in the video.

Nor does the danger end as children grow older. National health 8 officials tell us that children younger than teen-agers are apt to react to excessive violence with suicide, satanism, drug and alcohol abuse. Even grown-ups are not immune. One series of studies by researchers at the University of Wisconsin found that men exposed to films in which women are beaten, butchered, maimed and raped were significantly desensitized to the violence. Not only did they express less sympathy for the victims, they even approved of lesser penalties in hypothetical rape trials.

Sado-masochistic pornography is a kind of poison. Like most poisons, it probably cannot be totally eliminated, but it certainly could be labeled for what it is and be kept away from those who are most vulnerable. The largest record companies have agreed to this—in principle at least. In November 1985, the Recording Industry Association of America adopted my proposal to alert parents by having producers either put warning labels on records with explicitly sexual lyrics or display the lyrics on the outside of the record jackets. Since then, some companies have complied in good faith, although others have not complied at all.

This is where we parents must step in. We must let the industry know we're angry. We must press for uniform voluntary compliance with labeling guidelines. And we must take an active interest at home in what our children are watching and listening to. After all, we can hardly expect that the labels or printed lyrics alone will discourage young consumers.

Some parents may want to write to the record companies. Others can give their support to groups like the Parent Teacher Association, which have endorsed the labeling idea. All of us can use our purchasing power. We have more power than we think, and we must use it. For the sake of our children, we simply can't afford to slip back into apathy.

My concern for the health and welfare of children has nothing 12 to do with politics: It is addressed to conservatives and liberals alike. Some civil libertarians believe it is wrong even to raise these questions—just as some conservatives believe that the Government should police popular American culture. I reject both these views. I have no desire to restrain artists or cast a "chill" over popular culture. But I believe parents have First Amendment rights, too.

The fate of the family, the dignity of women, the mental health of children—these concerns belong to everyone. We must protect our children with choice, not censorship. Let's start working in our communities to forge a moral consensus for the 1990s. Children need our help, and we must summon the courage to examine the culture that shapes their lives.

Topics for Discussion and Writing

1. Analyze and evaluate Gore's opening paragraph.
2. Gore says she is not advocating censorship. In a sentence or two state what she *is* advocating. If you agree with her position, what can you add to it? If you disagree, what are the grounds for your disagreement?
3. Consider the songs of some prominent singer, perhaps Madonna, Sade, Michael Jackson, or Bruce Springsteen. Do you find them offensive in

any way? If so, explain. If not, explain why parents should not be distressed by the music of the person you have selected.

4.   Gore concentrates on rock lyrics, movies, and soap operas. Where else in our society are we given images of violence and of the degradation of women? Do you think that parents can protect their children from such images? If so, how?

Lynne Layton

Lynne Layton is a clinical psychologist and lecturer in Women's Studies at Harvard. This essay originally appeared in The Boston Globe.

What's Really behind the Madonna-Bashing?

I became a Madonna watcher largely because I was intrigued by what professional Madonna-watchers had to say about her. It's clear to me now that the way Madonna is written and spoken about is every bit as interesting as Madonna herself. Lately, there's been an increasing hostility toward Madonna in the press, a hostility that has a gendered edge and that often seems greater than its subject would warrant.

The September issue of *Spin* magazine called Madonna a "media whore," and that was months before the release of "Justify My Love." Also months before, on the occasion of Madonna's last visit to Boston for The Blonde Ambition Tour, she was trashed in the *Globe* by Mike Barnicle and David B. Wilson and sharply criticized in the *Herald* by Margery Eagan. Last week, she was trashed by Ed Siegel and more calmly critiqued by Ellen Goodman. Writers, talk-show hosts, anchor people of both genders seem honestly confused as to what all the fuss is about, little realizing that it is they who create much of the fuss and they who define what aspects of the phenomenon are going to be talked about.

So what is all the fuss this time around? Madonna, who I am convinced sincerely believes in the '60s philosophy that sexual freedom and honesty are the key to liberation (a philosophy that is itself a legacy of most 20th-century avant-garde movements), puts out a video that explores all varieties of sexual fantasy and experience, and the media goes berserk. MTV bans it but justifies their love by doing a two-day tribute to Madonna the weekend before the censored video is shown on "Nightline." Serious-minded media people are outraged that "Nightline" justifies this video by devoting a show to it.

What is the fuss about? Censorship? Only Madonna was talk- 4 ing about that. Madonna was absolutely correct to assert that MTV shows videos 24 hours a day that are violent and degrading to women—and there is not a peep about it in the popular press. Forrest Sawyer thought she was being facetious to suggest that MTV have a violent hour and a degradation-of-women hour—he's obviously never watched MTV.

And let's not think for a moment that this phenomenon is limited to MTV. As Jean Kilbourne's slide show on women and advertising, "Still Killing Us Softly," painfully demonstrates, ads in mainstream magazines (yes, the ones that litle kids can leaf through in any convenience store) contain sadomasochistic, violent images, most of which feature women as victims. (See, for example, Kikit ads.) In fact, as critic Kathy Myers suggests, sadistic and violent imagery from the world of art photography regularly enters fashion magazines via the work of male photographers who inhabit both worlds, such as Helmut Newton.

What is intriguing is that few critics have anything to say about issues of censorship or about Madonna's work, so caught up are they in how much money she makes and whether she's just doing what she does for money and publicity. It would be legitimate to question Madonna's view that the more open we are as a culture about sexuality, the less prey we will be to teen-age pregnancy and the spread of AIDS. It would be legitimate to critique her for her own brand of blasphemy; although rarely commented upon, most TV newscasts have prominently displayed the clip from "Like A Prayer," in which Madonna, not content with the adjunct status of bearing Christ's mother's name, cuts her hands in such a way as to embody herself as Christ. Is this what outrages? That a woman would portray herself as Christ? Perhaps—but it hasn't been mentioned.

No one has commented on what I take to be a direct attack on the church in "Justify My Love": As Madonna sings "Poor is the man whose pleasures depend on the permission of another," the video image is of Christ on the cross. The video ends with these same words written on the screen. Madonna's crusade for sexual liberation seems intimately connected with her sense that the church has set itself up as the arbiter of what pleasures are and are not permissible. And censors as well as media critics are taking on the same role as the church.

Perhaps one should examine the ways we are brought up in 8 church and family to understand why so much of contemporary popular and avant-garde art presents erotic, violent, and sado-masochistic images alongside religious images. Fantasies of domination and submission, victims and violators are not born of watching MTV; they come from the hurts and humiliations and inequities that take place right within our most cherished institutions—family, school, religion.

In the fervor to criticize Madonna for being a slut, for being purely concerned with image and money, critics do not even mention, let alone discuss seriously, what she is doing in her video. So I take it that what the fuss may really be about is a woman, a woman who runs her own show, who is enormously popular with young women and girls, a woman who dares unabashedly to display her sexuality and her sexual fantasies before the public, who dares visibly to enjoy it, and who dares to make a lot of money from it.

I suggest that what is at issue is her gender, because male stars such as Prince have done the same thing as Madonna for years—with not a peep from the press.

Take a look at the rhetoric of some of the male critics writing about her, and what you will see is an excess of anger that is, in my opinion, not commensurate to its subject matter. You'll see Mike Barnicle wondering "if they make a shoe big enough to fit over her fat, sick head?" You'll see David B. Wilson talking about her "cold, deliberate, premeditated, apparently interminable, eventually repulsive profanity that seems to capture the imagination of the American mob." You'll see and hear male critics repeat so often how much money she makes that you begin to wonder what feelings of inadequacy, envy, or competition Madonna's success evokes. You'll see Ed Siegel back up his own view that Madonna is an uninteresting conformist and money-grubber with a quote from Bret Easton Ellis—which seems in ironic bad taste coming just a few weeks after the announcement that Ellis' current book was dropped by Knopf because it contained excessive violence toward women.

And this brings us back to the question Madonna posed 12 on "Nightline," which, in my view is the relevant one: Why are images of degradation and violence toward women OK, almost mainstream, and images of two women or two men kissing taboo? Why is it that only Madonna was raising this question, not her critics?

This is indeed a hypocritical culture, and the hypocrisy has everything to do with the unequal gender relations and with an open distaste for any version of femininity that threatens not to know its place.

Topics for Discussion and Writing

1. In paragraph 5 Layton says that "mainstream magazines . . . contain sadomasochistic, violent images, most of which feature women as victims." Is this true? (Check through a few "mainstream magazines" to verify your response. If you do find such images, bring a few copies of at least one to class for class discussion.)

2. If you are familiar with Madonna's "Justify My Love," do you agree with Layton that Madonna is presenting "a direct attack on the church"?

3. In paragraphs 9–10 Layton says that Madonna has dared "to display her sexuality and her sexual fantasies before the public," just as Prince and other male stars have done. Do you agree that Madonna and Prince are in this respect alike? If you disagree, set forth the grounds of your disagreement.

4. If you already had some sense of Madonna, did this essay further your understanding of her? If you did not have much sense of her, do you now feel that you have read a reliable introduction? Explain.

5. In paragraph 8 Layton says that "erotic, violent, and sadomasochistic images" may have their roots in "our most cherished institutions—family, school, religion." How might you support or rebut this assertion?

Stephen King

Stephen King, with 50 million copies of his books in print, is one of America's most popular authors. King was born in Portland, Maine, in 1947. After graduating from the University of Maine he taught English in high school until he was able to devote himself full-time to writing. In addition to writing stories and novels—some of which have been made into films—he has written Danse Macabre, *a book that, like the essay we reprint here, discusses the appeal of horror.*

Why We Crave Horror Movies

I think that we're all mentally ill; those of us outside the asylums only hide it a little better—and maybe not all that much better, after all. We've all known people who talk to themselves, people who sometimes squinch their faces into horrible grimaces when they believe no one is watching, people who have some hysterical fear—of snakes, the dark, the tight place, the long drop . . . and, of course, those final worms and grubs that are waiting so patiently underground.

When we pay our four or five bucks and seat ourselves at tenth-row center in a theater showing a horror movie, we are daring the nightmare.

Why? Some of the reasons are simple and obvious. To show that we can, that we are not afraid, that we can ride this roller coaster. Which is not to say that a really good horror movie may not surprise a scream out of us at some point, the way we may scream when the roller coaster twists through a complete 360 or plows through a lake at the bottom of the drop. And horror movies, like roller coasters, have always been the special province of the young; by the time one turns 40 or 50, one's appetite for double twists or 360-degree loops may be considerably depleted.

We also go to re-establish our feelings of essential normality; the 4 horror movie is innately conservative, even reactionary. Freda Jackson as the horrible melting woman in *Die, Monster, Die!* confirms for us that no matter how far we may be removed from the beauty of a Robert Redford or a Diana Ross, we are still light-years from true ugliness.

And we go to have fun.

Ah, but this is where the ground starts to slope away, isn't it? Because this is a very peculiar sort of fun, indeed. The fun comes from seeing others menaced—sometimes killed. One critic has suggested that if pro football has become the voyeur's version of combat, then the horror film has become the modern version of the public lynching.

It is true that the mythic, "fairy-tale" horror film intends to take away the shades of gray. . . . It urges us to put away our more civilized and adult penchant for analysis and to become children again, seeing things in pure blacks and whites. It may be that horror movies provide psychic relief on this level because this invitation to lapse into simplicity, irrationality and even outright madness is extended so rarely. We are told we may allow our emotions a free rein . . . or no rein at all.

If we are all insane, then sanity becomes a matter of degree. If   8
your insanity leads you to carve up women like Jack the Ripper or the Cleveland Torso Murderer, we clap you away in the funny farm (but neither of those two amateur-night surgeons was ever caught, heh-heh-heh); if, on the other hand, your insanity leads you only to talk to yourself when you're under stress or to pick your nose on your morning bus, then you are left alone to go about your business . . . though it is doubtful that you will ever be invited to the best parties.

The potential lyncher is in almost all of us (excluding saints, past and present; but then, most saints have been crazy in their own ways), and every now and then, he has to be let loose to scream and roll around in the grass. Our emotions and our fears form their own body, and we recognize that it demands its own exercise to maintain proper muscle tone. Certain of these emotional muscles are accepted—even exalted—in civilized society; they are, of course, the emotions that tend to maintain the status quo of civilization itself. Love, friendship, loyalty, kindness—these are all the emotions that we applaud, emotions that have been immortalized in the couplets of Hallmark cards and in the verses (I don't dare call it poetry) of Leonard Nimoy.

When we exhibit these emotions, society showers us with positive reinforcement; we learn this even before we get out of diapers. When, as children, we hug our rotten little puke of a sister and give her a kiss, all the aunts and uncles smile and twit and cry, "Isn't he the sweetest little thing?" Such coveted treats as chocolate-covered graham crackers often follow. But if we deliberately slam the rotten little puke of a sister's fingers in the door, sanctions follow—angry remonstrance from parents, aunts and uncles; instead of a chocolate-covered graham cracker, a spanking.

But anticivilization emotions don't go away, and they demand periodic exercise. We have such "sick" jokes as, "What's the difference between a truckload of bowling balls and a truckload of dead babies?" (You can't unload a truckload of bowling balls with a pitchfork . . . a joke, by the way, that I heard originally from a ten-year-old). Such a joke may surprise a laugh or a grin out of us even as we recoil, a possibility that confirms the thesis: If we share a brotherhood of man, then we also share an insanity of man. None of which is intended as a defense of either the sick joke or insanity but merely as an explanation of why the best horror films, like the best fairy tales, manage to be reactionary, anarchistic, and revolutionary all at the same time.

The mythic horror movie, like the sick joke, has a dirty job to do.   12
It deliberately appeals to all that is worst in us. It is morbidity unchained, our most base instincts let free, our nastiest fantasies realized . . . and it all happens, fittingly enough, in the dark. For those reasons, good liberals often shy away from horror films. For myself, I like to see the most aggressive of them — *Dawn of the Dead*, for instance — as lifting a trap door in the civilized forebrain and throwing a basket of raw meat to the hungry alligators swimming around in that subterranean river beneath.

Why bother? Because it keeps them from getting out, man. It keeps them down there and me up here. It was Lennon and McCartney who said that all you need is love, and I would agree with that.

As long as you keep the gators fed.

Topics for Discussion and Writing

1. In paragraph 6 King, paraphrasing an unnamed critic, suggests that "the horror film has become the modern version of the public lynching." In your opinion, why did some people find excitement in a lynching? Does the horror film offer somewhat similar excitement(s)?

2. King suggests in paragraph 11 that we have within us a stock of "anticivilization emotions [that] don't go away, and they demand periodic exercise." What, if any, evidence are you aware of that supports this view?

3. In paragraph 11 King tells a joke about dead babies. He suggests that jokes of this sort "may surprise a laugh or a grin out of us even as we recoil." Analyze your own response to the joke, or to similar jokes. Did you laugh, or grin? Or was your response utterly different? If so, what was it?

4. In paragraphs 12 and 13 King says that horror movies serve a valuable social purpose. Do you think he has proved his point? What are the strengths (if any) and the weaknesses (if any) of his argument?
5. Read Tipper Gore's essay (page 541). Then respond to King's argument as you think she might. Or compare Hawley (page 520) with King on sick humor.

Gish Jen

In 1983 Gish Jen received a master of Fine Arts degree from the Iowa Writer's Workshop. She has published stories in The Atlantic Monthly *and elsewhere, and in 1991 published her first novel. The essay that we reprint appeared originally in* The New York Times *in 1991.*

Challenging the Asian Illusion

For a very long time, when people talked about race, they talked about black America and white America. Where did that put Asian-Americans?

Spike Lee touches on the Asian-American dilemma in "Do the Right Thing" when the Korean grocer, afraid of having his business attacked by rioting blacks, yells: "I not white! I black! Like you! Same!"

Unlike the grocer, though, my family and I identified mostly with white America, which, looking back, was partly wishful thinking, partly racism and partly an acknowledgment that, whatever else we did face, at least we did not have to contend with the legacy of slavery.

Yet we were not white. We were somehow borderline; we did 4 not quite belong. Now, not only has the number of Asian-Americans in this country doubled in the last decade, we are growing faster than any other ethnic group. How meaningful it will ultimately prove to lump the Hmong with the Filipinos with the Japanese remains to be seen. Still, to be perceived as a significant minority is a development for which I, at least, am grateful.

There is a sense that to be perceived at all, a minority group must be plagued with problems—a problem in itself, to be sure. But what about our problems—were they significant enough to warrant attention? Who cared, for instance, that we did not see outselves reflected on movie screens? Until recently, it did not occur to most of us that the absence of Asian and Asian-American images was symptomatic of a more profound invisibility.

Today, though, it is shocking to behold how little represented we have been, and in how blatantly distorted a manner. There has been some progress now that more Asian-Americans like David Henry Hwang and Philip Kan Gotanda have begun to write for stage and screen: also, some recent Caucasian-directed television shows, including "Shannon's Deal" and "Davis Rules," are breaking new ground.

For the most part, however, film, television and theater, from "Miss Saigon" to "Teen-Age Mutant Ninja Turtles," have persisted in perpetuating stereotypes. Mostly this has been through the portrayal of Asian characters; Asian-Americans have rarely been represented at all.

This invisibility is essentially linked to the process by which 8 fanciful ideas are superimposed onto real human beings. How are everyday Asians transformed into mysterious "Orientals," after all, if not by distance? Americans can be led to believe anything about people living in a far-off land, or even a distinctly unfamiliar place like Chinatown. It is less easy with a kid next door who plays hockey and air guitar.

Over the years, Asians have been the form onto which white writers have freely projected their fears and desires. That this is a form of colonialism goes almost without saying; it can happen only when the people whose images are appropriated are in no position to object.

For certainly anyone would object to being identified with a figure as heartlessly evil and preternaturally cunning as Fu Manchu, a brilliant but diabolical force set on taking over the world. The character's prototype was invented in 1916, in a climate of hysteria over the "threat" that Asian workers posed to native labor. We behold its likeness in figures like Odd Job in "Goldfinger" (1964); his influence can be seen in depictions of Chinatown as a den of iniquity in movies like "The Year of the Dragon" (1985) and "True Believer" (1988). "Chinatown" (1974) used it as a symbol of all that is rotten in the city of Los Angeles, despite the fact that no Chinese person had much to do with the evil turnings of the plot.

What fuels these images is xenophobia. In periods of heightened political tension, they tend to recur; in more secure times, they are replaced by more benign images. Charlie Chan for example, arose in 1926, shortly after the last of a series of laws restricting Chinese immigration had been passed and the "Yellow Peril" seemed to be over.

The benign images, however, are typically no more tied to reality than their malign counterparts; vilification is merely replaced by glorification. The aphorism-spouting Charlie Chan (played by Warner Oland, a white actor in yellowface) is godlike in his intelligence, the original Asian whiz kid; you would not be surprised to hear he had won a Westinghouse prize in his youth. More message than human being, he recalls the ever-smiling black mammy that proliferated during Reconstruction: Don't worry, he seems to say, no one's going to go making any trouble.

One Good Guy, But He's a Rat

In today's social climate of multi-culturalism, movies like "Rambo," which made the Vietnamese out to be so much cannon fodder, seem to be behind us, at least temporarily. Instead, reflecting the American preoccupation with Japan, there is "Teen-Age Mutant Ninja Turtle." Here the Japanese enemy gang leader is once again purely demonic and bestial, a hairless, barbaric figure who wears a metal claw for ornament. What gives the movie a more contemporary stamp is the fact that Master Splinter, the good-guy rodent leader of the Mutant Turtles, is also Japanese. It is as if Fu Manchu and Charlie Chan were cast into a single movie—seemingly presenting a balanced view of the Japanese as good and bad.

But the fact that the "good" Japanese is a rat means that slanty eyes belong to the bad guy. And as individuals the Japanese are still portrayed as sub- or superhuman, possessing fabulous abilities and arcane knowledge that center on (another contemporary twist) martial arts.

Is it a sign of a fitness-crazed age that this single aspect of Asian culture is so enthralling? So perennially popular are movies like "The Karate Kid" (1984) and this year's "Iron and Silk" that one begins to wonder whether Aisan males pop out of the womb doing mid-air gyrations. The audience marvels: How fantastic, these people! Meanwhile, the non-Asian roles are the more recognizably human ones.

Real humanity similarly eludes the Asian characters in the Broadway play "Miss Saigon." As in "Teen-Age Mutant Ninja Turtles," they are either simply evil or simply good, with the possible exception of the Engineer (Jonathan Pryce) who, loathsome as he is, seems more self-interested than evil. Half-white, he seems to be, correspondingly, halfway human. In contrast, Thuy, the major Vietnamese character, is portrayed as so inhuman that he would kill a child in cold blood. Is this what Communists do? Asians? When Kim (Lea Salonga), the heroine, shoots her erstwhile loyal fiancé, the audience applauds, feeling no more for him than for Rambo's victims. The subhuman brute has got what he deserved.

At the same time, the audience does feel, horribly, for Kim, who has been forced to pull the trigger and now must live with blood on her hands. What a fate for a paragon of virtue! She is Madame Butterfly unpinned from her specimen board and let loose to flutter around the room again: abandoned, virtuous, she waits faithfully for her white lover, only to discover that he has married. He returns for his son (it's always a son); she kills herself.

Isn't this a beautiful story? Annette Kolodny, a feminist critic, has observed that when the Western mind feels free to remake a place and people according to its liking, it conceives of that place and people as a woman. This has been nowhere so true as in the case of the "Orient," and correspondingly, no woman, it seems, has been portrayed as more exquisitely feminine than an Oriental.

Take any play in which both Oriental and Caucasian women appear—say, "South Pacific"—and it is immediately obvious which is more delicate, more willing to sacrifice for her man, more docile. Never mind that there are in the world real women who might object to having their image appropriated for such use.

But of course, women do object. I object, especially since the only possible end for this invented Butterfly is suicide. For how would the white characters go on with their lives?

It is an irony of stage history that a musical as conventional in   20
its use of the Butterfly story should follow so closely on the heels of another play that turns the same narrative on its head. The 1988 Broadway play "M. Butterfly" offers not just the "beautiful story" itself, but also a white man who has been taken in by it. So enthralled is René Gallimard by the idea of his Butterfly, the projection of his own desire, that he forgets there is a real person—Song Liling, a man and a spy—upon which his notions are imposed.

Ultimately, "M. Butterfly" makes clear that for the "game" of Orientalism, there is a price to pay, not only by those whose images are appropriated, but by the appropriators.

Do stereotypes lurk even here? It might seem so, but would a stereotype wonder, as does Song Liling, whether he and Gallimard might not continue on together, even after the truth has been revealed. When Song asks, "What do I do now?" he conveys how helpless he is too, how powerless. This is a human being. That he should be is maybe not so surprising, given that he was invented by David Henry Hwang, an Asian-American.

One Step Forward: Spoof the Stereotype

Are Asian-American writers the only hope for new forms of characterization? Perhaps, when even directors as intelligent as Woody Allen portray Chinatown as having opium dens. In his most recent movie, "Alice," Mr. Allen's recycling of an Aisan sage is likewise problematic. Could he not have created a spoof of a sage—a character who winked at the stereotype even as he played it—without any damage to the plot?

Spoofing the stereotype was the strategy taken last spring in 24 an episode of the now-cancelled television series "Shannon's Deal" that featured a pony-tailed Korean immigrant. Here were clear signs for hope: the immigrant at first appeared to be an all-knowing Charlie Chan, but turned out to be at once less and more. At moments way ahead of the investigator Shannon, he proved to be way behind at others; he knew all the aphorisms but had trouble passing the bar exam, and discussed his own tendency to drop pronouns.

Other signs of change include a jeans-wearing, face-making, poker-playing Japanese character in "Davis Rules." Unexotic Mrs. Yamagami (Tamayo Otsuki) even shows a sense of humor, characterizing a co-worker as "a rebel without a car." Similarly, in "Twin Peaks," the figure of Jocelyn (Joan Chen), evil as she is, does not stand in contrast to the good, white characters the way a female Fu Manchu—a dragon lady—might. Neither, certainly, is she any Butterfly. She is, within the show's offbeat context, just one of the gang.

All these characters are heartening, since they are not simply unexamined projections onto the Asian race. Still, as might be expected, directors like Wayne Wang and playwrights like Philip Kan Gotanda are not only more likely to present Asian-Americans in their work, but to present Asian-Americans who are not of the immigrant generation. In Mr. Wang's movie "Dim Sum" (1987) and Mr. Gotanda's film "The Wash" (1988), Asian-Americans are presented in far greater complexity than is typical of the mainstream media;

the characters seem more captured than constructed, more like flesh-and-blood than cartoons. This is partly a matter of their status as protagonists rather than peripheral figures.

And more images are needed if the few that exist now are not to become new stereotypes. Since the much publicized success of Connie Chung, for example, Asian-American anchorwomen have become a staple in films like "Year of the Dragon" and "Moscow on the Hudson." With real-life repercussions: the San Francisco newscaster Emerald Yeh tells of an interview with CNN, during which she was more or less asked why she couldn't do her hair like Connie Chung's.

Ridiculous, right? And yet such is the power of image. We would   28
not have to insist that images reflect life, except that all too often we ask life to reflect images.

Topics for Discussion and Writing

1. Until recently, Jen says (in paragraph 4), Asians and Asian-Americans did not care that they were not "reflected on movie screens," but in paragraph 6 she calls the same invisibility (or distortion) "shocking." Does she account for the change in attitude? Can you?

2. Jen argues that Asians, for the most part, have been stereotyped in films. How might you construct a counterargument that Caucasians too have been stereotyped, for the most part? What evidence might you offer?

3. In paragraph 23, Jen asks "Are Asian-American writers the only hope for new forms of characterization?" How does she answer this question? How would you?

4. In her final paragraph, what is Jen's point about the power of images? What does she seem to suggest that we do?

5. Describe and analyze the depiction of an Asian or Asian-American in a recent film, TV show, comic strip, or print advertisement.

Woody Allen

Woody Allen, born in Brooklyn in 1935, began writing comic monologues while he was in high school. He soon wrote for Sid Caesar and Art Carney, and then developed a nightclub act of his own. Although he still publishes an occasional story in The New York-er, *he is now engaged chiefly in writing and directing films and in acting in them.*

The Colorization of Films Insults Artists and Society

In the world of potent self-annihilation, famine and AIDS, terrorists and dishonest public servants and quack evangelists and contras and Sandinistas and cancer, does it really matter if some kid snaps on his TV and happens to see The Maltese Falcon in color? Especially if he can simply dial the color out and choose to view it in its original black and white?

I think it does make a difference and the ramifications of what's called colorization are not wonderful to contemplate. Simply put, the owners of thousands of classic American black and white films believe that there would be a larger public for the movies, and consequently more money, if they were reissued in color. Since they have computers that can change such masterpieces as *Citizen Kane* and *City Lights* and *It's A Wonderful Life* into color, it has become a serious problem for anyone who cares about these movies and has feelings about our image of ourselves as a culture.

I won't comment about the quality of the color. It's not good, but probably it will get better. Right now it's like elevator music. It has no soul. All faces are rendered with the same deadening pleasance. The choices of what colors people should be wearing or what colors rooms should be (all crucial artistic decisions in making a film) are left to caprices and speculations by computer technicians who are not qualified to make those choices.

Probably false, but not worth debating here, is the claim that 4 young people won't watch black and white. I would think they would, judging from the amount of stylish music videos and MTV ads that are done in black and white, undoubtedly after market research. The fact that audiences of all ages have been watching Charlie Chaplin, Humphrey Bogart, Jimmy Stewart, Fred Astaire—in fact, all the stars and films of the so-called Golden Age of Hollywood—in black and white for decades with no diminution of joy also makes me wonder about these high claims for color. Another point the coloroids make is that one can always view the original if one prefers. The truth is, however, that in practical terms, what will happen is that the color versions will be aired while token copies of the original black and white will lie around preserved in a vault, unpromoted and unseen.

Another aspect of the problem that one should mention (although it is not the crucial ground on which I will make my stand) is that American films are a landmark heritage that do our nation proud all over the world, and should be seen as they were intended to be. One would wince at defacing great buildings or paintings, and, in the case of movies, what began as a popular entertainment has, like jazz music, developed into a serious art form. Now, someone might ask: "Is an old Abbott and Costello movie art? Should it be viewed in the same way as *Citizen Kane?*" The answer is that it should be protected, because all movies are entitled to their personal integrity and, after all, who knows what future generations will regard as art works of our epoch?

Yet another question: "Why were directors not up in arms about cutting films for television or breaking them up for commercials, insulting them with any number of technical alterations to accommodate the television format?" The answer is that directors always hated these assaults on their work but were powerless to stop them. As in life, one lives with the first few wounds, because to do battle is an overwhelmingly time-consuming and pessimistic prospect.

Still, when the assaults come too often, there is a revolution. The outrage of seeing one's work transformed into color is so dramatically appalling, so "obvious"—as against stopping sporadically for commercials—that this time all the directors, writers and actors chose to fight.

But let me get to the real heart of the matter and to why I think 8 the issue is not merely one that affronts the parties directly involved but has a larger meaning. What's at stake is a moral issue and how our culture chooses to define itself. No one should be able to alter an artist's work in any way whatsoever, for any reason, without the artist's consent. It's really as simple as that.

John Huston has made it clear that he doesn't want *The Maltese Falcon* seen in color. This is his right as an artist and certainly must be his choice alone. Nor would I want to see my film *Manhattan* in color. Not if it would bring in 10 times the revenue. Not if all the audiences in the world begged or demanded to see it that way.

I believe the people who are coloring movies have contempt for the audience by claiming, in effect, that viewers are too stupid and too insensitive to appreciate black and white photography—that they must be given, like infants or monkeys, bright colors to keep them amused. They have contempt for the artsit, caring little for the moral right these directors have over their own creations. And, finally, they have contempt for society because they help define it as one that chooses to milk every last dollar out of its artists' work, even if it means mutilating the work and humiliating the culture's creative talent.

This is how we are viewed around the world and how we will be viewed by future generations. Most civilized governments abroad, realizing that their society is at least as much shaped and identified by its artists as by its businessmen, have laws to protect such things from happening. In our society, merchants are willing to degrade anything or anyone so long it brings in a financial profit. Allowing the colorization of films is a good example of our country's regard for its artists, and why I think the issue of moral rights requires legislative help and protection.

The recent Federal copyright decision says that if a human being uses a certain minimum amount of creativity in coloring a black and white film, the new color version is a separate work that can be copyrighted. In short, if a man colors *Citizen Kane*, it becomes a new movie that can be copyrighted. This must be changed. How? By making sure that Representative Richard A. Gephardt's film integrity bill is passed. It would legalize the moral rights of film artists and, in the process, make colorization without consent illegal.   12

It is, after all, a very short step to removing the score from *Gone With the Wind* and replacing it with a rock score under the mistaken notion that it will render it more enjoyable to young people.

Topics for Discussion and Writing

1. We find Allen's argumentative strategy worth analyzing. But first, restate in a sentence or two the point he is arguing and the occasion that prompted it. (Note that Allen reports the occasion in his next-to-last paragraph.) Now look at Allen's opening paragraph. What does it assume about his audience? What does Allen imply about himself in relation to his audience?

2. In paragraph 2 Allen contrasts two groups. How does he make sure that you will identify yourself with one group and not with the other?

3. In paragraph 3, what words or phrases strike you as particularly lively or persuasive?
4. In paragraph 4 Allen says that "the claim that young people won't watch black and white" is "not worth debating." What does the rest of the paragraph do? Again, what particularly effective words or phrases underscore the point?
5. To what emotions does Allen appeal in paragraph 5?
6. Now consider the substance of his argument. In paragraph 8 Allen says, "No one should be able to alter an artist's work in any way whatsoever, for any reason, without the artist's consent. It's really as simple as that." Do you agree? If so, would you agree to the following propositions? Why or why not?

    a. Producers should be prohibited from showing on television films intended for the theater, unless the producers have the consent of the film director.
    b. Similarly, filmmakers should be prohibted from filming a novel, play, opera, or ballet without the consent of the author or composer. If the author or composer is dead, well, that's unfortunate, but the work cannot be adapted to a film.

    What parallel strictures might govern the display of objects in museums, reproductions of works of art, and the translation of classic works of literature?
7. Finally, consider some black and white film that you admire. What do you think would be lost (or gained) by colorization? (If you have seen the original black and white film and also a colorized version, of course you are in a good position to make comparisons. But in any case you can make a "thought-experiment." You might, for example, imagine a colorized version of Woody Allen's *Manhattan*.)

James H. Cone

James H. Cone, Professor of Theology at Union Seminary, New York, and Lecturer in Systematic Theology at Woodstock College, is regarded as the founder of Black Theology, a movement that has had a profound influence not only in the United States but also in South Africa and in South America, where he influenced the founders of Liberation Theology. Cone's major writings are Spirituals and the Blues *(in which this essay first appeared in 1972),* Black Theology and Black Power *(1969),* A Black Theology of Liberation *(1970), and* Martin & Malcolm & America *(1991, a study of Martin Luther King, Jr., and Malcolm X).*

The Blues: A Secular Spiritual

Theologically, there is more to be said about the music of black people than what was revealed in the black spirituals. To be sure, a significant number of black people were confident that the God of Israel was involved in black history, liberating them from slavery and oppression. But not all blacks could accept the divine promises of the Bible as a satisfactory answer to the contradictions of black existence. They refused to adopt a God-centered perspective as the solution to the problem of black suffering. Instead, they sang, "Got the blues, and too dam' mean to cry."

The blues depict the "secular" dimension of black experience. They are "worldly" songs which tell us about love and sex, and about that other "mule kickin' in my stall." They tell us about the "Black Cat's Bones," "a Mojo hand," and "dese backbitin' womens tryin' fo' to steal my man." The blues are about black life and the sheer earth and gut capacity to survive in an extreme situation of oppression.

> I wrote these blues, gonna sing 'em as I please,
> I wrote these blues, gonna sing 'em as I please,
> I'm the only one like the way I'm singing' 'em,
> I'll swear to goodness ain't no one else to please

The Rise of the Blues

The exact date of the origin of the blues is difficult to determine. Most experts agree that they probably began to take form in the late nineteenth century.[1] But the spirit and mood of the blues have roots stretching back into slavery days and even to Africa. As with the spirituals, the Africanism of the blues is related to the *functional* character of West African music. And this is one of the essential ingredients of black music which distinguishes it from Western music and connects it with its African heritage. "The fact that American Negro music, like the African, is at the core of daily life explains the immemorial African quality of all Negro *folk* music in this country, if not of the Negro in exile everywhere."[2]

Black music then, is not an artistic creation for its own sake; 4 rather it tells us about the *feeling* and *thinking* of African people, and the kinds of mental adjustments they had to make in order to survive in an alien land. For example, the work songs were a means of heightening energy, converting labor into dances and games, and providing emotional excitement in an otherwise unbearable situation. The emphasis was on free, continuous, creative energy as produced in song.[3] A similar functional character applied to the slave seculars, ballads, spirituals, as well as the blues.

Slavery is the historical background of which the blues were created. From a theological perspective, the blues are closely related to the "slaves seculars." The "secular" songs of slavery were "non-religious," occasionally anti-religious, and were often called "devil songs" by religious folk. The "seculars" expressed the skepticism of black slaves who found it difficult to take seriously anything suggesting the religious faith of white preachers. Sterling Brown reported:

> Bible stories, especially the creation, the fall of Man, and the flood, were spoofed. 'Reign, Master Jesus, reign' became 'Rain Masser, rain hard! Rain flour and lard, and a big hog head, Down in my back yard.' After couplets of nonsense and ribaldry, slaves sang with their fingers crossed, or hopeless in defeat: 'Po' mourner, you shall be free, when de good Lord set you free.'[4]

While seculars were not strictly atheistic as defined by modern Western philosophy, they nontheless uncover the difficulties black people encountered when they attempted to relate white Christian categories to their situation of oppression.

The blues reflect the same existential tension. Taking form sometime after the Emancipation and Reconstruction, they invited black people to embrace the reality and truth of black experience. They express the "laments of folk Negroes over hard luck, 'careless' or unrequited love, broken family life, or general dissatisfaction with a cold and trouble-filled world."[5]

Because the blues ignore the "religious" concerns of the church, 8 many interpreters of black music make a sharp distinction between the blues and the spirituals. John W. Work's treatement is representative:

> The blues differ radically from the spirituals. . . . The spirituals are intensely religious, and the blues are just as intensely worldly. The spirituals sing of heaven, and of the fervent hope that after death the singer may enjoy the celestial joys to be found there. The blues singer has no interest in heaven, and not much hope in earth—a thoroughly

disillusioned individual. The spirituals were created in the church, the blues sprang from everyday life.[6]

Unfortunately, it is true that many black church people at first condemned the blues as vulgar and indecent. But that was because they did not understand them rightly. If the blues are viewed in the proper perspective, it is clear that their mood is very similar to the ethos of the spirituals. Indeed, I contend that the blues and the spirituals flow from the same bedrock of experience, and neither is an adequate interpretation of black life without the commentary of the other.

The blues are "secular spirituals."[7] They are *secular* in the sense that they confine their attention solely to the immediate and affirm the bodily expression of black soul, including its sexual manifestations. They are *spirituals* because they are impelled by the same search for the truth of black experience.

Yet despite the fact that the blues and the spirituals partake of the same Black Essence, there are important differences between them. The spirituals are *slave* songs, and they deal with historical realities that are pre-Civil War. They were created and sung by the group. The blues, while having some pre-Civil War roots, are essentially post-Civil War in consciousness. They reflect experiences that issued from Emancipation, the Reconstruction Period, and segregation laws.

Historically and theologically, the blues express conditions associated with the "burden of freedom." However, freedom in the blues is not simply the "existential freedom" defined by modern philosophy. Philosophical existentialism speaks of freedom in the context of absurdity and about the inability to reconcile the "strangeness of the world" and one's perception of human existence. But absurdity in the blues is factual, not conceptual. The blues, while not denying that the world was strange, described its strangeness in more concrete and vivid terms. Freedom took on historical specificity when contrasted with legal servitude. It meant that simple alternatives, which whites took for granted, became momentous options for newly "free" black slaves. It meant getting married, drinking gin, praising God—and expressing these historical possibilities in song.

The Emancipation decentralized the black population, and the Reconstruction gave black people a certain feeling of autonomy and self-reliance that they had not experienced during slavery. For the first time, many black people were free to move from town to town and from farm to farm without being restricted by slave codes and patrollers. They had leisure and the freedom to be alone and to reflect. But these options also revealed new limitations. To be sure, blacks had free time, but they also needed money for food and shelter.

> I never had to have no money befo',
> And now they want it everywhere I go.

The Hayes Compromise of 1877 led to the withdrawal of federal troops from the South and ended the hopes of black people becoming authentic participants in the political processes of America. In 1883 the United States Supreme Court declared the Civil Rights Act of 1875 as unconstitutional; and in 1896 it upheld the doctrine of "separate but equal" (Plessy vs. Ferguson), giving legal sanction to the dehumanizing aspects of white supremacy. By the end of the nineteenth century, the political disfranchisement of black people was complete. White people could still do to black people what they willed, just as in slavery days. This was the situation that created the blues.

During slavery the social movement of black people was limited, and the church served as the primary social unit for black expression. After the Civil War, the social mobility of blacks increased, and the church became only one of several places where blacks could meet and talk about the problems of black existence. Other "priests" of the community began to emerge alongside of the preachers and deacons; and other songs were sung in addition to the spirituals. The "new priests" of the black community were the blues men and women and their songs were the blues. Like the preacher in the church, they proclaimed the Word of black existence, depicting its joy and sorrow, love and hate, and the awesome burden of being "free" in a racist society when one is black.

> Oh, Ahm tired a dis mess,
> Oh, yes, Ahm tired a dis mess.

Toward a Definition of the Blues

What is the precise meaning of the blues? And how is that meaning 16 related to the experience of the black community? These questions are not easy to answer, because the blues do not deal with abstract ideas that can be analyzed from the perspective of "objective reason." They are not propositional truths *about* the black experience. Rather they are essential ingredients that define the *essence* of the black experience. And to understand them, it is necessary to view the blues as *a state of mind in relation to the Truth of the black experience.* This is what blues man Henry Townsend of St. Louis has in mind when he says: "When I sing the blues I sing the truth."[8]

The blues and Truth are one reality of the black experience. The blues are that "true feeling," says Henry Townsend.[9] In the words of Memphis Willie B.: "A blues is about something that's real. It is about what a man feels when his wife leaves him, or about some disappointment that happens to him that he can't do anything about. That's why none of these young boys can really sing the blues. They don't know about the things that go into a blues."[10]

The thing that goes into the blues is the experience of being black in a white racist society. It is that peculiar feeling that makes you know that there is something seriously wrong with the society, even though you may not possess the intellectual or political power to do anything about it. No black person can escape the blues, because the blues are an inherent part of black existence in America. To be black is to be blue.

For many people, a blues song is about sex or a lonely woman longing for her rambling man. However, the blues are more than that. To be sure, the blues involve sex and what that means for human bodily expression, but on a much deeper level.

> De blues ain't nothin'
> But a poor man's heart disease.

The blues experience always is an encounter with life, its trials and tribulations, its bruises and abuses—but not without benefit of the melody and rhythm of song.

The blues are an expression of fortitude in the face of a broken 20 existence. They emphasize the will to be, despite non-being as symbolized in racism and hate.

> Lord, going to sleep now for mama just got bad news,
> Lord, going to sleep now for mama just got bad news,
> To try to dream away my troubles, counting the blues.

The blues are a state of mind that affirms the essential worth of black humanity, even though white people attempted to define blacks as animals. The blues tell us about a people who refused to accept the absurdity of white society. Black people rebelled artistically, and affirmed through ritual, pattern, and form that they were human beings. "You never seen a mule sing, have you?" asked Big Bill (William Lee Conley) Broonzy.

The affirmation of self in the blues is the emphasis that connects them theologically with the spirituals. Like the spirituals, the blues affirm the somebodiness of black people, and they preserve the worth of black humanity through ritual and drama. The blues are a transformation of black life through the sheer power of song.

The blues feeling was not just a temporary "bad mood" that would soon pass away. The blues have to do with the structure and meaning of existence itself. Black people were asking questions about the nature of being and non-being, life and death. They knew that something was wrong; people were not created to be defined by others. And neither was it meant for a woman to be separated from her man. And Clara Smith pleads for a prescription for "de mean ole blues."

> So I ask yo', Doctor,
> See if yo can fin'
> Somethin' in yo' satchel
> To pacify my min'.
>
> Doctor! Doctor!
> Write me a prescription fo' dih blues.
> De mean ole blues.

Because the blues are rooted in the black perception of existence, they are historical. Historical experience, as interpreted by the black community, is the key to an understanding of the blues. Black people accepted the dictum: Truth is experience, and experience is the Truth. If it is lived and encountered, then it is real. There is no attempt in the blues to make philosophical distinctions between divine and human truth. That is why many blues people reject the contention that the blues are vulgar or dirty. As Henry Townsend puts it: "If I sing the blues and tell the truth, what have I done? What have I committed? I haven't lied."[11]

The blues also deal with the agony of love. The blues woman is the priestess and prophet of the people. She verbalizes the emotion for herself and the audience, articulating the stresses and strains of human relationships.

> My man left this morning, just about half past four.
> My man left this morning, just about half past four.
> He left a note on the pillow saying he couldn't use me no more.
>
> It's awful hard to take it, it was such a bitter pill.
> It's awful hard to take it, it was such a bitter pill.
> If the blues don't kill me that man's meanness will.

The blues are not abstract; they are concrete. They are intense and direct responses to the reality of black experience. They tell us about floods, pneumonia, and the train. The train was a symbol of escape from the harsh reality of the present. It was the freedom to move; and many blacks "got on board," expressing their liberated being.

Every aspect of black life was exemplified in the blues. The blues dealt with TB and other forms of sickness. They focused on guns, highways, and Greyhound buses, and the boll weevil—that little black bug that invaded Texas over fifty years ago and destroyed more than a billion dollars in cotton.

The blues were a living reality. They are a sad feeling and also a joyous mood. They are bitter but also sweet. They are funny and not so funny. The blues are not evil per se; rather they represent that sad feeling when a woman's man leaves or joy when he returns. They are part of that structure of reality in which human beings are condemned to live. And because the black person had to live in the midst of a broken existence, the reality of the blues was stark and real. [28]

> Well, the blues ain't nothin'
> But a workingman feelin' bad
> Well, it's one of the worst old feelins
> That any poor man's ever had.

The personification of the blues feeling and experience is most revealing: to black folk he is no shadow, but a person whose presence is inescapable.

I worry all day, I worry all night,
Everytime my man comes home he wants to fuss and fight.
When I pick up the paper to try to read the news,
Just when I'm satisfied, yonder comes the blues.

This blues person is no stranger, but somebody every black knows well. For "When I got up this mornin', [the] Blues [was] walking round my bed; I went to eat my breakfast, the blues was in my bread." And I said:

Good mornin', blues,
Blues, how do you do?
Yes, blues, how do you do?
I'm doin' all right,
Good mornin', how are you?

Notes

1. See LeRoi Jones, *Blues People* (New York: William Morrow and Co., 1963); Alain Locke, *The Negro and His Music* and *Negro Art: Past and Present* (New York: Arno Press, 1969); Charles Keil, *Urban Blues* (Chicago: The University of Chicago Press, 1916); Phyl Garland, *The Sound of Soul* (Chicago: Henry Regnery Co., 1969); Harold Courlander, *Negro Folk Music, U.S.A.* (New York: Columbia University Press, 1963); Eileen Southern, *The Music of Black Americans* (New York: W.W. Norton, 1971); Rudi Blesh, *Shining Trumpets* (New York: Collier Books, 1963); and *The Story of the Blues* (Philadelphia: Chilton Book Co., 1969); Samuel Charters, *The Bluesmen* (New York: Oak Publications, 1967); and *The Poetry of the Blues* (New York: Avon, 1963); Russell Ames, *The Story of American Folk Song* (New York: Grosset and Dunlap, 1960); and John A. and Alan Lomax, *Folk Song U.S.A.* The list of commentators on the blues could be extended but there are some of the important studies. For the lyrics, Oliver's *The Meaning of the Blues*, Charter's *Poetry of the Blues* and Sterling Brown's "The Blues" in *The Negro Caravan* and his "Blues" in L. Hughes and A. Bontemps, *Book of Negro Folklore,* are the most useful.
2. Rudi Blesh, *Shining Trumpets,* p. 47.
3. Blesh, p. 48.
4. Brown, "Negro Folk Expression" in A. Meier and E. Rudwick, *The Making of Black America,* p. 215.

5. Brown in *Negro Caravan*, p. 426.
6. John W. Work, *American Negro Songs and Spirituals* (New York: Bonanza Books, 1940), p. 28.
7. I am indebted to C. Eric Lincoln of Union Theological Seminary for this phrase.
8. Cited in Samuel Charters, *Poetry of the Blues*, p. 58.
9. Cited in Charters, p. 17.
10. Cited in Charters, p. 18.
11. Cited in Paul Oliver, *The Blues Tradition* (New York: Oak Publications, 1970), p. 47.

Topics for Discussion and Writing

1. In paragraph 10 Cone writes, "The blues are 'secular spirituals.'" The two words that Cone places within quotation marks might strike some people as contradictory. Explain in your own words what he means by the term. What, according to Cone, distinguishes the blues from spirituals?

2. In paragraph 12 Cone speaks of the "burden of freedom." What is meant by that seemingly paradoxical phrase?

3. In paragraph 15 Cone says that "other 'priests' of the black community began to emerge alongside of the preachers and deacons." What does he mean by "priests"?

4. In paragraph 18 Cone says, "The thing that goes into the blues is the experience of being black in a white racist society." Can you think of any blues that at least on the surface do *not* seem to reflect racist society—for instance, a song about an unfaithful lover? (In his next paragraph Cone says that for many of us a blues song is about "a lonely woman longing for a rambling man.") If you can think of such songs, do they refute Cone's point? Or do you think Cone adequately explains how even these songs support his argument? In any case, in your own words argue for or against Cone's position.

Garrison Keillor

Garrison Keillor was born in Anoka, Minnesota, in 1942 and was educated at the University of Minnesota. He achieved national fame as host of a radio program, "Prairie Home Companion," on which he told of the doings in the mythical town of Lake Wobegon, where "all the children are above average." Keillor has published several collections of stories and now devotes most of his time to writing.

The Tip-Top Club

The idea of pouring warm soapy water into overshoes and wearing them around the house to give yourself a relaxing footbath while you work is one that all fans of WLT's "The Tip-Top Club" seem to have remembered over the years, along with the idea that if you're depressed you should sit down and write a letter to yourself praising all of your good qualities, and the idea of puffing cigarette smoke at violets to prevent aphids.

Every evening, Sunday through Thursday at 10:00 P.M. ("and now . . . direct from the Tip-Top studio in downtown Minneapolis . . ."), WLT played the Tip-Top theme song—

Whenever you feel blue, think of something nice to do;
That's the motto of the Tip-Top crew.
Don't let it get you down, wear a smile and not a frown,
And you'll be feeling Tip-top too.

—and Bud Swenson came on the air with his friendly greeting: "Good evening, Tip-Toppers, and welcome to *your* show. This is your faithful recording secretary, chief cook and bottle-washer, Bud Swenson, calling the Club to order and waiting to hear from you." And of the hundreds of calls that came in on the Tip-Top line (847-8677, or T-I-P-T-O-P-S), and of the fifty or sixty that actually got on the air, many were from listeners who simply wanted Bud to know they were doing fine, feeling good, and enjoying the show. "And—oh yes," they might add, "we got our boots on," referring to overshoes.

Every night, Bud got at least one request for a copy of the poem a woman had written about writing a letter to yourself. It was called "Dear Me," it was a hundred and eight lines long, WLT mailed out 18,000 copies of it in the six months after it was written (May 18, 1956), and it began:

When I look around these days
And hear blame instead of praise
(For to bless is so much harder than to damn),
It makes me feel much better
To write myself a letter
And tell myself how good I really am.

Dear Me, Sorry, it's been
So long since I took pen
In hand and scribbled off a word or two.
I'm busy with my work and such,
But I need to keep in touch
Cause the very closest friend I have is you.

Through times of strife and toil,
You've always remained loyal
And stuck with me when other friends were far,
And because we are so close,
I think of you the most
And of just how near and dear to me you are.

As for puffing smoke at violets, it touched off a debate that lasted for years. For months after it was suggested by an elderly woman, Bud got call after call from listeners who said that smoke-puffing would *not* discourage aphids; that even if it would, there are *better* ways to discourage aphids; and, worse, that it might encourage young people to take up smoking. 4

The pro-puffers replied hotly that: (1) you don't have to *inhale* in order to *puff* on a plant; (2) the treatment should be given only once a week or so; and (3) anyone who wants to smoke probably will go ahead and do it *anyway*, violets or no violets.

As time passed, the issue became confused in the minds of some Tip-Toppers, who came to think that Bud himself was a smoker (he was not). To the very end (November 26, 1969), he got calls from listeners wanting to know if he didn't agree with them that smoking is a filthy habit. (He did.)

At Bud's retirement party, Roy Elmore, Jr., president of WLT, presented him with twenty-five potted violet plants, one for each year of service.

Controversy was the very thing that distinguished "The Tip-Top Club." It had none. Edgar Elmore, the founder of WLT, abhorred controversy, and the terms of his will bound his heir, Roy Jr., to abhor it also. Though Edgar never heard Bud's show, having died in 1940, eleven years before the Club was formed, he certainly would have enjoyed it very much, as Roy Jr. told Bud frequently. No conversation about religion or politics was permitted, nor were callers allowed to be pessimistic or moody on the air. If a person started in to be moody, he or she was told firmly and politely to hang up and *listen* to the show and it would cheer him or her up. Few had to be told. 8

Vacations and pets were favorite Tip-Top topics, along with household hints, children, gardening, memories of long ago, favorite foods, great persons, good health and how to keep it, and of course the weather. Even when the weather was bad, even in times of national crisis, the Tip-Toppers always came up with cheerful things to talk about.

One reason for the show's cheery quality and the almost complete absence of crank calls was Bud's phone policy. After the first years he never divulged the Tip-Top phone number over the air (nor, for that matter, over the phone). In fact, it was an unlisted number, and one could obtain it only from another Tip-Topper. This tended to limit participation to those who understood the rules and accepted them.

The main reason for the show's cheery quality was Bud himself and his radio personality. His voice wasn't deep but his style of speaking was warm and reassuring, and he always tried to look on the bright side, even as host of "The Ten o'Clock News" (started July 1, 1944). On the newscast, Bud played up features and human-interest stories and he skimmed over what he called "the grim stuff." He might devote fifteen seconds to a major earthquake and three minutes to a story about a chimpanzee whose finger paintings had been exhibited at a New York gallery and fooled all the critics. His approach offended a few listeners ("the *New York Times* crowd," he called them), but most people liked it. Bud pulled in fifty or sixty fan letters a week, more than all other WLT newscasters combined.

After reading a few headlines, he'd say, "Oh, here's something you might be interested in," and he'd tell about a dog that had actually learned to sing and sing on key, or read a story about the world's largest known tomato, or about a three-year-old kid who was a whiz at chess; and then he'd talk about a dog that *he* knew, or a kid *he* knew, or a tomato *he* had seen, and then he'd say, "Well, I don't know. Let me know what *you* think."

At first, some letters said, "What happened to the news?" but they quickly dwindled. ("Anger doesn't last," Roy Jr. said. "Only love is lasting. Angry people spout off once and then get over it. The people who love you are loyal to the end.") Most of the letters were about a story Bud had read: the letter writer described a similar experience that *he* had had, or quoted a poem or a saying that the story had reminded *her* of—and Bud made sure to read every one of those letters on the air. One day in the winter of 1950, Roy Jr. said, "It's time to close down the News. You need a new shingle."

According to Bud, the Tip-Top Club was the idea of a woman in St. Paul. "We love your show," she wrote in January 1951, "and feel that truly it is our show too. When I listen, as I do every night, I feel as if I am among friends and we are all members of the club that gathers around our radios. We share ideas and experiences, we inspire each other with beautiful thoughts, and I only wish I could meet personally every one of the wonderful people who also write to you, for when they write to you, they are truly writing to me also."

Bud read her letter on the air, and listeners responded favorably to the idea of a club. (Since he had often referred to his stories as "News-Toppers," Bud suggested the name Tip-Top Club and it stuck.)

Nobody at WLT quite remembers who came up with the phone   16
idea. WLT had been doing remote broadcasts over telephone lines for years, starting with the "WLT Barn Dance and Bean Feed" in 1938; all that needed to be done to put a telephone signal on the air was wrap the bare end of one wire around the bare end of another. One night, Bud's engineer, Harlan, did just that, and a woman's voice came on describing dark thunderstorm clouds moving east toward Minneapolis.

"Is it raining there yet?" asked Bud.

"No," she said, "but it will be, any minute now. But I've got my boots on!"

Roy Jr. was leery of the phone idea from the start. "Every foul-mouth in town will be slobbering into his telephone for the chance to get on the air," he told Bud. "Every creep who writes on toilet walls, every dummy, every drunken son-of-a-bitch from hell to breakfast. We'll be running a nuthouse. We'll lose our license in a week."

Then Harlan came forward with his tape loop. Harlan was one   20
who seldom cracked a smile, but when WLT bought its first tape recorders, two big Ampexes, in 1949, he was like a boy with a new toy. He recorded everything on tape, and he played around with it, and his favorite game was to play around with Bud's voice. At first, he got a kick out of playing Bud's voice at a faster speed so he sounded like a hysterical woman; then backward, which sounded like Russian; then slower, so Bud sounded drunk; and then Harlan

became fascinated with editing Bud. With a razor blade in hand, Harlan went through thousands of feet of Bud tape, finding a word here and a word there, and a vowel sound here and a consonant there making new words, and snipping and splicing hundreds of little bits of tape to form a few sentences spoken in Bud's own voice, in which Bud spoke, in his own warm and reassuring tones, about having carnal relations with dogs, cats, tomatoes, small boys, chimpanzees, overshoes, fruit jars, lawn mowers. It was disgusting, and also an amazing feat of patience. In two years, Harlan assembled just three minutes of Bud.

Harlan solved the problem of loonies by the simple trick of threading a continuous loop of tape through two machines sitting side by side. Bud and his telephone caller could be recorded on the first machine, which fed the tape into the second machine, which played it back on the air three seconds later. If the caller said anything not befitting the show, Harlan, listening to the first machine, would have three seconds in which to turn off the second. "Can't beat it," said Harlan. "I hit the button and they die like rats."

Nevertheless, Roy Jr. was on hand for the first taped show and supervised the Stop button personally. "I trust you," he told Harlan, "but the way you talk, you might not notice profanity until it is too late." Bud explained the tape loop on the air and invited calls as Roy Jr. hunched over the machine, his finger in position, like a ship's gunner waiting for incoming aircraft. The first caller was a man who wanted to know more about the loop and if it might have useful applications in the home. He got flustered in mid-call and stopped. On his radio at home, he heard his own voice, delayed by tape, saying what he had said three seconds before. "Please turn your radio down," Bud said. It was a line that he was to repeat thousands of times in the next eighteen years.

"This has been an historic event," Roy Jr. said proudly when the show was over. He had cut off just two calls, the first one after the words "What in hell—" and the second at the mention of the Pope ("Probably nothing, but I wasn't about to take chances," he explained to Harlan).

Most of the calls were about the tape loop, with all callers favoring its use, howbeit with some trepidation that a mechanical failure or employee carelessness might lead to tragedy. Several were worried that certain persons might try to fool Bud, opening their calls with a few innocuous remarks and then slipping in a fast one. ("Thanks for the tip," said Bud. "I'm confident we can handle them.")

Communists, people agreed, might be particularly adept at subverting the tape loop. Communists, one man reported, learned these techniques at special schools, including how to insinuate their beliefs into a conversation without anyone being the wiser. ("Appreciate your concern, sir, and, believe me, we'll be on guard.")

It was three weeks before Roy Jr. turned over the guard duty to Harlan and Alice the switchboard girl. Alice was to screen all callers: no kids, no foreign accents, and nobody who seemed unusually intense or determined to get on the air. Harlan was the second line of defense. Roy Jr. instructed him to listen carefully to each call and try to anticipate what the caller was driving at; and if the conversation should drift toward deep waters—hit the button. No politics. No religion except for general belief in the Almighty, thankfulness for His gifts, wonder at His creation, etc. No criticism of others, not even the caller's kith and kin. Roy Jr. didn't want them to get dragged into family squabbles and maybe have to give equal time to a miffed husband or mother-in-law giving *their* side of it. No promotion of products, services, clubs, fund drives, or events.

"What's left to talk about?" Harlan wondered. "Not a goddamn helluva lot."

And, at first, the Tip-Toppers seemed unsure of what to talk about too. "Just thought I'd call and say hi," one would say. "Great. What are you doing tonight?" Bud would ask. "Oh, not much," the caller would reply. "Just sitting here listening to the show." 28

Gradually, though, they loosened up, and when Bud said to a caller, "Tell me about yourself," the caller generally did. Most Tip-Toppers seemed to be older persons leading quiet lives and keeping busy with hobbies and children and grandchildren, and, judging from the interest in household hints, their homes were neat as a pin and in good repair. They were unfailingly courteous ("The distinguished gentleman who spoke earlier on cats was very well-informed on most points, but I feel he may have overlooked the fact that cats will not shed if brushed regularly"), and soon Harlan was taking his finger off the button and relaxing in the control room and even leaving for a smoke now and then. The few nuts who called in Alice soon recognized by voice—she enjoyed talking with them, and after a few conversations they always asked for her and not for Bud. They sent her gifts, usually pamphlets or books but occasionally a box of cookies or a cake, which, on Harlan's advice, she did not eat. Three months went by, and not a single nut got past the loop; Roy Jr. raised Bud's salary and even gave him a contract—six months with an option of renewing for three more.

"It is so pleasant in this day and age when we are subjected to so much dissension and mud-slinging to take a rest and listen to a show that follows the old adage 'If you can't say something nice, don't say anything at all,'" a woman wrote to Bud. "I am a faithful listener-in and now have a telephone in my bedroom so that I can participate after turning in. I go to sleep listening to the show, and I believe I sleep better knowing it is there."

Sleep was a major item on the Tip-Top agenda: how much is needed? how to get it? what position is best? Many scorned the eight-hour quota as wasteful and self-indulgent and said four or five is enough for any adult. "The secret of longevity is to stay out of bed," said one oldster.

Most members disagreed; they felt they needed more sleep, and one call asking for a cure for insomnia would set off an avalanche of sleep tips—warm milk, a hot bath, a brisk walk, a brief prayer, a mild barbiturate—each of which had gotten the caller through some difficult nights. A doctor (he called in often, usually to settle somebody's hash on the value of vitamins, chiropractic medicine, and vegetarian diets) offered the opinion that worry causes 95 percent of all sleeplessness. He suggested that Tip-Toppers who go to bed with restless thoughts should fill their minds instead with pleasant memories and plans for vacations.

As for vacations, there were strong voices in the Club who argued that a Minnesotan's vacation money should be kept at home, not spent abroad. The rest of the world, it was said, could be seen perfectly well in the pages of the *National Geographic*. There was general agreement, however, that the purpose of a vacation is to rest and enjoy yourself and not necessarily to visit family members or to catch up on work around the house.

Housework was important, though, a sure antidote for grief and worry and feeling sorry for yourself. To scrub a floor or paint a wall or make a pie was better than going to a psychiatrist. At the same time, there was no use taking more time than necessary to get the job done, and every job had its shortcuts. "What's a quick way to get bubble gum out of hair?" a woman would ask, and minutes later, a legion of women who had faced that very problem would rally to her side. Give the club a problem, and in short order the Club solved it, whether it be a wobbly table, a grape-juice stain, or a treacherous stair tread, and then it suggested two or three things you could do in the time you had saved, such as making lovely and useful gifts from egg cartons, Popsicle sticks, and bottle caps.

And then there were hobbies. Bud often asked callers, particularly the shyer ones, to talk about their hobbies. He *never* asked about their occupations, not after the first few times: the answers were always apologetic-sounding—"Oh, I'm just a truck driver," or "Oh, I just work for the Post Office." But ask someone what he did in his spare time and the answer might be good for five or ten minutes.

Club members tended to be collectors. It seemed as if every object of which there was more than one sort, type, shape, brand, color, or configuration was the object of some collector's affection. "I have matchbook covers from more than thirty-five countries." "Some of my fruit jars have been appraised at ten dollars and more." "I hope someday to open a license-plate museum." "I plan to donate my nails to the historical society."

Bird-watching, a sort of collecting, was also popular, and Bud had to put a damper on the bird people, they were so fanatical. One might call in and say, "I wonder if anyone out there can help me identify a bird I heard this morning. Its call sounded something like this—" and then whistle, *"twee-twee, twee-twee,"* and suddenly Alice was swamped with calls, some identifying the bird, some saying they had heard it too and didn't know what it was either, and others wondering if the bird's call perhaps wasn't more of a *"twee-it, twee-it."*

Five nights a week, from 10:00 P.M. to sign-off, Bud sat in Studio B behind a table, the earphones clamped on, and scribbled notes on a pad as one Tip-Topper after another poured it out. After the first few months of the tape loop, he quit reading news stories, and after the club had hit full stride, telephonically speaking, he himself said very little, aside from an occasional question. He became a listener. For eighteen years, from 1951 to 1969, he sat in the same chair, in the same position (slightly hunched, head down and supported with one hand, the other hand writing, feet on the floor), and heard the same stuff, until he seemed to lose whatever personality he had in the beginning. He became neutral. "A goddamn ghost," Harlan said. "When he comes in, I don't even see him anymore. He don't really exist, except on the air."

At the age of sixty-five, he quietly retired. He didn't mention his retirement on "The Tip-Top Club." Tip-Toppers didn't know he was gone until they tuned in one night and heard Wayne Bargy. Wayne was the only WLT announcer willing to take the show.

Others had subbed for Bud before when he took vacations and they noted a certain snideness, a meanness, among the Tip-Toppers, who implied in their conversations that the new man, while adequate, was certainly no Bud. "Bud would *know* that," a caller might say. "Bud wouldn't have said that." "Maybe I'll talk to Bud about it. When is Bud coming back?"

So one night out of the clear blue it was "The Tip-Top Club with Wayne Bargy," and one can only imagine the shock that Bud's fans felt to hear a new theme song (Simon and Garfunkel's "Sound of Silence") instead of the old Tip-Top song, and then Wayne Bargy delivering a tribute to Bud as if Bud were dead. He called him "an innovator" and "a genius" and "a man who was totally concerned about others." "I loved him," said Wayne. "He was a totally understanding, giving type of man. He was someone I could always talk to about my problems."

"Friends, I know you're as disappointed as I am that Bud won't be here with us anymore, and let me tell you, I'd give anything if he were, and I want to be honest with you and admit that I've never done this type of show before and I don't know how good I am at talking with people, and maybe some of you will even wonder what I'm doing in the radio business and I have to admit that you may have a point there, but I would rather be honest about this than sit here and pretend that I'm somebody that I'm not, because I think that honesty has a place in radio, I don't think a radio personality has to be some sort of star or an idol or anything, I think he can be a real person, and even if I should fail and would quit this show tomorrow, I'd still be satisfied knowing I had done it my way and not tried to be like somebody else."

The Tip-Toppers heard him out; there was a minute or so of lull at the switchboard (perhaps they were too dazed to dial, or else they were composing carefully what they would say); and then the first wave struck. Even Harlan was surprised by the abuse Wayne got.

First call: "Why wait until tomorrow? Why not quit tonight?" (Wayne: "Thanks for calling.") A man said: "Oh, don't worry that we'll consider you a star, Wayne. Don't worry about that for one minute!" (Wayne: "Okay, I won't.") A woman said it was the worst night of her life. (Wayne: "It's hard for all of us.") "You make me absolutely sick. You're the biggest mistake they've made down there!" ("I appreciate your honesty, sir. I don't necessarily agree with that statement, but I think it's important that you feel you can be honest with me.")

By midnight, Wayne had logged almost a hundred calls, most 44
of them quite brief and most cut off by Harlan. The longest exchange
was with a woman who wanted to know where Bud was. Wayne
said Bud had retired.

SHE: Then I'd like his number.
HE: I'm sorry?
SHE: I want Bud's phone number.
HE: I—ma'am, I wish I could give you that but I can't, it's against com-
pany policy. We don't give out announcers' home numbers to the
general public.
SHE: Well, *I'm* not the general public. I'm Grace Ritter and he knows
me even if you don't.
HE: I'm sorry, but—
SHE: And this is his show, and I think he has a right to know what
you're doing to it! (CLICK)

During the midnight newscast, Roy Jr. called and told Wayne
he was doing great. "I knew it'd be tough sledding the first night,"
he said, "but you stick in there. They're sore about Bud, but in three
weeks they'll get tired and give up and all you'll get is flowers."

It didn't work that way. For one thing, Wayne had little interest
in the old Tip-Top topics. He was divorced and lived in an efficiency
apartment (no lawn to keep up, no maintenance responsibilities)
and had no pets or children. His major interest was psychology.
"People fascinate me," he said ("You don't fascinate *me*," someone
said.) He read psychology books and talked about them on the air.
He said that he was undergoing therapy, and it had helped him to
understand himself better. ("What's to understand?")

His other interests were eating out in foreign restaurants, attending films, and planning a trip to the Far East. ("How about leaving tomorrow?") Occasionally, he got a friendly caller who also liked
Szechuan cuisine or Carl Rogers[1] or Woody Allen movies, and he
reached out and hung onto that call for dear life. Those calls would
last for fifteen, twenty minutes, as if the caller were an old college
chum he hadn't heard from in ages, but when he hung up, the Tip-
Toppers were waiting, more determined than ever.

---

[1] Carl R. Rogers (1902–87) was an American psychotherapist and the author of, among other
books, *On Becoming a Person.*

THEM: This show is so boring. You talk about stuff that nobody but you is interested in.

HIM: I really think you're mistaken about that, at least I hope you are, but more importantly, I think that I would have no business being here if I *didn't* talk about things that interest me, because, when all is said and done, I do have to be myself.

THEM: That's the problem, Wayne. Yourself. You're dull.

HIM: Well, I grant you I'm not slick or polished, and I'm not a comedian, but that's not my job. Basically, I'm a communicator, and whatever my faults or failures in relating to people, I do try to be positive.

THEM: You're positively boring.

HIM: Well, let's talk about that. Define your terms. What do you mean by "boring"?

What they meant was Wayne Bargy. For all he said about keep- 48 ing an open mind ("You got a hole in your head, Wayne!") and not condemning others by trying to understand people who may be different from ourselves ("You're different from everybody, Wayne! You're a different species!"), the Club kept a united front against him.

One night, Wayne casually mentioned that it was his first anniversary hosting the show. The switchboard sizzled. One man said it was time for Club members to take action, and before Harlan could cut him off he announced a time and place for the meeting.

Word came back that the Tip-Toppers had elected officers and were putting together a mailing list for a monthly newsletter. It was said the Club was assigning members to "listening squads" with each squad assigned two hours of "Wayne duty" a week. The squad members were responsible for listening to the show and calling in frequently. The newsletter printed a list of things to say.

It was harder on Harlan than on Wayne. Harlan had started to assemble a special Wayne Bargy tape, but he had no time to work on it. What with Wayne giving out the phone number every fifteen minutes, the show was attracting oddballs, in addition to the legions of Tip-Toppers, and Harlan was cutting calls off the air by the dozens. One night, after Wayne had talked about his divorce (he said that he and wife didn't "relate to each other sexually"), there passed a long half hour during which no call was fit to broadcast. "I was slapping them down like barnyard flies. We were up to our ears in crazies," said Harlan. "Finally, my finger got sore, and Alice pulled the plug on the switchboard and her and me sat down and had a cup of coffee and let that poor SOB sit and die by himself."

Wayne talked a long time that night. He said he'd had a typical 52
middle-class upbringing until he went to college, which opened his
mind up to new possibilities. He said he had gone into radio because it had tremendous possibilities for creative communication.
This show was a tremendous opportunity to get people to open up
their minds. He viewed himself as an educator of sorts.

"I'll be honest," he said. "This past year has been rough. There's
a lot of anger and violence out there—and I don't say people
shouldn't feel that way, but I do feel people should be willling to
change. Life is change. We all change. I've changed. Frankly, when
I started doing this show, I didn't come off very well. I didn't communicate well. I had a hard time relating to working-class people.
I think I've improved. I'm learning. I've put my feelings on the line,
and I've benefited from it. I'm going to keep on trying."

He did keep on trying, and the Tip-Toppers kept calling—"We
won't go away, Wayne!" they said, and he said, "I don't want you
to go away. I want you to stay and let's get to know each other."
That summer WLT did a survey that showed that most of the Tip-
Top Club audience was over forty (72 percent), the least desirable
age group to advertisers, and in July the station switched the Tip-
Top slot to what it called "a modified middle-of-the-road pop-rock
format" with a disc jockey who never talked except to give time,
temperature, and commercials. His name was Mickael Keske, but
he never said it on the air.

Topics for Discussion and Writing

1. Compare Bud and Wayne. Why is Bud a successful host and Wayne
   a failure?

2. We are told that Bud's "approach offended a few listeners ('the *New
   York Times* crowd,' he called them.)" What sort of people were offended
   by Bud's approach? And why do you suppose "the few nuts who called
   in" preferred talking to Alice rather than to Bud?

3. Moving from the story to real life, do you think that Keillor is making
   a valid point about talk-show hosts and audiences? Can you support
   your view with reference to real talk shows? Is Keillor making a serious
   point, or is he just kidding around? Or a little of each?

Stevie Smith

Stevie Smith (1902–71) was born Florence Margaret Smith in England. Her first book was a novel, published in 1936, but she is best known for her several volumes of poetry.

Not Waving but Drowning

Nobody heard him, the dead man,
But still he lay moaning:
I was much further out than you thought
And not waving but drowning.   4

Poor chap, he always loved larking
And now he's dead
It must have been too cold for him his heart gave way,
They said   8

Oh, no no no, it was too cold always
(Still the dead one lay moaning)
I was much too far out all my life
And not waving but drowning.   12

Topics for Discussion and Writing

1. The first line, "Nobody heard him, the dead man," is, of course, literally true. Dead men do not speak. In what other ways is it true?
2. Who are "they" whose voices we hear in the second stanza? What does the punctuation—or lack of it—in line 7 tell us of their feelings for the dead man? What effect is produced by the brevity of line 6? of line 8?
3. In the last stanza, does the man reproach himself, or others, or simply bemoan his fate? What was the cause of his death?

10
LAW AND ORDER

The Third of May, 1808
Francisco Goya

Flower Power
Bernie Boston, 1967

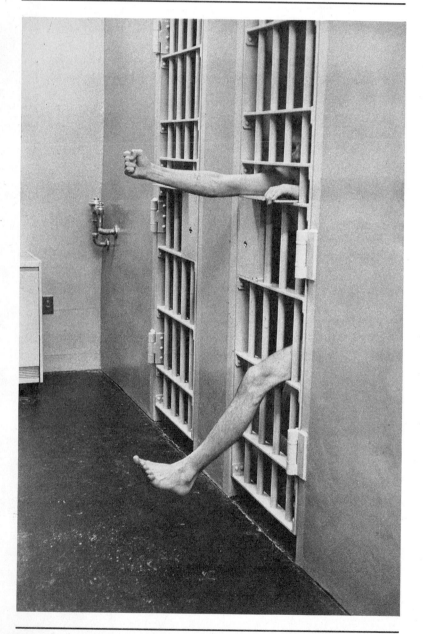

The Problem We All Live With
Norman Rockwell, 1964

Short Views

The trouble for the thief is not how to steal the bugle, but where to blow it.
African proverb

Whether there was ever a significant increase in crime and when it might have occurred is puzzling, since the phrase, "the land is full of bloody crimes and the city full of violence," did not appear in a recent Chicago newspaper but in a report on a crime wave in the promised land about 600 B.C. as recorded in Ezekiel VII:23. The logical possibility of an ever-increasing crime wave becomes more doubtful when we consider the biblical origin of humankind: Adam, Eve and Cain committed the worst offenses possible and after Abel was killed, all survivors—or 75 percent of the first four human beings—had criminal records. In spite of all righteous claims to the opposite, this crime wave seems to have subsided, never to reach its biblical heights again. It is simpler and more correct to state that crime has always existed but statistics have not.
Kurt Weis and Michael F. Milakovich

Whoever desires to found a state and give it laws, must start with assuming that all men are bad and ever ready to display their vicious nature, whenever they may find occasion for it.
Niccolò Machiavelli

It is questionable whether, when we break a murderer on the wheel, we aren't lapsing into precisely the mistake of the child who hits the chair he bumps into.
G. C. Lichtenberg

If a man were permitted to make all the ballads, he need not care who should make the laws of a nation.
Andrew Fletcher

Nature has given women so much power that the law has very wisely given them very little.
Samuel Johnson

588

I asked him whether, as a moralist, he did not think that the practice of the law, in some degree, hurt the nice feeling of honesty. JOHNSON. "Why no, Sir, if you act properly. You are not to deceive your clients with false representations of your opinion: you are not to tell lies to a judge." BOSWELL. "But what do you think of supporting a cause which you know to be bad?" JOHNSON. "Sir, you do not know it to be good or bad till the Judge determines it. I have said that you are to state facts fairly; so that your thinking, or what you call knowing, a cause to be bad, must be from reasoning, must be from your supposing your arguments to be weak and inconclusive. But, Sir, that is not enough. An argument which does not convince yourself, may convince the Judge to whom you urge it; and if it does convince him, why, then, Sir, you are wrong, and he is right. It is his business to judge; and you are not to be confident in your own opinion that a cause is bad, but to say all you can for your client, and then hear the Judge's opinion." BOSWELL. "But, Sir, does not affecting a warmth when you have no warmth, and appearing to be clearly of one opinion when you are in reality of another opinion, does not such dissimulation impair one's honesty? Is there not some danger that a lawyer may put on the same mask in common life, in the intercourse with his friends?" JOHNSON. "Why no, Sir. Everybody knows you are paid for affecting warmth for your client; and it is, therefore, properly no dissimulation: the moment you come from the bar you resume your usual behaviour. Sir, a man will no more carry the artifice of the bar into the common intercourse of society, than a man who is paid for tumbling upon his hands will continue to tumble upon his hands when he should walk on his feet."
James Boswell

One law for the ox and the ass is oppression.
William Blake

The law, in its majestic equality, forbids the rich as well as the poor to sleep under bridges, to beg in the streets, and to steal bread.
Anatole France

Decency, security and liberty alike demand that government officials shall be subjected to the same rules of conduct that are commands to the citizen. In a government of laws, existence of the government will be imperilled if it fails to observe the law scrupulously. Our Government is the potent, the omnipresent teacher. For good or for ill, it teaches the whole people by its example. Crime is contagious. If the Government becomes a lawbreaker, it breeds contempt for law; it invites every man to become a law unto himself; it invites anarchy. To declare that in the administration of the criminal law the end justifies the means—to declare that the Government may commit crimes in order to secure the conviction of a private criminal—would bring terrible retribution. Against that pernicious doctrine this Court should resolutely set its face.

Louis D. Brandeis

The trouble about fighting for human freedom is that you have to spend much of your life defending sons of bitches; for oppressive laws are always aimed at them originally, and oppression must be stopped in the beginning if it is to be stopped at all.

H. L. Mencken

Censorship upholds the dignity of the profession, know what I mean?

Mae West

Thomas Jefferson

Thomas Jefferson (1743–1826), governor of Virginia and the third president of the United States, devoted most of his adult life, until his retirement, to the service of Virginia and of the nation. The spirit and the wording of the Declaration are almost entirely Jefferson's.

The Declaration of Independence

In CONGRESS, July 4, 1776.
The Unanimous Declaration of the Thirteen United States of America.

When in the Course of human events, it becomes necessary for one people to dissolve the political bands which have connected them with another, and to assume among the powers of the earth, the separate and equal station to which the Laws of Nature and of Nature's God entitle them, a decent respect to the opinions of mankind requires that they should declare the causes which impel them to the separation.

We hold these truths to be self-evident, that all men are created equal, that they are endowed by their Creator with certain unalienable Rights, that among these are Life, Liberty and the pursuit of Happiness.

That to secure these rights, Governments are instituted among 4 Men, deriving their just powers from the consent of the governed.

That whenever any Form of Government becomes destructive of these ends, it is the Right of the People to alter or to abolish it, and to institute new Government, laying its foundation on such principles and organizing its powers in such form, as to them shall seem most likely to effect their Safety and Happiness. Prudence, indeed, will dictate that Governments long established should not be changed for light and transient causes; and accordingly all experience hath shewn, that mankind are more disposed to suffer, while evils are sufferable, than to right themselves by abolishing the forms to which they are accustomed. But when a long train of abuses and usurpations, pursuing invariably the same Object evinces a design to reduce them under absolute Despotism, it is their right, it is their duty, to throw off such Government, and to provide new Guards for their future security.

Such has been the patient sufferance of these Colonies; and such is now the necessity which constrains them to alter their former Systems of Government. The history of the present King of Great Britain is a history of repeated injuries and usurpations, all having in direct object the establishment of an absolute Tyranny over these States. To prove this, let Facts be submitted to a candid world.

He has refused his Assent to Laws, the most wholesome and necessary for the public good.

He has forbidden his Governors to pass Laws of immediate and 8 pressing importance, unless suspended in their operation till his Assent should be obtained; and when so suspended, he has utterly neglected to attend to them.

He has refused to pass other Laws for the accommodation of large districts of people, unless those people would relinquish the right of Representation in the Legislature, a right inestimable to them and formidable to tyrants only.

He has called together legislative bodies at places unusual, uncomfortable, and distant from the depository of their public Records, for the sole purpose of fatiguing them into compliance with his measures.

He has dissolved Representative Houses repeatedly, for opposing with manly firmness his invasions on the rights of people.

He has refused for a long time, after such dissolutions, to cause 12 others to be elected; whereby the Legislative powers, incapable of Annihilation, have returned to the People at large for their exercise; the State remaining in the mean time exposed to all the dangers of invasion from without, and convulsions within.

He has endeavoured to prevent the population of these States; for that purpose obstructing the Laws for Naturalization of Foreigners; refusing to pass others to encourage their migrations hither, and raising the conditions of new Appropriations of Lands.

He has obstructed the Administration of Justice, by refusing his Assent to Laws for establishing Judiciary powers.

He has made Judges dependent on his Will alone, for the tenure of their offices, and the amount and payment of their salaries.

He has erected a multitude of New Offices, and sent hither 16 swarms of Officers to harass our people, and eat out their substance.

He has kept among us, in times of peace, Standing Armies without the Consent of our legislatures.

He has affected to render the Military independent of and superior to the Civil power.

He has combined with others to subject us to a jurisdiction foreign to our constitution, and unacknowledged by our laws; giving his Assent to their Acts of pretended Legislation:

For Quartering large bodies of armed troops among us: 20

For Protecting them, by a mock Trial, from punishment for any Murders which they should commit on the Inhabitants of these States:

For cutting off our Trade with all parts of the world:

For imposing Taxes on us without our Consent:

For depriving us in many cases, of the benefits of Trial by Jury: 24

For transporting us beyond Seas to be tried for pretended offences:

For abolishing the free System of English Laws in a neighbouring Province, establishing therein an Arbitrary government, and enlarging its Boundaries so as to render it at once an example and fit instrument for introducing the same absolute rule into these Colonies:

For taking away our Charters, abolishing our most valuable Laws, and altering fundamentally the Forms of our Governments:

For suspending our own Legislatures, and declaring themselves 28 invested with power to legislate for us in all cases whatsoever.

He has abdicated Government here, by declaring us out of his Protection and waging War against us:

He has plundered our seas, ravaged our Coasts, burnt our towns, and destroyed the lives of our people.

He is at this time transporting large Armies of foreign Mercenaries to compleat the works of death, desolation and tyranny, already begun with circumstances of Cruelty & perfidy scarcely paralleled in the most barbarous ages, and totally unworthy the Head of a civilized nation.

He has constrained our fellow Citizens taken Captive on the high 32 Seas to bear Arms against their Country, to become the executioners of their friends and Brethren, or to fall themselves by their Hands.

He has excited domestic insurrections amongst us, and has endeavoured to bring on the inhabitants of our frontiers, the merciless Indian Savages, whose known rule of warfare, is an undistinguished destruction of all ages, sexes and conditions. In every stage of these Oppressions We have Petitioned for Redress in the most humble terms: Our repeated Petitions have been answered only by repeated injury. A Prince, whose character is thus marked by every act which may define a Tyrant, is unfit to be the ruler of a free people. Nor have We been wanting in attentions to our British brethren. We have warned them from time to time of attempts by their legislature to extend an unwarrantable jurisdiction over us. We have reminded them of the circumstances of our emigration and settlement here. We have appealed to their native justice and magnanimity, and we have conjured them by the ties of our common kindred to disavow these usurpations, which, would inevitably interrupt our connections and correspondence. They too have been deaf to the voice of justice and of consanguinity. We must, therefore, acquiesce in the necessity, which denounces our Separation, and hold them, as we hold the rest of mankind, Enemies in War, in Peace Friends.

We, THEREFORE, the Representatives of the UNITED STATES OF AMERICA, in General Congress Assembled, appealing to the Supreme Judge of the world for the rectitude of our intentions, do, in the Name and by Authority of the good People of these Colonies, solemnly publish and declare, That these United Colonies are, and of Right ought to be FREE AND INDEPENDENT STATES; that they are Absolved from all Allegiance to the British Crown, and that all political connection between them and the State of Great Britain, is and ought to be totally dissolved; and that as Free and Independent States, they have full Power to levy War, conclude Peace, contract Alliances, establish Commerce, and to do all other Acts and Things which Independent States may of right do.

And for the support of this Declaration, with a firm reliance on the protection of divine Providence, we mutually pledge to each other our Lives, our Fortunes and our sacred Honor.

Topics for Discussion and Writing

1. What audience is being addressed in the Declaration of Independence? Cite passages in the text that support your answer.

2. The Library of Congress has the original manuscript of the rough draft of the Declaration. This manuscript itself includes revisions that are indicated below, but it was later further revised. We print the first part of the second paragraph of the draft and, after it, the corresponding part of the final version. Try to account for the changes within the draft, and from the revised draft to the final version.

We hold these truths to be *self evident* ~~sacred & undeniable~~, that all men are created equal ~~& independent~~, that *they are endowed by their creator* ~~from that equal creation they derive equal~~ *with*

~~rights some of which are~~ *rights; that those* ~~in rights~~ inherent & inalienable, among ~~which~~ are ~~the preservation of~~ life, liberty, & the pursuit of happiness.

We hold these Truths to be self-evident, that all Men are created equal, that they are endowed by their Creator with certain unalienable Rights, that among these are Life, Liberty, and the Pursuit of Happiness.

In a paragraph evaluate the changes. Try to put yourself into Jefferson's mind and see if you can sense why Jefferson made the changes.

3. In a paragraph define *happiness*, and then in a second paragraph explain why, in your opinion, Jefferson spoke of "the pursuit of happiness" rather than of "happiness."

4. In "We Have No 'Right to Happiness'" (page 28) C. S. Lewis discusses the meaning of "the pursuit of happiness" in the Declaration, and a current misinterpretation of the phrase. How does he explain and define the phrase? How does his interpretation differ from what he considers an erroneous interpretation?

5. What assumptions lie behind the numerous specific reasons that are given to justify the rebellion? Set forth the gist of the argument of the Declaration using the form of reasoning known as a syllogism, which consists of a major premise (such as "All men are mortal"), a minor premise ("Socrates is a man"), and a conclusion ("Therefore, Socrates is mortal"). For a brief discussion of syllogisms, see pages 876–77 (deduction).

6. In a paragraph argue that the assertion that "all Men are created equal" is nonsense, or, on the other hand, that it makes sense.

7. If every person has an unalienable right to life, how can capital punishment be reconciled with the Declaration of Independence? You need not in fact be a supporter of capital punishment; simply offer the best defense you can think of, in an effort to make it harmonious with the Declaration.

Martin Luther King, Jr.

Martin Luther King, Jr. (1929–68), clergyman and civil rights leader, achieved national fame in 1955–56 when he led the boycott against segregated bus lines in Montgomery, Alabama. His policy of passive resistance succeeded in Montgomery, and King then organized the Southern Christian Leadership Conference in order to extend his efforts. In 1964 he was awarded the Nobel Peace Prize, but he continued to encounter strong opposition. On April 4,1968, while in Memphis to support striking sanitation workers, he was shot and killed.

Nonviolent Resistance

Oppressed people deal with their oppression in three characteristic ways. One way is acquiescence: the oppressed resign themselves to their doom. They tacitly adjust themselves to oppression, and thereby become conditioned to it. In every movement toward freedom some of the oppressed prefer to remain oppressed. Almost 2800 years ago Moses set out to lead the children of Israel from the slavery of Egypt to the freedom of the promised land. He soon discovered that slaves do not always welcome their deliverers. They become accustomed to being slaves. They would rather bear those ills they have, as Shakespeare pointed out, than flee to others that they know not of. They prefer the "fleshpots of Egypt" to the ordeals of emancipation.

There is such a thing as the freedom of exhaustion. Some people are so worn down by the yoke of oppression that they give up. A few years ago in the slum areas of Atlanta, a Negro guitarist used to sing almost daily: "Ben down so long that down don't bother me." This is the type of negative freedom and resignation that often engulfs the life of the oppressed.

But this is not the way out. To accept passively an unjust system is to cooperate with that system; thereby the oppressed become as evil as the oppressor. Noncooperation with evil is as much a moral obligation as is cooperation with good. The oppressed must never allow the conscience of the oppressor to slumber. Religion reminds every man that he is his brother's keeper. To accept injustice or segregation passively is to say to the oppressor that his actions are morally right. It is a way of allowing his conscience to fall asleep. At this moment the oppressed fails to be his brother's keeper. So acquiescence—while often the easier way—is not the moral way. It is the way of the coward. The Negro cannot win the respect of his oppressor by acquiescing; he merely increases the oppressor's arrogance and contempt. Acquiescence is interpreted as proof of the Negro's inferiority. The Negro cannot win the respect of the white people of the South or the peoples of the world if he is willing to sell the future of his children for his personal and immediate comfort and safety.

A second way that oppressed people sometimes deal with oppression is to resort to physical violence and corroding hatred. Violence often brings about momentary results. Nations have frequently won their independence in battle. But in spite of temporary victories, violence never brings permanent peace. It solves no social problem; it merely creates new and more complicated ones. 4

Violence as a way of achieving racial justice is both impractical and immoral. It is impractical because it is a descending spiral ending in destruction for all. The old law of an eye for an eye leaves everybody blind. It is immoral because it seeks to humiliate the opponent rather than win his understanding; it seeks to annihilate rather than to convert. Violence is immoral because it thrives on hatred rather than love. It destroys community and makes brotherhood impossible. It leaves society in monologue rather than dialogue. Violence ends by defeating itself. It creates bitterness in the survivors and brutality in the destroyers. A voice echoes through time saying to every potential Peter, "Put up your sword." History is cluttered with the wreckage of nations that failed to follow his command.

If the American Negro and other victims of oppression succumb to the temptation of using violence in the struggle for freedom, future generations will be the recipients of a desolate night of bitterness, and our chief legacy to them will be an endless reign of meaningless chaos. Violence is not the way.

The third way open to oppressed people in their quest for freedom is the way of nonviolent resistance. Like the synthesis in Hegelian philosophy, the principle of nonviolent resistance seeks to reconcile the truths of two opposites—acquiescence and violence—while avoiding the extremes and immoralities of both. The nonviolent resister agrees with the person who acquiesces that one should not be physically aggressive toward his opponent; but he balances the equation by agreeing with the person of violence that evil must be resisted. He avoids the nonresistance of the former and the violent resistance of the latter. With nonviolent resistance, no individual or group need submit to any wrong, nor need anyone resort to violence in order to right a wrong.

It seems to me that this is the method that must guide the actions of the Negro in the present crisis in race relations. Through nonviolent resistance the Negro will be able to rise to the noble height of opposing the unjust system while loving the perpetrators of the system. The Negro must work passionately and unrelentingly for full stature as a citizen, but he must not use inferior methods to gain it. He must never come to terms with falsehood, malice, hate, or destruction. 8

Nonviolent resistance makes it possible for the Negro to remain in the South and struggle for his rights. The Negro's problem will not be solved by running away. He cannot listen to the glib suggestion of those who would urge him to migrate en masse to other sections of the country. By grasping his great opportunity in the South he can make a lasting contribution to the moral strength of the nation and set a sublime example of courage for generations yet unborn.

By nonviolent resistance, the Negro can also enlist all men of good will in his struggle for equality. The problem is not a purely racial one, with Negroes set against whites. In the end, it is not a struggle between people at all, but a tension between justice and injustice. Nonviolent resistance is not aimed against oppressors but against oppression. Under its banner consciences, not racial groups, are enlisted.

If the Negro is to achieve the goal of integration, he must organize himself into a militant and nonviolent mass movement. All three elements are indispensable. The movement for equality and justice can only be a success if it has both a mass and militant character; the barriers to be overcome require both. Nonviolence is an imperative in order to bring about ultimate community.

A mass movement of militant quality that is not at the same time   12
committed to nonviolence tends to generate conflict, which in turn breeds anarchy. The support of the participants and the sympathy of the uncommitted are both inhibited by the threat that bloodshed will engulf the community. This reaction in turn encourages the opposition to threaten and resort to force. When, however, the mass movement repudiates violence while moving resolutely toward its goal, its opponents are revealed as the instigators and practitioners of violence if it occurs. Then public support is magnetically attracted to the advocates of nonviolence, while those who employ violence are literally disarmed by overwhelming sentiment against their stand.

Only through a nonviolent approach can the fears of the white community be mitigated. A guilt-ridden white minority lives in fear that if the Negro should ever attain power, he would act without restraint or pity to revenge the injustices and brutality of the years. It is something like a parent who continually mistreats a son. One day that parent raises his hand to strike the son, only to discover that the son is now as tall as he is. The parent is suddenly afraid— fearful that the son will use his new physical power to repay his parent for all the blows of the past.

The Negro, once a helpless child, has now grown up politically, culturally, and economically. Many white men fear retaliation. The job of the Negro is to show them that they have nothing to fear, that the Negro understands and forgives and is ready to forget the past. He must convince the white man that all he seeks is justice, *for both himself and the white man.* A mass movement exercising nonviolence is an object lesson in power under discipline, a demonstration to the white community that if such a movement attained a degree of strength, it would use its power creatively and not vengefully.

Nonviolence can touch men where the law cannot reach them. When the law regulates behavior it plays an indirect part in molding public sentiment. The enforcement of the law is itself a form of peaceful persuasion. But the law needs help. The courts can order desegregation of the public schools. But what can be done to mitigate the fears, to disperse the hatred, violence, and irrationality gathered around school integration, to take the initiative out of the hands of racial demagogues, to release respect for the law? In the end, for laws to be obeyed, men must believe they are right.

Here nonviolence comes in as the ultimate form of persuasion. 16 It is the method which seeks to implement the just law by appealing to the conscience of the great decent majority who through blindness, fear, pride, or irrationality have allowed their consciences to sleep.

The nonviolent resisters can summarize their message in the following simple terms: We will take direct action against injustice without waiting for other agencies to act. We will not obey unjust laws or submit to unjust practices. We will do this peacefully, openly, cheerfully because our aim is to persuade. We adopt the means of nonviolence because our end is a community at peace with itself. We will try to persuade with our words, but if our words fail, we will try to persuade with our acts. We will always be willing to talk and seek fair compromise, but we are ready to suffer when necessary and even risk our lives to become witnesses to the truth as we see it.

The way of nonviolence means a willingness to suffer and sacrifice. It may mean going to jail. If such is the case the resister must be willing to fill the jail houses of the South. It may even mean physical death. But if physical death is the price that a man must pay to free his children and his white brethren from a permanent death of the spirit, then nothing could be more redemptive.

Topics for Discussion and Writing

1. In the first paragraph, the passage about Moses and the children of Israel is not strictly necessary; the essential idea of the paragraph is stated in the previous sentence. Why, then, does King add this material? And why the quotation from Shakespeare?

2. Pick out two or three sentences that seem to you to be especially effective and analyze the sources of their power. You can choose either isolated sentences or (because King often effectively links sentences with repetition of words or of constructions) consecutive ones.

3. In a paragraph set forth your understanding of what nonviolent resistance is. Use whatever examples from your own experience or reading you find useful. In a second paragraph, explain how Maya Angelou's "Graduation" (page 191) offers an example of nonviolent resistance.

Linda M. Hasselstrom

Linda M. Hasselstrom, a South Dakota rancher, writer, and environmentalist, has wielded a gun as a last resort, but she has never used it. Her essay first appeared in High Country News *and later appeared in a somewhat longer form in a collection of her essays,* Land Circle: Writings Collected from the Land *(Golden Co.: Fulcrum, 1991).*

Ms. Hasselstrom has asked us to indicate that her choices for self-defense are based on a particular set of circumstances, that she does not advocate handgun ownership, and that she is not a member of any group that advocates handgun use.

A Peaceful Woman Explains Why She Carries a Gun

I am a peace-loving woman. But several events in the past 10 years have convinced me I'm safer when I carry a pistol. This was a personal decision, but because handgun possession is a controversial subject, perhaps my reasoning will interest others.

I live in western South Dakota on a ranch 25 miles from the nearest large town: for several years I spent winters alone here. As a free-lance writer, I travel alone a lot—more than 100,000 miles by car in the last four years. With women freer than ever before to travel alone, the odds of our encountering trouble seem to have risen. And help, in the West, can be hours away. Distances are great, roads are deserted, and the terrain is often too exposed to offer hiding places.

A woman who travels alone is advised, usually by men, to protect herself by avoiding bars and other "dangerous situations," by approaching her car like an Indian scout, by locking doors and windows. But these precautions aren't always enough. I spent years following them and still found myself in dangerous situations. I began to resent the idea that just because I am female, I have to be extra careful.

A few years ago, with another woman, I camped for several weeks in the West. We discussed self-defense, but neither of us had taken a course in it. She was against firearms, and local police told us Mace was illegal. So we armed ourselves with spray cans of deodorant tucked into our sleeping bags. We never used our improvised Mace because we were lucky enough to camp beside people who came to our aid when men harassed us. But on one occasion

4

we visited a national park where our assigned space was less than 15 feet from other campers. When we returned from a walk, we found our closest neighbors were two young men. As we gathered our cooking gear, they drank beer and loudly discussed what they would do to us after dark. Nearby campers, even families, ignored them; rangers strolled past, unconcerned. When we asked the rangers point-blank if they would protect us, one of them patted my shoulder and said, "Don't worry, girls. They're just kidding." At dusk we drove out of the park and hid our camp in the woods a few miles away. The illegal spot was lovely, but our enjoyment of that park was ruined. I returned from the trip determined to reconsider the options available for protecting myself.

At that time, I lived alone on the ranch and taught night classes in town. Along a city street I often traveled, a woman had a flat tire, called for help on her CB radio, and got a rapist who left her beaten. She was afraid to call for help again and stayed in her car until morning. For that reason, as well as because CBs work best along line-of-sight, which wouldn't help much in the rolling hills where I live, I ruled out a CB.

As I drove home one night, a car followed me. It passed me on a narrow bridge while a passenger flashed a blinding spotlight in my face. I braked sharply. The car stopped, angled across the bridge, and four men jumped out. I realized the locked doors were useless if they broke the windows of my pickup. I started forward, hoping to knock their car aside so I could pass. Just then another car appeared, and the men hastily got back in their car. They continued to follow me, passing and repassing. I dared not go home because no one else was there. I passed no lighted houses. Finally they pulled over to the roadside, and I decided to use their tactic: fear. Speeding, the pickup horn blaring, I swerved as close to them as I dared as I roared past. It worked: they turned off the highway. But I was frightened and angry. Even in my vehicle I was too vulnerable.

Other incidents occurred over the years. One day I glanced out a field below my house and saw a man with a shotgun walking toward a pond full of ducks. I drove down and explained that the land was posted. I politely asked him to leave. He stared at me, and the muzzle of the shotgun began to rise. In a moment of utter clarity I realized that I was alone on the ranch, and that he could shoot me and simply drive away. The moment passed; the man left.

One night, I returned home from teaching a class to find deep   8
tire ruts in the wet ground of my yard, garbage in the driveway,
and a large gas tank empty. A light shone in the house; I couldn't
remember leaving it on. I was too embarrassed to drive to a neighboring ranch and wake someone up. An hour of cautious exploration convinced me the house was safe, but once inside, with the
doors locked, I was still afraid. I kept thinking of how vulnerable
I felt, prowling around my own house in the dark.

My first positive step was to take a kung fu class, which teaches
evasive or protective action when someone enters your space
without permission. I learned to move confidently, scanning for possible attackers. I learned how to assess danger and techniques for
avoiding it without combat.

I also learned that one must practice several hours a day to be
good at kung fu. By that time I had married George; when I practiced with him, I learned how *close* you must be to your attacker
to use martial arts, and decided a 120-pound woman dare not let
a six-foot, 220-pound attacker get that close unless she is very, very
good at self-defense. I have since read articles by several women
who were extremely well trained in the martial arts, but were raped
and beaten anyway.

I thought back over the times in my life when I had been attacked or threatened and tried to be realistic about my own behavior,
searching for anything that had allowed me to become a victim.
Overall, I was convinced that I had not been at fault. I don't believe
myself to be either paranoid or a risk-taker, but I wanted more protection.

With some reluctance I decided to try carrying a pistol. George   12
had always carried one, despite his size and his training in martial
arts. I practiced shooting until I was sure I could hit an attacker who
moved close enough to endanger me. Then I bought a license from
the county sheriff, making it legal for me to carry the gun concealed.

But I was not yet ready to defend myself. George taught me
that the most important preparation was mental: convincing myself I could actually *shoot a person*. Few of us wish to hurt or kill
another human being. But there is no point in having a gun—in fact,
gun possession might increase your danger—unless you know you
can use it. I got in the habit of rehearsing, as I drove or walked,
the precise conditions that would be required before I would shoot
someone.

People who have not grown up with the idea that they are capable of protecting themselves—in other words, most women—might have to work hard to convince themselves of their ability, and of the necessity. Handgun ownership need not turn us into gunslingers, but it can be part of believing in, and relying on, *ourselves* for protection.

To be useful, a pistol has to be available. In my car, it's within instant reach. When I enter a deserted rest stop at night, it's in my purse, with my hand on the grip. When I walk from a dark parking lot into a motel, it's in my hand, under a coat. At home, it's on the headboard. In short, I take it with me almost everywhere I go alone.

Just carrying a pistol is no protection; avoidance is still the best   16 approach to trouble. Subconsciously watching for signs of danger, I believe I've become more alert. Handgun use, not unlike driving, becomes instinctive. Each time I've drawn my gun—I have never fired it at another human being—I've simply found it in my hand.

I was driving the half-mile to the highway mailbox one day when I saw a vehicle parked about midway down the road. Several men were standing in the ditch, relieving themselves. I have no objection to emergency urination, but I noticed they'd dumped several dozen beer cans in the road. Besides being ugly, cans can slash a cow's feet or stomach.

The men noticed me before they finished and made quite of performance out of zipping their trousers while walking toward me. All four of them gathered around my small foreign car, and one of them demanded what the hell I wanted.

"This is private land. I'd appreciate it if you'd pick up the beer cans."

"What beer cans?" said the belligerent one, putting both hands   20 on the car door and leaning in my window. His face was inches from mine, and the beer fumes were strong. The others laughed. One tried the passenger door, locked; another put his foot on the hood and rocked the car. They circled, lightly thumping the roof, discussing my good fortune in meeting them and the benefits they were likely to bestow upon me. I felt very small and very trapped and they knew it.

"The ones you just threw out," I said politely.

"I don't see no beer cans. Why don't you get out here and show them to me, honey?" said the belligerent one, reaching for the handle inside my door.

"Right over there," I said, still being polite, "—there, and over there." I pointed with the pistol, which I'd slipped under my thigh. Within one minute the cans and the men were back in the car and headed down the road.

I believe this incident illustrates several important principles. The [24] men were trespassing and knew it; their judgment may have been impaired by alcohol. Their response to the polite request of a woman alone was to use their size, numbers, and sex to inspire fear. The pistol was a response in the same language. Politeness didn't work; I couldn't match them in size or number. Out of the car, I'd have been more vulnerable. The pistol just changed the balance of power. It worked again recently when I was driving in a desolate part of Wyoming. A man played cat-and-mouse with me for 30 miles, ultimately trying to run me off the road. When his car passed mine with only two inches to spare, I showed him my pistol, and he disappeared.

When I got my pistol, I told my husband, revising the old Colt slogan. "God made men *and women,* but Sam Colt made them equal." Recently I have seen a gunmaker's ad with a similar sentiment. Perhaps this is an idea whose time has come, though the pacifist inside me will be saddened if the only way women can achieve equality is by carrying weapons.

We must treat a firearm's power with caution. "Power tends to corrupt, and absolute power corrupts absolutely," as a man (Lord Acton) once said. A pistol is not the only way to avoid being raped or murdered in today's world, but, intelligently wielded, it can shift the balance of power and provide a measure of safety.

Topics for Discussion and Writing

1. In her first eight paragraphs, Hasselstrom sketches the kinds of experiences that ultimately caused her to carry a gun. Do you find her account of those experiences persuasive? Do they, in your opinion, justify her decision? If not, why not?

2. In paragraph 13 Hasselstrom introduces an idea that perhaps takes a reader by surprise. Do you think it is true, by and large, that a person who decides to carry a gun must, by means of "rehearsing," prepare himself or herself to use it? Whether or not you think it is true, what is the effect of her introducing this idea? Does it make her account more, or less, persuasive?

3. In paragraphs 17–24 Hasselstrom recounts an episode when her gun frightened off several belligerent and probably slightly intoxicated men.

Do you think that this episode serves (as Hasselstrom doubtless thinks it does) as clear support for her position? What counter-argument(s) can you imagine?
4. What devices does Hasselstrom use, as a writer, to convince her reader that she is not aggressive or gun-crazy?

Barbara Ehrenreich

Barbara Ehrenreich, born in Butte, Montana, in 1941, and educated at Reed College and at Rockefeller University, has taught at the State University of New York in Old West-bury. The author of several books, since 1982 she has been a fellow of the Institute of Policy Studies in Washington, D.C. We print a portion of an essay from New York Woman *magazine.*

Angry Young Men

Recall the roar of commentary that followed the murderous 1989 assault on a 28-year-old woman jogging in Central Park. Every detail of the assailants' lives was sifted for sociological significance: Were they poor? How poor? Students or dropouts? From families with two parents or one?

Yet weeks before the East Harlem "posse" attacked a jogger, suburbanites in nearby Long Island were shaken by two murders that were, if anything, even more inexplicably vicious than the assault in Central Park. In early March the body of 13-year-old Kelly Tinyes was found in the basement of a house just down the block from her own. She had been stabbed, strangled, and hit with a blunt instrument before being mutilated with a bayonet. A few weeks later 14-year-old Jessica Manners was discovered along the side of a road in East Setauket, strangled to death, apparently with her own bra, and possibly sexually assaulted.

Suspects have been apprehended. Their high school friends, parents, and relatives have been interviewed. Their homes and cars have been searched, their photos published. We know who they hung out with and what they did in their spare time. But on the scale of large social meanings, these crimes don't rate. No one is demanding that we understand—or condemn—the white communities that nourished the killers. No one is debating the roots of violence in the land of malls and tract homes. In the city, apparently, crime is construed as something "socioeconomic." Out here it's merely "sick."

But East Setauket is not really all that far from East Harlem. If 4 something is festering in the ghetto, something very similar is gnawing away in middle-income suburbs. A "way of life," as the cliché goes, is coming to an end, and in its place a mean streak is opening up and swallowing everything in its path. Economists talk about "deindustrialization" and "class polarization." I think of it as the problem of marginal men: They are black and white, Catholic and Pentecostal, rap fans and admirers of techno-pop. What they have in common is that they are going nowhere—nowhere legal, that is.

Consider the suspects in the Long Island murders. Twenty-one-year-old Robert Golub, in whose basement Kelly Tinyes was killed, is described- in *Newsday* as an "unemployed body-builder." When his high school friends went off to college, he stayed behind in his parents' home in Valley Stream. For a while he earned a living driving a truck for a cosmetics firm, but he lost that job, in part because of his driving record: His license has been suspended 12 times since 1985. At the time of the murder Golub had been out of work for several months, constructing a life around his weight-lifting routine and his dream of becoming an entrepreneur.

Christopher Loliscio, the suspect in the Manners case, is 19 and, like Golub, lives with his parents. He has been in trouble before, charged with third-degree assault and "menacing" in an altercation that took place on the campus of the State University at Stony Brook. Loliscio does not attend college himself. He is employed as a landscaper.

The suburbs are full of young white men like Golub and Loliscio. If they had been born 20 years earlier, they might have found steady work in decent-paying union jobs, married early, joined the volunteer fire department, and devoted their leisure to lawn maintenance. But the good blue-collar jobs are getting sparser, thanks to "deindustrialization." Much of what's left is likely to be marginal, low-paid work. Nationwide, the earnings of young white men dropped 18 percent between 1973 and 1986, making those at the low end of the wage scale less than desirable marriage prospects.

Landscaping, for example—a glamorous term for raking and 8 mowing—pays four to five dollars an hour; truck driving for a small firm is in the same range; not enough to pay for a college education, a house, or even a midsize wedding reception at the VFW hall.

And even those modest perquisites of life in the sub-yuppie class have become, in some sense, "not enough." On Long Island the culture that once sustained men in blue-collar occupations is crumbling as more affluent settlers move in, filling the vacant lots with their new $750,000 homes. In my town, for example, the last five years saw the bowling alley close and the blue-collar bar turn into a pricey dining spot. Even the volunteer fire department is having trouble recruiting. The prestigious thing to join is a $500-a-year racquetball club; there's just not much respect anymore for putting out fires.

So the marginal man lives between two worlds—one that he aspires to and one that is dying—neither of which he can afford. Take "Rick," the 22-year-old son of family friends. His father is a machinist in an aerospace plant that hasn't hired anyone above the floor-sweeping level for years now. Not that Rick has ever shown any interest in his father's trade. For one thing, he takes too much pride in his appearance to put on the dark green, company-supplied work clothes his father has worn for the past 20 years. Rick has his own kind of uniform: pleated slacks, high-tops, Italian knit cardigans, and a $300 leather jacket, accessorized with a gold chain and earring stud.

To his parents, Rick is a hardworking boy for whom things just don't seem to work out. Right now he has a gig doing valet parking at a country club. The tips are good, and he loves racing around the lot in the Porsches and Lamborghinis of the stockbroker members. But the linchpin of his economic strategy is living at home, with his parents and sisters, in the same room he's occupied since third grade. This arrangement is less than ideal for his social life. Besides, Rick is a long way from being able to afford even a cramped, three-bedroom house like his family home; given the choice, he'd rather have a new Camaro anyway. So Rick's girlfriends tend to move on rapidly, looking for men who might someday have a chance in the real estate market.

If this were the '70s, Rick might have dropped out; he might 12 have taken up marijuana, the Grateful Dead, and vague visions of a better world. But like so many of his contemporaries in the '80s, Rick isn't rebellious. He has no problem with "the system," which, in his mind, embraces every conceivable hustle, legal or illegal. He can't imagine demanding better jobs or a living wage when there's easy money to be made elsewhere. Two years ago he made a tidy bundle dealing coke in a local dance club, bought a $20,000 car, and smashed it up. Now he spends his evenings working as a bouncer in an illegal gambling joint—his parents still think he's out "dancing"—and is proud of the handgun he's got stowed in his glove compartment.

Someday Rick will use that gun, and I'll probably be the first to say—like Robert Golub's friends—"but he isn't the kind of person who would hurt *anyone.*" Except that even now I can sense the danger in him. He's smart enough to know he's only a cut-rate copy of the upscale young men in *GQ* ads and MTV commercials whom he is trying to emulate. Viewed from Wall Street or Southampton, he's a peon, a member of the invisible underclass that parks cars, waits on tables, and is satisfied with a $5 tip and an occasional remark about the weather.

He's also proud. And there's nowhere for him to put that pride except into the politics of gesture: the macho stance, the 75-mph takeoff down the expressway, and, eventually, maybe, the drawn gun. Jobs are the liberal solution; conservatives would throw in "traditional values." But what the marginal men—from Valley Stream to Bedford-Stuyvesant—need most of all is *respect.* If they can't find that in work, or in a working-class lifestyle that is no longer honored, they'll extract it from someone weaker—a girlfriend, a random jogger, a neighbor, perhaps just any girl. They'll find a victim.

Topics for Discussion and Writing

1. In her first three paragraphs Ehrenreich compares murders that took place in New York City and on Long Island, New York. What is the point of the comparison?

2. In paragraph 4 Ehrenreich speaks of "deindustrialization," "class polarization," and "the problem of marginal men." Again, what is her point? If you are not clear about the point, how might Ehrenreich have helped you to understand it?

3. In paragraphs 5–7 what relationship does Ehrenreich imply between the job market and criminal behavior? Do you find this relationship probable, or plausible? What other connections might there be between being unemployed or being unemployable and criminal behavior?

4. Ehrenreich's essay is called "Angry Young Men," and she mentions young women (other than murder victims) only briefly, at the end of paragraph 11. Can Ehrenreich's thesis—that the drying-up of blue-collar jobs has had a profound effect on young men—also be applied to young women?

5. Ehrenreich states her thesis most fully, and most clearly, in her final paragraph. Do you believe it? If not, why not?
6. In paragraph 10 Ehrenreich sketches the portrait of a young man who illustrates her thesis. Drawing on your experience—or maybe your imagination—write a paragraph describing a comparable person.

Byron R. White

In January 1985 a majority of the United States Supreme Court, in a case called New Jersey v. T.L.O. *(a student's initials), ruled 6–3 that a school official's search of a student who is suspected of disobeying a school regulation does not violate the Fourth Amendment's protection against unreasonable searches and seizures.*

The case originated thus: an assistant principal in a New Jersey high school opened the purse of a fourteen-year-old girl who had been caught violating school rules by smoking in the lavatory. The girl denied that she ever smoked, and the assistant principal thought that the contents of her purse would show whether or not she was lying. The purse was found to contain cigarettes, marijuana, and some notes that seemed to indicate that she sold marijuana to other students. The school then called the police.

The case went through three lower courts; almost five years after the event occurred, the case reached the Supreme Court. Associate Justice Byron R. White wrote the majority opinion, joined by Chief Justice Warren E. Burger and by Associate Justices Lewis F. Powell, Jr., William H. Rehnquist, and Sandra Day O'Connor. Associate Justice Harry A. Blackmun concurred in a separate opinion. Associate Justice William J. Brennan, Jr., John Paul Stevens, and Thurgood Marshall dissented in part.

The Majority Opinion of the Supreme Court in *New Jersey* v *T.L.O* [On the Right to Search Students]

In determining whether the search at issue in this case violated the Fourth Amendment, we are faced initially with the question whether that amendment's prohibition on unreasonable searches and seizures applies to searches conducted by public school officials. We hold that it does.

It is now beyond dispute that "the Federal Constitution, by virtue of the 14th Amendment, prohibits unreasonable searches and seizures by state officers." Equally indisputable is the proposition that the 14th Amendment protects the rights of students against encroachment by public school officials.

On reargument, however, the State of New Jersey has argued that the history of the Fourth Amendment indicates that the amendment was intended to regulate only searches and seizures carried out by law enforcement officers; accordingly, although public school officials are concededly state agents for purposes of the 14th Amendment, the Fourth Amendment creates no rights enforceable against them.

But this Court has never limited the amendment's prohibition   4 on unreasonable searches and seizures to operations conducted by the police. Rather, the Court has long spoken of the Fourth Amendment's strictures as restraints imposed upon "governmental action"—that is, "upon the activities of sovereign authority." Accordingly, we have held the Fourth Amendment applicable to the activities of civil as well as criminal authorities: building inspectors, OSHA inspectors, and even firemen entering privately owned premises to battle a fire, are all subject to the restraints imposed by the Fourth Amendment.

Notwithstanding the general applicability of the Fourth Amendment to the activities of civil authorities, a few courts have concluded that school officials are exempt from the dictates of the Fourth Amendment by virtue of the special nature of their authority over schoolchildren. Teachers and school administrators, it is said, act *in loco parentis* [i.e., in place of a parent] in their dealings with students: their authority is that of the parent, not the State, and is therefore not subject to the limits of the Fourth Amendment.

Such reasoning is in tension with contemporary reality and the teachings of this Court. We have held school officials subject to the commands of the First Amendment, and the Due Process Clause of the 14th Amendment. If school authorities are state actors for purposes of the constitutional guarantees of freedom of expression and due process, it is difficult to understand why they should be deemed to be exercising parental rather than public authority when conducting searches of their students.

In carrying out searches and other disciplinary functions pursuant to such policies, school officials act as representatives of the State, not merely as surrogates for the parents, and they cannot claim the parents' immunity from the strictures of the Fourth Amendment.

To hold that the Fourth Amendment applies to searches con-   8 ducted by school authorities is only to begin the inquiry into the standards governing such searches. Although the underlying command of the Fourth Amendment is always that searches and seizures be reasonable, what is reasonable depends on the context within which a search takes place.

[Standard of Reasonableness]

The determination of the standard of reasonableness governing any specific class of searches requires balancing the need to search against the invasion which the search entails. On one side of the balance are arrayed the individual's legitimate expectations of privacy and personal security; on the other, the government's need for effective methods to deal with breaches of public order.

We have recognized that even a limited search of the person is a substantial invasion of privacy. A search of a child's person or of a closed purse or other bag carried on her person, no less than a similar search carried out on an adult, is undoubtedly a severe violation of subjective expectations of privacy.

Of course, the Fourth Amendment does not protect subjective expectations of privacy that are unreasonable or otherwise "illegitimate." The State of New Jersey has argued that because of the pervasive supervision to which children in the schools are necessarily subject, a child has virtually no legitimate expectation of privacy in articles of personal property "unnecessarily" carried into a school. This argument has two factual premises: (1) the fundamental incompatibility of expectations of privacy with the maintenance of a sound educational environment; and (2) the minimal interest of the child in bringing any items of personal property into the school. Both premises are severely flawed.

Although this Court may take notice of the difficulty of maintaining discipline in the public schools today, the situation is not so dire that students in the schools may claim no legitimate expectations of privacy. 12

[Privacy and Discipline]

Against the child's interest in privacy must be set the substantial interest of teachers and administrators in maintaining discipline in the classroom and on school grounds. Maintaining order in the classroom has never been easy, but in recent years, school disorder has often taken particularly ugly forms; drug use and violent crime in the schools have become major social problems. Accordingly, we have recognized that maintaining security and order in the schools requires a certain degree of flexibility in school disciplinary procedures, and we have respected the value of preserving the informality of the student-teacher relationship.

How, then, should we strike the balance between the schoolchild's legitimate expectations of privacy and the school's equally legitimate need to maintain an environment in which learning can take place? It is evident that the school setting requires some easing of the restrictions to which searches by public authorities are ordinarily subject. The warrant requirement, in particular, is unsuited to the school environment; requiring a teacher to obtain a warrant before searching a child suspected of an infraction of school rules (or of the criminal law) would unduly interfere with the maintenance of the swift and informal disciplinary procedures needed in the schools. We hold today that school officials need not obtain a warrant before searching a student who is under their authority.

The school setting also requires some modification of the level of suspicion of illicit activity needed to justify a search. Ordinarily, a search—even one that may permissibly be carried out without a warrant—must be based upon "probable cause" to believe that a violation of the law has occurred. However, "probable cause" is not an irreducible requirement of a valid search.

[Balancing of Interests]

The fundamental command of the Fourth Amendment is that searches and seizures be reasonable, and although "both the concept of probable cause and the requirement of a warrant bear on the reasonableness of a search, . . . in certain limited circumstances neither is required." Thus, we have in a number of cases recognized the legality of searches and seizures based on suspicions that, although "reasonable," do not rise to the level of probable cause. Where a careful balancing of governmental and private interests suggests that the public interest is best served by a Fourth Amendment standard of reasonableness that stops short of probable cause, we have not hesitated to adopt such a standard. 16

We join the majority of courts that have examined this issue in concluding that the accommodation of the privacy interests of schoolchildren with the substantial need of teachers and administrators for freedom to maintain order in the schools does not require strict adherence to the requirement that searches be based on probable cause to believe that the subject of the search has violated or is violating the law.

Rather, the legality of a search of a student should depend simply on the reasonableness, under all the circumstances, of the search. Determining the reasonableness of any search involves a twofold inquiry; first, one must consider "whether the . . . action was justified at its inception," second, one must determine whether the search as actually conducted "was reasonably related in scope to the circumstances which justified the interference in the first place."

Under ordinary circumstances, a search of a student by a teacher or other school official will be "justified at its inception" when there are reasonable grounds for suspecting that the search will turn up evidence that the student has violated or is violating either the law or the rules of the school. Such a search will be permissible in its scope when the measures adopted are reasonably related to the objectives of the search and not excessively intrusive in light of the age and sex of the student and the nature of the infraction.

This standard will, we trust, neither unduly burden the efforts of 20
school authorities to maintain order in their schools nor authorize unrestrained intrusions upon the privacy of schoolchildren. By focusing attention on the question of reasonableness, the standard will spare teachers and school administrators the necessity of schooling themselves in the niceties of probable cause and permit them to regulate their conduct according to the dictates of reason and common sense. At the same time, the reasonableness standard should insure that the interests of students will be invaded no more than is necessary to achieve the legitimate end of preserving order in the schools.

There remains the question of the legality of the search in this case. We recognize that the "reasonable grounds" standard applied by the New Jersey Supreme Court in its consideration of this question is not substantially different from the standard that we have adopted today. Nonetheless, we believe that the New Jersey court's application of that standard to strike down the search of T.L.O.'s purse reflects a somewhat crabbed notion of reasonableness. Our review of the facts surrounding the search leads us to conclude that the search was in no sense unreasonable for Fourth Amendment purposes. [End of majority opinion][2]

---

[2] Questions on this selection appear on page 614.

John Paul Stevens

Dissent in the Case of
New Jersey v. *T.L.O.*

The majority holds that "a search of a student by a teacher or other school official will be 'justified at its inception' when there are reasonable grounds for suspecting that the search will turn up evidence *that the student has violated or is violating either the law or the rules of the school.*"

This standard will permit teachers and school administrators to search students when they suspect that the search will reveal evidence of [violation of] even the most trivial school regulation or precatory guideline for students' behavior. For the Court, a search for curlers and sunglasses in order to enforce the school dress code is apparently just as important as a search for evidence of heroin addiction or violent gang activity.

A standard better attuned to this concern would permit teachers and school administrators to search a student when they have reason to believe that the search will uncover *evidence that the student is violating the law or engaging in conduct that is seriously disruptive of school order or the educational process.*

A standard that varies the extent of the permissible intrusion 4 with the gravity of the suspected offense is also more consistent with common-law experience and this Court's precedent. Criminal law has traditionally recognized a distinction between essentially regulatory offenses and serious violations of the peace, and graduated the response of the criminal justice system depending on the character of the violation.

Topics for Discussion and Writing

1. In the majority opinion Justice White says (paragraph 14) that it is "evident that the school setting requires some easing of the restrictions to which searches by public authorities are ordinarily subject." Does White offer evidence supporting what he says is "evident"? List the evidence, if you can find it in White, or if you can think of any.

2. In paragraph 20 Justice White writes of a "reasonableness standard." What does he mean by this phrase? (See paragraphs 18–20.)

3. Considering your own experience of school life as well as the arguments of Justice White and Justice Stevens, do you, on the whole, agree with the majority decision or with the dissent? What, in your opinion, are the chief issues? Explain.

4. Some forty years before this case, Justice Robert H. Jackson argued that the schools have a special responsibility for adhering to the Constitution: "That they are educating the young for citizenship is reason for scrupulous protection of constitutional freedoms of the individual, if we are not to strangle the free mind at its source and teach youth to discount important principles of our government as mere platitudes." Similarly, in 1967 in an analogous case involving another female pupil, Justice Brennan argued that "The lesson the school authorities taught her that day will undoubtedly make a greater impression than the one her teacher had hoped to convey. . . . Schools cannot expect their students to learn the lessons of good citizenship when the school authorities themselves disregard the fundamental principles underpinning our constitutional freedoms." Do you find these arguments compelling? Why, or why not?

Derek Bok

Derek Bok was born in 1930 in Bryn Mawr, Pennsylvania, and was educated at Stanford and Harvard, where he received a law degree. He taught law at Harvard, then served as dean of the law school, and held the office of president of Harvard from 1971 to 1991. The essay that we give here was published in a Boston newspaper, prompted by the display of Confederate flags hung from the window of a dormitory room.

Protecting Freedom of Expression at Harvard

For several years, universities have been struggling with the problem of trying to reconcile the rights of free speech with the desire to avoid racial tension. In recent weeks, such a controversy has sprung up at Harvard. Two students hung Confederate flags in public view, upsetting students who equate the Confederacy with slavery. A third student tried to protest the flags by displaying a swastika.

These incidents have provoked much discussion and disagreement. Some students have urged that Harvard require the removal of symbols that offend many members of the community. Others reply that such symbols are a form of free speech and should be protected.

Different universities have resolved similar conflicts in different ways. Some have enacted codes to protect their communities from forms of speech that are deemed to be insensitive to the feelings of other groups. Some have refused to impose such restrictions.

It is important to distinguish between the appropriateness of such communications and their status under the First Amendment. The fact that speech is protected by the First Amendment does not necessarily mean that it is right, proper, or civil. I am sure that the vast majority of Harvard students believe that hanging a Confederate flag in public view—or displaying a swastika in response—is insensitive and unwise because any satisfaction it gives to the students who display these symbols is far outweighed by the discomfort it causes to many others.   4

I share this view and regret that the students involved saw fit to behave in this fashion. Whether or not they merely wished to manifest their pride in the South—or to demonstrate the insensitivity of hanging Confederate flags by mounting another offensive symbol in return—they must have known that they would upset many fellow students and ignore the decent regard for the feelings of others so essential to building and preserving a strong and harmonious community.

To disapprove of a particular form of communication, however, is not enough to justify prohibiting it. We are faced with a clear example of the conflict between our commitment to free speech and our desire to foster a community founded on mutual respect. Our society has wrestled with this problem for many years. Interpreting the First Amendment, the Supreme Court has clearly struck the balance in favor of free speech.

While communities do have the right to regulate speech in order to uphold aesthetic standards (avoiding defacement of buildings) or to protect the public from disturbing noise, rules of this kind must be applied across the board and cannot be enforced selectively to prohibit certain kinds of messages but not others.

Under the Supreme Court's rulings, as I read them, the display of swastikas or Confederate flags clearly falls within the protection of the free-speech clause of the First Amendment and cannot be forbidden simply because it offends the feelings of many members   8 of the community. These rulings apply to all agencies of government, including public universities.

Although it is unclear to what extent the First Amendment is enforceable against private institutions, I have difficulty understanding why a university such as Harvard should have less free speech than the surrounding society—or than a public university.

One reason why the power of censorship is so dangerous is that it is extremely difficult to decide when a particular communication is offensive enough to warrant prohibition or to weigh the degree of offensiveness against the potential value of the communication. If we begin to forbid flags, it is only a short step to prohibiting offensive speakers.

I suspect that no community will become humane and caring by restricting what its members can say. The worst offenders will simply find other ways to irritate and insult.

In addition, once we start to declare certain things "offensive," 12 with all the excitement and attention that will follow, I fear that much ingenuity will be exerted trying to test the limits, much time will be expanded trying to draw tenuous distinctions, and the resulting publicity will eventually attract more attention to the offensive material than would ever have occurred otherwise.

Rather than prohibit such communications, with all the resulting risks, it would be better to ignore them, since students would then have little reason to create such displays and would soon abandon them. If this response is not possible—and one can understand why—the wisest course is to speak with those who perform insensitive acts and try to help them understand the effects of their actions on others.

Appropriate officials and faculty members should take the lead, as the Harvard House Masters have already done in this case. In talking with students, they should seek to educate and persuade, rather than resort to ridicule or intimidation, recognizing that only persuasion is likely to produce a lasting, beneficial effect. Through such effects, I believe that we act in the manner most consistent with our ideals as an educational institution and most calculated to help us create a truly understanding, supportive community.

Topics for Discussion and Writing

1. In paragraph 8 Bok argues that "the display of swastikas or of Confederate flags clearly falls within the free-speech clause of the First

Amendment and cannot be forbidden simply because it offends the feelings of many members of the community." Suppose someone replied thus: "The display of swastikas or of Confederate flags—symbols loaded with meaning—is, to a Jew or an African-American, at least equivalent to a slap in the face. Such a display is, in short, an act of violence." What would you reply, and how would your support your response?

2.   Do you find Bok persuasive? Support your answer with evidence about the points of his argument and his techniques of argument.

3.   What rules, if any, does your school have concerning limitations of speech? What rules, if any, would you propose?

4.   Compare Bok with Hawley (page 520) on reasons for and against limitations on students' freedom of speech.

Robert Satter

Before being appointed a judge of the court of common pleas, Robert Satter was a prominent lawyer in Connecticut, and a Connecticut State Representative. He is now a judge on the Connecticut Superior Court.

For several decades Satter has been a member of the Writers Group, a dozen people who meet monthly and discuss each other's writing. In his preface to the book from which our selection is drawn, Satter says that the Writers Group "shaped this book by their constructive criticism."

Whom to Believe?

The phone rings in my chambers a few minutes after ten. The calendar judge for the civil part of Hartford Superior Court is on the line.

"Bob, I'm sending you a court case to try. *Romano* v. *Costello.* Your clerk is bringing you the file. The lawyers say it's a short trial."

A court case means I will hear it without a jury and I alone will determine the facts, resolve the issues of law, and render a final judgment. Determining the facts is often the most difficult.

The facts of the case are the conclusions drawn from the evidence. The evidence is mainly in the form of testimony, so finding the facts requires assessing not only what witnesses say on the stand, but which are telling the truth. Since people on each side of a case often give contradictory versions of the same event, the subtext of a trial is credibility—which witnesses, and to what extent, are to be believed. I suspect it will be so in the trial being sent to me.

Certain kinds of cases are required to be tried by a judge alone. Among them are so-called equity actions, in which one party seeks an injunction to forbid the other party from doing an illegal or harmful act or seeks to compel the other party to specifically perform a contract. Others are appeals from decisions of administrative agencies. Actually, any case can be tried to the court without a jury if the parties so desire and they often do when they want a quicker hearing, or when the issues are complicated and they do not trust a jury to decide them. Businessmen in particular prefer to have their commercial and corporate controversies resolved by judges.

The lawyers appear at my chambers. I know them both as hardworking practitioners. We chat informally for a few moments, I calling them by their first names. I glance at the complaint in the file. It alleges that the plaintiff has loaned the defendant $10,000; the defendant has failed to pay on time; the plaintiff demands damages equal to the amount of the loan plus interest and costs.

"Do you have a defense?" I ask the defendant's lawyer.

"You bet, Your Honor. My client claims—" 8

"Wait a minute," the plaintiff's lawyer interrupts, bristling, "we can't discuss the case before the judge who's going to hear it."

"Take it easy, fellows. I just want to know what the issue is. Any chance of settling the case? If so, I will send you to another judge who can help you reach an agreement."

The trying judge in a court case cannot get involved in settlement negotiations with the attorneys. He may learn facts not admissible into evidence or learn the parties' compromise positions, which may improperly influence his ultimate decision.

Both lawyers shake their heads. The plaintiff's attorney says, 12 "We've tried to settle, Judge, but there's no chance. The case has to be tried."

"Okay, let's try it," I say.

The next moment I am on the bench. The courtroom is small and spare, as unpretentious as the waiting room of a rural railroad station. None of the splendor of a jury courtroom. Aside from the court clerk and reporter, the only others present are the two lawyers and their clients. I have just finished bantering with the lawyers and am now conducting the trial with strict formality. I am amazed at how quickly all of us assume our roles.

Since this is a court case, lawyers will forgo the hammy vaudeville gestures they pull before jurors: the dramatic thrusting of a document at the witness as if piercing his heart; the rolling of the eyes upward and the incredulous shaking of the head at the witness's last answer. They will also eschew hackneyed tactics, such as asking witnesses called by the other attorney whether they talked to the attorney before testifying. They know judges understand that lawyers must speak to witnesses in order to prepare them for trial. If the attorney's do engage in such playacting, I will say, "Counsel, please don't waste my time with this nonsense. Let's get on with the case."

I also try court cases differently from jury cases. For example, although the rules of evidence are supposed to be applied alike in both, I, and most judges, apply them with less rigor in court cases. The analogy can be made between the difference in adult conversation when children are in the room and when they are out of earshot. In court cases, where there is no jury, I tend to be more liberal in letting in evidence that the rules might exclude as unreliable, because, as an experienced trier, I feel capable of disregarding such evidence.

The plaintiff's attorney motions to his client to take the stand. The clerk asks the short, gray-haired man to raise his right hand and intones, "You solemnly swear that the evidence you shall give, concerning the case now in question, shall be the truth, the whole truth, and nothing but the truth, so help you God?"

"I do."

"Give your name and address."

"Frank Romano, Thirty-nine Preston Street, Hartford."

The witness takes his seat in the chair on the raised stand next to the bench. He sits stiffly, ceaselessly kneading his thick hands in his lap. Under questioning by his attorney, he testifies that his niece's husband wanted to start a sidewalk construction business. "That's Joe," he says, pointing to the defendant. "He asked me to loan him ten thousand dollars, and promised to pay me back in two years. I was glad to help him get going in a new business."

The $10,000 check to the order of Joseph Costello is introduced into evidence; it has been duly endorsed and cashed. Mr. Romano's lawyer asks:

"Was your agreement with Costello in writing?"

"No. I trusted him. He was my *paisan*."[1]

Mr. Romano concludes by saying that after three years he demanded payment, and when it was not forthcoming, he started this suit.

---

[1] *paisan* fellow countryman (Italian)

I have been listening and observing the witness. I notice that he holds his head slantwise and seems to speak into space rather than directly to his lawyer.

The defendant's attorney begins his cross-examination of Romano by eliciting from him that he has no children and Joe's wife, Felicia, is his favorite niece. Then the lawyer asks, "Didn't you really give the money to Mr. Costello so he could provide a better living for Felicia?"

"Yes, I wanted to help Felicia. But the money was a loan to Joe." 28

"Yet you waited three years to ask for the money back when you said the loan was for two years, isn't that so?"

"I wanted to see if Joe would pay me back on his own."

"Isn't it a fact that you didn't demand payment until after Joe left Felicia and started the divorce?"

"That had nothing to do with it," Mr. Romano retorts angrily. 32 "It was a loan, and I wanted my money back."

After both counsel finish with the witness, I have a question to ask him. Although in a jury case I intervene as little as possible in order to permit the attorneys to convince the jury in their own way, in court cases they have to convince me, and the decision is my responsibility. I am more interested in finding out all the information that will help me decide than I am in protecting the trial strategy of the lawyers. So I ask from the bench, "Tell me, Mr. Romano, if there had not been a divorce between Joe and Felicia, would you still be asking for the money?"

"Well, Judge . . . I don' . . . I love Felicia. . . . " Mr. Romano looks at his attorney. "But it was a loan, Judge," he says in a rising voice. "Joe promised to pay me back, and he didn't."

Mr. Costello is called by his attorney to the stand. He is a muscular man of about thirty, with wavy black hair and blue eyes. The clerk recites: "You solemnly swear that the evidence you shall give, concerning the case now in question, shall be the truth, the whole truth, and nothing but the truth, so help you God?"

"I do." 36

He is at ease on the witness chair, but I notice he speaks slightly out of the side of his mouth. After some preliminary questions, his lawyer asks, "What was the arrangement concerning the ten thousand dollars with your uncle-in-law?"

"He knew I was going into the construction business and offered to help me. I said I didn't know if I could pay him back. He said, 'Don't worry about it, Joe. This is a gift. Felicia is my favorite niece. I'm glad to help her in this way.' I thanked him. A few days later he gave me the check."

"What happened next?" asks his lawyer.

"Three years later Felicia and I got divorced. Then for the first 40 time he starting pestering me for the money. I woulda paid him just to get him off my back. But the business is barely breaking even, and I just don't have the dough."

Cross-examination does not shake the essentials of his story. That is the case. Simple set of facts. The only thing difficult is the decision.

Was the money given as a loan or a gift? Whom am I to believe, the uncle or the nephew? On what basis can I decide who was telling the truth?

In olden days the sworn oath of a witness as a God-fearing man was thought to assure his telling the truth. Now God is not so feared. We rely on the tendency of people generally to be truthful, on the professional ethics of lawyers not to suborn perjury, and on the weapon of cross-examination. In practice, all are slender reeds.

Professor John Henry Wigmore, leading authority on evidence, 44 warns of the latent errors in oral testimony of "Perception, Recollection or Narration." Witnesses may testify erroneously because they perceive an event incompletely, recall it imperfectly, or tell it inaccurately. Clues to such errors can sometimes be revealed by artful cross-examination. However, the best of cross-examination can rarely crack deliberate perjury or its next of kin, the conscious shading of the truth by a witness out of his own self-interest. Here the uncle and nephew have equal self-interest to remember the facts in the way that favored each of them.

Can I decide credibility on my observations of the demeanor of the uncle and nephew on the stand: the uncle's tenseness, his way of never looking at his lawyer; the nephew's ease, his manner of speaking out of the side of his mouth? Can I, in Shakespeare's felicitous words, "find the mind's construction in the face"? Are the external signs—squints of the eye, twitches in the cheek, nervous gestures of the hands—reliable clues of the speaker's truth or falsity?

I know so little about the uncle and nephew. The uncle has been on the stand about thirty minutes, the nephew twenty. A friend who served on a jury once complained about his lack of information about the background of the witnesses.

"What did you want to know?" I asked.

"For one thing, what people who know the witness think of him. 48 People like his neighbors, his pastor, his banker. For another, what kind of person the witness is. Things like does he pay his debts, give to charities, drink to excess."

"But," I protested, "that would open up so many areas that the trial would never end."

Yet my friend was right in his essential point. Witnesses on the stand appear two-dimensional. Rarely is the third dimension of their character revealed.

Forced to decide in the uncle-nephew case, I choose to believe the nephew. It rings truer to me that the divorce, and not the original understanding about the money, is the real reason the uncle wants to be repaid. I do so despite the uncle's heated denial. But my decision in favor of the nephew has no solid, objectve basis; it is founded not on analysis, but on a hunch.

Topics for Discussion and Writing

1. In paragraph 4 Satter writes, "The facts of a case are the conclusions drawn from the evidence." How does this definition differ from what we ordinarily expect "facts" to mean?

2. In paragraph 16, after admitting that—despite the rules—he tries court cases differently from jury cases, Satter offers an analogy in order to justify his behavior. Do you find the analogy (and the explanation) adequate or inadequate? Why?

3. In paragraph 45 Satter wonders whether, in the words of King Duncan in *Macbeth* (1.4.13–14), he can "find the mind's construction in the face." (In fact, Duncan says that one *cannot* find the mind in the face.) Satter talks about the demeanor of the two witnesses, and in the final paragraph says that he decided on "a hunch," and that the nephew's story "rings truer." Do you suppose that the men's appearances influenced his decision, or simply that the nephew's *story* (and not the *way* he told the story) sounded truer? If you had been the judge, would you have taken into account the manner in which each witness testified? Why?

Edward I. Koch

Edward I. Koch, born in 1924 in New York City, was educated at City College and at New York University Law School. Active in Democratic politics, Mr. Koch served as mayor of New York from 1978 to 1989. This essay appeared in The New Republic, *a publication that usually has a liberal slant.*

Death and Justice: How Capital Punishment Affirms Life

Last December a man named Robert Lee Willie, who had been convicted of raping and murdering an 18-year-old woman, was executed in the Louisiana state prison. In a statement issued several minutes before his death, Mr. Willie said: "Killing people is wrong. . . . It makes no difference whether it's citizens, countries, or governments. Killing is wrong." Two weeks later in South Carolina, an admitted killer named Joseph Carl Shaw was put to death for murdering two teenagers. In an appeal to the governor for clemency, Mr. Shaw wrote: "Killing is wrong when I did it. Killing is wrong when you do it. I hope you have the courage and moral strength to stop the killing."

It is a curiosity of modern life that we find ourselves being lectured on morality by cold-blooded killers. Mr. Willie previously had been convicted of aggravated rape, aggravated kidnapping, and the murders of a Louisiana deputy and a man from Missouri. Mr. Shaw committed another murder a week before the two for which he was executed, and admitted mutilating the body of the 14-year-old girl he killed. I can't help wondering what prompted these murderers to speak out against killing as they entered the death-house door. Did their newfound reverence for life stem from the realization that they were about to lose their own?

Life is indeed precious, and I believe the death penalty helps to affirm this fact. Had the death penalty been a real possibility in the minds of these murderers, they might well have stayed their hand. They might have shown moral awareness before their victims died, and not after. Consider the tragic death of Rosa Velez, who happened to be home when a man named Luis Vera burglarized her apartment in Brooklyn. "Yeah, I shot her," Vera admitted. "She knew me, and I knew I wouldn't go to the chair."

During my 22 years in public service, I have heard the pros and cons of capital punishment expressed with special intensity. As a district leader, councilman, congressman, and mayor, I have represented constituencies generally thought of as liberal. Because I support the death penalty for heinous crimes of murder, I have sometimes been the subject of emotional and outraged attacks by voters who find my position reprehensible or worse. I have listened to their ideas. I have weighed their objections carefully. I still support the death penalty. The reasons I maintain my position can be best understood by examining the arguments most frequently heard in opposition.

1. *The death penalty is "barbaric."* Sometimes opponents of capital punishment horrify with tales of lingering death on the gallows, of faulty electric chairs, or of agony in the gas chamber. Partly in response to such protests, several states such as North Carolina and Texas switched to execution by lethal injection. The condemned person is put to death painlessly, without ropes, voltage, bullets, or gas. Did this answer the objections of death penalty opponents? Of course not. On June 22, 1984, *The New York Times* published an editorial that sarcastically attacked the new "hygienic" method of death by injection, and stated that "execution can never be made humane through science." So it's not the method that really troubles opponents. It's the death itself they consider barbaric.

Admittedly, capital punishment is not a pleasant topic. However, one does not have to like the death penalty in order to support it any more than one must like radical surgery, radiation, or chemotherapy in order to find necessary these attempts at curing cancer. Ultimately we may learn how to cure cancer with a simple pill. Unfortunately, that day has not yet arrived. Today we are faced with the choice of letting the cancer spread or trying to cure it with the methods available, methods that one day will almost certainly be considered barbaric. But to give up and do nothing would be far more barbaric and would certainly delay the discovery of an eventual cure. The analogy between cancer and murder is imperfect, because murder is not the "disease" we are trying to cure. The disease is injustice. We may not like the death penalty, but it must be available to punish crimes of cold-blooded murder, cases in which any other form of punishment would be inadequate and, therefore, unjust. If we create a society in which injustice is not tolerated, incidents of murder—the most flagrant form of injustice—will diminish.

2. *No other major democracy uses the death penalty.* No other major democracy—in fact, few other countries of any description—are plagued by a murder rate such as that in the United States. Fewer and fewer Americans can remember the days when unlocked doors

were the norm and murder was a rare and terrible offense. In America the murder rate climbed 122 percent between 1963 and 1980. During that same period, the murder rate in New York City increased by almost 400 percent, and the statistics are even worse in many other cities. A study at M.I.T. showed that based on 1970 homicide rates a person who lived in a large American city ran a greater risk of being murdered than an American soldier in World War II ran of being killed in combat. It is not surprising that the laws of each country differ according to differing conditions and traditions. If other countries had our murder problem, the cry for capital punishment would be just as loud as it is here. And I daresay that any other major democracy where 75 percent of the people supported the death penalty would soon enact it into law.

3. *An innocent person might be executed by mistake.* Consider the work of Hugo Adam Bedau, one of the most implacable foes of capital punishment in this country. According to Mr. Bedau, it is "false sentimentality to argue that the death penalty should be abolished because of the abstract possibility that an innocent person might be executed." He cites a study of the 7,000 executions in this country from 1893 to 1971, and concludes that the record fails to show that such cases occur. The main point, however, is this. If government functioned only when the possibility of error didn't exist, government wouldn't function at all. Human life deserves special protection, and one of the best ways to guarantee that protection is to assure that convicted murderers do not kill again. Only the death penalty can accomplish this end. In a recent case in New Jersey, a man named Richard Biegenwald was freed from prison after serving 18 years for murder; since his release he has been convicted of committing four murders. A prisoner named Lemuel Smith, who while serving four life sentences for murder (plus two life sentences for kidnapping and robbery) in New York's Green Haven Prison, lured a woman corrections officer into the chaplain's office and strangled her. He then mutilated and dismembered her body. An additional life sentence for Smith is meaningless. Because New York has no death penalty statute, Smith has effectively been given a license to kill.

But the problem of multiple murder is not confined to the nation's penitentiaries. In 1981, 91 police officers were killed in the line of duty in this country. Seven percent of those arrested in the cases that have been solved had a previous arrest for murder. In New York

City in 1976 and 1977, 85 persons arrested for homicide had a previous arrest for murder. Six of these individuals had two previous arrests for murder, and one had four previous murder arrests. During those two years the New York police were arresting for murder persons with a previous arrest for murder on the average of one every 8.5 days. This is not surprising when we learn that in 1975, for example, the median time served in Massachusetts for homicide was less than two-and-a-half years. In 1976 a study sponsored by the Twentieth Century Fund found that the average time served in the United States for first-degree murder is ten years. The median time served may be considerably lower.

4. *Capital punishment cheapens the value of human life.* On the contrary, it can be easily demonstrated that the death penalty strengthens the value of human life. If the penalty for rape were lowered, clearly it would signal a lessened regard for the victims' suffering, humiliation, and personal integrity. It would cheapen their horrible experience, and expose them to an increased danger of recurrence. When we lower the penalty for murder, it signals a lessened regard for the value of the victim's life. Some critics of capital punishment, such as columnist Jimmy Breslin, have suggested that a life sentence is actually a harsher penalty for murder than death. This is sophistic nonsense. A few killers may decide not to appeal a death sentence, but the overwhelming majority make every effort to stay alive. It is by exacting the highest penalty for the taking of human life that we affirm the highest value of human life.

5. *The death penalty is applied in a discriminatory manner.* This factor no longer seems to be the problem it once was. The appeals process for a condemned prisoner is lengthy and painstaking. Every effort is made to see that the verdict and sentence were fairly arrived at. However, assertions of discrimination are not an argument for ending the death penalty but for extending it. It is not justice to exclude everyone from the penalty of the law if a few are found to be so favored. Justice requires that the law be applied equally to all.

6. *Thou Shalt Not Kill.* The Bible is our greatest source of moral [12] inspiration. Opponents of the death penalty frequently cite the sixth of the Ten Commandments in an attempt to prove that capital punishment is divinely proscribed. In the original Hebrew, however, the Sixth Commandment reads, "Thou Shalt Not Commit Murder," and the Torah specifies capital punishment for a variety of offenses. The biblical viewpoint has been upheld by philosophers throughout

history. The greatest thinkers of the 19th century—Kant, Locke, Hobbes, Rousseau, Montesquieu, and Mill—agreed that natural law properly authorizes the sovereign to take life in order to vindicate justice. Only Jeremy Bentham was ambivalent. Washington, Jefferson, and Franklin endorsed it. Abraham Lincoln authorized executions for deserters in wartime. Alexis de Tocqueville, who expressed profound respect for American institutions, believed that the death penalty was indispensable to the support of social order. The United States Constitution, widely admired as one of the seminal achievements in the history of humanity, condemns cruel and inhuman punishment, but does not condemn capital punishment.

7. *The death penalty is state-sanctioned murder.* This is the defense with which Messrs. Willie and Shaw hoped to soften the resolve of those who sentenced them to death. By saying in effect, "You're no better than I am," the murderer seeks to bring his accusers down to his own level. It is also a popular argument among opponents of capital punishment, but a transparently false one. Simply put, the state has rights that the private individual does not. In a democracy, those rights are given to the state by the electorate. The execution of a lawfully condemned killer is no more an act of murder than is legal imprisonment an act of kidnapping. If an individual forces a neighbor to pay him money under threat of punishment, it's called extortion. If the state does it, it's called taxation. Rights and responsibilities surrendered by the individual are what give the state its power to govern. This contract is the foundation of civilization itself.

Everyone wants his or her rights, and will defend them jealously. Not everyone, however, wants responsibilities, especially the painful responsibilities that come with law enforcement. Twenty-one years ago a woman named Kitty Genovese was assaulted and murdered on a street in New York. Dozens of neighbors heard her cries for help but did nothing to assist her. They didn't even call the police. In such a climate the criminal understandably grows bolder. In the presence of moral cowardice, he lectures us on our supposed failings and tries to equate his crimes with our quest for justice.

The death of anyone—even a convicted killer—diminishes us all. But we are diminished even more by a justice system that fails to function. It is an illusion to let ourselves believe that doing away with capital punishment removes the murderer's deed from our conscience. The rights of society are paramount. When we protect guilty lives, we give up innocent lives in exchange. When opponents of capital punishment say to the state: "I will not let you kill in my name," they are also saying to murderers: "You can kill in your *own* name as long as I have an excuse for not getting involved."

It is hard to imagine anything worse than being murdered while 16 neighbors do nothing. But something worse exists. When those same neighbors shrink back from justly punishing the murderer, the victim dies twice.

Topics for Discussion and Writing

1. Koch is, of course, writing an argument. He wants to persuade his readers. Beginning with paragraph 5, he states the opposition's arguments and tries to refute them. But why did he include his first four paragraphs? What, as persuasion, does each contribute?

2. In paragraph 6, Koch compares our use of capital punishment to our use of "radical surgery, radiation, or chemotherapy." Do you find this analogy impressive—or not—and why? (Note that in this paragraph Koch goes on to say that "the analogy between cancer and murder is imperfect." Should he, then, not have used it?)

3. At the end of paragraph 6, Koch says: "If we create a society in which injustice is not tolerated, incidents of murder—the most flagrant form of injustice—will diminish." Has the earlier part of the paragraph prepared us for this statement?

4. Why, or why not, are you persuaded by Koch's second argument, about the likelihood that if other countries had high rates of murder they too would enact the death penalty?

5. In paragraph 9, Koch speaks of "murder" and then of "homicide." Are these two the same? If not, *why* is Koch bringing in statistics about homicide?

6. In paragraph 12, Koch lists authorities who supported the death penalty. Some of these, for instance Washington and Jefferson, also owned slaves. What can be said in behalf of, and what can be said against, Koch's use of these authorities?

7. In paragraph 15, Koch puts a sentence into the mouths of his opponents. *Is* this what his opponents are in effect saying or thinking?

8. If you have read Schwarzschild's remarks opposing capital punishment, below, write an essay indicating which essay you think is a better piece of persuasive writing. Note that it is not a matter of which position you subscribe to; in your essay you are concerned only with the essays as examples of persuasive writing.

Henry Schwarzschild

Henry Schwarzschild was the director of the National Coalition Against the Death Penalty. The material that we print is an excerpt from his statement submitted at the hearing in 1978 before the Subcommittee on Criminal Justice of the Committee on the Judiciary, House of Representatives, 95th Congress, 2nd Session.

In Opposition to Death Penalty Legislation

You know the classic arguments about the merits of the death penalty:

Its dubious and unproved value as a deterrent to violent crime;

The arbitrariness and mistakes inevitable in any system of justice instituted and administered by fallible human beings;

The persistent and ineradicable discrimination on grounds of race, class, and sex in its administration in our country's history (including the present time);

The degrading and hurtful impulse toward retribution and revenge that it expresses;

The barbarousness of its process (whether by burning at the stake, by hanging from the gallows, by frying in the electric chair, by suffocating in the gas chamber, by shooting at the hands of a firing squad, or by lethal injection with a technology designed to heal and save lives);

Even the deeply distorting and costly effect the death penalty has upon the administration of the courts, upon law enforcement, and upon the penal institutions of the country.

Let me therefore concentrate my remarks upon a few selected issues about which much unclarity exists in the public mind, in the media, and even in many legislative chambers.

I want to discuss these issues in the context of the evident support of public opinion for the reintroduction of capital punishment in the country. Let me be candid: For the past few years, public opinion polls, whether national or regional, have tended to reflect a substantial majority of the American people affirming their support for the death penalty, to the level of between 65 percent and 75 percent—enough to make many an elected official surrender his or her religious or moral principles against capital punishment. As little as twenty years ago, the polls reflected almost precisely the opposite distribution of views in the country. It is not hard to infer what has turned the American people back toward support of so atavistic and demonstrably useless a criminal sanction. The causes are (a) the rising rate of violent crime in the past two decades, (b) the increasing panic about the rising crime rate, together with a justified (as well as exaggerated) fear for the safety of lives and property, (c) the understandable reaction to a terrible series of assassinations and attempted assassinations of our national leaders and other prominent personalities (President John Kennedy, Senator Robert Kennedy, the Rev. Dr. Martin Luther King Jr., Governor George Wallace, Malcolm X, Medgar Evers, and others), (d) the rise of international terrorism, including aircraft hijackings and the murder of prominent political and business leaders as well as the random political killings of innocent victims, (e) many years of the effective discontinuation of capital punishment and the remoteness from actual experience of its horrors, and finally (f) a largely subliminal but sometimes almost articulated racism that attributes most violent criminality to the minority community, that knows quite well that the poor and the black are most often the subjects of the death penalty, and that thinks that's just the way it ought to be.

What, then, are the rational answers to this series of partly understandable and partly impermissible misconceptions in the American public? 4

True, violent crime has risen sharply in the past two decades, but to begin with it has been abundantly demonstrated by social research that the availability of the death penalty has no effect whatsoever upon the rate of violent crime; to the contrary, there is some scientific evidence that death sentences imposed and carried out may, for peculiar reasons of social and psychic pathology, be an incentive to further acts of violence in the society. Furthermore, while the rates of most major, violent felonies have been rising—most probably by reason of increased urbanization, social mobility, economic distress, and the like—the rate of non-negligent homicide has been rising at a rate *slower* than the other major felonies, and non-negligent homicide is, of course, the only crime for which the death penalty has been declared constitutionally permissible by the Supreme Court. The crisis in violent crime, such as it is, has therefore been least acute in the area of homicide. Indeed, in the past three years, the murder rate in this country has actually been declining. Thirdly, there is an appalling number of about 20,000 non-negligent homicides in this country per year. But we would have to return to the condition of the mid-1950s to execute as many as one hundred persons per year, and even that would constitute only one in every two hundred murderers. In other words, we have always picked quite arbitrarily a tiny handful of people among those convicted of murder to be executed, not those who have committed the most heinous, the most revolting, the most destructive murders, but always the poor, the black, the friendless, the life's losers, those without competent, private attorneys, the illiterate, those despised or ignored by the community for reasons having nothing to do with their crime. Ninety-nine and one-half percent of all murderers were never executed—and the deterrent value (which very likely does not exist at all in any case) is reduced to invisibility by the overwhelming likelihood that one will not be caught, or not be prosecuted, or not be tried on a capital charge, or not be convicted, or not be sentenced to death, or have the conviction or sentence reversed on appeal, or have one's sentence commuted.

And if we took the other course and eliminated those high chances of not being executed, but rather carried out the death penalty for every murder, then we should be executing 400 persons per week, every week of the month, every month of the year—and that, Mr. Chairman, should strike even the most ardent supporters of the death penalty as a bloodbath, not as a civilized system of criminal justice.

Assassinations and terrorism are well known to be undeterrable by the threat of the death penalty. They are acts of political desperation or political insanity, always committed by people who are at least willing, if not eager, to be martyrs to their cause. Nor would executing terrorists be a preventive against the subsequent taking of hostages for the purpose of setting political assassins or terrorists free. There would of course be a considerable interval of time between arrest and execution, at least for the purpose of trial and the accompanying processes of law, and during that time their fellow activists would have a far more urgent incentive for taking hostages, since not only the freedom but the very lives of their arrested and sentenced colleagues would be at stake. Let me only respectfully add that distinguished fellow citizens of ours such as Senator Edward Kennedy and Ms. Coretta King, who have suffered terrible sadness in their lives at the hands of assassins, are committed opponents of the death penalty.

There has been only one execution in the United States since 8 1967, that of Gary Mark Gilmore, by a volunteer firing squad in Utah on January 17, 1977. Gilmore's execution troubled the public conscience less than it might have otherwise because of his own determination to die. The public and perhaps the legislators of our states and in the Congress have forgotten in a decade that was virtually without executions what sort of demoralizing and brutalizing spectacle executions are. There are now enough people on death row in the country to stage one execution each and every single day for more than a year, to say nothing of the other people who are liable to be sentenced to death during that time. We will again know the details of men crazed with fear, screaming like wounded animals, being dragged from the cell, against their desperate resistance, strapped into the electric chair, voiding their bowels and bladder, being burned alive, almost breaking the restraints from the impact of the high voltage, with their eyeballs popping out of their sockets, the smell of their burning flesh in the nostrils of the witnesses. The ghastly experience of men being hanged, their heads half torn off their bodies, or of the slow strangulation in the gas chamber, or of the press sticking their fingers into the bloody bullet holes of the chair in which Gilmore sat to be executed by rifles, or the use of forcible injection by a paralyzing agent—these reports will not ennoble the image of the United States of America that wants to be the defender of human rights and decency in a world that has largely given up the death penalty as archaic.

No one in this Committee surely is guilty of that shoddiest of all impulses toward capital punishment, namely the sense that white, middle-class people, irrespective of their crime, in fact hardly ever get sentenced to death and in such an extremely rare case are virtually never executed. You, Mr. Chairman and Members, and I and probably everyone in this hearing room are in fact absolutely immune, no matter what ghastly crime we might commit, from the likelihood of being executed for it. The penalty of death is imposed almost entirely upon members of what the distinguished social psychologist Kenneth B. Clark has referred to as "the lower status elements of American society."

Blacks have always constituted a dramatically disproportionate number of persons executed in the United States, far beyond their share of capital crimes, and even as we sit here today they represent half of the more than 500 persons on the death rows of our state prisons. Indeed, not only the race of the criminal is directly proportional to the likelihood of his being sentenced to death and executed but the race of the victim of the crime as well. The large majority of criminal homicides are still disasters between people who have some previous connection with each other (as husband and wife, parent and child, lovers, business associates, and the like), and murder is therefore still largely an intra-racial event, i.e. black on black or white on white. Yet while half the people under sentence of death right now are black (showing egregious discrimination on the grounds of the race of the murderer), about 85 percent of their victims were white.

In other words, it is far more likely to get the murderer into the electric chair or the gas chamber if he has killed a white person than if he had killed a black person, quite irrespective of his own race. (I say "he" in this context for good reason: the death penalty is also highly discriminatory on grounds of sex. Of the 380 death-row inmates in the country today, only two are women, and even they are far more likely objects of executive commutation of their death sentences than their male counterparts.)

Let me add here that, to the extent to which fear of crime and greater exposure to it, combined with inadequate police protection and more callous jurisprudence, has made the minority communities also voice increasing support for the death penalty, they have not yet fully realized that the death penalty will not protect them from what they (and all of us) rightly fear but that their support of capital punishment will only put their brothers and husbands and sons in jeopardy of being killed by the same state that has been unable properly to protect their lives, their rights, or their property to begin with. 12

In sum: The public is deeply uninformed about the real social facts of the death penalty and is responding to the seemingly insoluble problem of crime by a retreat to the hope that an even more severe criminal penalty will stem the tide of violence. But it will not. We do not know what will. Judges and lawyers do not know, philosophers and criminologists don't, not even civil libertarians or legislators know the answer—if any of us did, we would have long since accomplished our purpose of reducing crime to the irreducible minimum. But legislators are not therefore entitled to suborn illusory solutions merely because they would garner widespread though uninformed public approval, in order to signal to the electorate that they are "tough on crime." Capital punishment does not deal with crime in any useful fashion and in fact deludes the public into an entirely false sense of greater security about that complex social problem. The death penalty is a legislative way of avoiding rather than dealing with the problem of crime, and the American public will come to learn this very dramatically and tragically if the Congress should unwisely enact the bill before you today.

Two final words about public support for the death penalty.

There are strong indications that the public in great numbers answers in the affirmative when asked whether they support capital punishment because they want a death penalty law on the books in the hope that this threat will deter criminals from committing violent crimes. Many, perhaps most, of the people who support the enactment of the death penalty do not want executions and would be horrified at being asked to sentence a living human being to a premeditated, ceremonial, legally sanctioned killing. They want deterrence, not electrocutions; prevention, not lethal injections; safety, not firing squads. But a re-enactment by this Congress of a federal death penalty statute will give them at best only electrocutions or lethal injections or firing squads, but neither deterrence nor crime prevention nor safety from violence.

The last stand of supporters for the death penalty, when all the ¹⁶ other arguments have been rebutted or met, is that of retribution or revenge, the proposition that a murderer has forfeited his life and that we should kill him as an act of abstract equity, irrespective of whether executions serve any social purpose whatsoever. We do not need to preach to each other here this morning, but it is important to have it said once more that civilized societies have instituted systems of justice precisely in order to overcome private acts of retribution and revenge and that they have done so with the understanding that social necessity and social usefulness will be the guideposts of their punishments. Since there has never been and cannot be a showing of social usefulness or social necessity for capital punishment, the virtually unanimous voices of the religious community of our land, our leading thinkers and social analysts, in unison with enlightened opinion for hundreds, perhaps thousands, of years should guide your actions on this matter. Whatever the understandable, bitter, vengeful impulses might be of any of us who suffer the disastrous tragedy of having someone we love or respect murdered by pathological or cruel killers, the society's laws are written not to gratify those impulses but to channel them into helpful, healing, and life-sustaining directions. Gratifying the impulse for revenge is not the business of a government that espouses the humane and liberating ideas expressed in our Declaration of Independence and Constitution. It would be rather a return to the darkest instincts of mankind. It would be arrogating unto the state, unto government, either the god-like wisdom to judge who shall live and who shall die or else the totalitarian arrogance to make that judgment. We, as a nation, have foresworn that idolatry of the state that would justify either of these grounds for the legally sanctioned killing of our fellow citizens, of any human being, except perhaps in personal or national self-defense.

Mr. Chairman: The question before the country and before the Congress ultimately is whether it is the right of the state, with premeditation, with the long foreknowledge of the victim, under color of law, in the name of all of us, with great ceremony, and to the approval of many angry people in our land, to kill a fellow citizen, a fellow human being, to do that which we utterly condemn, which we utterly abhor in him for having done. What does the penalty, after all, say to the American people and to our children? That killing is all right if the right people do it and think they have a good enough reason for doing it! That is the rationale of every pathological murderer walking the street: he thinks he is the right person to do it and has a good reason for doing his destructive deed. How can a thoughtful and sensible person justify killing people who kill people to teach that killing is wrong? How can you avert your eyes from the obvious: that the death penalty and that executions in all their bloody and terrible reality only aggravate the deplorable atmosphere of violence, the disrespect for life, and brutalization of ourselves that we need to overcome?

If the death penalty were shown, or even could be shown, to be socially necessary or even useful, I would personally still have a deep objection to it. But those who argue for its re-enactment have not and cannot meet the burden of proving its necessity or usefulness. At the very least, before you kill a human being under law, do you not have to be absolutely certain that you are doing the right thing? But how can you be sure that the criminal justice system has worked with absolute accuracy in designating this single person to be the guilty one, that this single person is the one that should be killed, that killing him is the absolutely right thing to do? You cannot be sure, because human judgment and human institutions are demonstrably fallible. And you cannot kill a man when you are not absolutely sure. You can (indeed sometimes you must) make sure that he is incapacitated from repeating his crime, and we obviously accomplish that by ways other than killing him. And while there is fallibility there also, death is different: it is final, irreversible, barbarous, brutalizing to all who come into contact with it. That it is a very hurtful model for the United States to play in the world, it is a very hurtful model for a democratic and free government to play for its people.

Topics for Discussion and Writing

1. In the first paragraph, what is Schwarzschild getting at when he says that administration of the death penalty has been discriminatory?
2. In paragraph 5 Schwarzschild points out that even when capital punishment was relatively common, "ninety-nine and one-half percent of all murderers were never executed." Assuming the truth of this statement, is it inherently unjust to execute the remaining half of one percent?
3. In paragraph 8 Schwarzschild briefly describes some of the horrible physical responses of persons about to be executed. If one believes that the death penalty serves a useful purpose as a deterrent, should one argue (against Schwarzschild) that executions ought to be televised, so that they would have a maximum effect as deterrents?
4. What is Schwarzchild's chief point in paragraph 16? What counter-arguments can you imagine offering?
5. What is Schwarzchild's strategy in his next-to-last paragraph?
6. Evaluate Schwarzschild's final paragraph as a piece of persuasion.
7. If you have read Koch's essay (page 624) supporting the death penalty, indicate which of Koch's arguments, if any, Schwarzschild does not face.

Stephen Chapman

Stephen Chapman was on the staff of New Republic, *where this essay was first published.*

The Prisoner's Dilemma

If *the punitive laws of Islam were applied for only one year, all the devastating injustices would be uprooted. Misdeeds must be punished by the law of retaliation: cut off the hands of the thief; kill the murderers; flog the adulterous woman or man. Your concerns, your "humanitarian" scruples are more childish than reasonable. Under the terms of Koranic law, any judge fulfilling the seven requirements (that he have reached puberty, be a believer, know the Koranic laws perfectly, be just, and not be affected by amnesia, or be a bastard, or be of the female sex) is qualified to be a judge* *in any type of case. He can thus judge and dispose of twenty trials in a single day, whereas the Occidental justice might take years to argue them out.*

From *Sayings of the Ayatollah Khomeini* (Bantam Books)

One of the amusements of life in the modern West is the opportunity to observe the barbaric rituals of countries that are attached to the customs of the dark ages. Take Pakistan, for example, our newest ally and client state in Asia. Last October President Zia, in harmony with the Islamic fervor that is sweeping his part of the world, revived the traditional Moslem practice of flogging lawbreakers in public. In Pakistan, this qualified as mass entertainment, and no fewer than 10,000 law-abiding Pakistanis turned out to see justice done to 26 convicts. To Western sensibilities the spectacle seemed barbaric—both in the sense of cruel and in the sense of pre-civilized. In keeping with Islamic custom each of the unfortunates—who had been caught in prostitution raids the previous night and summarily convicted and sentenced—was stripped down to a pair of white shorts, which were painted with a red stripe across the buttocks (the target). Then he was shackled against an easel, with pads thoughtfully placed over the kidneys to prevent injury. The floggers were muscular, fierce-looking sorts—convicted murderers, as it happens—who paraded around the flogging platform in colorful loincloths. When the time for the ceremony began, one of the floggers took a running start and brought a five-foot stave down across the first victim's buttocks, eliciting screams from the convict and murmurs from the audience. Each of the 26 received from five to 15 lashes. One had to be carried from the stage unconscious.

Flogging is one of the punishments stipulated by Koranic law, which has made it a popular penological device in several Moslem countries, including Pakistan, Saudi Arabia, and, most recently, the Ayatollah's Iran. Flogging, or *ta'zir*, is the general punishment prescribed for offenses that don't carry an explicit Koranic penalty. Some crimes carry automatic *hadd* punishment—stoning or scourging (a severe whipping) for illicit sex, scourging for drinking alcoholic beverages, amputation of the hands for theft. Other crimes—as varied as murder and abandoning Islam—carry the death penalty (usually carried out in public). Colorful practices like these have given the Islamic world an image in the West, as described by historian G. H. Jansen, "of blood dripping from the stumps of amputated hands and from the striped backs of malefactors, and piles of stones barely concealing the battered bodies of adulterous couples." Jansen, whose book *Militant Islam* is generally effusive in its praise of Islamic practices, grows squeamish when considering devices like flogging, amputation, and stoning. But they are given enthusiastic endorsement by the Koran itself.

Such traditions, we all must agree, are no sign of an advanced civilization. In the West, we have replaced these various punishments (including the death penalty in most cases) with a single device. Our custom is to confine criminals in prison for varying lengths of time. In Illinois, a reasonably typical state, grand theft carries a punishment of three to five years; armed robbery can get you from six to 30. The lowest form of felony theft is punishable by one to three years in prison. Most states impose longer sentences on habitual offenders. In Kentucky, for example, habitual offenders can be sentenced to life in prison. Other states are less brazen, preferring the more genteel sounding "indeterminate sentence," which allows parole boards to keep inmates locked up for as long as life. It was under an indeterminate sentence of one to 14 years that George Jackson served 12 years in California prisons for committing a $70 armed robbery. Under a Texas law imposing an automatic life sentence for a third felony conviction, a man was sent to jail for life last year because of three thefts adding up to less than $300 in property value. Texas also is famous for occasionally imposing extravagantly long sentences, often running into hundreds or thousands of years. This gives Texas a leg up on Maryland, which used to sentence some criminals to life plus a day—a distinctive if superfluous flourish.

The punishment *intended* by Western societies in sending their   4
criminals to prison is the loss of freedom. But, as everyone knows, the actual punishment in most American prisons is of a wholly different order. The February 2 riot at New Mexico's state prison in Santa Fe, one of several bloody prison riots in the nine years since the Attica bloodbath, once again dramatized the conditions of life in an American prison. Four hundred prisoners seized control of the prison before dawn. By sunset the next day 33 inmates had died at the hands of other convicts and another 40 people (including five guards) had been seriously hurt. Macabre stories came out of prisoners being hanged, murdered with blow-torches, decapitated, tortured, and mutilated in a variety of gruesome ways by drug-crazed rioters.

The Santa Fe penitentiary was typical of most maximum-security facilities, with prisoners subject to overcrowding, filthy conditions, and routine violence. It also housed first-time, non-violent offenders, like check forgers and drug dealers, with murderers serving life sentences. In a recent lawsuit, the American Civil Liberties Union called the prison "totally unfit for human habitation." But the ACLU says New Mexico's penitentiary is far from the nation's worst.

That American prisons are a disgrace is taken for granted by experts of every ideological stripe. Conservative James Q. Wilson has criticized our "[c]rowded, antiquated prisons that require men and women to live in fear of one another and to suffer not only deprivation of liberty but a brutalizing regimen." Leftist Jessica Mitford has called our prisons "the ultimate expression of injustice and inhumanity." In 1973 a national commission concluded that "the American correctional system today appears to offer minimum protection to the public and maximum harm to the offender." Federal courts have ruled that confinement in prisons in 16 different states violates the constitutional ban on "cruel and unusual punishment."

What are the advantages of being a convicted criminal in an advanced culture? First there is the overcrowding in prisons. One Tennessee prison, for example, has a capacity of 806, according to accepted space standards, but it houses 2300 inmates. One Louisiana facility has confined four and five prisoners in a single six-foot-by-six-foot cell. Then there is the disease caused by overcrowding, unsanitary conditions, and poor or inadequate medical care. A federal appeals court noted that the Tennessee prison had suffered frequent outbreaks of infectious diseases like hepatitis and tuberculosis. But the most distinctive element of American prison life is its constant violence. In his book *Criminal Violence, Criminal Justice*, Charles Silberman noted that in one Louisiana prison, there were 211 stabbings in only three years, 11 of them fatal. There were 15 slayings in a prison in Massachusetts between 1972 and 1975. According to a federal court, in Alabama's penitentiaries (as in many others), "robbery, rape, extortion, theft and assault are everyday occurrences."

At least in regard to cruelty, it's not at all clear that the system of punishment that has evolved in the West is less barbaric than the grotesque practices of Islam. Skeptical? Ask yourself: would you rather be subjected to a few minutes of intense pain and considerable public humiliation, or to be locked away for two or three years in a prison cell crowded with ill-tempered sociopaths? Would you rather lose a hand or spend 10 years or more in a typical state prison? I have taken my own survey on this matter. I have found no one who does not find the Islamic system hideous. And I have found no one who, given the choices mentioned above, would not prefer its penalties to our own.

The great divergence between Western and Islamic fashions in punishment is relatively recent. Until roughly the end of the 18th century, criminals in Western countries rarely were sent to prison. Instead they were subjected to an ingenious assortment of penalties. Many perpetrators of a variety of crimes simply were executed, usually by some imaginative and extremely unpleasant method involving prolonged torture, such as breaking on the wheel, burning at the stake, or drawing and quartering. Michel Foucault's book *Discipline and Punish: The Birth of the Prison* notes one form of capital punishment in which the condemned man's "belly was opened up, his entrails quickly ripped out, so that he had time to see them, with his own eyes, being thrown on the fire; in which he was finally decapitated and his body quartered." Some criminals were forced to serve on slave galleys. But in most cases various corporal measures such as pillorying, flogging, and branding sufficed.

In time, however, public sentiment recoiled against these measures. They were replaced by imprisonment, which was thought to have two advantages. First, it was considered to be more humane. Second, and more important, prison was supposed to hold out the possibility of rehabilitation — purging the criminal of his criminality — something that less civilized punishments did not even aspire to. An 1854 report by inspectors of the Pennsylvania prison system illustrates the hopes nurtured by humanitarian reformers:

> Depraved tendencies, characteristic of the convict, have been restrained by the absence of vicious association, and in the mild teaching of Christianity, the unhappy criminal finds a solace for an involuntary exile from the comforts of social life. If hungry, he is fed; if naked, he is clothed; if destitute of the first rudiments of education, he is taught to read and write; and if he has never been blessed with a means of livelihood, he is schooled in a mechanical art, which in after life may be to him the source of profit and respectability. Employment is not his toil nor labor, weariness. He embraces them with alacrity, as contributing to his moral and mental elevation.

Imprisonment is now the universal method of punishing criminals in the United States. It is thought to perform five functions, each of which has been given a label by criminologists. First, there is simple *retribution*: punishing the lawbreaker to serve society's sense of justice and to satisfy the victims' desire for revenge. Second, there is *specific deterrence:* discouraging the offender from misbehaving in the future. Third, *general deterrence:* using the offender as an example to discourage others from turning to crime. Fourth, *prevention:* at least during the time he is kept off the streets, the criminal cannot victimize other members of society. Finally, and most important, there is rehabilitation: reforming the criminal so that when he returns to society he will be inclined to obey the laws and able to make an honest living.

How satisfactorily do American prisons perform by these criteria? Well, of course, they do punish. But on the other scores they don't do so well. Their effect in discouraging future criminality by the prisoner or others is the subject of much debate, but the soaring rates of the last 20 years suggest that prisons are not a dramatically effective deterrent to criminal behavior. Prisons do isolate convicted criminals, but only to divert crime from ordinary citizens to prison guards and fellow inmates. Almost no one contends anymore that prisons rehabilitate their inmates. If anything, they probably impede rehabilitation by forcing inmates into prolonged and almost exclusive association with other criminals. And prisons cost a lot of money. Housing a typical prisoner in a typical prison costs far more than a stint at a top university. This cost would be justified if prisons did the job they were intended for. But it is clear to all that prisons fail on the very grounds—humanity and hope of rehabilitation—that caused them to replace earlier, cheaper forms of punishment. 12

The universal acknowledgment that prisons do not rehabilitate criminals has produced two responses. The first is to retain the hope of rehabilitation but do away with imprisonment as much as possible and replace it with various forms of "alternative treatment," such as psychotherapy, supervised probation, and vocational training. Psychiatrist Karl Menninger, one of the principal critics of American penology, has suggested even more unconventional approaches, such as "a new job opportunity or a vacation trip, a course of reducing exercises, a cosmetic surgical operation or a herniotomy, some night school courses, a wedding in the family (even one for the patient!), an inspiring sermon." This starry-eyed approach naturally has produced a backlash from critics on the right, who think that it's time to abandon the goal of rehabilitation. They argue that prisons perform an important service just by keeping criminals off the streets, and thus should be used with that purpose alone in mind.

So the debate continues to rage in all the same old ruts. No one, of course, would think of copying the medieval practices of Islamic nations and experimenting with punishments such as flogging and amputation. But let us consider them anyway. How do they compare with our American prison system in achieving the ostensible objectives of punishment? First, do they punish? Obviously they do, and in a uniquely painful and memorable way. Of course any sensible person, given the choice, would prefer suffering these punishments to years of incarceration in a typical American prison. But presumably no Western penologist would criticize Islamic punishments on the grounds that they are not barbaric enough. Do they deter crime? Yes, and probably more effectively than sending convicts off to prison. Now we read about a prison sentence in the newspaper, then think no more about the criminal's payment for his crimes until, perhaps, years later we read a small item reporting his release. By contrast, one can easily imagine the vivid impression it would leave to be wandering through a local shopping center and to stumble onto the scene of some poor wretch being lustily flogged. And the occasional sight of an habitual offender walking around with a bloody stump at the end of his arm no doubt also would serve as a forceful reminder that crime does not pay.

Do flogging and amputation discourage recidivism? No one knows whether the scars on his back would dissuade a criminal from risking another crime, but it is hard to imagine that corporal measures could stimulate a higher rate of recidivism than already exists. Islamic forms of punishment do not serve the favorite new right goal of simply isolating criminals from the rest of society, but they may achieve the same purpose of making further crimes impossible. In the movie *Bonnie and Clyde*, Warren Beatty successfully robs a bank with his arm in a sling, but this must be dismissed as artistic license. It must be extraordinarily difficult, at the very least, to perform much violent crime with only one hand.

Do these medieval forms of punishment rehabilitate the crimi- 16 nal? Plainly not. But long prison terms do not rehabilitate either. And it is just as plain that typical Islamic punishments are no crueler to the convict than incarceration in the typical American state prison.

Of course there are other reasons besides its bizarre forms of punishment that the Islamic system of justice seems uncivilized to the Western mind. One is the absence of due process. Another is the long list of offenses—such as drinking, adultery, blasphemy, "profiteering," and so on—that can bring on conviction and punishment. A third is all the ritualistic mumbo-jumbo in pronouncements of Islamic law (like that talk about puberty and amnesia in the Ayatollah's quotation at the beginning of this article). Even in these matters, however, a little cultural modesty is called for. The vast majority of American criminals are convicted and sentenced as a result of plea bargaining, in which due process plays almost no role. It has been only half a century since a wave of religious fundamentalism stirred this country to outlaw the consumption of alcoholic beverages. Most states also still have laws imposing austere constraints on sexual conduct. Only two weeks ago the *Washington Post* reported that the FBI had spent two and a half years and untold amounts of money to break up a nationwide pornography ring. Flogging the clients of prostitutes, as the Pakistanis did, does seem silly. But only a few months ago Mayor Koch of New York was proposing that clients caught in his own city have their names broadcast by radio stations. We are not so far advanced on such matters as we often like to think. Finally, my lawyer friends assure me that the rules of jurisdiction for American courts contain plenty of petty requirements and bizarre distinctions that would sound silly enough to foreign ears.

Perhaps it sounds barbaric to talk of flogging and amputation, and perhaps it is. But our system of punishment also is barbaric, and probably more so. Only cultural smugness about their system and willful ignorance about our own make it easy to regard the one as cruel and the other as civilized. We inflict our cruelties away from public view, while nations like Pakistan stage them in front of 10,000 onlookers. Their outrages are visible; ours are not. Most Americans can live their lives for years without having their peace of mind disturbed by the knowledge of what goes on in our prisons. To choose imprisonment over flogging and amputation is not to choose human kindness over cruelty, but merely to prefer that our cruelties be kept out of sight, and out of mind.

Public flogging and amputation may be more barbaric forms of punishment than imprisonment, even if they are not more cruel. Society may pay a higher price for them, even if the particular criminal does not. Revulsion against officially sanctioned violence and infliction of pain derives from something deeply ingrained in the Western conscience, and clearly it is something admirable. Grotesque displays of the sort that occur in Islamic countries probably breed a greater tolerance for physical cruelty, for example, which prisons do not do precisely because they conceal their cruelties. In fact it is our admirable intolerance for calculated violence that makes it necessary for us to conceal what we have not been able to do away with. In a way this is a good thing, since it holds out the hope that we may eventually find a way to do away with it. But in another way it is a bad thing, since it permits us to congratulate ourselves on our civilized humanitarianism while violating its norms in this one area of our national life.

Topics for Discussion and Writing

1. What is the effect of juxtaposing the epigraph (the quotation at the top of the essay) with the first paragraph? By the time we finish the first paragraph, do we feel confident that the Ayatollah has been put into his place? Having read the entire essay, how would you explain Chapman's strategy in beginning the way he begins?
2. Consider the two systems of punishment, and make a list of the pros and cons for each, drawing on Chapman's essay but adding any other points that you can think of.
3. Despite apparent disclaimers, implied for example by using the word "barbaric" when speaking of Islamic punishments, is Chapman in fact arguing that we adopt a system of punishment more or less similar to the Islamic system? If not, what *is* he arguing? What do you think is the chief message that he wishes to convey?
4. In paragraph 8, Chapman says that the persons whom he surveyed preferred the Islamic punishments to our own. Ask a dozen or so people to read Chapman's essay, at least up to this point, and find out their preferences. In 500 words report the result of your survey, including some effective quotations.

Jean-Bertrand Aristide

Jean-Bertrand Aristide was elected President of Haiti in 1990, in the first fair election in the country's history. Born into an impoverished farming family, he would ordinarily have grown up illiterate, but his father died when Jean-Bertrand was only three months old, and his mother, who became a merchant, saw to it that her son was educated. After graduating from the national university, where he majored in psychology, he studied theology abroad and was ordained in 1982. An outspoken foe of the tyrannical Duvalier regime, he was immensely popular among the people but was strongly opposed not only by the government but also by the church hierarchy and by the government that followed Duvalier's fall. In 1988 his church was burned to the ground while the police looked on; and although thirteen people lost their lives, Aristide escaped. When at last an honest election could be held, he won almost 70% of the vote. On 30 September, 1991, less than eight months after taking office, he was deposed in a military rebellion.

A selection of Aristide's sermons has been published, entitled In the Parish of the Poor *(1990). The material that we print was part of a sermon, and was reprinted in* The New York Times.

Disobey the Rules

Haiti is a prison. In that prison, there are rules you must abide by, or suffer the pain of death. One rule is: Never ask for more than what the prison warden considers your share. Never ask for more than a cupful of rice and a drink of dirty water each day, or each week. Another rule is: Remain in your cell. Though it is crowded and stinking and full of human refuse, remain there, and do not complain. That is your lot.

Another rule is: Do not organize. Do not speak to your fellow prisoners about your plight. Every time you get two cups of rice, another prisoner will go hungry. Every time another prisoner gets two drinks of dirty water, you will go thirsty. Hate your fellow man.

Another rule is: Accept your punishment silently. Do not cry out. You are guilty. The warden has decreed it. Live in silence until you die. Never try to escape, for escape means a certain return to this prison, and worse cruelty, worse torture. If you dare to escape in your little boat, the corrections officer from the cold country to the north will capture you and send you back to eke out your days within your eternal prison, which is Haiti.

Fort Dimanche is Haiti. Fort Dimanche is Latin American today. Latin America and Haiti today are Fort Dimanche. Fort Dimanche spits out bullets and tear gas and death. It spews rules, regulations, law, order, decree and death. It vomits on us a system of cruelty, repression, exploitation, misery, and death. If we live by its rules, we will certainly perish beneath its whip.

I say: Disobey the rules. Ask for more. Leave your wretchedness behind. Organize with your brothers and sisters. Never accept the hand of fate. Keep hope alive. Refuse the squalor of the parishes of the poor. Escape the charnel house, and move toward life. Fill the parishes of the poor with hope and meaning and life. March out of the prison, down the hard and pitiless road toward life, and you will find the parishes of the poor gleaming and sparkling with joy in the sunrise at the road's end. Children with strong bodies will run with platefuls of rice and beans to greet their starving saviors. That is your reward. Along that hard and pitiless road toward life, death comes as an honor. But life in the charnel house is a disgrace, an affront to humankind.

Topic for Discussion and Writing

Aristide's message to Haiti's impoverished and illiterate masses is clear. Can you account for its appeal outside of Haiti? Do you find in it any relevance to your own life?

Jeffrey W. Leppo and Robert J. Bryan

Jeffrey W. Leppo, a 35-year-old Seattle lawyer, was preparing to argue a civil case in May when he learned that the trial date had been postponed until Oct. 1 — the day after he was to return from his honeymoon.

Desperate to salvage his wedding plans, Mr. Leppo filed a motion with the trial judge in Federal District Court in Tacoma, Wash., requesting that the trial be further postponed, until Oct. 8. Here are excerpts from his motion and the Judge's order.

Get Me to the Church on Time, Your Honor

I. Introductlon

Jeffrey W. Leppo ("Counsel") respectfully requests that this Court reconsider its decision to amend the trial date of this litigation to Oct. 1, 1990. Counsel requests that the trial begin one week later on Oct. 8, 1990.

II. Marital Facts

Counsel bases this motion upon the following uncontroverted facts:

It has taken Counsel over 34 years to find someone whom he loves and who loves him.

Counsel became engaged on Jan. 31, 1990, at a time when this matter was set for trial beginning May 21, 1990.   4

Scheduling for a wedding, especially one involving the concurrence of two out-of-town families and the Roman Catholic Church, requires considerable advance planning.

Counsel's honeymoon was scheduled for Sept. 11 through Sept. 30, 1990. On very solid information and belief, Counsel believes his betrothed will feel very irritated, ignored [and] offended if the honeymoon must be cancelled, delayed or cut short. Counsel further believes such feelings would be justified.

Counsel is loath to begin what he very sincerely hopes and intends to be his one and only marriage by offending his bride-to-be, in-laws, associated friends, and the Roman Catholic Church.

III. Prayer for Relief

The merits of this motion are founded upon common notions of respect, fairness and compassion. Accordingly, they speak for themselves. Nevertheless, one point bears further brief discussion. [8]

After completing four months of marriage preparation classes approved by the parish priest of Counsel's betrothed, Counsel has been informed that his proposed marriage is now blessed and sacred to the Roman Catholic Church. Counsel is not exactly sure what this means, but is convinced after experiencing the prescribed preparation that the Roman Catholic Church has little sense of humor about such matters. Counsel seriously suspects that it would be a Mortal Sin (in secular terms, a "Big Mistake") to disappoint the Roman Catholic Church at this point in time.

Accordingly, Counsel respectfully offers the eternal gratitude of himself, his heirs, his assigns and his issue (if any there be), in return for the Court's compassion. Counsel warrants that this eternal gratitude will be far more valuable a gift should he be so fortunate as to spend his days on Earth in the state of Marital Bliss and the Everlasting in a state of heavenly repose.

> DATED this 29th day of May, 1990.
> Jeffry W. Leppo
> Counsel of Record for Plaintiff
> Port of Tacoma

Order

In this court's 20 years of judicial experience, counsel's motion for reconsideration is unprecedented in its creativity and urgency. In a spirit of cooperation with Mr. Leppo's efforts to avoid eternal damnation and to please (and appease) his intended, their families and friends, as well as the Roman Catholic Church, it is hereby

ORDERED that the Port of Tacoma's Motion for Reconsideration of Second-Amended Trial Date is GRANTED and the trial date of this case is hereby continued to October 9, 1990.

> DATED this 31st day of May, 1990.
> By Robert J. Bryan
> United States District Judge

Mr. Leppo's marrige to Robin McManamin, a property manager in Seattle, took place as scheduled on Sept. 8. Their honeymoon was in Bali and Indonesia.

Yesterday Mr. Leppo was in Federal District Court in Tacoma, where Judge Bryan was hearing the case that almost pre-empted a wedding: Port of Tacoma v. Asarco Incorporated, a New Jersey corporation, and other defendants.

Topics for Discussion and Writing

1. Consult the entry on "parody" in A Writer's Glossary (page 882). Evaluate "Get Me to The Church on Time" as parody, being as specific as you can.
2. File a motion requesting the appropriate authority to postpone an exam, lengthen a recess, raise a wage, accompany you to a concert—or whatever you most earnestly desire. Your motion, like Leppo's, should have an Introduction, a Facts section, a Prayer for Relief, and a respectful tone.
3. We have no further questions.

Mitsuye Yamada

Mitsuye Yamada, the daughter of Japanese immigrants to the United States, was born in Japan in 1923, during her mother's return visit to her native land. Yamada was raised in Seattle, but in 1942 she and her family were incarcerated and then relocated in a camp in Idaho, when Executive Order 9066 gave military authorities the right to remove any and all persons from "military areas." In 1954 she became an American citizen. A professor of English at Cypress Junior College in San Luis Obispo, California, she is the author of poems and stories.

To the Lady

The one in San Francisco who asked:
Why did the Japanese Americans let
the government put them in
those camps without protest?

Come to think of it I   5
    should've run off to Canada
    should've hijacked a plane to Algeria
    should've pulled myself up from my
    bra straps
    and kicked'm in the groin   10
    should've bombed a bank
    should've tried self-immolation
    should've holed myself up in a
    woodframe house
    and let you watch me   15
    burn up on the six o'clock news
    should've run howling down the street
    naked and assaulted you at breakfast
    by AP wirephoto
    should've screamed bloody murder   20
    like Kitty Genovese[1]

    Then
YOU would've
    come to my aid in shining armor
    laid yourself across the railroad track   25

---

[1] **Kitty Genovese** In 1964 Kitty Genovese of Kew Gardens, New York, was stabbed to death when she left her car and walked toward her home. Thirty-eight persons heard her screams, but no one came to her assistance.

marched on Washington
tatooed a Star of David on your arm
written six million enraged
letters to Congress

But we didn't draw the line   30
anywhere
law and order Executive Order 9066[2]
social order moral order internal order

YOU let'm
I let'm   35
All are punished.

[1976]

Topics for Discussion and Writing

1. Has the lady's question (lines 2–4) ever crossed your mind? If so, what answers did you think of?
2. What, in effect, is the speaker really saying in lines 5–21? And in lines 24–29?
3. Explain the last line.

---

[2] **Executive Order 9066** an authorization, signed in 1941 by President Franklin D. Roosevelt, allowing military authorities to relocate Japanese and Japanese-Americans who resided on the Pacific Coast of the United States

11

IDENTITIES

Grandfather and Grandchildren Awaiting Evacuation Bus
Dorothea Lange

Behind the Bar, Birney, Montana
Marion Post Wolcott, 1941

Short Views

In every known society, the male's need for achievement can be recognized. Men may cook, or weave, or dress dolls or hunt hummingbirds, but if such activities are appropriate occupations of men, then the whole society, men and women alike, votes them as important. When the same occupations are performed by women, they are regarded as less important.

Margaret Mead

There is no female mind. The brain is not an organ of sex. As well speak of a female liver.

Charlotte Perkins Gilman

This has always been a man's world, and none of the reasons hitherto brought forward in explanation of this fact has seemed adequate.

Simone de Beauvoir

We all have been put into categories which fix us in a position which lasts the whole of our lives. Girls are called "feminine" beings and are taught the appropriate feminine behavior; boys are labelled "masculine" and have their behavior defined for them too. No one escapes. Failure to conform to our assigned behavior means that we feel wrong and bad about ourselves. We are not encouraged to break the laws of sex and gender; and certainly no one questions whether the demands of society are contrary to the demands of being human. There ought to be questions asked, though. For what society does is not in our best interest as persons. Society's interest is concerned with how effective we will be as economic and political and cultural supports, not how human we will be.

Heather Formaini

America is God's crucible, the great melting pot where all the races of Europe are melting and re-forming.

Israel Zangwill

No metaphor can capture completely the complexity of ethnic dynamics in the U. S. "Melting pot" ignores the persistence and reconfiguration of ethnicity over the generations. "Mosaic," much more apt for pluralistic societies such as Kenya or India, is too static a metaphor; it fails to take into account the easy penetration of many ethnic boundaries. Nor is "salad bowl" appropriate; the ingredients of a salad bowl are mixed but do not change. "Rainbow" is a tantalizing metaphor, but rainbows disappear. "Symphony," like "rainbow," implies near perfect harmony; both fail to take into account the variety and range of ethnic conflict in the United States.

The most accurately descriptive metaphor, the one that best explains the dynamics of ethnicity, is "kaleidoscope." American ethnicity is kaleidoscopic, i.e. "complex and varied, changing form, pattern, color . . . continually shifting from one set of relations to another; rapidly changing." When a kaleidoscope is in motion, the parts give the appearance of rapid change and extensive variety in color and shape and in their interrelationships. The viewer sees an endless variety of variegated patterns, just as takes place on the American ethnic landscape.
Lawrence Fuchs

We have room for but one language here and that is the English language, for we intend to see that the crucible turns out our people as Americans, of American nationality and not as dwellers in a polyglot boarding house, and we have room for but one loyalty and that is a loyalty to the American people.
Theodore Roosevelt

I cannot say too often — any man who carries a hyphen about him carries a dagger which he is ready to plunge into the vitals of the Republic.
Woodrow Wilson

Capitalism is a machine for the suppression of one class by another.
Vladimir I. Lenin

Through our own efforts and concerted good faith in learning to know, thus to respect, the wonderfully rich and diverse subcom-

munities of America, we can establish a new vision of America: a place where "community" may mean many things, yet retains its deeper spiritual significance. We may even learn to coincide with the 500th anniversary of the "discovery" of America by Columbus, that America, in its magnificent variety, has yet to be discovered.
Joyce Carol Oates

I have a dream that my four little children will one day live in a nation where they will not be judged by the color of their skin but by the content of their character.
Martin Luther King, Jr.

Dorothy Sayers

Dorothy Sayers (1893–1957), English writer, was one of the first women to get a degree from Oxford University, when in 1915 she was awarded first-class honors in medieval literature. After graduating, she taught and worked as a copy writer in an advertising agency, while she was writing novels. Her first detective novel, Whose Body? *(1923), introduced Lord Peter Wimsey, who reappeared in ten later novels. His success enabled her to devote herself full-time to being a writer. Her interest in medieval literature continued, however, and she published a number of essays on the topic, as well as essays on political, social, and religious matters, and a translation of most of Dante's* Divine Comedy.*

When Sayers first published "Are Women Human?" in 1947, she identified it as an "Address given to a Women's Society, 1938."

Are Women Human?

When I was asked to come and speak to you, your Secretary made the suggestion that she thought I must be interested in the feminist movement. I replied—a little irritably, I am afraid—that I was not sure I wanted to identify myself," as the phrase goes, with feminism, and that the time for "feminism," in the old-fashioned sense of the word, had gone past. In fact, I think I went so far as to say that, under present conditions, an aggressive feminism might do more harm than good. As a result I was, perhaps not unnaturally, invited to explain myself.

I do not know that it is very easy to explain, without offence or risk of misunderstanding, exactly what I do mean, but I will try.

The question of "sex-equality" is, like all questions affecting human relationships, delicate and complicated. It cannot be settled by loud slogans or hard-and-fast assertions like "a woman is as good as a man"—or "woman's place is the home"—or "women ought not to take men's jobs." The minute one makes such assertions, one finds one has to qualify them. "A woman is as good as a man" is as meaningless as to say, "a Kaffir is as good as a Frenchman" or "a poet is as good as an engineer" or "an elephant is as good as a racehorse"—it means nothing whatever until you add: "at doing what?" In a religious sense, no doubt, the Kaffir is as valuable in the eyes of God as a Frenchman—but the average Kaffir is probably less skilled in literary criticism than the average Frenchman, and the average Frenchman less skilled than the average Kaffir in tracing the spoor of big game. There might be exceptions on either side: it is largely a matter of heredity and education. When we balance the poet against the engineer, we are faced with a fundamental difference of temperament—so that here our question is complicated by the enormous social problem whether poetry or engineering is "better" for the State, or for humanity in general. There may be people who would like a world that was all engineers or all poets—but most of us would like to have a certain number of each; though here again, we should all differ about the desirable proportion of engineering to poetry. The only provison we should make is that people with dreaming and poetical temperaments should not entangle themselves in engines, and that mechanically-minded persons should not issue booklets of bad verse. When we come to the elephant and the racehorse, we come down to bedrock physical differences—the elephant would make a poor showing in the Derby, and the unbeaten Eclipse himself would be speedily eclipsed by an elephant when it came to hauling logs.

That is so obvious that it hardly seems worth saying. But it is the 4 mark of all movements, however well-intentioned, that their pioneers tend, by much lashing of themselves into excitement, to lose sight of the obvious. In reaction against the age-old slogan, "woman is the weaker vessel," or the still more offensive, "woman is a divine creature," we have, I think, allowed ourselves to drift into asserting that "a woman is as good as a man," without always pausing to think what exactly we mean by that. What, I feel, we ought to mean is something so obvious that it is apt to escape attention altogether, viz: not that every woman is, in virtue of her sex, as strong, clever, artistic, level-headed, industrious, and so forth as any man that can be mentioned; but, that a woman is just as much an ordinary human being as a man, with the same individual preferences, and with just as much right to the tastes and preferences of an individual. What is repugnant to every human being is to be reckoned always as a member of a class and not as an individual person. A certain amount of classification is, of course, necessary for practical purposes: there is no harm in saying that women, as a class, have smaller bones than men, wear lighter clothing, have more hair on their heads and less on their faces, go more pertinaciously to church or the cinema, or have more patience with small and noisy babies. In the same way, we may say that stout people of both sexes are commonly better-tempered than thin ones, or that university dons of both sexes are more pedantic in their speech than agricultural labourers, or that Communists of both sexes are more ferocious than Fascists—or the other way round. What is unreasonable and irritating is to assume that *all* one's tastes and preferences have to be conditioned by the class to which one belongs. That has been the very common error into which men have frequently fallen about women—and it is the error into which feminist women are, perhaps, a little inclined to fall into about themselves.

Take, for example, the very usual reproach that women nowadays always want to "copy what men do." In that reproach there is a great deal of truth and a great deal of sheer, unmitigated, and indeed quite wicked nonsense. There are a number of jobs and pleasures which men have in times past cornered for themselves. At one time, for instance, men had a monopoly of classical education. When the pioneers of university training for women demanded that women should be admitted to the universities, the cry went up at once: "Why should women want to know about Aristotle?" The answer is NOT that *all* women would be the better for knowing about Aristotle—still less, as Lord Tennyson[1] seemed to think, that they would be more companionable wives for their husbands if they did know about Aristotle—but simply: "What women want as a class is irrelevant. *I* want to know about Aristotle. It is true that most women care nothing about him, and a great many male undergraduates turn pale and faint at the thought of him—but I, eccentric individual that I am, do want to know about Aristotle, and I submit that there is nothing in my shape or bodily functions which need prevent my knowing about him."

---

[1] **Aristotle . . . Lord Tennyson** Aristotle (384–322 B.C.) was a Greek philosopher; Tennyson (1809–92) was a Victorian poet. (All notes to this selection are by the editors.)

That battle was won, and rightly won, for women. But there is a sillier side to the university education of women. I have noticed lately, and with regret, a tendency on the part of the women's colleges to "copy the men" on the side of their failings and absurdities, and this is not so good. Because the constitution of the men's colleges is autocratic, old-fashioned, and in many respects inefficient, the women are rather inclined to try and cramp their own collegiate constitutions—which were mapped out on freer democratic lines—into the mediaeval mould of the men's—and that is unsound. It contributes nothing to the university and it loses what might have been a very good thing. The women students, too, have a foolish trick of imitating and outdoing the absurdities of male undergraduates. To climb in drunk after hours and get gated[2] is silly and harmless if done out of pure high spirits: if it is done "because the men do it," it is worse than silly, because it is not spontaneous and not even amusing.

Let me give one simple illustration of the difference between the right and the wrong kind of feminism. Let us take this terrible business—so distressing to the minds of bishops—of the women who go about in trousers. We are asked: "Why do you want to go about in trousers? They are extremely unbecoming to most of you. You only do it to copy the men." To this we may very properly reply: "It is true that they are unbecoming. Even on men they are remarkably unattractive. But, as you men have discovered for yourselves, they are comfortable, they do not get in the way of one's activities like skirts and they protect the wearer from draughts about the ankles. As a human being, I like comfort, and dislike draughts. If the trousers do not attract you, so much the worse; for the moment I do not want to attract you. I want to enjoy myself as a human being. and why not? As for copying you, certainly you thought of trousers first and to that extent we must copy you. But we are not such abandoned copy-cats as to attach these useful garments to our bodies with braces. There we draw the line. These machines of leather and elastic are unnecessary and unsuited to the female form. They are, moreover, hideous beyond description. And as for indecency—of which you sometimes accuse the trousers—we at least can take our coats off without becoming the half-undressed bedroom spectacle that a man presents in his shirt and braces."

[2] **gated** confined within the college gates

So that when we hear that women have once more laid hands 8
upon something which was previously a man's sole privilege, I think
we have to ask ourselves: is this trousers or is it braces? Is it something useful, convenient, and suitable to a human being as such?
Or is it merely something unnecessary to us, ugly, and adopted
merely for the sake of collaring the other fellow's property? These
jobs and professions, now. It is ridiculous to take on a man's job
just in order to be able to say that "a woman has done it—yah!" The
only decent reason for tackling any job is that it is *your* job and *you*
want to do it.

At this point, somebody is likely to say: "Yes, that is all very
well. But it *is* the woman who is always trying to ape the man. She
is the inferior being. You don't as a rule find the men trying to take
the women's jobs away from them. They don't force their way into
the household and turn women out of their rightful occupations."

Of course they do not. They have done it already.

Let us accept the idea that women should stick to their own
jobs—the jobs they did so well in the good old days before they
started talking about votes and women's rights. Let us return to the
Middle Ages and ask what we should get then in return for certain
political and educational privileges which we should have to
abandon.

It is a formidable list of jobs: the whole of the spinning industry, 12
the whole of the dyeing industry, the whole of the weaving industry. The whole catering industry and—which would not please Lady
Astor,[3] perhaps—the whole of the nation's brewing and distilling.
All the preserving, pickling, and bottling industry, all the bacon-
curing. And (since in those days a man was often absent from home
for months together on war or business) a very large share in the
management of landed estates. Here are the women's jobs—and
what has become of them? They are all being handled by men. It
is all very well to say that woman's place is the home—but modern
civilisation has taken all these pleasant and profitable activities out
of the home, where the women looked after them, and handed them
over to big industry, to be directed and organised by men at the
head of large factories. Even the dairy-maid in her simple bonnet
has gone, to be replaced by a male mechanic in charge of a mechanical milking plant.

---

[3] **Lady Astor** Nancy Astor (1879–1964), American-born British politician. She was the first
woman elected to the British House of Commons. In her years as a Conservative, she was known
as a foe of alcohol and as a champion of women's rights and child welfare.

Now, it is very likely that men in big industries do these jobs better than the women did them at home. The fact remains that the home contains much less of interesting activity than it used to contain. What is more, the home has so shrunk to the size of a small flat that—even if we restrict woman's job to the bearing and rearing of families—there is no room for her to do even that. It is useless to urge the modern woman to have twelve children, like her grandmother. Where is she to put them when she has got them? And what modern man wants to be bothered with them? It is perfectly idiotic to take away women's traditional occupations and then complain because she looks for new ones. Every woman is a human being—one cannot repeat that too often—and a human being *must* have occupation, if he or she is not to become a nuisance to the world.

I am not complaining that the brewing and baking were taken over by the men. If they can brew and bake as well as women or better, then by all means let them do it. But they cannot have it both ways. If they are going to adopt the very sound principle that the job should be done by the person who does it best, then that rule must be applied universally. If the women make better office-workers than men, they must have the office work. If any individual woman is able to make a first-class lawyer, doctor, architect, or engineer, then she must be allowed to try her hand at it. Once lay down the rule that the job comes first and you throw that job open to every individual, man or woman, fat or thin, tall or short, ugly or beautiful, who is able to do that job better than the rest of the world.

Now, it is frequently asserted that, with women, the job does not come first. What (people cry) are women doing with this liberty of theirs? What woman really prefers a job to a home and family? Very few, I admit. It is unfortunate that they should so often have to make the choice. A man does not, as a rule, have to choose. He gets both. In fact, if he wants the home and family, he usually has to take the job as well, if he can get it. Nevertheless, there have been women, such as Queen Elizabeth and Florence Nightingale, who had the choice, and chose the job and made a success of it. And there have been and are many men who have sacrificed their careers for women—sometimes like Antony or Parnell,[4] very disastrously.

---

[4] **Antony or Parnell**   Marc Antony (c. 83 B.C.–30 B.C.), lover and political ally of Cleopatra, was conquered by Octavian. Charles Stewart Parnell (1846–91), Irish politician, fell from power because of the scandal evoked by his affair with a married woman, "Kitty" O'Shea.

When it comes to a *choice,* then every man or woman has to choose as an individual human being, and, like a human being, take the consequences.

As human beings! I am always entertained—and also irritated— by the newsmongers who inform us, with a bright air of discovery, that they have questioned a number of female workers and been told by one and all that they are "sick of the office and would love to get out of it." In the name of God, what human being is *not,* from time to time, heartily sick of the office and would *not* love to get out of it? The time of female officeworkers is daily wasted in sympathising with disgruntled male colleagues who yearn to get out of the office. No human being likes work—not day in and day out. Work is notoriously a curse—and if women *liked* everlasting work they would not be human beings at all. *Being* human beings, they like work just as much and just as little as anybody else. They dislike perpetual washing and cooking just as perpetual typing and standing behind shop counters. Some of them prefer typing to scrubbing—but that does not mean that they are not, as human beings, entitled to damn and blast the typewriter when they feel that way. The number of men who daily damn and blast typewriters is incalculable; but that does not mean that they would be happier doing a little plain sewing. Nor would the women.

I have admitted that there are very few women who would put their job before every earthly consideration. I will go further and assert that there are very few men who would do it either. In fact, there is perhaps only one human being in a thousand who is passionately interested in his job for the job's sake. The difference is that if that one person in a thousand is a man, we say, simply, that he is passionately keen on his job; if she is a woman, we say she is a freak. It is extraordinarily entertaining to watch the historians of the past, for instance, entangling themselves in what they were pleased to call the "problem" of Queen Elizabeth. They invented the most complicated and astonishing reasons both for her success as a sovereign and for her tortuous matrimonial policy. She was the tool of Burleigh, she was the tool of Leicester, she was the fool of Essex: she was diseased, she was deformed, she was a man in disguise. She was a mystery, and must have some extraordinary solution. Only recently has it occurred to a few enlightened people that the solution might be quite simple after all. She might be one of the rare people who were born into the right job and put that job first. Whereupon a whole series of riddles cleared themselves up by magic. She was in love with Leicester—why didn't she marry him? Well, for the very same reason that numberless kings have not married their lovers—because it would have thrown a spanner into the wheels of the State machine. Why was she so blood-thirsty and unfeminine as to sign the death-warrant of Mary Queen of Scots? For much the same reasons that induced King George V to say that if the House of Lords did not pass the Parliament Bill he would create enough new peers to force it through—because she was, in the measure of her time, a constitutional sovereign, and knew that there was a point beyond which a sovereign could not defy Parliament. Being a rare human being with her eye to the job, she did what was necessary; being an ordinary human being, she hesitated a good deal before embarking on unsavoury measures— but as to feminine mystery, there is no such thing about it, and no-body, had she been a man, would have thought either her states-manship or her humanity in any way mysterious. Remarkable they were—but she was a very remarkable person. Amont her most remarkable achievements was that of showing that sovereignty was one of the jobs for which the right kind of woman was particularly well fitted.

Which brings us back to this question of what jobs, if any, are women's jobs. Few people would go so far as to say that all women are well fitted for all men's jobs. When people do say this, it is par-ticularly exasperating. It is stupid to insist that there are as many female musicians and mathematicians as male—the facts are other-wise, and the most we can ask is that if a Dame Ethel Smyth or a Mary Somerville[5] turns up, she shall be allowed to do her work without having aspersions cast either on her sex or her ability. What we ask is to be human individuals, however peculiar and unex-pected. It is no good saying: "You are a little girl and therefore you ought to like dolls"; if the answer is, "But I don't," there is no more to be said. Few women happen to be natural born mechanics; but if there is one, it is useless to try and argue her into being some-thing different. What we must *not* do is to argue that the occasional appearance of a female mechanical genius proves that all women would be mechanical geniuses if they were educated. They would not.

Where, I think, a great deal of confusion has arisen is in a failure to distinguish between special *knowledge* and special *ability*. There are certain questions on which what is called "the woman's point

---

[5] **Smyth . . . Somerville** Ethel Smyth (1858–1944), a composer of music, was a vigorous suffragist; Mary Somerville (1780–1872) wrote on astronomy and physics.

of view" is valuable, because they involve special *knowledge*. Women should be consulted about such things as housing and domestic architecture because, under present circumstances, they have still to wrestle a good deal with houses and kitchen sinks and can bring special knowledge to the problem. Similarly, some of them (though not all) know more about children than the majority of men, and their opinion, *as women,* is of value. In the same way, the opinion of colliers is of value about coal-mining, and the opinion of doctors is valuable about disease. But there are other questions—as for example, about literature or finance—on which the "woman's point of view" has no value at all. In fact, it does not exist. No special knowledge is involved, and a woman's opinion on literature or finance is valuable only as the judgment of an individual. I am occasionally desired by congenital imbeciles and the editors of magazines to say something about the writing of detective fiction "from the woman's point of view." To such demands, one can only say, "Go away and don't be silly. You might as well ask what is the female angle on an equilateral triangle."

In the old days it used to be said that women were unsuited   20
to sit in Parliament, because they "would not be able to think imperially." That, if it meant anything, meant that their views would be cramped and domestic—in short, "the woman's point of view." Now that they *are* in Parliament, people complain that they are a disappointment: they vote like other people with their party and have contributed nothing to speak of from "the woman's point of view"—except on a few purely domestic questions, and even then they are not all agreed. It looks as though somebody was trying to have things both ways at once. Even critics must remember that women are human beings and obliged to think and behave as such. I can imagine a "woman's point of view" about town-planning, or the education of children, or divorce, or the employment of female shop-assistants, for here they have some special knowledge. But what in thunder is the "woman's point of view" about the devaluation of the franc or the abolition of the Danzig Corridor?[6] Even where women have special knowledge, they may disagree among themselves like other specialists. Do doctors never quarrel or scientists disagree? Are women really *not human,* that they should be expected to toddle along all in a flock like sheep? I think that people should be allowed to drink as much wine and beer as they can

---

[6] **the Danzig Corridor** After World War I the victorious allies promised Poland access to the sea (a "corridor") through Danzig (Gdansk), a city populated chiefly by Germans.

afford and is good for them; Lady Astor thinks nobody should be allowed to drink anything of the sort. Where is the "woman's point of view"? Or is one or the other of us unsexed? If the unsexed one is myself, then I am unsexed in very good company. But I prefer to think that women are human and differ in opinion like other human beings. This does not mean that their opinions, as individual opinions, are valueless; on the contrary, the more able they are the more violently their opinions will be likely to differ. It only means that you cannot ask for "the woman's point of view," but only for the woman's special knowledge—and this, like all special knowledge, is valuable, though it is no guarantee of agreement.

"What," men have asked distractedly from the beginning of time, "what on earth do women want?" I do not know that women, *as* women, want anything in particular, but as human beings they want, my good men, exactly what you want yourselves: interesting occupation, reasonable freedom for their pleasures, and a sufficient emotional outlet. What form the occupation, the pleasures, and the emotion may take, depends entirely upon the individual. You know that this is so with yourselves—why will you not believe that it is so with us. The later D. H. Lawrence, who certainly cannot be accused of underrating the importance of sex and talked a good deal of nonsense upon the subject, was yet occasionally visited with shattering glimpses of the obvious. He said in one of his *Assorted Articles:*

> Man is willing to accept woman as an equal, as a man in skirts, as an angel, a devil, a baby-face, a machine, an instrument, a bosom, a womb, a pair of legs, a servant, an encyclopaedia, an ideal or an obscenity; the one thing he won't accept her as is a human being, a real human being of the feminine sex.

"Accepted as a human being!"—yes; not as a inferior class and not, I beg and pray all feminists, as a superior class—not, in fact, as a class at all, except in a useful context. We are much too much inclined in these days to divide people into permanent categories, forgetting that a category only exists for its special purpose and must be forgotten as soon as that purpose is served. There is a fundamental difference between men and women, but it is not the only fundamental difference in the world. There is a sense in which my charwoman and I have more in common than either of us has with, say, Mr. Bernard Shaw: on the other hand, in a discussion about art and literature, Mr. Shaw and I should probably find we had more fundamental interests in common than either of us had with my

charwoman. I grant that, even so, he and I should disagree fero-
ciously about the eating of meat—but that is not a difference between
the sexes—on that point, that late Mr. G. K. Chesterton would have
sided with me against the representative of his own sex. Then there
are points on which I, and many of my own generation of both sexes,
should find ourselves heartily in agreement: but on which the rising generation of young men and women would find us too incom-
prehensibly stupid for words. A difference of age is as fundamental as a difference of sex; and so is a difference of nationality. *All*
categories, if they are insisted upon beyond the immediate purpose
which they serve, breed class antagonism and disruption in the state,
and that is why they are dangerous.

The other day, in the "Heart-to-Heart" column of one of our
popular newspapers, there appeared a letter from a pathetic gentleman about a little disruption threatening his married state. He
wrote:

> I have been married eleven years and think a great deal of the wed-
> ding anniversary. I remind my wife a month in advance and plan to
> make the evening a success. But she does not share my keenness, and,
> if I did not remind her, would let the day go by without a thought of
> its significance. I thought a wedding anniversary meant a lot to a
> woman. Can you explain this indifference?

Poor little married gentleman, nourished upon generalisations— 24
and convinced that if his wife does not fit into the category of "a
woman" there must be something wrong! Perhaps she resents being
dumped into the same category as all the typical women of the comic
stories. If so, she has my sympathy. "A" woman—not an individual person, disliking perhaps to be reminded of the remorseless
flowing-by of the years and the advance of old age—but "a" woman,
displaying the conventional sentimentalities attributed to her unfortunate and ridiculous sex.

A man once asked me—it is true that it was at the end of a very
good dinner, and the compliment conveyed may have been due to
that circumstance—how I managed in my books to write such natural
conversation between men when they were by themselves. Was I,
by any chance, a member of a large, mixed family with a lot of male
friends? I replied that, on the contrary, I was an only child and had
practically never seen or spoken to any men of my own age till I
was about twenty-five. "Well," said the man, "I shouldn't have
expected a woman [meaning me] to have been able to make it so

convincing." I replied that I had coped with this difficult problem by making my men talk, as far as possible, like ordinary human beings. This aspect of the matter seemed to surprise the other speaker; he said no more, but took it away to chew it over. One of these days it may quite likely occur to him that women, as well as men, when left to themselves, talk very much like human beings also.

Indeed, it is my experience that both men and women are fundamentally human, and that there is very little mystery about either sex, except the exasperating mysteriousness of human beings in general. And though for certain purposes it may still be necessary, as it undoubtedly was in the immediate past, for women to band themselves together, as women, to secure recognition of their requirements as a sex, I am sure that the time has now come to insist more strongly on each woman's—and indeed each man's—requirements as an individual person. It used to be said that women had no *esprit de corps;*[7] we have proved that we have—do not let us run into the opposite error of insisting that there is an aggressively feminist "point of view" about everything. To oppose one class perpetually to another—young against old, manual labour against brain-worker, rich against poor, woman against man—is to split the foundations of the State; and if the cleavage runs too deep, there remains no remedy but force and dictatorship. If you wish to preserve a free democracy, you must base it—not on classes and categories, for this will land you in the totalitarian State, where no one may act or think except as the member of the category. You must base it upon the individual Tom, Dick, and Harry, on the individual Jack and Jill—in fact, upon you and me.

Topics for Discussion and Writing

1. Sayers talk was delivered to an English audience in 1938. Are some of her points irrelevant to an American audience in the 1990s? If so, which points?

2. In paragraph 18 Sayers assumes that there are, generally, some differences in aptitude between men and women. What examples does she offer? Do you agree that there are such differences, in these areas or others? Why, or why not?

[7] *esprit de corps* French, meaning enthusiasm among members of a group for each other and for the group

3. In paragraph 19 Sayers says that on certain issues, such as "literature and finance," the "'woman's point of view' has no value at all." Do you agree? Why, or why not? (Before responding, reread the entire paragraph.)
4. In paragraph 4 Sayers writes, "What is repugnant to every human being is to be reckoned always as a member of a class and not as an individual person." If you have experienced such repugnance, recount your experience.

Margaret Mead

Margaret Mead (1901–79), born in Philadelphia and educated at Barnard College and Columbia University, was for decades the best-known anthropologist in the United States. During her long career she served as curator of ethnology at the American Museum of Natural History and as adjunct professor of anthropology at Columbia, but her fame was established early, with Coming of Age in Samoa *(1928), a study that focused on adolescent girls. Among her many books are* The Changing Culture of an Indian Tribe *(1932),* Male and Female *(1949),* Continuities in Cultural Evolution *(1964), and an autobiographical account of her early years,* Blackberry Winter *(1972).*

Why Do We Speak of Feminine Intuition?

The term *intuition* is used to describe knowledge that seems to appear full-blown. It is knowledge that appears in a nonrational way, the steps leading to which are unrecognizable and difficult to articulate, either for the knower or for those who watch the knower. *Feminine intuition* is used to describe those intuitive understandings that seem to come more easily and quickly to women by virtue of their sex. While the term usually applies to some aspect of human relationships, when used without the qualifier *feminine* it may apply to any kind of knowledge, the source of which is obscure.

Following its use in everyday life in our own society, one can often detect the term's comic element. For instance, a man, coming home tired and disgruntled, slams the car door shut, kicks a misplaced boot away from the door, slams the door, walks into the living room, and throws down his coat in an inappropriate place. His wife asks: "What's the matter, dear)" and he answers in wonder:

"How did you know anything was the matter?" By extension, men who pay attention to the moods of others or pick up minimal cues from the behavior of others are said to have an "almost feminine type of intuition."

Although cultures differ in the extent to which they articulate comments on gender differences in perception, certain universals seem evident. Girls not only learn to talk earlier than boys, but they also learn to talk about different things; they learn the names for relationships and learn to comment on the behavior and motives of those around them. Even if, as in Samoa, speculation about the motives of others is discouraged and masked under the blanket diagnosis *musu* (unwilling), girls still make the diagnosis earlier. Little girls also imitate their mothers' tone of voice, nag, cajole, and insinuate (often with comic effect) in tones that are fully identifiable as those of women.

Methodologically, as a cultural anthropologist, I look first at available cross-cultural behavior and do not turn to psychological explanations until the cultural ones are exhausted. If girls seem universally to display this kind of behavior, the next question may be, are there any cultures in which boys also display this behavior? We do not have extremely detailed studies investigating this point, but the material we do have on prerevolutionary Russians—both males and females—suggests that both displayed an extremely alert sense of the unavowed intentions and motives of others: this seems to be related to their generalized expectation that children of both sexes identify temperamentally with both parents and that children of each sex could internalize characteristics of the other. Thus, it was said that a boy learned tenderness from his mother, and a girl learned a masculine-type bravery from her father. While certain qualities of personality were thought to be gender-linked, these could also be learned; but a lively alertness to the undeclared or unrecognized motives of others was still felt to be a feminine attribute that could be learned by men.

Fortune telling, an occupation that requires tremendous attention to the small cues given by strangers, tends to be regarded as a female occupation. When comparing methods of reading the future as practiced by men versus women, the male methods tend more often to be supported by props—dice, divining bones, haruspicy*—while women are able to "see" the future in tea leaves,

---

* **haruspicy** the art of foretelling the future by interpreting the entrails of sacrificial animals. (Editors' note)

in the palm, or in handwriting. But all of these techniques can be, and sometimes are, practiced by men, whether they are gender-linked or not.

Another occupation in which a high degree of sensitivity and attention to small, imperfectly verbalized or nonverbalized cues is necessary is child psychiatry or child psychoanalysis. Because the ordinary approach to the patient by way of speech is often not available in dealing with children, toys, tools, and test objects are used instead to allow the child to be active, to run away, cower on the floor, batter the analyst with his fists, or manipulate miniature objects, thereby allowing communication where no words are possible. One stylized form of such communication procedure is an objective test called the Lowenfeld World Technique.[1] Here, a child (or an adult) is presented with a set of miniatures of the real world (horses, cows, motor cars, houses, people, post boxes), a few fantasy objects (witches, dragons), a box of sand, and a pail of water; the child is then told to make a world. The therapist watches, records, and assists (when skill or the search for an appropriate animal fails) as the patient communicates to himself or herself, feelings and views of the world hitherto inaccessible to both therapist and patient. This procedure is related to the kind of self-illumination that comes from a daydream or a dream or (for someone skilled in self-analysis) from a poem or a painting. The finished creation embodies the same kind of knowledge that, when apprehended in the behavior or expressive work of another, we call intuition.

In my long and articulate relationship to child analysts, it has been my experience that women find this kind of therapeutic or psychological enterprise more congenial and less tiring than do men, that men tend to abandon it earlier and turn to analyzing adults who deal with children, rather than children themselves. It appears that male and female analysts use different approaches to observing and participating communicably in the behavior of small children; males identify with the child, try to feel what the child feels, and respond in terms of postures and attitudes that, having experienced themselves, they can analyze. In this respect, their behavior is much like the behavior they are taught when they become aware of a countertransference. Women, on the other hand, can watch small children as one of them or in the role of mother or nurse, alert to the

---

[1] See Notes, page 679, for all notes to this selection. — Ed.)

smallest indication of a child's needs. In tracing back, I have found that those men who are as successful as women in being able to tolerate long periods of watching children have learned this from women—either from women analysts, women anthropologists, or, as in two striking cases (in childhood and adolescence), from twin sisters.

There is also some cross-cultural evidence that considerable dif- 8
ferences exist in the types of gender-linked behavior that can be tested with instruments and the extent to which test results can be modified by immediate experience. Thus, Kate Franck, in her gender test, found that boys who had been recently chastised tended to emit the same type of passive responses to the test stimuli that were usually associated with those of girls.[2] I found that among the Tchambuli of Chambri Lake, in New Guinea, where women play a much more active role than is customary and men are more dependent upon display and responsiveness, the small girls and small boys also behaved in opposite ways. Whereas among the other South Pacific peoples I have studied, small girls are usually absorbed in the care of babies by the time they are ten and less curious and interested in the world about them, less willing than the boys to participate in the unfamiliar activities of the field anthropologist, among the Tchambuli it was the small girls who maintained their curiosity and alertness to the outside world, while the boys withdrew into an emphasis on their own bodies and their own feelings.

Thus, the material we have suggests that although males can learn to show and to use "feminine" intuition, and girls can learn to inhibit it, as a rule girls and boys learn to apprehend the behavior of others (as well as the "meaning" of some products of behavior) in different ways.

This difference can be ascribed to the difference in the way in which male and female children experience the early period in life when they are cared for almost exclusively by women. Women, if watched carefully, handle, bathe, feed, caress, lull, and stimulate male and female babies differently; although wide individual, temperamental, class, and caste differences are also found (for example, a lower-class nurse will differentiate between upper-class nurslings and her own children).

But with all due allowance for such differences, women tend to treat female infants as like themselves and males as different—as small creatures who should be taught different kinds of activity. Correspondingly, male and female infants respond to the difference in gender of those who are holding and caring for them early in life (as early as two months), but here again, it is difficult to tell whether this is an instinctive response to smell, or style of movement, or rather a response to the difference in the child-directed behavior of the caretaker.

A recurrent example of differential treatment of infants by women is that while girls are encouraged to lean passively against their mothers, boys are encouraged to face their mothers actively and later to move away from them. (Erikson found that in analyzing children's play productions, girls tend to build a back or supporting wall, while boys built towers or scenes of activity in open spaces.[3]) Stated simply, female infants are cared for primarily by others like themselves, males by others who are unlike themselves; girls are encouraged to identify, in posture and pace, with their female nurses, boys are forbidden to make this identification—are pushed off their mothers' laps and encouraged to move out and away. Girls learn on their mothers' laps to explore and master the environment around them.[4]

In cases where drawing or painting have been introduced experimentally from outside the culture (as I did among the Manus[5]) or by stranger artists (as was done in Bali[6]), girls draw as women do, while boys' drawings are immediately recognizable as male (girls drawing beadwork or cake, boys drawing fishermen, warriors, or *kris* dancers). Where, however, traditional styles of drawing exist, these spontaneous differences do not appear. Thus, among the Latmul, where there are highly developed and stylized ways of representing males and females, both boys and girls alike drew in an adult male style. On the other hand, among the Arapesh, where women amuse themselves by drawing stick figures on bark, both boys and girls drew in a female style.[7]

Thus, while girl children learn to identify with their mothers, boys learn *not* to identify with their mothers. Furthermore, girls actually identify with the process of mothering—a process that paradoxically means a lack of identification with the nursling being mothered. Successful mothering requires that a woman (or a man who plays this role) learn not to identify with the infant needing care; not to project his or her own needs on the infant, but to be alert to the infant's actual needs.

When a boy is pushed off his mother's lap, he is also pushed away from identifying with the needs of others. He is given the message: be yourself; do not respond to the arms that have held you. As a result, we have the paradox that a female child learns from her mother (or nurse) how to be attentive to the needs of another, while a male child is left with identification as his only access to these needs. The psychic cost of this difference in upbringing is vividly apparent in the case of male versus female analysts of children; the male analyst attempts to understand child patients by identification, involving expensive regression and the struggle to overcome it, while the female analyst has available either identification or the position of a watchful, attentive nurse or mother.

So far I have suggested that the capacity to be attentive to the other is a function of the way children are reared in the care of women. It may be, however, that the capacity to attend to another is a function of a much deeper process related to a woman's experience of the process of gestation during which she must physiologically relate to a being that is other—sometimes very much other—than herself. It need not be that the actual experience of pregnancy is necessary for the development of feminine intuition, for although many women do not bear children, all women were born of women and almost all have been reared by women who have borne children—their own mothers. The permission to lean back and identify with her mother, which is given to a girl, may well be, therefore, the permission (or the invitation) to identify with a mother's capacity for relating to another in the deepest possible way.

If it is merely the postnatal experience that is operative in shaping the capacities of male and female children, then a change in life style in which young fathers take as much care of infants as do young mothers should make it possible for both boys and girls to identify with a like parent and differentiate themselves from the opposite gender parent. This might be accompanied by less of a need (on the part of mothers) to push their sons away from them, as sons instead would be drawn towards their fathers. The mothering behavior, even if rooted at the very deepest level in the process of gestation, would become at least partly available to male children also.[8] But these are speculations about the future.

In the world humankind has known for the last million years or so, infants have been breastfed, carried, and cared for primarily by women; it is from females that males and females learn different things. Under primitive conditions of child rearing, the child of a mother who cannot relate successfully to her child, or whose child cannot thrive on her milk, will die; children of women who cannot see their child as "other"—hungry, sleepy, and thirsty in its own rhythm, not in hers—would not survive.[9] Thus, feminine intuition, as the capacity to attend to (rather than identify with), would be perpetuated from generation to generation whether structurally related to women's child bearing functions or not.

There is a further theoretical possibility. Given that some temperaments (of which there are both male and female versions) are innately responsive to the needs and desires of others, while other temperaments are not, if both men and women are expected to conform to a nonresponsive temperamental style, intuition would be less pronounced as a characteristic of feminine behavior.[10] But the sheer necessity of caring for an infant whose needs are different from her own might still force the unresponsive woman, or the woman who was fitted (by cultural pressure) into an unresponsive mold, to attend to infants and children and so learn to be attentive to the needs and desires of others.

A further speculation involves the way in which men and women have treated the external world; while men impose their wills upon it, bending it to their purposes, women's greater historical tendency is to adapt to the environment within which they find themselves. The historical division of labor between hunting and gathering did, of course, predispose women to watch where the berries and bulbs grew and where to return to find them; men were occupied in the pursuit of game. Here again we cannot be certain that even 50,000 years of one type of food producing practice rather than another would result in the selection of men and women who differed from one another. Similarly, the fact that women in our society have done best in those areas that require listening and looking, while men have excelled in those areas where they impose a form upon the world, may reflect some basic difference, or may be merely a historical residue of earlier ages. We do know women in many cultures are more field dependent than men.[11]

From a different angle, we might ask how is intuition preserved and cultivated? Can it be extinguished in women? Can it be cultivated in men? If, at present, it is habitual behavior for women reared by women, what kind of childrearing and teaching by women of boys or young men might open the way for males to have more access to intuitive types of behavior? Is recognition of pattern in fact a form of feminine intuition, which when practiced by males, is something that they have learned from women? Could intuitive behavior, once freed from its anchorage in maternal behavior, be made readily available to both boys and girls?

Is the fear of using intuition (among Euro-American scientists, for example) simply a fear of being feminine, of surrendering to the nature of an observed set of phenomena instead of building up information from carefully devised logical steps? I have known brilliant men who felt somehow guilty when they arrived at some important insight intuitively. They have felt constrained to return laboriously to as assumed ignorance and reconstruct, step by step, the knowledge they already had.

This was, in fact, the history of the enormously expensive study on the authoritarian personality. When all the complicated instruments had been applied and analyzed, we were right where we first started when Else Frenkel-Brunswik wrote her "intuitive" article.[12]

These are all possibilities that need exploration. We also need to know more about transexuals—those who appear to be male children who have so closely and physically identified with their mothers, and have been so closely identified as female by their mothers, that their feelings and movements are feminine rather than masculine.[13] We need information on children who have been cared for by members of both sexes from birth. We need much more material on the way in which small infants learn to distinguish sex, on the appearance of the earliest forms of sex-typed behavior, and to correlate these with the kind of work that John Money is doing.[14] We need to look at the work of Alan Lomax, who has found that differences in musical style vary with the role of women in food production.[15]

Until we know a great deal more, we won't be able to say much that is definite about feminine intuition.

Notes

1. Margaret Lowenfeld, "The World Technique," *Topical Problems in Psychotherapy* 3(1960): 248–63.
2. Kate Franck, "Preference for Sex Symbols and Their Personality Correlation," *Genetic Psychology Monographs* 33, no. 2 (1946): 73–123.
3. Erik H. Erikson, "Sex Differences in the Play Configurations of American Adolescents," in *Childhood in Contemporary Cultures,* eds., Margaret Mead and Martha Wolfenstein (Chicago: University of Chicago Press, 1955), pp. 324–41.
4. Margaret Mead, *Male and Female: A Study of the Sexes in a Changing World* (New York: Morrow, 1949).
5. ——, *Growing Up in New Guinea: A Comparative Study of Primitive Education* (New York: Morrow, 1930).

6. ——, "Research on Primitive Children," in *Manual of Child Psychology*, ed., Leonard Carmichael (New York: Wiley, 1946), pp. 667–706.

7. ——, "The Bark Paintings of the Mountain Arapesh of New Guinea," in *Technique and Personality in Primitive Art*, Museum of Primitive Art Lecture Series No. 3 (New York: The Museum of Primitive Art, 1963), pp. 8–43.

8. ——, "A Note on the Evocative Character of the Rorschach Test," in *Toward a Discovery of the Person: The First Bruno Klopfer Memorial Symposium, and Carl G. Jung Centennial Symposium* (Burbank, Calif.: Monograph of the Society for Personality Assessment, 1974), pp. 62–7.

9. ——, "Changing Patterns of Parent-Child Relations in an Urban Culture" *International Journal of Psycho-Analysts* 38, part 6 (1957): 369–78.

10. ——, *Sex and Temperament in Three Primitive Societies* (New York: Morrow, 1935); Mead, Margaret. *Blackberry Winter: My Earlier Years* (New York: Morrow, 1972).

11. Helen Lewis, *The Psychic War in Men and Women* (New York: New York University Press, 1976).

12. T. W. Aderno et al, *The Authoritarian Personality* (New York: Harper & Row, 1950).

13. Robert Stoller, *Sex and Gender: On the Development of Masculinity and Femininity* (New York: Science House, 1968).

14. John Money and Anke Ehrhardt, *Man and Woman, Boy and Girl* (Baltimore: Johns Hopkins University, 1972).

15. Alan Lomax, "A Note on Feminine Factors in Culture History," in *Being Female: Reproduction, Power and Change*, ed., Dana Raphael (The Hague: Mouton, 1975).

Topics for Discussion and Writing

1. If you had been asked to define "intuition," what definition might you have offered? And how would you have defined "feminine intuition"? Do you find your definition and Mead's reasonably consistent, or did her article offer you some surprises?

2. What does Mead imply in paragraph 3 about the source of what little girls talk about and how they talk? Is there any reason to suppose that the same source is unavailable to little boys?

3. In paragraph 4 Mead refers to evidence that in prerevolutionary Russia (that is, before the Communist revolution) parents generally

3. expected children of both sexes to identify with both parents. Can you speculate as to why this might be so?
4. In paragraph 12 Mead says that while "girls are encouraged to identify, in posture and pace, with their female nurses, boys are forbidden to make this identification." Do you recall ever seeing or hearing about such behavior? If so, describe the episode.
5. From this article, what do you know about Mead's characteristic ways of forming a hypothesis and testing it? Does intuition appear to play a role at any stage?
6. Compare Mead with Gould (681–87) on the role of intuition in science.

Stephen Jay Gould

Stephen Jay Gould, born in 1941, is a professor of geology at Harvard University, where he teaches paleontology, biology, and the history of science. The essays he has written for the magazine Natural History *have been collected in five highly readable books.*

Women's Brains

In the Prelude to *Middlemarch*, George Eliot lamented the unfulfilled lives of talented women:

> Some have felt that these blundering lives are due to the inconvenient indefiniteness with which the Supreme Power has fashioned the natures of women: if there were one level of feminine incompetence as strict as the ability to count three and no more, the social lot of women might be treated with scientific certitude.

Eliot goes on to discount the idea of innate limitation, but while she wrote in 1872, the leaders of European anthropometry were trying to measure "with scientific certitude" the inferiority of women. Anthropometry, or measurement of the human body, is not so fashionable a field these days, but it dominated the human sciences for much of the nineteenth century and remained popular until intelligence testing replaced skull measurement as a favored device for making invidious comparisons among races, classes, and sexes. Craniometry, or measurement of the skull, commanded the most attention and respect. Its unquestioned leader, Paul Broca (1824–80), professor of clinical surgery at the Faculty of Medicine in Paris, gathered a school of disciples and imitators around himself. Their work, so meticulous and apparently irrefutable, exerted great influence and won high esteem as a jewel of nineteenth-century science.

Broca's work seemed particularly invulnerable to refutation. Had he not measured with the most scrupulous care and accuracy? (Indeed, he had. I have the greatest respect for Broca's meticulous procedure. His numbers are sound. But science is an inferential exercise, not a catalog of facts. Numbers, by themselves, specify nothing. All depends upon what you do with them.) Broca depicted himself as an apostle of objectivity, a man who bowed before facts and cast aside superstition and sentimentality. He declared that "there is no faith, however respectable, no interest, however legitimate, which must not accommodate itself to the progress of human knowledge and bend before truth." Women, like it or not, had smaller brains than men and, therefore, could not equal them in intelligence. This fact, Broca argued, may reinforce a common prejudice in male society, but it is also a scientific truth. L. Manouvrier, a black sheep in Broca's fold, rejected the inferiority of women and wrote with feeling about the burden imposed upon them by Broca's numbers:

> Women displayed their talents and their diplomas. They also invoked philosophical authorities. But they were opposed by *numbers* unknown to Condorcet or to John Stuart Mill. These numbers fell upon poor women like a sledge hammer, and they were accompanied by commentaries and sarcasms more ferocious than the most misogynist imprecations of certain church fathers. The theologians had asked if women had a soul. Several centuries later, some scientists were ready to refuse them a human intelligence.

Broca's argument rested upon two sets of data: the larger brains of men in modern societies, and a supposed increase in male superiority through time. His most extensive data came from autopsies performed personally in four Parisian hospitals. For 292 male brains, he calculated an average weight of 1,325 grams; 140 female brains averaged 1,144 grams for a difference of 181 grams, or 14 percent of the male weight. Broca understood, of course, that part of this difference could be attributed to the greater height of males. Yet he made no attempt to measure the effect of size alone and

actually stated that it cannot account for the entire difference because we know, a priori, that women are not as intelligent as men
(a premise that the data were supposed to test, not rest upon):

> We might ask if the small size of the female brain depends exclusively
> upon the small size of her body. Tiedemann has proposed this expla-
> nation. But we must not forget that women are, on the average, a little
> less intelligent than men, a difference which we should not exagger-
> ate but which is, nonetheless, real. We are therefore permitted to sup-
> pose that the relatively small size of the female brain depends in part
> upon her physical inferiority and in part upon her intellectual inferiority.

In 1873, the year after Eliot published *Middlemarch*, Broca measured the cranial capacities of prehistoric skulls from L'Homme Mort
cave. Here he found a difference of only 99.5 cubic centimeters between males and females, while modern populations range from
129.5 to 220.7. Topinard, Broca's chief disciple, explained the increasing discrepancy through time as a result of differing evolutionary
pressures upon dominant men and passive women:

> The man who fights for two or more in the struggle for existence, who
> has all the responsibility and the cares of tomorrow, who is constantly
> active in combating the environment and human rivals, needs more
> brain than the woman whom he must protect and nourish, the seden-
> tary woman, lacking any interior occupations, whose role is to raise
> children, love, and be passive.

In 1879, Gustave Le Bon, chief misogynist of Broca's school, used
these data to publish what must be the most vicious attack upon
women in modern scientific literature (no one can top Aristotle).
I do not claim his views were representative of Broca's school, but
they were published in France's most respected anthropological journal. Le Bon concluded

> In the most intelligent races, as among the Parisians, there are a large
> number of women whose brains are closer in size to those of gorillas
> than to the most developed male brains. This inferiority is so obvious
> that no one can contest it for a moment; only its degree is worth dis-
> cussion. All psychologists who have studied the intelligence of women,
> as well as poets and novelists, recognize today that they represent
> the most inferior forms of human evolution and that they are closer
> to children and savages than to an adult, civilized man. They excel in

fickleness, inconstancy, absence of thought and logic, and incapacity to reason. Without doubt there exist some distinguished women, very superior to the average man, but they are as exceptional as the birth of any monstrosity, as, for example, of a gorilla with two heads; consequently, we may neglect them entirely.

Nor did Le Bon shrink from the social implications of his views. He was horrified by the proposal of some American reformers to grant women higher education on the same basis as men:

A desire to give them the same education, and, as a consequence, to propose the same goals for them, is a dangerous chimera. . . . The day when, misunderstanding the inferior occupations which nature has given her, women leave the home and take part in our battles; on this day a social revolution will begin, and everything that maintains the sacred ties of the family will disappear.

Sound familiar?*

I have reexamined Broca's data, the basis for all this derivative 8 pronouncement, and I find his numbers sound but his interpretation ill-founded, to say the least. The data supporting his claim for increased difference through time can be easily dismissed. Broca based his contention on the samples from L'Homme Mort alone— only seven male and six female skulls in all. Never have so little data yielded such far ranging conclusions.

In 1888, Topinard published Broca's more extensive data on the Parisian hospitals. Since Broca recorded height and age as well as brain size, we may use modern statistics to remove their effect. Brain weight decreases with age, and Broca's women were, on average, considerably older than his men. Brain weight increases with height, and his average man was almost half a foot taller than his average woman. I used multiple regression, a technique that allowed me to assess simultaneously the influence of height and age upon brain size. In an analysis of the data for women, I found that, at average male height and age, a woman's brain would weigh 1,212 grams. Correction for height and age reduces Broca's measured difference of 181 grams by more than a third, to 113 grams.

---

* When I wrote this essay, I assumed that Le Bon was a marginal, if colorful, figure. I have since learned that he was a leading scientist, one of the founders of social psychology, and best known for a seminal study on crowd behavior, still cited today (*La psychologie des foules*, 1895), and for his work on unconscious motivation.

I don't know what to make of this remaining difference because I cannot assess other factors known to influence brain size in a major way. Cause of death has an important effect: degenerative disease often entails a substantial diminution of brain size. (This effect is separate from the decrease attributed to age alone.) Eugene Schreider, also working with Broca's data, found that men killed in accidents had brains weighing, on average, 60 grams more than men dying of infectious diseases. The best modern data I can find (from American hospitals) records a full 100-gram difference between death by degenerative arteriosclerosis and by violence or accident. Since so many of Broca's subjects were very elderly women, we may assume that lengthy degenerative disease was more common among them than among the men.

More importantly, modern students of brain size still have not agreed on a proper measure for eliminating the powerful effect of body size. Height is partly adequate, but men and women of the same height do not share the same body build. Weight is even worse than height, because most of its variation reflects nutrition rather than intrinsic size—fat versus skinny exerts little influence upon the brain. Manouvrier took up this subject in the 1880s and argued that muscular mass and force should be used. He tried to measure this elusive property in various ways and found a marked difference in favor of men, even in men and women of the same height. When he corrected for what he called "sexual mass," women actually came out slightly ahead in brain size.

Thus, the corrected 113-gram difference is surely too large; the true figure is probably close to zero and may as well favor women as men. And 113 grams, by the way, is exactly the average difference between a 5 foot 4 inch and a 6 foot 4 inch male in Broca's data. We would not (especially us short folks) want to ascribe greater intelligence to tall men. In short, who knows what to do with Broca's data? They certainly don't permit any confident claim that men have bigger brains than women. 12

To appreciate the social role of Broca and his school, we must recognize that his statements about the brains of women do not reflect an isolated prejudice toward a single disadvantaged group. They must be weighed in the context of a general theory that supported contemporary social distinctions as biologically ordained. Women, blacks, and poor people suffered the same disparagement, but women bore the brunt of Broca's argument because he had easier access to data on women's brains. Women were singularly denigrated but they also stood as surrogates for other disenfranchised groups. As one of Broca's disciples wrote in 1881: "Men of the black races have a brain scarcely heavier than that of white women." This juxtaposition extended into many other realms of anthropological argument, particularly to claims that, anatomically and emotionally, both women and blacks were like white children—and that white children, by the theory of recapitulation, represented an ancestral (primitive) adult stage of human evolution. I do not regard as empty rhetoric the claim that women's battles are for all of us.

Maria Montessori did not confine her activities to educational reform for young children. She lectured on anthropology for several years at the University of Rome, and wrote an influential book entitled *Pedagogical Anthropology* (English edition, 1913). Montessori was no egalitarian. She supported most of Broca's work and the theory of innate criminality proposed by her compatriot Cesare Lombroso. She measured the circumference of children's heads in her schools and inferred that the best prospects had bigger brains. But she had no use for Broca's conclusions about women. She discussed Manouvrier's work at length and made much of his tentative claim that women, after proper correction of the data, had slightly larger brains than men. Women, she concluded, were intellectually superior, but men had prevailed heretofore by dint of physical force. Since technology has abolished force as an instrument of power, the era of women may soon be upon us: "In such an epoch there will really be superior human beings, there will really be men strong in morality and in sentiment. Perhaps in this way the reign of women is approaching, when the enigma of her anthropological superiority will be deciphered. Woman was always the custodian of human sentiment, morality and honor."

This represents one possible antidote to "scientific" claims for the constitutional inferiority of certain groups. One may affirm the validity of biological distinctions but argue that the data have been misinterpreted by prejudiced men with a stake in the outcome, and that disadvantaged groups are truly superior. In recent years, Elaine Morgan has followed this strategy in her *Descent of Woman,* a speculative reconstruction of human prehistory from the woman's point of view— and as farcical as more famous tall tales by and for men.

I prefer another strategy. Montessori and Morgan followed Broca's philosophy to reach a more congenial conclusion. I would rather label the whole enterprise of setting a biological value upon groups for what it is: irrelevant and highly injurious. George Eliot well appreciated the special tragedy that biological labeling imposed 16 upon members of disadvantaged groups. She expressed it for people like herself—women of extraordinary talent. I would apply it more widely—not only to those whose dreams are flouted but also to those who never realize that they may dream—but I cannot match her prose. In conclusion, then, the rest of Eliot's prelude to *Middlemarch*:

> The limits of variation are really much wider than anyone would imagine from the sameness of women's coiffure and the favorite love stories in prose and verse. Here and there a cygnet is reared uneasily among the ducklings in the brown pond, and never finds the living stream in fellowship with its own oary-footed kind. Here and there is born a Saint Theresa, foundress of nothing, whose loving heartbeats and sobs after an unattained goodness tremble off and are dispersed among hindrances instead of centering in some long-recognizable deed.

Topics for Discussion and Writing

1. What is your understanding of anthropometry from paragraph 2? According to Gould, what does intelligence testing have in common with anthropometry? Characterize his attitude toward both. How does he reveal his attitude in this paragraph?
2. In paragraph 3, what does Gould mean when he says, "But science is an inferential exercise, not a catalog of facts"?
3. In paragraph 13 Gould says, "I do not regard as empty rhetoric the claim that women's battles are for all of us." What does he mean? What foundation for this opinion have this paragraph and paragraph 2 provided?
4. Who was Maria Montessori and what does her work have to do with Gould's argument? If her relevance is not entirely clear to you, or was not on first reading, what might Gould have done to make it clearer?
5. What, according to Gould, are the social consequences of what he calls in paragraph 16 "biological labeling"? If on the whole you agree with him, what is the basis of your agreement?
6. In paragraph 13 Gould refers to the "social role of Broca and his school." What does he mean by that? On the basis of this essay (and others of Gould's that you may have read) formulate in a sentence or two the social role of Gould.

Anna Quindlen

For nearly three years Anna Quindlen wrote, for The New York Times, *"Life in the '30s," a strikingly frank column about being thirty-something. The column stopped in 1988, and later Quindlen started a new weekly column in the* Times, *"Public & Private," in which she discussed such national matters as the budget in a highly personal way. We reprint one of her recent columns.*

The Glass Half Empty

My daughter is 2 years old today. She is something like me, only better. Or at least that is what I like to think. If personalities had colors, hers would be red.

Little by little, in the 20 years between my eighteenth birthday and her second one, I had learned how to live in the world. The fact that women were now making 67 cents for every dollar a man makes — well, it was better than 1970, wasn't it, when we were making only 59 cents? The constant stories about the underrepresentation of women, on the tenure track, in the film industry, in government, everywhere, had become commonplace. The rape cases. The sexual harassment stories. The demeaning comments. Life goes on. Where's your sense of humor?

Learning to live in the world meant seeing the glass half full. Ann Richards was elected Governor of Texas instead of a good ol' boy who said that if rape was inevitable, you should relax and enjoy it. The police chief of Houston is a pregnant woman who has a level this-is-my-job look and a maternity uniform with stars on the shoulder. There are so many opportunities unheard of when I was growing up.

And then I had a daughter and suddenly I saw the glass half empty. And all the rage I thought had cooled, all those how-dare-you-treat-us-like-that days, all of it comes back when I look at her, and especially when I hear her say to her brothers, "Me too."

4

When I look at my sons, it is within reason to imagine all the world's doors open to them. Little by little some will close, as their individual capabilities and limitations emerge. But no one is likely to look at them and mutter: "I'm not sure a man is right for a job at this level. Doesn't he have a lot of family responsibilities?"

Every time a woman looks at her daughter and thinks "She can be anything" she knows in her heart, from experience, that it's a lie. Looking at this little girl, I see it all, the old familiar ways of a world that still loves Barbie. Girls aren't good at math, dear. He needs the money more than you, sweetheart; he's got a family to support. Honey—this diaper's dirty.

It is like looking through a telescope. Over the years I learned to look through the end that showed things small and manageable. This is called a sense of proportion. And then I turned the telescope around, and all the little tableaus rushed at me, vivid as ever.

That's called reality.

8

We soothe ourselves with the gains that have been made. There are many role models. Role models are women who exist—and are photographed often—to make other women feel better about the fact that there aren't really enough of us anywhere, except in the lowest-paying jobs. A newspaper editor said to me not long ago, with no hint of self-consciousness, "I'd love to run your column, but we already run Ellen Goodman." Not only was there a quota, there was a quota of one.

My daughter is ready to leap into the world, as though life were chicken soup and she a delighted noodle. The work of Prof. Carol Gilligan of Harvard suggests that some time after the age of 11 this will change, that even this lively little girl will pull back, shrink, that her constant refrain will become "I don't know." Professor Gilligan says the culture sends a message: "Keep quiet and notice the absence of women and say nothing." A smart 13-year-old said to me last week, "Boys don't like it if you answer too much in class."

Maybe someday, years from now, my daughter will come home and say, "Mother, at college my professor acted as if my studies were an amusing hobby and at work the man who runs my department puts his hand on my leg and to compete with the man who's in the running for my promotion who makes more than I do I can't take time to have a relationship but he has a wife and two children and I'm smarter and it doesn't make any difference and some guy tried to jump me after our date last night." And what am I supposed to say to her?

I know?

12

You'll get used to it?

No. Today is her second birthday and she has made me see fresh this two-tiered world, a world that, despite all our nonsense about postfeminism, continues to offer less respect and less opportunity for women than it does for men. My friends and I have learned to live with it, but my little girl deserves better. She has given me my anger back, and I intend to use it well.

That is her gift to me today. Some birthday I will return it to her, because she is going to need it.

Topics for Discussion and Writing

1. In paragraph 6, after saying that we live in "a world that still loves Barbie," Quindlen clarifies her assertion by offering some bits of conversation. Drawing on your own experience, do you agree that our world "still loves Barbie"? Support your view. (If you agree, give some additional bits of conversation.)
2. In paragraph 9 Quindlen mentions Ellen Goodman, with the obvious implication that Goodman fills the editor's quota for women. Read Goodman's article (page 400) and consider the possibility that the editor has in mind not a quota for women but a quota for a certain *kind of essay.* Argue for or against this view, calling attention to qualities in the two essays.
3. In paragraph 11 Quindlen asks what she is supposed to say to her daughter's difficult questions. What do you think she *should* say? Why?
4. Consider Quindlen's beginning and ending paragraphs, and evaluate them.

Scott Russell Sanders

Scott Russell Sanders first published this essay in Milkweek Chronicle, *Spring/Summer 1984, and then reprinted it in his book,* Paradise of Bombs.

The Men We Carry in Our Minds . . . and how they differ from the real lives of most men

This must be a hard time for women." I say to my friend Anneke. "They have so many paths to choose from, and so many voices calling them."

"I think it's a lot harder for men," she replies.

"How do you figure that?"

"The women I know feel excited, innocent, like crusaders in a just cause. The men I know are eaten up with guilt."

"Women feel such pressure to be everything, do everything," I say. "Career, kids, art, politics. Have their babies and get back to the office a week later. It's as if they're trying to overcome a million years' worth of evolution in one lifetime."

"But we help one another. And we have this deep-down sense that we're in the *right*—we've been held back, passed over, used— while men feel they're in the wrong. Men are the ones who've been discredited, who have to search their souls."

I search my soul. I discover guilty feelings aplenty—toward the poor, the Vietnamese, Native Americans, the whales, an endless list of debts. But toward women I feel something more confused, a snarl of shame, envy, wary tenderness, and amazement. This muddle troubles me. To hide my unease I say, "You're right, it's tough being a man these days."

"Don't laugh," Anneke frowns at me. "I wouldn't be a man for anything. It's much easier being the victim. All the victim has to do is break free. The persecutor has to live with his past."

How deep is that past? I find myself wondering. How much of an inheritance to I have to throw off?

When I was a boy growing up on the back roads of Tennessee and Ohio, the men I knew labored with their bodies. They were marginal farmers, just scraping by, or welders, steelworkers, carpenters; they swept floors, dug ditches, mined coal, or drove trucks, their forearms ropy with muscle; they trained horses, stoked furnaces, made tires, stood on assembly lines wrestling parts onto cars and refrigerators. They got up before light, worked all day long whatever the weather, and when they came home at night they looked as though somebody had been whipping them. In the evenings and on weekends they worked on their own places, tilling gardens that were lumpy with clay, fixing broken-down cars, hammering on houses that were always too drafty, too leaky, too small.

The bodies of the men I knew were twisted and maimed in ways visible and invisible. The nails of their hands were black and split, the hands tattooed with scars. Some had lost fingers. Heavy lifting had given many of them finicky backs and guts weak from hernias. Racing against conveyor belts had given them ulcers. Their ankles and knees ached from years of standing on concrete. Anyone who had worked for long around machines was hard of hearing. They squinted, and the skin of their faces was creased like the leather of old work gloves. There were times, studying them, when I dreaded growing up. Most of them coughed, from dust or cigarettes, and most of them drank cheap wine or whiskey, so their eyes looked bloodshot and bruised. The fathers of my friends always seemed older than the mothers. Men wore out sooner. Only women lived into old age.

As a boy I also knew another sort of men, who did not sweat   12
and break down like mules. They were soldiers, and so far as I could tell they scarcely worked at all. But when the shooting started, many of them would die. This was what soldiers were *for*, jsut as a hammer was for driving nails.

Warriors and toilers: these seemed, in my boyhood vision, to be the chief destinies for men. They weren't the only destinies, as I learned from having a few male teachers, from reading books, and from watching television. But the men on television—the politicians, the astronauts, the generals, the savvy lawyers, the philosophical doctors, the bosses who gave orders to both soldiers and laborers—seemed as remote and unreal to me as the figures in Renaissance tapestries. I could no more imagine growing up to become one of these cool, potent creatures that I could imagine becoming a prince.

A nearer and more hopeful example was that of my father, who had escaped from a red-dirt farm to a tire factory, and from the assembly line to the front office. Eventually he dressed in a white shirt and tie. He carried himself as if he had been born to work with his mind. But his body, remembering the earlier years of slogging work, began to give out on him in his fifties, and it quit on him entirely before he turned 65.

A scholarship enabled me not only to attend college, a rare enough feat in my circle, but even to study in a university meant for the children of the rich. Here I met for the first time young men who had assumed from birth that they would lead lives of comfort and power. And for the first time I met women who told me that men were guilty of having kept all the joys and privileges of the earth for themselves. I was baffled. What privileges? What joys? I thought about the maimed, dismal lives of most of the men back home. What had they stolen from their wives and daughters? The right to go five days a week, 12 months a year, for 30 or 40 years to a steel mill or a coal mine? The right to drop bombs and die in war? The right to feel every leak in the roof, every gap in the fence, every cough in the engine as a wound they must mend? The right to feel, when the layoff comes or the plant shuts down, not only afraid but ashamed?

I was slow to understand the deep grievances of women. This was because, as a boy, I had envied them. Before college, the only people I had ever known who were interested in art or music or literature, the only ones who read books, the only ones who ever seemed to enjoy a sense of ease and grace were the mothers and daughters. Like the menfolk, they fretted about money, they scrimped and made do. But, when the pay stopped coming in, they were not the ones who had failed. Nor did they have to go to war, and that seemed to me a blessed fact. By comparison with the narrow, ironclad days of fathers, there was an expansiveness, I thought, in the days of mothers. They went to see neighbors, to shop in town, to run errands at school, at the library, at church. No doubt, had I looked harder at their lives, I would have envied them less. It was not my fate to become a woman, so it was easier for me to see the graces. I didn' see, then, what a prison a house could be, since houses seemed to me brighter, handsomer places than any factory. I did not realize—because such things were never spoken of—how often women suffered from men's bullying. Even then I could see how exhausting it was for a mother to cater all day to the needs of young children. But if I had been asked, as a boy, to choose between tending a baby and tending a machine, I think I would have chosen the baby. (Having now tended both, I know I would choose the baby.)

So I was baffled when the women at college accused me and my sex of having cornered the world's pleasures. I think something like my bafflement has been felt by other boys (and by girls as well) who grew up in dirt-poor farm country, in mining country, in black ghettos, in Hispanic barrios, in the shadows of factories, in Third World nations—any place where the fate of men is just as grim and bleak as the fate of women.

When the women I met at college thought about the joys and privileges of men, they did not carry in their minds the sort of men I had known in my childhood. They thought of their fathers, who were bankers, physicians, architects, stockbrokers, the big wheels of the big cities. They were never laid off, never short of cash at month's end, never lined up for welfare. These fathers made decisions that mattered. They ran the world.

The daughters of such men wanted to share in this power, this glory. So did I. They yearned for a say over their future, for jobs worthy of their abilities, for the right to live at peace, unmolested, whole. Yes, I thought, yes yes. The difference between me and these daughters was that they saw me, because of my sex, as destined from birth to become like their fathers, and therefore as an enemy to their desires. But I knew better. I wasn't an enemy, in fact or in feeling. I was an ally. If I had known, then, how to tell them so, would they have believed me? Would they now?

Topics for Discussion and Writing

1. Look at Sander's introductory paragraphs (1–9). What do you think he hoped to accomplish by these paragraphs? To put it another way, suppose the essay began with paragraph 10, "When I was a boy growing up. . . ." What would be changed or lost?

2. Look at the second sentence of paragraph 10. It's a rather long sentence, with three independent clauses and lists of parallel phrases. How would you describe the verbs he uses? What effect does the structure of the sentence produce?

3. What is the topic sentence of paragraph 11? How does Sanders develop the paragraph, and what does the paragraph contribute to his argument?

4. What advantages did women enjoy that Sanders says he envied when he was a boy? What disadvantages does he mention (in paragraph 15)? What disadvantages does he *not* mention?

5. In paragraphs 16, 17, and 18, Sanders shifts from focusing on issues of gender to issues of class. How has he prepared us for this shift?

6. Evaluate Sanders' argument. How would you answer the questions he poses in his final paragraph?

7. When you were growing up, which lives seemed to have the most advantages or disadvantages, those of men or of women? Why did you think so? Did your opinion change as you grew older? Explain.

Robert Bly

Robert Bly was born on a farm in Minnesota. He studied mathematics at Harvard and then came home to live on the farm—but not to work it, to the dismay of his father and the neighbors. He turned to writing poetry, supporting himself by working as a transla- tor and by giving occasional readings and lectures on myths. In these readings he chanted, played drums, put on masks, and in time developed programs that made him a leader in the men's movement that seeks to recover the masculine identity (and energy) that allegedly has been suppressed since the industrial revolution because a boy no longer serves a sort of apprenticeship working at his fathers' side. In Bly's version, the move- ment aims at "bringing the interior warriors back to life."

Bly has set forth his ideas at length in an immensely popular book, Iron John, *in which he offers an elaborate explanation of each phase of a Grimm fairy tale. Briefly, the story of Iron John is this: a king imprisons a wild man in a cage, but a boy releases the man, learns from the man the secrets of regaining manhood, and eventually marries the princess.*

Men's Initiation Rites

The ancient rites of male initiation were complicated and subtle experiences which could be imagined better as a continual spiral than as a walk down a road. The spiral could be described as a year which repeats itself in seasons. The four seasons of male development amount to four stages, four steps and four events, though we all know that seasons run into each other, and repeat.

The four seasons, or stages, I'll discuss here are bonding with and separation from the mother; bonding with and separation from the father; finding of the male mother; and the interior marriage or marriage with the Hidden Woman.

Bonding with and Separation from Mother

The first event is bonding with the mother and separation from the mother. Bonding of the son with the mother usually gets quite well in this country, though we could distinguish between instantane- ous birth-bonding and a later, slower emotional bonding. The med- ical profession has adopted birth practices involving harsh lights, steel tables, painful medicines and, most harmful of all, the infant's isolation for long periods, all of which damage the birth bond. Joseph Chilton Pearce has written of that movingly in *The Magical Child* (Dell). Mothers can sometimes repair that bonding later by careful attention to their sons' needs, by praise, carrying, talking, protecting, comforting—and many mothers do exactly that. Most American men achieve a successful bonding with the mother. It is the *separation* from the mother that doesn't go well.

When the world of men is submerged in the world of technology and business, it seems to the boy that cool excitement lies there, and warm excitement with the mother; money with the father, food with the mother; anxiety with the father, assurance with the mother; conditional love with the father, and unconditional love with the mother. All over the United States we meet women whose 35-year-old sons are still living at home. One such woman told me that her divorce brought her freedom from the possessiveness of her husband, who wanted her home every night, etc. But she had noticed last week that her son said, "Why are you going out so much in the evenings?" In recent years the percentage of adult sons still living at home has increased; and we can see much other evidence of the difficulty the male feels in breaking with the mother: the guilt often felt toward the mother; the constant attempt, usually unconscious, to be a nice boy; lack of male friends; absorption in boyish flirtation with women; attempts to carry women's pain, and be their comforters; efforts to change a wife into a mother; abandonment of discipline for "softness and gentleness"; a general confusion about maleness. These qualities are all simple human characteristics, and yet when they, or a number of them, appear together, they point toward a failure in the very first stage of initiation. Ancient initiation practice, still going on in many parts of the world, solve this problem decisively through active intervention by the older males. Typically, when three or four boys in a tribe get to be eight to 12 years old, a group of older men simply appears at the houses one night, and takes them from their mothers, with whom the boys never live again. They may return, but often with faces covered with ash, to indicate that they are now "dead" to their mothers, who in their part return this play by crying out in mourning when they see their sons again, and acting out rituals otherwise done for the dead.

Bonding with and Separation from Father

The second season of initiation is bonding with the father and separation from the father. Before the Industrial Revolution this event took place with most sons. But this bonding requires many hours in which the bodies of the father and son sit, stand or work close to each other, within a foot or two. The average father in the United

States talks to his son less than 10 minutes a day. And that talk may be talk from a distance, such as "Is your room cleaned up?" or "Are you on drugs?" As we know, the psyche of the child interprets the death of a parent personally; that is, the psyche regards it as a failure on the child's part: "If I had been worthy, my parent would not have died." So the psyche of the small son interprets without question the father's absence from the house for hours and hours each day as evidence of the same unworthiness. The German psychiatrist Alexander Mitscherlich in his book *Society Without the Father* (Tavistock Publications) gives an image still more startling. He declares that when a son does not witness his father at work through the day and through the year, a hole develops in the son's psyche, and that hole fills with demons. Dustin Hoffman played such a son in *Marathon Man:* The son does not bond with the father then, but on the contrary a magnetic repulsion takes place, for by secret processes the father becomes associated in the son's mind with demonic energy, cold evil, Nazis, concentration camp guards, evil capitalists, agents of the CIA, powers of world conspiracy. Some of the fear felt in the '60s by young leftist men ("Never trust anyone over 30") came from that well of demons.

The severance that the Norwegian immigrant male, for example, experienced when he lost his old language in which feelings naturally expressed themselves—and the Polish immigrant, and the German immigrant—affected the ability of these men to talk to their sons, and their sons to their sons. We might add to that the frontier mentality, whose pressure of weather, new land, building, plowing, etc. left almost all feeling activities—music appreciation, novel reading, poetry recital—to women. This request to women that they carry on "feeling" activities obviously deepened the crisis, because the boy then learns cultural feeling, verbal feeling, discrimination of feeling almost entirely from his mother. Bonding requires physical closeness, a sense of protection, approval of one's very being, conversation in which feelings and longings can step out, and some attention which the young male can feel as *care for the soul*. The boy in the United States receives almost all of these qualities, if he receives them at all, from the mother, and so his bonding talkes place with her, not with the father. If bonding with the father does not take place, how can separation from the father take place? There are many exceptions to this generalization, of course, but most of the exceptions I met were in men who worked in some physical way with their fathers, as carpenters, woodcutters, musicians, farmers, etc.

American men in general cannot achieve separation from the father because they have not achieved bonding with the father; or more exactly, our bonding with the father goes on slowly, bit by bit, often beginning again, after the remoteness of adolescence, at the age of 35 or so; and of course this gradual bonding over many years slows up the separation as well, so that the American man is often 40 or 45 before the first two events of initiation have taken place completely enough to be felt as events. The constant attempt by young males working in popular music to play a music their fathers never played or heard suggests an inability to bond with their fathers. The fathers in their turn feel puzzled, rejected, inadequate and defeated. So many American fathers if they answer the phone when a son or daughter calls will usually say after a moment: "Here is your mother."

Male Mother

A third event in the ancient male initiation was the appearance of the male mother, and we'll call that the essential event. John Layard, who gained much of his knowledge of male initiation from his years with the Stone-Age tribes of Malekula, declares in his study, called *The Celtic Quest* (Spring Publications) that Arthur was a male mother. "Arthur" may have been the name traditionally given to such an initiator centuries before he came King Arthur. In the ancient Mabinogion story "Culhwch and Olwen," Arthur is the keeper of a castle to which the young male initiate gains entry. Though male, Arthur's kingdon, Layard says, "has to be 'entered' as though it were a woman." Layard continues: "This entry into the male world which is a 'second mother' is what all initiation rites are concerned with." When Arthur has accepted the invader, he details the things he will not give to the young man, which are ship, cloak, sword, shield, dagger and Guinevere, his wife. He then asks the boy, "What do you want?" Culhwch says, "I want my hair trimmed." Then "Arthur took a golden comb and shears with loops of silver, and combed his head." The younger male places his head, or his consciousness, into the hands of an older man he trusts, and by that act he is symbolically freed from his bonds both to his mother and to his father.

Our culture lacks the institution of the male mother: The [8] memory of it seems to have dropped into forgetfulness. We receive only one birth, from the mother, even though Jesus insisted on the importance of a second birth. We lose the meaning of his metaphor by interpreting it as a conversion experience. It was a new birth from the male, and it is possible that Jesus himself provided this second birth to young men. The Australian aborigines to this day arrange an experience of male birth that the sons do not forget: They construct a sort of tunnel of sticks and brush 20 to 30 feet long, and at the proper moment put the boys in at one end, and receive them, surrounded by the tremendous male noise of the bullroarers, at the other end, and immediately declare them to be born out of the male body for once and for all—a new boy, a new body, a new spirit, a man at last.

This experience, of course, implies the willingness of the older males to become male mothers, and so exhibit the protectiveness, self-sacrificing generosity and soul-caring that the female mother traditionally shows. In Africa, males of the Kikuyu tribe take boys who are hungry and terrified, after a day's fasting, and sit them down among adult males around a fire late at night. Each adult male then cuts his arm with a knife and lets his blood flow into a gourd which is passed on to the young boys to drink, so that they can see and taste the depth of the older males' love for them. By this single ceremony, the boy is asked to shift from female milk to male blood.

It is Arthur's kindness, savvy, spiritual energy, his store of psychic knowledge, his willingness to lead, guide and welcome the young male which we lack in American ritual, when, for example, the initiating power is held by sergeants, priests or corporate executives. The qualities I've mentioned above cannot appear together, or only rarely, in those three roles because we have forgotten the male mother role. We need to rethink the purpose of a male mother and how he achieves that purpose. The old apprentice system in crafts and arts through the Middle Ages and Renaissance accomplished initiation for some young men, but the mass university lectures of today cannot provide it—nor can workshop classes of 20. Pablo Casals was a male mother to some young men; William Carlos Williams[1] to others, and there are always a few marvelous teachers or woodsmen here and there who understand the concept and embody it. By and large, however, one would say that if the American male does achieve the first two events—bonding with and separation from the mother, bonding with and separation from the father—he will come up short on this third step. A man needs to

---

[1] **Pablo Casals . . . William Carlos Williams** Casals (1876–1973) was a Spanish cellist; Williams (1883–1963) was an American physician and poet (Editors' note)

look decisively for a male mother, but he cannot look if the culture has not even retained the concept in its storehouse of possibilities. The men around Arthur were healthy because he nourished them, and they expected it.

The Invisible Czarina

We notice that the male mother, or primary initiator, is not one's personal father; so by this third step, the male passes beyond the realm of his personal mother and father. He also expands his conception of women beyond the roles of wife, girlfriend, mistress, chick, movie actress, model. The predominant figure in the fourth stage is the Invisible Czarina, or Elena the Wise, as some Russian fairy tales call her, and in the fourth season it is the man's task to marry her. Edward Schieffel, in *Rituals of Manhood,* writing about contemporary male rituals in New Guinea, reports that in the Kaluli tribe the young boys sometimes find in the pool below a waterfall during ceremonies a "stone bride," which they can identify because it moves on its own. We see here again a connection being made with a secret, powerful and usually helpful woman who is not a living woman. The fourth step does not aim then at a hardening or intensification of maleness, but rather at a deepening of feeling toward the religious life. We can immediately see the connection with the worship of the woman in Arthurian legend, the image of Mona Lisa in Italy, "Diotima" in Socrates' Greece, and lunar substance that contributes to the creation of "gold" that is the aim of alchemy. The "woman by the well" preserves in many European fairy tales and in the New Testament the memory of the Hidden Woman. In Celtic initiation, Arthur guides the young male toward the marriage with her; she is in fact the Olwen ("white race" or "track of the moon") mentioned in the title of the Celtic story, "Culhwch and Olwen."

The fourth season therefore represents an astonishing leap into the other world and a love for the radiance of the yin.[2] Initiation results in less dependence on living women or "strong" women, less fear of the feminine and creation of the more balanced older man that Zen and Tibetan traditions, to name only these two, aim at. Western culture has retained a dim memory of his fourth stage; and when most men today ima gine initiation, a fourth stage like

12

---

[2] **yin** In East Asian thought, *yin* is a female cosmic element or force that is complementary to *yang,* a masculine force. *Yin* is associated with the moon, *yang* with the sun. (Editors' note)

this is probably not a part of their imaginative scenario, even though the Wild Man story or "Iron Hans" ends like so many Grimm Brothers tales, in a marriage. The 20th-century Spanish poet Antonio Machado retained a very lively memory of Elena or the Hidden Woman, about whom he wrote a number of poems. This poem he wrote around 1900:

> Close to the road we sit down one day.
> our whole life now amounts to time, and our sole concern
> the attitudes of despair that we adopt
> while we wait. But She will not fail to arrive.

I want to emphasize that the ancient view of male development implies a spiral movement rather than a linear passage through clearly defined stages, with a given stage finished once and for all. As men, we go through all stages in a shallow way, then go back, live in several stages at once, go through them all with slightly less shallowness, return again to our parents, bond and separate once more, find a new male mother, and so on and so on. The old initiation systems having been destroyed, and their initiators gone, no step is ever done cleanly, just as we don't achieve at 12 a clean break with our mothers. So a quality of male initiation as we live it in the culture is a continual returning. Gradually and messily over many years a man achieves this complicated or subtle experience; it is very slow.

Topics for Discussion and Writing

1. In paragraph 2 Bly says that the medical profession has adopted birth practices that are "harmful." Do you agree? How would you go about verifying (or rebutting) his charge?

2. In paragraph 3 Bly says that "In recent years the percentage of adult sons still living at home has increased." Assuming the truth of the assertion, can you think of any reasons to account for the phenomenon, beyond the reason(s) implied by Bly? If so, what are they?

3. Is Bly saying in paragraph 5 that "feeling activities"—his examples include music appreciation, novel reading, poetry recital—cannot include such traditionally male activities as hunting, fishing, house-building, and farming. If he is saying this, do you agree with him? If he is not saying this, what *is* he saying?

4. In paragraph 6 Bly suggests that young male musicians play music that their "fathers never played or heard" because they were unable "to bond with their fathers." What other reasons might there be?

5. In paragraph 8 Bly describes an Australian aborginal ritual. Assuming that his description is accurate, what do you imagine young males learn from such a ritual about how they are to regard women and about traits that may be thought to be feminine?

6. If you are a male and are over, say, 40, has your life included someone comparable to what Bly calls the male mother? If you are not a male over 40, can you think of someone—perhaps a parent or other older relative or neighbor—whose life seems to have been shaped in part by a male mother? If so, describe the relationship.

7. In paragraph 11, in the section headed "The Invisible Czarina," Bly lists the roles that form a young man's conception of women. What roles are conspicuously absent? Do these omissions diminish his argument, in your opinion, or strengthen it?

Paul Theroux

Paul Theroux was born in 1941 in Medford, Massachusetts, and was educated at the University of Maine, the University of Massachusetts, and Syracuse University. He served as a Peace Corps volunteer in Africa and has spent much of his adult life abroad, in Africa, Asia, Europe, and Central America. Though best known as a novelist and writer of travel books, he is also a poet and essayist. This essay originally appeared in The New York Times Magazine.

The Male Myth

There is a pathetic sentence in the chapter "Fetishism" in Dr. Norman Cameron's book *Personality Development and Psychopathology*. It goes: "Fetishists are nearly always men; and their commonest fetish is a woman's shoe." I cannot read that sentence without thinking that it is just one more awful thing about being a man—and perhaps it is the most important thing to know about us.

I have always disliked being a man. The whole idea of manhood in America is pitiful, a little like having to wear an ill-fitting coat for one's entire life. (By contrast, I imagine femininity to be an oppressive sense of nakedness.) Even the expression "Be a man!" strikes me as insulting and abusive. It means: Be stupid, be unfeeling, obedient and soldierly, and stop thinking. Man means "manly"—how can one think "about men" without considering the terrible ambition of manliness? And yet it is part of every man's life.

It is a hideous and crippling lie; it not only insists on difference and connives at superiority, it is also by its very nature destructive— emotionally damaging and socially harmful.

The youth who is subverted, as most are, into believing in the masculine ideal is effectively separated from women—it is the most savage tribal logic—and he spends the rest of his life finding women a riddle and a nuisance. Of course, there is a female version of this male affliction. It begins with mothers encouraging little girls to say (to other adults), "Do you like my new dress?" In a sense, girls are traditionally urged to please adults with a kind of coquettishness, while boys are enjoined to behave like monkeys toward each other. The 9-year-old coquette proceeds to become womanish in a subtle power game in which she learns to be sexually indispensable, socially decorative and always alert to a man's sense of inadequacy.

Femininity—being ladylike—implies needing a man as witness   4
and seducer; but masculinity celebrates the exclusive company of men. That is why it is so grotesque; and that is also why there is no manliness without inadequacy—because it denies men the natural friendship of women.

It is very hard to imagine any concept of manliness that does not belittle women, and it begins very early. At an age when I wanted to meet girls—let's say the treacherous years of 13 to 16—I was told to take up a sport, get more fresh air, join the Boy Scouts, and I was urged not to read so much. It was the 1950's and, if you asked too many questions about sex, you were sent to camp—boy's camp, of course; the nightmare. Nothing is more unnatural or prisonlike than a boys' camp, but if it were not for them, we would have no Elks' Lodges, no poolrooms, no boxing matches, no marines.

And perhaps no sports as we know them. Everyone is aware of how few in number are the athletes who behave like gentlemen. Just as high-school basketball teaches you how to be a poor loser, the manly attitude toward sports seems to be little more than a recipe for creating bad marriages, social misfits, moral degenerates, sadists, latent rapists and just plain louts. I regard high-school sports as a drug far worse than marijuana, and it is the reason that the average tennis champion, say, is a pathetic oaf.

Any objective study would find the quest for manliness essentially right wing, puritanical, cowardly, neurotic and fueled largely by a fear of women. It is also certainly philistine. There is no book hater like a Little League coach. But, indeed, all the creative arts are obnoxious to the manly ideal, because at their best the arts are pursued by uncompetitive and essentially solitary people. It makes it very hard for a creative youngster, for any boy who expresses the desire to be alone seems to be saying that there is something wrong with him.

It ought to be clear by now that I have an objection to the way we turn boys into men. It does not surprise me that when the President of the United States has his customary weekend off, he dresses like a cowboy—it is both a measure of his insecurity and his willingness to please. In many ways, American culture does little more for a man than prepare him for modeling clothes in the L. L. Bean catalogue. I take this as a personal insult because for many years I found it impossible to admit to myself that I wanted to be a writer. It was my guilty secret, because being a writer was incompatible with being a man.

There are people who might deny this, but that is because the American writer, typically, has been so at pains to prove his manliness. But first there was a fear that writing was not a manly profession—indeed, not a profession at all. (The paradox in American letters is that it has always been easier for a woman to write and for a man to be published.) Growing up, I had thought of sports as wasteful and humiliating, and the idea of manliness as a bore. My wanting to become a writer was not a flight from that oppressive role playing, but I quickly saw that it was at odds with it. Everything in stereotyped manliness goes against the life of the mind. The Hemingway personality is too tedious to go into here, but certainly it was not until this aberrant behavior was examined by feminists in the 1960's that any male writer dared question the pugnacity in Hemingway's fiction. All that bullfighting and arm-wrestling and elephant shooting diminished Hemingway as a writer: One cannot be a male writer without first proving that one is a man.

It is normal in America for a man to be dismissive or even somewhat apologetic about being a writer. Various factors make it easier. There is a heartiness about journalism that makes it acceptable—journalism is the manliest form of American writing and, therefore, the profession the most independent-minded women seek (yes, it is an illusion, but that is my point). Fiction writing is equated with a kind of dispirited failure and is only manly when it produces wealth. Money is masculinity. So is drinking. Being a drunkard is another assertion, if misplaced, of manliness. The American male writer is traditionally proud of his heavy drinking. But we are also very literal-minded people. A man proves his manhood in America in old-fashioned ways. He kills lions, like Hemingway; or he hunts ducks, like Nathanael West; or he makes pronouncements, like "A man should carry enough knife to defend himself with," as James Jones is said to have once told an interviewer. And we are familiar with the lengths to which Norman Mailer is prepared, in his endearing way, to prove that he is just as much a monster as the next man.

When the novelist John Irving was revealed as a wrestler, people took him to be a very serious writer. But what interests me is that it is inconceivable that any woman writer would be shown in such a posture. How surprised we would be if Joyce Carol Oates were revealed as a sumo wrestler or Joan Didion enjoyed pumping iron. "Lives in New York City with her three children" is the typical woman-writer's biographical note, for just as the male writer must prove he has achieved a sort of muscular manhood, the woman writer—or rather her publicists—must prove her motherhood.

There would be no point in saying any of this if it were not 12 generally accepted that to be a man is somehow—even now in feminist-influenced America—a privilege. It is on the contrary an unmerciful and punishing burden. Being a man is bad enough; being manly is appalling. It is the sinister silliness of men's fashions that inspires the so-called dress code of the Ritz-Carlton Hotel in Boston. It is the institutionalized cheating in college sports. It is a pathetic and primitive insecurity.

And this is also why men often object to feminism, but are afraid to explain why: Of course women have a justified grievance, but most men believe—and with reason—that their lives are much worse.

Topics for Discussion and Writing

1. In paragraph 6 Theroux says that "high school basketball teaches you how to be a poor loser." Think about this, and then write a paragraph that in effect offers a definition of a "poor loser" but that also shows how a high school sport teaches one to be a poor loser.
2. Theroux speaks of "the Hemingway personality" and of "the pugnacity in Hemingway's fiction." If you have read a work by Hemingway, write a paragraph in which you explain (to someone unfamiliar with Hemingway) what Theroux is talking about.
3. Let's assume that a reader says he or she doesn't quite understand Theroux's final paragraph. Write a paragraph explaining it.

4. Theroux makes some deliberately provocative statements, for example:

> Nothing is more unnatural or prisonlike than a boys' camp.

> Everyone is aware of how few in number are the athletes who behave like gentlemen.

> The quest for manliness . . . [is] fueled largely by a fear of women.

Choose one such statement from the essay and consider what you would need to do to argue effectively against it. You needn't produce the argument, but simply consider how such an argument might be constructed.

Dennis Altman

We print an excerpt from an article that originally appeared in the New Internationalist *in November, 1989.*

Why Are Gay Men So Feared?

Gay men are the victims of insults, prejudice, abuse, violence, sometimes murder. Why are gay men hated by so many other men? Some maintain that homosexuality is unnatural or a threat to the family. But celibacy is also unnatural, yet nuns and priests are not regularly attacked. And there is also a good case to be made that homosexuality actually *strengthens* the family by liberating some adults from childbearing duties and so increasing the pool of adults available to look after children.

But the real objection to homosexuality (and lesbianism) is undoubtedly more deep-seated: It is threatening because it seems to challenge the conventional roles governing a person's sex, and the female and male roles in society. The assertion of homosexual identity clearly challenges the apparent naturalness of gender roles.

Men are particularly prone to use anger and violence against those they think are undermining their masculinity. And it is here that we can find at least some of the roots of homophobia and gay-bashing.

As Freud understood, most societies are built upon a set of rela- 4 tionships between men: Most powerful institutions like parliaments and business corporations are male-dominated. And this "male bonding" demands a certain degree of sexual sublimation.

In many societies, the links between men are much stronger than the relations that link them to women. But these bonds are social rather than individual, and for this reason need to be strictly governed. Armies, for example, depend upon a very strong sense of male solidarity, though this does not allow for too close an emotional tie between any *specific* pair of men.

Thus the most extreme homophobia is often found among tightly knit groups of men, who need to deny any sexual component to their bonding as well as boost their group solidarity by turning violently on "fags" or "queers," who are defined as completely alien. This is a phenomenon found among teenage gangs, policemen, and soldiers. A particularly prominent example of this was Germany's Nazi Party, which shortly after coming to power purged those of its members who were tempted to turn the hypermasculinity of Nazism into an excuse for overt homosexual behavior.

Many observers of sexual violence have argued that the most virulent queer-basher is attacking the homosexual potential in himself—a potential that he has learned to suppress. Because homosexuality is "un-masculine," those who struggle with feelings of homosexuality (often unacknowledged) will be particularly tempted to resolve them through "masculine" expressions of violence. In court cases involving violence against gay men, the idea of preserving one's male honor is often pleaded as a defense.

Homophobia has effects that go far beyond those individuals 8 against whom it is directed. Like racism and sexism, it is an expression of hatred that harms the perpetrator as well as the victim; the insecurities, fears, and sexual hang-ups that lead young men to go out looking for "fags" to beat up are dangerous to the entire society.

Those societies that are best able to accept homosexuals are also societies that are able to accept assertive women and gentle men, and they tend to be less prone to the violence produced by hypermasculinity.

Topics for Discussion and Writing

1. Before you read this essay, had it occurred to you that gay men are "feared"? What other attitudes toward gay men does Altman suggest?

2. Does Altman believe that homosexuality is unnatural? Does he offer any evidence that it either is or is not unnatural? How, in this context, might *natural* and *unnatural* be defined?
3. In a sentence or two state the answer that Altman gives to the question that he poses in his title. How convincing do you find it?
4. Does the logic of Altman's argument lead you to infer that lesbians are feared? Do you think they *are* feared? What do you think that Altman might say in reply to this question?

Lindsy Van Gelder

Lindsy Van Gelder was born in 1942 and educated at Northwestern University and Sarah Lawrence College. After graduating she worked as a newspaper reporter and (since 1977) as a staff writer for Ms., where the present essay first appeared.

Marriage as a Restricted Club

Several years ago, I stopped going to weddings. In fact, I no longer celebrate the wedding anniversaries or engagements of friends, relatives, or anyone else, although I might wish them lifelong joy in their relationships. My explanation is that the next wedding I attend will be my own—to the woman I've loved and lived with for nearly six years.

Although I've been legally married to a man myself (and come close to marrying two others), I've come, in these last six years with Pamela, to see heterosexual marriage as very much a restricted club. (Nor is this likely to change in the near future, if one can judge by the recent clobbering of what was actually a rather tame proposal to recognize "domestic partnerships" in San Francisco.) Regardless of the *reason* people marry—whether to save on real estate taxes or qualify for married students housing or simply to express love—lesbians and gay men can't obtain the same results should they desire to do so. It seems apparent to me that few friends of Pamela's and mine would even join a club that excluded blacks, Jews, or women, much less assume that they could expect their black, Jewish, or female friends to toast their new status with champagne. But probably no other stand of principle we've ever made in our lives has been so misunderstood, or caused so much bad feeling on both sides.

Several people have reacted with surprise to our views, it never having occurred to them that gay people *can't* legally marry. (Why on earth did they think that none of us had bothered?) The most common reaction, however, is acute embarrassment, followed by a denial of our main point—that the about-to-be-wed person is embarking on a privileged status. (One friend of Pamela's insisted that lesbians are "lucky" not to have to agonize over whether or not to get married.) So wrapped in gauze is the institution of marriage, so ingrained the expectation that brides and grooms can enjoy the world's delighted approval, that it's hard for me not to feel put on the defensive for being so mean-spirited, eccentric, and/or politically rigid as to boycott such a happy event.

Another question we've fielded more than once (usually from   4
our most radical friends, both gay and straight) is why we'd want to get married in the first place. In fact, I have mixed feelings about registering my personal life with the state, but—and this seems to me to be the essence of radical politics—I'd prefer to be the one making the choice. And while feminists in recent years have rightly focused on puncturing the Schlaflyite myth of the legally protected homemaker, it's also true that marriage does confer some very real dollars-and-cents benefits. One example of inequity is our inability to file joint tax returns, although many couples, both gay and straight, go through periods when one partner in the relationship is unemployed or makes considerably less money than the other. At one time in our relationship, Pamela—who is a musician—was between bands and earning next to nothing. I was making a little over $37,000 a year as a newspaper reporter, a salary that put me in the 42 percent tax bracket—about $300 a week taken out of my paycheck. If we had been married, we could have filed a joint tax return and each paid taxes on half my salary, in the 25 or 30 percent bracket. The difference would have been nearly $100-a-week in our pockets.

Around the same time, Pamela suffered a months'-long illness which would have been covered by my health insurance if she were my spouse. We were luckier than many; we could afford it. But on top of the worry and expense involved (and despite the fact that intellectually we believe in the ideal of free medical care for everyone), we found it almost impossible to avoid internalizing a sense of personal failure—the knowledge that *because of who we are, we can't take care of each other.* I've heard of other gay people whose lovers were deported because they couldn't marry them and enable them to become citizens; still others who were barred from intensive-care units where their lovers lay stricken because they weren't "immediate family."

I would never begrudge a straight friend who got married to save a lover from deportation or staggering medical bills, but the truth is that I no longer sympathize with most of the less tangible justifications. This includes the oft-heard "for the sake of the children" argument, since (like many gay people, especially women) I *have* children, and I resent the implication that some families are more "legitimate" than others. (It's important to safeguard one's children's rights to their father's property, but a legal contract will do the same thing as marriage.)

But the single most painful and infuriating rationale for marriage, as far as I'm concerned, is the one that goes: "We wanted to stand up and show the world that we've made a *genuine* commitment." When one is gay, such sentiments are labeled "flaunting." My lover and I almost never find ourselves in public settings outside the gay ghetto where we are (a) perceived to be a couple at all (people constantly ask us if we're sisters, although we look nothing like each other), and (b) valued as such. Usually we're forced to choose between being invisible and being despised. "Making a genuine commitment" in this milieu is like walking a highwire without a net—with most of the audience not even watching and a fair segment rooting for you to fall. A disproportionate number of gay couples do.

I think it's difficult for even my closest, most feminist straight women friends to empathize with the intensity of my desire to be recognized as Pamela's partner. (In fact, it may be harder for feminists to understand than for others; I know that when I was straight, I often resented being viewed as one half of a couple. My struggle was for an independent identity, not the cojoined one I now crave.) But we are simply not considered *authentic,* and the reminders are constant. Recently at a party, a man I'd known for years spied me across the room and came over to me, arms outstretched, big happy-to-see-you grin on his face. Pamela had a gig that night and wasn't at the party; my friend's wife was there but in another room, and I hadn't seen her yet. "How's M——?" I asked the man. "Oh, she's fine," he replied, continuing to smile pleasantly. "Are you and Pam still together?"

Our sex life itself is against the law in many states, of course, and like all lesbians and gay men, we are without many other rights, both large and small. (In Virginia, for instance, it's technically against the law for us to buy liquor.) But as a gay couple. we are also most likely to be labeled and discriminated against in those very settings that, for most heterosexual Americans, constitute the most relaxed and personal parts of life. Virtually every tiny public act of togetherness—from holding hands on the street to renting a hotel room to dancing—requires us constantly to risk humiliation (I think, for example, of the two California women who were recently thrown out of a restaurant that had special romantic tables for couples), sexual harassment (it's astonishing how many men can't resist coming on to a lesbian couple), and even physical assault. A great deal of energy goes into just expecting possible trouble. It's a process which, after six years, has become second nature for me—but occasionally, when I'm in Provincetown or someplace else with a large lesbian population, I experience the *absence* of it as a feeling of virtual weightlessness.

What does all this have to do with my friends' weddings? Obviously, I can't expect my friends to live my life. But I do think that lines are being drawn in this "pro-family" Reagan era, and I have no choice about what side I'm placed on. My straight friends do, and at the very least, I expect them to acknowledge that. I certainly expect them to understand why I don't want to be among the rice-throwers and well-wishers at their weddings; beyond that, I would hope that they would commit themselves to fighting for my rights—preferably in personally visible ways, like marching in gay pride parades. But I also wish they wouldn't get married, period. And if that sounds hard-nosed, I hope I'm only proving my point—that not being able to marry isn't a minor issue.

Not that my life would likely be changed as the result of any individual straight person's symbolic refusal to marry. (Nor, for that matter, do all gay couples want to be wed.) But it's a political reality that heterosexual live-together couples are among our best tactical allies. The movement to repeal state sodomy laws has profited from the desire of straight people to keep the government out of *their* bedrooms. Similarly, it was a heterosexual New York woman who went to court several years ago to fight her landlord's demand that she either marry her live-in boyfriend or face eviction for violating a lease clause prohibiting "unrelated" tenants—and whose struggle led to the recent passage of a state rent law that had ramifications for thousands of gay couples, including Pamela and me.

The right wing has seized on "homosexual marriage" as its 12
bottom-line scare phrase in much the same way that "Would you
want your sister to marry one?" was brandished 25 years ago. *They*
see marriage as their turf. And so when I see feminists crossing into
that territory of respectability and "sinlessness," I feel my buffer zone
slipping away. I feel as though my friends are taking off their arm-
bands, leaving me exposed.

Topics for Discussion and Writing

1. Evaluate Van Gelder's title and opening paragraph. Did the title and
    the first sentence attract your attention, and, if so, did the rest of the
    first paragraph continue to hold it? Why, or why not?

2. In paragraphs 4 and 5 Van Gelder gives some concrete details to sup-
    port her point that members of the club receive benefits. Do you agree
    that fairness requires that gay and lesbian couples (and unmarried het-
    erosexual couples) receive the same benefits? (By the way, *why* does
    society grant certain benefits to married heterosexual couples? What
    good reasons, if any, can you think of?)

3. As paragraph 10 indicates, the essay was written during the "Reagan
    era." Do you think the climate has changed since then?

4. In paragraph 10 Van Gelder says that she expects her friends "to un-
    derstand" why she is not among the guests at their weddings. Do you
    understand why, or do you think she does not really explain why her
    inability legally to marry Pamela should influence her view of heterosex-
    ual marriage?

Beverly Cronin

Beverly Cronin is a member of the staff of The Boston Globe, *the newspaper in which this column appeared in 1991.*

Here's What
Happened . . .

The private life of a disabled person can, with just a few words, become the topic of a public exchange.

"What happened to you?" can never be dispatched quickly and neatly when the question is addressed to someone like me who uses crutches. The telling would take a couple of days.

So for the sake of expediency, as well as privacy, I dispense stock answers to the curious who ask about my crutches and one leg.

"I had an accident," is quick and dirty, even if not entirely ac-   4
curate. But it's also not without its perils. Everyone who asks really just wants to recount his or her own accident or that of someone near and dear.

Recently a sales clerk in a coffee shop interrupted the rhythm of serving customers to shape the question that intrudes almost daily.

"What happened to you?"

"I had an accident."

"Oh. My son had an accident, too. He was run over by a train   8
and lost his leg. Now he's been dead five years."

It was a sunny day when I entered the bakery, but not quite so bright when I left. All I had wanted was a cup of coffee.

Some inquiries are serious requests for information disguised as ridiculous questions.

A few months ago I was wrestling with the copying machine in my local library, just minding my own business and inserting my coins.

A man approached.   12

"Do you have multiple sclerosis?"

"Excuse me?"

"Do you have multiple sclerosis?"

Well, I could still hear, anyway.   16

"I hope not," I said. "I have one leg. Why?"

713

It turned out that this man's wife had recently been diagnosed with multiple sclerosis and was apparently devastated over it. He said that she refused to leave her wheelchair and would not go out in public. He had been trying in vain to coax her into using crutches. What he really was asking me was for a primer on crutch walking. So I helped him out with some details, including the pros and cons of axillary versus forearm style crutches.

He was immensely grateful. He even copied the name and address of the manufacturer from a label on my crutch and said he was going to order a pair. He wanted them ready for the moment when his wife decided that it is not a source of shame to be physically disabled.

Children always react by pointing or stating the obvious: 20 "Mommy, that lady has one leg." This is refreshing. It's a fact. Their inquiring minds are easily satisfied. They want to know if it hurts. No. And although they don't articulate it, they want to know if it can happen to them. When I say, "Don't worry, it's not going to happen to you," they're ready to tackle their next task.

The mothers do not recover as easily. They're usually red-faced and bumble over an apology. Some fathers are likewise flustered, as in the case of a colleague whose daughter got down on the floor to peer up my skirt. She just had to see for herself. This is perfectly understandable. Many children do this, I told her dad.

Some people want to compare notes. They deserve the courtesy of a straight answer.

Then there are the ones who deserve what they get.

"I was on safari in Africa . . . hungry hippo . . . nearest doc- 24 tor . . . three days on a dirt road . . ."

"I was swimming off the coast of Australia . . . ravenous alligators . . . sharks . . . miraculous rescue . . . bathing suit torn to shreds."

"I was just out for a walk one starry night . . . green glow in the sky . . . eerie sounds . . . Martians . . ."

Then there was the time when I was about 14. I told a woman in Connecticut that I was hit by a bus. (Not true.)

She knew all the gory details.   28

"I know, dear, I read all about it in the paper."

Topics for Discussion and Writing

1. Explain the irony of the title. (You may want to check the glossary, page 880–81, on "irony.")

2. Cronin does not disclose how she became disabled. Why not? Should she have?
3. Cronin suggests, through her examples, several reasons for the question "What happened to you?" What are the reasons? Do they cover the territory, or can you think of others? She also suggests the variety of her responses to the questions. From her responses, how would you characterize her own attitude toward her disability?
4. The article does not have an apparent occasion; that is, Cronin does not explain what caused her to write it. Why, in your opinion, might she have written it?
5. Reading the article and responding to the above questions might have disclosed your own response to disabilities—of others, or possibly your own. If so, write a paragraph, a journal entry, or an essay, examining your response.
6. Cronin calls herself disabled and, following her lead, we have also used the words "disabled" and "disability" above. But these words have recently been called into question. All people, we sometimes hear today, are "differently abled"—some can speak Spanish and some can't, some have great physical strength and some don't, some have the use of only one leg or of no legs, and some don't, and so on. What is your opinion of the use of words like "disabled" or "handicapped" or even "crippled," and of newer descriptions such as "physically challenged" and "differently abled"? Do you find Cronin's use of the word "disabled" appropriate or not?

Zora Neale Hurston

Zora Neale Hurston (1891?–1960) was brought up in Eatonville, Florida, a town said to be the first all-black self-governing town in the United States. Her early years were spent working at odd jobs (domestic servant, manicurist, waitress), but she managed to attend Howard University and then, with the aid of a scholarship, entered Barnard College, where she was the first black student. At Barnard, influenced by the anthropologists Franz Boas and Ruth Benedict, she set out to study the folklore of Eatonville. Later she published several volumes of folklore, as well as stories, novels, and an autobiography (the source of our selection) called Dust Tracks on a Road *(1942).*

In the 1950s her writing seemed reactionary, almost embarrassing in an age of black protest, and she herself—working as a domestic, a librarian, and a substitute teacher—was almost forgotten. She died in a county welfare home in Florida and was buried in an unmarked grave. In the 1980s Hurston was, so to speak, rediscovered, partly because of the attention given to her by Alice Walker.

A Conflict of Interest

An incident happened that made me realize how theories go by the board when a person's livelihood is threatened. A man, a Negro, came into the shop one afternoon and sank down in Banks's chair. Banks was the manager and had the first chair by the door. It was so surprising that for a minute Banks just looked at him and never said a word. Finally, he found his tongue and asked, "What do you want?"

"Hair-cut and shave," the man said belligerently.

"But you can't get no hair-cut and shave here. Mr. Robinson[1] has a fine shop for Negroes on U Street near Fifteenth," Banks told him.

"I know it, but I want one here. The Constitution of the United 4 States—"

But by that time, Banks had him by the arm. Not roughly, but he was helping him out of his chair, nevertheless.

"I don't know how to cut your hair," Banks objected. "I was trained on straight hair. Nobody in here knows how."

"Oh, don't hand me that stuff!" the crusader snarled. "Don't be such an Uncle Tom."

"Run on, fellow. You can't get waited on in here." 8

"I'll stay right here until I do. I know my rights. Things like this have got to be broken up. I'll get waited on all right, or sue the place."

"Go ahead and sue," Banks retorted. "Go on uptown, and get your hair cut, man. Don't be so hard-headed for nothing."

"I'm getting waited on right here!"

"You're next, Mr. Powell," Banks said to a waiting customer. 12 "Sorry, mister, but you better go on uptown."

"But I have a right to be waited on wherever I please," the Negro said, and started towards Updyke's chair which was being emptied. Updyke whirled his chair around so that he could not sit down and stepped in front of it. "Don't you touch *my* chair!" Updyke glared. "Go on about your business."

But instead of going, he made to get into the chair by force.

"Don't argue with him! Throw him out of here!" somebody in the back cried. And in a minute, barbers, customers all lathered and hair half cut, and porters, were all helping to throw the Negro out.

[1] **Robinson** George Robinson, an African-American, owned a chain of barber shops. Most of his shops catered to whites in Washington, D.C. (Editors' note)

The rush carried him way out into the middle of G Street and flung him down. He tried to lie there and be a martyr, but the roar of oncoming cars made him jump up and scurry off. We never heard any more about it. I did not participate in the mêlée, but I wanted him thrown out, too. My business was threatened.

It was only that night in bed that I analyzed the whole thing and realized that I was giving sanction to Jim Crow, which theoretically, I was supposed to resist. But here were ten Negro barbers, three porters and two manicurists all stirred up at the threat of our living through loss of patronage. Nobody thought it out at the moment. It was an instinctive thing. That was the first time it was called to my attention that self-interest rides over all sorts of lines. I have seen the same thing happen hundreds of times since, and now I understand it. One sees it breaking over racial, national, religious and class lines. Anglo-Saxon against Anglo-Saxon, Jew against Jew, Negro against Negro, and all sorts of combinations of the three against other combinations of the three. Offhand, you might say that we fifteen Negroes should have felt the racial thing and served him. He was one of us. Perhaps it would have been a beautiful thing if Banks had turned to the shop crowded with customers and announced that this man was going to be served like everybody else even at the risk of losing their patronage, with all of the other employees lined up in the center of the floor shouting, "So say we all!" It would have been a stirring gesture, and made the headlines for a day. Then we could all have gone home to our unpaid rents and bills and things like that. I could leave school and begin my wanderings again. The "militant" Negro who would have been the cause of it all, would have perched on the smuddled-up wreck of things and crowed. Nobody ever found out who or what he was. Perhaps he did what he did on the spur of the moment, not realizing that serving him would have ruined Mr. Robinson, another Negro who had got what he had the hard way. For not only would the G Street shop have been forced to close, but the F Street shop and all of his other six downtown shops. Wrecking George Robinson like that on a "race" angle would have been ironic tragedy. He always helped out any Negro who was trying to do anything progressive as far as he was able. He had no education himself, but he was for it. He would give any Howard University student a job in his shops if they could qualify, even if it was only a few hours a week.

So I do not know what was the ultimate right in this case. I do know how I felt at the time. There is always something fiendish and loathsome about a person who threatens to deprive you of your way of making a living. That is just human-like, I reckon.

Topics for Discussion and Writing

1. Hurston published this account in 1942, and she was writing about an event that had taken place a couple of decades earlier. Given the period, and given Hurston's analysis of her action, do you find her behavior understandable and excusable, or do you think that she is rationalizing cowardice? Explain.

2. Words like "outrageous," "ironic," "pathetic," and even "tragic" probably can be appropriately applied to this episode. Would you agree, however, that, as Hurston narrates it, it also has comic elements? If so, explain.

3. Hurston argues that self-interest overrides "racial, national, religious, and class lines." Do you agree? Does she persuade you that at least in this incident it was true, or might there have been other reasons for the employees' actions?

Gloria Naylor

Gloria Naylor, university teacher and essayist and novelist, holds an M.A. in Afro-American Studies from Yale University. Her first novel, The Women of Brewster Place *(1983), won an American Book Award. "A Question of Language" originally appeared in* The New York Times.

A Question of Language

Language is the subject. It is the written form with which I've managed to keep the wolf away from the door and, in diaries, to keep my sanity. In spite of this, I consider the written word inferior to the spoken, and much of the frustration experienced by novelists is the awareness that whatever we manage to capture in even the most transcendent passages falls far short of the richness of life. Dialogue achieves its power in the dynamics of a fleeting moment of sight, sound, smell, and touch.

I'm not going to enter the debate here about whether it is language that shapes reality or vice versa. That battle is doomed to be waged whenever we seek intermittent reprieve from the chicken and egg dispute. I will simply take the position that the spoken word, like the written word, amounts to a nonsensical arrangement of sounds or letters without a consensus that assigns "meaning." And building from the meanings of what we hear, we order reality. Words themselves are innocuous; it is the consensus that gives them true power.

I remember the first time I heard the word *nigger*. In my third-grade class, our math tests were being passed down the rows, and as I handed the papers to a little boy in back of me, I remarked that once again he had received a much lower mark than I did. He snatched his test from me and spit out that word. Had he called me a nymphomaniac or a necrophiliac, I couldn't have been more puzzled. I didn't know what a nigger was, but I knew that whatever it meant, it was something he shouldn't have called me. This was verified when I raised my hand, and in a loud voice repeated what he had said and watched the teacher scold him for using a "bad" word. I was later to go home and ask the inevitable question that every black parent must face—"Mommy, what does 'nigger' mean?"

And what exactly did it mean? Thinking back, I realize that this 4 could not have been the first time the word was used in my presence. I was part of a large extended family that had migrated from the rural South after World War II and formed a close-knit network that gravitated around my maternal grandparents. Their ground-floor apartment in one of the buildings they owned in Harlem was a weekend mecca for my immediate family, along with countless aunts, uncles, and cousins who brought along assorted friends. It was a bustling and open house with assorted neighbors and tenants popping in and out to exchange bits of gossip, pick up an old quarrel or referee the ongoig checkers game in which my grandmother cheated shamelessly. They were all there to let down their hair and put up their feet after a week of labor in the factories, laundries, and shipyards of New York.

Amid the clamor, which could reach deafening proportions— two or three conversations going on simultaneously, punctuated by the sound of a baby's crying somewhere in the back rooms or out on the street—there was still a rigid set of rules about what was said and how. Older children were sent out of the living room when it was time to get into the juicy details about "you-know-who" up on the third floor who had gone and gotten herself "p•r•e•g•n•a•n•t!" But my parents, knowing that I could spell well beyond my years, always demanded that I follow the others out to play. Beyond sexual misconduct and death, everything else was considered harmless for our young ears. And so among the anecdotes of the triumphs and disappointments in the various workings of their lives, the word *nigger* was used in my presence, but it was set within contexts and inflections that caused it to register in my mind as some thing else.

In the singular, the word was always applied to a man who had distinguished himself in some situation that brought their approval for his strength, intelligence, or drive:

"Did Johnny really do that?"

"I'm telling you, that nigger pulled in $6,000 of overtime last year. Said he got enough for a down payment on a house."   8

When used with a possessive adjective by a woman—"my nigger"—it became a term of endearment for husband or boyfriend. But it could be more than just a term applied to a man. In their mouths it became the pure essence of manhood—a disembodied force that channeled their past history of struggle and present survival against the odds into a victorious statement of being: "Yeah, that old foreman found out quick enough—you don't mess with a nigger."

In the plural, it became a description of some group within the community that had overstepped the bounds of decency as my family defined it: Parents who neglected their children, a drunken couple who fought in public, people who simply refused to look for work, those with excessively dirty mouths or unkempt households were all "trifling niggers." This particular circle could forgive hard times, unemployment, the occasional bout of depression—they had gone through all of that themselves—but the unforgivable sin was lack of self-respect.

A woman could never be a *nigger* in the singular, with its connotation of confirming worth. The noun *girl* was its closest equivalent in that sense, but only when used in direct address and regardless of the gender doing the addressing. *Girl* was a token of respect for a woman. The one-syllable word was drawn out to sound like three in recognition of the extra ounce of wit, nerve or daring that the woman had shown in the situation under discussion.

"G•i•r•l, stop. You mean you said that to his face?"   12

But if the word was used in a third-person reference or shortened so that it almost snapped out of the mouth, it always involved some element of communal disapproval. And age became an important factor in these exchanges. It was only between individuals of the same generation, or from an older person to a younger (but never the other way around), that "girl" would be considered a compliment.

I don't agree with the argument that use of the word *nigger* at this social stratum of the black community was an internalization of racism. The dynamics were the exact opposite: the people in my grandmother's living room took a word that whites used to signify worthlessness or degradation and rendered it impotent. Gathering there together, they transformed *nigger* to signify the varied and complex human beings they knew themselves to be. If the word was to disappear totally from the mouths of even the most liberal of white society, no one in that room was naïve enough to believe it would disappear from white minds. Meeting the word head-on, they proved it had absolutely nothing to do with the way they were determined to live their lives.

So there must have been dozens of times that the word *nigger* was spoken in front of me before I reached the third grade. But I didn't "hear" it until it was said by a small pair of lips that had already learned it could be a way to humiliate me. That was the word I went home and asked my mother about. And since she knew that I had to grow up in America, she took me in her lap and explained.

Topics for Discussion and Writing

1. Why, according to Naylor (in paragraph 1) is written language inferior to spoken language? Can you think of any way or any circumstance in which written language is superior? How does Naylor's essay support her position here? Or does it?

2. In paragraph 2 Naylor says "Words themselves are innocuous; it is the consensus that gives them true power." What does this mean? In the rest of the essay Naylor discusses meanings of the word "nigger." To what extent does her discussion demonstrate that consensus "assigns meaning" and gives words power.

3. If as a child you were the victim of an ethnic slur, explain how you reacted to it and how others (perhaps a parent or teacher) reacted to it. Or, if you ever delivered an ethnic slur, explain how you felt then, and how you feel now, about the incident or incidents.

Lorene Cary

Lorene Cary was brought up in Yeadon, Pennsylvania, a Philadelphia suburb that she characterizes as "an enclave of black professionals." In 1971, when she was 14, she applied to St. Paul's, a distinguished preparatory school in New Hampshire. (Until 1971 the school had admitted only male students.) She was accepted and entered St. Paul's in 1972 as a member of the class of '74.

After graduating from St. Paul's she earned a bachelor's and a master's degree at the University of Pennsylvania, taught at St. Paul's, worked as a writer for Time, *and served as an associate editor for* TV Guide. *She has also published short fiction, and has served as a trustee of St. Paul's.*

We give (under titles of our own) two selections from her memoir, Black Ice *(1991). The first describes her first visit home (after three months at St. Paul's), where she rejoins her two closest friends, Karen and Ruthie. The passage also mentions Fumiko, a Japanese student at St. Paul's. The second excerpt recounts experiences of Cary's senior year. Bruce Chan, a Chinese-American student at St. Paul's, had introduced Cary to Fumiko.*

Two Excerpts from *Black Ice*

I. Real Life

I visited Karen and Ruthie. They asked how St. Paul's was, and whether or not I liked it. I wanted to answer them honestly. I wanted them to know how my life had changed so that we could sit down in the dim light of Karen's living room and talk about it. But I did not have enough words or time to make them see it and feel it with me, and besides, nobody, not even my best friends, cared as much about St. Paul's as its students. Nobody else lived there. They lived, as we Paulies joked, in the real world.

Fumiko told them in her halting English that St. Paul's was "very hard." I agreed, and once they laughed, I broke into the monologue that I repeated, with variations according to the audience, for years: "First of all, you've got to understand that the teachers are all a little screwy. You've got to be to stay in a place like that for twenty years. These are the people who decided to opt out of real life at some point, and they are set loose on us twenty-four hours a day.

"OK? You got the picture? There is no escape from these people. They are out to *improve* you: how you read, how you write, how you run, how you look, what you say at the dinner table, how you *think*. You see what I mean by no escape? Meanwhile, back at the dorm, the white kids are blasting the hardest hard rock you've ever heard. . . ."

Later, I figured, when I understood the school better, then I could talk to them seriously about it. For now, I wanted to make them laugh. I wanted to entertain. I didn't dare risk being boring or snobbish or cry-babyish about my new school. I didn't want to lose them.

"Now you tell me about everybody at Yeadon. How was the new majorette squad this season? Did Mr. Cenatempo let you do flaming batons this year?"

Each time we began a new subject, I needed them to fill me in on facts, and I had to fill Fumiko in. I didn't know what they'd just read in English, or who had sung the solos in this year's *Messiah*, or what prank Bob Bailey had pulled in science lab. Too much exposition weighed down our conversation. We couldn't anticipate each other anymore or jump back and forth between subjects until we landed in intimate territory. I was with my friends, but I could not get the full pleasure of them. I wanted to weep with frustration.

Two nights before we returned to school, I stayed up by myself drinking my mother's Christmas liqueur late into the night. I decided to level with myself. My new friends and I knew each other's daily routines, but we had no history—and no future, I thought, when we all went back to our real lives. But back in real life, Karen and Ruthie and I, once past the memories, had to work hard just to keep talking. At my own house I felt as if I were fighting for a new position in the family order, while Mama pretended not to notice and Dad maybe didn't notice for real. Everywhere I went I felt out of place. The fact was that I had left home in September gleeful and smug. I took it as divine justice that now I felt as if I no longer belonged anywhere.

II. Sojourner

During the winter term Bruce Chan, who had drafted me to look after Fumiko on the first day of my Fifth Form, suggested that we begin tutoring some of the younger students in English. He also delegated me to write a letter of protest to the English department for what we thought was prejudice against the incoming students of color. (One teacher, by way of correcting a young student's paper, commented on the pattern of grammatical errors and warned the boy that he'd have to work to overcome his black English. We suspected, after reading several papers, that our teachers judged typically black "errors" more harshly than others, and that once obsessed by idiom they lost sight of black students' ideas.) A few days later I gritted my teeth as Bruce edited my letter in red pen. I remember delivering the rewritten version to the department chairman, who responded that he and the other teachers worked hard to be as sensitive as possible to the needs of all the students, but that he would urge his teachers, as he had been doing, to even greater consideration.

The tutoring was equally frustrating. Students brought us their papers during free periods before class. They wanted us to tidy things up, plug in big words. They did not come with a rough draft, as we asked, prepared to rethink and rewrite.

The best I could do, I decided, was to try to build their confidence rather than tear it down. I tried to pick out their original ideas and show them that these, the scary ones, were worth writing about.

"Forget your notes; put them away until exams. Thc papers are yours. It's how *you* read the same old story that that man has been teaching for twenty years. He's waiting for *you* to see it fresh. And you *can*. You've brought a whole bunch of new ideas that haven't been here until now."

When the girl left, I heard my own words. I had never said   12
them before, never even thought them. I sat in my room grinning. More than anything I had said while I stood nervously trying to solicit discussion on blues lyrics, a half-hour with that girl and her no-thesis, no-introduction, no-proper-conclusion paper had shown me that I, too, had something to give to St. Paul's. I had come not just with my hat in my hand, a poorly shod scholarship girl, but as a sojourner bearing gifts, which were mine to give or withhold.

No doubt, the appearance of Miss Clinton that year gave me strength. The new black Spanish teacher was in her early twenties. She was dark and thin with high pockets and a high bark of a laugh if you caught her in a funny mood outside of class. In class was a different matter. She would step outside the classroom, kick the doorstop with one sensible shoe, and say clearly over her shoulder: "*¡Listos, ya!*"

Her mouth with its pointed top lip was beautiful when she spoke, and the language came out bright and precise: "Ready, now!" Those of us who were not in her class stood in the sunny hallway in the modern-languages wing of the Schoolhouse on purpose to hear her. We yelped when she said it—not *ahora*, meaning now, but *¡ya!* Immediately! She was tough.

"Hell, no, they're not ready," we'd say as we walked back to the Reading Room across the hall.

"They're not *even* ready."   16

"They will never be ready."

"They better get ready."

"Forget it. Those guys are smoked. *Smoked!*"

The other teachers did not treat Miss Clinton with conde-   20
scending politeness (as many did another young black teacher).I
could not tell whether they offered her friendship, but I could see
that they gave her respect.

And no mistaking she was black. Now and then Miss Clinton
drove into town to buy greens—fresh greens in Concord—and she'd
boil a big pot. It stunk up her tiny dormitory; it seeped into the Indian tapestries on students' walls. On Saturday evening I watched
her dance to her new Marvin Gaye album, and I realized how lonely
she might be, this energetic young woman, for a companion. But
she neither hid it from us nor slopped it onto us to carry.

I took courage from her, as much as I dared, and yet I feared
her, too. I feared judgment that never came.

"You should stop by more often," she said as I stirred her pot
and moistened my face in the steam.

Buoyed up by Miss Clinton, my head crammed with the liter-   24
ature I was teaching under Mr. Lederer, who spent his sabbatical
year teaching in a North Philadelphia high school, I began to feel
more confident in the inevitable racial discussions in classes, at
Seated Meal, after visitors' talks. I took the offensive and bore my
gifts proudly. What the discussions concerned specifically, who was
there, where they took place, I do not remember. I do recall hearing the same old Greek-centered, European-centered assumptions
of superiority. Might made right. I had my stories about Chaka
Zulu[1] from my Harvard evening course (and I knew they worshipped Harvard!). Nothing mattered. I was like a child again, trying to argue that I was still somebody—I am Somebody! as we
shouted back to Jesse Jackson on the television—even though black
people had been slaves, even though we hadn't had the dignity to
jump off the boats en masse or die from tuberculosis like the Indians. More facts. I wanted more facts to show that it wasn't all fair
now, that the resources that kept them here, ruddy and well-tutored,
as healthy as horses, had been grabbed up in some greedy, obscene,
unfair competition years before.

---

[1] **Chaka Zulu** a famous Zulu warrior who, at his death in 1828, ruled all of what is now Natal (Editors' note)

"Even if my great-grandfather did own slaves, it's not fair to hold me responsible."

Fair. Fair. Fair. They shouted fair, as if fair had anything to do with it, and I had no facts to wipe their words away. I had no words for their trust funds, capital gains, patrimonies, legacies, bequests. My mind screamed profanities. I had no other words. They had taken them and made them into lies.

That's how I felt the night I left a racial discussion with a girl named India Bridgeman. A group of black girls had once asked her to take the role of plantation overseer in a student choreographed dance. I'd kept in my head the image of her as she danced around the slaves with a whip, her classical ballet training showing in every movement. She'd visited England as a member of St. Paul's varsity field hockey team. She was an acolyte who knew the rituals of high mass: where to walk, what to carry. I knew her through Janie, but mostly I envied her from a distance as a symbol, a collection of accomplishments that I did not possess.

We continued the debate into the Upper and then up the stairs to 28 her room. She turned toward me, and I saw India the dancer. She pivoted on the balls of her feet, calf muscles bunched, sternum up. On her forehead was a light brown spot that I had thought she penciled on as an affected beauty mark. (It was a mole.) She had clear eyes, kissy lips, and big, dramatic movements. "Wait, wait a minute! Wait, wait, wait, wait!" India talked like that.

"I get it," she said. "I get it. You know how when you *get* something that you've never been able to know before?"

I nodded, but I resisted her enthusiasm, and the spontaneous humility of this sudden expansiveness. India translated what I had been saying into different words, and I listened, dumb-founded to hear them. It was clear that she, too, knew how it felt to be an outsider. I had never suspected it. India told me about her life growing up in Manhattan, and her own estrangement from many of our schoolmates. We talked until we grew hungry.

"Isn't there anything to eat, anywhere?" India jumped up from the floor, where we'd been sitting, and walked across the room to her stash. "All I've got is mayonnaise," she said as if the world would end. "Hold everything! I know I had some crackers, too. Do you think that's gross, just putting mayonnaise on crackers?"

"Are you kidding? I was raised on mayonnaise. And mayon- 32 naise, not that cheap-ass salad dressing." I cut my eyes to the little jar in her hand. She whooped with laughter.

"What would you have done if I'd been holding some 'cheap-ass salad dressing'?"

"I would have died. But really, that stuff—"

"I know, I know, it's awful," she agreed.

"My mother makes mayonnaise sandwiches. My whole family 36 does. And my grandmother! God forbid she should have a few drinks. You should see what she does. *That's* awful."

I had not talked to other girls at St. Paul's about my grand-mother. India laughed with me, but solicitously, watchfully, as if to judge how much I could take, or how far beneath the surface of humor lay the shame.

"My *other* grandmother," I said, having risked as much as I dared just then, "sends me care packages, and I think I have some juice. Do you like pear nectar?"

"Not really."

"I used to love it. I don't have the heart to tell her I'm not so 40 crazy about it now."

"I know. It's like they get one thing that they know makes you happy, and they'll buy it for you for the rest of your life." She stopped eating a cracker. "Oh, that's so dear. That's so beautiful that your grandmother does that. Do you have anymore?"

"Sure. It's hot, though."

"Oh, let's get it. Let's drink to—what do you call her?"

"Nana."   44

"Let's drink to Nana."

We tiptoed to my room, and I pulled my pantry box out from underneath my bed. "Do you like sardines?" I whispered.

"Why not?"

India and I talked often and late into the night after that. We raged together at St. Paul's School—at its cliques and competitive-ness; its ambivalence toward its new female members; its smugness and certainty and power. We talked about families and boyfriends, girls we liked and girls we didn't. We laughed at how we had ap-peared to each other the year before. Our talk was therapeutic, pri-vate, and as intense as romance. It was for me the first triumph of love over race.

Topics for Discussion and Writing

1.   Analyze Cary's opening three paragraphs. How does the first paragraph reveal Cary's estrangement from her old friends? In the next paragraphs

she describes her teachers at St. Paul's. What is her attitude toward them? Is she contemptuous or fond of them? Is complaining or boasting? Why is it difficult to tell exactly how she does feel?

2. In paragraph 7 Cary refers to "our real lives" and "real life." In paragraph 3, she also uses the words "real life," and paragraph 1 ends with the words "real world." Why do you suppose these words keep cropping up as she remembers this episode in her life? (Have you ever felt that part of your life was real or unreal? Do you remember the circumstances?)

3. In paragraph 12, Cary sees herself as "a sojourner bearing gifts." What were the gifts? And why do you suppose she uses this slightly odd language to describe them?

4. In the section of her memoir to which we have given the title "Sojourner," Cary writes about tutoring younger students in English, the arrival of Miss Clinton (a new teacher), participating in discussions of racism, and the beginning of a new friendship. Why do these reminiscences come in the same section? What unifies them?

5. How do you interpret Cary's final sentence?

Studs Terkel

Studs Terkel was born Louis Terkel in New York City in 1912. He was brought up in Chicago and graduated from the University of Chicago. Terkel has been an actor, playwright, columnist, and disc jockey, but he is best known as the man who makes books out of tape recordings of people he gets to talk. Elsewhere in The Little, Brown Reader *we reprint interviews from his book called* Workers *(1974); below we print an interviews from* American Dreams: Lost and Found *(1980).*

Stephen Cruz

He *is thirty-nine.*

"The family came in stages from Mexico. Your grandparents usually came first, did a little work, found little roots, put together a few bucks, and brought the family in, one at a time. Those were the days when controls at the border didn't exist as they do now."

You just tried very hard to be whatever it is the system wanted of you. I was a good student and, as small as I was, a pretty good athlete. I was well liked, I thought. We were fairly affluent, but we lived down where all the trashy whites were. It was the only housing we could get. As kids, we never understood why. We did everything right. We didn't have those Mexican accents, we were never on welfare. Dad wouldn't be on welfare to save his soul. He woulda died first. He worked during the depression. He carries that pride with him, even today.

Of the five children, I'm the only one who really got into the business world. We learned quickly that you have to look for opportunities and add things up very quickly. I was in liberal arts, but as soon as Sputnik went up, well, golly, hell, we knew where the bucks were. I went right over to the registrar's office and signed up for engineering. I got my degree in '62. If you had a master's in business as well, they were just paying all kinds of bucks. So that's what I did. Sure enough, the market was super. I had fourteen job offers. I could have had a hundred if I wanted to look around.

I never once associated these offers with my being a minority. I   4 was aware of the Civil Rights Act of 1964, but I was still self-confident enough to feel they wanted me because of my abilities. Looking back, the reason I got more offers than the other guys was because of the government edict. And I thought it was because I was so goddamned brilliant. (Laughs.) In 1962, I didn't get as many offers as those who were less qualified. You have a tendency to blame the job market. You just don't want to face the issue of discrimination.

I went to work with Procter & Gamble. After about two years, they told me I was one of the best supervisors they ever had and they were gonna promote me. Okay, I went into personnel. Again, I thought it was because I was such a brilliant guy. Now I started getting wise to the ways of the American Dream. My office was glass-enclosed, while all the other offices were enclosed so you couldn't see into them. I was the visible man.

They made sure I interviewed most of the people that came in. I just didn't really think there was anything wrong until we got a new plant manager, a southerner. I received instructions from him on how I should interview blacks. Just check and see if they smell, okay? That was the beginning of my training program. I started asking: Why weren't we hiring more minorities? I realized I was the only one in a management position.

I guess as a Mexican I was more acceptable because I wasn't really black. I was a good compromise. I was visibly good. I hired a black secretary, which was *verboten*. When I came back from my vacation, she was gone. My boss fired her while I was away. I asked why and never got a good reason.

Until then, I never questioned the American Dream. I was con-   8
vinced if you worked hard, you could make it. I never considered
myself different. That was the trouble. We had been discriminated
against a lot, but I never associated it with society. I considered it
an individual matter. Bad people, my mother used to say. In '68
I began to question.

I was doing fine. My very first year out of college, I was making twelve thousand dollars. I left Procter & Gamble because I really
saw no opportunity. They were content to leave me visible, but my
thoughts were not really solicited. I may have overreacted a bit, with
the plant manager's attitude, but I felt there's no way a Mexican
could get ahead here.

I went to work for Blue Cross. It's 1969. The Great Society is
in full swing. Those who never thought of being minorities before
are being turned on. Consciousness raising is going on. Black programs are popping up in universities. Cultural identity and all that.
But what about the one issue in this country: economics? There were
very few management jobs for minorities, especially blacks.

The stereotypes popped up again. If you're Oriental, you're real
good in mathematics. If you're Mexican, you re a happy guy to have
around, pleasant but emotional. Mexicans are either sleeping or
laughing all the time. Life is just one big happy kind of event.
Mañana. Good to have as part of the management team, as long as
you weren't allowed to make decisions.

I was thinking there were two possibilities why minorities were   12
not making it in business. One was deep, ingrained racism. But there
was still the possibility that they were simply a bunch of bad
managers who just couldn't cut it. You see, until now I believed
everything I was taught about the dream: the American businessman is omnipotent and fair. If we could show these turkeys there's
money to be made in hiring minorities, these businessmen—good
managers, good decision makers—would respond. I naïvely thought
American businessmen gave a damn about society, that given a
choice they would do the right thing. I had that faith.

I was hungry for learning about decision-making criteria. I was
still too far away from top management to see exactly how they were
working. I needed to learn more. Hey, just learn more and you'll
make it. That part of the dream hadn't left me yet. I was still cling-
ing to the notion of work your ass off, learn more than anybody
else, and you'll get in that sphere.

During my fifth year at Blue Cross, I discovered another flaw
in the American Dream. Minorities are as bad to other minorities

as whites are to minorities. The strongest weapon the white manager had is the old divide and conquer routine. My mistake was thinking we were all at the same level of consciousness.

I had attempted to bring together some blacks with the other minorities. There weren't too many of them anyway. The Orientals never really got involved. The blacks misunderstood what I was presenting, perhaps I said it badly. They were on the cultural kick: a manager should be crucified for saying "Negro" instead of "black." I said as long as the Negro or the black gets the job, it doesn't mean a damn what he's called. We got into a huge hassle. Management, of course, merely smiled. The whole struggle fell flat on its face. It crumpled from divisiveness. So I learned another lesson. People have their own agenda. It doesn't matter what group you're with, there is a tendency to put the other guy down regardless.

The American Dream began to look so damn complicated, I began to think: Hell, if I wanted, I could just back away and reap the harvest myself. By this time, I'm up to twenty-five thousand dollars a year. It's beginning to look good, and a lot of people are beginning to look good. And they're saying: "Hey, the American Dream, you got it. Why don't you lay off?" I wasn't falling in line. 16

My bosses were telling me I had all the "ingredients" for top management. All that was required was to "get to know our business." This term comes up all the time. If I could just warn all minorities and women whenever you hear "get to know our business," they're really saying "fall in line." Stay within that fence, and glory can be yours. I left Blue Cross disillusioned. They offered me a director's job at thirty thousand dollars before I quit.

All I had to do was behave myself. I had the "ingredients" of being the good Chicano, the equivalent of the good nigger. I was smart. I could articulate well. People didn't know by my speech patterns that I was of Mexican heritage. Some tell me I don't look Mexican, that I have a certain amount of Italian, Lebanese, or who knows. (Laughs.)

One could easily say: "Hey, what's your bitch? The American Dream has treated you beautifully. So just knock it off and quit this crap you're spreading around." It was a real problem. Every time I turned around, America seemed to be treating me very well.

Hell, I even thought of dropping out, the hell with it. Maybe get a job in a factory. But what happened? Offers kept coming in. I just said to myself: God, isn't this silly? You might as well take the bucks and continue looking for the answer. So I did that. But each time I took the money, the conflict in me got more intense, not less. 20

Wow, I'm up to thirty-five thousand a year. This is a savings and loan business. I have faith in the executive director. He was the kind of guy I was looking for in top management: understanding, humane, also looking for the formula. Until he was up for consideration as executive v.p. of the entire organization. All of a sudden everything changed. It wasn't until I saw this guy flip-flop that I realized how powerful vested interests are. Suddenly he's saying: "Don't rock the boat. Keep a low profile. Get in line." Another disappointment.

Subsequently, I went to work for a consulting firm. I said to myself: Okay, I've got to get close to the executive mind. I need to know how they work. Wow, a consulting firm.

Consulting firms are saving a lot of American businessmen. They're doing it in ways that defy the whole notion of capitalism. They're not allowing these businesses to fail. Lockheed was successful in getting U.S. funding guarantees because of the efforts of consulting firms working on their behalf, helping them look better. In this kind of work, you don't find minorities. You've got to be a proven success in business before you get there.

The American Dream, I see now, is governed not by education, opportunity, and hard work, but by power and fear. The higher up in the organization you go, the more you have to lose. The dream is *not* losing. This is the notion pervading America today: Don't lose. 24

When I left the consulting business, I was making fifty-five thousand dollars a year. My last performance appraisal was: You can go a long way in this business, you can be a partner, but you gotta know our business. It came up again. At this point, I was incapable of being disillusioned any more. How easy it is to be swallowed up by the same set of values that governs the top guy. I was becoming that way. I was becoming concerned about losing that fifty grand or so a year. So I asked other minorities who had it made. I'd go up and ask 'em: "Look, do you owe anything to others?" The answer was: "We owe nothing to anybody." They drew from the civil rights movement but felt no debt. They've quickly forgotten how it happened. It's like I was when I first got out of college. Hey, it's really me, I'm great. I'm as angry with these guys as I am with the top guys.

Right now, it's confused. I've had fifteen years in the business world as "a success." Many Anglos would be envious of my progress. Fifty thousand dollars a year puts you in the one or two top percent of all Americans. Plus my wife making another thirty thousand. We had lots of money. When I gave it up, my cohorts looked at me not just as strange, but as something of a traitor. "You're screwing it up for all of us. You're part of our union, we're the elite, we should govern. What the hell are you doing?" So now I'm looked at suspiciously by my peer group as well.

I'm teaching at the University of Wisconsin at Platteville. It's nice. My colleagues tell me what's on their minds. I got a farm next-door to Platteville. With farm prices being what they are (laughs), it's a losing proposition. But with university work and what money we've saved, we're gonna be all right.

The American Dream is getting more elusive. The dream is being   28 governed by a few people's notion of what the dream is. Sometimes I feel it's a small group of financiers that gets together once a year and decides all the world's issues.

It's getting so big. The small-business venture is not there any more. Business has become too big to influence. It can't be changed internally. A counterpower is needed.

Topics for Discussion and Writing

1. In paragraph 9, Cruz refers to "The Great Society." What is (or was) "The Great Society" and how is it relevant to Cruz's story? If you aren't sure what The Great Society was, what can you learn about it from this pararaph, or others in Cruz's account?

2. In paragraphs 13 and 14 Cruz says he discovered that "Minorities are as bad to other minorities as whites are to minorities." Does this view come as a surprise to you? Or have you had experiences that tend to confirm it? Conversely, have you had experiences that tend to refute it? Explain.

3. In paragraph 17 Cruz says, "If I could just warn all minorities and women whenever you hear 'get to know the business,' they're really saying 'fall in line.' Stay within that fence . . ." If someone were to tell you "get to know the business" how else might you interpret it? Do you agree with Cruz that the message you were being given would depend on whether or not you were a member of a minority culture or a woman?

4. Cruz frequently cites The American Dream. What is Cruz's idea of the American Dream and what has disillusioned him with it? Do you find yourself in sympathy with his complaints? Why or why?

5. Suppose you were in a position to offer Cruz a job in management, how would you evaluate him as a candidate? You might try to do this by writing a memo to your supervisor, arguing Cruz's strengths and weaknesses and making a recommendation to hire or not. (You can take as much license as you need to invent the company, your position in it, the job opening, and the resumé Cruz has presented.)

Courtesy Amy Tan

Amy Tan

Amy Tan was born in 1952 in Oakland, California, two-and-a-half years after her parents had emigrated from China. She attended Linfield College in Oregon and then California State University at San Jose, where she shifted her major from premedical studies to English. After earning a master's degree in linguistics from San Jose, Tan worked as a language consultant and then as a freelance business writer. In 1985, having decided to try her hand at fiction, she joined the Squaw Valley Community of Writers, a fiction workshop. In 1989 she published her first novel, The Joy Luck Club, *a collection of sixteen interwoven stories. In 1991 she published a second novel,* The Kitchen God's Wife.*

    The essay that we reprint appeared in* Life *magazine in April, 1991.*

Snapshot: Lost Lives of Women

When I first saw this photo as a child, I thought it was exotic and remote, of a faraway time and place, with people who had no connection to my American life. Look at their bound feet! Look at that funny lady with the plucked forehead!

The solemn little girl is, in fact, my mother. And leaning against the rock is my grandmother, Jingmei. "She called me Baobei," my mother told me. "It means Treasure."

The picture was taken in Hangzhou, and my mother believes the year was 1922, possibly spring or fall, judging by the clothes. At first glance, it appears the women are on a pleasure outing.

But see the white bands on their skirts? The white shoes? They are in mourning. My mother's grandmother, known to the others as Divong, "The Replacement Wife," has recently died. The women have come to this place, a Buddhist retreat, to perform yet another ceremony for Divong. Monks hired for the occasion have chanted the proper words. And the women and little girl have walked in circles clutching smoky sticks of incense. They knelt and prayed, then burned a huge pile of spirit money so that Divong might ascend to a higher position in her new world.

This is also a picture of secrets and tragedies, the reasons that warnings have been passed along in our family like heirlooms. Each of these women suffered a terrible fate, my mother said. And they were not peasant women but big city people, very modern. They went to dance halls and wore stylish clothes. They were supposed to be the lucky ones.

Look at the pretty woman with her finger on her cheek. She is my mother's second cousin, Nunu Aiji, "Precious Auntie." You cannot see this, but Nunu Aiyi's entire face was scarred from smallpox. Lucky for her, a year or so after this picture was taken, she received marriage proposals from two families. She turned down a lawyer and married another man. Later she divorced her husband, a daring thing for a woman to do. But then, finding no means to support herself or her young daughter, Nunu eventually accepted the lawyer's second proposal—to become his number two concubine. "Where else could she go?" my mother asked. "Some people said she was lucky the lawyer still wanted her."

Now look at the small woman with a sour face (*third from left*). There's a reason that Jyou Ma, "Uncle's Wife," looks this way. Her husband, my great-uncle often complained that his family had chosen an ugly woman for his wife. To show his displeasure, he often insulted Jyou Ma's cooking. One time Great-Uncle tipped over a pot of boiling soup, which fell all over his niece's four-year-old neck and nearly killed her. My mother was the little niece, and she still has that soup scar on her neck. Great-Uncle's family eventually chose a pretty woman for his second wife. But the complaints about Jyou Ma's cooking did not stop.

Doomma, "Big Mother," is the regal-looking woman seated on   8
a rock. (The woman with the plucked forehead, far left, is a servant, remembered only as someone who cleaned but did not cook.)
Doomma was the daughter of my great-grandfather and Nu-pei,
"The Original Wife." She was shunned by Divong, "The Replacement Wife," for being "too strong," and loved by Divong's daughter, my grandmother. Doomma's first daughter was born with a
hunchback—a sign, some said, of Doomma's own crooked nature.
Why else did she remarry, disobeying her family's orders to remain
a widow forever? And why did Doomma later kill herself, using
some mysterious means that caused her to die slowly over three
days? "Doomma died the same way she lived," my mother said,
"strong, suffering lots."

Jingmei, my own grandmother, lived only a few more years after
this picture was taken. She was the widow of a poor scholar, a man
who had the misfortune of dying from influenza when he was about
to be appointed a vice-magistrate. In 1924 or so, a rich man, who
liked to collect pretty women, raped my grandmother and thereby
forced her into becoming one of his concubines. My grandmother,
now an outcast, took her young daughter to live with her on an island outside of Shanghai. She left her son behind, to save his face.
After she gave birth to another son she killed herself by swallowing
raw opium buried in the New Year's rice cakes. The young daughter who wept at her deathbed was my mother.

At my grandmother's funeral, monks tied chains to my mother's
ankles so she would not fly away with her mother's ghost. "I tried to
take them off," my mother said. "I was her treasure. I was her life."

My mother could never talk about any of this, even with her
closest friends. "Don't tell anyone," she once said to me. "People
don't understand. A concubine was like some kind prostitute. My
mother was a good woman, high-class. She had no choice."

I told her I understood.   12

"How can you understand?" she said, suddenly angry. "You
did not live in China then. You do not know what it's like to have
no position in life. I was her daughter. We had no face! We belonged
to nobody! This is a shame I can never push off my back." By the
end of the outburst, she was crying.

On a recent trip with my mother to Beijing, I learned that my
uncle found a way to push the shame off his back. He was the son
my grandmother left behind. In 1936 he joined the Communist
party—in large part, he told me, to overthrow the society that forced
his mother into concubinage. He published a story about his mother.

I told him I had written about my grandmother in a book of fiction. We agreed that my grandmother is the source of strength running through our family. My mother cried to hear this.

My mother believes my grandmother is also my muse, that she helps me write. "Does she still visit you often?" she asked while I was writing my second book. And then she added shyly, "Does she say anything about me?"

"Yes," I told her. "She has lots to say. I am writing it down."   16

This is the picture I see when I write. These are the secrets I was supposed to keep. These are the women who never let me forget why stories need to be told.

Topics for Discussion and Writing

1. Consider the title of this essay. Why are the women's lives described as "lost lives"? Can you imagine a companion piece, "Lost Lives of Men"? If not, why not?

2. In paragraph 5, what does Tan communicate by "And they were not peasant women, but big city people, very modern"? What does she imply about the lives of those who *were* peasants?

3. In the fifth paragraph and in the last, Tan refers to "secrets" that she "was supposed to keep." What were the secrets? Why does she reveal them?

4. In the first paragraph Tan reports, "When I first saw this photo as a child, I thought it was exotic and remote, of a faraway time and place, with people who had no connection to my American life." What does she imply in this paragraph about their "connection to [her] American life" now? Where in the essay is that connection revealed or explained?

5. If you are lucky enough to have photographs of your ancestors, explore the images of the people in them and what you have been told about their lives. Do you feel "connected" or not? Explain.

Liliana Heker

Liliana Heker, born in Argentina in 1943, achieved fame in 1966 with the publication of her first book. She has continued to write fiction, and she has also been influential in her role as the editor of a literary magazine. "The Stolen Party," first published in Spanish in 1982, was translated and printed in Other Fires: Short Fiction by Latin American Women *(1985), edited and translated by Alberto Manguel.*

The Stolen Party

As soon as she arrived she went straight to the kitchen to see if the monkey was there. It was: what a relief! She wouldn't have liked to admit that her mother had been right. *Monkeys at a birthday?* her mother had sneered. *Get away with you, believing any nonsense you're told!* She was cross, but not because of the monkey, the girl thought; it's just because of the party.

"I don't like you going," she told her. "It's a rich people's party."

"Rich people go to Heaven too," said the girl, who studied religion at school.

"Get away with Heaven," said the mother. "The problem with you, young lady, is that you like to fart higher than your ass." 4

The girl didn't approve of the way her mother spoke. She was barely nine, and one of the best in her class.

"I'm going because I've been invited," she said. "And I've been invited because Luciana is my friend. So there."

"Ah yes, your friend," her mother grumbled. She paused. "Listen, Rosaura," she said at last. "That one's not your friend. You know what you are to them? The maid's daughter, that's what."

Rosaura blinked hard: she wasn't going to cry. Then she yelled: 8 "Shut up! You know nothing about being friends!"

Every afternoon she used to go to Luciana's house and they would both finish their homework while Rosaura's mother did the cleaning. They had their tea in the kitchen and they told each other secrets. Rosaura loved everything in the big house, and she also loved the people who lived there.

"I'm going because it will be the most lovely party in the whole world, Luciana told me it would. There will be a magician, and he will bring a monkey and everything."

The mother swung around to take a good look at her child, and pompously put her hands on her hips.

"Monkeys at a birthday?" she said. "Get away with you, believ- 12 ing any nonsense you're told!"

Rosaura was deeply offended. She thought it unfair of her mother to accuse other people of being liars simply because they were rich. Rosaura too wanted to be rich, of course. If one day she managed to live in a beautiful palace, would her mother stop loving her? She felt very sad. She wanted to go to that party more than anything else in the world.

"I'll die if I don't go," she whispered, almost without moving her lips.

And she wasn't sure whether she had been heard, but on the morning of the party she discovered that her mother had starched her Christmas dress. And in the afternoon, after washing her hair, her mother rinsed it in apple vinegar so that it would be all nice and shiny. Before going out, Rosaura admired herself in the mirror, with her white dress and glossy hair, and thought she looked terribly pretty.

Señora Ines also seemed to notice. As soon as she saw her, she said:

"How lovely you look today, Rosaura."

Rosaura gave her starched skirt a slight toss with her hands and 16 walked into the party with a firm step. She said hello to Luciana and asked about the monkey. Luciana put on a secretive look and whispered into Rosaura's ear: "He's in the kitchen. But don't tell anyone, because it's a surprise."

Rosaura wanted to make sure. Carefully she entered the kitchen and there she saw it: deep in thought, inside its cage. It looked so funny that the girl stood there for a while, watching it, and later, every so often, she would slip out of the party unseen and go and admire it. Rosaura was the only one allowed into the kitchen. Señora Ines had said: "You yes, but not the others, they're much too boisterous, they might break something." Rosaura had never broken anything. She even managed the jug of orange juice, carrying it from the kitchen into the dining room. She held it carefully and didn't spill a single drop. And Señora Ines had said: "Are you sure you can manage a jug as big as that?" Of course she could manage. She wasn't a butterfingers, like the others. Like that blonde girl with the bow in her hair. As soon as she saw Rosaura, the girl with the bow had said:

"And you? Who are you?"

"I'm a friend of Luciana," said Rosaura.

"No," said the girl with the bow, "you are not a friend of Lu- 20 ciana because I'm her cousin and I know all her friends. And I don't know you."

"So what," said Rosaura. "I come here every afternoon with my mother and we do our homework together."

"You and your mother do your homework together?" asked the girl, laughing.

"I and Luciana do our homework together," said Rosaura, very seriously.

The girl with the bow shrugged her shoulders.   24

"That's not being friends," she said. "Do you go to school together?"

"No."

"So where do you know her from?" said the girl, getting impatient.

Rosaura remembered her mother's words perfectly. She took a   28
deep breath.

"I'm the daughter of the employee," she said.

Her mother had said very clearly: "If someone asks, you say you're the daughter of the employee; that's all." She also told her to add: "And proud of it." But Rosaura thought that never in her life would she dare say something of the sort.

"What employee?" said the girl with the bow. "Employee in a shop?"

"No," said Rosaura angrily. "My mother doesn't sell anything in   32
any shop, so there."

"So how come she's an employee?" said the girl with the bow.

Just then Señora Ines arrived saying *shh shh*, and asked Rosaura if she wouldn't mind helping serve out the hotdogs, as she knew the house so much better than the others.

"See?" said Rosaura to the girl with the bow, and when no one was looking she kicked her in the shin.

Apart from the girl with the bow, all the others were delight-   36
ful. The one she liked best was Luciana, with her golden birthday crown; and then the boys. Rosaura won the sack race, and nobody managed to catch her when they played tag. When they split into two teams to play charades, all the boys wanted her for their side. Rosaura felt she had never been so happy in all her life.

But the best was still to come. The best came after Luciana blew out the candles. First the cake. Señora Ines had asked her to help pass the cake around, and Rosaura had enjoyed the task immensely, because everyone called out to her, shouting "Me, me!" Rosaura remembered a story in which there was a queen who had the power of life or death over her subjects. She had always loved that, having the power of life or death. To Luciana and the boys she gave the largest pieces, and to the girl with the bow she gave a slice so thin one could see through it.

After the cake came the magician, tall and bony, with a fine red cape. A true magician: he could untie handkerchiefs by blowing on them and make a chain with links that had no openings. He could guess what cards were pulled out from a pack, and the monkey was his assistant. He called the monkey "partner." "Let's see here, partner," he would say, "turn over a card." And, "Don't run away, partner: time to work now."

The final trick was wonderful. One of the children had to hold the monkey in his arms and the magician said he would make him disappear.

"What, the boy?" they all shouted.   40

"No, the monkey!" shouted back the magician.

Rosaura thought that this was truly the most amusing party in the whole world.

The magician asked a small fat boy to come and help, but the small fat boy got frightened almost at once and dropped the monkey on the floor. The magician picked him up carefully, whispered something in his ear, and the monkey nodded almost as if he understood.

"You mustn't be so unmanly, my friend," the magician said to   44
the fat boy.

"What's unmanly?" said the fat boy.

The magician turned around as if to look for spies.

"A sissy," said the magician. "Go sit down."

Then he stared at all the faces, one by one. Rosaura felt her heart   48
tremble.

"You, with the Spanish eyes," said the magician. And everyone saw that he was pointing at her.

She wasn't afraid. Neither holding the monkey, nor when the magician made him vanish; not even when, at the end, the magician flung his red cape over Rosaura's head and uttered a few magic words . . . and the monkey reappeared, chattering happily, in her arms. The children clapped furiously. And before Rosaura returned to her seat, the magician said:

"Thank you very much, my little countess."

She was so pleased with the compliment that a while later, when   52
her mother came to fetch her, that was the first thing she told her.

"I helped the magician and he said to me, 'Thank you very much, my little countess.'"

It was strange because up to then Rosaura had thought that she was angry with her mother. All along Rosaura had imagined that she would say to her: "See that the monkey wasn't a lie?" But instead she was so thrilled that she told her mother all about the wonderful magician.

Her mother tapped her on the head and said: "So now we're a countess!"

But one could see that she was beaming. 56

And now they both stood in the entrance, because a moment ago Señora Ines, smiling, had said: "Please wait here a second."

Her mother suddenly seemed worried.

"What is it?" she asked Rosaura.

"What is what?" said Rosaura. "It's nothing; she just wants to 60 get the presents for those who are leaving, see?"

She pointed at the fat boy and at a girl with pigtails who were also waiting there, next to their mothers. And she explained about the presents. She knew, because she had been watching those who left before her. When one of the girls was about to leave, Señora Ines would give her a bracelet. When a boy left, Señora Ines gave him a yo-yo. Rosaura preferred the yo-yo because it sparkled, but she didn't mention that to her mother. Her mother might have said: "So why don't you ask for one, you blockhead?" That's what her mother was like. Rosaura didn't feel like explaining that she'd be horribly ashamed to be the odd one out. Instead she said:

"I was the best-behaved at the party."

And she said no more because Señora Ines came out into the hall with two bags, one pink and one blue.

First she went up to the fat boy, gave him a yo-yo out of the 64 blue bag, and the fat boy left with his mother. Then she went up to the girl and gave her a bracelet out of the pink bag, and the girl with the pigtails left as well.

Finally she came up to Rosaura and her mother. She had a big smile on her face and Rosaura liked that. Señora Ines looked down at her, then looked up at her mother, and then said something that made Rosaura proud:

"What a marvelous daughter you have, Herminia."

For an instant, Rosaura thught that she'd give her two presents: the bracelet and the yo-yo. Señora Ines bent down as if about to look for something. Rosaura also leaned forward, stretching out her arm. But she never completed the movement.

Señora Ines didn't look in the pink bag. Nor did she look in the 68 blue bag. Instead she rummaged in her purse. In her hand appeared two bills.

"You really and truly earned this," she said handing them over. "Thank you for all your help, my pet."

Rosaura felt her arms stiffen, stick close to her body, and then she noticed her mother's hand on her shoulder. Instinctively she pressed herself against her mother's body. That was all. Except her eyes. Rosaura's eyes had a cold, clear look that fixed itself on Señora Ines's face.

Señora Ines, motionless, stood there with her hand outstretched. As if she didn't dare draw it back. As if the slightest change might shatter an infinitely delicate balance.

Topics for Discussion and Writing

1. The first paragraph tells us, correctly, that Rosaura's mother is wrong about the monkey. By the time the story is over, is the mother right about anything? If so, what?
2. Characterize Señora Ines. Why does she offer Rosaura money instead of a yo-yo or a bracelet? By the way, do you assume she is speaking deceptively when she tells Rosaura that she bars other children from the kitchen on the grounds that "they might break something"? On what do you base your view?
3. What do you make of the last paragraph? Why does Señora Ines stand with her hand outstretched, "as if she didn't dare draw it back"? What "infinitely delicate balance" might be shattered?

Pat Mora

Pat Mora did her undergraduate work at Texas Western College, and then earned a master's degree at the University of Texas at El Paso, where she then served as Assistant to the Vice President for Academic Affairs, Director of the University Museum, and then (1981–89) as Assistant to the President. She has published essays on Hispanic culture as well as a children's book, Tomás and the Library Lady, *but she is best known for her books of poems. Mora has received several awards, including one from the Southwest Council of Latin American Studies.*

Immigrants

wrap their babies in the American flag,
feed them mashed hot dogs and apple pie,
name them Bill and Daisy,
buy them blonde dolls that blink blue
eyes or a football and tiny cleats   5

before the baby can even walk,
speak to them in thick English,
    hallo, babee, hallo.
whisper in Spanish or Polish
when the babies sleep, whisper   10
in a dark parent bed, that dark
parent fear, "Will they like
our boy, our girl, our fine american
boy, our fine american girl?"

[1986]

Topics for Discussion and Writing

1. To say that someone—for example, a politician—"wraps himself in the American flag" is to suggest disapproval or even anger or contempt. What behavior does the phrase usually describe? What does Mora mean when she says that immigrants "wrap their babies in the American flag"?
2. What do you suppose is Mora's attitude toward the immigrants? Do you think the poet fully approves of their hopes? On what do you base your answer?
3. Does Mora's description of the behavior of immigrants ring true of the immigrant group you are part of or know best? What is your attitude toward their efforts to assimilate? Explain in an essay of 750–1000 words.

12
Articles of Faith

The Creation of Adam
Michelangelo

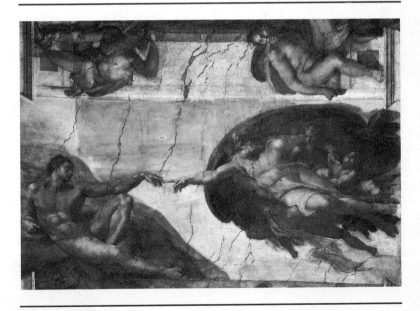

The Creation of Adam (detail)
Michelangelo

Priest Kensu Achieving Enlightenment
While Catching a Shrimp
Kao, 14th Century

Tokyo National Museum, Orion Press/Art Resource, NY

Short Views

A little philosophy inclineth man's mind to atheism, but depth in philosophy bringeth men's minds about to religion.
Francis Bacon

Religion is the opium of the people.
Karl Marx

If one wishes to form a true estimate of the full grandeur of religion, one must keep in mind what it undertakes to do for men. It gives them information about the source and origin of the universe, it assures them of protection and final happiness amid the changing vicissitudes of life, and it guides their thoughts and motions by means of precepts which are backed by the whole force of its authority.
Sigmund Freud

Religion is an attempt to get control over the sensory world, in which we are placed, by means of the wish-world, which we have developed inside us as a result of biological and psychological necessities.
Sigmund Freud

The language of "sonship," "brotherhood," "fellowship," "good Christian men," which pervades liturgy, prayerbooks and hymnbooks, . . . alienates women in their specific identity as women. Many women and most men are not aware of the alienation which is produced by the structures of English grammar. In pronouns and many other words, the male specific and the generic coincide. Thus when a word which is both male specific and generic is used, men naturally identify, whereas women can only identify by denying their specific identity as female.

To be sure, the image of woman is not entirely excluded from the language of Christian liturgy and theology. The church has been portrayed as a woman, referred to as "She," and discussed in feminine categories. But language applied to the church embodies sexual stereotypes and reflects and reinforces the secondary status of women. "She" receives life, sustenance and power from "her"

relation to a male Christ and is clearly subordinated to him. Women's identification with the church has not led to an elevation of their status, but rather has set the seal on their subordination.
                                Carol Christ and Marilyn Collins

To stand on one leg and prove God's existence is a very different thing from going down on one's knees and thanking him for it.
                                Soren Kierkegaard

Ethiopians have gods with snub noses and black hair; Thracians have gods with gray eyes and red hair.
                                Xenophanes of Colophon

God offers to every mind its choice between truth and repose. Take which you please; you can never have both. Between these, as a pendulum, man oscillates. He in whom the love of repose predominates will accept the first creed, the first philosophy, the first political party he meets—most likely his father's. He gets rest, commodity, reputation; but he shuts the door of truth. He in whom the love of truth predominates will keep himself aloof from all the moorings, afloat. He will abstain from dogmatism, and recognize all the opposite negations between which, as walls, his being is swung. He submits to the inconvenience of suspense and imperfect opinions, but he is a candidate for truth, as the other is not, and respects the highest law of his being.
                                Ralph Waldo Emerson

We cannot know whether we love God, although there may be strong reasons for thinking so, but there can be no doubt about whether we love our neighbor or no.
                                Saint Theresa

To the [Hebrew] biblical mind, man is above all a commanded being, a being of whom demands may be made. The central problem is not, What is being? but rather, What is required of me?
                                Abraham Heschel

The Sabbath lays down a judgment on the fundamental issues of our civilization and, specifically, demands restraint, dignity, reticence, and silent rest—not commonplace virtues. . . . The Sabbath . . . calls into question the foundations of the life of one dimension only, asking how people can imagine that all there is is what they see just now.
                                Jacob Neusner

"What," it will be questioned, "When the sun rises do you not see a round disk of fire somewhat like a guinea?" O no no, I see an In- numerable Company of the Heavenly Host crying, "Holy holy holy is the Lord God Almighty." I question not my corporeal or vegeta- tive eye any more than I would question a window concerning sight. I look through it and not with it.
William Blake

I feel no need for any other faith than my faith in human beings. Like Confucius of old, I am so absorbed in the wonder of earth and the life upon it that I cannot think of heaven and the angels. I have enough for this life. If there is no other life, then this one has been enough to make it worth being born, myself a human being.
Pearl Buck

Langston Hughes

Langston Hughes (1902–67) was the first black American writer to establish an interna- tional reputation. Enormously versatile, he wrote poems, plays, stories, novels, children's books, filmscripts, autobiographies, and essays. Hughes also exerted a great influence on American literature by organizing poetry readings for black writers, and by founding three theater groups. The following selection comes from his autobiography, The Big Sea *(1940).*

Salvation

I was saved from sin when I was going on thirteen. But not really saved. It happened like this. There was a big revival at my Auntie Reed's church. Every night for weeks there had been much preaching, singing, praying, and shouting, and some very hardened sinners had been brought to Christ, and the membership of the church had grown by leaps and bounds. Then just before the revival ended, they held a special meeting for children, "to bring the young lambs to the fold." My aunt spoke of it for days ahead. That night I was escorted to the front row and placed on the mourners' bench with all the other young sinners, who had not yet been brought to Jesus.

My aunt told me that when you were saved you saw a light, and something happened to you inside! And Jesus came into your life! And God was with you from then on! She said you could see and hear and feel Jesus in your soul. I believed her. I had heard a great many old people say the same thing and it seemed to me they ought to know. So I sat there calmly in the hot, crowded church, waiting for Jesus to come to me.

The preacher preached a wonderful rhythmical sermon, all moans and shouts and lonely cries and dire pictures of hell, and then he sang a song about the ninety and nine safe in the fold, but one little lamb was left out in the cold. Then he said: "Won't you come? Won't you come to Jesus? Young lambs, won't you come?" And he held out his arms to all us young sinners there on the mourners' bench. And the little girls cried. And some of them jumped up and went to Jesus right away. But most of us just sat there.

A great many old people came and knelt around us and prayed, 4 old women with jet-black faces and braided hair, old men with work-gnarled hands. And the church sang a song about the lower lights are burning, some poor sinners to be saved. And the whole building rocked with prayer and song.

Still I kept waiting to *see* Jesus.

Finally all the young people had gone to the altar and were saved, but one boy and me. He was a rounder's son named Westley. Westley and I were surrounded by sisters and deacons praying. It was very hot in the church, and getting late now. Finally Westley said to me in a whisper: "God damn! I'm tired o' sitting here. Let's get up and be saved." So he got up and was saved.

Then I was left all alone on the mourners' bench. My aunt came and knelt at my knees and cried, while prayers and songs swirled all around me in the little church. The whole congregation prayed for me alone, in a mighty wail of moans and voices. And I kept waiting serenely for Jesus, waiting, waiting—but he didn't come. I wanted to see him, but nothing happened to me. Nothing! I wanted something to happen to me, but nothing happened.

I heard the songs and the minister saying: "Why don't you 8 come? My dear child, why don't you come to Jesus? Jesus is waiting for you. He wants you. Why don't you come? Sister Reed, what is this child's name?"

"Langston," my aunt sobbed.

"Langston, why don't you come? Why don't you come and be saved? Oh, Lamb of God! Why don't you come?"

Now it was really getting late. I began to be ashamed of myself, holding everything up so long. I began to wonder what God thought about Westley, who certainly hadn't seen Jesus either, but who was now sitting proudly on the platform, swinging his knickerbockered legs and grinning down at me, surrounded by deacons and old women on their knees praying. God had not struck Westley dead for taking his name in vain or for lying in the temple. So I decided that maybe to save further trouble, I'd better lie, too, and say that Jesus had come, and get up and be saved.

So I got up.   12

Suddenly the whole room broke into a sea of shouting, as they saw me rise. Waves of rejoicing swept the place. Women leaped in the air. My aunt threw her arms around me. The minister took me by the hand and led me to the platform.

When things quieted down, in a hushed silence, punctuated by a few ecstatic "Amens," all the new young lambs were blessed in the name of God. Then joyous singing filled the room.

That night, for the last time in my life but one—for I was a big boy twelve years old—I cried. I cried, in bed alone, and couldn't stop. I buried my head under the quilts, but my aunt heard me. She woke up and told my uncle I was crying because the Holy Ghost had come into my life, and because I had seen Jesus. But I was really crying because I couldn't bear to tell her that I had lied, that I had deceived everybody in the church, and I hadn't seen Jesus, and that now I didn't believe there was a Jesus any more, since he didn't come to help me.

Topics for Discussion and Writing

1. Is this piece amusing, or serious, or both? Explain.
2. How would you characterize the style or voice of the first three sentences? Childlike? Sophisticated? How would you characterize the final sentence? How can you explain the change in style or tone?
3. Why does Hughes bother to tell us, in paragraph 11, that Westley was "swinging his knickerbockered legs and grinning"? Do you think that Westley, too, may have cried that night? Give your reasons.
4. Is the episode told from the point of view of someone "going on thirteen," or from the point of view of a mature man? Consult the entry on "persona" in the Glossary. One way to answer this question about point of view is to describe Hughes's persona in this essay. Does the essay strike you as in some ways "a performance"? If so, who is the audience—or who might be the ideal audience for this performance?

George Washington

Although George Washington (1732–99) issued the proclamation of "a day of public thanks-giving and prayer" in the first year of his presidency, the first Thanksgiving Day had been celebrated long before, in 1621, in accordance with a proclamation by Governor William Bradford of Plymouth Colony. Bradford's proclamation, issued in thanks for a harvest after a severe winter, was enacted in a feast of wild turkeys, shared by the colonists and neighboring Indians. In subsequent years the holiday was observed only irregularly until Washington's proclamation of 1789, but even after this proclamation the custom was observed only occasionally. In 1863 Lincoln revived it, setting the date as the last Thursday in November. In 1941 Franklin Delano Roosevelt moved the holiday to the third Thursday, but later in the year Congress passed a joint resolution setting it on the fourth Thursday.

A 1789 Proclamation

Whereas it is the duty of all Nations to acknowledge the providence of Almighty God, to obey his will, to be grateful for his benefits, and humbly to implore his protection and favor, and Whereas both Houses of Congress have by their joint Committee requested me "to recommend to the People of the United States a day of public thanks-giving and prayer to be observed by acknowledging with grateful hearts the many signal favors of Almighty God, especially by affording them an opportunity peaceably to establish a form of government for their safety and happiness."

Now therefore I do recommend and assign Thursday the 26th day of November next to be devoted by the People of these States to the service of that great and glorious Being, who is the beneficent Author of all the good that was, that is, or that will be. That we may then all unite in rendering unto him our sincere and humble thanks, for his kind care and protection of the People of this country previous to their becoming a Nation, for the signal and manifold mercies, and the favorable interpositions of his providence, which we experienced in the course and conclusion of the late war, for the great degree of tranquillity, union, and plenty, which we have since enjoyed, for the peaceable and rational manner in which we have been enabled to establish constitutions of government for our safety and happiness, and particularly the national One now lately instituted, for the civil and religious liberty with which we are blessed, and the means we have of acquiring and diffusing useful knowledge and in general for all the great and various favors which he hath been pleased to confer upon us.

And also that we may then unite in most humbly offering our prayers and supplications to the great Lord and Ruler of Nations and beseech him to pardon our national and other transgressions, to enable us all, whether in public or private stations, to perform our several and relative duties properly and punctually, to render our national government a blessing to all the People, by constantly being a government of wise, just and constitutional laws, discreetly and faithfully executed and obeyed, to protect and guide all Sovereigns and Nations (especially such as have shown kindness unto us) and to bless them with good government, peace, and control. To promote the knowledge and practice of true religion and virtue, and the increase of science among them and Us, and generally to grant unto all Mankind such a degree of temporal prosperity as he alone knows to be best.

Topics for Discussion and Writing

1. Washington lists among benefits attributed to God "the civil and religious liberty with which we are blessed" (paragraph 4). Does our "civil and religious liberty" not guarantee separation of church and state, which a national day of "public thanksgiving and prayer" might be thought to violate? What issues might be involved in a debate on this question, and what is your position on them?

2. Note the many references in Washington's speech to the intervention of God in national affairs. In the religious worship most familiar to you, is God thought of in such terms as, for example, "Ruler of Nations" (paragraph 3)?

3. In your experience, to what extent is Thanksgiving observed both as a national and religious holiday? Compare it to other national holidays such as the Fourth of July or Veterans Day. Or compare it to a national holiday you are familiar with in another country.

4. Imitating Washington's style, proclaim a holiday, for instance the Fourth of July, or Washington's birthday (or your own birthday).

Jon D. Levenson

Jon D. Levenson is a professor of Jewish studies at the Harvard Divinity School. We reprint an essay that originally appeared in The New York Times.

The Good Friday-
Passover Connection

This year, as Good Friday comes to an end, Passover will begin, and Jews all over the world will sit down to the seder, the ceremonial banquet that commemorates and re-enacts the exodus from Egypt. Though Good Friday and Passover rarely overlap, the connection between them is more than coincidence.

According to three of the four Gospels in the New Testament, the trial and execution of Jesus took place on the first day of Passover; that would mean the meal of the previous evening—the Last Supper—would have been a kind of seder itself. (Jewish holidays begin at sundown.) But according to the Gospel of John, Good Friday, the day of the Crucifixion, fell on the day before Passover, exactly as it does this year, and that would mean the Last Supper was not a seder in any sense.

That the Crucifixion took place at Passover time has deeply influenced the way in which Christians conceive of Jesus. In the Gospel of John, it is reported that because of the prohibition in the Book of Exodus against breaking bones in the paschal lamb, the sacrifice offered on the first night of Passover, Jesus's legs were not broken during the Crucifixion. And in the early church, the idea was pervasive that Jesus was not only the son of God but also the lamb whose blood provided protection from the forces of destruction. Although the application of these two ideas to Jesus crosses the line between Judaism and Christianity, the conjunction of the ideas grows out of Jewish sources.

In the Hebrew Bible, the theme of the sacrifice of the special son centers on Isaac. His father, Abraham, bound him on an altar in fearsome obedience to God's command to make of him a burnt offering. When Abraham passed his test of obedience, God rescinded the command, and Abraham sacrificed a sheep in his son's stead. The affinities with the story of Passover, in which the blood of the lamb prevents the death of the Israelites' first-born sons, is obvious.

758

Jubilees, a Jewish book written about two centuries before the execution of Jesus, makes the connection explicit. It reports that the binding of Isaac took place at Passover time and that the holiday itself was instituted by Abraham upon Abraham's return.

While Christians were transferring the Passover theology to Jesus, Jews continued developing the association of Isaac's near-sacrifice with the same holiday. "When I see the blood [of the lamb], I will pass over you," reads Exodus.

A rabbinic source from early in the common era comments, "I see the blood of the binding of Isaac"—implying that some of the son's blood really was shed. Another rabbinic source has Abraham asking God to "remember the binding of Isaac and consider it as if his ashes were piled up on the altar so that you will forgive his descendants and rescue them from affliction."

Ironically, much of that affliction has historically come about because of the story of Good Friday. Probably no words in any scriptures have wrought move havoc than the words the New Testament reports as those of the Jewish crowd at the trial of Jesus: "His blood be on us, and on our children." It is thus hardly surprising that, traditionally, Christian violence against Jews often erupted at this time of year. In England in 1144, for example, the discovery on Good Friday eve of the dead body of a Christian boy led to anti-Jewish riots and the murder of a prominent Jew. 8

The blood libel—the idea that Jews murder gentile children to use their blood in matzoh, the unleavened bread of Passover—was once especially widespread in Christendom. The superstition was condemned in 1247 by Pope Innocent IV, who noted that as a result of this popular belief, the fate of the Jews in his own time was "perhaps worse than that of their fathers in Egypt." Yet the blood libel endured into modern times, and echoes of it have been heard even in recent years.

The relationship of Good Friday to Passover is thus subtle and complex. The Christian holiday is rooted in the Jewish one in ways that are not incidental, and the two occasions share important symbols and points of theology. Yet the differences are also important.

It must not be overlooked that the great claim of the early church was not that its gospel had continued the Jewish Torah[1] but that the gospel had superseded Torah, and that the church superseded the people of Israel, the Jews.

---

[1] **Torah** the first five books of the Hebrew Bible (Editors' note)

"Once, the slaying of the sheep was precious," wrote St. Melito,   12
a bishop of the second century, "but it is worthless now because
of the life of the Lord." As for the Jews, they were, he wrote, only
a "preliminary sketch" that was "made void" by the appearance of
the church, "the repository of the reality."

But today, when Jews sit down to the seder, they are making
the opposite statement—that the rites of the Torah are not obsolete,
nor the Jewish people about to disappear. In recent decades, some
Christian groups—and by no means only the most liberal ones—
have repudiated the classic supersessionist theology. But even this
repudiation emphasizes the gulf that lies between these two great
traditions.

Good Friday and Passover thus bear eloquent witness not only
to important similarities between Judaism and Christianity but also
to the importance of the differences. Wise Jews and wise Christians
will want to keep both the similarities and the differences in mind,
especially in this season.

Topics for Discussion and Writing

1. In paragraph 6 Levenson says that early Christians engaged in "trans-
    ferring the Passover theology to Jesus." Exactly what does he mean?
2. Much of Levenson's essay is devoted to sketching the history or tradi-
    tion behind Passover. What, however, would you say Levinson's thesis
    is, and how is this sketch relevant to the thesis?
3. What is the significance of Passover today for Jews of your acquain-
    tance? That is, what does it mean, in their eyes—what does it *do* for
    them when they celebrate it?
4. In paragraph 4 Levenson refers to "the Hebrew Bible," a collection of
    writings that until recently was usually known as "the Old Testament."
    Why do you suppose Levenson (like many other people today) prefers
    the term "Hebrew Bible"?

Irving Kristol

Irving Kristol (b. 1920), a professor at New York University and coeditor of the journal
The Public Interest, *describes himself as a "neoconservative." According to Kristol, in*
Reflections of a Neoconservative *(1984), neoconservatism is "a current of thought emerging out of the academic-intellectual world and provoked by disillusionment with contemporary liberalism." The following essay appeared in* The New York Times.

Room for Darwin
and the Bible

The argument over whether (or how) the scientific theory of evolution should be taught in our public schools, as against the religious doctrine of "creationism," generates high passions. The consequence, alas, is that the debate has become a dogmatic crusade on both sides, and our educators, school administrators and textbook publishers find themselves trapped in the middle.

It should not be this way. It is largely a pointless conflict, because its terms have been erroneously formulated. There is no single theory of evolution as taught in our elementary or high-school biology textbooks. And the religious doctrine of creation is a more complicated affair than many of our believing Christians think it is.

Practically all biologists, when they engage in scientific discourse, assume that the earth's species were not created by divine command. As scientists, they could not make any other assumption. But they agree on little else—a fact which our textbooks are careful to ignore, lest it give encouragement to the religious. There is no doubt that most of our textbooks are still written as participants in the "warfare" between science and religion that is our heritage from the 19th century. And there is also little doubt that it is this pseudo-scientific dogmatism that has provoked the current religious reaction.

The majority of our biologists still accept, and our textbooks still teach, the "neo-Darwinian synthesis"—Darwin's original teaching as modified by modern genetics. We all know this theory: Living creatures emerged by evolution from inert matter and the original species evolved over time into the species we are familiar with—including, of course, our own species, homo sapiens. The mechanism of this evolution is "survival of the fittest," speeded up by the occasional genetic mutation. 4

Though this theory is usually taught as an established scientific truth, it is nothing of the sort. It has too many lacunae. Geological evidence does not provide us with the spectrum of intermediate species we would expect. Moreover, laboratory experiments reveal how close to impossible it is for one species to evolve into another, even allowing for selective breeding and some genetic mutation. There is unquestionably evolution *within* species: every animal breeder is engaged in exemplifying this enterprise. But the gradual transformation of the population of one species into another is a biological hypothesis, not a biological fact.

Moreover, today a significant minority of distinguished biologists and geneticists find this hypothesis incredible and insist that evolution must have proceeded by "quantum jumps," caused by radical genetic mutation. This copes with some of the problems generated by neo-Darwinist orthodoxy, but only to create others. We just don't know of any such "quantum jumps" that create new species, since most genetic mutations work against the survival of the individual. So this is another hypothesis—no less plausible than the orthodox view, but still speculative.

And there are other speculations about evolution, some by Nobel prize-winning geneticists, that border on the bizarre—for example, that life on earth was produced by spermatozoa from outer space. In addition, many younger biologists (the so-called "cladists") are persuaded that the differences among species—including those that seem to be closely related—are such as to make the very concept of evolution questionable.

So "evolution" is no simple established scientific orthodoxy, and 8 to teach it as such is an exercise in dogmatism. It is reasonable to suppose that if evolution were taught more cautiously, as a congolomerate idea consisting of conflicting hypotheses rather than as an unchallengeable certainty, it would be far less controversial. As things now stand, the religious fundamentalists are not far off the mark when they assert that evolution, as generally taught, has an unwarranted anti-religious edge to it.

"Creation" is a matter of faith, not science. Such faith is perfectly defensible, theologically. Indeed, many learned and sophisticated religious thinkers—Soren Kierkegaard and Karl Barth, most notably—have argued that "a leap of faith" is in some sense a "natural" and preordained fulfillment of the human condition. Such writings may well be read with profit in college courses on religion, but are inappropriate to the lower school grades. And in any case such theological analysis, establishing the grounds of faith, has nothing to do with the study of biology.

Moreover, even if one wished to teach "creationism" in a high-school course in religion, one would quickly find oneself in a booby-trap. Exposing the doctrine to literate, inquiring minds results in all sorts of intellectual complications. For such minds, theologians have offered all kinds of subtle and sophisticated interpretations—

analogical, symbolic, esoteric and mystical. Such theological discussions, expressed in the rhetoric and imagery associated with a particular creed, are best left to parochial schools or to the churches.

The current teaching of evolution in our public schools does indeed have an ideological bias against religious belief—teaching as "fact" what is only hypothesis. But religious instruction in our public schools is something we have carefully avoided for most of American history, for the good and obvious reasons that in a pluralist society, theological issues can so easily become a focus of conflict. If believing Christians are persuaded that their children are not exposed to anti-religious instruction, one may reasonably hope that they will feel comfortable once again with this American tradition.

Topics for Discussion and Writing

1. The theory of evolution, Kristol says in paragraph 5, that is "usually taught as an established truth . . . is nothing of the sort." How does he support this assertion?
2. In paragraph 9 Kristol gives reasons for not teaching Creationism in high school. What are his reasons, and how convincing do you find them?
3. In paragraph 8 and again in his final paragraph Kristol suggests that evolution as it is now taught in high school has an antireligious tinge. If you studied evolution in high school, did your experience confirm Kristol's assertion? If so, now that you have read Kristol's essay, do you think that the subject could have been taught *without* such a tinge?

William James

William James (1842–1910), the older brother of the novelist Henry James, was one of the founders of the discipline of psychology in the United States. As he once remarked, the first lectures he ever heard on the subject were the ones he delivered in the 1870s.

James studied philosophy, science, and then medicine at Harvard University during the Civil War. In 1869–70 he suffered extreme depression and experienced a nervous collapse, but he emerged from it with the conviction that only a belief in freedom of the will gives life meaning. This essay comes from a collection of James's essays called The Will to Believe *(1897).*

Religious Faith

Religion has meant many things in human history; but when from now onward I use the word I mean to use it in the supernaturalist sense, as declaring that the so-called order of nature, which constitutes this world's experience, is only one portion of the total universe, and that there stretches beyond this visible world an unseen world of which we now know nothing positive, but in its relation to which the true significance of our present mundane life consists. A man's religious faith (whatever more special items of doctrine it may involve) means for me essentially his faith in the existence of an unseen order of some kind in which the riddles of the natural order may be found explained. In the more developed religions the natural world has always been regarded as the mere scaffolding or vestibule of a truer, more eternal world, and affirmed to be a sphere of education, trial, or redemption. In these religions, one must in some fashion die to the natural life before one can enter into life eternal. The notion that this physical world of wind and water, when the sun rises and the moon sets, is absolutely and ultimately the divinely aimed-at and established thing, is one which we find only in very early religions. . . . It is this natural religion (primitive still, in spite of the fact that poets and men of science whose good-will exceeds their perspicacity keep publishing it in new editions tuned to our contemporary ears) that, as I said a while ago, has suffered definitive bankruptcy in the opinion of a circle of persons, among whom I must count myself, and who are growing more numerous every day. For such persons the physical order of nature, taken simply as science knows it, cannot be held to reveal any one harmonious spiritual intent. It is mere *weather*, as Chauncey Wright called it, doing and undoing without end.

Now, I wish to make you feel, if I can in the short remainder of this hour, that we have a right to believe the physical order to be only a partial order; that we have a right to supplement it by an unseen spiritual order which we assume on trust, if only thereby life may seem to us better worth living again. But as such a trust will seem to some of you sadly mystical and execrably unscientific, I must first say a word or two to weaken the veto which you may consider that science opposes to our act.

There is included in human nature an ingrained naturalism and materialism of mind which can only admit facts that are actually tangible. Of this sort of mind the entity called "science" is the idol. Fondness for the word "scientist" is one of the notes by which you may know its votaries; and its short way of killing any opinion that it disbelieves in is to call it "unscientific." It must be granted that there is no slight excuse for this. Science has made such glorious leaps in the last three hundred years, and extended our knowledge of nature so enormously both in general and in detail; men of science, moreover, have as a class displayed such admirable virtues — that it is no wonder if the worshippers of science lose their head. In this very University, accordingly, I have heard more than one teacher say that all the fundamental conceptions of truth have already been found by science, and that the future has only the details of the picture to fill in. But the slightest reflection on the real conditions will suffice to show how barbaric such notions are. They show such a lack of scientific imagination, that it is hard to see how one who is actively advancing any part of science can make a mistake so crude. Think how many absolutely new scientific conceptions have arisen in our own generation, how many new problems have been formulated that were never thought of before, and then cast an eye upon the brevity of science's career. It began with Galileo, not three hundred years ago. Four thinkers since Galileo, each informing his successor of what discoveries his own lifetime had seen achieved, might have passed the torch of science into our hands as we sit here in this room. Indeed, for the matter of that, an audience much smaller than the present one, an audience of some five or six score people, if each person in it could speak for his own generation, would carry us away to the black unknown of the human species, to days without a document or monument to tell their tale. Is it credible that such a mushroom knowledge, such a growth overnight as this, *can* represent more than the minutest glimpse of what the universe will really prove to be when adequately understood? No! our science is a drop, our ignorance a sea. Whatever else be certain, this at least is certain — that the world of our present natural knowledge *is* enveloped in a larger world of *some* sort of whose residual properties we at present can frame no positive idea.

Agnostic positivism,[1] of course, admits this principle theoretically in the most cordial terms, but insists that we must not turn it to any practical use. We have no right, this doctrine tells us, to dream dreams, or suppose anything about the unseen part of the

[1] A belief that human knowledge must be based on sense perceptions (Editors' note)

universe, merely because to do so may be for what we are pleased to call our highest interests. We must always wait for sensible evidence for our beliefs; and where such evidence is inaccessible we must frame no hypotheses whatever. Of course this is a safe enough position *in abstracto*. If a thinker had no stake in the unknown, no vital needs, to live or languish according to what the unseen world contained, a philosophic neutrality and refusal to believe either one way or the other would be his wisest cue. But, unfortunately, neutrality is not only inwardly difficult, it is also outwardly unrealizable, where our relations to an alternative are practical and vital. This is because, as the psychologists tell us, belief and doubt are living attitudes, and involve conduct on our part. Our only way, for example, of doubting, or refusing to believe, that a certain thing *is*, is continuing to act as if it were *not*. If, for instance, I refuse to believe that the room is getting cold, I leave the windows open and light no fire just as if it still were warm. If I doubt that you are worthy of my confidence, I keep you uninformed of all my secrets just as if you were *un*worthy of the same. If I doubt the need of insuring my house, I leave it uninsured as much as if I believed there were no need. And so if I must not believe that the world is divine, I can only express that refusal be declining ever to act distinctively as if it were so, which can only mean acting on certain critical occasions as if it were *not* so, or in an irreligious way. There are, you see, inevitable occasions in life when inaction is a kind of action, and must count as action, and when not to be for is to be practically against; and in all such cases strict and consistent neutrality is an unattainable thing.

And, after all, is not this duty of neutrality where only our inner interests would lead us to believe, the most ridiculous of commands? Is it not sheer dogmatic folly to say that our inner interests can have no real connection with the forces that the hidden world may contain? In other cases divinations based on inner interests have proved prophetic enough. Take science itself! Without an imperious inner demand on our part for ideal logical and mathematical harmonies, we should never have attained to proving that such harmonies lie hidden between all the chinks and interstices of the crude natural world. Hardly a law has been established in science, hardly a fact ascertained, which was not first sought after, often with sweat and blood, to gratify an inner need. Whence such needs come from we do not know: we find them in us, and biological psychology so far only classes them with Darwin's "accidental variations." But the inner need of believing that this world of nature is a sign of some thing more spiritual and eternal than itself is just as strong and authoritative in those who feel it, as the inner need of uniform laws of causation ever can be in a professionally scientific head. The toil of many generations has proved the latter need prophetic. Why *may* not the former one be prophetic, too? And if needs of ours outrun the visible universe, why *may* not that be a sign than an invisible universe is there? What, in short, has authority to debar us from trusting our religious demands? Science as such assuredly has no authority, for she can only say what is, not what is not; and the agnostic "thou shalt not believe without coercive sensible evidence" is simply an expression (free to any one to make) of private personal appetite for evidence of a certain peculiar kind.

Now, when I speak of trusting our religious demands, just what do I mean by "trusting"? Is the word to carry with it license to define in detail an invisible world, and to anathematize and excommunicate those whose trust is different? Certainly not! Our faculties of belief were not primarily given us to make orthodoxies and heresies withal; they were given us to live by. And to trust our religious demands means first of all to live in the light of them, and to act as if the invisible world which they suggest were real. It is a fact of human nature, that men can live and die by the help of a sort of faith that goes without a single dogma or definition. The bare assurance that this natural order is not ultimate but a mere sign or vision, the external staging of a many-storied universe, in which spiritual forces have the last word and are eternal—this bare assurance is to such men enough to make life seem worth living in spite of every contrary presumption suggested by its circumstances on the natural plane. Destroy this inner assurance, however, vague as it is, and all the light and radiance of existence is extinguished for these persons at a stroke. Often enough the wild-eyed look at life—the suicidal mood—will then set in.

And now the application comes directly home to you and me. Probably to almost every one of us here the most adverse life would seem well worth living, if we only could be *certain* that our bravery and patience with it were terminating and eventuating and bearing fruit somewhere in an unseen spiritual world. But granting we are not certain, does it then follow that a bare trust in such a world is a fool's paradise and lubberland, or rather that it is a living attitude in which we are free to indulge? Well, we are free to trust at our own risks anything that is not impossible, and that can bring analogies to bear in its behalf. That the world of physics is probably not absolute, all the converging multitude of arguments that make in favor of idealism tend to prove; and that our whole physical life may lie soaking in a spiritual atmosphere, a dimension of being that we at present have no organ for apprehending, is vividly suggested to us by the analogy of the life of our domestic animals. Our dogs, for example, are in our human life but not of it. They witness hourly the outward body of events whose inner meaning cannot, by any possible operation, be revealed to their intelligence—events in which they themselves often play the cardinal part. My terrier bites a teasing boy, for example, and the father demands damages. The dog may be present at every step of the negotiations, and see the money paid, without an inkling of what it all means, without a suspicion that it has anything to do with *him;* and he never *can* know in his natural dog's life. Or take another case which used greatly to impress me in my medical-student days. Consider a poor dog whom they are vivisecting in a laboratory. He lies strapped on a board and shrieking at his executioners, and to his own dark consciousness is literally in a sort of hell. He cannot see a single redeeming ray in the whole business; and yet all these diabolical-seeming events are often controlled by human intentions with which, if his poor benighted mind could only be made to catch a glimpse of them, all that is heroic in him would religiously acquiesce. Healing truth, relief to future sufferings of beast and man, are to be bought by them. It may be genuinely a process of redemption. Lying on his back on the board there he may be performing a function incalculably higher than any that prosperous canine life admits of; and yet, of the whole performance, this function is the one portion that must remain absolutely beyond his ken.

Now turn from this to the life of man. In the dog's life we see 8 the world invisible to him because we live in both worlds. In human life, although we only see our world, and his within it, yet encompassing both these worlds a still wider world may be there, as unseen by us as our world is by him; and to believe in that world *may* be the most essential function that our lives in this world have to perform. But *"may* be! *may* be!" one now hears the positivist contemptuously exclaim; "what use can a scientific life have for maybes?" Well, I reply, the "scientific" life itself has much to do with maybes, and human life at large has everything to do with them. So far as man stands for anything, and is productive or originative at all, his entire vital function may be said to have to deal with maybes. Not a victory is gained, not a deed of faithfulness or courage is done, except upon a maybe; not a service, not a sally of generosity, not a scientific exploration or experiment or textbook, that may not be a mistake. It is only by risking our persons from one hour to another that we live at all. And often enough our faith beforehand in an uncertified result *is the only thing that makes the result come true.* Suppose, for instance, you are climbing a mountain, and have worked yourself into a position from which the only escape is by a terrible leap. Have faith that you can successfully make it, and your feet are nerved to its accomplishment. But mistrust yourself, and think of all the sweet things you have heard the scientists say of *maybes,* and you will hesitate so long that, at least, all unstrung and trembling, and launching yourself in a moment of despair, you roll in the abyss. In such a case (and it belongs to an enormous class), the part of wisdom as well as of courage is to *believe what is in the line of your needs,* for only by such belief is the need fulfilled. Refuse to believe, and you shall indeed be right, for you shall irretrievably perish. But believe, and again you shall be right, for you shall save yourself. You make one or the other of two possible universes true by your trust or mistrust—both universes having been only *maybes,* in this particular, before you contributed your act.

Now, it appears to me that the question whether life is worth living is subject to conditions logically much like these. It does, indeed, depend on you *the liver.* If you surrender to the nightmare view and crown the evil edifice by your own suicide, you have indeed made a picture totally black. Pessimism, completed by your act, is true beyond a doubt, so far as your world goes. Your mistrust of life has removed whatever worth your own enduring existence might have given to it; and now, throughout the whole sphere of possible influence of that existence, the mistrust has proved itself to have had divining power. But suppose, on the other hand, that instead of giving way to the nightmare view you cling to it that this world is not the *ultimatum.* Suppose you find yourself a very well-spring, as Wordsworth says, of—

> Zeal, and the virtue to exist by faith
> As soldiers live by courage; as, by strength
> Of heart, the sailor fights with roaring seas.

Suppose, however thickly evils crowd upon you, that your unconquerable subjectivity proves to be their match, and that you find a more wonderful joy than any passive pleasure can bring in trusting ever in the larger whole. Have you not now made life worth living on these terms? What sort of a thing would life really be, with your qualities ready for a tussle with it, if it only brought fair weather and gave these higher faculties of yours no scope? Please remember that optimism and pessimism are definitions of the world, and that our own reactions on the world, small as they are in bulk, are integral parts of the whole thing, and necessarily help to determine the definition. They may even be the decisive elements in determining the definition. A large mass can have its unstable equilibrium overturned by the addition of a feather's weight; a long phrase may have its sense reversed by the addition of the three letters *n-o-t*. This life *is* worth living, we can say, *since it is what we make it, from the moral point of view*; and we are determined to make it from that point of view, so far as we have anything to do with it, a success.

Now, in this description of faiths that verify themselves I have assumed that our faith in an invisible order is what inspires those efforts and that patience which make this visible order good for moral men. Our faith in the seen world's goodness (goodness now meaning fitness for successful moral and religious life) has verified itself by leaning on our faith in the unseen world. But will our faith in the unseen world similarly verify itself? Who knows?

Once more it is a case of *maybe*; and once more *maybes* are the essence of the situation. I confess that I do not see why the very existence of an invisible world may not in part depend on the personal response which any one of us may make to the religious appeal. God himself, in short, may draw vital strength and increase of very being from our fidelity. For my own part, I do not know what the sweat and blood and tragedy of this life mean, if they mean anything short of this. If this life be not a real fight, in which something is eternally gained for the universe by success, it is no better than a game of private theatricals from which one may withdraw at will. But it *feels* like a real fight—as if there were something really wild in the universe which we, with all our idealities and faithfulnesses, are needed to redeem; and first of all to redeem our own hearts from atheisms and fears. For such a half-wild, half-saved universe our nature is adapted. The deepest thing in our nature is the *Binnenleben*[2] (as a German doctor lately has called it), this dumb region of the heart in which we dwell alone with our willingness and unwillingness, our faiths and fears. As through the cracks and crannies of caverns those waters exude from the earth's bosom which then form the fountain-heads of springs, so in these crepuscular depths of personality the sources of all our outer deeds and decisions take their rise. Here is our deepest organ of communication

---

[2] Interior life (Editors' note)

with the nature of things; and compared with these concrete movements of our soul all abstract statements and scientific arguments—the veto, for example, which the strict positivist pronounces upon our faith—sound to us like the mere chatterings of the teeth. For here possibilities, not finished facts, are the realities with which we have actively to deal; and to quote my friend William Salter, of the Philadelphia Ethical Society, "as the essence of courage is to stake one's life on a possibility, so the essence of faith is to believe that the possibility exists."

These, then, are my last words to you: Be not afraid of life. Believe that life *is* worth living, and your belief will help create the fact. The "scientific proof" that you are right may not be clear before the day of judgment (or some stage of being which that expression may serve to symbolize) is reached. But the faithful fighter of this hour, or the beings that then and there will represent them, may then turn to the faint-hearted, who here decline to go on, with words like those with which Henry IV[3] greeted the tardy Crillon after a great victory had been gained: "Hang yourself, brave Crillon! We fought at Arques, and you were not there." 12

Topics for Discussion and Writing

1. From the first two paragraphs, what can you infer about James's audience? How would you characterize his relationship to the audience and the tone he established? Is his tone formal, or informal? Are he and his listeners on an equal footing? Does he expect that they will share most of his opinions and beliefs, or only some, or none?

2. James mentions the words "science" and "scientist" several times in his opening paragraphs, expecially in paragraph 3. What is his attitude toward science? Is it mostly favorable, or critical, or mixed? How is science related to "natural religion," which he discussed in paragraph 1? And in paragraph 3, what argument (which he will further develop in paragraph 5) is suggested by the phrase "worshippers of science"?

3. In paragraph 4, what is James's argument against agnosticism? What is the *tone* of his remarks in this paragraph?

4. James frequently uses comparisons in building his argument. Read the entry on "analogy" in the Glossary, and then note the comparisons James makes that qualify as analogies. Do you find these analogies effective, or perhaps even persuasive? Is there anything about his subject matter that particularly lends itself to the use of analogy?

---

[3] Henry IV of France put down a rebellion at the battle of Arques, 1589. (Editors' note)

Will Herberg

*Will Herberg (1901–77) was, in his youth, a Marxist who was active in the labor move-
ment in the United States. In middle age he became an anti-Communist, and he grew
increasingly interested in religion. Deeply moved by the writings of Reinhold Niebuhr,
Herberg thought of converting to Christianity, but Niebuhr urged him to remain true to
his Jewish roots. Herberg followed Niebuhr's advice, and went on to edit a volume of
writings by the Jewish philosopher Martin Buber. He also wrote two books:* Judaism
and Modern Man *(1951) and* Protestant-Catholic-Jew *(1955). A portion of this second
book, a sociological study, is reprinted here.*

Religiosity and Religion

Religion is taken very seriously in present-day America,
in a way that would have amazed and chagrined the "advanced"
thinkers of half a century ago, who were so sure that the ancient
superstition was bound to disappear very shortly in the face of the
steady advance of science and reason. Religion has not disappeared;
it is probably more pervasive today, and in many ways more influential, than it has been for generations. The only question is: What
kind of religion is it? What is its content? What is it that Americans
believe in when they are religious?

"The 'unknown God' of Americans seems to be faith itself."[1]
What Americans believe in when they are religious is . . . religion
itself. Of course, religious Americans speak of God and Christ, but
what they seem to regard as really redemptive is primarily religion,
the "positive" attitude of believing. It is this faith in faith, this religion
that makes religion its own object, that is the outstanding characteristic of contemporary American religiosity. Daniel Poling's
formula: "I began saying in the morning two words, 'I believe'—
those two words *with nothing added* . . ."[2] (emphasis not in original) may be taken as the classic expression of this aspect of American faith.

On the social level, this faith in religion involves the conviction,
quite universal among Americans today, that every decent and virtuous nation is religious, that religion is the true basis of national
existence and therefore presumably the one sure resource for the
solution of all national problems.[3] On the level of personal life, the
American faith in religion implies not only that every right-minded
citizen is religious, but also that religion (or faith) is a most effica-
cious device for getting what one wants in life.[4] "Jesus," the Rev.

Irving E. Howard assures us, "recommended faith as a technique for getting results. . . . Jesus recommended faith as a way to heal the body and to remove any of the practical problems that loom up as mountains in a man's path."[5]

As one surveys the contemporary scene, it appears that the   4 "results" Americans want to get out of faith are primarily "peace of mind," happiness, and success in worldly achievement. Religion is valued too as a means of cultural enrichment.

Prosperity, success, and advancement in business are the obvious ends for which religion, or rather the religious attitude of "believing," is held to be useful.[6] There is ordinarily no criticism of the ends themselves in terms of the ultimate loyalties of a God-centered faith, nor is there much concern about what the religion or the faith is all about, since it is not the content of the belief but the attitude of believing that is felt to be operative.

Almost as much as worldly success, religion is expected to produce a kind of spiritual euphoria, the comfortable feeling that one is all right with God. Roy Eckardt calls this the cult of "divine-human chumminess" in which God is envisioned as the "Man Upstairs," a "Friendly Neighbor," Who is always ready to give you the pat on the back you need when you happen to feel blue. "Fellowship with the Lord is, so to say, an extra emotional jag that keeps [us] happy. The 'gospel' makes [us] 'feel real good.'"[7] Again, all sense of the ambiguity and precariousness of human life, all sense of awe before the divine majesty, all sense of judgment before the divine holiness, is shut out; God is, in Jane Russell's inimitable phrase, a "livin' Doll." What relation has this kind of god to the biblical God Who confronts sinful man as an enemy before He comes out to meet repentant man as a Savior? Is this He of Whom we are told, "It is a fearful thing to fall into the hands of the living God" (Heb. 10:31)? The measure of how far contemporary American religiosity falls short of the authentic tradition of Jewish-Christian faith is to be found in the chasm that separates Jane Russell's "livin' Doll" from the living God of Scripture.

The cultural enrichment that is looked for in religion varies greatly with the community, the denomination, and the outlook and status of the church members. Liturgy is valued as aesthetically and emotionally "rewarding," sermons are praised as "interesting" and "enjoyable," discussions of the world relations of the church are welcomed as "educational," even theology is approved of as "thought provoking." On another level, the "old-time religion" is cherished by certain segments of the population because it so obviously enriches their cultural life.

But, in the last analysis, it is "peace of mind" that most Americans expect of religion. "Peace of mind" is today easily the most popular gospel that goes under the name of religion; in one way or another it invades and permeates all other forms of contemporary religiosity. It works in well with the drift toward other-direction characteristic of large sections of American society, since both see in adjustment the supreme good in life. What is desired, and what is promised, is the conquest of insecurity and anxiety, the overcoming of inner conflict, the shedding of guilt and fear, the translation of the self to the painless paradise of "normality" and "adjustment"! Religion, in short, is a spiritual anodyne designed to allay the pains and vexations of existence.

It is this most popular phase of contemporary American religiosity that has aroused the sharpest criticism in more sophisticated theological circles. The Most Rev. Patrick A. O'Boyle, Catholic archbishop of Washington, has warned that although "at first glance piety seems to be everywhere . . ." many persons appear to be "turning to religion as they would to a benign sedative to soothe their minds and settle their nerves."[8] Liston Pope emphasizes that the approach of the "peace of mind" school is not only "very dubious on psychological grounds," but its "identification [with] the Christian religion . . . is of questionable validity."[9] Roy Eckardt describes it as "religious narcissism," in which "the individual and his psycho-spiritual state occupy the center of the religious stage" and piety is made to "concentrate on its own navel."[10] I have myself spoken of it as a philosophy that would "dehumanize man and reduce his life to the level of sub-human creation which knows neither sin nor guilt."[11] It encourages moral insensitivity and social irresponsibility, and cultivates an almost lascivious preoccupation with self. The church becomes a kind of emotional service station to relieve us of our worries: "Go to church—you'll feel better," "Bring your troubles to church and leave them there" (slogans on subway posters urging church attendance). On every ground, this type of religion is poles apart from authentic Jewish-Christian spirituality which, while it knows of the "peace that passeth understanding" as the gift of God, promotes a "divine discontent"[12] with things as they are and a "passionate thirst for the future,"[13] in which all things will be renewed and restored to their right relation to God.[14]

The burden of this criticism of American religion from the point of view of Jewish-Christian faith is that contemporary religion is so naively, so innocently *man-centered*. Not God, but man—man in his individual and corporate being—is the beginning and end of the spiritual system of much of present-day American religiosity. In this kind of religion there is no sense of transcendence, no sense of the nothingness of man and his works before a holy God; in this kind of religion the values of life, and life itself, are not submitted to Almighty God to judge, to shatter, and to reconstruct; on the contrary, life, and the values of life, are given an ultimate sanction by being identified with the divine. In this kind of religion it is not man who serves God, but God who is mobilized and made to serve man and his purposes—whether these purposes be economic prosperity, free enterprise, social reform, democracy, happiness, security, or "peace of mind." God is conceived as man's "omnipotent servant,"[15] faith as a sure-fire device to get what we want. The American is a religious man, and in many cases personally humble and conscientious. But religion as he understands it is not something that makes for humility or the uneasy conscience: it is something that reassures him about the essential rightness of everything American, his nation, his culture, and himself; something that validates his goals and his ideals instead of calling them into question; something that enhances his self-regard instead of challenging it; something that feeds his self-sufficiency instead of shattering it; something that offers him salvation on easy terms instead of demanding repentance and a "broken heart." Because it does all these things, his religion, however sincere and well-meant, is ultimately vitiated by a strong and pervasive idolatrous element.

Notes

1. Reinhold Niebuhr, "Religiosity and the Christian Faith," *Christianity and Crisis*, Vol. XIV, No. 24, January 24, 1955.
2. Daniel A. Poling, "A Running Start to Every Day," *Parade: The Sunday Picture Magazine*, September 19, 1954.
3. At the Conference on the Spiritual Foundations of Our Democracy, held in Washington, D.C., in November 1954, Monsignor George G. Higgins, director of the social action department of the National Catholic Welfare Conference, issued a sharp warning against the widespread notion that a "return to God" on the part of the American people was in itself sufficient to solve all national problems, without the necessity of resorting to

responsible and informed thinking on the "secular" level, on the level of institutions and social strategies. His warning was echoed by others at the conference.

4. For a critique of this conception of religion, see H. Richard Niebuhr, "Utilitarian Christianity," *Christianity and Crisis*, Vol. VI, No. 12, July 8, 1946.

5. Howard, "Random Reflections," *Christian Economics*, March 8, 1955.

6. This is the burden of the philosophy of "positive thinking" so effectively expounded by Norman Vincent Peale, and may be documented in any of Dr. Peale's many writings. For example: "How do you practice faith? First thing every morning, before you arise, say out loud, 'I believe,' three times" (*The Power of Positive Thinking* [Prentice-Hall, 1952], p. 154). For a sharp criticism of this philosophy, see Miller, "Some Negative Thinking about Norman Vincent Peale," *The Reporter*, January 13, 1955, see also Paul Hutchinson, "Have We a 'New' Religion?" *Life*, April 11, 1955, pp. 148–157. A penetrating critique of the Peale gospel of "positive thinking" by a Catholic theologian will be found in Gustave Weigel, "Protestantism as a Catholic Concern," *Theological Studies*, Vol. XVI, No. 2, June 1955. A Jewish version of the same cult of "faith in faith" may be found in Louis Binstock, *The Power of Faith* (Prentice-Hall, 1952). Declares Rabbi Binstock: "You, like everyone else, have access to a great storehouse of dynamic power on which you can draw. . . . That storehouse is *Faith*. Not religion. Not your immortal soul. Not this House of Worship. Not God. But—FAITH" (p. 4). For a critical review of this book, see Herberg, "Faith and Idolatry," *The Pastor*, Vol. XVI, No. 3, November 1952. One of the oldest and most respectable of Protestant denominations recently ran a newspaper advertisement in which the readers were told that "there are times in life when faith alone protects" and were urged to attend church because "regular church attendance helps you build your own personal reserve of faith." Neither God nor Christ was anywhere mentioned.

7. "The Cult of the 'Man Upstairs.' A rhapsodic inquiry greets us from the TV screen and the radio: 'Have you talked to the Man Upstairs?' God is a friendly neighbor who dwells in the apartment just above. Call on him any time, especially if you are feeling a little blue. He does not get upset over your little faults. He understands. . . . Thus is the citizenry guided to divine-human chumminess. . . . Fellowship with the Lord is, so to say,

an extra emotional jag that keeps him [the individual] happy. The 'gospel' makes him 'feel real good'" (Eckardt, "The New Look in American Piety," *The Christian Century*, November 17, 1954). A strong strain of this "divine-human chumminess" is to be found in certain aspects of American revivalistic religion; there, too, the gospel makes you "feel real good." "What today's cult of reassurance most lacks—and indeed disavows—is a sense of life's inevitable failures. Here is the point at which it stands in starkest contrast to the teaching of America's most searching contemporary theologian, Reinhold Niebuhr. . . . There is one central idea in his writing which . . . is validated by universal experience. This is his contention that all human effort, however noble, however achieving contains within it an element of failure. Perhaps one reason Americans say they cannot understand Niebuhr is because their minds simply will not harbor this fact that all success is dogged by failure" (Hutchinson, "Have We a 'New' Religion?" *Life*, April 11, 1955, p. 148).

 8. Address at the forty-first annual meeting of the Association of American Colleges, held in Washington, January 1955, as reported in *New York Herald Tribune*, January 12, 1955.

 9. Address at the dinner meeting of the broadcasting and film commission of the National Council of Churches, New York City, March 1, 1955 (unpublished). See also Hutchinson, "Have We a 'New' Religion?" *Life*, April 11, 1955, pp. 147–148; Hutchinson calls it the "cult of reassurance."

10. Eckardt, "The New Look in American Piety," *The Christian Century*, November 17, 1954.

11. Herberg, *Judaism and Modern Man: An Interpretation of Jewish Religion* (Farrar, Straus, and Young, 1951), p. 29.

12. "I most emphatically prefer a divine discontent to peace of mind. . . . Are you satisfied with the state of the world? Are you content with the behavior of modern man? Have you reached the point where soporific relaxation is the real goal, where more than anything else you want rest and quiet and protection from stimulation? . . . If that's what you want, count me out. . . . God pity me on the day when I have lost my restlessness! God forgive me on the day when I'm satisfied! God rouse me up if ever I am so dull, insensitive, lazy, complacent, phlegmatic, and apathetic as to be at peace!" (Warren Weaver, "Peace of Mind," *The Saturday Review*, December 11, 1954). Mr. Weaver is director of the division of natural sciences of the Rockefeller Foundation.

13. Ernst Renan is reported to have described the "true Israelite" as a man "torn with discontent and possessed with a passionate thirst for the future."

14. "We are undoubtedly in the midst of a widespread and powerful revival of religion. There is, however, a real danger of this spiritual current running up against a steep wall of compulsive escapism and becoming a giant pool of stagnation and futility, instead of a vital tide of constructive energy and new creative work" (Charles W. Lowry, co-chairman of the Foundation for Religious Action, Washington, D.C., in a press release of the Foundation, issued June 10, 1954).

15. The phrase is from Jules H. Masserman, "Faith and Delusion in Psychotherapy: The Ur-Defenses of Man," *The American Journal of Psychiatry*, Vol. 110, No. 5, November 1953. For a critique of the theological aspects of Masserman's thesis, see Herberg, "Biblical Faith and Natural Religion," *Theology Today*, Vol. XI, No. 4, January 1955.

Topics for Discussion and Writing

1. Herberg several times uses the word "religiosity." How does religiosity differ from religion? What are Herberg's objections to religiosity?

2. What evidence in the "contemporary scene" (paragraph 4) do you find to confirm Herberg's thesis, or to reject it? Look for evidence, as he does, in sermons, magazine articles, TV programs, or advertisements. Cite specific instances.

3. Herberg writes: "Prosperity, success, and advancement in business are the obvious ends for which . . . the religious attitude of 'believing' . . . is held to be useful," and he suggests that "there is ordinarily no criticism of [these] ends" as appropriate to a "Godcentered faith" (paragraph 5). Do you believe that faith *is* useful in achieving success and prosperity? How might one argue that it is? How might one argue that success in business is an inappropriate goal for religious faith?

4. Herberg is unhappy that many Americans simply have "faith in faith" (paragraph 2). Does William James's essay (page 763–71), written long before Herberg's, provide an adequate answer to Herberg? Explain?

5. Explain what Herberg means by "idolatrous" in his last sentence.

Wilfred Cantwell Smith

Wilfred Cantwell Smith was born in Toronto in 1916 and educated at the University of Toronto and at Princeton University. After working from 1941 to 1949 with Muslims in India, he returned to Canada where he taught Islamic studies at McGill University from 1949 to 1963. From 1964 he taught religion at Harvard University until he retired.

Muslims

Almost any visitor to India interested in the religious life of its people will note a striking difference architecturally between a Hindu temple and a Muslim mosque. The temple is apt to be ornate, even florid. Its involute complexity suggests that truth is much more elaborate than one had supposed, and denies nothing, not even incongruity. Very different is the stark simplicity of the Muslim place of worship. The mighty Imperial Mosque in Delhi, for example, is a structure whose artistic impressiveness and power come from the use of straight lines and simple curves, splendidly graceful and yet austerely disciplined. Certainly it is brilliantly conceived and its impact is immediate: one grasps at once the balance and dignity, the spacious reverence, the serenity of its straightforward affirmation. Its architect's vision of the glory of God, and of man's service due to Him, is evidently an ordered vision.

Such a point is confirmed if one has the privilege of witnessing a service in such a mosque, especially at one of the great festival prayers, where perhaps a hundred thousand people array themselves in neat lines and bow in precise unison as token of their personal and corporate submission to the will of God, which is definite and sure.

A similar contrast can be seen in the realm of doctrine. For a Hindu, there are various systems of ideas, involute, elaborate, and always tentative, from among which he may choose. In contrast, the Muslim community symbolizes its belief in probably the simplest, tidiest creed in all the world. I am sure that you have all heard it: "There is no god but God, and Muhammad is God's apostle." The Muslims themselves refer to this simply as "the two words," or even "the word." And while this may be carrying compression just a trifle far, still its two pithy clauses are, certainly, as succinct and clean as one could hope to find.

Because of its centrality, and its neatness, this simple creed may   4
well provide us with the item for our consideration of the Muslims. As with other religious communities, so with the Islamic, we choose

one element from out of the formal pattern of their faith, in the hope that, exploring it, we may find that it can lead us, if not to the heart of their religious life, at least into its precincts, and can suggest something of the richness of what lies behind. What better emblem of the Muslim's faith, for our purposes, than this crystallized creed, which the Muslims themselves have chosen to sum up their belief? To repeat this creed is, formally, to become a Muslim; perhaps to understand it is to understand a Muslim. Or let me put the point more realistically: to begin to understand it may be to go some distance, at least, towards understanding the position of those whose faith it typifies.

In suggesting the coherence and simplicity of the Muslim confession of faith, I do not wish to suggest that it is limited or lacks profundity. A mosque may be very intricately decorated—fine interlacing arabesques and the endlessly delicate complexities of an elaborate calligraphy usually embroider the arches and the walls—yet these decorations, however ornate in themselves, are regularly held in strict subordination to an over-all pattern that is essentially simple, so that detail is organized into a coherent unity. Similarly in the realm of doctrine. The Muslim world has produced its philosophers and theologians, constructing elaborate systems of ideas—the names of Avicenna and Averroes are probably the best known in the West, but there are many others also who worked out in careful detail considerable structures of thought. And there were also meticulously elaborate systems of law, comprehensive and ramified. But again, these were subordinate to the higher truth, the simpler truth, of the creed.

As one gets closer to truth, one gets closer to God; and God is one. He is majestic, mighty, awesome, merciful, and many other things, but above all, for the Muslim, He is one. Every other sin, the theologians affirm, may be forgiven man, but not that of *shirk*, polytheism, the failure to recognize that the final truth and power of the universe is one.

Before we turn to questions of meaning, which are of course our chief concern, let us note a few points about the formula as a formula. I suppose that every effective religious symbol is not only inexhaustibly meaningful in what it stands for, but is also in some ways intrinsically interesting in itself. This one certainly is. We have already remarked that it is short. It is also pungent and crisp. In the original Arabic—the language in which it is always used, no matter what the actual language of the people concerned, from

Indonesian to African Swahili, from South Indian Malayalam to Turkish—in Arabic it is resonant and rolling, packing quite a punch. It so happens that of the fifteen syllables, about half begin with an l sound, or end with it, or both. This liquid alliteration, added to the rhyme, and to a very marked rhythm, is quite forceful. *Lā-'i-lā-ha-'il-lal-lāh; Mu-ham-ma-dur-ra-sū-lul-lāh.*

Then there is a calligraphic point. In the Arabic alphabet, which 8 is anyway highly decorative, it so happens that this particular set of words when written out is strikingly patterned, and lends itself to very picturesque presentation.

The formula is certainly in constant service. For example, it is whispered in the ears of the newborn baby, so that its affirmation may be the first words that a Muslim shall hear on entering this world. And between then and its use at his funeral, he will hear it, and pronounce it, often and often and often. And apart from its ceremonial and—as it were—sacred use, it can be found in every-day affairs also. I remember a scene in India some years ago when my wife and I were one summer at a mountain resort in the Himalayas, and were out for a hike in the hills; we came upon a work-gang busy in the construction of a rude mountain road. It was, of course, all hand labor; they had crushed the stones with hammers, and were now rolling them with a large and very heavy roller. Rather in the fashion of sailors working to a sea shanty, they were rhythmically pulling this heavy roller in spurts of concerted effort: the foreman would sing out *Lā ilāha illa 'llāh*, and the rest of the gang, then, would put their shoulders to the ropes and with a heave would respond *Muhammadur rasūlu 'llāh*. This went on and on, as they continued to work, with a will and with good strong heaves. *Lā ilāha illa 'llāh* he would chant; *Muhammadur rasūlu 'llāh* would come the vigorous response. Such a scene represents, of course, a kind of living in which a split into religious and secular has not come—or has not yet come—to segment life. At a different level, of course, are the formal ceremonies in the weekly service of some of the Islamic Sufi orders, in which the initiate devotees will induce a mystic ecstasy or trance by the solemn and rhythmic repetition or incantation of the formula.

Between these two comes a religious use such as that by the *mu'azzin* in his call to prayer five times a day, whose sonorous recitative from the minaret punctuates village or town life and summons the faithful to turn for a moment from their routine affairs to the life of the spirit.

I have called this creed a symbol; and in some ways it plays in Muslim life a role similar to that played, for instance, for Christians by the cross. Nonetheless it is not a pictorial sign but a verbal one, and this itself is significant and appropriate. The role of linguistic form, of words, in Islamic religious life is quite special. I have already spoken of the written word—calligraphy—as a typical Muslim art form. This community has carried the decorative use of writing probably further than has any other people. And take revelation itself. In the Christian case this takes the form of a person, whereas for the Muslim it too is verbal. In the Qur'an, God makes himself and His purpose known to man in the form of words. It is altogether appropriate, then, that the chief symbol of Islam should also be verbal.

So far, I have allowed myself to follow the usual Western practice of calling this two-phrase synopsis of the Muslim's faith a "creed." For to do this is not altogether misleading, though you will have seen that its place in Muslim life is only partly correlative with that of the creed for us. It is time now, however, to modify this still further. We need to see more carefully ways in which the faith of other people is expressed in patterns that do not quite correspond to our own—or even to what we expect of them. 12

In some ways, then, the "two words" of the Islamic assertion do constitute a creed, a statement of belief, but in other ways they do not; and the Muslims do not themselves call this formula a creed. They call it, rather, a "witness." Regularly the statement is preceded by the words "I bear witness that" there is no god . . . and so on. And even when these actual terms are not employed, an idea of witnessing is involved, and can be quite basic. The Islamic has been one of the three great missionary communities in human history (along with the Buddhist and the Christian); and the idea of bearing witness to his faith is quite central to a Muslim's attitudes. His assertion is not so much an affirmation of belief, as a proclamation— of conviction. And in a subtle fashion, there is involved here a point that I rather imagine is more basic in all religious life perhaps than is usually recognized. It is this: that it is not so much that the Muslim *believes* that God is one, and Muhammad is His prophet, as it is that he takes this for granted. He presupposes it, and goes on from there. From his own point of view, one might almost say that, so far as he is concerned, he *knows* that these things are so, and what he is doing is simply announcing them, bearing witness to them.

The same kind of thing is true, I think, of all religious life. One distorts a Christian's faith, for example, by saying simply that he believes Jesus Christ to be divine, to be the son of God. He would rather say that he recognizes this—these are the facts, and he has been fortunate enough to see them. In the Christian case the matter has been somewhat complicated by the use in Western languages of a single verb, *credo*, "I believe," and so on, both for intellectual belief (belief that) and for religious faith (belief in)—though men of faith have insisted that the two things are different. Anyway, I feel that true faith has already begun to crumble a bit, if it has not actually gone, as soon as people have reduced what used to be the data, the presuppositions, of their world view to a set of true-or-false propositions—I mean, when what was once the presupposed context or intellectual background for a transcending religious faith becomes rather the foreground of intellectual belief. This is one of the fundamental troubles in the modern world, and one of the fundamental problems arising from a recognition of religious diversity—that what used to be unconscious premises become, rather, scrutinized intellectualizations. At this new level the believer himself begins to wonder if he really "believes," in this new sense (and often enough finds that he actually does not).

In the Islamic case, as in the Jewish, the word of God is, fundamentally, an imperative. And even the proclamation of God's oneness is in some ways more a command, to worship Him alone, than merely an invitation to believe that He is there alone. Faith differs from belief in many ways, and goes beyond it; one way is that faith in God's oneness is a recognition of His unique and exclusive authority, and an active giving of oneself to it. Like the Christian, the classical Muslim theologian has seen faith as a commitment. He would understand at once St. James in the New Testament writing, "You believe that God is one? You do well: the devils also believe—and tremble." To a truly religious man, the question is not one merely of belief, but of doing something about it.

Having said that, however, we on the outside may still ask what the presuppositions are; what belief is presumed, for those who do go on to commitment. 16

We find ourselves having come round, then, to the question that we earlier postponed, the question of the meaning of the "two words." What does it mean to say "There is no god but God, and Muhammad is His apostle"? What does it mean, that is, to a Muslim—to someone to whom these two clauses are not merely true, but profoundly and cosmically true, are the two most important and final truths in the world, and the most crucial for man and his destiny?

Let us look at each in turn.

To say that there is one God, and that He alone is to be worshipped, means at its most immediate, as it meant in pagan Arabia when it was first proclaimed, a rejection of polytheism and idolatry. When Muhammad captured Mecca in A.D. 630, and set up Islam in triumph, he gave a general amnesty to the human beings there who had resisted his cause and were now defeated, but he smashed without quarter the idols—three hundred and sixty of them, it is said—in the shrine of the Ka'bah, the figures of the pagans' gods. From that day to this, Islam has been uncompromising in its doctrine of monotheism, and its insistence on transcendence: God the Creator and Judge is Lord of all the universe, is high above all his creatures and beyond them, and beyond all their imaginings—and certainly beyond all their representations. Other deities, it asserts, are but the figments of men's wayward imagination, are unadulterated fiction; they just do not exist. Man must not bow down to them nor worship them, or look to them for help, or think about them. God is God alone; on this point Islam is emphatic, positive, and clear.

Historically, as the Islamic movement has spread, across the   20
centuries, from Arabia through the Near East and into Central Asia and has penetrated China, into India and South-East Asia, across Africa and still today is spreading down into Africa, it has met polytheism in many forms, has attacked it and replaced it. Like the Church in the Roman Empire and Northern Europe, and later in the Americas, so Islam in large parts of the world has superseded polytheistic practice and thought with monotheistic.

At a subtler level, for those capable of seeing it, the doctrine has meant also at times, and certainly ought to mean, a rejection of human tyranny. God alone is to be worshipped, to be served. For the man for whom this faith is sufficiently vivid, this can mean that no earthly power, no human figure, deserves or can legitimately claim man's allegiance; and any attempt to impose a purely human yoke on man's neck is an infringement not only of human dignity but of cosmic order, and to submit to it would be sin. Admittedly there has been, especially in periods of decline, an alternative interpretation whereby God's governance of affairs is taken as determining not what ought to be but what is. This view has led to fatalism—a passive acceptance of whatever happens. Perhaps you will feel that I am intruding my own predilections here in siding with those Muslims who have taken rather the activist line, asserting God's will as something to be striven for, as was done more widely in Islam's earlier centuries, and is beginning to be done again in our own day. You will agree, in any case, that it is legitimate and proper, in interpreting other men's faith as in one's own, to try to see it at its best and highest. That at least is what I am trying to do throughout these talks.

There is still a third level of meaning, which was stressed particularly by the Sufi mystics in the medieval period, and is beginning to get wide support today. According to this view, to worship God alone is to turn aside from false gods not only in the concrete sense of idols and religious polytheism, but also in the subtler sense of turning aside from a moral polytheism, from false values—the false gods of the heart. To pursue merely earthly goals, to value them, to give them one's allegiance and in a sense to worship them—goals such as wealth, prestige, sex, national aggrandizement, comfort, or all the other distractions and foibles of human life— this, says the sensitive Muslim conscience, like the sensitive Christian or Jewish one, is to infringe the principle of monotheism. Similarly, to look for help to purely mundane forces, to rely upon armies or clever stratagems, to trust anything that is not intrinsically good—this is to have more than one god. The affirmation that God alone is to be worshipped means, for the man of true piety and rigorous sincerity, that no other objective must claim man's effort or loyalty; he must fear no other power, honor no other prize, pursue no other goal.

I would mention, finally, one other interpretation of the "no god but God" phrase, one that again has been put forward by some of the mystics. This one has not been widespread, even among these; yet I mention it because I personally find it attractive, and it shows the kind of thing that can be done. This particular view is in line with the general position taken by the mystics that the religious life is a process, a movement in faith. According to this interpretation, then, the statement that "there is no god but God" is to be taken in stages. No man, this reading suggests, can legitimately and truly say "God" who has not previously said, and meant, "no god." To arrive at true faith, one must first pass through a stage of unbelief. "There is no god": this comes first, and must be lived through in all sincerity, and all terror. A person brought up in a religious tradition must have seen through that tradition, its forms and fancies, its shams and shibboleths; he must have learned the bleakness of atheism, and have experienced its meaninglessness and eventually its dread. Only such a person is able to go on, perhaps only years later, to a faith that is without superficiality and without merely cheap and secondhand glibness. If one has said "there is no god" with the anguish of a genuine despair, one may then, with God's grace, go on to say ". . . but God," and say it with the ecstasy of genuine insight.

Let us turn, next, to the second proposition: "Muhammad is   24
the apostle of God." The first thing to grasp here is that this is a statement not about Muhammad's status but about his function. The Islamic concept of apostle, or prophet, is quite special; and one is misled if one too readily assumes that this corresponds to ideas familiar to us in the West. The underlying notion here, and it is tacitly presupposed by the formulation, is that God has something to say to mankind, and has from time to time chosen certain persons in various communities through whom to say it; the assertion here is that Muhammad was one of those persons. It too, then, is in significant degree, and even primarily, a statement about God. As the theologians worked it out, it involves the conviction that God is not essentially passive, inscrutable, content to remain transcendent; rather than from all eternity, and as part of His very nature, He is the kind of God who has something to say to mankind. What He has to say is what we would call the moral law. When He created the universe and when He created man, He did not exactly create the moral law, for this comes closer to being, rather, a part of Himself,—but anyway He ordained it, or set it forth, and He created man to receive it, free and responsible to carry it out.

This is the first affirmation. The second is that He communicated this moral law to mankind. He did not leave man to grope about in the dark, to discover for himself, by his own efforts, what he could. No; God Himself acted, and spoke—spoke through the mouth of the prophets and apostles, beginning with Adam, that is, from the very beginning of history. Religion is nowadays sometimes spoken of as man's search for God. On this, the Islamic position is like the Jewish and the Christian, rejecting such a view emphatically, and asserting rather that God takes the initiative. As Micah put it, in our Judeo-Christian tradition, "He hath *shown* thee, O man, what is good. . . ." Man's business in the religious life is not a quest but a response.

Thirdly, in the message that God communicated is to be found, in the Muslim view, not what is true so much, though of course they do hold this, but what is *right*. The position differs from the Christian in that it is a revelation *from* God, more than *of* God. The apostle or prophet is one who conveys to men the message that God wants them to know; namely, how they should live. Accordingly out of the message theoreticians and systematizers have extracted and constructed a law, finally elaborated in all detail and ultimately turned into a static system.

One last point, and with this I close. I said a moment ago that the phrase "Muhammad is the apostle of God" is a statement not about Muhammad's status so much as about his function. Let me elaborate this just a little. The position stands over against the quite different Christian orientation, which sees the person of Christ as central and ultimate, pre-existent and divine. Muslims also posit a central and ultimate truth, pre-existent and divine, namely the Qur'an—not a person but a book, or better, what the book says. Muhammad plays in the Islamic scheme the role played in the Christian system by St. Paul or St. Peter; namely, that of an apostle who proclaims among men God's gift to them, which in the Islamic case is the scripture. In contrast to the Christian conviction, you might almost say that the Muslims' affirmation about their prophet is not a statement about Muhammad's person at all, but about the Qur'an and "what Muhammad brought." To say that he is an apostle, sent by God, is to affirm these things that we have noted, about God, and about the kind of universe that we live in, and about the human situation, and morality; and then within that framework it is to assert further that the message purveyed by Muhammad is authentic. If you believe this, then you are accepting as incumbent upon you in an ultimate moral sense the practical duties that flow from this tradition. For you are recognizing the obligation to perform them as not of human origin but of divine. Those of us for whom the content of morality is not defined in this historical source should nonetheless not allow this to obscure from us the cosmic things that those inspired from this source are saying about morality, about man, and about God.

Topics for Discussion and Writing

1. Consider the first three paragraphs as a piece of writing. Are they clear? If so, by what means did the author achieve clarity? If they are not clear, what are the causes of the obscurity?

2. In paragraph 14 Smith distinguishes between "belief in" and "belief that." Suppose a friend did not quite get Smith's point. Clarify it for this friend.

3. In paragraph 15 Smith says, "To a truly religious man, the question is not one merely of belief, but of doing something about it." (Presumably "doing something" means more than making an occasional monetary

contribution to the church, and more than attending church sporadically or even regularly.) Do you think Smith is going too far here? Do you know many people who, by this standard, are "truly religious"? If so—and of course you yourself may be such a person—what do they do?

4. In the West, Muslims (or followers of Islam) are often called Muhammadans (or Mohammedans). Why is the term "Muhammadan" offensive to Muslims? Why is the term not comparable to "Christian"? (Notice that Smith touches on this point in paragraph 27.)

5. Taking the criteria set forth in the first paragraph, where a Hindu temple is contrasted with a Muslim mosque, what does a Gothic cathedral suggest, contrasted with a New England Protestant church or with a southwest adobe Roman Catholic church?

D. T. Suzuki

D[aisetz] T[eitaro] Suzuki (1870–1966) was one of Japan's leading writers on Zen Buddhism. He occasionally visited the United States, where he taught, lectured, and wrote. He is still regarded as the foremost interpreter of Zen Buddhism to the West.

Zen is the Japanese word for a school of Buddhism derived from China, where it was called Ch'an. In this essay Suzuki tries to explain satori, "enlightenment" or "awakening." The awakening is from a world of blind strivings (including those of reason and morality); the awakened being, free from a sense of the self in opposition to all other things, perceives the unity of all things. (When Suzuki was asked how it feels to have attained satori, he replied, "Just like ordinary everyday experience, except about two inches off the ground.")

What Is Zen?

The object of Zen training consists in making us realize that Zen is our daily experience and that it is not something put in from the outside. Tennō Dōgo (T'ien-huang Tao-wu, 748–807) illustrates the point most eloquently in his treatment of a novice monk, while an unknown Japanese swordmaster demonstrates it in the more threatening manner characteristic of his profession. Tennō Dōgo's story runs as follows:

Dōgo had a disciple called Sōshin (Ch'ung-hsin). When Sōshin was taken in as a novice, it was perhaps natural of him to expect lessons in Zen from his teacher the way a schoolboy is taught at school. But Dōgo gave him no special lessons on the subject, and this bewildered and disappointed Sōshin. One day he said to the master, "It is some time since I came here, but not a word has been given me regarding the essence of the Zen teaching." Dōgo replied, "Since your arrival I have ever been giving you lessons on the matter of Zen discipline."

"What kind of lesson could it have been?"

"When you bring me a cup of tea in the morning, I take it; when you serve me a meal, I accept it; when you bow to me I return it with a nod. How else do you expect to be taught in the mental discipline of Zen?"

Sōshin hung his head for a while, pondering the puzzling words of the master. The master said, "If you want to see, see right at once. When you begin to think, you miss the point."

The swordsman's story is this:

When a disciple came to a master to be disciplined in the art of sword-play, the master, who was in retirement in his mountain hut, agreed to undertake the task. The pupil was made to help him gather kindling, draw water from the nearby spring, split wood, make fires, cook rice, sweep the rooms and the garden, and generally look after his household. There was no regular or technical teaching in the art. After some time the young man became dissatisfied, for he had not come to work as servant to the old gentleman, but to learn the art of swordsmanship. So one day he approached the master and asked him to teach him. The master agreed.

The result was that the young man could not do any piece of work with any feeling of safety. For when he began to cook rice early in the morning, the master would appear and strike him from behind with a stick. When he was in the midst of his sweeping, he would be feeling the same sort of blow from somewhere, some unknown direction. He had no peace of mind, he had to be always on the *qui vive.* Some years passed before he could successfully dodge the blow from wherever it might come. But the master was not quite satisfied with him yet.

One day the master was found cooking his own vegetables over an open fire. The pupil took it into his head to avail himself of this opportunity. Taking up his big stick, he let it fall over the head of the master, who was then stooping over the cooking pan to stir its contents. But the pupil's stick was caught by the master with the cover of the pan. This opened the pupil's mind to the secrets of the art, which had hitherto been kept from him and to which he had so far been a stranger. He then, for the first time, appreciated the unparalleled kindness of the master.

The secrets of perfect swordsmanship consist in creating a certain frame or structure of mentality which is made always ready to respond instantly, that is, im-mediately, to what comes from the outside. While technical training is of great importance, it is after all something artificially, consciously, calculatingly added and acquired. Unless the mind that avails itself of the technical skill somewhat attunes itself to a state of the utmost fluidity or mobility, anything acquired or superimposed lacks spontaneity of natural growth. This state prevails when the mind is awakened to a *satori*. What the swordsman aimed at was to make the disciple attain to this realization. It cannot be taught by any system specifically designed for the purpose, it must simply grow from within. The master's system was really no system in the proper sense. But there was a "natural" method in his apparent craziness, and he succeeded in awakening in his young disciple's mind something that touched off the mechanism needed for the mastery of swordsmanship.

Dōgo the Zen master did not have to be attacking his disciple all the time with a stick. The swordsman's object was more definite and limited to the area of the sword, whereas Dōgo wanted to teach by getting to the source of being from which everything making up our daily experience ensues. Therefore, when Sōshin began to reflect on the remark Dōgo made to him, Dōgo told him: "No reflecting whatever. When you want to see, see im-mediately. As soon as you tarry [that is, as soon as an intellectual interpretation or mediation takes place], the whole thing goes awry." This means that, in the study of Zen, conceptualization must go, for as long as we tarry at this level we can never reach the area where Zen has its life. The door of enlightenment-experience opens by itself as one finally faces the deadlock of intellectualization.

We now can state a few things about Zen in a more or less summary way:

1. Zen discipline consists in attaining enlightenment (or *satori*, in Japanese).

2. *Satori* finds a meaning hitherto hidden in our daily concrete particular experiences, such as eating, drinking, or business of all kinds.

3. The meaning thus revealed is not something added from the outside. It is in being itself, in becoming itself, in living itself. This is called, in Japanese, a life of *kono-mama* or *sono-mama*.[1] Kono- or sonomama means the "isness" of a thing. Reality in its isness.

---

[1] *Kono* is "this," *sono* "that" and *mama* means "as-it-is-ness." Kono-mama or sono-mama thus corresponds to the Sanskrit *tathatā*, "suchness," and to the Chinese *chih-mo* or *shih-mo*.

4. Some may say, "There cannot be any meaning in mere isness." But this is not the view held by Zen, for according to it, isness is the meaning. When I see into it I see it as clearly as I see myself reflected in a mirror.

5. This is what made Hō Koji (P'ang Chü-shih), a lay disciple of the eighth century, declare:

> How wondrous this, how mysterious!
> I carry fuel, I draw water.

The fuel-carrying or the water-drawing itself, apart from its utilitarianism, is full of meaning; hence its "wonder," its "mystery."

6. Zen does not, therefore, indulge in abstraction or in conceptualization. In its verbalism it may sometimes appear that Zen does this a great deal. But this is an error most commonly entertained by those who do not at all know Zen.

7. *Satori* is emancipation, moral, spiritual, as well as intellectual. When I am in my isness, thoroughly purged of all intellectual sediments, I have my freedom in its primary sense.

8. When the mind, now abiding in its isness—which, to use Zen verbalism, is not isness—and thus free from intellectual complexities and moralistic attachments of every description, surveys the world of the senses in all its multiplicities, it discovers in it all sorts of values hitherto hidden from sight. Here opens to the artist a world full of wonders and miracles.

9. The artist's world is one of free creation, and this can come only from intuitions directly and im-mediately rising from the isness of things, unhampered by senses and intellect. He creates forms and sounds out of formlessness and soundlessness. To this extent, the artist's world coincides with that of Zen.

10. What differentiates Zen from the arts is this: While the artists have to resort to the canvas and brush or mechanical instruments or some other mediums to express themselves, Zen has no need of things external, except "the body" in which the Zen-man is so to speak embodied. From the absolute point of view this is not quite correct; I say it only in concession to the worldly way of saying things. What Zen does is to delineate itself on the infinite canvas of time and space the way the flying wild geese cast their shadow on the water below without any idea of doing so, while the water reflects the geese just as naturally and unintentionally.

11. The Zen-man is an artist to the extent that, as the sculptor chisels out a great figure deeply buried in a mass of inert matter, the Zen-man transforms his own life into a work of creation, which exists, as Christians might say, in the mind of God.

Topics for Discussion and Writing

1. In paragraph 2 Suzuki first uses the word "im-mediately." Why does he add the hyphen? (Check a dictionary if you don't know the Latin origin of the word.)
2. Suzuki in this essay is teaching the meaning of Zen. How does he go about teaching? How successful do you find his methods?
3. In paragraph 13 Suzuki says that the artist, like the enlightened person, works from "intuition" and is "unhampered by senses and intellect." What do you understand him to mean by intuition? What value does the work of art have for the artist? Does it have the same value for us?

Nancy E. Auer Falk

Nancy Falk is Professor of Religion at Western Michigan University. The essay that we reprint appeared originally in The Perennial Dictionary of World Religions *(originally entitled* Abingdon Dictionary of Living Religions*). The book, designed for the nonspecialist, includes about 1600 articles on the histories and beliefs of many religions practiced today.*

Women: Status and Role in World Religions

The difference between men and women has been a source of fascination for many of the world's religious traditions. On the one hand, the simultaneous opposition, yet complementarity of the sexes has been taken as a model and symbol for a whole series of other pairings: for example, matter and spirit, instinct and intellect, chaos and order, change and permanence. On the other hand, the biological roles of the sexes have, for many religious traditions, evidenced different modes of creative power operating in the world. Thus religions have recognized male and female divinities, who give and take life and order in ways distinctive to their sex. But men and women themselves have also been experienced as reservoirs of creative, and sometimes threatening, sacral forces. All of these perceptions have carried implications for women's status vis-à-vis men, and they have also helped shape the roles that women have been able to, or encouraged to, develop.

But here we come to a puzzling problem. Many tribal religions, and apparently also many of ancient times, have drawn upon women's sacred and symbolic values to weave rich fabrics of cosmic and ritual balance. In such traditions women often assume roles as significant ritual functionaries, shamans, and seers. The world's largest and most successful religions, however, have often used the same values to exclude women from many important arenas of religious life and to justify their practical subordination to men. The reasons for this apparent reversal are complex, but the facts are indisputable. As a normal rule, in the great religious traditions of the world, women have been expected to play a role, religious and social, second to that of men.

Until very recent times, however, such considerations have only rarely discouraged women from active participation in the religious arenas allotted to them, such as the women's orders of Christianty, Buddhism, and Jainism, as well as corresponding lay communities. Women have furthermore generated their own rites and cults, as in the so-called "calendrical" rites of Hinduism and in the "vows" undertaken by women in Islam. Women have also risen to prominence as saints, prophets, and scholars; while in some traditions vestiges of older patterns remain in the activities of female mediums and diviners.

1. **Judaism.** Judaism, oldest of the West's major living religions, [4] draws on an ancient patriarchal heritage shaped in part by responses to competing ancient Near Eastern traditions in which women played conspicuous cultic roles. In the ancient Hebrew laws women were viewed as potential sources of pollution, through the menstrual flow and the impurities of childbirth. But as mother, a woman was also essential for both the biological and cultural continuity of the chosen people. In a tradition that continues to place great emphasis on the family unit as matrix of most religious life, the domestic role has remained the Jewish woman's central opportunity for religious service. As wife and household manager, a woman frees her husband and sons for prayer and study of the Torah—while Jewish law has exempted her from these same central duties. She administers the dietary laws and lights the candles that usher in the

Sabbath. As mother she bears children to perpetuate the Jewish community and is responsible for instilling in her sons the desire to study Torah.

In traditional rabbinic Judaism women had no formal role in public life or in the life of the synagogue. Despite all influences to the contrary, rare women achieved fame for their scholarship (cf. Bruria, wife of Rabbi Meir). More ancient Hebrew records preserve the memory of a few women prophets, such as Miriam the sister of Moses, the "judge" Deborah, and the prophetess Huldah. In much more recent times women won unusual prominence in Hasidism, with a number achieving the role of *rebee*, or spiritual leader.

2. **Christianity.** "In Christ," says the apostle Paul, "there is neither male nor female" (Gal. 3:28). But Christ's church has furthered discrimination between the sexes ever since the same apostle told women to keep their hair covered and their mouths closed in church.

Much of the traditional Christian attitude toward women can be traced to the dualism, inherited from the Greek world, that has shaped Christian thought since the tradition's earliest centuries. Spirit and matter, soul and body, are separate and in conflict. Woman is more "carnal"; hence, like other things of the flesh, she should be kept subordinate. This same dualistic thinking led, in Roman Catholic Christianity, to a significant denigration of married women—i.e., those most directly implicated in carnal life—as opposed to virgins—i.e., those who denied the claims of their bodies for the sake of spiritual development.

Christian custom continued menstrual and childbirth taboos [8] inherited in part from its Jewish parent; these were once an important contributing factor to the Catholic tradition's long-standing refusal to ordain women to the priesthood. However, nonclerical orders for women have existed since very early Christian times and have pursued a broad range of vocations, from service to secluded contemplation.

Within their allotted "places" women have made massive contributions to Christianity. Women were very prominent in the early church, and have remained important as laywomen until the present day. Christian women became martyrs, and later famous saints and mystics. At times, women's orders have had twice the membership of their male counterparts.

3. **Islam.** The revelation to Muhammad that gave rise to Islam called for a massive restructuring of the social order. In Islam's early

years this effectively improved the status of women, placing new restraints on divorce and polygamy and requiring husbands to support their wives, as well as bringing women the right to inherit and retain control of their dowries. The Qur'ān still taught, nontheless, that "men are in charge of women, because Allah hath made the one of them to excel the other" (Sura 4:34; trans. M. M. Pickthall). To temper the dangers of sexual attraction and also to protect women followers of the faith from insult, the Qur'ān called for modesty in the form of covering one's inner dress and ornaments in public. In time, however, and under pressure of local custom, such teachings were cited to justify demands that women be veiled from head to foot in public. In some regions, and especially among the upper social classes, women were totally secluded in the home (*purdah*). Muslim popular culture also preserved strict menstrual taboos; among other prohibitions, these excluded from the mosques both menstruating women and those who had recently given birth. Menstrual taboos also closed to women some religious offices, such as that of Imam, or prayer leader.

As in Christianity and in many other new religions that challenge repressive establishments, women were very prominent in the early Muslim community; in later centuries some once again became prominent scholars. Women such as the mystic poetess Rabia were important to the Sufi orders; a number of these had women's branches and convents from very early times. Even though largely restricted to the home, many women of traditional Muslim countries have elaborated their own religious networks and practices, transmitting religious instruction and holding gatherings in their homes.

4. **Hinduism.** Considerations of status and role for any group 12 in Hindu society are largely determined by the ancient conception of *Dharma*. This conception communicates simultaneously the image of a sacred, all-embracing, and organic cosmic order and the belief that any individual's preeminent duty is to fulfill the "place" that one inherits within it. Dharma precepts identified a woman's place as wife and mother; traditionally a woman was out of place, anomalous, unless this role was achieved. The dharma teachings further stipulated that a woman should always be subordinated to some male: in childhood, to her father; in maturity, to her husband; and in old age, to her sons. A married woman was instructed to take her husband as her god. She also observed numerous menstrual taboos to shield him and her family from her pollution.

Woman's dharma excluded her from virtually all public roles, including the priesthood practiced by the Brahmin caste; for many centuries women could not learn or recite Hinduism's sacred language, Sanskrit.

At the same time, a woman who fulfilled perfectly the discipline of her "place" was thought to win considerable, even superhuman, power. As in Judaism, motherhood acquired an exaggerated honor. From very ancient times a married Hindu woman has been considered a ritual unit with her husband. Thus she shares with him responsibility for many observances performed in the home as well as the merit of his religious accomplishments. An extensive cycle of domestic rituals concerned with the family's well-being has become almost exclusively women's religious province.

If a woman's "place" was lost, through her husband's death or his decision to enter an ascetic life, she again became anomalous. A widow was extremely inauspicious and was expected, in effect, to become invisible. An ascetic's wife enjoyed a theoretically higher status; but practically her position remained ambiguous. As with men, any woman whose domestic responsibilities have been completed is allowed to take up the ascetic life. Some women have exercised this option; but for the most part they have enjoyed less honor than male ascetics. In contrast, a few women have been very important in Hindu devotional movements which claim that all cases and both sexes have equal access to their chosen deity and to salvation.

5. **Buddhism** shares with Christianity the somewhat paradoxical position of assuming an equal potential for spiritual development of men and women, while affirming inequity between the sexes at the beginning of the spiritual path. The Buddhist position, however, is not based on the saving grace of deity, but rather on the workings of karma, or cosmic justice, which traces all inequities of birth to the effects of deeds in previous lives. This position has required that women be given equal opportunities with men to follow Buddhism's path of renunciation; this was institutionalized in early Buddhist days by the founding of parallel orders for monks and nuns. At the same time, the initial sexual inequity has justified a practical subordination of women to men; this, too, has found institutional expression both in Buddhist norms for domestic life and in the men's and women's monastic rules: the most notorious example is the stipulation that monks must always be treated as senior to nuns.

For a variety of reasons not yet well known, the order of Buddhist nuns did not fare equally well in all regions where Buddhism   16 became established. In India, after several prosperous centuries, it faded into obscurity; in Sri Lanka the succession of Theravāda ordination for nuns apparently died out before it could be transmitted to Southeast Asia. However, the order became quite powerful in China and remained a significant force in Chinese Buddhism until the Maoist revolution; it continues to be important in the Taiwanese exile community.

Surprisingly, after the founding years, Buddhist nuns in India left little impression as communal leaders and scholars. In China, Buddhist laywomen attached to the courts achieved distinction for their scholarship. Laywoman-donors have been prominent throughout the Buddhist tradition, with the first, much-cited example set by the celebrated merchant's daughter Visākhā.

6. **East Asia.** The history of woman's fate in the interlocking traditions of East Asia is at the same time the most intriguing and the most problematic. All evidence suggests that women were once a very significant part of religious life in East Asia. The early importance of powerful medium-priestesses called *miko* is well documented in Japan; vestiges still remain in the female priesthood of the imperial shrine at Isé and in the role of female mediums and ascetics in popular Shintō practice. Woman shaman-seers remain active in other popular traditions throughout East Asia, and there is reason to believe that they, too, once enjoyed more prestigious positions. Early Taoist teachings, therefore, may have continued an ancient tradition when they proclaimed ideals of cosmic balance (yin and yang) and of "becoming female" to the Tao. But real women were also important to the Taoist Heavenly Masters sect, achieving the rank of priestess and consequent deification.

Confucianism, which came to dominate both Chinese and other East Asian social theory, moved firmly in the opposite direction. In its grand cosmic hierarchy, earth's subordination to heaven became the model for woman's subordination to man. Marriage was the normative state for a woman, and submission to husband the appropriate expression of cosmic piety for a wife. In various times and regions the Confucian norm was interpreted with varying degrees of severity. But by the nineteenth century it was cited to condone the severe oppression of Chinese women that moved various reformers to call for their liberation.

As in most other traditions taboos surrounding menstruation 20 and childbirth additionally shaped the lives of East Asian women. Japan still preserves remnants of menstrual taboos and exclusions. But the folk tradition in China has, perhaps, carried its unease with women's generative processes to the greatest extreme; unless a woman's offspring performed a special rite to redeem her, the mother could expect to be immersed for a time in a pool of blood in hell when she died. A menstruating woman could not participate in any family rites; furthermore, a woman retained enough residual pollution to prevent her from officiating at the rights of major family gods during other times as well.

7. **The contemporary scene.** The twentieth century has, of course, seen numerous changes in women's status and role, both within and beyond the confines of organized religion. In large part such changes are attributable to the twin forces of secular ideology, which often calls into question traditional religious norms and values, and the political and social revolution which has often been its by-product.

In the Christian and Jewish traditions an important phenomenon has been the emergence and growing influence of a feminist critique. While some feminists are increasingly alienated from traditional religions that they regard as male-centered and male-dominated, others have worked within the traditions for reform of offending imagery and institutional strictures. One by-product has been women's increasing access to roles that were formerly closed. Thus, Reform Judaism now ordains woman rabbis, Angelican women have won ordination to the priesthood, and women are entering various branches of the Protestant ministry in increasing numbers.

Traditional Islamic restrictions on women have also been subjected to searching critique, often influenced by Western secular values. In many modern Islamic nations women have put aside the veil and gained access to education, as well as positions of leadership in secular, and especially professional life. Sometimes, however, changes emerging too quickly have provoked a religious backlash.

The liberation of women in the People's Republic of China was 20 a secular development, brought about by a revolution that overturned most traditional religious norms. But a striking phenomenon in other regions of South and East Asia has been new prominence for women in roles of religious leadership. Woman gurus, as well as women's associations and/or orders, have been important in several Hindu movements of the twentieth century. In Japan, woman founders of so-called "New Religions" such as Tenri-Kyō and Risshō Kōseikai have renewed the charismatic vocations and style of the old shamanic tradition. Women have also been newly active in Buddhism. Thus the order of Taiwanese Mahāyāna nuns has extended a branch to the United States, while women in Thailand have reestablished the ordination of nuns in their own Theravāda tradition.

Bibliography

Materials on this topic are sparse for some traditions and times, and scattered throughout many sources. For cross-cultural approaches, see N. Falk and R. Gross, eds., *Unspoken Worlds: Women's Religious Lives in Non-Western Cultures* (1980) and D. L. Carmody, *Women and World Religions* (1979). Valuable information on individual traditions can be found in the following: for Christianity and Judaism, R. R. Ruether, ed., *Religion and Sexism* (1974); for Islam, E. W. Fernea and B. Q. Bezirgan, eds., *Middle Eastern Muslim Women Speak* (1977); for the period of Buddhist origins, as recorded in Pali literature, I. B. Horner, *Women under Primitive Buddhism* (1930); for Sanskrit and Chinese Buddhist sources, D. Paul, *Women in Buddhism* (1980). For women under Hindu dharma the best starting point is still two older and somewhat ponderous works: J. J. Meyer, *Sexual Life in Ancient India* (1930) and S. R. Sastri, *Women in the Sacred Laws* (1953). For Japan, see H. Okano, *Die Stellung der Frau im Shinto* (1976); also for excellent accounts of contemporary women shamans, C. Blacker, *The Catalpa Bow* (1975). China presents the most difficult problem, for resources in Western languages are still very fragmentary; but see R. H. van Gulik, *Sexual Life in Ancient China* (1961); also, E. Ahern, "The Power and Pollution of Chinese Women," in M. Wolf and R. Witke, eds., *Women in Chinese Society* (1975), pp. 19–24.

Topics for Discussion and Writing

1. In her first paragraph Falk lists a series of pairings that she claims have been modeled after differences between men and women. Read aloud the pairings (in the second sentence). Which word in each pair is associated with women and which with men? How do you account for these associations?

2. Do you think that differences between men and women are responsible for discrimination against women in most world religions? Or do you think

that discrimination against women is responsible for their status and role in world religions? How does Falk seem to answer this question?

3. Consider a world in which men menstruated and bore children. Do you think that these functions would be the subject of religious taboos, as they now are?

4. Are you able to verify any of Falk's assertions about the status and role of women in a particular religion? Is the status of women currently changing or not? What changes would you like to see?

5. Does your experience allow you to discuss a topic—for instance the status of women in Navaho religion or in Voodoo—that Falk does not mention? If so, write a paragraph or two that might have been incorporated into her article.

Renita Weems

Renita Weems, a minister and writer, teaches at Vanderbilt Divinity School in Nashville, Tennessee. She is the author of Just a Sister Away *(a collection of feminist essays on the women in the Bible) as well as other essays. We reprint an essay that originally appeared in* Ms.

Whispering Hope

Something is missing, something inarticulate, yet conspicuous: something ancient and precious; something so basic to our survival that its absence leaves us spiritually dazed. It's been missing for so long, we've forgotten its name.

I'm a minister, and I know that this thing so sorely missing in our lives and in our society is more than just religion. We are a religiously moody nation. Our religiosity often surfaces when we are feeling especially insecure or threatened cosmically by such things as nuclear war, Communists, and a failing economy, or more personally by such things as the deterioration of relationships, the fear of aging, or the outbreak of a fatal disease. Any one of these may be just cause for concern, but if these alone are the kinds of things that evoke religious reflection among Americans, then religion is not enough to guide us through this labyrinth. We have only to look around us in our country, where there has always been a curious mixture of the sacred and the secular, to see that religion is rarely any better than its adherents.

Yet, after having said that religion per se isn't what's missing, and after listening to folks editorialize and pontificate about morals, ethics, and values, it is comforting to know that we are still tuned in enough to realize that whatever this missing something is, it belongs to that vicinity of the psyche that our decent job, nice cars, and cozy condominiums have not been able to fill. Some inner voice keeps quietly whispering, telling us that this void we feel may not be religious, but it is profoundly spiritual. And at the risk of sounding like one of those anxiety-ridden medieval Protestant theologians who seem to have taken perverse delight in rehearsing our fallen state, it may be time to admit that in spite of this country's religiosity, despite our noblest efforts to march, protest, and petition our way into a better society, we find ourselves having lived just long enough, having been bombarded with so many horrible stories of atrocity, bloodshed, hatred, senseless and systematic violence and murder that we've become inured to and no longer repulsed by evil—especially the evil without ourselves. And, more sadly, many of us have lost or are rapidly losing our ability to protect ourselves against evil.

Stuffed on one of the dusty shelves in my study is a photograph   4 and an article about a young Atlanta woman named Mozella Dansby. I keep them because her story reminds me of my own capacity for and vulnerability to evil. On Friday, April 24, 1987, Mozella Dansby, a bookkeeper at the Georgia Power Company, walked into her office, pulled out a gun, and shot and wounded two of her supervisors. And then this 31-year-old woman, wife, and mother pointed the gun to her own head and pulled the trigger. The newspapers reported that she'd been distraught, that once again she'd been passed over for a promotion on her job at the utility company.

Anyone who knows what it feels like to be humiliated and betrayed, no doubt understands what could have fueled Mozella Dansby's rage and despair. Haven't we all spent at least one night dreaming of revenge, envisioning what it would be like to break a particularly loathsome ex-lover's kneecaps, run over a long-time adversary; berating ourselves for what we did not say; reliving the moment of our greatest humiliation? At some point, we have all been to that edge of despair. And some of us have even tarried there far longer than was wise. Most of us, after a whole lot of shrieking and a modest amount of reflecting, have peered over the edge and chosen not to jump. But not Mozella Dansby.

The news of the attempted murders and her suicide left me numb for days. For Mozella was not a total stranger to me—I grew up with members of her family. Unwillingly, I found myself dwelling on the feelings of humiliation and rage, the sense of betrayal that evidently drove Mozella to plot revenge and contemplate suicide; and I was horrified at how easily those same feelings surfaced within me, often at the slightest provocation. Mozella's act of rage reminded me how dangerously close I, like so many of us, live to the edge. For there are days when my own sanity and insanity are just a stone's throw away from each other. Perhaps it is the nature of life itself—equally likely it is a comment upon the culture in which we live—but the distance between hope and hopelessness feels like it's shortening these days. Maybe it's me, maybe I'm not as well informed as I think I am, but has there always been such a high incidence of suicide and mass slayings, so much physical and emotional violence as there is today? I look at the photograph of Mozella and I wonder what has prevented me, you, any and all of us from leaping over the edge and reaching for a gun?

Almost a week elapsed between the time Mozella found out she'd been denied the promotion and the time she fired those shots. A week is a long time to dream of killing someone. Didn't anyone sense her torment? Wasn't there some friend somewhere who suddenly felt propelled to call her in the middle of one of her restless nights: "Girl, you've been on my mind. Something told me to call you." Where were her support systems?

Evil is too mammoth a thing to war against alone. Why couldn't 8 she find solace in the talks she'd had with her husband? According to Dwight Dansby, Mozella had taken the day before off from work to look for a new job and had come home cheerful and optimistic. He later discovered that was the day she bought the gun. Why hadn't the sight and sounds and smell, the very feel of her two small children as she prepared them for bed that Thursday night, or awakened them that fateful Friday morning, or the touch of her husband's lips as she gave him "a strange long kiss" been enough to ease her torment and pull her back from the abyss?

Without a lifeline Mozella wrapped all the hopes she'd once had for a better life for herself and her family around a .38-caliber revolver and stuffed them and that gun in her purse. In that same pocketbook she left a note that read: "I think this was something that needed to be done. They didn't do [a friend] or myself fair about the job and they had to be stopped. I know everyone is saying this goes on everywhere and always will. But I think this will give other supervisors and managers something to think about before someone else is done unfairly."

It was not until the fourth reading of that letter that I could finally hear Mozella explain why she *chose* to jump over the edge. *I know everyone is saying this goes on everywhere and always will.* Evidently, it wasn't just the fact that she'd been passed over for a job. One which had been given to a white man instead, though her employer later admitted she was eminently qualified for it. That was crushing, but survivable. What drove Mozella to take up that gun was being told that there was nothing more to look forward to except more crushing. "This is the way things are." "Get used to it." "You can't do a thing about it." "Why fight it?" "It doesn't hurt so much if you don't think about it." Though sympathetic, people were telling her to simply accept the inevitability of evil. But the thing she didn't know, because there was no one around to tell her, is that evil can be as deceptive as it is repulsive: it takes as much evil in us to confront it sometimes as it does to inflict it. Which explains why her only perfect aim was at her own head.

If, as some suppose, our grandparents were more moral, more forbearing than ourselves, what might Mozella's grandmother have done differently? First, she would have cried. Then she might have sprinkled strange dust across the doorway of Georgia Power. And then after staying up all night rocking and praying, she would have washed her face, combed her hair, and told her granddaughter, "Baby, two wrong's don't make a right." What would have kept Mozella's grandmother from buying a gun? I suspect it would have been mostly a stubborn hope. That irrational, nay, *trans*rational believe that life *is* worth living and that—with more marching, strategizing, and praying—no matter how slowly, the wheels of justice do grind. That fighting hope that makes all of us live beyond what we can immediately see and touch. It makes us pick up those placards and march for the ERA one more time, petition for justice in South Africa one more time, try love one more time, and pray for peace—one more time. Even though we may never live to see their dawning—justice is still just. It's the same hope that kept Mozella's great-great grandmother chopping away at that cotton and inching her way to freedom, even though she knew she'd probably die a slave. It's why caged birds sing. Because they know they were born to fly. And because hope is rarely our first response, it takes sometimes the prompting, presence, and stubbornness of others, their hope in us, to keep us from jumping. Faith beckons us to stare evil in the face, even the evil within ourselves, and refuse it our hope.

As I am writing this, the early morning bells from the church 12 up the street are ringing out an unfamiliar hymn and I am haunted by the words of the Grand Inquisitor, Dostoyevsky's brilliant tortured old priest in *The Brothers Karamazov,* who badgers and accuses the Christ of having grossly, and hence cruelly, overestimated human nature. By asking humankind to follow his example, the priest remonstrates, Christ had only frustrated them and in essence driven them mad. And then there are the words of that same Christ to his small band of followers on the night of his own betrayal, "There will be those who will deliver you up to be killed, thinking they are doing God's will." And when I look in the eyes of fallen politicians, self-righteous evangelists, unrepentant heads of state, racist feminists, chauvinistic liberals, liberal conservatives, conservative liberals, a torn Pope, those who bomb abortion clinics and others who protest the sacrifice of a baboon in order to save the life of Baby Doe, I wonder if the tortured priest is not right. Have we gone mad from the exhausting effort to be moral?

And yet, there is an altar deep within all of us, an altar that eventually demands an encounter with something profoundly Incorruptible. Call it the soul, if you will. And there are regions in the human heart and spaces in the human mind that modern technology and liberal rationalism have not been able to gratify. And I know that it is our incessant quest to build something upon that altar, to find something to fill that void, something Holy, something Incorruptible that is our only hope.

Topics for Discussion and Writing

1. "Something is missing," the essay begins. The rest of the first paragraph describes the "something" in various ways without naming it. The second paragraph says what it is not. Do we ever learn what it is? If so, how and where do we learn it?

2. What is the point of Mozella Dansby's story, as Weems tells it? How does she secure our interest in Mozella's story and our empathy with Mozella?

3. In response to rage and despair, Weems says, in paragraph 5, "Most of us, after a whole lot of shrieking and a modest amount of reflecting, have peered over the edge and chosen not to jump." In the same paragraph she says "Haven't we all spent at least one night dreaming of revenge, envisioning what it would be like to break a particularly loathsome ex-lover's kneecaps, run over a long-time adversary; berating ourselves for what we did not say; reliving the moment of our greatest humiliation?" Whether or not you have ever dreamt of breaking an ex-lover's kneecaps, do you feel included by this paragraph or excluded? How does the fact that Weems is a minister affect the way you respond to this and other apparently self-revelatory passages?

4. Characterize Weems's style and evaluate its effectiveness.
5. If you have ever experienced humiliation, betrayal, rage, or despair, experiences and feelings frequently referred to in this article, how have you handled those feelings? Is religion a solace? Is friendship? Or do you have ways of cutting these feelings off, or avoiding them? Explain.
6. Write a 500-word essay on the worst thing that ever happened to you.

Chewing Blackbones

Nothing is known about Chewing Blackbones except that he was a Blackfoot Indian described in 1953 as "an elderly grandfather . . . [who] could tell the old tales only in the old Blackfoot language." Ella E. Clark collected this tale in 1953 and published it in her 1966 collection, Indian Legends from the Northern Rockies.

Old Man and Old Woman
A Blackfoot Indian Myth Retold

Long, long ago, there were only two persons in the world: Old Man and Old Woman. One time when they were traveling about the earth, Old Woman said to Old Man, "Now let us come to an agreement of some kind. Let us decide how the people shall live when they shall be on the earth."

"Well," replied Old Man, "I am to have the first say in everything."

"I agree with you," said Old Woman. "That is I if I may have the second say."

Then Old Man began his plans. "The women will have the duty   4 of tanning the hides. They will rub animals' brains on the hides to make them soft and scrape them with scraping tools. All this they will do very quickly, for it will not be hard work."

"No," said Old Woman, "I will not agree to this. They must tan hides in the way you say; but it must be very hard work, so that the good workers may be found out."

"Well," said Old Man, "we will let the people have eyes and mouths, straight up and down in their faces."

"No," replied Old Woman, "let us not have them that way. We will have the eyes and mouths in the faces, as you say, but they shall be set crosswise."

"Well," said Old Man, "the people shall have ten fingers on each hand."

"Oh, no!" replied Old Woman. "That will be too many. They will be in the way. There will be four fingers and one thumb on each hand."

So the two went on until they had provided for everything in the lives of the people who were to be.

"What shall we do about life and death?" asked Old Woman. "Should the people live forever, or should they die?"

Old Woman and Old Man had difficulty agreeing about this. Finally Old Man said, "I will tell you what we will do. I will throw a buffalo chip into the water. If it floats, the people will die for four days and then come to life again; if it sinks, they will die forever." 12

So he threw a buffalo chip into the water, and it floated.

"No," said Old Woman, "we will not decide in that way. I will throw this rock into the water. If it floats, the people will die for four days; if it sinks, they will die forever."

Then Old Woman threw the rock into the water, and it sank to the bottom.

"There," said she. "It is better for the people to die forever. If they did not, they would not feel sorry for each other, and there would be no sympathy in the world." 16

"Well," said Old Man, "let it be that way."

After a time, Old Woman had a daughter, who soon became sick and died. The mother was very sorry then that they had agreed that people should die forever. "Let us have our say over again," she said.

"No," replied Old Man. "Let us not change what we have agreed upon."

And so people have died ever since.

Topics for Discussion and Writing

1. Do we think of Old Man and Old Woman as people or as gods? Explain.
2. Though briefly sketched, Old Man and Old Woman are distinct characters. What are the important differences between them?
3. The dialogue helps to characterize Old Man and Old Woman. What other function does it serve?
4. If the story ended six sentences earlier (after Old Man says: "Well . . . let it be that way"), the myth would still provide an explanation of why people die. What would be lost?

Katherine Anne Porter

Katherine Anne Porter (1890–1980) had the curious habit of inventing details in her life, but it is true that she was born in a log cabin in Indian Creek, Texas, that she was originally named Callie Russell Porter, that her mother died when the child was two years old, and that Callie was brought up by her maternal grandmother in Kyle, Texas. She was sent to convent schools, where, in her words, she received a "strangely useless and ornamental education." When she was sixteen she left school, married (and soon divorced), and worked as a reporter, first in Texas and later in Denver and Chicago. She moved around a good deal, both within the United States and abroad; she lived for a while in Mexico, Belgium, Switzerland, France, and Germany.

Even as a child she was interested in writing, but she did not publish her first story until she was 33. She wrote essays and one novel (Ship of Fools), but she is best known for her stories. Porter's Collected Stories won the Pulitzer Prize and the National Book Award in 1965.

The Jilting of Granny Weatherall

She flicked her wrist neatly out of Doctor Harry's pudgy careful fingers and pulled the sheet up to her chin. The brat ought to be in knee breeches. Doctoring around the country with spectacles on his nose! "Get along now, take your schoolbooks and go. There's nothing wrong with me."

Doctor Harry spread a warm paw like a cushion on her forehead where the forked green vein danced and made her eyelids twitch. "Now, now, be a good girl, and we'll have you up in no time."

"That's no way to speak to a woman nearly eighty years old just because she's down. I'd have you respect your elders, young man."

"Well, Missy, excuse me." Doctor Harry patted her cheek. "But I've got to warn you, haven't I? You're a marvel, but you must be careful or you're going to be good and sorry."

"Don't tell me what I'm going to be. I'm on my feet now, morally speaking. It's Cornelia. I had to go to bed to get rid of her."

Her bones felt loose, and floated around in her skin, and Doctor Harry floated like a balloon around the foot of the bed. He floated and pulled down his waistcoat and swung his glasses on a cord. "Well, stay where you are, it certainly can't hurt you."

"Get along and doctor your sick," said Granny Weatherall. "Leave a well woman alone. I'll call for you when I want you. . . .

Where were you forty years ago when I pulled through milk-leg and double pneumonia? You weren't even born. Don't let Cornelia lead you on," she shouted, because Doctor Harry appeared to float up to the ceiling and out. "I pay my own bills, and I don't throw my money away on nonsense!"

She meant to wave good-bye, but it was too much trouble. Her 8
eyes closed of themselves, it was like a dark curtain drawn around the bed. The pillow rose and floated under her, pleasant as a hammock in a light wind. She listened to the leaves rustling outside the window. No, somebody was swishing newspapers: no, Cornelia and Doctor Harry were whispering together. She leaped broad awake, thinking they whispered in her ear.

"She was never like this, *never* like this!" "Well, what can we expect?" "Yes, eighty years old. . . . "

Well, and what if she was? She still had ears. It was like Cornelia to whisper around doors. She always kept things secret in such a public way. She was always being tactful and kind. Cornelia was dutiful; that was the trouble with her. Dutiful and good: "So good and dutiful," said Granny, "and I'd like to spank her." She saw herself spanking Cornelia and making a fine job of it.

"What'd you say, Mother?"

Granny felt her face tying up in hard knots.   12

"Can't a body think, I'd like to know?"

"I thought you might want something."

"I do. I want a lot of things. First off, go away and don't whisper."

She lay and drowsed, hoping in her sleep that the children 16
would keep out and let her rest a minute. It had been a long day. Not that she was tired. It was always pleasant to snatch a minute now and then. There was always so much to be done, let me see: tomorrow.

Tomorrow was far away and there was nothing to trouble about. Things were finished somehow when the time came; thank God there was always a little margin over for peace; then a person could spread out the plan of life and tuck in the edges orderly. It was good to have everything clean and folded away, with the hair brushes and tonic bottles sitting straight on the white embroidered linen: the day started without fuss and the pantry shelves laid out with rows of jelly glasses and brown jugs and white stone-china jars and blue whirligigs and words painted on them: coffee, tea, sugar, ginger, cinnamon, allspice: and the bronze clock with the lion on top nicely dusted off. The dust that lion could collect in twenty-four hours! The box in the attic with all those letters tied up, she'd have to go through that tomorrow. All those letters—George's letters and John's letters and her letters to them both—lying around for the children to find afterwards made her uneasy. Yes, that would be tomorrow's business. No use to let them know how silly she had been once.

While she was rummaging around she found death in her mind and it felt clammy and unfamiliar. She had spent so much time preparing for death there was no need for bringing it up again. Let it take care of itself now. When she was sixty she had felt very old, finished, and went around making farewell trips to see her children and grandchildren, with a secret in her mind: This is the very last of your mother, children! Then she made her will and came down with a long fever. That was all just a notion like a lot of other things, but it was lucky too, for she had once for all got over the idea of dying for a long time. Now she couldn't be worried. She hoped she had better sense now. Her father had lived to be one hundred and two years old and had drunk a noggin of strong hot toddy at his last birthday. He told the reporters it was his daily habit, and he owed his long life to that. He had made quite a scandal and was very pleased about it. She believed she'd just plague Cornelia a little.

"Cornelia! Cornelia!" No footsteps, but a sudden hand on her cheek. "Bless you, where have you been?"

"Here, Mother."   20

"Well, Cornelia, I want a noggin of hot toddy."

"Are you cold, darling?"

"I'm chilly, Cornelia. Lying in bed stops the circulation. I must have told you that a thousand times."

Well, she could just hear Cornelia telling her husband that   24
Mother was getting a little childish and they'd have to humor her. The thing that most annoyed her was that Cornelia thought she was deaf, dumb, and blind. Little hasty glances and tiny gestures tossed around her and over her head saying, "Don't cross her, let her have her way, she's eighty years old," and she sitting there as if she lived in a thin glass cage. Sometimes Granny almost made up her mind to pack up and move back to her own house where nobody could remind her every minute that she was old. Wait, wait, Cornelia, till your own children whisper behind your back!

In her day she had kept a better house and had got more work done. She wasn't too old yet for Lydia to be driving eighty miles for advice when one of the children jumped the track, and Jimmy still dropped in and talked things over: "Now, Mammy, you've a good business head, I want to know what you think of this? . . ." Old. Cornelia couldn't change the furniture around without asking. Little things, little things! They had been so sweet when they were little. Granny wished the old days were back again with the children young and everything to be done over. It had been a hard pull, but not too much for her. When she thought of all the food she had cooked, and all the clothes she had cut and sewed, and all the gardens she had made—well, the children showed it. There they were, made out of her, and they couldn't get away from that. Sometimes she wanted to see John again and point to them and say, Well, I didn't do so badly, did I? But that would have to wait. That was for tomorrow. She used to think of him as a man, but now all the children were older than their father, and he would be a child beside her if she saw him now. It seemed strange and there was something wrong in the idea. Why, he couldn't possibly recognize her. She had fenced in a hundred acres once, digging the post holes herself and clamping the wires with just a negro boy to help. That changed a woman. John would be looking for a young woman with the peaked Spanish comb in her hair and the painted fan. Digging post holes changed a woman. Riding country roads in the winter when women had their babies was another thing: sitting up nights with sick horses and sick negroes and sick children and hardly ever losing one. John, I hardly ever lost one of them! John would see that in a minute, that would be something he could understand, she wouldn't have to explain anything!

It made her feel like rolling up her sleeves and putting the whole place to rights again. No matter if Cornelia was determined to be everywhere at once, there were a great many things left undone on this place. She would start tomorrow and do them. It was good to be strong enough for everything, even if all you made melted and changed and slipped under your hands, so that by the time you finished you almost forgot what you were working for. What was it I set out to do? she asked herself intently, but she could not remember. A fog rose over the valley, she saw it marching across the creek swallowing the trees and moving up the hill like an army of ghosts. Soon it would be at the near edge of the orchard, and then it was time to go in and light the lamps. Come in, children, don't stay out in the night air.

Lighting the lamps had been beautiful. The children huddled up to her and breathed like little calves waiting at the bars in the twilight. Their eyes followed the match and watched the flame rise and settle in a blue curve, then they moved away from her. The lamp was lit, they didn't have to be scared and hang on to mother any more. Never, never, never more. God, for all my life I thank Thee. Without Thee, my God, I could never have done it. Hail, Mary, full of grace.

I want you to pick all the fruit this year and see that nothing is 28 wasted. There's always someone who can use it. Don't let good things rot for want of using. You waste life when you waste good food. Don't let things get lost. It's bitter to lose things. Now, don't let me get to thinking, not when I am tired and taking a little nap before supper. . . .

The pillow rose about her shoulders and pressed against her heart and the memory was being squeezed out of it: oh, push down that pillow, somebody: it would smother her if she tried to hold it. Such a fresh breeze blowing and such a green day with no threats in it. But he had not come, just the same. What does a woman do when she has put on the white veil and set out the white cake for a man and he doesn't come? She tried to remember. No, I swear he never harmed me but in that. He never harmed me but in that . . . and what if he did? There was the day, the day, but a whirl of dark smoke rose and covered it, crept up and over into the bright field where everything was planted so carefully in orderly rows. That was hell, she knew hell when she saw it. For sixty years she had prayed against remembering him and against losing her soul in the deep pit of hell, and now the two things were mingled in one and the thought of him was a smoky cloud from hell that moved and crept in her head when she had just got rid of Doctor Harry and was trying to rest a minute. Wounded vanity, Ellen, said a sharp voice in the top of her mind. Don't let your wounded vanity get the upper hand of you. Plenty of girls get jilted. You were jilted, weren't you? Then stand up to it. Her eyelids wavered and let in streamers of blue-gray light like tissue paper over her eyes. She must get up and pull the shades down or she'd never sleep. She was in bed again and the shades were not down. How could that happen? Better turn over, hide from the light, sleeping in the light gave you nightmares. "Mother, how do you feel now?" and a stinging wetness on her forehead. But I don't like having my face washed in cold water!

Hapsy? George? Lydia? Jimmy? No, Cornelia, and her features were swollen and full of little puddles. "They're coming, darling, they'll all be here soon." Go wash your face, child, you look funny.

Instead of obeying, Cornelia knelt down and put her head on the pillow. She seemed to be talking but there was no sound. "Well, are you tongue-tied? Whose birthday is it? Are you going to give a party?"

Cornelia's mouth moved urgently in strange shapes. "Don't do   32
that, you bother me, daughter."

"Oh, no, Mother. Oh, no. . . ."

Nonsense. It was strange about children. They disputed your every word. "No what, Cornelia?"

"Here's Doctor Harry."

"I won't see that boy again. He just left five minutes ago."   36

"That was this morning, Mother. It's night now. Here's the nurse."

"This is Doctor Harry, Mrs. Weatherall. I never saw you look so young and happy!"

"Ah, I'll never be young again—but I'd be happy if they'd let me lie in peace and get rested."

She thought she spoke up loudly, but no one answered. A warm   40
weight on her forehead, a warm bracelet on her wrist, and a breeze went on whispering, trying to tell her something. A shuffle of leaves in the everlasting hand of God. He blew on them and they danced and rattled. "Mother, don't mind, we're going to give you a little hypodermic." "Look here, daughter, how do ants get in this bed? I saw sugar ants yesterday." Did you send for Hapsy too?

It was Hapsy she really wanted. She had to go a long way back through a great many rooms to find Hapsy standing with a baby on her arm. She seemed to herself to be Hapsy also, and the baby on Hapsy's arm was Hapsy and himself and herself, all at once, and there was no surprise in the meeting. Then Hapsy melted from within and turned flimsy as gray gauze and the baby was a gauzy shadow, and Hapsy came up close and said, "I thought you'd never come," and looked at her very searchingly and said, "You haven't changed a bit!" They leaned forward to kiss, when Cornelia began whispering from a long way off, "Oh, is there anything you want to tell me? Is there anything I can do for you?"

Yes, she had changed her mind after sixty years and she would like to see George. I want you to find George. Find him and be sure to tell him I forgot him. I want him to know I had my husband just the same and my children and my house like any other woman. A good house too and a good husband that I loved and fine children out of him. Better than I hoped for even. Tell him I was given back everything he took away and more. Oh, no, oh, God, no, there was something else besides the house and the man and the children. Oh, surely they were not all? What was it? Something not given back. . . . Her breath crowded down under her ribs and grew into a monstrous frightening shape with cutting edges; it bored up into her head, and the agony was unbelievable: Yes, John, get the doctor now, no more talk, my time has come.

When this one was born it should be the last. The last. It should have been born first, for it was the one she had truly wanted. Everything came in good time. Nothing left out, left over. She was strong, in three days she would be as well as ever. Better. A woman needed milk in her to have her full health.

"Mother, do you hear me?"   44

"I've been telling you—"

"Mother, Father Connolly's here."

"I went to Holy Communion only last week. Tell him I'm not so sinful as all that."

"Father just wants to speak to you."   48

He could speak as much as he pleased. It was like him to drop in and inquire about her soul as if it were a teething baby, and then stay on for a cup of tea and a round of cards and gossip. He always had a funny story of some sort, usually about an Irishman who made his little mistakes and confessed them, and the point lay in some absurd thing he would blurt out in the confessional showing his struggles between native piety and original sin. Granny felt easy about her soul. Cornelia, where are your manners? Give Father Connolly a chair. She had her secret comfortable understanding with a few favorite saints who cleared a straight road to God for her. All as surely signed and sealed as the papers for the new Forty Acres. Forever . . . heirs and assigns forever. Since the day the wedding cake was not cut, but thrown out and wasted. The whole bottom dropped out of the world, and there she was blind and sweating and nothing under her feet and the walls falling away. His hand had caught her under the breast, she had not fallen, there was the freshly polished floor with the green rug on it, just as before. He had cursed like a sailor's parrot and said, "I'll kill him for you." Don't lay a hand on him, for my sake leave something to God. "Now, Ellen, you must believe what I tell you. . . ."

So there was nothing, nothing to worry about any more, except sometimes in the night one of the children screamed in a nightmare, and they both hustled out shaking and hunting for the matches and calling, "There, wait a minute, here we are!" John, get the doctor now, Hapsy's time has come. But there was Hapsy standing by the bed in a white cap. "Cornelia, tell Hapsy to take off her cap. I can't see her plain."

Her eyes opened very wide and the room stood out like a picture she had seen somewhere. Dark colors with the shadows rising toward the ceiling in long angles. The tall black dresser gleamed with nothing on it but John's picture, enlarged from a little one, with John's eyes very black when they should have been blue. You never saw him, so how do you know how he looked? But the man insisted the copy was perfect, it was very rich and handsome. For a picture, yes, but it's not my husband. The table by the bed had a linen cover and a candle and a crucifix. The light was blue from Cornelia's silk lampshades. No sort of light at all, just frippery. You had to live forty years with kerosene lamps to appreciate honest electricity. She felt very strong and she saw Doctor Harry with a rosy nimbus around him.

"You look like a saint, Doctor Harry, and I vow that's as near as   52 you'll ever come to it."

"She's saying something."

"I heard you, Cornelia. What's all this carrying on?"

"Father Connolly's saying—"

Cornelia's voice staggered and bumped like a cart in a bad road.   56 It rounded corners and turned back again and arrived nowhere. Granny stepped up in the cart very lightly and reached for the reins, but a man sat beside her and she knew him by his hands, driving the cart. She did not look in his face, for she knew without seeing, but looked instead down the road where the trees leaned over and bowed to each other and a thousand birds were singing a Mass. She felt like singing too, but she put her hand in the bosom of her dress and pulled out a rosary, and Father Connolly murmured Latin in a very solemn voice and tickled her feet. My God, will you stop that nonsense? I'm a married woman. What if he did run away and leave me to face the priest by myself? I found another a whole world better. I wouldn't have exchanged my husband for anybody except St. Michael himself, and you may tell him that for me with a thank you in the bargain.

Light flashed on her closed eyelids, and a deep roaring shook her. Cornelia, is that lightning? I hear thunder. There's going to be a storm. Close all the windows. Call the children in. . . ."Mother, here we are, all of us." "Is that you, Hapsy?" "Oh, no, I'm Lydia. We drove as fast as we could." Their faces drifted above her, drifted away. The rosary fell out of her hands and Lydia put it back. Jimmy tried to help, their hands fumbled together, and Granny closed two fingers around Jimmy's thumb. Beads wouldn't do, it must be something alive. She was so amazed her thoughts ran round and round. So, my dear Lord, this is my death and I wasn't even thinking about it. My children have come to see me die. But I can't, it's not time. Oh, I always hated surprises. I wanted to give Cornelia the amethyst set—Cornelia, you're to have the amethyst set, but Hapsy's to wear it when she wants, and, Doctor Harry, do shut up. Nobody sent for you. Oh, my dear Lord, do wait a minute. I meant to do something about the Forty Acres, Jimmy doesn't need it and Lydia will later on, with that worthless husband of hers. I meant to finish the altar cloth and send six bottles of wine to Sister Borgia for her dyspepsia. I want to send six bottles of wine to Sister Borgia, Father Connolly, now don't let me forget.

Cornelia's voice made short turns and tilted over and crashed. "Oh, Mother, oh, Mother, oh, Mother. . . ."

"I'm not going, Cornelia. I'm taken by surprise. I can't go."

You'll see Hapsy again. What about her? "I thought you'd never 60 come." Granny made a long journey outward, looking for Hapsy. What if I don't find her? What then? Her heart sank down and down, there was no bottom to death, she couldn't come to the end of it. The blue light from Cornelia's lampshade drew into a tiny point in the center of her brain, it flickered and winked like an eye, quietly it fluttered and dwindled. Granny lay curled down within herself, amazed and watchful, staring at the point of light that was herself; her body was now only a deeper mass of shadow in an endless darkness and this darkness would curl around the light and swallow it up, God, give a sign!

For the second time there was no sign. Again no bridegroom and the priest in the house. She could not remember any other sorrow because this grief wiped them all away. Oh, no, there's nothing more cruel than this—I'll never forgive it. She stretched herself with a deep breath and blew out the light.

Topics for Discussion and Writing

1. Who is Hapsy? What do we know about her? *How* do we know these things?

2. How would you describe Granny Weatherall? In what ways does her name suit her?

3. The final paragraph begins: "For the second time there was no sign." What happened the first time? What is happening now? How are the

two events linked? (The paragraph alludes to Christ's parable of the bridegroom, in Matthew 25: 1–13. If you are unfamiliar with the parable, read it in the Gospel according to St. Matthew.)
4. What do you think happens in the last line of the story.

Emily Dickinson

Emily Dickinson (1830–86) was born into a proper New England family in Amherst, Massachusetts. Although she spent her seventeenth year a few miles away, at Mount Holyoke Seminary (now Mount Holyoke College), in her twenties and thirties she left Amherst only five or six times, and in her last twenty years she may never have left her house. Her brother was probably right when he said that having seen something of the rest of the world — she had visited Washington with her father, when he was a member of Congress — "she could not resist the feeling that it was painfully hollow. It was to her so thin and unsatisfying in the face of the Great Realities of Life." Dickinson lived with her parents (a somewhat reclusive mother and an austere, remote father) and a younger sister; a married brother lived in the house next door. She did, however, form some passionate attachments, to women as well as men, but there is no evidence that they found physical expression. By the age of twelve Dickinson was writing witty letters, but she apparently did not write more than an occasional poem before her late twenties. At her death — she died in the house where she was born — she left 1,775 poems, only seven of which had been published (anonymously) during her lifetime.

This World is not Conclusion

This World is not Conclusion.
A Species stands beyond —
Invisible, as Music —
But positive, as Sound — 4
It beckons, and it baffles —
Philosophy — dont know —
And through a Riddle, at the last —
Sagacity, must go — 8
To guess it, puzzles scholars —
To gain it, Men have borne
Contempt of Generations
And Crucifixion, shown — 12
Faith slips — and laughs, and rallies —
Blushes, if any see —

Plucks at a twig of Evidence—
And asks a Vane, the way—   16
Much Gesture, from the Pulpit—
Strong Hallelujahs roll—
Narcotics cannot still the Tooth
That nibbles at the soul—   20

[c.1862]

Topics for Discussion and Writing

1. Given the context of the first two lines, what do you think "Conclusion" means in the first line?
2. Although white spaces here are not used to divide the poem into stanzas, the poem seems to be constructed in units of four lines each. Summarize each four-line unit in a sentence or two.
3. Compare your summaries with those of a classmate. If you substantially disagree, reread the poem to see if, on reflection, one or the other of you seems in closer touch with the poem. Or does the poem (or some part of it) allow for two very different interpretations?
4. In the first four lines the speaker seems (to use a word from line 4) quite "positive." Do some or all of the following stanzas seem less positive? If so, which—and what makes you say so?
5. How do you understand "Much Gesture, from the Pulpit" (line 17)? Would you agree with a reader who said that the line suggests a *lack* of deep conviction? Explain.

13
Classic Essays

Jonathan Swift

Jonathan Swift (1667–1745) was born in Ireland of an English family. He was ordained in the Church of Ireland in 1694, and in 1714 he became dean of St. Patrick's Cathedral, Dublin. He wrote abundantly on political and religious topics, often motivated (in his own words) by "savage indignation." It is ironic that Gulliver's Travels, *the masterpiece by this master of irony, is most widely thought of as a book for children.*

From the middle of the sixteenth century the English regulated the Irish economy so that it would enrich England. Heavy taxes and other repressive legislation impoverished Ireland, and in 1728, the year before Swift wrote "A Modest Proposal," Ireland was further weakened by a severe famine. Swift, deeply moved by the injustice, the stupidity, and the suffering that he found in Ireland, adopts the disguise or persona of an economist and offers an ironic suggestion on how Irish families may improve their conditions.

A Modest Proposal

For Preventing the Children of Poor People
in Ireland from Being a Burden to Their
Parents or Country, and for Making Them
Beneficial to the Public

It is a melancholy object to those who walk through this great town or travel in the country, when they see the streets, the roads, and cabin doors, crowded with beggars of the female sex, followed by three, four, or six children, all in rags and importuning every passenger for an alms. These mothers, instead of being able to work for their honest livelihood, are forced to employ all their time in strolling to beg sustenance for their helpless infants: who as they grow up either turn thieves for want of work, or leave their dear native country to fight for the pretender in Spain, or sell themselves to the Barbadoes.

I think it is agreed by all parties that this prodigious number of children in the arms, or on the backs, or at the heels of their mothers, and frequently of their fathers, is in the present deplorable state of the kingdom a very great additional grievance; and, therefore, whoever could find out a fair, cheap, and easy method of making these children sound, useful members of the commonwealth, would deserve so well of the public as to have his statue set up for a preserver of the nation.

But my intention is very far from being confined to provide only for the children of professed beggars; it is of a much greater extent, and shall take in the whole number of infants at a certain age who are born of parents in effect as little able to support them as those who demand our charity in the streets.

As to my own part, having turned my thoughts for many years 4 upon this important subject, and maturely weighed the several schemes of our projectors, I have always found them grossly mistaken in their computation. It is true, a child just dropped from its dam may be supported by her milk for a solar year, with little other nourishment; at most not above the value of 2s.,[1] which the mother may certainly get, or the value in scraps, by her lawful occupation of begging; and it is exactly at one year old that I propose to provide for them in such a manner as instead of being a charge upon their parents or the parish, or wanting food and raiment for the rest of their lives, they shall on the contrary contribute to the feeding, and partly to the clothing, of many thousands.

There is likewise another great advantage in my scheme, that it will prevent those voluntary abortions, and that horrid practice of women murdering their bastard children, alas! too frequent among us! sacrificing the poor innocent babes I doubt more to avoid the expense than the shame, which would move tears and pity in the most savage and inhuman breast.

The number of souls in this kingdom being usually reckoned one million and a half, of these I calculate there may be about 200,000 couple whose wives are breeders; from which number I subtract 30,000 couple who are able to maintain their own children (although I apprehend there cannot be so many, under the present distress of the kingdom); but this being granted, there will remain 170,000 breeders. I again subtract 50,000 for those women who miscarry, or whose children die by accident or disease within the year. There only remain 120,000 children of poor parents annually born. The question therefore is, how this number shall be reared and provided for? which, as I have already said, under the present situation of affairs, is utterly impossible by all the methods hitherto proposed. For we can neither employ them in handicraft or agriculture; we neither build houses (I mean in the country) nor cultivate land; they can very seldom pick up a livelihood by stealing, till they arrive at six years old, except where they are of towardly parts; although I confess they learn the rudiments much earlier; during which time they can, however, be properly looked upon only as probationers;

---

[1] 2s. = two shillings. Later in the essay, "£" and "l" stand for pounds and "d" for pence. (Editors' note)

as I have been informed by a principal gentleman in the county of
Cavan, who protested to me that he never knew above one or two
instances under the age of six, even in a part of the kingdom so
renowned for the quickest proficiency in that art.

I am assured by our merchants, that a boy or a girl before twelve
years old is no saleable commodity; and even when they come to
this age they will not yield above 31. or 31. 2s. 6d. at most on the
exchange; which cannot turn to account either to the parents or kingdom, the charge of nutriment and rags having been at least four
times that value.

I shall now therefore humbly propose my own thoughts, which   8
I hope will not be liable to the least objection.

I have been assured by a very knowing American of my acquaintance in London, that a young healthy child well nursed is at a year
old a most delicious, nourishing, and wholesome food, whether
stewed, roasted, baked, or broiled; and I make no doubt that it will
equally serve in a fricassee or a ragout.

I do therefore humbly offer it to public consideration that of the
120,000 children already computed, 20,000 may be reserved for
breed, whereof only one-fourth part to be males; which is more than
we allow to sheep, black cattle, or swine; and my reason is, that
these children are seldom the fruits of marriage, a circumstance not
much regarded by our savages; therefore one male will be sufficient
to serve four females. That the remaining 100,000 may, at a year
old, be offered in sale to the persons of quality and fortune through
the kingdom; always advising the mother to let them suck plenti-
fully in the last month, so as to render them plump and fat for a
good table. A child will make two dishes at an entertainment for
friends; and when the family dines alone, the fore or hind quarter
will make a reasonable dish, and seasoned with a little pepper or
salt will be very good boiled on the fourth day, especially in winter.

I have reckoned upon a medium that a child just born will weigh
12 pounds, and in a solar year, if tolerably nursed, will increase to
28 pounds.

I grant this food will be somewhat dear, and therefore very   12
proper for landlords, who, as they have already devoured most of
the parents, seem to have the best title to the children.

Infant's flesh will be in season throughout the year, but more
plentiful in March, and a little before and after: for we are told by
a grave author, an eminent French physician, that fish being a prolific diet, there are more children born in Roman Catholic countries

about nine months after Lent than at any other season; therefore, reckoning a year after Lent, the markets will be more glutted than usual, because the number of popish infants is at least three to one in this kingdom: and therefore it will have one other collateral advantage, by lessening the number of papists among us.

I have already computed the charge of nursing a beggar's child (in which list I reckon all cottagers, laborers, and four-fifths of the farmers) to be about 2s. per annum, rags included; and I believe no gentleman would repine to give 10s. for the carcass of a good fat child, which, as I have said, will make four dishes of excellent nutritive meat, when he has only some particular friend or his own family to dine with him. Thus the squire will learn to be a good landlord, and grow popular among the tenants; the mother will have 8s. net profit, and be fit for work till she produces another child.

Those who are more thrifty (as I must confess the times require) may flay the carcass; the skin of which artificially dressed will make admirable gloves for ladies, and summer boots for fine gentlemen.

As to our city of Dublin, shambles may be appointed for this 16 purpose in the most convenient parts of it, and butchers we may be assured will not be wanting: although I rather recommend buying the children alive, and dressing them hot from the knife as we do roasting pigs.

A very worthy person, a true lover of his country, and whose virtues I highly esteem, was lately pleased in discoursing on this matter to offer a refinement upon my scheme. He said that many gentlemen of this kingdom, having of late destroyed their deer, he conceived that the want of venison might be well supplied by the bodies of young lads and maidens, not exceeding fourteen years of age nor under twelve; so great a number of both sexes in every country being now ready to starve for want of work and service; and these to be disposed of by their parents, if alive, or otherwise by their nearest relations. But with due deference to so excellent a friend and so deserving a patriot, I cannot be altogether in his sentiments; for as to the males, my American acquaintance assured me from frequent experience that their flesh was generally tough and lean, like that of our schoolboys by continual exercise, and their taste disagreeable; and to fatten them would not answer the charge. Then as to the females, it would, I think, with humble submission be a loss to the public, because they soon would become breeders themselves: and besides, it is not improbable that some scrupulous people might be apt to censure such a practice (although indeed very unjustly), as a little bordering upon cruelty; which, I confess, has always been with me the strongest objection against any project, how well soever intended.

But in order to justify my friend, he confessed that this expedient was put into his head by the famous Psalmanazar, a native of the island Formosa, who came from thence to London about twenty years ago: and in conversation told my friend, that in his country when any young person happened to be put to death, the executioner sold the carcass to persons of quality as a prime dainty; and that in his time the body of a plump girl of fifteen, who was crucified for an attempt to poison the emperor, was sold to his imperial majesty's prime minister of state, and other great mandarins of the court, in joints from the gibbet, at 400 crowns. Neither indeed can I deny, that if the same use were made of several plump young girls in this town, who without one single groat to their fortunes cannot stir abroad without a chair, and appear at the playhouse and assemblies in foreign fineries which they never will pay for, the kingdom would not be the worse.

Some persons of a desponding spirit are in great concern about that vast number of poor people, who are aged, diseased, or maimed, and I have been desired to employ my thoughts what course may be taken to ease the nation of so grievous an encumbrance. But I am not in the least pain upon that matter, because it is very well known that they are every day dying and rotting by cold and famine, and filth and vermin, as fast as can be reasonably expected. And as to the young laborers, they are now in as hopeful a condition: they cannot get work, and consequently pine away for want of nourishment, to a degree that if at any time they are accidentally hired to common labor, they have not strength to perform it; and thus the country and themselves are happily delivered from the evils to come.

I have too long digressed, and therefore shall return to my subject. I think the advantages by the proposal which I have made are obvious and many, as well as of the highest importance.

For first, as I have already observed, it would greatly lessen the number of papists, with whom we are yearly overrun, being the principal breeders of the nation as well as our most dangerous enemies; and who stay at home on purpose to deliver the kingdom to the Pretender, hoping to take their advantage by the absence of so many good Protestants, who have chosen rather to leave their country than stay at home and pay tithes against their conscience to an Episcopal curate.

Secondly, The poor tenants will have something valuable of their own, which by law may be made liable to distress and help to pay their landlord's rent, their corn and cattle being already seized, and money a thing unknown.

Thirdly, Whereas the maintenance of 100,000 children from two years old and upward, cannot be computed at less than 10s. a-piece per annum, the nation's stock will be thereby increased £50,000 per annum, beside the profit of a new dish introduced to the tables of all gentlemen of fortune in the kingdom who have any refinement in taste. And the money will circulate among ourselves, the goods being entirely of our own growth and manufacture.

Fourthly, The constant breeders beside the gain of 8s. sterling 24 per annum by the sale of their children, will be rid of the charge of maintaining them after the first year.

Fifthly, This food would likewise bring great custom to taverns, where the vintners will certainly be so prudent as to procure the best receipts for dressing it to perfection, and consequently have their houses frequented by all the fine gentlemen, who justly value themselves upon their knowledge in good eating; and a skilful cook who understands how to oblige his guests, will contrive to make it as expensive as they please.

Sixthly, This would be a great inducement to marriage, which all wise nations have either encouraged by rewards or enforced by laws and penalties. It would increase the care and tenderness of mothers toward their children, when they were sure of a settlement for life to the poor babes, provided in some sort by the public, to their annual profit instead of expense. We should see an honest emulation among the married women, which of them would bring the fattest child to the market. Men would become as fond of their wives during the time of their pregnancy as they are now of their mares in foal, their cows in calf, their sows when they are ready to farrow; nor offer to beat or kick them (as is too frequent a practice) for fear of a miscarriage.

Many other advantages might be enumerated. For instance, the addition of some thousand carcasses in our exportation of barreled beef, the propagation of swine's flesh, and improvement in the art of making good bacon, so much wanted among us by the great destruction of pigs, too frequent at our table; which are no way comparable in taste or magnificence to a well-grown, fat, yearling child, which roasted whole will make a considerable figure at a lord mayor's feast or any other public enertainment. But this and many others I omit, being studious of brevity.

Supposing that 1,000 families in this city would be constant cus-   28
omers for infants' flesh, besides others who might have it at merry-
meetings, particularly at weddings and christenings, I compute that
Dublin would take off annually about 20,000 carcasses; and the rest
of the kingdom (where probably they will be sold somewhat
cheaper) the remaining 80,000.

I can think of no one objection that will possibly be raised against
this proposal, unless it should be urged that the number of people
will be thereby much lessened in the kingdom. This I freely own,
and it was indeed one principal design in offering it to the world.
I desire the reader will observe, that I calculate my remedy for this
one individual kingdom of Ireland and for no other that ever was,
is, or I think ever can be upon earth. Therefore let no man talk to
me of other expedients: of taxing our absentees at 5s. a pound: of
using neither clothes nor household furniture except what is of our
own growth and manufacture: of utterly rejecting the materials and
instruments that promote foreign luxury: of curing the expensive-
ness of pride, vanity, idleness, and gaming in our women: of introducing a vein of parsimony, prudence, and temperance: of learning to love our country, in the want of which we differ even from
Laplanders and the inhabitants of Topinamboo: of quitting our ani-
mosities and factions, nor acting any longer like the Jews, who were
murdering one another at the very moment their city was taken:
of being a little cautious not to sell our country and conscience for
nothing: of teaching landlords to have at least one degree of mercy
toward their tenants: lastly, of putting a spirit of honesty, industry,
and skill into our shopkeepers; who, if a resolution could now be
taken to buy only our native goods, would immediately unite to
cheat and exact upon us in the price, the measure, and the goodness, nor could ever yet be brought to make one fair proposal of
just dealing, though often and earnestly invited to it.

Therefore, I repeat, let no man talk to me of these and the like
expedients, till he has at least some glimpse of hope that there will
be ever some hearty and sincere attempt to put them in practice.

But as to myself, having been wearied out for many years with
offering vain, idle, visionary thoughts, and at length utterly despair-
ing of success, I fortunately fell upon this proposal; which, as it is
wholly new, so it has something solid and real, of no expense and
little trouble, full in our own power, and whereby we can incur no
danger in disobliging England. For this kind of commodity will not
bear exportation, the flesh being of too tender a consistence to admit

a long continuance in salt, although perhaps I could name a country which would be glad to eat up our whole nation without it.

After all, I am not so violently bent upon my own opinion as to reject any offer proposed by wise men, which shall be found equally innocent, cheap, easy, and effectual. But before something of that kind shall be advanced in contradiction to my scheme, and offering a better, I desire the author or authors will be pleased maturely to consider two points. First, as things now stand, how they will be able to find food and raiment for 100,000 useless mouths and backs. And secondly, there being a round million of creatures in human figure throughout this kingdom, whose subsistence put into a common stock would leave them in debt 200,000,0001. sterling, adding those who are beggars by profession to the bulk of farmers, cottagers, and laborers, with the wives and children who are beggars in effect; I desire those politicians who dislike my overture, and may perhaps be so bold as to attempt an answer, that they will first ask the parents of these mortals, whether they would not at this day think it a great happiness to have been sold for food at a year old in the manner I prescribe, and thereby have avoided such a perpetual scene of misfortunes as they have since gone through by the oppression of landlords, the impossibility of paying rent without money or trade, the want of common sustenance, with neither house nor clothes to cover them from the inclemencies of the weather, and the most inevitable prospect of entailing the like or greater miseries upon their breed for ever. 32

I profess, in the sincerity of my heart, that I have not the least personal interest in endeavoring to promote this necessary work, having no other motive than the public good of my country, by advancing our trade, providing for infants, relieving the poor, and giving some pleasure to the rich. I have no children by which I can propose to get a single penny; the youngest being nine years old, and my wife past child-bearing.

Topics for Discussion and Writing

1. Characterize the pamphleteer (not Swift but his persona) who offers his "modest proposal." What sort of man does he think he is? What sort of man do we regard him as? Support your assertions with evidence.
2. In the first paragraph the speaker says that the sight of mothers begging is "melancholy." In this paragraph what assumption does the

speaker make about women that in part gives rise to this melancholy? Now that you are familiar with the entire essay, explain Swift's strategy in his first paragraph.

3. Explain the function of the "other expedients" (listed in paragraph 29).
4. How might you argue that although this satire is primarily ferocious, it also contains some playful touches? What specific passages might support your argument?

E. M. Forster

E[dward] M[organ] Forster (1879–1970) was born in London and was graduated from King's College, Cambridge. He traveled widely and lived for a while in India, but most of his life was spent back at King's College. His best-known novel, A Passage to India *(1926), is alluded to in the first line of the essay that we reprint.*

My Wood

A few years ago I wrote a book which dealt in part with the difficulties of the English in India. Feeling that they would have had no difficulties in India themselves, the Americans read the book freely. The more they read it the better it made them feel, and a checque to the author was the result. I bought a wood with the checque. It is not a large wood—it contains scarcely any trees, and it is intersected, blast it, by a public footpath. Still, it is the first property that I have owned, so it is right that other people should participate in my shame, and should ask themselves, in accents that will vary in horror, this very important question: What is the effect of property upon the character? Don't let's touch economics; the effect of private ownership upon the community as a whole is another question—a more important question, perhaps, but another one. Let's keep on psychology. If you own things, what's their effect on you? What's the effect on me of my wood?

In the first place, it makes me feel heavy. Property does have this effect. Property produces men of weight, and it was a man of weight who failed to get into the Kingdom of Heaven. He was not wicked, that unfortunate millionaire in the parable, he was only stout; he stuck out in front, not to mention behind, and as he wedged himself this way and that in the crystalline entrance and bruised his well-fed flanks, he saw beneath him a comparatively slim camel passing through the eye of a needle and being woven into the robe of God. The Gospels all through couple stoutness and slowness. They point out what is perfectly obvious, yet seldom realized: that if you have a lot of things you cannot move about a lot, that furniture requires dusting, dusters require servants, servants require insurance stamps, and the whole tangle of them makes you think twice before you accept an invitation to dinner or go for a bathe in the Jordan. Sometimes the Gospels proceed further and say with Tolstoy that property is sinful; they approach the difficult ground of asceticism here, where I cannot follow them. But as to the immediate effects of property on people, they just show straightforward logic. It produces men of weight. Men of weight cannot, by definition, move like the lightning from the East unto the West, and the ascent of a fourteen-stone[1] bishop into a pulpit is thus the exact antithesis of the coming of the Son of Man. My wood makes me feel heavy.

In the second place, it makes me feel it ought to be larger.

The other day I heard a twig snap in it. I was annoyed at first, for I thought that someone was blackberrying, and depreciating the value of the undergrowth. On coming nearer, I saw it was not a man who had trodden on the twig and snapped it, but a bird, and I felt pleased. My bird. The bird was not equally pleased. Ignoring the relation between us, it took fright as soon as it saw the shape of my face, and flew straight over the boundary hedge into a field, the property of Mrs. Henessy, where it sat down with a loud squawk. It had become Mrs. Henessy's bird. Something seemed grossly amiss here, something that would not have occurred had the wood been larger. I could not afford to buy Mrs. Henessy out, I dared not murder her, and limitations of this sort beset me on every side. Ahab did not want that vineyard—he only needed it to round off his property, preparatory to plotting a new curve—and all the land around my wood has become necessary to me in order to round off the wood. A boundary protects. But—poor little thing—the boundary ought in its turn to be protected. Noises on the edge of it. Children throw stones. A little more, and then a little more, until we reach the sea. Happy Canute! Happier Alexander! And after all, why should even the world be the limit of possession? A rocket containing a Union Jack, will, it is hoped, be shortly fired at the moon. Mars. Sirius. Beyond which . . . But these immensities ended by

4

[1] 196-pound. (Editors' note)

saddening me. I could not suppose that my wood was the destined nucleus of universal dominion—it is so very small and contains no mineral wealth beyond the blackberries. Nor was I comforted when Mrs. Henessy's bird took alarm for the second time and flew clean away from us all, under the belief that it belonged to itself.

In the third place, property makes its owner feel that he ought to do something to it. Yet he isn't sure what. A restlessness comes over him, a vague sense that he has a personality to express—the same sense which, without any vagueness, leads the artist to an act of creation. Sometimes I think I will cut down such trees as remain in the wood, at other times I want to fill up the gaps between them with new trees. Both impulses are pretentious and empty. They are not honest movements towards money-making or beauty. They spring from a foolish desire to express myself and from an inability to enjoy what I have got. Creation, property, enjoyment form a sinister trinity in the human mind. Creation and enjoyment are both very very good, yet they are often unattainable without a material basis, and at such moments property pushes itself in as a substitute, saying, "Accept me instead—I'm good enough for all three." It is not enough. It is, as Shakespeare said of lust, "The expense of spirit in a waste of shame": it is "Before, a joy proposed; behind, a dream." Yet we don't know how to shun it. It is forced on us by our economic system as the alternative to starvation. It is also forced on us by an internal defect in the soul, by the feeling that in property may lie the germs of self-development and of exquisite or heroic deeds. Our life on earth is, and ought to be, material and carnal. But we have not yet learned to manage our materialism and carnality properly; they are still entangled with the desire for ownership, where (in the words of Dante) "Possession is one with loss."

And this brings us to our fourth and final point: the blackberries.

Blackberries are not plentiful in this meager grove, but they are easily seen from the public footpath which traverses it, and all too easily gathered. Foxgloves, too—people will pull up the foxgloves, and ladies of an educational tendency even grub for toadstools to show them on the Monday in class. Other ladies, less educated, roll down the bracken in the arms of their gentlemen friends. There is paper, there are tins. Pray, does my wood belong to me or doesn't it? And, if it does, should I not own it best by allowing no one else to walk there? There is a wood near Lyme Regis, also cursed by a public footpath, where the owner has not hesitated on this point. He has built high stone walls each side of the path, and has spanned it by bridges, so that the public circulate like termites while he gorges on the blackberries unseen. He really does own his wood, this able chap. Dives in Hell did pretty well, but the gulf dividing him from Lazarus could be traversed by vision, and nothing traverses it here.[2] And perhaps I shall come to this in time. I shall wall in and fence out until I really taste the sweets of property. Enormously stout, endlessly avaricious, pseudo-creative, intensely selfish, I shall weave upon my forehead the quadruple crown of possession until those nasty Bolshies come and take it off again and thrust me aside into the outer darkness.

Topic for Discussion and Writing

Much of the strength of the essay lies in its concrete presentation of generalities. Note, for example, that the essay is called "My Wood," but we might say that the general idea of the essay is "The Effect of Property on Owners." Forster gives four effects, chiefly through concrete statements. Put these four effects into four general statements.

Virginia Woolf

Virginia Woolf (1882–1941) was born in London into an upper-middle class literary family. In 1912 she married a writer, and with him she founded the Hogarth Press, whose important publications included not only books by T. S. Eliot but her own novels.
This essay was originally a talk delivered in 1931 to The Women's Service League.

Professions for Women

When your secretary invited me to come here, she told me that your Society is concerned with the employment of women and she suggested that I might tell you something about my own professional experiences. It is true I am a woman; it is true I am

---

[2] According to Christ's parable in Luke 16:19–26, the rich man (unnamed, but traditionally known as Dives) at whose gate the poor man Lazarus had begged was sent to hell, from where he could see Lazarus in heaven. (Editors' note)

employed, but what professional experiences have I had? It is difficult to say. My profession is literature; and in that profession there are fewer experiences for women than in any other, with the exception of the stage—fewer, I mean, that are peculiar to women. For the road was cut many years ago—by Fanny Burney, by Aphra Behn, by Harriet Martineau, by Jane Austen, by George Eliot—many famous women, and many more unknown and forgotten, have been before me, making the path smooth, and regulating my steps. Thus, when I came to write, there were very few material obstacles in my way. Writing was a reputable and harmless occupation. The family peace was not broken by the scratching of a pen. No demand was made upon the family purse. For ten and sixpence one can buy paper enough to write all the plays of Shakespeare—if one has a mind that way. Pianos and models, Paris, Vienna and Berlin, masters and mistresses, are not needed by a writer. The cheapness of writing paper is, of course, the reason why women have succeeded as writers before they have succeeded in the other professions.

But to tell you my story—it is a simple one. You have only got to figure to yourselves a girl in a bedroom with a pen in her hand. She had only to move that pen from left to right—from ten o'clock to one. Then it occurred to her to do what is simple and cheap enough after all—to slip a few of those pages into an envelope, fix a penny stamp in the corner, and drop the envelope in the red box at the corner. It was thus that I became a journalist; and my effort was rewarded on the first day of the following month—a very glorious day it was for me—by a letter from an editor containing a check for one pound ten shillings and sixpence. But to show you how little I deserve to be called a professional woman, how little I know of the struggles and difficulties of such lives, I have to admit that instead of spending that sum upon bread and butter, rent, shoes and stockings, or butcher's bills, I went out and bought a cat—a beautiful cat, a Persian cat, which very soon involved me in bitter disputes with my neighbors.

What could be easier than to write articles and to buy Persian cats with the profits? But wait a moment. Articles have to be about something. Mine, I seem to remember, was about a novel by a famous man. And while I was writing this review, I discovered that if I were going to review books I should need to do battle with a certain phantom. And the phantom was a woman, and when I came to know her better I called her after the heroine of a famous poem, The Angel in the House. It was she who used to come between me and my paper when I was writing reviews. It was she who bothered me and wasted my time and so tormented me that at last I killed her. You who come of a younger and happier generation may not have heard of her—you may not know what I mean by the Angel in the House. I will describe her as shortly as I can. She was intensely sympathetic. She was immensely charming. She was utterly unselfish. She excelled in the difficult arts of family life. She sacrificed herself daily. If there was chicken, she took the leg; if there was a draught she sat in it—in short she was so constituted that she never had a mind or a wish of her own but preferred to sympathize always with the minds and wishes of others. Above all—I need not say it—she was pure. Her purity was supposed to be her chief beauty—her blushes, her great grace. In those days—the last of Queen Victoria—every house had its Angel. And when I came to write I encountered her with the very first words. The shadow of her wings fell on my page; I heard the rustling of her skirts in the room. Directly, that is to say, I took my pen in hand to review that novel by a famous man, she slipped behind me and whispered: "My dear, you are a young woman. You are writing about a book that has been written by a man. Be sympathetic; be tender; flatter; deceive; use all the arts and wiles of our sex. Never let anybody guess that you have a mind of your own. Above all, be pure." And she made as if to guide my pen. I now record the one act for which I take some credit to myself, though the credit rightly belongs to some excellent ancestors of mine who left me a certain sum of money—shall we say five hundred pounds a year?—so that it was not necessary for me to depend solely on charm for my living. I turned upon her and caught her by the throat. I did my best to kill her. My excuse, if I were to be had up in a court of law, would be that I acted in self-defense. Had I not killed her she would have killed me. She would have plucked the heart out of my writing. For, as I found, directly I put pen to paper, you cannot review even a novel without having a mind of your own, without expressing what you think to be the truth about human relations, morality, sex. And all these questions, according to the Angel in the House, cannot be dealt with freely and openly by women; they must charm, they must conciliate, they must—to put it bluntly—tell lies if they are to succeed. Thus, whenever I felt the shadow of her wing or the radiance of her halo upon my page, I took up the inkpot and flung it at her. She died hard. Her fictitious nature was of great assistance to her. It is far harder to kill a phantom than a reality. She was always creeping back when I thought I had despatched her. Though I flatter myself that I killed her in the end, the struggle was severe; it took much time that had better have been spent upon learning Greek grammar; or in roaming the world in search of adventures. But it was a real experience; it was an experience that was bound to befall all women writers at that time. Killing the Angel in the House was part of the occupation of a woman writer.

But to continue my story. The Angel was dead; what then remained? You may say that what remained was a simple and common object—a young woman in a bedroom with an inkpot. In other words, now that she had rid herself of falsehood, that young woman had only to be herself. Ah, but what is "herself"? I mean, what is a woman? I assure you, I do not know. I do not believe that you know. I do not believe that anybody can know until she has expressed herself in all the arts and professions open to human skill. That indeed is one of the reasons why I have come here—out of respect for you, who are in process of showing us by your experiments what a woman is, who are in process of providing us, by your failures and successes, with that extremely important piece of information.

But to continue the story of my professional experiences. I made one pound ten and six by my first review; and I bought a Persian cat with the proceeds. Then I grew ambitious. A Persian cat is all very well, I said; but a Persian cat is not enough. I must have a motor car. And it was thus that I became a novelist—for it is a very strange thing that people will give you a motor car if you will tell them a story. It is a still stranger thing that there is nothing so delightful in the world as telling stories. It is far pleasanter than writing reviews of famous novels. And yet, if I am to obey your secretary and tell you my professional experiences as a novelist, I must tell you about a very strange experience that befell me as a novelist. And to understand it you must try first to imagine a novelist's state of mind. I hope I am not giving away professional secrets if I say that a novelist's chief desire is to be as unconscious as possible. He has to induce in himself a state of perpetual lethargy. He wants life to proceed with the utmost quiet and regularity. He wants to see the same faces, to read the same books, to do the same things day after day, month after month, while he is writing, so that nothing may break the illusion in which he is living—so that nothing may disturb or disquiet the mysterious nosings about, feelings round, darts, dashes and sudden discoveries of that very shy and illusive spirit, the imagination. I suspect that this state is the same both for men and women. Be that as it may, I want you to imagine me writing a novel in a state of trance. I want you to figure to yourselves a girl sitting with a pen in her hand, which for minutes, and indeed for hours, she never dips into the inkpot. The image that comes to my mind when I think of this girl is the image of a fisherman lying sunk in dreams on the verge of a deep lake with a rod held out over the water. She was letting her imagination sweep unchecked round every rock and cranny of the world that lies submerged in the depths of our unconscious being. Now came the experience, the experience that I believe to be far commoner with women writers than with men. The line raced through the girl's fingers. Her imagination had rushed away. It had sought the pools, the depths, the dark places where the largest fish slumber. And then there was a smash. There was an explosion. There was foam and confusion. The imagination had dashed itself against something hard. The girl was roused from her dream. She was indeed in a state of the most acute and difficult distress. To speak without figure she had thought of something, something about the body, about the passions which it was unfitting for her as a woman to say. Men, her reason told her, would be shocked. The consciousness of what men will say of a woman who speaks the truth about her passions had roused her from her artist's state of unconsciousness. She could write no more. The trance was over. Her imagination could work no longer. This I believe to be a very common experience with women writers—they are impeded by the extreme conventionality of the other sex. For though men sensibly allow themselves great freedom in these respects, I doubt that they realize or can control the extreme severity with which they condemn such freedom in women.

These then were two very genuine experiences of my own. These were two of the adventures of my professional life. The first— killing the Angel in the House—I think I solved. She died. But the second, telling the truth about my own experiences as a body, I do not think I solved. I doubt that any woman has solved it yet. The obstacles against her are still immensely powerful—and yet they are very difficult to define. Outwardly, what is simpler than to write books? Outwardly, what obstacles are there for a woman rather than for a man? Inwardly, I think the case is very different; she has still many ghosts to fight, many prejudices to overcome. Indeed it will be a long time still, I think, before a woman can sit down to write a book without finding a phantom to be slain, a rock to be dashed against. And if this is so in literature, the freest of all professions for women, how is it in the new professions which you are now for the first time entering?

Those are the questions that I should like, had I time, to ask you. And indeed, if I have laid stress upon these professional experiences of mine, it is because I believe that they are, though in different forms, yours also. Even when the path is nominally open—when there is nothing to prevent a woman from being a doctor, a lawyer, a civil servant—there are many phantoms and obstacles, as I believe, looming in her way. To discuss and define them is I think of great value and importance; for thus only can the labor be shared, the difficulties be solved. But besides this, it is necessary also to discuss the ends and the aims for which we are fighting, for which we are doing battle with these formidable obstacles. Those aims cannot be taken for granted; they must be perpetually questioned and examined. The whole position, as I see it—here in this hall surrounded by women practising for the first time in history I know not how many different professions—is one of extraordinary interest and importance. You have won rooms of your own in the house hitherto exclusively owned by men. You are able, though not without great labor and effort, to pay the rent. You are earning your five hundred pounds a year. But this freedom is only a beginning; the room is your own, but it is still bare. It has to be furnished; it has to be decorated; it has to be shared. How are you going to furnish it, how are you going to decorate it? With whom are you going to share it, and upon what terms? These, I think, are questions of the utmost importance and interest. For the first time in history you are able to ask them; for the first time you are able to decide for yourselves what the answers should be. Willingly would I stay and discuss those questions and answers—but not tonight. My time is up; and I must cease.

Topics for Discussion and Writing

1. How would you characterize Woolf's tone, especially her attitude toward her subject and herself, in the first paragraph?

2. What do you think Woolf means when she says (paragraph 3): "It is far harder to kill a phantom than a reality"?

3. Woolf conjectures (paragraph 6) that she has not solved the problem of "telling the truth about my own experiences as a body." Is there any reason to believe that today a woman has more difficulty than a man in telling the truth about the experiences of the body?

4. In paragraph 7 Woolf suggests that phantoms as well as obstacles impede women from becoming doctors and lawyers. What might some of these phantoms be?

5. This essay is highly metaphoric. Speaking roughly (or, rather, as pre-cisely as possible), what is the meaning of the metaphor of "rooms" in the final paragraph? What does Woolf mean when she says: "The room is your own, but it is still bare. . . . With whom are you going to share it, and upon what terms?"

6. Evaluate the last two sentences. Are they too abrupt and mechanical? Or do they provide a fitting conclusion to the speech?

George Orwell

George Orwell (1903–50) was the pen name adopted by Eric Blair, an Englishman born in India. Orwell was educated at Eton, in England, but in 1921 he went back to the East and served for five years as a police officer in Burma. He then returned to Europe, doing odd jobs while writing novels and stories. In 1936 he fought in the Spanish Civil War on the side of the Republicans, an experience reported in Homage to Catalonia *(1938). His last years were spent writing in England.*

Shooting an Elephant

In Moulmein, in Lower Burma, I was hated by large num-bers of people—the only time in my life that I have been important enough for this to happen to me. I was sub-divisional police officer of the town, and in an aimless, petty kind of way anti-European feeling was very bitter. No one had the guts to raise a riot, but if a European woman went through the bazaars alone somebody would probably spit betel juice over her dress. As a police officer I was an obvious target and was baited whenever it seemed safe to do so. When a nimble Burman tripped me up on the football field and the referee (another Burman) looked the other way, the crowd yelled with hideous laughter. This happened more than once. In the end the sneering yellow faces of young men that met me every-where, the insults hooted after me when I was at a safe distance, got badly on my nerves. The young Buddhist priests were the worst of all. There were several thousands of them in the town and none of them seemed to have anything to do except stand on street corners and jeer at Europeans.

All this was perplexing and upsetting. For at that time I had already made up my mind that imperialism was an evil thing and the sooner I chucked up my job and got out of it the better. Theoretically—and secretly, of course—I was all for the Burmese and all against their oppressors, the British. As for the job I was doing, I hated it more bitterly than I can perhaps make clear. In a job like that you see the dirty work of Empire at close quarters. The wretched prisoners huddling in the stinking cages of the lock-ups, the grey, cowed faces of the long-term convicts, the scarred buttocks of the men who had been flogged with bamboos—all these oppressed me with an intolerable sense of guilt. But I could get nothing into perspective. I was young and ill-educated and I had had to think out my problems in the utter silence that is imposed on every Englishman in the East. I did not even know that the British Empire is dying, still less did I know that it is a great deal better than the younger empires that are going to supplant it. All I knew was that I was stuck between my hatred of the empire I served and my rage against the evil-spirited little beasts who tried to make my job impossible. With one part of my mind I thought of the British Raj as an unbreakable tyranny, as something clamped down, in *saecula saeculorum*,[1] upon the will of the prostrate peoples; with another part I thought that the greatest joy in the world would be to drive a bayonet into a Buddhist priest's guts. Feelings like these are normal by-products of imperialism; ask any Anglo-Indian official, if you can catch him off duty.

One day something happened which in a roundabout way was enlightening. It was a tiny incident in itself, but it gave me a better glimpse than I had had before of the real nature of imperialism—the real motives for which despotic governments act. Early one morning the sub-inspector at a police station the other end of town rang me up on the 'phone and said that an elephant was ravaging the bazaar. Would I please come and do something about it? I did not know what I could do, but I wanted to see what was happening and I got on to a pony and started out. I took my rifle, an old .44 Winchester and much too small to kill an elephant, but I thought the noise might be useful *in terrorem*.[2] Various Burmans stopped me on the way and told me about the elephant's doings. It was not, of course, a wild elephant, but a tame one which had gone "must." It had been chained up, as tame elephants always are when their attack of "must" is due, but on the previous night it had broken its chain and escaped. Its mahout, the only person who could manage it when it was in that state, had set out in pursuit, but had taken

[1] For world without end. (Editors' note)
[2] As a warning. (Editors' note)

the wrong direction and was now twelve hours' journey away, and in the morning the elephant had suddenly reappeared in the town. The Burmese population had no weapons and were quite helpless against it. It had already destroyed somebody's bamboo hut, killed a cow and raided some fruit-stalls and devoured the stock; also it had met the municipal rubbish van and, when the driver jumped out and took to his heels, had turned the van over and inflicted violences upon it.

The Burmese sub-inspector and some Indian constables were   4 waiting for me in the quarter where the elephant had been seen. It was a very poor quarter, a labyrinth of squalid bamboo huts, thatched with palmleaf, winding all over a steep hillside. I remember that it was a cloudy, stuffy morning at the beginning of the rains. We began questioning the people as to where the elephant had gone and, as usual, failed to get any definite information. That is invariably the case in the East; a story always sounds clear enough at a distance, but the nearer you get to the scene of events the vaguer it becomes. Some of the people said that the elephant had gone in one direction, some said that he had gone in another, some professed not even to have heard of any elephant. I had almost made up my mind that the whole story was a pack of lies, when we heard yells a little distance away. There was a loud, scandalized cry of "Go away, child! Go away this instant!" and an old woman with a switch in her hand came round the corner of a hut, violently shooing away a crowd of naked children. Some more women followed, clicking their tongues and exclaiming; evidently there was something that the children ought not to have seen. I rounded the hut and saw a man's dead body sprawling in the mud. He was an Indian, a black Dravidian coolie, almost naked, and he could not have been dead many minutes. The people said that the elephant had come suddenly upon him round the corner of the hut, caught him with its trunk, put its foot on his back and ground him into the earth. This was the rainy season and the ground was soft, and his face had scored a trench a foot deep and a couple of yards long. He was lying on his belly with arms crucified and head sharply twisted to one side. His face was coated with mud, the eyes wide open, the teeth bared and grinning with an expression of unendurable agony. (Never tell me, by the way, that the dead look peaceful. Most of the corpses I have seen looked devilish.) The friction of the great beast's foot had stripped the skin from his back as neatly as one skins a rabbit. As soon as I saw the dead man I sent an orderly to a friend's house nearby to borrow an elephant rifle. I had already sent back the pony, not wanting it to go mad with fright and throw me if it smelt the elephant.

The orderly came back in a few minutes with a rifle and five cartridges, and meanwhile some Burmans had arrived and told us that the elephant was in the paddy fields below, only a few hundred yards away. As I started forward practically the whole population of the quarter flocked out of the houses and followed me. They had seen the rifle and were all shouting excitedly that I was going to shoot the elephant. They had not shown much interest in the elephant when he was merely ravaging their homes, but it was different now that he was going to be shot. It was a bit of fun to them, as it would be to an English crowd; besides they wanted the meat. It made me vaguely uneasy. I had no intention of shooting the elephant—I had merely sent for the rifle to defend myself if necessary—and it is always unnerving to have a crowd following you. I marched down the hill, looking and feeling a fool, with the rifle over my shoulder and an evergrowing army of people jostling at my heels. At the bottom, when you got away from the huts, there was a metalled road and beyond that a miry waste of paddy fields a thousand yards across, not yet ploughed but soggy from the first rains and dotted with coarse grass. The elephant was standing eight yards from the road, his left side towards us. He took not the slightest notice of the crowd's approach. He was tearing up bunches of grass, beating them against his knees to clean them and stuffing them into his mouth.

I had halted on the road. As soon as I saw the elephant I knew with perfect certainty that I ought not to shoot him. It is a serious matter to shoot a working elephant—it is comparable to destroying a huge and costly piece of machinery—and obviously one ought not to do it if it can possibly be avoided. And at that distance, peacefully eating, the elephant looked no more dangerous than a cow. I thought then and I think now that his attack of "must" was already passing off; in which case he would merely wander harmlessly about until the mahout came back and caught him. Moreover, I did not in the least want to shoot him. I decided that I would watch him for a little while to make sure that he did not turn savage again, and then go home.

But at that moment, I glanced round at the crowd that had followed me. It was an immense crowd, two thousand at the least and growing every minute. It blocked the road for a long distance on either side. I looked at the sea of yellow faces above the garish clothes—faces all happy and excited over this bit of fun, all certain that the elephant was going to be shot. They were watching me as they would watch a conjuror about to perform a trick. They did not like me, but with the magical rifle in my hands I was momentarily worth watching. And suddenly I realized that I should have to shoot the elephant after all. The people expected it of me and I had got to do it; I could feel their two thousand wills pressing me forward, irresistibly. And it was at this moment, as I stood there with the rifle in my hands, that I first grasped the hollowness, the futility of the white man's dominion in the East. Here was I, the white man with his gun, standing in front of the unarmed native crowd— seemingly the leading actor of the piece; but in reality I was only an absurd puppet pushed to and fro by the will of those yellow faces behind. I perceived in this moment that when the white man turns tyrant it is his own freedom that he destroys. He becomes a sort of hollow, posing dummy, the conventionalized figure of a sahib. For it is the condition of his rule that he shall spend his life in trying to impress the "natives," and so in every crisis he has got to do what the "natives" expect of him. He wears a mask, and his face grows to fit it. I had got to shoot the elephant. I had committed myself to doing it when I sent for the rifle. A sahib has got to act like a sahib; he has got to appear resolute, to know his own mind and do definite things. To come all that way, rifle in hand, with two thousand people marching at my heels, and then to trail feebly away, having done nothing—no, that was impossible. The crowd would laugh at me. And my whole life, every white man's life in the East, was one long struggle not to be laughed at.

But I did not want to shoot the elephant. I watched him beating his bunch of grass against his knees, with that preoccupied grandmotherly air that elephants have. It seemed to me that it would be murder to shoot him. At that age I was not squeamish about killing animals, but I had never shot an elephant and never wanted to. (Somehow it always seems worse to kill a *large* animal.) Besides, there was the beast's owner to be considered. Alive, the elephant was worth at least a hundred pounds; dead, he would only be worth the value of his tusks, five pounds, possibly. But I had got to act quickly. I turned to some experienced-looking Burmans who had been there when we arrived, and asked them how the elephant had been behaving. They all said the same thing: he took no notice of you if you left him alone, but he might charge if you went too close to him.

It was perfectly clear to me what I ought to do. I ought to walk up to within, say, twenty-five yards of the elephant and test his behavior. If he charged, I could shoot; if he took no notice of me, it would be safe to leave him until the mahout came back. But also I knew that I was going to do no such thing. I was a poor shot with a rifle and the ground was soft mud into which one would sink at every step. If the elephant charged and I missed him, I should have about as much chance as a toad under a steam-roller. But even then I was not thinking particularly of my own skin, only of the watchful yellow faces behind. For at that moment, with the crowd watching me, I was not afraid in the ordinary sense, as I would have been if I had been alone. A white man mustn't be frightened in front of "natives"; and so, in general, he isn't frightened. The sole thought in my mind was that if anything went wrong those two thousand Burmans would see me pursued, caught, trampled on and reduced to a grinning corpse like that Indian up the hill. And if that happened it was quite probable that some of them would laugh. That would never do. There was only one alternative. I shoved the cartridges into the magazine and lay down on the road to get a better aim.

The crowd grew very still, and a deep, low, happy sigh, as of people who see the theatre curtain go up at last, breathed from innumerable throats. They were going to have their bit of fun after all. The rifle was a beautiful German thing with cross-hair sights. I did not then know that in shooting an elephant one would shoot to cut an imaginary bar running from ear-hole to ear-hole. I ought, therefore, as the elephant was sideways on, to have aimed straight at his earhole; actually I aimed several inches in front of this, thinking the brain would be further forward.

When I pulled the trigger I did not hear the bang or feel the kick—one never does when a shot goes home—but I heard the devilish roar of glee that went up from the crowd. In that instant, in too short a time, one would have thought, even for the bullet to get there, a mysterious, terrible change had come over the elephant. He neither stirred nor fell, but every line of his body had altered. He looked suddenly stricken, shrunken, immensely old, as though the frightful impact of the bullet had paralysed him without knocking him down. At last, after what seemed a long time—it might have been five seconds, I dare say—he sagged flabbily to his knees. His mouth slobbered. An enormous senility seemed to have settled upon him. One could have imagined him thousands of years old. I fired again into the same spot. At the second shot he did not collapse but climbed with desperate slowness to his feet and stood weakly upright, with legs sagging and head drooping. I fired a third time.

That was the shot that did for him. You could see the agony of it jolt his whole body and knock the last remnant of strength from his legs. But in falling he seemed for a moment to rise, for as his hind legs collapsed beneath him he seemed to tower upward like a huge rock toppling, his trunk reaching skywards like a tree. He trumpeted, for the first and only time. And then down he came, his belly towards me, with a crash that seemed to shake the ground even where I lay.

I got up. The Burmans were already racing past me across the mud. It was obvious that the elephant would never rise again, but he was not dead. He was breathing very rhythmically with long rattling gasps, his great mound of a side painfully rising and falling. His mouth was wide open. I could see far down into caverns of pale pink throat. I waited a long time for him to die, but his breathing did not weaken. Finally I fired my two remaining shots into the spot where I thought his heart must be. The thick blood welled out of him like red velvet, but still he did not die. His body did not even jerk when the shots hit him, the tortured breathing continued without a pause. He was dying, very slowly and in great agony, but in some world remote from me where not even a bullet could damage him further. I felt I had to put an end to that dreadful noise. It seemed dreadful to see the great beast lying there, powerless to move and yet powerless to die, and not even to be able to finish him. I sent back for my small rifle and poured shot after shot into his heart and down his throat. They seemed to make no impression. The tortured gasps continued as steadily as the ticking of a clock.

In the end I could not stand it any longer and went away. I heard later that it took him half an hour to die. Burmans were bringing dahs and baskets even before I left, and I was told they had stripped his body almost to the bones by the afternoon.

Afterwards, of course, there were endless discussions about the shooting of the elephant. The owner was furious, but he was only an Indian and could do nothing. Besides, legally I had done the right thing, for a mad elephant has to be killed, like a mad dog, if its owner fails to control it. Among the Europeans opinion was divided. The older men said I was right, the younger men said it was a damn shame to shoot an elephant for killing a coolie, because the elephant was worth more than any damn Coringhee coolie. And afterwards I was very glad that the coolie had been killed; it put me legally in the right and it gave me sufficient pretext for shooting the elephant. I often wondered whether any of the others grasped that I had done it solely to avoid looking a fool.

Topics for Discussion and Writing

1. How does Orwell characterize himself at the time of the events he describes? What evidence in the essay suggests that he wrote it some years later?

2. Orwell says that the incident was "enlightening." What does he mean? Picking up this clue, state in a sentence or two the main point of the essay.

3. Compare Orwell's description of the dead coolie (page 839) with his description of the death of the elephant (pages 842–43). Why does Orwell devote more space to the death of the elephant?

4. How would you describe the tone of the last paragraph, particularly of the last two sentences? Do you find the paragraph an effective conclusion? Explain.

May Sarton

May Sarton, born in Belgium in 1912, was brought to the United States in 1916; in 1924 she became a citizen. A teacher of writing and a distinguished writer herself, she has received numerous awards for her fiction, poetry, and essays.

The Rewards of Living a Solitary Life

The other day an acquaintance of mine, a gregarious and charming man, told me he had found himself unexpectedly alone in New York for an hour or two between appointments. He went to the Whitney and spent the "empty" time looking at things in solitary bliss. For him it proved to be a shock nearly as great as falling in love to discover that he could enjoy himself so much alone.

What had he been afraid of, I asked myself? That, suddenly alone, he would discover that he bored himself, or that there was, quite simply, no self there to meet? But having taken the plunge, he is now on the brink of adventure; he is about to be launched into his own inner space, space as immense, unexplored, and sometimes frightening as outer space to the astronaut. His every perception will come to him with a new freshness and, for a time, seem startlingly original. For anyone who can see things for himself with a naked eye becomes, for a moment or two, something of a genius.

With another human being present vision becomes double vision, inevitably. We are busy wondering, what does my companion see or think of this, and what do I think of it? The original impact gets lost, or diffused.

"Music I heard with you was more than music."[1] Exactly. And therefore music *itself* can only be heard alone. Solitude is the salt of personhood. It brings out the authentic flavor of every experience.

"Alone one is never lonely: the spirit adventures, walking / In   4 a quiet garden, in a cool house, abiding single there."

Loneliness is most acutely felt with other people, for with others, even with a lover sometimes, we suffer from our differences of taste, temperament, mood. Human intercourse often demands that we soften the edge of perception, or withdraw at the very instant of personal truth for fear of hurting, or of being inappropriately present, which is to say naked, in a social situation. Alone we can afford to be wholly whatever we are, and to feel whatever we feel absolutely. That is a great luxury!

For me the most interesting thing about a solitary life, and mine has been that for the last twenty years, is that it becomes increasingly rewarding. When I can wake up and watch the sun rise over the ocean, as I do most days, and know that I have an entire day ahead, uninterrupted, in which to write a few pages, take a walk with my dog, lie down in the afternoon for a long think (why does one think better in a horizontal position?), read and listen to music, I am flooded with happiness.

I am lonely only when I am overtired, when I have worked too long without a break, when for the time being I feel empty and need filling up. And I am lonely sometimes when I come back home after a lecture trip, when I have seen a lot of people and talked a lot, and am full to the brim with experience that needs to be sorted out.

Then for a little while the house feels huge and empty, and I   8 wonder where my self is hiding. It has to be recaptured slowly by watering the plants, perhaps, and looking again at each one as though it were a person, by feeding the two cats, by cooking a meal.

It takes a while, as I watch the surf blowing up in fountains at the end of the field, but the moment comes when the world falls away, and the self emerges again from the deep unconscious, bringing back all I have recently experienced to be explored and slowly understood, when I can converse again with my hidden powers, and so grow, and so be renewed, till death do us part.

[1] "Music . . . music" a line from Conrad Aiken's *Bread and Music* (1914)

Topics for Discussion and Writing

1. The essay opens with an anecdote about an acquaintance of the author's. Why are we told at the outset that he is "a gregarious and charming man"?

2. In paragraph 2 Sarton compares inner space with outer space. And in paragraph 3 she writes, "Solitude is the salt of personhood." How do you interpret these metaphors? How do they enrich her main point, that solitude is rewarding?

3. What does Sarton mean when in her first paragraph she says, "Anyone who can see things for himself with a naked eye becomes, for a moment or two, something of a genius"? Does your own experience confirm her comment? Explain.

4. What phrase in the last paragraph connects the ending with the first paragraph?

5. Drawing on Sarton's essay, in a paragraph explain the distinction between being "alone" and being "lonely."

6. In an essay of about 500 words explain the difference between loving and being in love.

Joan Didion

Joan Didion, a fifth-generation Californian, was born in Sacramento in 1934. In 1956 she was graduated from the University of California, Berkeley, and in the same year she published her first story and won a contest sponsored by Vogue *magazine. Since then she has written essays, stories, screenplays, and novels. All of her writing, she says, is an "act of saying I, of imposing oneself upon other people, of saying* listen to me, see it my way, change your mind."*

On Going Home

I am home for my daughter's first birthday. By "home" I do not mean the house in Los Angeles where my husband and I and the baby live, but the place where my family is, in the Central Valley of California. It is a vital although troublesome distinction. My husband likes my family but is uneasy in their house, because once there I fall into their ways, which are difficult, oblique, deliberately inarticulate, not my husband's ways. We live in dusty houses ("D-U-S-T," he once wrote with his finger on surfaces all over the house, but no one noticed it) filled with mementos quite without value to him (what could the Canton dessert plates mean to him?

how could he have known about the assay scales, why should he care if he did know?), and we appear to talk exclusively about people we know who have been committed to mental hospitals, about people we know who have been booked on drunk-driving charges, and about property, particularly about property, land, price per acre and C-2 zoning and assessments and freeway access. My brother does not understand my husband's inability to perceive the advantage in the rather common real-estate transaction known as "sale-leaseback," and my husband in turn does not understand why so many of the people he hears about in my father's house have recently been committed to mental hospitals or booked on drunk-driving charges. Nor does he understand that when we talk about sale-leasebacks and right-of-way condemnations we are talking in code about the things we like best, the yellow fields and the cottonwoods and the rivers rising and falling and the mountain roads closing when the heavy snow comes in. We miss each other's points, have another drink and regard the fire. My brother refers to my husband, in his presence, as "Joan's husband." Marriage is the classic betrayal.

Or perhaps it is not any more. Sometimes I think that those of us who are now in our thirties were born into the last generation to carry the burden of "home," to find in family life the source of all tension and drama. I had by all objective accounts a "normal" and a "happy" family situation, and yet I was almost thirty years old before I could talk to my family on the telephone without crying after I had hung up. We did not fight. Nothing was wrong. And yet some nameless anxiety colored the emotional charges between me and the place that I came from. The question of whether or not you could go home again was a very real part of the sentimental and largely literary baggage with which we left home in the fifties; I suspect that it is irrelevant to the children born of the fragmentation after World War II. A few weeks ago in a San Francisco bar I saw a pretty young girl on crystal take off her clothes and dance for the cash prize in an "amateur-topless" contest. There was no particular sense of moment about this, none of the effect of romantic degradation, of "dark journey," for which my generation strives so assiduously. What sense could that girl possibly make of, say, *Long Day's Journey into Night*? Who is beside the point?

That I am trapped in this particular irrelevancy is never more apparent to me than when I am home. Paralyzed by the neurotic lassitude engendered by meeting one's past at every turn, around every corner, inside every cupboard, I go aimlessly from room to room. I decide to meet it head-on and clean out a drawer, and I spread the contents on the bed. A bathing suit I wore the summer I was seventeen. A letter of rejection from *The Nation,* an aerial photograph of the site for a shopping center my father did not build in 1954. Three teacups handpainted with cabbage roses and signed "E. M.," my grandmother's initials. There is no final solution for letters of rejection from *The Nation* and teacups hand-painted in 1900. Nor is there any answer to snapshots of one's grandfather as a young man on skis, surveying around Donner Pass in the year 1910. I smooth out the snapshot and look into his face, and do and do not see my own. I close the drawer, and have another cup of coffee with my mother. We get along very well, veterans of a guerrilla war we never understood.

Days pass. I see no one. I come to dread my husband's evening 4 call, not only because he is full of news of what by now seems to me our remote life in Los Angeles, people he has seen, letters which require attention, but because he asks what I have been doing, suggests uneasily that I get out, drive to San Francisco or Berkeley. Instead I drive across the river to a family graveyard. It has been vandalized since my last visit and the monuments are broken, overturned in the dry grass. Because I once saw a rattlesnake in the grass I stay in the car and listen to a country-and-Western station. Later I drive with my father to a ranch he has in the foothills. The man who runs his cattle on it asks us to roundup, a week from Sunday, and although I know that I will be in Los Angeles I say, in the oblique way my family talks, that I will come. Once home I mention the broken monuments in the graveyard. My mother shrugs.

I go to visit my great-aunts. A few of them think now that I am my cousin, or their daughter who died young. We recall an anecdote about a relative last seen in 1948, and they ask if I still like living in New York City. I have lived in Los Angeles for three years, but I say that I do. The baby is offered a horehound drop, and I am slipped a dollar bill "to buy a treat." Questions train off, answers are abandoned, the baby plays with the dust motes in a shaft of afternoon sun.

It is time for the baby's birthday party; a white cake, strawberry-marshmallow ice cream, a bottle of champagne saved from another party. In the evening, after she has gone to sleep, I kneel beside the crib and touch her face, where it is pressed against the slats, with mine. She is an open and trusting child, unprepared for and unaccustomed to the ambushes of family life, and perhaps it is just as well that I can offer her little of that life. I would like to give her more. I would like to promise her that she will grow up with a sense of her cousins and of rivers and of her great-grandmother's teacups, would like to pledge her a picnic on a river with fried chicken and her hair uncombed, would like to give her *home* for her birthday, but we live differently now and I can promise her nothing like that. I give her a xylophone and a sundress from Madeira, and promise to tell her a funny story.

Topics for Discussion and Writing

1. Didion reveals that members of her family are difficult, inarticulate, poor housekeepers, and so forth. Do you find these revelations about her family distasteful? Would you mind seeing in print similarly unflattering things you had written about your own family? How might such revelations be justified? Are they justified in this essay?

2. Summarize the point of paragraph 2. Do you find Didion's speculations about the difference between her generation and succeeding generations meaningful? Are they accurate for your generation?

3. Do you think that growing up necessarily involves estrangement from one's family?

Alice Walker

Alice Walker was born in 1944 in Eatonton, Georgia, where her parents eked out a living as sharecroppers and dairy farmers; her mother also worked as a domestic. (In a collection of essays, In Search of Our Mothers' Gardens [1984], Walker celebrates women who, like her mother, passed on a "respect for the possibilities [of life] — and the will to grasp them.") Walker attended Spelman College in Atlanta, and in 1965 finished her undergraduate work at Sarah Lawrence College near New York City. She then became active in the welfare rights movement in New York and in the voter registration movement in Georgia. Later she taught writing and literature in Mississippi, at Jackson State College and Tougaloo College, and at Wellesley College, the University of Massachusetts, and Yale University.

Walker has written essays, poetry, and fiction. Her best-known novel, The Color Purple (1982), won a Pulitzer Prize and the National Book Award. She has said that her chief concern is "exploring the oppressions, the insanities, the loyalties, and the triumphs of black women."

In Search of Our Mothers' Gardens

I

I *described her own nature and temperament. Told how they needed a larger life for their expression. . . . I pointed out that in lieu of proper channels, her emotions had overflowed into paths and dissipated them. I talked beautifully I thought, about an art that would be born, an art that would open the way for women the likes of her. I asked her to hope, and build up an inner life against the coming of that day. . . . I sang, with a strange quiver in my voice, a promise song.*

—"Avey," Jean Toomer, Cane

The poet speaking to a prostitute who falls asleep while he's talking—

When the poet Jean Toomer walked through the South in the early twenties, he discovered a curious thing: Black women whose spirituality was so intense, so deep, so *unconscious*, they were themselves unaware of the richness they held. They stumbled blindly through their lives: creatures so abused and mutilated in body, so dimmed and confused by pain, that they considered themselves unworthy even of hope. In the selfless abstractions their bodies became to the men who used them, they became more than "sexual objects," more even than mere women: they became Saints. Instead of being perceived as whole persons, their bodies became shrines; what was thought to be their minds became temples suitable for worship. These crazy "Saints" stared out at the world, wildly, like lunatics—or quietly, like suicides; and the "God" that was in their gate was as mute as a great stone.

Who were these "Saints"? These crazy, loony, pitiful women?

Some of them without a doubt, were our mothers and grand-   4
mothers.

In the still heat of the post-Reconstruction South, this is how they seemed to Jean Toomer: exquisite butterflies trapped in an evil honey, toiling away their lives in an era, a century, that did not acknowledge them, except as "the *mule* of the world." They dreamed dreams that no one knew—not even themselves, in any coherent fashion—and saw visions no one could understand. They wandered or sat about the countryside crooning lullabies to ghosts, and drawing the mother of Christ in charcoal on courthouse walls.

They forced their minds to desert their bodies and their striving spirits sought to rise, the frail whirlwinds from the hard red clay. And when those frail whirlwinds fell, in scattered particles, upon the ground, no one mourned. Instead, men lit candles to celebrate the emptiness that remained, as people do who enter a beautiful but vacant space to resurrect a God.

Our mothers and grandmothers, some of them: moving to music not yet written. And they waited.

They waited for a day when the unknown thing that was in them 8 would be made known; but guessed, somehow in their darkness, that on the day of their revelation they would be long dead. Therefore to Toomer they walked, and even ran, in slow motion. For they were going nowhere immediate, and the future was not yet within their grasp. And men took our mothers and grandmothers, "but got no pleasure from it." So complex was their passion and their calm.

To Toomer, they lay vacant and fallow as autumn fields, with harvest time never in sight: and he saw them enter loveless marriages, without joy; and become prostitutes, without resistance; and become mothers of children without fulfillment.

For these grandmothes and mothers of ours were not "Saints," but Artists; driven to a numb and bleeding madness by the springs of creativity in them for which there was no release. They were Creators, who lived lives of spiritual waste, because they were so rich in spirituality—which is the basis of Art—that the strain of enduring their unused and unwanted talent drove them insane. Throwing away this spirituality was their pathetic attempts to lighten the soul to a weight their work-worn, sexually abused bodies could bear.

What did it mean for a Black woman to be an artist in our grandmothers' time? In our great-grandmothers' day? It is a question with an answer cruel enough to stop the blood.

Did you have a genius of a great-great-grandmother who died 12 under some ignorant and depraved white overseer's lash? Or was she required to bake biscuits for a lazy backwater tramp, when she cried out in her soul to paint watercolors of sunsets, or the rain falling on the green and peaceful pasturelands? Or was her body broken and forced to bear children (who were more often that not sold away from her)—eight, ten, fifteen, twenty children—when her one joy was the thought of modeling heroic figures of Rebellion, in stone or clay?

How was the creativity of the Black woman kept alive, year after year and century after century, when for most of the years Black people have been in America, it was a punishable crime for a Black person to read or write? And the freedom to paint, to sculpt, to expand the mind with action, did not exist. Consider, if you can bear to imagine it, what might have been the result of singing, too, had been forbidden by law. Listen to the voices of Bessie Smith, Billie Holiday, Nina Simone, Roberta Flack, and Aretha Franklin, among others, and imagine those voices muzzled for life. Then you may begin to comprehend the lives of our "crazy," "Sainted" mothers and grandmothers. The agony of the lives of women who might have been Poets, Novelists, Essayists, and Short Story Writers (over a period of centuries), who died with their real gifts stifled within them.

And, if this were the end of the story, we would have cause to cry out in my paraphrase of Okot p'Bitek's great poem:

> O, my clanswomen
> Let us call cry together!
> Come,
> Let us mourn the death of our mother,
> The death of a Queen
> The ash that was produced
> By a great fire!
> O this homestead is utterly dead
> Close the gates
> With *lacari* thorns,
> For our mother
> The creator of the Stool is lost!
> And all the young women
> Have perished in the wilderness.[1]

But this is not the end of the story, for all the young women—our mothers and grandmothers, *ourselves*—have not perished in the wilderness. And if we ask ourselves why, and search for and find the answer, we will know beyond all efforts to erase it from our minds, just exactly who, and of what, we Black American women are.

One example, perhaps the most pathetic, most misunderstood one, can provide a backdrop for our mothers' work: Phillis Wheatley, a slave in the 1700s. 16

---

[1] Okot p'Bitek, *Song of Lawino: An Africa Lament* (Nairobi: East African Publishing House, 1966)

Virginia Woolf, in her book, *A Room of One's Own*, wrote that in order for a woman to write fiction she must have two things, certainly: a room of her own (with a key and lock) and enough money to support herself.

What then are we to make of Phillis Wheatley, a slave, who owned not even herself? This sickly, frail, Black girl who required a servant of her own at times—her health was so precarious—and who, had she been white, would have been easily considered the intellectual superior of all the women and most of the men in the society of her day.

Virginia Woolf wrote further, speaking of course not of our Phillis, that "any woman born with a great gift in the sixteenth century [insert *eighteenth century*, insert *Black woman*, insert *born or made a slave*] would certainly have gone crazed, shot herself, or ended her days in some lonely cottage outside the village, half witch, half wizard [insert *Saint*,] feared and mocked at. For it needs little skill and psychology to be sure that a highly gifted girl who had tried to use her gift for poetry would have been so thwarted and hindered by contrary instincts [add *chains, guns, the lash, the ownership of one's body by someone else, submission to an alien religion,*] that she must have lost her health and sanity to a certainty."

The key words, as they relate to Phillis, are "contrary instincts." 20 For when we read the poetry of Phillis Wheatley—as when we read the novels of Nella Larsen or the oddly false-sounding autobiography of that freest of all Black women writers, Zora Hurston— evidence of "contrary instincts" is everywhere. Her loyalties were completely divided, as was, without question, her mind.

But how could this be otherwise? Captured at seven, a slave of wealthy, doting whites who instilled in her the "savagery" of the Africa they "rescued" her from . . . one wonders if she was even able to remember her homeland as she had known it, or as it really was.

Yet, because she did try to use her gift for poetry in a world that made her a slave, she was "so thwarted and hindered by . . . contrary instincts that she . . . lost her health. . . . " In the last years of her brief life, burdened not only with the need to express her gift but also with a penniless, friendless "freedom" and several small children for whom she was forced to do strenuous work to feed, she lost her health, certainly. Suffering from malnutrition and neglect and who knows what mental agonies, Phillis Wheately died.

So torn by "contrary instincts" was Black, kidnapped, enslaved Phillis that her description of "the Goddess"—as she poetically called the Liberty she did not have—is ironically, cruelly humorous. And, in fact, has held Phillis up to ridicule for more than a century. It is usually read prior to hanging Phillis's memory as that of a fool. She wrote:

> The Goddess comes, she moves divinely fair,
> Olive and laurel binds her *golden* hair:
> Wherever shines this native of the skies,
> Unnumber'd charms and recent graces rise.

[Emphasis mine]

It is obvious that Phillis, the slave, combed the "Goddess's" hair 24 every morning; prior, perhaps, to bringing in the milk, or fixing her mistress's lunch. She took her imagery from one one thing she saw elevated above all others.

With the benefit of hindsight we ask, "How could she?"

But at last, Phillis, we understand. No more snickering when your stiff, struggling, ambivalent lines are forced on us. We know now that you were not an idiot nor a traitor; only a sickly little Black girl, snatched from your home and country and made a slave; a woman who still struggled to sing the song that was your gift, although in a land of barbarians who praised you for your bewildered tongue. It is not so much what you sang, as that you kept alive, in so many of our ancestors, *the notion of song*.

II

Black women are called, in the folklore that so aptly identifies one's status in society, "the *mule* of the world," because we have been handed the burdens that everyone else—*everyone* else—refused to carry. We have been called "Matriarchs," "Superwomen," and "Mean and Evil Bitches." Not to mention "Castrators" and "Sapphire's Mama." When we have pleaded for understanding, our character has been distorted; when we have asked for simple caring, we have been handed empty inspirational appellations, then stuck in the farthest corner. When we have asked for love, we have been given children. In short, even our plainer gifts, our labors of fidelity and love, have been knocked down our throats. To be an Artist and a Black woman, even today, lowers our status in many respects, rather than raises it: and yet, Artists we will be.

Therefore we must fearlessly pull out of ourselves and look 28 at and identify with our lives the living creativity some of our great-grandmothers were not allowed to know. I stress *some* of them because it is well known that the majority of our great-grandmothers knew, even without "knowing" it, the reality of their spirituality, even if they didn't recognize it beyond what happened in the singing at church—and they never had any intention of giving it up.

How they did it: those millions of Black women who were not Phillis Wheatley, or Lucy Terry or Frances Harper or Zora Hurston or Nella Larsen or Bessie Smith—nor Elizabeth Catlett, nor Katherine Dunham, either—brings me to the title of this essay, "In Search of Our Mothers' Gardens," which is a personal account that is yet shared, in its theme and its meaning, by all of us. I found, while thinking about the far-reaching world of the creative Black woman, that often the truest answer to a question that really matters can be found very close.

In the late 1920s my mother ran away from home to marry my father. Marriage, if not running away, was expected of seventeen-year-old girls. By the time she was twenty, she had two children and was pregnant with a third. Five children later, I was born. And this is how I came to know my mother: she seemed a large, soft, loving-eyed woman who was rarely impatient in our home. Her quick, violent temper was on view only a few times a year, when she battled with the white landlord who had the misfortune to suggest to her that her children did not need to go to school.

She made all the clothes we wore, even my brothers' overalls. She made all the towels and sheets we used. She spent the summers canning vegetables and fruits. She spent the winter evenings making quilts enough to cover all our beds.

During the "working" day, she labored beside—not behind— 32 my father in the fields. Her day began before sunup, and did not end until late at night. There was never a moment for her to sit down, undisturbed, to unravel her own private thoughts; never a time free from interruption—by work or the noisy inquiries of her many children. And yet, it is to my mother—and all our mothers who were not famous—that I went in search of the secret of what has fed that muzzled and often mutilated, but vibrant, creative spirit that the Black woman has inherited, and that pops out in wild and unlikely places to this day.

But when, you will ask, did my overworked mother have time to know or care about feeding the creative spirit?

The answer is so simple that many of us have spent years discovering it. We have constantly looked high, when we should have looked high—and low.

For example: in the Smithsonian Institution in Washington, D.C., there hangs a quilt unlike any other in the world. In fanciful, inspired, and yet simple and identifiable figures, it portrays the story of the Crucifixion. It is considered rare, beyond price. Though it follows no known pattern of quiltmaking, and though it is made of bits and pieces of worthless rags, it is obviously the work of a person of powerful imagination and deep spiritual feelings. Below this quilt I saw a note that says it was made by "an anonymous Black woman in Alabama, a hundred years ago."

If we could locate this "anonymous" Black woman from 36 Alabama, she would turn out to be one of our grandmothers—an artist who left her mark in the only materials she could afford, and in the only medium her position in society allowed her to use.

As Virginia Woolf wrote further, in *A Room of One's Own*:

"Yet genius of a sort must have existed among women as it must have existed among the working class. [Change this to *slaves* and *the wives and daughters of sharecroppers*.] Now and again an Emily Brontë or a Robert Burns [change this to *a Zora Hurston or a Richard Wright*] blazes out and proves its presence. But certainly it never got itself on to paper. When, however, one reads of a witch being ducked, of a woman possessed by devils [or *Sainthood*], of a wise woman selling herbs [our rootworkers], or even a very remarkable man who had a mother, then I think we are on the track of a suppressed poet, of some mute and inglorious Jane Austen. . . . Indeed, I would venture to guess that Anon, who wrote so many poems without singing them, was often a woman. . . ."

And so our mothers and grandmothers have, more often than not anonymously, handed on the creative spark, the seed of the flower they themselves never hoped to see: or like a sealed letter they could not plainly read.

And so it is, certainly, with my own mother. Unlike Ma Rainey's 40 songs, which retained their creator's name even while blasting forth from Bessie Smith's mouth, no song or poem will bear my mother's name. Yet so many of the stories that I write, that we all write, are my mother's stories. Only recently did I fully realize this: that through years of listening to my mother's stories of her life, I have absorbed not only the stories themselves, but something of the manner in which she spoke, something of the urgency that involves the knowledge that her stories—like her life—must be recorded. It is probably for this reason that so much of what I have written is about characters whose counterparts in real life are so much older than I am.

But the telling of these stories, which came from my mother's lips as naturally as breathing, was not the only way my mother showed herself as an artist. For stories, too, were subject to being distracted, to dying without conclusion. Dinners must be started, and cotton must be gathered before the big rains. The artist that was and is my mother showed itself to me only after many years. This is what I finally noticed:

Like Mem, a character in *The Third Life of Grange Copeland,* my mother adorned with flowers whatever shabby house we were forced to live in. And not just your typical straggly country stand of zinnias, either. She planted ambitious gardens — and still does — with over fifty different varieties of plants that bloom profusely from early March until later November. Before she left home for the fields, she watered her flowers, chopped up the grass, and laid out new beds. When she returned from the fields she might divide clumps of bulbs, dig a cold pit, uproot and replant roses, or prune branches from her taller bushes or trees — until night came and it was too dark to see.

Whatever she planted grew as if by magic, and her fame as a grower of flowers spread over three counties. Because of her creativity with her flowers, even my memories of poverty are seen through a screen of blooms — sunflowers, petunias, roses, dahlias, forsythia, spirea, delphiniums, verbena . . . and on and on.

And I remember people coming to my mother's yard to be given cuttings from her flowers; I hear again the praise showered on her because whatever rocky soil she landed on, she turned into a garden. A garden so brilliant with colors, so original in its design, so magnificient with life and creativity, that to this day people drive by our house in Georgia — perfect strangers and imperfect strangers — and ask to stand or walk among my mother's art. 44

I notice that it is only when my mother is working in her flowers that she is radiant, almost to the point of being invisible — except as Creator: hand and eye. She is involved in work her soul must have. Ordering the universe in the image of her personal conception of Beauty.

Her face, as she prepares the Art that is her gift, is a legacy of respect she leaves to me, for all that illuminates and cherishes life. She had handed down respect for the possibilities — and the will to grasp them.

For her, so hindered and intruded upon in so many ways, being an artist has still been a daily part of her life. This ability to hold on, even in very simple ways, is work Black women have done for a very long time.

This poem is not enough, but it is something, for the woman   48
who literally covered the holes in our walls with sunflowers:

They were women then
My mama's generation
Husky of voice—Stout of
Step
With fists as well as
Hands
How they battered down
Doors
And ironed
Starched white
Shirts
How they led
Armies
Headragged Generals
Across mined
Fields
Booby-trapped
Ditches
To discover books
Desks
A place for us
How they knew what we
Must know
Without knowing a page
Of it
Themselves.

Guided by my heritage of love and beauty and a respect for
strength—in search of my mother's garden, I found my own.

And perhaps in Africa over two hundred years ago, there was
just such a mother; perhaps she painted vivid and daring decorations in oranges and yellows and greens on the walls of her hut;
perhaps she sang—in a voice like Roberta Flack's—*sweetly* over the
compounds of her village; perhaps she wove the most stunning mats
or told the most ingenious stories of all the village story-tellers.
Perhaps she was herself a poet—though only her daughter's name
is signed to the poems that we know.

Perhaps Phillis Wheatley's mother was also an artist.

Perhaps in more than Phillis Wheatley's biological life is her   52
mother's signature made clear.

Topics for Discussion and Writing

1. Can you justify the great shift in tone between "their gaze was as mute as a great stone" and "loony" (second and third paragraphs)? If so, how?
2. Explain Walker's assertion (paragraph 10) that "these grandmothers and mothers of ours were not 'Saints,' but Artists." In this view, what are the qualities of an artist?
3. Pick out two or three sentences that strike you as especially interesting, either because of what they say or because of the way they say it (or both), and try to account for their appeal.
4. Explain the last sentence of the essay.
5. Outline the organization of this essay; that is, list in order the main topics and then explain the relationships between these parts. Then, in one or two sentences, summarize Walker's thesis or argument.

Peter Singer

Peter Singer teaches philosophy at Monash University in Melbourne, Australia. This essay originally appeared, in 1973, as a review of Animals, Men and Morals, *edited by Stanley and Roslind Godlovitch and John Harris.*

Animal Liberation

I

We are familiar with Black Liberation, Gay Liberation, and a variety of other movements. With Women's Liberation some thought we had come to the end of the road. Discrimination on the basis of sex, it has been said, is the last form of discrimination that is universally accepted and practiced without pretense, even in those liberal circles which have long prided themselves on their freedom from racial discrimination. But one should always be wary of talking of "the last remaining form of discrimination." If we have learned anything from the liberation movements, we should have learned how difficult it is to be aware of the ways in which we discriminate until they are forcefully pointed out to us. A liberation movement demands an expansion of our moral horizons, so that practices that were previously regarded as natural and inevitable are now seen as intolerable.

Animals, Men and Morals is a manifesto for an Animal Liberation movement. The contributors to the book may not all see the issue this way. They are a varied group. Philosophers, ranging from professors to graduate students, make up the largest contingent. There are five of them, including the three editors, and there is also an extract from the unjustly neglected German philosopher with an English name, Leonard Nelson, who died in 1927. There are essays by two novelist/critics, Brigid Brophy and Maureen Duffy, and another by Muriel the Lady Dowding, widow of Dowding of Battle of Britain fame and the founder of "Beauty Without Cruelty," a movement that campaigns against the use of animals for furs and cosmetics. The other pieces are by a psychologist, a botanist, a sociologist, and Ruth Harrison, who is probably best described as a professional campaigner for animal welfare.

Whether or not these people, as individuals, would all agree that they are launching a liberation movement for animals, the book as a whole amounts to no less. It is a demand for a complete change in our attitudes to nonhumans. It is a demand that we cease to regard the exploitation of other species as natural and inevitable, and that, instead, we see it as a continuing moral outrage. Patrick Corbett, Professor of Philosophy at Sussex University, captures the spirit of the book in his closing words:

> . . . We require now to extend the great principles of liberty, equality and fraternity over the lives of animals. Let animal slavery join human slavery in the graveyard of the past.

The reader is likely to be skeptical. "Animal Liberation" sounds 4
more like a parody of liberation movements than a serious objective. The reader may think: We support the claims of blacks and women for equality because blacks and women really are equal to whites and males—equal in intelligence and in abilities, capacity for leadership, rationality, and so on. Humans and nonhumans obviously are not equal in these respects. Since justice demands only that we treat equals equally, unequal treatment of humans and nonhumans cannot be an injustice.

This is a tempting reply, but a dangerous one. It commits the nonracist and non-sexist to a dogmatic belief that blacks and women really are just as intelligent, able, etc., as whites and males—and no more. Quite possibly this happens to be the case. Certainly attempts to prove that racial or sexual differences in these respects have a genetic origin have not been conclusive. But do we really want to stake our demand for equality on the assumption that there are no genetic differences of this kind between the different races or sexes? Surely the appropriate response to those who claim to have found evidence for such genetic differences is not to stick to the belief that there are no differences, whatever the evidence to the contrary; rather one should be clear that the claim to equality does not depend on IQ. Moral equality is distinct from factual equality. Otherwise it would be nonsense to talk of the equality of human beings, since humans, as individuals, obviously differ in intelligence and almost any ability one cares to name. If possessing greater intelligence does not entitle one human to exploit another, why should it entitle humans to exploit nonhumans?

Jeremy Bentham expressed the essential basis of equality in his famous formula: "Each to count for one and none for more than one." In other words, the interests of every being that has interests are to be taken into account and treated equally with the like interests of any other being. Other moral philosophers, before and after Bentham, have made the same point in different ways. Our concern for others must not depend on whether they possess certain characteristics, though just what that concern involves may, of course, vary according to such characteristics.

Bentham, incidentally, was well aware that the logic of the demand for racial equality did not stop at the equality of humans. He wrote:

The day *may* come when the rest of the animal creation may acquire those rights which never could have been withholden from them but by the hand of tyranny. The French have already discovered that the blackness of the skin is no reason why a human being should be abandoned without redress to the caprice of a tormentor. It may one day come to be recognized that the number of the legs, the villosity of the skin, or the termination of the *os sacrum*, are reasons equally insufficient for abandoning a sensitive being to the same fate. What else is it that should trace the insuperable line? Is it the faculty of reason, or perhaps the faculty of discourse? But a full-grown horse or dog is beyond comparison a more rational, as well as a more conversable animal, than an infant of a day, or a week, or even a month, old. But suppose they were otherwise, what would it avail? The question is not, Can they *reason?* nor Can they *talk?* but, Can they *suffer?*[1]

[1] *The Principles of Morals and Legislation*, ch. XVII, sec. 1, footnote to paragraph 4

Surely Bentham was right. If a being suffers, there can be no moral justification for refusing to take that suffering into consideration, and, indeed, to count it equally with the like suffering (if rough comparisons can be made) of any other being.

So the only question is: Do animals other than man suffer? 8 Most people agree unhesitatingly that animals like cats and dogs can and do suffer, and this seems also to be assumed by those laws that prohibit wanton cruelty to such animals. Personally, I have no doubt at all about this and find it hard to take seriously the doubts that a few people apparently do have. The editors and contributors of *Animals, Men and Morals* seem to feel the same way, for although the question is raised more than once, doubts are quickly dismissed each time. Nevertheless, because this is such a fundamental point, it is worth asking what grounds we have for attributing suffering to other animals.

It is best to begin by asking what grounds any individual human has for supposing that other humans feel pain. Since pain is a state of consciousness, a "mental event," it can never be directly observed. No observations, whether behavioral signs such as writhing or screaming or physiological or neurological recordings, are observations of pain itself. Pain is something one feels, and one can only infer that others are feeling it from various external indications. The fact that only philosophers are ever skeptical about whether other humans feel pain shows that we regard such inference as justifiable in the case of humans.

Is there any reason why the same inference should be unjustifiable for other animals? Nearly all the external signs which lead us to infer pain in other humans can be seen in other species, especially "higher" animals such as mammals and birds. Behavioral signs—writhing, yelping, or other forms of calling, attempts to avoid the source of pain, and many others—are present. We know, too, that these animals are biologically similar in the relevant respects, having nervous systems like ours which can be observed to function as ours do.

So the grounds for inferring that these animals can feel pain are nearly as good as the grounds for inferring other humans do. Only nearly, for there is one behavioral sign that humans have but nonhumans, with the exception of one or two specially raised chimpanzees, do not have. This, of course, is a developed language. As the quotation from Bentham indicates, this has long been regarded as an important distinction between man and other animals. Other animals may communicate with each other, but not in the way we do. Following Chomsky, many people now mark this distinction by saying that only humans communicate in a form that is governed by rules of syntax. (For the purposes of this argument, linguists allow those chimpanzees who have learned a syntactic sign language to rank as honorary humans.) Nevertheless, as Bentham pointed out, this distinction is not relevant to the question of how animals ought to be treated, unless it can be linked to the issue of whether animals suffer.

This link may be attempted in two ways. First, there is a hazy line of philosophical thought, stemming perhaps from some doctrines associated with Wittgenstein, which maintains that we cannot meaningfully attribute states of consciousness to beings without language. I have not seen this argument made explicit in print, though I have come across it in conversation. This position seems to me very implausible, and I doubt that it would be held at all if it were not thought to be a consequence of a broader view of the significance of language. It may be that the use of a public, rule-governed language is a precondition of conceptual thought. It may even be, although personally I doubt it, that we cannot meaningfully speak of a creature having an intention unless that creature can use a language. But states like pain, surely, are more primitive than either of these, and seem to have nothing to do with language.

Indeed, as Jane Goodall points out in her study of chimpanzees, when it comes to the expression of feelings and emotions, humans tend to fall back on non-linguistic modes of communication which are often found among apes, such as a cheering pat on the back, an exuberant embrace, a clasp of hands, and so on.[2] Michael Peters makes a similar point in his contribution to *Animals, Men and Morals* when he notes that the basic signals we use to convey pain, fear, sexual arousal, and so on are not specific to our species. So there seems to be no reason at all to believe that a creature without language cannot suffer.

The second, and more easily appreciated way of linking language and the existence of pain is to say that the best evidence that we can have that another creature is in pain is when he tells us that he is. This is a distinct line of argument, for it is not being denied that a non-language-user conceivably could suffer, but only that we could know that he is suffering. Still, this line of argument seems

---

[2] Jane van Lawick-Goodall, *In the Shadow of Man* (Houghton Mifflin, 1971), p. 225

to me to fail, and for reasons similar to those just given. "I am in pain" is not the best possible evidence that the speaker is in pain (he might be lying) and it is certainly not the only possible evidence. Behavioral signs and knowledge of the animal's biological similarity to ourselves together provide adequate evidence that animals do suffer. After all, we would not accept linguistic evidence if it contradicted the rest of the evidence. If a man was severely burned, and behaved as if he were in pain, writhing, groaning, being very careful not to let his burned skin touch anything, and so on, but later said he had not been in pain at all, we would be more likely to conclude that he was lying or suffering from amnesia than that he had not been in pain.

Even if there were stronger grounds for refusing to attribute pain to those who do not have a language, the consequences of this refusal might lead us to examine these grounds unusually critically. Human infants, as well as some adults, are unable to use language. Are we to deny that a year-old infant can suffer? If not, how can language be crucial? Of course, most parents can understand the responses of even very young infants better than they understand the responses of other animals, and sometimes infant responses can be understood in the light of later development.

This, however, is just a fact about the relative knowledge we have of our own species and other species, and most of this knowledge is simply derived from closer contact. Those who have studied the behavior of other animals soon learn to understand their responses at least as well as we understand those of an infant. (I am not referring to Jane Goodall's and other well-known studies of apes. Consider, for example, the degree of understanding achieved by Tinbergen from watching herring gulls.[3] Just as we can understand infant human behavior in the light of adult human behavior, so we can understand the behavior of other species in the light of our own behavior (and sometimes we can understand our own behavior better in the light of the behavior of other species).

The grounds we have for believing that other mammals and birds suffer are, then, closely analogous to the grounds we have for believing that other humans suffer. It remains to consider how far down the evolutionary scale this analogy holds. Obviously it becomes poorer when we get further away from man. To be more precise would require a detailed examination of all that we know about

[3] N. Tinbergen, *The Herring Gull's World* (Basic Books, 1961)

other forms of life. With fish, reptiles, and other vertebrates the analogy still seems strong, with molluscs like oysters it is much weaker. Insects are more difficult, and it may be that in our present state of knowledge we must be agnostic about whether they are capable of suffering.

If there is no moral justification for ignoring suffering when it occurs, and it does occur in other species, what are we to say of our attitudes toward these other species? Richard Ryder, one of the contributors to *Animals, Men and Morals,* uses the term "speciesism" to describe the belief that we are entitled to treat members of other species in a way in which it would be wrong to treat members of our own species. The term is not euphonious, but it neatly makes the analogy with racism. The non-racist would do well to bear the analogy in mind when he is inclined to defend human behavior toward nonhumans. "Shouldn't we worry about improving the lot of our own species before we concern ourselves with other species?" he may ask. If we substitute "race" for "species" we shall see that the question is better not asked. "Is a vegetarian diet nutritionally adequate?" resembles the slave-owner's claim that he and the whole economy of the South would be ruined without slave labor. There is even a parallel with skeptical doubts about whether animals suffer, for some defenders of slavery professed to doubt whether blacks really suffer in the way whites do.

I do not want to give the impression, however, that the case for Animal Liberation is based on the analogy with racism and no more. On the contrary, *Animals, Men and Morals* describes the various ways in which humans exploit nonhumans, and several contributors consider the defenses that have been offered, including the defense of meat-eating mentioned in the last paragraph. Sometimes the rebuttals are scornfully dismissive, rather than carefully designed to convince the detached critic. This may be a fault, but it is a fault that is inevitable, given the kind of book this is. The issue is not one on which one can remain detached. As the editors state in their Introduction:

> Once the full force of moral assessment has been made explicit there can be no rational excuse left for killing animals, be they killed for food, science, or sheer personal indulgence. We have not assembled this book to provide the reader with yet another manual on how to make brutalities less brutal. Compromise, in the traditional sense of the term, is simple unthinking weakness when one considers the actual reasons for our crude relationships with the other animals.

The point is that on this issue there are few critics who are gen- 20
uinely detached. People who eat pieces of slaughtered nonhumans every day find it hard to believe that they are doing wrong;
and they also find it hard to imagine what else they could eat. So
for those who do not place nonhumans beyond the pale of morality, there comes a stage when further argument seems pointless,
a stage at which one can only accuse one's opponent of hypocrisy
and reach for the sort of sociological account of our practices and
the way we defend them that is attempted by David Wood in his
contribution to this book. On the other hand, to those unconvinced
by the arguments, and unable to accept that they are merely rationalizing their dietary preferences and their fear of being thought
peculiar, such sociological explanations can only seem insultingly
arrogant.

II

The logic of speciesism is most apparent in the practice of experimenting on nonhumans in order to benefit humans. This is because the issue is rarely obscured by allegations that nonhumans
are so different from humans that we cannot know anything about
whether they suffer. The defender of vivisection cannot use this argument because he needs to stress the similarities between man and
other animals in order to justify the usefulness to the former of experiments on the latter. The researcher who makes rats choose between starvation and electric shocks to see if they develop ulcers
(they do) does so because he knows that the rat has a nervous system very similar to man's, and presumably feels an electric shock
in a similar way.

Richard Ryder's restrained account of experiments on animals
made me angrier with my fellow men than anything else in this
book. Ryder, a clinical psychologist by profession, himself ex-
perimented on animals before he came to hold the view he puts forward in his essay. Experimenting on animals is now a large industry, both academic and commercial. In 1969, more than 5 million
experiments were performed in Britain, the vast majority without
anesthetic (though how many of these involved pain is not known).
There are no accurate U.S. figures, since there is no federal law on
the subject, and in many cases no state law either. Estimates vary
from 20 million to 200 million. Ryder suggests that 80 million may
be the best guess. We tend to think that this is all for vital medical

research, but of course it is not. Huge numbers of animals are used in university departments from Forestry to Psychology, and even more are used for commercial purposes, to test whether cosmetics can cause skin damage, or shampoos eye damage, or to test food additives or laxatives or sleeping pills or anything else.

A standard test for foodstuffs is the "LD50." The object of this test is to find the dosage level at which 50 percent of the test animals will die. This means that nearly all of them will become very sick before finally succumbing or surviving. When the substance is a harmless one, it may be necessary to force huge doses down the animals, until in some cases sheer volume or concentration causes death.

Ryder gives a selection of experiments, taken from recent scientific journals. I will quote two, not for the sake of indulging in gory details, but in order to give an idea of what normal researchers think they may legitimately do to other species. The point is not that the individual researchers are cruel men, but that they are behaving in a way that is allowed by our speciesist attitudes. As Ryder points out, even if only 1 percent of the experiments involve severe pain, that is 50,000 experiments in Britain each year, or nearly 150 every day (and about fifteen times as many in the United States, if Ryder's guess is right). Here then are two experiments:

> O. S. Ray and R. J. Barrett of Pittsburgh gave electric shocks to the feet of 1,042 mice. They then caused convulsions by giving more intense shocks through cup-shaped electrodes applied to the animals' eyes or through pressure spring clips attached to their ears. Unfortunately some of the mice who "successfully completed Day One training were found sick or dead prior to testing on Day Two." [*Journal of Comparative and Physiological Psychology*, 1969, vol. 67, pp. 110–116]

> At the National Institute for Medical Research, Mill Hill, London, W. Feldberg and S. L. Sherwood injected chemicals into the brains of cats—"with a number of widely different substances, recurrent patterns of reaction were obtained. Retching, vomiting, defaecation, increased salivation and greatly accelerated respiration leading to panting were common features." . . .
> The injection into the brain of a large dose of Tubocuraine caused the cat to jump "from the table to the floor and then straight into its cage, where it started calling more and more noisily whilst moving about restlessly and jerkily . . . finally the cat fell with legs and neck flexed, jerking in rapid clonic movements, the condition being that of a major [epileptic] convulsion . . . within a few seconds the cat got up, ran for a few yards at high speed and fell in another fit. The whole process

24

was repeated several times within the next ten minutes, during which the cat lost faeces and foamed at the mouth."

This animal finally died thirty-five minutes after the brain injection. [*Journal of Physiology*, 1954, vol. 123, pp. 148–167]

There is nothing secret about these experiments. One has only to open any recent volume of a learned journal, such as the *Journal of Comparative and Physiological Psychology*, to find full descriptions of experiments of this sort, together with the results obtained— results that are frequently trivial and obvious. The experiments are often supported by public funds.

It is a significant indication of the level of acceptability of these practices that, although these experiments are taking place at this moment on university campuses throughout the country, there has, so far as I know, not been the slightest protest from the student movement. Students have been rightly concerned that their universities should not discriminate on grounds of race or sex, and that they should not serve the purposes of the military or big business. Speciesism continues undisturbed, and many students participate in it. There may be a few qualms at first, but since everyone regards it as normal, and it may even be a required part of a course, the student soon becomes hardened and, dismissing his earlier feelings as "mere sentiment," comes to regard animals as statistics rather than sentient beings with interests that warrant consideration.

Argument about vivisection has often missed the point because it has been put in absolutist terms: Would the abolitionist be prepared to let thousands die if they could be saved by experimenting on a single animal? The way to reply to this purely hypothetical question is to pose another: Would the experimenter be prepared to experiment on a human orphan under six months old, if it were the only way to save many lives? (I say "orphan" to avoid the complication of parental feelings, although in doing so I am being overfair to the experimenter, since the nonhuman subjects of experiments are not orphans.) A negative answer to this question indicates that the experimenter's readiness to use nonhumans is simple discrimination, for adult apes, cats, mice, and other mammals are more conscious of what is happening to them, more self-directing, and, so far as we can tell, just as sensitive to pain as a human infant. There is no characteristic that human infants possess that adult mammals do not have to the same or a higher degree.

(It might be possible to hold that what makes it wrong to 28 experiment on a human infant is that the infant will in time develop into more than the nonhuman, but one would then, to be consistent, have to oppose abortion, and perhaps contraception, too, for the fetus and the egg and sperm have the same potential as the infant. Moreover, one would still have no reason for experimenting on a nonhuman rather than a human with brain damage severe enough to make it impossible for him to rise above infant level.)

The experimenter, then, shows a bias for his own species whenever he carries out an experiment on a nonhuman for a purpose that he would not think justified him in using a human being at an equal or lower level of sentience, awareness, ability to be self-directing, etc. No one familiar with the kind of results yielded by these experiments can have the slightest doubt that if this bias were eliminated the number of experiments performed would be zero or very close to it.

III

If it is vivisection that shows the logic of speciesism most clearly, it is the use of other species for food that is at the heart of our attitudes toward them. Most of *Animals, Men and Morals* is an attack on meat-eating—an attack which is based solely on concern for nonhumans, without reference to arguments derived from considerations of ecology, macrobiotics, health, or religion.

The idea that nonhumans are utilities, means to our ends, pervades our thought. Even conservationists who are concerned about the slaughter of wild fowl but not about the vastly greater slaughter of chickens for our tables are thinking in this way—they are worried about what we would lose if there were less wildlife. Stanley Godlovitch, pursuing the Marxist idea that our thinking is formed by the activities we undertake in satisfying our needs, suggests that man's first classification of his environment was into Edibles and Inedibles. Most animals came into the first category, and there they have remained.

Man may always have killed other species for food, but he has never exploited them so ruthlessly as he does today. Farming has succumbed to business methods, the objective being to get the highest possible ratio of output (meat, eggs, milk) to input (fodder, labor costs, etc.). Ruth Harrison's essay "On Factory Farming" gives an account of some aspects of modern methods, and of the unsuccessful British campaign for effective controls, a campaign which was sparked off by her *Animal Machines* (Stuart: London, 1964). 32

Her article is in no way a substitute for her earlier book. This is a pity since, as she says, "Farm produce is still associated with mental pictures of animals browsing in the fields . . . of hens having a last forage before going to roost. . . ." Yet neither in her article nor elsewhere in *Animals, Men and Morals* is this false image replaced by a clear idea of the nature and extent of factory farming. We learn of this only indirectly, when we hear of the code of reform proposed by an advisory committee set up by the British government.

Among the proposals, which the government refused to implement on the grounds that they were too idealistic, were: *"Any animals should at least have room to turn around freely."*

Factory farm animals need liberation in the most literal sense. Veal calves are kept in stalls five feet by two feet. They are usually slaughtered when about four months old, and have been too big to turn in their stalls for at least a month. Intensive beef herds, kept in stalls only proportionately larger for much longer periods, account for a growing percentage of beef production. Sows are often similarly confined when pregnant, which, because of artificial methods of increasing fertility, can be most of the time. Animals confined in this way do not waste food by exercising, nor do they develop unpalatable muscle.

"A dry bedded area should be provided for all stock." Intensively kept 36 animals usually have to stand and sleep on slatted floors without straw, because this makes cleaning easier.

"Palatable roughage must be readily available to all calves after one week of age." In order to produce the pale veal housewives are said to prefer, calves are fed on an all-liquid diet until slaughter, even though they are long past the age at which they would normally eat grass. They develop a craving for roughage, evidenced by attempts to gnaw wood from their stalls. (For the same reason, their diet is deficient in iron.)

"Battery cages for poultry should be large enough for a bird to be able to stretch one wing at a time." Under current British practice, a cage for four or five laying hens has a floor area of twenty inches by eighteen inches, scarcely larger than a double page of the *New York Review of Books.* In this space, on a sloping wire floor (sloping so the eggs roll down, wire so the dung drops through) the birds live for a year or eighteen months while artificial lighting and temperature conditions combine with drugs in their food to squeeze the maximum number of eggs out of them. Table birds are also sometimes kept in cages. More often they are reared in sheds, no less crowded.

Under these conditions all the birds' natural activities are frustrated, and they develop "vices" such as pecking each other to death. To prevent this, beaks are often cut off, and the sheds kept dark.

How many of those who support factory farming by buying its produce know anything about the way it is produced? How many have heard something about it, but are reluctant to check up for fear that it will make them uncomfortable? To non-speciesists, the typical consumer's mixture of ignorance, reluctance to find out the truth, and vague belief that nothing really bad could be allowed seems analogous to the attitudes of "decent Germans" to the death camps.

There are, of course, some defenders of factory farming. Their 40 arguments are considered, though again rather sketchily, by John Harris. Among the most common: "Since they have never known anything else, they don't suffer." This argument will not be put by anyone who knows anything about animal behavior, since he will know that not all behavior has to be learned. Chickens attempt to stretch wings, walk around, scratch, and even dustbathe or build a nest, even though they have never lived under conditions that allowed these activities. Calves can suffer from maternal deprivation no matter at what age they were taken from their mothers. "We need these intensive methods to provide protein for a growing population." As ecologists and famine relief organizations know, we can produce far more protein per acre if we grow the right vegetable crop, soy beans for instance, than if we use the land to grow crops to be converted into protein by animals who use nearly 90 percent of the protein themselves, even when unable to exercise.

There will be many readers of this book who will agree that factory farming involves an unjustifiable degree of exploitation of sentient creatures, and yet will want to say that there is nothing wrong with rearing animals for food, provided it is done "humanely." These people are saying, in effect, that although we should not cause animals to suffer, there is nothing wrong with killing them.

There are two possible replies to this view. One is to attempt to show that this combination of attitudes is absurd. Roslind Godlovitch takes this course in her essay, which is an examination of some common attitudes to animals. She argues that from the combination of "animal suffering is to be avoided" and "there is nothing wrong with killing animals" it follows that all animal life ought to be exterminated (since all sentient creatures will suffer to some degree at some point in their lives). Euthanasia is a contentious issue only because we place some value on living. If we did not, the least amount of suffering would justify it. Accordingly, if we deny that we have a duty to exterminate all animal life, we must concede that we are placing some value on animal life.

This argument seems to me valid, although one could still reply that the value of animal life is to be derived from the pleasures that life can have for them, so that, provided their lives have a balance of pleasure over pain, we are justified in rearing them. But this would imply that we ought to produce animals and let them live as pleasantly as possible, without suffering.

At this point, one can make the second of the two possible   44 replies to the view that rearing and killing animals for food is all right so long as it is done humanely. This second reply is that so long as we think that a nonhuman may be killed simply so that a human can satisfy his taste for meat, we are still thinking of nonhumans as means rather than as ends in themselves. The factory farm is nothing more than the application of technology to this concept. Even traditional methods involve castration, the separation of mothers and their young, the breaking up of herds, branding or ear-punching, and of course transportation to the abattoirs and the final moments of terror when the animal smells blood and senses danger. If we were to try rearing animals so that they lived and died without suffering, we should find that to do so on anything like the scale of today's meat industry would be a sheer impossibility. Meat would become the prerogative of the rich.

I have been able to discuss only some of the contributions to this book, saying nothing about, for instance, the essays on killing for furs and for sport. Nor have I considered all the detailed questions that need to be asked once we start thinking about other species in the radically different way presented by this book. What, for instance, are we to do about genuine conflicts of interest like rats biting slum children? I am not sure of the answer, but the essential point is just that we do see this as a conflict of interests, that we recognize that rats have interests too. Then we may begin to think about other ways of resolving the conflict—perhaps by leaving out rat baits that sterilize the rats instead of killing them.

I have not discussed such problems because they are side issues compared with the exploitation of other species for food and for experimental purposes. On these central matters, I hope that I have said enough to show that this book, despite its flaws, is a challenge to every human to recognize his attitudes to nonhumans as a form of prejudice no less objectionable than racism or sexism. It is a challenge that demands not just a change of attitudes, but a change in our way of life, for it requires us to become vegetarians.

Can a purely moral demand of this kind succeed? The odds are certainly against it. The book holds out no inducements. It does not tell us that we will become healthier, or enjoy life more, if we cease exploiting animals. Animal Liberation will require greater altruism on the part of mankind than any other liberation movement, since animals are incapable of demanding it for themselves, or of protesting against their exploitation by votes, demonstrations, or bombs. Is man capable of such genuine altruism? Who knows? If this book does have a significant effect, however, it will be a vindication of all those who have believed that man has within himself the potential for more than cruelty and selfishness.

Topics for Discussion and Writing

1. Reread Singer's first seven paragraphs carefully, observing how he leads us to see that "animal liberation" is not a joke. It will help you to understand his strategy if for each of his paragraphs you write one sentence either summarizing the paragraph or commenting on what it accomplishes in his argument.

2. What grounds does Singer find for attributing suffering to nonhumans? List the arguments he offers to dismiss the relevance of a developed language. Why does he find it necessary to offer these arguments?

3. Does Singer attribute the capacity to feel pain to all species? Explain.

4. How does Singer define speciesism? To what extent does he use the analogy of speciesism to racism?

5. What is vivisection? Why, according to Singer, *must* defenders of vivisection also defend speciesism? Why do many of us who would not be willing to defend speciesism tolerate or even participate in experiments on animals?

6. What use of animals does Singer analyze beginning with paragraph 30? Why does he reserve this discussion for the last part of his essay? Why does he offer more detailed and more concrete examples in this section than in the second part, beginning with paragraph 21?

7. When Singer wrote "Animal Liberation," more than 20 years ago, he used language that would now be described as sexist. In paragraph 8, for example, he wrote "Do animals other than man suffer?" where he might today write "Do animals other than human beings suffer?" How would you revise his concluding paragraph to avoid sexist language?

APPENDIX

A Writer's Glossary

analogy. An analogy (from the Greek *analogos,* proportionate, resembling) is a kind of comparison. Normally an analogy compares substantially different kinds of things and reports several points of resemblance. A comparison of one city with another ("New York is like Chicago in several ways") does not involve an analogy because the two things are not substantially different. And a comparison giving only one resemblance is usually not considered an analogy ("Some people, like olives, are an acquired taste"). But if we claim that a state is like a human body, and we find in the state equivalents for the brain, heart, and limbs, we are offering an analogy. Similarly, one might construct an analogy between feeding the body with food and supplying the mind with ideas: the diet must be balanced, taken at approximately regular intervals, in proper amounts, and digested. An analogy may be useful in explaining the unfamiliar by comparing it to the familiar ("The heart is like a pump . . ."), but of course the things compared are different, and the points of resemblance can go only so far. For this reason, analogies cannot prove anything, though they are sometimes offered as proof.

analysis. Examination of the parts and their relation to the whole.

argument. Discourse in which some statements are offered as reasons for other statements. Argument, then, like emotional appeal and wit, is a form of persuasion, but argument seeks to persuade by appealing to reason. (See *deduction,* pages 876–77.)

audience. The writer's imagined readers. An essay on inflation written for the general public—say, for readers of *Newsweek*—will assume less specialized knowledge than will an essay written for professional economists—say, the readers of *Journal of Economic History.* In general, the imagined audience in a composition course is *not* the instructor (though in fact the instructor may be the only reader of the essay); the imagined audience usually is the class, or, to put it a little differently, someone rather like the writer but without the writer's specialized knowledge of the topic.

cliché.   Literally, a *cliché* was originally (in French) a stereotype or an electrotype plate for printing; in English the word has come to mean an oft-repeated expression such as "a sight for sore eyes," "a heartwarming experience," "the acid test," "a meaningful relationship," "last but not least." Because these expressions implicitly claim to be impressive or forceful, they can be distinguished from such unpretentious common expressions as "good morning," "thank you," and "see you tomorrow." Clichés in fact are not impressive or forceful; they strike the hearer as tired, vague, and unimaginative.

compare/contrast.   Strictly speaking, to compare is to examine in order to show similarities. (It comes from the Latin *comparare*, "to pair," "to match.") To contrast is to set into opposition in order to show differences. (It comes from the Latin *contra*, "against," and *stare*, "to stand.") But in ordinary usage a comparison may include not only similarities but also differences. (For a particular kind of comparison, emphasizing similarities, see *analogy*.) In comparing and contrasting, a writer usually means not simply to list similarities or differences but to reveal something clearly, by calling attention either to its resemblances to something we might not think it resembles, or to its differences from something we might think it does resemble.

connotation.   The associations that cluster around a word. "Mother" has connotations that "female parent" does not have, yet both words have the same denotation or explicit meaning.

convention.   An agreed-on usage. Beginning each sentence with a capital letter is a convention.

deduction.   Deduction is the process of reasoning from premises to a logical conclusion. Here is the classic example: "All men are mortal" (the major premise); "Socrates is a man" (the minor premise); "therefore Socrates is mortal" (the conclusion). Such an argument, which takes two truths and joins them to produce a third truth, is called a *syllogism* (from Greek for "a reckoning together"). Deduction (Latin for "lead down from") moves from a general statement to a specific application; it is, therefore, the opposite of *induction* (page 880), which moves from specific instances to a general conclusion.

Notice that if a premise of a syllogism is not true, one can reason logically yet can come to a false conclusion. Example: "All teachers are members of a union"; "Jones is a teacher"; "therefore Jones is a member of a union." Although the process of reasoning is correct here, the major premise is false — all teachers are *not* members of a union — and so the conclusion is worthless. Jones may or may not be a member of the union.

Another point: some arguments superficially appear logical but are not. Let's take this attempt at a syllogism: "All teachers of Spanish know that in Spanish *hoy* means 'today'" (major premise); "John knows that in Spanish *hoy* means 'today'" (minor premise); "therefore John is a teacher of Spanish" (conclusion). Both of the premises are correct, but the conclusion does not follow. What's wrong? Valid deduction requires that the subject or condition of the major premise (in this case, teachers of Spanish) appear also in the minor premise, but here it does not. The minor premise should be "John is a teacher of Spanish," and the valid conclusion, of course, would be "therefore John knows that *hoy* means 'today.'"

denotation. The explicit meaning of a word, as given in a dictionary, without its associations. "Daytime serial" and "soap opera" have the same denotation, though "daytime serial" probably has a more favorable connotation (see *connotation*).

description. Discourse that aims chiefly at producing a sensory response (usually a mental image) to, for example, a person, object, scene, taste, smell, and so on. A descriptive essay, or passage in an essay, uses concrete words (words that denote observable qualities such as "hair" and "stickiness") and it uses specific language (words such as "basketball" rather than "game," and "steak, potatoes, and salad" rather than "hearty meal").

diction. Choice of words. Examples: between "car," "auto," and "automobile," between "lie" and "falsehood," between "can't" and "cannot."

euphemism. An expression such as "passed away" for "died," used to avoid realities that the writer finds unpleasant. Thus, oppressive governments "relocate people" (instead of putting them in concentration camps).

evaluation. Whereas an interpretation seeks to explain the meaning, an evaluation judges worth. After we interpret a difficult piece of writing we may evaluate it as not worth the effort.

explication. An attempt to reveal the meaning by calling attention to implications, such as the connotations of words and the tone conveyed by the brevity or length of a sentence. Unlike a paraphrase, which is a rewording or rephrasing in order to set forth the gist of the meaning, an explication is a commentary that makes explicit what is implicit. If we paraphrased the beginning of the Gettysburg Address (page 465), we might turn "Four score and seven years ago our fathers brought forth" into "Eighty-seven years ago our ancestors established," or some such statement. In an explication, however, we would mention that "four score" evokes the language of the Bible, and that the biblical echo helps to establish the solemnity and holiness of the occasion. In an explication we would also mention that "fathers" initiates a chain of images of birth, continued in "conceived in liberty," "any nation so conceived," and "a new birth." (See Highet's explication of the Gettysburg Address, page 466.)

exposition.   An expository essay is chiefly concerned with giving information—how to register for classes, the causes of the French Revolution, or the tenets of Zen Buddhism. The writer of exposition must, of course, have a point of view (an attitude or a thesis), but because exposition—unlike persuasion—does not assume that the reader's opinion differs from the writer's, the point of view in exposition often is implicit rather than explicit.

general and **specific** (or **particular**).   A general word refers to a class or group; a specific (particular) word refers to a member of the class or group. Example: "vehicle" is general compared with "automobile" or with "motorcycle." But "general" and "specific" are relative. "Vehicle" is general when compared to "automobile," but "vehicle" is specific when compared to "machine," for "machine" refers to a class or group that includes not only vehicles but clocks, typewriters, and dynamos. Similarly, although "automobile" is specific in comparison with "vehicle," "automobile" is general in comparison with "Volkswagen" or "sportscar."

generalization.   A statement relating to every member of a class or category, or, more loosely, to most members of a class or category. Example: "Students from Medford High are well prepared." Compare: (1) "Janet Kuo is well prepared" (a report of a specific condition); (2) "Students from Medford High are well prepared" (a low-level generalization, because it is limited to one school); (3) "Students today are well prepared" (a high-level generalization, covering many people in many places).

imagery and symbolism.   When we read "rose," we may more or less call to mind a picture of a rose, or perhaps we are reminded of the odor or texture of a rose. Whatever in a piece of writing appeals to any of our senses (including sensations of heat and pressure as well as of sight, smell, taste, touch, sound) is an image. In short, images are the sensory content of a work, whether literal (the roses discussed in an essay on rose-growing) or figurative (a comparison, in a poem, of a girl to a rose). It is usually easy to notice images in literature, particularly in poems, which often include comparisons such as "I wandered lonely as a cloud," "a fiery eye," and "seems he a dove? His feathers are but borrowed." In literature, imagery (again, literal as well as figurative) plays a large part in communicating the meaning of the work. For instance, in *Romeo and Juliet* abundant imagery of light and dark reenforces the conflict between life and death. Juliet especially is associated with light (Romeo says, "What light through yonder window breaks? It is the east and Juliet is the sun"), and at the end of the play, when the lovers have died, we are told that the morning is dark: "The sun for sorrow will not show his head."

If we turn from imaginative literature to the essay, we find, of course, that descriptive essays are rich in images. But other kinds of essays, too, may make use of imagery—and not only by literal references to real people or things. Such essays may use figures of speech, as Thoreau does when he says that the imagination as well as the body should "both sit down at the same table." The imagination, after all, does not literally sit down at a table—but Thoreau personifies the imagination, seeing it as no less concrete than the body.

The distinction between an image and a symbol is partly a matter of emphasis and partly a matter of a view of reality. If an image is so insisted on that we feel that the writer sees it as highly significant in itself and also as a way of representing something else, we can call it a symbol. In Henry James's words, symbolism is the presentation "of objects casting . . . far behind them a shadow more curious . . . than the apparent figure." A symbol is what it is, and yet it is also much more. We may feel that a passage about the railroad, emphasizing its steel tracks and its steel cars, its speed and its noise, may be not only about the railroad but also about industrialism and, even further, about an entire way of life—a way of thinking and feeling—that came into being in the nineteenth century.

A symbol, then, is an image so loaded with significance that it is not simply literal, and it does not simply stand as a figure for something else; it is both itself *and* something else that it richly suggests, a kind of manifestation of something too complex or too elusive to be otherwise revealed. In a symbol, Thomas Carlyle wrote, "the Infinite is made to blend with the Finite, to stand visible, and as it were, attainable there." Still, having said all of this, one must add that the distinction between image and symbol is not sharp, and usage allows us even to say such things as, "The imagery of light symbolizes love," meaning that the imagery stands for or represents or is in part about love.

induction.   Reasoning from the particular to the general, or drawing a conclusion about all members of a class from a study of some members of the class. Every elephant I have seen is grayish, so by induction (from Latin, "lead into," "lead up to") I conclude that all elephants are grayish. Another example: I have met ten graduates of Vassar College and all are females, so I conclude that all Vassar graduates are females. This conclusion, however, happens to be incorrect; a few years ago Vassar began to admit males, and so although male graduates are relatively few they do exist. Induction is valid only if the sample is representative.

Because one can rarely be certain that it is representative, induced conclusions are usually open to doubt. Still, we live our lives largely by induction; we have dinner with a friend, we walk the dog, we write home for money—all because these actions have produced certain results in the past and we assume that actions of the same sort will produce results consistent with our earlier findings. Nelson Algren's excellent advice must have been arrived at inductively: "Never eat at a place called Mom's, and never play cards with a man called Doc."

interpretation.   An explanation of the meaning. If we see someone clench his fist and tighten his mouth, we may interpret these signs as revealing anger. When we say that in the New Testament the passage alluding to the separation of sheep from goats is to be understood as referring to the saved and the damned, we are offering an interpretation.

irony.   In *verbal irony*, the meaning of the words intentionally contradicts the literal meaning, as in "that's not a very good idea," where the intended meaning is "that's a terrible idea."

Irony, in distinction from sarcasm, employs at least some degree of wit or wryness. Sarcasm reveals contempt obviously and heavily, usually by asserting the opposite of what is meant: "You're a great guy" (if said sarcastically) means "It's awful of you to do this to me." Notice that the example of irony we began with was at least a trifle more ingenious than this sarcastic remark, for the sarcasm here simply is the opposite of what is meant, whereas our example of verbal irony is not quite the opposite. The opposite of "that's not a very good idea" is "that is a very good idea," but clearly (in our example) the speaker's meaning is something else. Put it this way: sarcasm is irony at its crudest, and finer irony commonly uses overstatement or especially understatement, rather than a simple opposite. (For a brief discussion of the use of irony in satire, see the entry on satire, pages 883–84.)

If the speaker's words have an unintentional double meaning, the irony may be called *dramatic irony:* a character, about to go to bed, says, "I think I'll have a sound sleep," and dies in her sleep. Similarly, an action can turn dramatically ironic: a character seeks to help a friend and unintentionally harms her. Finally, a situation can be ironic: thirsty sailors are surrounded by water that cannot be drunk.

All these meanings of irony are held together, then, by the sense of a somewhat bitter contrast.

jargon.   Technical language used inappropriately or inexactly. "Viable" means "able to survive." To speak of "a viable building" is to use jargon. "A primary factor in my participation in the dance" is jargon if what is meant is "I dance because. . . ."

metaphor.   Words have literal meanings: a lemon is a yellow, egg-shaped citrus fruit; to drown is to suffocate in water or other fluid. But words can also have metaphoric meanings: we can call an unsatisfactory automobile a lemon, and we can say that we are drowning in paperwork. Metaphoric language is literally absurd; if we heed only the denotation it is clearly untrue, for an automobile cannot be a kind of citrus fruit, and we cannot drown in paperwork. (Even if the paper literally suffocated someone, the death could not be called a drowning.) Metaphor, then, uses not the denotation of the word but the associations, the connotations. Because we know that the speaker is not crazy, we turn from the literal meaning (which is clearly untrue) to the association.

myth.   (1) A traditional story dealing with supernatural beings or with heroes, often accounting for why things are as they are. Myths tell of the creation of the world, the creation of man, the changes of the season, the achievements of heroes. A Zulu myth, for example, explains that rain is the tears of a god weeping for a beloved slain bird. *Mythology* is a system or group of such stories, and so we speak of Zulu mythology, or Greek mythology, or Norse mythology. (2) Mark Schorer, in *William Blake*, defines myth as "a large controlling image that gives philosophic meaning to the facts of ordinary life. . . . All real convictions involve a mythology. . . . Wars may be described as the clash of mythologies." In this sense, then, a myth is not a traditional story we do not believe, but any idea, true or false, to which people subscribe. Thus, one can speak of the "myth" of democracy or of communism.

narration. Discourse that recounts a real or a fictional happening. An anecdote is a narrative, and so is a history of the decline and fall of the Roman Empire. Narration may, of course, include substantial exposition ("four possible motives must be considered") and description ("the horse was an old gray mare"), but the emphasis is on a sequence of happenings ("and then she says to me, . . . ").

parable. A parable is a short narrative from which a moral or a lesson can be drawn. A parable may, but need not, be an allegory wherein, say, each character stands for an abstraction that otherwise would be hard to grasp. Usually the parable lacks the *detailed* correspondence of an allegory.

paradox. An apparent self-contradiction, such as "He was happiest when miserable."

paraphrase. A rewording of a passage, usually in order to clarify the meaning. A paraphrase is a sort of translating within the same language; it can help to make clear the gist of the passage. But one must recognize the truth of Robert Frost's charge that when one paraphrases a line of good writing one puts it "in other and worse English." Paraphrase should not be confused with *explication*, pages 877–78.

parody. A parody (from the Greek "counter song") seeks to amuse by imitating the style—the diction, the sentence structure—of another work, but normally the parody substitutes a very different subject. Thus, it might use tough-guy Hemingway talk to describe not a bullfighter but a butterfly catcher. Often a parody of a writer's style is a good-natured criticism of it.

persona. The writer or speaker in a role adopted for a specific audience. When Abraham Lincoln wrote or spoke, he sometimes did so in the persona of commander in chief of the Union army, but at other times he did so in the persona of the simple man from Springfield, Illinois. The persona is a mask put on for a performance (*persona* is the Latin word for mask). If mask suggests insincerity, we should remember that whenever we speak or write we do so in a specific role—as friend, or parent, or teacher, or applicant for a job, or whatever. Although Lincoln was a husband, a father, a politician, a president, and many other things, when he wrote a letter or speech he might write solely as one of these; in a letter to his son, the persona (or, we might say, personality) is that of father, not that of commander in chief. The distinction between the writer (who necessarily fills many roles) and the persona who writes or speaks a work is especially useful in talking about satire, because the satirist often invents a mouthpiece very different from himself. The satirist—say, Jonathan Swift—may be strongly opposed to a view, but his persona (his invented essayist) may favor the view; the reader must perceive that the real writer is ridiculing the invented essayist.

persuasion.   Discourse that seeks to change a reader's mind. Persuasion usually assumes that the writer and the reader do not agree, or do not fully agree, at the outset. Persuasion may use logical argument (appeal to reason), but it may also try to win the reader over by other means—by appeal to the emotions, by wit, by geniality.

rhetoric.   Although in much contemporary usage the word's meaning has sadly decayed to "inflated talk or writing," it can still mean "the study of elements such as content, structure, and cadence in writing or in speech." In short, in the best sense rhetoric is the study of the art of communicating with words.

satire.   A work ridiculing identifiable objects in real life, meant to arouse in the reader contempt for its object. Satire is sometimes distinguished from comedy in that comedy aims simply to evoke amusement, whereas satire aims to bring about moral reform by ridicule. According to Alexander Pope, satire "heals with morals what it hurts with wit." Satire sometimes uses invective (direct abuse), but if the invective is to entertain the reader it must be witty, as in a piling up of ingenious accusations. Invective, however, is probably less common in satire than is irony, a device in which the tone somehow contradicts the words. For instance, a speaker may seem to praise ("well, that's certainly an original idea that you have"), but we perceive that she is ridiculing a crackpot idea. Or the satirist may invent a naive speaker (a persona) who praises, but the praise is really dispraise because a simpleton offers it; the persona is sincere but the writer is ironic and satiric. Or, adopting another strategy, the writer may use an apparently naive persona to represent the voice of reason; the persona dispassionately describes actions that we take for granted (a political campaign), and through this simple, accurate, rational description we see the irrationality of our behavior. (For further comments on irony, see pages 880–81.)

style.   A distinctive way of expression. If we see a picture of a man sitting on a chair, we may say that it looks like a drawing for a comic book, or we may say that it looks like a drawing by Rembrandt or Van Gogh or Andrew Wyeth. We have come to recognize certain ways of expression—independent of the content—as characteristic of certain minds. The content, it can be said, is the same—a man sitting in a chair—but the creator's way of expressing the content is individual.

Similarly, "Four score and seven years ago" and "Eighty-seven years ago" are the same in content; but the styles differ, because "Four score and seven years ago" distinctively reflects a mind familiar with the Bible and an orator speaking solemnly. Many people (we include ourselves) believe that the content is not the same if the expression is not the same. The "content" of "Four score and seven years ago" includes suggestions of the Bible and of God-fearing people not present in "eighty-seven years ago." In this view, a difference in style is a difference in content and therefore a difference in meaning. Surely it is true that in the work of the most competent writers, those who make every word count, one cannot separate style and content.

Let C. S. Lewis have the next-to-last word: "The way for a person to develop a style is (a) to know exactly what he wants to say, and (b) to be sure he is saying exactly that. The reader, we must remember, does not start by knowing what we mean. If our words are ambiguous, our meaning will escape him. I sometimes think that writing is like driving sheep down a road. If there is any gate open to the left or the right the readers will most certainly go into it." And let the Austrian writer Karl Kraus have the last word: "There are two kinds of writers, those who are and those who aren't. With the first, content and form belong together like soul and body; with the second, they match each other like body and clothes."

summary.   The word "summary" is related to "sum," to the total something adds up to. (The Greeks and Romans counted upward, and wrote the total at the top.) A summary is a condensation or abridgment briefly giving the reader the gist of a longer work. Here are a few principles that govern summaries:

1. A summary is much briefer than the original. It is not a paraphrase—a word-by-word translation of someone's words into your own—for a paraphrase is usually at least as long as the original, whereas a summary is rarely longer than one-fourth the original, and may even be much briefer, perhaps giving in a sentence or two an entire essay.

2. A summary usually achieves its brevity by omitting almost all the concrete details of the original, presenting only the sum that the details add up to.

3. A summary is accurate; it has no value if it misrepresents the point of the original.

4. The writer of a summary need not make the points in the same order as that of the original. In fact, a reader is occasionally driven to write a summary because the original author does not present the argument in an orderly sequence; the summary is an attempt to disengage the author's argument from the confusing presentation.

5. A summary normally is written in the present tense, because the writer assumes that although the author wrote the piece last year or a hundred years ago, the piece speaks to us today. (In other words, the summary is explicitly or implicitly prefaced by "He says," and all that follows is in the present tense.)

6. Because a summary is openly based on someone else's views, not your own, you need not use quotation marks around any words that you take from the original.

Here is a summary of this entry on "summary":

A summary is a condensation or abridgment. These are some characteristics: (1) it is rarely more than one-fourth as long as the original; (2) its brevity is usually achieved by leaving out most of the concrete details of the original; (3) it is accurate; (4) it may rearrange the organization of the original, especially if a rearrangement will make things clearer; (5) it normally is in the present tense; (6) quoted words need not be enclosed in quotation marks.

thesis. The writer's position or attitude; the proposition advanced.

thesis statement.   A sentence or two summarizing the writer's position or attitude. An essay may or may not have an explicit thesis statement.

tone.   The prevailing spirit of an utterance. The tone may be angry or bitter or joyful or solemn, or expressive of any similar mood or emotion. Tone usually reflects the writer's attitude toward the subject, the audience, and the self. (For further comments on tone, see pages 23–25.)

ACKNOWLEDGMENTS

Woody Allen. "The Colorization of Films Insults Artists and Society," *The New York Times,* June 26, 1987. Copyright © 1987 by The New York Times Company. Reprinted by permission.

Dennis Altman. "Why Are Gay Men So Feared?" *The New Internationalist,* November, 1989. Reprinted by permission of *The New Internationalist.*

Maya Angelou. "Graduation" from *I Know Why the Caged Bird Sings* by Maya Angelou. Copyright © 1969 by Maya Angelou. Reprinted by permission of Random House, Inc.

Anonymous. "Confessions of an Erstwhile Child" from *The New Republic,* June 15, 1974. Reprinted by permission of *The New Republic,* © 1974, The New Republic, Inc.

Jean Bertrand Aristide. "Disobey the Rules" from *In the Parish of the Poor: Writings from Haiti by Jean Bertrand Aristide,* translated by Amy Wilentz. Copyright © 1990 by Orbis Books. Reprinted by permission of Orbis Books, Maryknoll, New York.

Alexandra Armstrong. "Starting a Business." Reprinted by permission from the March 1988 issue of *Ms.* Magazine.

W. H. Auden. "The Almighty Dollar." Copyright © 1962 by W. H. Auden. Reprinted from *The Dyer's Hand and Other Essays* by W. H. Auden by permission of Random House, Inc. and Faber and Faber Ltd. "Work, Labor, and Play" from *A Certain World* by W. H. Auden. Copyright © 1970 by W. H. Auden. Reprinted by permission of Curtis Brown, Ltd. "The Unknown Citizen." Copyright © 1940 and renewed 1968 by W. H. Auden. Reprinted from *W. H. Auden: Collected Poems,* edited by Edward Mendelson, by permission of Random House, Inc. and Faber and Faber Ltd.

Toni Cade Bambara. "The Lesson" from *Gorilla, My Love* by Toni Cade Bambara. Copyright © 1972 by Toni Cade Bambara. Reprinted by permission of Random House, Inc.

Mary Field Belenky et al. "Reminiscences of College" from *Women's Ways of Knowing: The Development of Self, Voice, and Mind* by Mary Field Belenky, Blythe McVicker Clinchy, Nancy Rule Goldberger, and Jill Mattuck Tarule. Copyright © 1986 by Basic Books, Inc. Reprinted by permission of Basic Books, Inc., a division of HarperCollins Publishers.

Warren Bennis. "Time to Hang Up the Old Sports Clichés," in *The New York Times,* July 5, 1987. Reprinted by permission of the author.

Black Elk. "High Horse's Courting" (pp. 67–76) and "War Games" (pp. 14–15, 59–60) from John G. Neihart, *Black Elk Speaks.* Copyright 1932, © 1959, 1972 by John G. Neihart. Reprinted by permission of the John G. Neihart Trust.

Robert Bly. "Men's Initiation Rites" reprinted by permission of Georges Borchardt, Inc., on behalf of the author. Copyright © 1986 by Robert Bly.

Derek Bok. "Protecting Freedom of Expression at Harvard" from *The Boston Globe,* March 25, 1991, p. 15. Reprinted by permission of the author.

Judy Brady. "Why I Want a Wife" from *Ms.* Magazine, Vol. 1, No. 1. (December 31, 1971). Reprinted by permission of the author.

Lorene Cary. Excerpts from pp. 98–100, 194–199 of *Black Ice* by Lorene Cary. Copyright © 1991 by Lorene Cary. Reprinted by permission of Alfred A. Knopf, Inc.

Stephen Chapman. "The Prisoner's Dilemma" from *The New Republic,* March 8, 1980. Reprinted by permission of *The New Republic,* © 1980, The New Republic Inc.

Chewing Blackbones. "Old Man and Old Woman" from *Indian Legends from the Northern Rockies,* by Ella E. Clark. Copyright © 1966 by the University of Oklahoma Press.

Lyrics on page 201 from James Weldon Johnson, "Lift Ev'ry Voice and Sing" (James Weldon Johnson, J. Rosamond Johnson). Use by permission of Edward B. Marks Music Company.

Elizabeth Joseph. "My Husband's Nine Wives" in *The New York Times*, May 23, 1991. Copyright © 1991 by The New York Times Company. Reprinted by permission.

Pauline Kael. "High School and Other Forms of Madness" from *Deeper into Movies* by Pauline Kael. Reprinted by permission of Curtis Brown, Ltd. Copyright © 1973 by Pauline Kael.

Robert W. Keidel. "A New Game for Managers to Play" in *The New York Times*, December 5, 1985. Copyright © 1985 by The New York Times Company. Reprinted by permission.

Garrsion Keillor. "Something from the Sixties." Reprinted by permission of Ellen Levine Literary Agency, Inc. Copyright © 1984 by Garrison Keillor. First published in the April 9, 1984 issue of *The New Yorker*. "The Tip-Top Club" copyright © 1981 by Garrison Keillor, from *Happy to Be Here* by Garrison Keillor. Used by permission of Viking Penguin, a division of Penguin Books USA Inc.

Evelyn Fox Keller. "Women in Science: An Analysis of a Social Problem," *Harvard Magazine*, October 1974. Copyright © 1974 Harvard Magazine. Reprinted by permission.

Jamaica Kincaid. "Girl from *At the Bottom of the River* by Jamaica Kincaid. Copyright © 1978, 1983 by Jamaica Kincaid. Reprinted by permission of Farrar, Straus & Giroux, Inc.

Martin Luther King, Jr. "Nonviolent Resistance" from pp. 211–216 in *Stride toward Freedom* by Martin Luther King, Jr. Copyright © 1958 by Martin Luther King, Jr. Reprinted by permission of HarperCollins Publishers, Inc.

Stephen King. "Why We Crave Horror Movies." Copyright © 1982 by Stephen King. Originally appeared in *Playboy*. Reprinted by permission of Arthur B. Greene.

Edward I. Koch. "Death and Justice: How Capital Punishment Affirms Life" from *The New Republic*, April 15, 1985. Reprinted by permission of *The New Republic*, © 1985, The New Republic, Inc.

Irving Kristol. "Room for Darwin and the Bible" in *The New York Times*, May 23, 1991. Copyright © 1991 by The New York Times Company. Reprinted by permission.

Robin Lakoff. "You Are What You Say" from *Ms.* Magazine. July 1974. Reprinted by permission of the author.

Barbara Lawrence. "Four-Letter Words Can Hurt You" in *The New York Times*, October 27, 1973. Copyright © 1973 by The New York Times Company. Reprinted by permission.

Lynne Layton. "What's Really behind the Madonna-Bashing?" in *The Boston Globe*, December 16, 1990, p. A15. Reprinted by permission of the author.

B. Aisha Lemu. "In Defense of Polygamy" from B. Aisha Lemu and Fatima Heerin, *Women in Islam.* © Islamic Council of Europe, 1978/1398 A. H. Reprinted by permission of The Islamic Foundation, 223 London Road, Leicester LE2 1ZE, U.K.

Jeffrey W. Leppo and Robert J. Bryan. "Get Me to the Church on Time, Your Honor" in *The New York Times*, December 7, 1990. Copyright © 1990 by The New York Times Company. Reprinted by permission.

Jon D. Levenson. "The Good Friday–Passover Connection" in *The New York Times*, March 29, 1991. Copyright © 1991 by The New York Times Company. Reprinted by permission.

C. S. Lewis. "We Have No 'Right to Happiness'" from *God in the Dock* by C. S. Lewis, copyright © 1970 by C. S. Lewis Pte Ltd., reproduced by permission of HarperCollins Publishers Ltd., London.

Patricia Nelson Limerick. "The Phenomenon of Phantom Students: Diagnosis and Treatment" from *The Harvard Gazette*, November 11, 1983. Reprinted by permission of the author.

Malcolm X. "The Shoeshine Boy." from *The Autobiography of Malcolm X* by Malcolm X, with Alex Haley. Copyright © 1964 by Alex Haley and Malcolm X, © 1965 by Alex Haley and Betty Shabazz. Reprinted by permission of Random House, Inc.

Marya Mannes. "Television Advertising: The Splitting Image" from *Saturday Review,* November 4, 1970. Copyright © 1970 by Marya Mannes. Reprinted by permission.

Julie Matthaei. "Political Economy and Family Policy." Reprinted from Union for Radical Political Economics, *The Imperiled Economy, Book II: Through the Safety Net,* copyright 1988. Reprinted by permission of the author and the Union for Radical Political Economics.

Margaret Mead. "Why Do We Speak of Feminine Intuition?" in *Anima,* Spring 1975. Reprinted by permission.

Pat Mora. "Immigrants" from *Borders* by Pat Mora, 1986. Reprinted by permission of Arte Publico Press.

Sir Thomas More. "Work and Play in Utopia." Reprinted from *Utopia* by Sir Thomas More, A Nort London.

George Orwell. "Politics and the English Language," copyright 1946 by Sonia Brownell Orwell and renewed 1974 by Sonia Orwell. "Shooting an Elephant," copyright 1950 by Sonia Brownell Orwell and renewed 1978 by Sonia Pitt-Rivers, both from *Shooting an Elephant and Other Essays* by George Orwell. Reprinted by permission of the estate of the late Sonia Brownell Orwell, Martin Secker & Warburg Ltd. and Harcourt Brace Jovanovich, Inc.

Noel Perrin. "A Part-Time Marriage" in *The New York Times,* September 9, 1984. Copyright © 1984 by The New York Times Company. Reprinted by permission.

J. H. Plumb. "The Dying Family" from *In the Light of History* by J. H. Plumb, published by Houghton Mifflin Company and Penguin Books Ltd. Copyright © 1972 by J. H. Plumb. Reprinted by permission of Sir John Plumb.

Letty Cottin Pogrebin. "Consequences" in *The New York Times,* June 2, 1991. Copyright © 1991 by The New York Times Company. Reprinted by permission.

Katherine Anne Porter. "The Jilting of Granny Weatherall" from The Flowering Judas and Other Stories, copyright 1930 and renewed 1958 by Katherine Anne Porter, reprinted by permission of Harcourt Brace Jovanovich, Inc.

Neil Postman. "Order in the Classroom" from Teaching as a Conserving Activity by Neil Postman. Copyright © 1979 by Neil Postman. Used by permission of Delacorte Press, a division of Bantam Doubleday Dell Publishing Group, Inc.

Anna Quindlen. "The Glass Half Empty" in *The New York Times,* November 22, 1990. Copyright © 1990 by The New York Times Company. Reprinted by permission.

Diane Ravitch. "Multiculturalism: E Pluribus Plures" in *The Key Reporter,* Autumn 1990. Reprinted by permission of the author and Phi Beta Kappa Society.

Adrienne Rich. "Claiming an Education" is reprinted from *On Lies, Secrets and Silence, Selected Prose 1966–1978* by Adrienne Rich by permission of W. W. Norton & Company, Inc. Copyright © 1979 by W. W. Norton & Company, Inc.

Bertrand Russell, "Work" reprinted from *The Conquest of Happiness* by Bertrand Russell with the permission of Liveright Publishing Corporation and Routledge. Copyright 1930 by Horace Liveright, Inc. Copyright renewed 1958 by Bertrand Russell.

Scott Russell Sanders. "The Men We Carry in Our Minds . . . and how they differ from the real lives of most men." Copyright © 1984 by Scott Russell Sanders; first appeared in *Milkweed Chronicle;* reprinted by permission of the author and the author's agent, Virginia Kidd.

May Sarton. "The Rewards of Living a Solitary Life," in *The New York Times*, April 6, 1974. Copyright © 1974 by The New York Times Company. Reprinted by permission.

Robert Satter. "Whom to Believe?" from *Doing Justice* by Judge Robert Satter. Copyright © 1990 by Robert Satter. Reprinted by permission of Simon & Schuster.

Dorothy L. Sayers. "Are Women Human?" from *Unpopular Opinions* by Dorothy L. Sayers. Reprinted by permission of David Higham Associates.

Felice N. Schwartz. "The 'Mommy Track' Isn't Anti-Woman" in *The New York Times*, March 22, 1989. Copyright © 1989 by The New York Times Company. Reprinted by permission.

Peter Singer. "Animal Liberation" from *The New York Review of Books*, April 5, 1973. Copyright © 1973 by Peter Singer. Reprinted by permission of the author.

Theodore Sizer. "Principals' Questions" from *Horace's Compromise* by Theodore Sizer. Copyright © 1984 by Theodore Sizer. Reprinted by permission of Houghton Mifflin Company. All rights reserved.

Stevie Smith. "Not Waving But Drowning" in Stevie Smith, Collected Poems of Stevie Smith. Copyright 1972 by Stevie Smith. Reprinted by permission of New Directions Publishing Corporation.

Wilfred Cantwell Smith. "Muslims" from *The Faith of Other Men* by Wilfred Cantwell Smith. Copyright © 1962 by Wilfred Cantwell Smith. Printed by arrangement with NAL Penguin Inc.

Gloria Steinem. "The Importance of Work" from *Outrageous Acts and Everyday Rebellions* by Gloria Steinem. Copyright © 1983 by Gloria Steinem, © 1984 by East Toledo Productions, Inc. Reprinted by permission of Henry Holt and Company, Inc.

Daisetz Teitara Suzuki. "What is Zen?" from *Zen and Japanese Culture*, Bollingen Series 44. Copyright © 1959 by Princeton University Press, © renewed 1987. Excerpt, pp. 13–18, reprinted with permission of Princeton University Press.

Amy Tan. "Snapshot: Lost Lives of Women" in *Life*, April 1991, pp. 90–91. Reprinted by permission of the author and the author's agent, Sandra Dijkstra Literary Agency. The photograph accompanying this selection is owned by Amy Tan.

Deborah Tannen. "The Workings of Conversational Style" and notes from p. 202 of *That's Not What I Meant* by Deborah Tannen. Copyright © 1986 by Deborah Tannen. Reprinted by permission of William Morrow & Company, Inc.

Studs Terkel. "Three Workers" from *Working: People Talk about What They Do All Day and How They Feel about What They Do* by Studs Terkel. Copyright © 1972, 1974 by Studs Terkel. "Stephen Cruz" from *American Dreams: Lost and Found* by Studs Terkel. Copyright © 1980 by Studs Terkel. Reprinted by permission of Pantheon Books, a division of Random House, Inc.

Paul Theroux. "The Male Myth" in *The New York Times*, November 27, 1983. Copyright © 1983 by The New York Times Company. Reprinted by permission.

Lewis Thomas. "The Art of Teaching Science." First appeared in *The New York Times*, March 14, 1982. Copyright © 1982 by Dr. Lewis Thomas. Reprinted by permission.

Bill Totten. "Eigyoman" in an advertising supplement in *The New York Times*, 1991. Reprinted by permission of Kodansha America, Inc.

Florence Trefethen. "Points of a Lifelong Triangle; Reflections of an Adoptive Mother." *The Washington Post*, January 29, 1991. Reprinted by permission of the author.

John Updike. "A & P" from *Pigeon Feathers and Other Stories* by John Updike. Copyright © 1962 by John Updike. Reprinted by permission of Alfred A. Knopf, Inc. Originally appeared in *The New Yorker*.

Lindsy van Gelder. "Marriage as a Restricted Club" originally appeared in *Ms.*, February 1984. Reprinted by permission of the author.

Alice Walker. "In Search of Our Mothers' Gardens" from *In Search of Our Mothers' Gardens*, *copyright* © 1974 by Alice Walker, reprinted by permission of Harcourt Brace Jovanovich, Inc.

Renita Weems. "Whispering Hope" (*Ms.*, December 1987). Reprinted by permission of the author.

E. B. White. "Education" from pp. 52–54 in "Education—March 1939" in *One Man's Meat* by E. B. White. Copyright 1939, 1967 by E. B. White. Reprinted by permission of HarperCollins Publishers, Inc.

Merry White. "Japanese Education: How Do They Do It?" reprinted with permission of the author from *The Public Interest*, No. 76 (Summer 1984), pp. 87–101. © 1984 by National Affairs, Inc.

Marie Winn. "The End of Play" from *Children without Childhood* by Marie Winn. Copyright © 1981, 1983 by Marie Winn. Reprinted by permission of Pantheon Books, a division of Random House, Inc.

Virginia Woolf. "Professions for Women" from *The Death of the Moth and Other Essays* by Virginia Woolf. Copyright © 1942 by Harcourt Brace Jovanovich, Inc. and renewed 1970 by Marjorie T. Parsons, Executrix, reprinted by permission of Harcourt Brace Jovanovich, Inc. and Random Century Group.

Wu-tsu Fa-yen. "Zen and the Art of Burglary" from Daisetz T. Suzuki, *Zen and Japanese Culture*, Bollingen Series 44. Copyright © 1959 by Princeton University Press, renewed © 1987. Reprinted by permission of Princeton University Press.

Index

Titles of illustrations are enclosed in quotation marks.